NEW CENTURY BIBLE
COMMENTARY

General Editors

RONALD E. CLEMENTS
(Old Testament)

MATTHEW BLACK
(New Testament)

Numbers

THE NEW CENTURY BIBLE COMMENTARIES

EXODUS (J. P. Hyatt)
DEUTERONOMY (A. D. H. Mayes)
JOSHUA, JUDGES, RUTH (John Gray)
1 AND 2 KINGS, Volumes 1 and 2 (Gwilym H. Jones)
1 AND 2 CHRONICLES (H. G. Williamson)
EZRA, NEHEMIAH, AND ESTHER (D. J. Clines)
JOB (H. H. Rowley)
PSALMS, Volumes 1 and 2 (A. A. Anderson)
PROVERBS (R. N. Whybray)
ECCLESIASTES (R. N. Whybray)
ISAIAH 1–39 (R. E. Clements)
ISAIAH 40–66 (R. N. Whybray)
JEREMIAH (Douglas Rawlinson Jones)
LAMENTATIONS (Iain W. Provan)
EZEKIEL (John W. Wevers)
THE GOSPEL OF MATTHEW (David Hill)
THE GOSPEL OF MARK (Hugh Anderson)
THE GOSPEL OF LUKE (E. Earle Ellis)
THE GOSPEL OF JOHN (Barnabas Lindars)
THE ACTS OF THE APOSTLES (William Neil)
ROMANS, Second Edition (Matthew Black)
1 AND 2 CORINTHIANS (F. F. Bruce)
GALATIANS (Donald Guthrie)
EPHESIANS (C. Leslie Mitton)
PHILIPPIANS (Ralph P. Martin)
COLOSSIANS AND PHILEMON (Ralph P. Martin)
1 AND 2 THESSALONIANS (I. Howard Marshall)
PASTORAL EPISTLES (A. T. Hanson)
HEBREWS (R. McL. Wilson)
1 PETER (Ernest Best)
JAMES, JUDE, AND 2 PETER (E. M. Sidebottom)
JOHANNINE EPISTLES (K. Grayson)
THE BOOK OF REVELATION (G. R. Beasley-Murray)

Other titles are in preparation

NEW CENTURY BIBLE
COMMENTARY

Based on the Revised Standard Version

NUMBERS

ERYL W. DAVIES

Marshall Pickering
An Imprint of HarperCollins*Publishers*

WILLIAM B. EERDMANS PUBLISHING COMPANY, GRAND RAPIDS

Marshall Pickering is an Imprint of
HarperCollins*Religious*
Part of HarperCollins*Publishers*
77–85 Fulham Palace Road, London W6 8JB

First published 1995 in Great Britain by Marshall Pickering
and in the United States by Wm. B. Eerdmans Publishing Co.,
225 Jefferson Avenue, S.E., Grand Rapids, Michigan 49503.

1 3 5 7 9 10 8 6 4 2

A catalogue record for this book is
available from the British Library

Marshall Pickering ISBN 0-551-02835-1
Eerdmans ISBN 0-8028-0790-9

Typeset in Great Britain by
Rowland Phototypesetting Ltd, Bury St Edmunds, Suffolk
Printed in the United States of America
for Marshall Pickering and Wm. B. Eerdmans

CONTENTS

PREFACE

Like all commentaries, the present work rests on the labours of many scholars, both past and present. To those familiar with the literature on the book of Numbers, my indebtedness to all who have worked in this area of the Old Testament will be only too apparent. In the study of Numbers there are both profound questions and comparatively insignificant details upon which commentators hold entirely differing opinions. I have endeavoured, so far as it has been practicable within the limitations of space, to combine a general outline of the views of others with some modest conclusions of my own.

I should like to express my thanks to Professor R. E. Clements for his kind invitation to contribute this volume to the New Century Bible Commentary series, and for his much valued advice and guidance during all the stages of its preparation. Much of the commentary was written during two terms' sabbatical leave in 1991, and I am indebted to the authorities of the University of Wales, Bangor, for making this possible, and to my colleagues in the School of Theology and Religious Studies for undertaking my university duties while I was away. It is a pleasure to thank Professor Gwilym H. Jones, the head of the School, for his unstinting support and personal encouragement not only during this particular project but throughout my academic career. I am also grateful to Mr Ed Ball of the University of Nottingham, and to my colleague, the Revd Dr Margaret E. Thrall, for their kindness in reading through the entire manuscript, and for redeeming it from both errors of judgment and infelicities of style. Their constructive criticisms and suggestions are responsible for many improvements upon the version which first came into their hands. Successive drafts of the present commentary have been typed by Mrs Beti Llewellyn, and – not for the first time – I am very much indebted to her for her patience and perseverance.

The book is dedicated to my wife, Eirian, who has been a constant source of support and encouragement, and to my two daughters, Manon and Llinos, who provided some very welcome diversion from the often arduous tasks of writing and research.

ERYL W. DAVIES, August 1994

ABBREVIATIONS

BIBLICAL
OLD TESTAMENT *(OT)*

Gen.	Jg.	1 Chr.	Ps.	Lam.	Ob.	Hag.
Exod.	Ru.	2 Chr.	Prov.	Ezek.	Jon.	Zech.
Lev.	1 Sam.	Ezr.	Ec.	Dan.	Mic.	Mal.
Num.	2 Sam.	Neh.	Ca.	Hos.	Nah.	
Dt.	1 Kg.	Est.	Isa.	Jl	Hab.	
Jos.	2 Kg.	Job	Jer.	Am.	Zeph.	

APOCRYPHA *(Apoc.)*

1 Esd.	Tob.	Ad. Est.	Sir.	S 3 Ch.	Bel	1 Mac.
2 Esd.	Jdt.	Wis.	Bar.	Sus.	Man.	2 Mac.
			E. Jer.			

NEW TESTAMENT *(NT)*

Mt.	Ac.	Gal.	1 Th.	Tit.	1 Pet.	3 Jn
Mk	Rom.	Eph.	2 Th.	Phm.	2 Pet.	Jude
Lk.	1 C.	Phil.	1 Tim.	Heb.	1 Jn	Rev.
Jn	2 C.	Col.	2 Tim.	Jas	2 Jn	

GENERAL

AASOR	*Annual of the American Schools of Oriental Research*
ABR	*Australian Biblical Review*
AI	*Ancient Israel: Its Life and Institutions,* R. de Vaux (ET by J. McHugh), London, 1961
AJBI	*Annual of the Japanese Biblical Institute*
AJSL	*American Journal of Semitic Languages and Literatures*
AJT	*American Journal of Theology*
Akkad.	Akkadian
AnBib	*Analecta Biblica*
ANET	*Ancient Near Eastern Texts Relating to the Old Testament,* ed. J. B. Pritchard, Princeton, 1969³
Ant.	Josephus, *The Antiquities of the Jews*
AOAT	*Alter Orient und Altes Testament*
Arab.	Arabic
Aram.	Aramaic

ASOR	*American Schools of Oriental Research*
ASTI	*Annual of the Swedish Theological Institute*
ATD	*Das Alte Testament Deutsch*
AThANT	*Abhandlungen zur Theologie des Alten und Neuen Testaments*
AV	*Authorized Version* (King James Version)
BA	*Biblical Archaeologist*
BAR	*Biblical Archaeological Review*
BASOR	*Bulletin of the American Schools of Oriental Research*
BBB	*Bonner Biblische Beiträge*
BDB	*Hebrew and English Lexicon of the Old Testament,* F. Brown, S. R. Driver and C. A. Briggs (eds), Oxford, 1952²
BHS	*Biblia Hebraica Stuttgartensia,* ed. K. Elliger and W. Rudolph, Stuttgart, 1977
Bib	*Biblica*
BibR	*Biblical Research*
BIES	*Bulletin of the Israel Exploration Society*
BJRL	*Bulletin of the John Rylands Library*
BJS	*Brown Judaic Studies*
BT	*The Bible Translator*
BTB	*Biblical Theology Bulletin*
BWANT	*Beiträge zur Wissenschaft vom Alten und Neuen Testament*
BZ	*Biblische Zeitschrift*
BZAW	*Beihefte zur Zeitschrift für die Alttestamentliche Wissenschaft*
BZNW	*Beihefte zur Zeitschrift für die Neutestamentliche Wissenschaft*
CB	*Century Bible*
CBC	*Cambridge Bible Commentary*
CBOTS	*Coniectanea Biblica, Old Testament Series*
CBQ	*Catholic Biblical Quarterly*
CH	The Code of Hammurabi
CJT	*Canadian Journal of Theology*
DOTT	*Documents from Old Testament Times,* ed. D. Winton Thomas, London, 1958
DSB	*Daily Study Bible*
EAEHL	*Encyclopedia of Archaeological Excavations in the Holy Land,* i–iv, ed. M. Avi-Yonah, Oxford, 1975–8
ET	English translation
ETL	*Ephemerides Theologicae Lovanienses*
EvTh	*Evangelische Theologie*

EvQ	*Evangelical Quarterly*
ExpT	*Expository Times*
FRLANT	*Forschungen zur Religion und Literatur des Alten und Neuen Testaments*
Gk	Greek
G–K	*Gesenius' Hebrew Grammar*, rev. E. Kautzsch, ed. A. E. Cowley, Oxford, 1910^2
HAR	*Hebrew Annual Review*
HAT	*Handbuch zum Alten Testament*
HDB	Hastings' *Dictionary of the Bible*, i–iv, Edinburgh, 1898–1902
Heb.	Hebrew
HKAT	*Handkommentar zum Alten Testament*
HSM	*Harvard Semitic Monographs*
HTR	*Harvard Theological Review*
HUCA	*Hebrew Union College Annual*
ICC	*International Critical Commentary*
IDB	*Interpreter's Dictionary of the Bible*, i–iv, ed. G. A. Buttrick *et al.*, Nashville, New York, 1962
IDBSup	*Interpreter's Dictionary of the Bible Supplementary Volume*, ed. K. Crim, Nashville, New York, 1976
IEJ	*Israel Exploration Journal*
IJH	*Israelite and Judaean History*, ed. J. H. Hayes and J. M. Miller, *OTL*, London, 1977
Int	*Interpretation*
JAAR	*Journal of the American Academy of Religion*
JAOS	*Journal of the American Oriental Society*
JB	*Jerusalem Bible*
JBL	*Journal of Biblical Literature*
JBS	*Jerusalem Bible Studies*
JCS	*Journal of Cuneiform Studies*
JETS	*Journal of the Evangelical Theological Society*
JJS	*Journal of Jewish Studies*
JNES	*Journal of Near Eastern Studies*
JNWSL	*Journal of Northwest Semitic Languages*
JPOS	*Journal of the Palestine Oriental Society*
JPS	*The Jewish Publication Society*
JQR	*Jewish Quarterly Review*
JSJ	*Journal for the Study of Judaism*
JSOT	*Journal for the Study of the Old Testament*

JSOTS	*Journal for the Study of the Old Testament Supplement Series*
JSS	*Journal of Semitic Studies*
JTS	*Journal of Theological Studies*
K–B	*Lexicon in Veteris Testamenti Libros*, ed. L. Köhler and W. Baumgartner, Leiden, 1953
KHAT	*Kurzer Hand-Commentar zum Alten Testament*
LXX	The Greek Septuagint Version
LXX^L	The Lucianic Recension
MAL	Middle Assyrian Laws
MS, MSS	Manuscript(s)
MT	The Massoretic Text of the Old Testament
NCB	*New Century Bible*
NEB	*New English Bible*
NIV	*New International Version*
NJPS	*New Jewish Publication Society Translation*
NovT	*Novum Testamentum*
NPC	*Peake's Commentary on the Bible*, rev. edn, M. Black and H. H. Rowley, London, 1962
NRSV	*New Revised Standard Version*
OLZ	*Orientalistische Literaturzeitung*
Or	*Orientalia*
OTL	*Old Testament Library*
OTS	*Oudtestamentische Studiën*
PEFQS	*Palestine Exploration Fund, Quarterly Statement*
PEQ	*Palestine Exploration Quarterly*
PJB	*Palästina-Jahrbuch*
PSB	*Princeton Seminary Bulletin*
RB	*Revue Biblique*
REB	*Revised English Bible*
RevQ	*Revue de Qumran*
RSV	*Revised Standard Version*
RV	*Revised Version*
Sam.	Samaritan Pentateuch
SB	*Sources Bibliques*
SBL	*Society of Biblical Literature*
SBLDS	*Society of Biblical Literature Dissertation Series*
SBLMS	*Society of Biblical Literature Monograph Series*
SBT	*Studies in Biblical Theology*
ScrHier	*Scripta Hierosolymitana*
SEÅ	*Svensk Exegetisk Årsbok*

SJT	*Scottish Journal of Theology*
SNTSMS	*Society for New Testament Studies Monograph Series*
Syr.	Syriac
Targ.	Targum
TBC	*Torch Bible Commentaries*
TDOT	*Theological Dictionary of the Old Testament*, ed. G. J. Botterweck and H. Ringgren (ET by J. T. Willis), Grand Rapids, Michigan, 1974–
TLZ	*Theologische Literaturzeitung*
TynB	*Tyndale Bulletin*
UF	*Ugarit-Forschungen*
Ugar.	Ugaritic
Vsns	The (Ancient) Versions
VT	*Vetus Testamentum*
VTS	*Supplements to Vetus Testamentum*
Vulg.	The Vulgate Version
WAI	*The World of Ancient Israel*, ed. R. E. Clements, Cambridge, 1989
WBC	*Word Biblical Commentary*
WEC	*Wycliffe Exegetical Commentary*
WMANT	*Wissenschaftliche Monographien zum Alten und Neuen Testament*
WO	*Die Welt des Orients*
ZAW	*Zeitschrift für die Alttestamentliche Wissenschaft*
ZDMG	*Zeitschrift der deutschen Morgenländischen Gesellschaft*
ZDPV	*Zeitschrift des deutschen Palästina-Vereins*
ZTK	*Zeitschrift für Theologie und Kirche*

BIBLIOGRAPHY

COMMENTARIES (*cited in text by author's name only*)

Baentsch, B., *Exodus, Leviticus, Numeri, HKAT* 2, Göttingen, 1903.

Binns, L. E., *The Book of Numbers*, London, 1927.

Budd, P. J., *Numbers, WBC* 5, Waco, Texas, 1984.

Dillmann, A., *Numeri, Deuteronomium und Josua*, Leipzig, 1886.

Gray, G. B., *A Critical and Exegetical Commentary on Numbers, ICC*,
   Edinburgh, 1903.

Harrison, R. K., *Numbers, WEC*, Chicago, 1990.

Heinisch, P., *Das Buch Numeri*, Bonn, 1936.

Holzinger, H., *Numeri, KHAT* 4, Tübingen and Leipzig, 1903.

Keil, C. F., *Biblischer Commentar über die Bücher Mose's*, ii, Leipzig, 1870.

Kennedy, A. R. S., *Leviticus and Numbers, CB*, n.d.

Levine, B. A., *Numbers 1–20, Anchor Bible*, London and New York, 1993.

L'Heureux, C. E., 'Numbers', *The New Jerome Biblical Commentary*,
   ed. R. E. Brown, J. A. Fitzmyer and R. E. Murphy, London,
   1990², pp. 80–93.

Maarsingh, B., *Numbers: A Practical Commentary* (ET by J. Vriend),
   Grand Rapids, Michigan, 1987.

Marsh, J., 'Numbers', *The Interpreter's Bible*, ii, New York,
   Nashville, 1953, pp. 142–308.

McNeile, A. H., *The Book of Numbers*, Cambridge, 1911.

Milgrom, J., *The JPS Torah Commentary: Numbers*, New York, 1990.

Noth, M., *Numbers. A Commentary* (ET by J. D. Martin), *OTL*,
   London, 1968.

Riggans, W., *Numbers, DSB*, Edinburgh, 1983.

Snaith, N. H., *Leviticus and Numbers, NCB*, London, 1967.

Snaith, N. H., 'Numbers', *NPC*, 1962, pp. 254–68.

Sturdy, J., *Numbers, CBC*, Cambridge, 1972.

de Vaulx, J., *Les Nombres, SB*, Paris, 1972.

Wenham, G. J., *Numbers, TBC*, London, 1982.

SPECIAL STUDIES (*cited in text by author's name only*)

Fritz, V., *Israel in der Wüste. Traditionsgeschichtliche Untersuchung der
   Wüstenüberlieferung des Jahwisten*, Marburg, 1970.

Kellermann, D., *Die Priesterschrift von Numeri 1:1 bis 10:10; literarkritisch und traditionsgeschichtlich untersucht*, Berlin, 1970.
Paterson, J. A., *The Book of Numbers*, Leipzig, 1900.
Rudolph, W., *Der "Elohist" von Exodus bis Josua*, *BZAW* 68, Berlin, 1938.

OTHER SOURCES

Abba, R., 'The Origin and Significance of Hebrew Sacrifice', *BTB* 7 (1977), pp. 123–38.
Aberbach, M., and Smolar, L., 'Aaron, Jeroboam, and the Golden Calves', *JBL* 86 (1967), pp. 129–40.
Aharoni, Y., 'Forerunners of the Limes: Iron Age Fortresses in the Negev', *IEJ* 17 (1967), pp. 1–17; 'Excavations at Tel Arad', *IEJ* 17 (1967), pp. 233–49; *The Land of the Bible* (ET by A. F. Rainey), London, 1967; 'Arad: Its Inscriptions and Temple', *BA* 31 (1968), pp. 2–32; 'Arad', *EAEHL*, i, 1975, pp. 74–89 (with R. Amiran).
Ahuis, F., *Autorität im Umbruch: Ein formgeschichtlicher Beitrag zur Klärung der literarischen Schichtung und der zeitgeschichtlichen Bezüge von Num 16 und 17* (Calwer Theologische Monographien), Stuttgart, 1983.
Albright, W. F., 'The Home of Balaam', *JAOS* 35 (1915), pp. 386–90; 'Researches of the School in Western Judaea', *BASOR* 15 (1924), pp. 2–11; 'The Administrative Divisions of Israel and Judah', *JPOS* 5 (1925), pp. 17–54; *From the Stone Age to Christianity: Monotheism and the Historical Process*, Baltimore, 1940; 'The Oracles of Balaam', *JBL* 63 (1944), pp. 207–33; 'The List of Levitic Cities', *Louis Ginzberg Jubilee Volume*, New York, 1945, pp. 49–73; *Archaeology and the Religion of Israel*, Baltimore, 1946[2]; 'Some Important Recent Discoveries: Alphabetic Origins and the Idrimi Statue', *BASOR* 118 (1950), pp. 11–20; 'Jethro, Hobab and Reuel in Early Hebrew Tradition', *CBQ* 25 (1963), pp. 1–11; *Yahweh and the Gods of Canaan*, London, 1968; 'Midianite Donkey Caravans', *Translating and Understanding the Old Testament. Essays in Honor of H. G. May*, ed. H. T. Frank and W. L. Reed, New York and Nashville, 1970, pp. 197–205; 'From the Patriarchs to Moses: II. Moses out of Egypt', *BA* 36 (1973), pp. 48–76.
Allegro, J. M., 'The Meaning of the Phrase *šetūm hā'ayin* in Num. XXIV 3, 15', *VT* 3 (1953), pp. 78–9; 'Further Messianic

References in Qumran Literature', *JBL* 75 (1956), pp. 174–87.

Alt, A., 'Festungen und Levitenorte im Lande Juda', *Kleine Schriften zur Geschichte des Volkes Israel*, ii, Munich, 1953, pp. 306–15.

Althann, R., 'Numbers 21, 30b in the Light of the Ancient Versions and Ugaritic', *Bib* 66 (1985), pp. 568–71.

Anderson, G. A., *Sacrifices and Offerings in Ancient Israel*, HSM 41, Atlanta, Georgia, 1987.

Arden, E., 'How Moses Failed God', *JBL* 76 (1957), pp. 50–2.

Auerbach, E., 'Die Feste im alten Israel', *VT* 8 (1958), pp. 1–18.

Auld, A. G., *Joshua, Moses and the Land*, Edinburgh, 1980.

Aurelius, E., *Der Fürbitter Israels: Eine Studie zum Mosebild im Alten Testament*, CBOTS 27, Stockholm, 1988.

Avi-Yonah, M., 'Medeba', *EAEHL*, iii, pp. 819–23.

Barkay, G., 'The Divine Name Found in Jerusalem', *BAR* 9/2 (1983), pp. 14–19; *Ketef Hinnom. A Treasure Facing Jerusalem's Walls*, The Israel Museum, Jerusalem, 1986.

Barnouin, M., 'Tableaux numériques du Livre des Nombres', *RB* 76 (1969), pp. 351–64; 'Les Recensements du Livre des Nombres et l'Astronomie Babylonienne', *VT* 27 (1977), pp. 280–303.

Barr, J., 'The Image of God in the Book of Genesis – A Study of Terminology', *BJRL* 51 (1968–9), pp. 11–26; '*Migraš* in the Old Testament', *JSS* 29 (1984), pp. 15–31.

Bartlett, J. R., 'The Edomite King-List of Genesis XXXVI. 31–39 and I Chron. I. 43–50', *JTS*, N.S., 16 (1965), pp. 301–14; 'The Land of Seir and the Brotherhood of Edom', *JTS*, N.S., 20 (1969), pp. 1–20; 'The Historical Reference of Numbers XXI. 27–30', *PEQ* 101 (1969), pp. 94–100. 'The Use of the Word *rōʾš* as a Title in the Old Testament', *VT* 19 (1969), pp. 1–10; 'Sihon and Og, Kings of the Amorites', *VT* 20 (1970), pp. 257–77; 'The Rise and Fall of the Kingdom of Edom', *PEQ* 104 (1972), pp. 26–37; 'The Brotherhood of Edom', *JSOT* 4 (1977), pp. 2–27; 'The Conquest of Sihon's Kingdom: A Literary Re-examination', *JBL* 97 (1978), pp. 347–51.

Baskin, J. R., *Pharaoh's Counsellors: Job, Jethro and Balaam in Rabbinic and Patristic Tradition*, BJS 47, Chico, California, 1983.

Batto, B. F., 'The Covenant of Peace: A Neglected Ancient Near Eastern Motif', *CBQ* 49 (1987), pp. 187–211.

Batten, L. W., *A Critical and Exegetical Commentary on the Books of Ezra and Nehemiah, ICC*, Edinburgh, 1913.

Baumgarten, J. M., 'The Sabbath Trumpets in 4Q493 M^c', *RevQ* 12 (1985–7), pp. 555–9.

Bechtel, L. M., 'Shame as a Sanction of Social Control in Biblical Israel: Judicial, Political, and Social Shaming', *JSOT* 49 (1991), pp. 47–76.

Beentjes, P. C., 'Inverted Quotations in the Bible: A Neglected Stylistic Pattern', *Bib* 63 (1982), pp. 506–23.

Beer, G., 'Miscellen: 1. Das Stehenlassen der Pe'ā Lev. 19, 9. 2. Die Bitterkräuter beim Paschafest. 3. Der Wein beim Paschafest. Zu Jeremia 4, 31', *ZAW* 31 (1911), pp. 152–4.

Beirne, D., 'A Note on Numbers 11, 4', *Bib* 44 (1963), pp. 201–3.

Beltz, W., *Die Kaleb-Traditionen im Alten Testament, BWANT* V/18, Stuttgart, 1964.

Ben-Barak, Z., 'Inheritance by Daughters in the Ancient Near East', *JSS* 25 (1980), pp. 22–33.

Bergman, A., 'The Israelite Tribe of Half-Manasseh', *JPOS* 16 (1936), pp. 224–54.

Bertman, S., 'Tasseled Garments in the Ancient East Mediterranean', *BA* 24 (1961), pp. 119–28.

Bewer, J. A., 'The Literary Problems of the Balaam Story in Numb., Chaps. 22–24', *AJT* 9 (1905), pp. 238–62; 'The Original Significance of the Rite of the Red Cow in Numbers XIX', *JBL* 24 (1905), pp. 41–4.

Binns, L. E., 'Midianite Elements in Hebrew Religion', *JTS* 31 (1930), pp. 337–54.

Blank, S. H., 'The Curse, Blasphemy, the Spell and the Oath', *HUCA* 23, Pt. I (1950–1), pp. 73–95.

Blenkinsopp, J., 'Structure and Style in Judges 13–16', *JBL* 82 (1963), pp. 65–76; *The Pentateuch: An Introduction to the First Five Books of the Bible*, London, 1992.

Bodenheimer, F. S., 'The Manna of Sinai', *BA* 10 (1947), pp. 2–6.

de Boer, P. A. H., 'Numbers VI 27', *VT* 32 (1982), pp. 3–13.

Böhl, F. M. Th., '*bên ha'arbayim*', *OLZ* 18 (1915), pp. 321–4.

Boorer, S., *The Promise of the Land as Oath, BZAW* 205, Berlin and New York, 1992.

Bokser, B. Z., 'Hidden Meanings in the Writings of Rabbi Kook', *Proceedings of the American Academy for Jewish Research 44*, Jerusalem, 1977, pp. 19–27.

Bowman, J., 'Did the Qumran Sect Burn the Red Heifer?', *RevQ*
    1 (1958), pp. 73–84.
Brettler, M. Z., *God is King: Understanding an Israelite Metaphor*,
    JSOTS 76, Sheffield, 1989.
Brichto, H. C., 'The Case of the Šōṭā and a Reconsideration of
    Biblical "Law"', *HUCA* 46 (1975), pp. 55–70.
Bright, J., *A History of Israel*, London, second revised edn, 1972.
Brin, G., 'The Firstling of Unclean Animals', *JQR* 68 (1977–8),
    pp. 1–15.
Brockington, L. H., *The Hebrew Text of the Old Testament*, Oxford
    and Cambridge, 1973.
Brueggemann, W., 'The Kerygma of the Priestly Writers', *ZAW*
    84 (1972), pp. 397–414.
Budde, K., 'Kleinigkeiten zu den historischen Volksliedern des
    A.T.', *Transactions of the Tenth International Congress of Orientalists*,
    pt. III, Geneva, 1894, pp. 16–18; 'The Song of the Well',
    New World 4 (1895), pp. 136–44.
Buis, P., 'Qadesh, un Lieu Maudit?', *VT* 24 (1974), pp. 268–85.
Burney, C. F., *The Book of Judges*, London, 1920².
Burns, R. J., *Has the Lord Indeed Spoken Only Through Moses?*, *SBLDS*
    84, 1987.
Butler, T. C., 'An Anti-Moses Tradition', *JSOT* 12 (1979), pp. 9–15.
Caquot, A., and Lemaire, A., 'Les textes araméens de Deir 'Alla',
    Syria 54 (1977), pp. 189–208.
Cardascia, G., 'L'ordalie par le Fleuve dans les "Lois
    Assyriennes"', *Festschrift für Wilhelm Eilers*, ed. by
    G. Wiessner, Wiesbaden, 1967, pp. 19–36.
Carmichael, C., 'A New View of the Origin of the Deuteronomic
    Credo', *VT* 19 (1969), pp. 273–89.
Cartledge, T. W., 'Were Nazirite vows Unconditional?', *CBQ* 51
    (1989), pp. 409–22; *Vows in the Hebrew Bible and the Ancient Near
    East*, *JSOTS* 147, Sheffield, 1992.
Cazelles, H., 'La Dîme Israélite et les Textes de Ras Shamra', *VT*
    1 (1951), pp. 131–4; 'David's Monarchy and the Gibeonite
    Claim', *PEQ* 87 (1955), pp. 165–75. *Le Deutéronome*, Paris, 1966.
Cheyne, T. K., 'Some Critical Difficulties in the Chapters on
    Balaam', *ExpT* 10 (1898–9), pp. 399–402; 'Further Remarks
    on the Hebrew Word *degel*', *JQR* 11 (1898–9), pp. 232–6.
Childs, B. S., 'The Etiological Tale Re-examined', *VT* 24 (1974),

pp. 387–97; *Introduction to the Old Testament as Scripture*, London, 1979.

Christensen, D. L., 'Num 21:14–15 and the Book of the Wars of Yahweh', *CBQ* 36 (1974), pp. 359–60.

Clark, I., 'Balaam's Ass: Suture or Structure?', *Literary Interpretations of Biblical Narratives*, ii (ed. K. R. R. Gros Louis), Abingdon, Nashville, 1982, pp. 137–44.

Clements, R. E., *Abraham and David. Genesis XV and its Meaning for Israelite Tradition*, *SBT*² 5, London, 1967.

Clines, D. J. A., *The Theme of the Pentateuch*, JSOTS 10, Sheffield, 1978.

Coats, G. W., *Rebellion in the Wilderness*, Nashville, New York, 1968; 'Balaam: Sinner or Saint?', *BibR* 18 (1973), pp. 21–29 (reprinted in G. W. Coats, ed., *Saga, Legend, Tale, Novella, Fable: Narrative Forms in Old Testament Literature*, *JSOTS* 35, Sheffield, 1985, pp. 56–62); 'Conquest Traditions in the Wilderness Theme', *JBL* 95 (1976), pp. 177–90; 'Legendary Motifs in the Moses Death Reports', *CBQ* 39 (1977), pp. 34–44; 'The Way of Obedience: Traditio-Historical and Hermeneutical Reflections on the Balaam Story', *Semeia* 24 (1982), pp. 53–79; 'Humility and Honor; A Moses Legend in Numbers 12', *Art and Meaning: Rhetoric in Biblical Literature* (ed. D. J. A. Clines, D. M. Gunn and A. J. Hauser), *JSOTS* 19, Sheffield, 1982, pp. 97–107; *Moses. Heroic Man, Man of God*, *JSOTS* 57, Sheffield, 1988.

Cochrane, R. G., *Biblical Leprosy: A Suggested Interpretation*, London, 1961.

Cody, A., *A History of Old Testament Priesthood*, AnBib 35, Rome, 1969.

Cohen, R., 'Excavations at Kadesh-barnea, 1976–78', *BA* 44 (1981), pp. 93–107.

Cooper, A., 'The "Euphemism" in Numbers 12:12. A Study in the History of Interpretation', *JJS* 32 (1981), pp. 56–64.

Coppens, J., 'Les Oracles de Biléam: Leur Origine Littéraire et leur Portée Prophétique', *Mélanges Eugène Tisserant*, i, Città del Vaticano, Biblioteca Apostolica Vaticana, 1964, pp. 67–79.

Cornill, C. H., 'Beiträge zur Pentateuchkritik', *ZAW* 11 (1891), pp. 1–34.

Craigie, P. C., 'The Conquest and Early Hebrew Poetry', *TynB* 20 (1969), pp. 76–94.

Cross, F. M., *Canaanite Myth and Hebrew Epic*, London, 1973.

Daiches, S., 'Balaam – a Babylonian *bārū*', *Hilprecht Anniversary*

Volume: Studies in Assyriology and Archaeology, Leipzig, 1909,
   pp. 60–70.
Daube, D., *The New Testament and Rabbinic Judaism*, London, 1956.
David, M., 'Die Bestimmungen über die Asylstädte in Josua XX',
   OTS 9 (1951), pp. 30–48.
Davies, E. W., 'The Meaning of *qesem* in Prv 16, 10', *Bib* 61 (1980),
   pp. 554–6; *Prophecy and Ethics: Isaiah and the Ethical Traditions
   of Israel, JSOTS* 16, Sheffield, 1981; 'Inheritance Rights and
   the Hebrew Levirate Marriage', *VT* 31 (1981), pp. 138–44,
   257–68; 'Ruth IV 5 and the Duties of the Gō'ēl', *VT* 33 (1983),
   pp. 231–4; 'The Meaning of *pî šnayim* in Deuteronomy XXI
   17', *VT* 36 (1986), pp. 341–7; 'Land: its Rights and
   Privileges', *WAI*, Cambridge, 1989, pp. 349–69; 'The
   Inheritance of the First-Born in Israel and the Ancient Near
   East', *JSS* 38 (1993), pp. 175–91.
Davies, G. I., 'Hagar, El-Heǧra and the Location of Mount Sinai',
   VT 22 (1972), pp. 152–63; 'The Wilderness Itineraries: A
   Comparative Study', *TynB* 25 (1974), pp. 46–81; *The Way of
   the Wilderness*, Cambridge, 1979; 'The Wilderness Itineraries
   and the Composition of the Pentateuch', *VT* 33 (1983), pp. 1–13.
Davies, M. Ll., 'Levitical Leprosy: Uncleanness and the Psyche',
   ExpT 99 (1987–8), pp. 136–9.
Dearman, J. A., 'The Location of Jahaz', *ZDPV* 100 (1984),
   pp. 122–5.
Delcor, M., 'Quelques cas de survivances du Vocabulaire Nomade
   en Hébreu Biblique', *VT* 25 (1975), pp. 307–22; 'Le Texte de
   Deir 'Alla et les Oracles Bibliques de Bala'am', *VTS* 32
   (Congress Volume, Vienna, 1980), Leiden, 1981, pp. 52–73.
Delekat, L., 'Zum Hebräischen Wörterbuch', *VT* 14 (1964), pp. 7–
   66; *Asylie und Schutzorakel am Zionheiligtum*, Leiden, 1967.
Delitzsch, F., *The Hebrew Language in the Light of Assyrian Research*,
   London and Edinburgh, 1883.
Dhorme, P., 'Les Amorrhéens', *RB* 40 (1931), pp. 161–84.
Driver, G. R., *The Assyrian Laws*, Oxford, 1935 (with J. C. Miles);
   The Babylonian Laws, i, Oxford, 1952; ii, 1955 (with J. C.
   Miles); 'Ordeal by Oath at Nuzi', *Iraq* 7 (1940), pp. 132–8
   (with J. C. Miles); 'Misreadings in the Old Testament', *WO*
   1 (1947–52), pp. 234–8; 'Two Problems in the Old Testament
   Examined in the Light of Assyriology', *Syria* 33 (1956),
   pp. 70–8; 'Three Technical Terms in the Pentateuch', *JSS* 1

(1956), pp. 97–105; *Aramaic Documents of the Fifth Century B.C.*, Oxford, revised edn, 1957.

Driver, S. R., *A Critical and Exegetical Commentary on Deuteronomy, ICC*, Edinburgh, 1896²; *The Book of Genesis*, London, 1916¹⁰.

Edelman, D., 'Saul's Battle against Amaleq (1 Sam. 15)', *JSOT* 35 (1986), pp. 71–84.

Eissfeldt, O., *Erstlinge und Zehnten im Alten Testament*, Leipzig, 1917; 'Jahwe als König', *ZAW*, N.F., 5 (1928), pp. 81–105; *Hexateuch-Synopse: Die Erzählung der fünf Bücher Mose und des Buches Josua mit dem Anfange des Richterbuches*, 1962; *The Old Testament: An Introduction* (ET by P. R. Ackroyd), Oxford, 1966; 'Protektorat der Midianiter über Ihre Nachbarn im Letzten Viertel des 2. Jahrtausends V. Chr.', *JBL* 87 (1968), pp. 383–93; 'Renaming in the Old Testament', in *Words and Meanings: Essays Presented to David Winton Thomas* (ed. P. R. Ackroyd and B. Lindars), Cambridge, 1968, pp. 69–79.

Eitan, I., *A Contribution to Biblical Lexicography*, New York, 1924.

Elliger, K., *Leviticus, HAT* I/4, Tübingen, 1966.

Eltester, W., 'Der siebenarmige Leuchter und der Titusbogen', *Judentum Urchristentum Kirche* (J. Jeremias *Festschrift*), ed. W. Eltester, *BZNW* 26 (1964), pp. 62–76.

Esh, Sh., 'Variant Readings in Mediaeval Hebrew Commentaries', *Textus* 5 (1966), pp. 84–92.

Ewald, H., *The History of Israel*, ii (ET by R. Martineau), London, 1876³.

Fichtner, J., 'Die Etymologische Ätiologie in den Namengebungen der geschichtlichen Bücher des Alten Testaments', *VT* 6 (1956), pp. 372–96.

Finesinger, S. B., 'Musical Instruments in OT', *HUCA* 3 (1926), pp. 21–76; 'The Shofar', *HUCA* 8–9 (1931–2), pp. 193–228.

Fishbane, M., 'Accusations of Adultery: A Study of Law and Scribal Practice in Numbers 5:11–31', *HUCA* 45 (1974), pp. 25–45; 'Form and Reformulation of the Biblical Priestly Blessing', *JAOS* 103 (1983), pp. 115–21; *Biblical Interpretation in Ancient Israel*, Oxford, 1985.

Fisher, L. R., 'A New Ritual Calendar from Ugarit', *HTR* 63 (1970), pp. 485–501.

Fohrer, G., *Introduction to the Old Testament* (ET by D. Green), London, 1970.

Franken, H. J., 'Texts from the Persian Period from Tell Deir 'Allā', *VT* 17 (1967), pp. 480–1.

Freedman, D. N., 'Archaic Forms in Early Hebrew Poetry', *ZAW*, N.F., 31 (1960), pp. 101–7; 'The Aaronic Benediction (Numbers 6:24–26)', *No Famine in the Land* (J. L. McKenzie *Festschrift*), ed. J. W. Flanagan and A. W. Robinson, Missoula, Montana, 1975, pp. 35–48; 'Pottery, Poetry, and Prophecy: An Essay on Biblical Poetry', *JBL* 96 (1977), pp. 5–26; ' "Who is like thee among the gods?" The Religion of Early Israel', *Ancient Israelite Religion: Essays in Honor of Frank Moore Cross* (ed. P. D. Miller, P. D. Hanson and S. Dean McBride), Philadelphia, 1987, pp. 315–35.

Frick, F. S., *The City in Ancient Israel*, *SBLDS* 36, Missoula, Montana, 1977.

Fritz, V., 'Arad in der biblischen Überlieferung und in der Liste Schoschenks I.', *ZDPV* 82 (1966), pp. 331–42.

Frymer, T. S., 'Ordeal, Judicial', *IDBSup*, pp. 638–40.

Frymer-Kensky, T., 'The Strange Case of the Suspected Sotah (Numbers V 11–31)', *VT* 34 (1984), pp. 11–26.

Galil, G., 'The Sons of Judah and the Sons of Aaron in Biblical Historiography', *VT* 35 (1985), pp. 488–95.

Gardiner, A., *Egypt of the Pharaohs: An Introduction*, Oxford, 1961.

Gaster, T. H., 'Two Textual Emendations', *ExpT* 78 (1966–7), p. 267.

Gemser, B., 'Der Stern aus Jakob (Num 24:17)', *ZAW*, N. F., 2 (1925), pp. 301–2.

Geraty, L. T., 'Heshbon: The First Casualty in the Israelite Quest for the Kingdom of God', *The Quest for the Kingdom of God: Studies in Honor of George E. Mendenhall* (ed. H. B. Huffmon, F. A. Spina and A. R. W. Green), Indiana, 1983, pp. 239–48.

Gertner, M., 'The Masorah and the Levites: An Essay in the History of a Concept', *VT* 10 (1960), pp. 241–72.

Gevirtz, S., *Patterns in the Early Poetry of Israel*, Chicago, Illinois, 1963

Gilbert, M. (and Pisano, S.), 'Psalm 110 (109), 5–7', *Bib* 61 (1980), pp. 343–56.

Ginzberg, L., *The Legends of the Jews*, i–vii, Philadelphia, 1909–38.

Glueck, N., 'Explorations in Eastern Palestine, I', *AASOR* 14 (1933–4), pp. 1–114; 'Some Ancient Towns in the Plains of Moab', *BASOR* 91 (1943), pp. 7–26.

Golka, F. W., 'The Aetiologies in the Old Testament', *VT* 26 (1976), pp. 410–28; *VT* 27 (1977), pp. 36–47.

Goodenough, E. R., 'The Menorah among Jews of the Roman World', *HUCA* 23, pt. II (1950–1), pp. 449–92.

Gooding, D. W., 'On the Use of the LXX for Dating Midrashic Elements in the Targums', *JTS*, N.S., 25 (1974), pp. 1–11.

Gordon, C. H., 'Parallèles Nouziens aux lois et coutumes de l'Ancien Testament', *RB* 44 (1935), pp. 34–41.

Gordon, R. P., 'Compositeness, Conflation and the Pentateuch', *JSOT* 51 (1991), pp. 57–69.

Gottwald, N. K., *The Tribes of Yahweh: A Sociology of the Religion of Liberated Israel, 1250–1050 B.C.E.*, London, 1979.

Goudoever, J. van, *Biblical Calendars*, Leiden, 1961².

Gradwohl, R., 'Das "Fremde Feuer" von Nadab und Abihu', *ZAW*, N.F., 34 (1963), pp. 288–96.

Gray, G. B., *Studies in Hebrew Proper Names*, London, 1896. 'The Meaning of the Hebrew Word *degel*', *JQR* 11 (1898–9), pp. 92–101; 'The Nazirite', *JTS* 1 (1899–1900), pp. 201–11; *Sacrifice in the Old Testament: Its Theory and Practice*, Oxford, 1925.

Gray, J., 'The Desert Sojourn of the Hebrews and the Sinai-Horeb Tradition', *VT* 4 (1954), pp. 148–54.

Greenberg, M., 'The Biblical Conception of Asylum', *JBL* 78 (1959), pp. 125–32; 'Some Postulates of Biblical Criminal Law', *Yehezkel Kaufmann Jubilee Volume* (ed. M. Haran), Jerusalem, 1960, pp. 5–28; 'City of Refuge', *IDB*, i, 1962, pp. 638–9; 'Idealism and Practicality in Numbers 35:4–5 and Ezekiel 48', *JAOS* 88 (1968), pp. 59–66; 'More Reflections on Biblical Criminal Law', *ScrHier* 31 (1986), Jerusalem, pp. 1–17.

Grelot, P., 'La dernière étape de la rédaction sacerdotale', *VT* 6 (1956), pp. 174–89.

Gressmann, H., *Mose und seine Zeit. Ein Kommentar zu den Mose-Sagen*, Göttingen, 1913.

Gross, W., *Bileam: Literar- und Formkritische Untersuchung der Prosa in Num 22–24*, Munich, 1974.

Grossfeld, B., 'The Translation of Biblical Hebrew *pāqad* in the Targum, Peshitta, Vulgate and Septuagint', *ZAW* 96 (1984), pp. 83–101.

Gruber, M. I., 'The Many Faces of Hebrew *nj' pānîm*, "lift up the face"', *ZAW* 95 (1983), pp. 252–60.

Guillaume, A., 'A Note on Numbers xxiii 10', *VT* 12 (1962),
    pp. 335–7.
Gunn, D. M., 'The "Battle Report": Oral or Scribal Convention?',
    JBL 93 (1974), pp. 513–8.
Gunneweg, A. H. J., *Leviten und Priester*, *FRLANT* 89, Göttingen, 1965.
Haak, R. D., 'A Study and New Interpretation of *QṢR NPŠ*', *JBL*
    101 (1982), pp. 161–7.
Hackett, J. A., *The Balaam Text from Deir ʿAllā*, *HSM* 31, Chico,
    California, 1980; 'The Dialect of the Plaster Text from Tell
    Deir ʿAlla', *Or* 53 (1984), pp. 57–65; 'Some Observations on
    the Balaam Tradition at Deir ʿAllā', *BA* 49 (1986), pp. 216–
    22; 'Religious Traditions in Israelite Transjordan', *Ancient
    Israelite Religion: Essays in Honor of Frank Moore Cross* (ed. P. D.
    Miller, P. D. Hanson, and S. Dean McBride), Philadelphia,
    1987, pp. 125–36.
Halbe, J., 'Passa-Massot im deuteronomischen Festkalender',
    ZAW 87 (1975), pp. 147–68.
Hanson, H. E., 'Num. XVI 30 and the Meaning of *BĀRĀ*", *VT*
    22 (1972), pp. 353–9.
Hanson, P. D., 'The Song of Heshbon and David's *NÎR*', *HTR* 61
    (1968), pp. 297–320.
Haran, M., 'The Nature of the "ʾOhel Moʿedh" in Pentateuchal
    Sources', *JSS* 5 (1960), pp. 50–65; 'The Uses of Incense in
    the Ancient Israelite Ritual', *VT* 10 (1960), pp. 113–29; 'The
    Gibeonites, the Nethinim and the Sons of Solomon's Servants',
    VT 11 (1961), pp. 159–69; 'Studies in the Account of the
    Levitical Cities', *JBL* 80 (1961), pp. 45–54, 156–65; 'From
    Early to Classical Prophecy: Continuity and Change', *VT* 27
    (1977), pp. 385–97; *Temples and Temple Service in Ancient Israel*,
    Oxford, 1978.
Harrison, R. K., 'The Biblical Problem of Hyssop', *EvQ* 26 (1954),
    pp. 218–24.
Hauser, A. J., 'Israel's Conquest of Palestine: A Peasants'
    Rebellion?' *JSOT* 7 (1978), pp. 2–19.
Henke, O., 'Zur Lage von Beth Peor', *ZDPV* 75 (1959), pp. 155–63.
Hentschke, R., *Satzung und Setzender: Ein Beitrag zur israelitischen
    Rechtsterminologie*, *BWANT* V/3, Stuttgart, 1963.
Herrmann, S., *A History of Israel in Old Testament Times* (ET by
    J. Bowden), London, 1975.
Hertz, J. H., 'Numbers xxiii. 9*b*, 10', *ExpT* 45 (1933–4), p. 524.

Hoftijzer, J., 'The Prophet Balaam in a 6th Century Aramaic Inscription', *BA* 39 (1976), pp. 11–17; *Aramaic Texts from Deir 'Alla* (ed. with G. van der Kooij), Leiden, 1976; *The Balaam Text from Deir 'Alla Re-evaluated* (ed. with G. van der Kooij), Leiden, 1991.

Horst, F., 'Recht und Religion im Bereich des A.T.', *EvTh* 16 (1956), pp. 49–75.

Hort, G., 'The Death of Qorah', *ABR* 7 (1959), pp. 2–26.

van Houten, C., *The Alien in Israelite Law*, *JSOTS* 107, Sheffield, 1991.

Hulse, E. V., 'The Nature of Biblical "Leprosy" and the Use of Alternative Medical Terms in Modern Translations of the Bible', *PEQ* 107 (1975), pp. 87–105.

Humbert, P., 'Die literarische Zweiheit des Priester–Codex in der Genesis', *ZAW*, N.F., 17 (1940–1), pp. 30–57.

Hurvitz, A., 'The Usage of šeš and bûṣ in the Bible and its Implication for the Date of P', *HTR* 60 (1967), pp. 117–21; 'The Evidence of Language in Dating the Priestly Code', *RB* 81 (1974), pp. 24–56.

Irwin, W. A., 'Qrî' ê Ha-'edhah', *AJSL* 57 (1940), pp. 95–7.

Jackson, B. S., *Essays in Jewish and Comparative Legal History*, Leiden, 1975.

Jagersma, H., 'Some Remarks on the Jussive in Numbers 6, 24–26', *Von Kanaan bis Kerala (Fest. J. P. M. van der Ploeg)*, ed. W. C. Delsman et al., *AOAT*, Neukirchen-Vluyn, 1982, pp. 131–6.

Jaroš, K., *Die Stellung des Elohisten zur Kanaanäischen Religion, Orbis Biblicus et Orientalis* 4, Freiburg and Göttingen, 1974.

Jastrow, M., 'The "Nazir" Legislation', *JBL* 33 (1914), pp. 266–85.

Jenks, A. W., *The Elohist and North Israelite Traditions*, *SBLMS* 22, Missoula, Montana, 1977.

Jobling, D., *The Sense of Biblical Narrative*, *JSOTS* 7, Sheffield, 1978; 'The Jordan a Boundary: A Reading of Numbers 32 and Joshua 22', *Society of Biblical Literature, 1980 Seminar Papers* (ed. P. J. Achtemeier), Chico, California, 1980, pp. 183–207.

Johnson, A. R., '*māšāl*', *Wisdom in Israel and in the Ancient Near East* (ed. M. Noth and D. Winton Thomas), *VTS* 3, Leiden, 1955, pp. 162–9; *The One and the Many in the Israelite Conception of God*, Cardiff, 1961²; *The Cultic Prophet in Ancient Israel*, Cardiff, 1962²; *Sacral Kingship in Ancient Israel*, Cardiff, 1967.

Johnson, M. D., *The Purpose of the Biblical Genealogies*, SNTSMS 8, Cambridge, 1969.

Joines, K. R., 'Winged Serpents in Isaiah's Inaugural Vision', *JBL* 86 (1967), pp. 410–15; 'The Bronze Serpent in the Israelite Cult', *JBL* 87 (1968), pp. 245–56; *Serpent Symbolism in the Old Testament*, Haddonfield, New Jersey, 1974.

Jones, G. H., 'The Concept of Holy War', *WAI*, Cambridge, 1989, pp. 299–321.

Kallai, Z., 'The Wandering-Traditions from Kadesh-Barnea to Canaan: A Study in Biblical Historiography', *JJS* 33 (1982), pp. 175–84; 'The Southern Border of the Land of Israel – Pattern and Application', *VT* 37 (1987), pp. 438–45.

Kapelrud, A. S., 'How Tradition Failed Moses', *JBL* 76 (1957), p. 242.

Kaufman, S. A., 'The Aramaic Texts from Deir 'Allā', *BASOR* 239 (1980), pp. 71–4.

Kaufmann, Y., *The Biblical Account of the Conquest of Palestine* (ET by M. Dagut), Jerusalem, 1953.

Kellermann, D., 'Bemerkungen zum Sündopfergesetz in Num 15, 22ff.', *Wort und Geschichte. Festschrift für Karl Elliger zum 70 Geburtstag*, ed. H. Gese and H. P. Rüger, Neukirchen-Vluyn, 1973, pp. 107–14.

Kiuchi, N., *The Purification Offering in the Priestly Literature*, *JSOTS* 56, Sheffield, 1987.

Knierim, R., *Die Hauptbegriffe für Sünde im Alten Testament*, Gütersloh, 1965.

Kohata, F., 'Die priesterschriftliche Überlieferungsgeschichte von Numeri XX 1–13', *AJBI* 3 (1977), pp. 3–34.

König, E., 'Number', *HDB*, iii, pp. 560–67.

Kramer, S. N., 'Ur-Nammu Law Code', *Or*, N.S., 23 (1954), pp. 40–51.

Kraus, H. J., 'Zur Geschichte des Passah – Massot – Festes im AT', *EvTh* 18 (1958), pp. 47–67; *Worship in Israel* (ET by G. Buswell), Oxford, 1966.

Kselman, J. S., 'A Note on Numbers XII 6–8', *VT* 26 (1976), pp. 500–5.

Kuenen, A., *An Historico-Critical Inquiry into the Origin and Composition of the Hexateuch* (ET by P. H. Wicksteed), London, 1886.

Kuschke, A., 'Die Lagervorstellung der priesterschriftlichen Erzälung', *ZAW*, N.F., 22 (1951), pp. 74–105.

Kutsch, E., 'Erwägungen zur Geschichte der Passafeier und des Massotfestes', *ZTK* 55 (1958), pp. 1–35.

Laughlin, J. C. H., 'The "Strange Fire" of Nadab and Abihu', *JBL* 95 (1976), pp. 559–65.

Lee, J. A. L., 'Equivocal and Stereotyped Renderings in the LXX', *RB* 87 (1980), pp. 104–17.

Leggett, D. A., *The Levirate and Goel Institutions in the Old Testament*, Cherry Hill, New Jersey, 1974.

Lehmann, M. R., 'Biblical Oaths', *ZAW* 81 (1969), pp. 74–92.

Lehming, S., 'Versuch zu Num 16', *ZAW*, N.F., 33 (1962), pp. 291–321.

Leiman, S. Z., 'The Inverted *Nuns* at Numbers 10:35–36 and the Book of Eldad and Medad', *JBL* 93 (1974), pp. 348–55.

Lemaire, A., 'Galaad et Makîr', *VT* 31 (1981), pp. 39–61; 'Fragments from the Book of Balaam Found at Deir 'Alla', *BAR* 11 (1985), pp. 27–39.

Levine, B. A., 'The Netînîm', *JBL* 82 (1963), pp. 207–12; 'The Descriptive Tabernacle Texts of the Pentateuch', *JAOS* 85 (1965), pp. 307–18; 'Numbers. Book of', *IDBSup*, Abingdon, Nashville, 1976, pp. 631–5; 'More on the Inverted *Nuns* of Num. 10:35–36', *JBL* 95 (1976), pp. 122–4; 'The Deir 'Alla Plaster Inscriptions', *JAOS* 101 (1981), pp. 195–205; 'The Balaam Inscription from Deir 'Alla: Historical Aspects', *Biblical Archaeology Today: Proceedings of the International Congress on Biblical Archaeology, Jerusalem, April 1984*, Jerusalem, 1985, pp. 326–39.

L'Heureux, C. E., 'The *y'lîdê hārāpā'* – A Cultic Association of Warriors', *BASOR* 221 (1976), pp. 83–5.

Liebreich, L. J., 'The Songs of Ascents and the Priestly Blessing', *JBL* 74 (1955), pp. 33–6.

Liedke, G., *Gestalt und Bezeichnung alttestamentlicher Rechtssätze*, *WMANT* 39, 1971.

Limburg, J., 'The Root *rîḇ* and the Prophetic Lawsuit Speeches', *JBL* 88 (1969), pp. 291–304.

Lindblom, J., 'Lot-casting in the Old Testament', *VT* 12 (1962), pp. 164–78; *Prophecy in Ancient Israel*, Oxford, 1973[5].

Lipiński, E., ''Urīm and Tummīm', *VT* 20 (1970), pp. 495–6.

Liver, J., 'Korah, Dathan and Abiram', *Studies in the Bible* (ed. Ch. Rabin), *ScrHier* 8 (1961), Jerusalem, pp. 189–217.

Lods, A., *Israel: From its Beginnings to the Middle of the Eighth Century* (ET by S. H. Hooke), London, 1932.

Loewe, R., 'Divine Frustration Exegetically Frustrated – Numbers 14:34 *t^enū'ātî*', *Words and Meanings: Essays Presented to David Winton Thomas*, ed. P. R. Ackroyd and B. Lindars, Cambridge, 1968, pp. 137–58; 'Abraham Ibn Ezra on Numbers xiv:34', *JJS* 21 (1970), pp. 65–8.

Loewenstamm, S. E., 'The Death of the Upright and the World to Come', *JJS* 16 (1965), pp. 183–6.

Lohfink, N., 'Darstellungskunst und Theologie in Dtn 1,6–3,29', *Bib* 41 (1960), pp. 105–34; '*ḥāram*', *TDOT*, v, 1986, pp. 180–99.

Long, B. O., *The Problem of Etiological Narrative in the Old Testament*, *BZAW* 108, Berlin, 1968; 'The Effect of Divination upon Israelite Literature', *JBL* 92 (1973), pp. 489–97.

Loretz, O., 'Altorientalischer Hintergrund sowie Inner- und Nachbiblische Entwicklung des aaronitischen Segens (Num 6, 24–26)', *UF* 10 (1978), pp. 115–19.

Lust, J., 'Balaam, an Ammonite', *ETL* 54 (1978), pp. 60–1.

Maag, V., 'Malkût Jhwh', *VTS* 7 (Congress Volume, Oxford, 1959), Leiden, 1960, pp. 129–53.

Mace, D. R., *Hebrew Marriage. A Sociological Study*, London, 1953.

McCarter, P. Kyle, 'The Balaam Texts from Deir 'Allā: The First Combination', *BASOR* 239 (1980), pp. 49–60.

McCarthy, D. J., 'The Symbolism of Blood and Sacrifice', *JBL* 88 (1969), pp. 166–76; *Old Testament Covenant. A Survey of Current Opinions*, Oxford, 1972; 'Further Notes on the Symbolism of Blood and Sacrifice', *JBL* 92 (1973), pp. 205–10.

McConville, J. G., *Law and Theology in Deuteronomy*, *JSOTS* 33, Sheffield, 1984.

McEvenue, S. E., 'A Source-Critical Problem in Num 14, 26–38', *Bib* 50 (1969), pp. 453–65; *The Narrative Style of the Priestly Writer*, *AnBib* 50, Rome, 1971.

McKane, W., 'Poison, Trial by Ordeal and the Cup of Wrath', *VT* 30 (1980), pp. 474–92.

Mackay, C., 'The North Boundary of Palestine', *JTS* 35 (1934), pp. 22–40.

McKeating, H., 'The Development of the Law on Homicide in Ancient Israel', *VT* 25 (1975), pp. 46–68.

McKenzie, J. L., 'The Elders in the Old Testament', *Bib* 40 (1959), pp. 522–40.

Maclaurin, E. C. B., 'Anak/ ANAX', *VT* 15 (1965), pp. 468–74.

Magonet, J., 'The Korah Rebellion', *JSOT* 24 (1982), pp. 3–25.

Malamat, A., 'The Danite Migration and the Pan-Israelite Exodus-Conquest: A Biblical Narrative Pattern', *Bib* 51 (1970), pp. 1–16; "AMM L⁽ʿ⁾ḄĀḌĀḌ YIŠKŌN: A Report from Mari and an Oracle of Balaam', *JQR* 76 (1985), pp. 47–50.

Malina, B. J., *The Palestinian Manna Tradition*, Leiden, 1968.

Maneschg, H., *Die Erzählung von der ehernen Schlange (Num 21, 4–9) in der Auslegung der frühen jüdischen Literatur: Eine traditionsgeschichtliche Studie*, Frankfurt, 1981.

Mann, T. W., 'Theological Reflections on the Denial of Moses', *JBL* 98 (1979), pp. 481–94.

Margaliot, M., 'The Transgression of Moses and Aaron – Num. 20:1–13', *JQR* 74 (1983), pp. 196–228; 'Literary, Historical and Religious Aspects of the Balaam Narrative, Numbers 22–24', *Proceedings of the Tenth World Congress of Jewish Studies, Jerusalem, August 16–24, 1989*, Jerusalem, 1990, pp. 75–82.

Mauchline, J., 'The Balaam-Balak Songs and Saga', *Studia Semitica et Orientalia, ii. Presentation Volume to William Barron Stevenson* (ed. C. J. Mullo Weir), Glasgow, 1945, pp. 73–94; 'Gilead and Gilgal: Some Reflections on the Israelite Occupation of Palestine', *VT* 6 (1956), pp. 19–33.

May, H. G., 'The Relation of the Passover to the Festival of Unleavened Cakes', *JBL* 55 (1936), pp. 65–82.

Mayes, A. D. H., *Israel in the Period of the Judges*, SBT² 29, London, 1974; *Deuteronomy*, NCB, London, 1979.

Mazar, B., 'The Cities of the Priests and the Levites', *VTS* 7 (1959 Congress Volume, Oxford), Leiden, 1960, pp. 193–205; 'The Cities of the Territory of Dan', *IEJ* 10 (1960), pp. 65–77; 'The Sanctuary of Arad and the Family of Hobab the Kenite', *JNES* 24 (1965), pp. 297–303.

Meek, T. J., 'Some Emendations in the Old Testament', *JBL* 48 (1929), pp. 162–8.

Mendenhall, G. E., 'The Census Lists of Numbers 1 and 26', *JBL* 77 (1958), pp. 52–66; 'The Hebrew Conquest of Palestine', *BA* 25 (1962), pp. 66–87; *The Tenth Generation: The Origins of the Biblical Tradition*, London, 1973.

Mettinger, T. N. D., *Solomonic State Officials. A Study of the Civil Government Officials of the Israelite Monarchy*, CBOTS 5, Lund, 1971.

Meyer, E., 'Kritik der Berichte über die Eroberung Palästinas', ZAW 1
    (1881), pp. 117–46.
Meyers, C., 'Kadesh Barnea: Judah's Last Outpost', BA 39 (1976),
    pp. 148–51; The Tabernacle Menorah: A Synthetic Study of a
    Symbol from the Biblical Cult, ASOR 2, Missoula, Montana, 1976.
Milgrom, J., Studies in Levitical Terminology I, Berkeley, 1970; 'Sin-
    Offering or Purification-Offering?', VT 21 (1971), pp. 237–9;
    'The Alleged Wave-Offering in Israel and in the Ancient Near
    East', IEJ 22 (1972), pp. 33–8; 'Priestly Terminology and
    the Political and Social Structure of Pre-monarchic Israel',
    JQR 69 (1978), pp. 65–81; 'Korah's Rebellion: A Study in
    Redaction', De la Tôrah au Messie (Fest. H. Cazelles), ed. M.
    Carrez, Desclée, 1981, pp. 135–46; 'The Paradox of the Red
    Cow (Num. XIX)', VT 31 (1981), pp. 62–72; 'The Case of
    the Suspected Adulteress, Numbers 5:11–31: Redaction and
    Meaning', The Creation of Sacred Literature: Composition and
    Redaction of the Biblical Text, ed. R. E. Friedman, Berkeley, Los
    Angeles and London, 1981, pp. 69–75; 'The Levitic Town:
    An Exercise in Realistic Planning', JJS 33 (1982), pp. 185–8;
    'The Two Pericopes on the Purification Offering', The Word
    of the Lord shall go Forth, Festschrift D. N. Freedman, ed. C. L.
    Meyers and M. O'Connor, Winona Lake, Indiana, 1983,
    pp. 211–5; 'Magic, Monotheism and the Sin of Moses', The
    Quest for the Kingdom of God: Studies in Honor of George E.
    Mendenhall, ed. H. B. Huffmon, F. A. Spina and A. R. W.
    Green, Winona Lake, Indiana, 1983, pp. 251–65; 'On the
    Suspected Adulteress (Numbers V 11–31)', VT 35 (1985),
    pp. 368–9; 'The Chieftains' Gifts: Numbers, Chapter 7', HAR
    9 (1985), pp. 221–5; 'The Structures of Numbers: Chapters
    11–12 and 13–14 and their Redaction. Preliminary
    Gropings', Judaic Perspectives on Ancient Israel, ed. J. Neusner,
    B. A. Levine and E. S. Frerichs, Philadelphia, 1987, pp. 49–
    61; 'The Rebellion of Korah, Numbers 16–18: A Study in
    Tradition History', Society of Biblical Literature 1988 Seminar
    Papers (ed. D. J. Lull), Atlanta, Georgia, 1989, pp. 570–3.
Miller, J. M., 'The Israelite Occupation of Canaan', IJH, 1977,
    pp. 213–84; A History of Ancient Israel and Judah (with J. H.
    Hayes), London, 1986; 'The Israelite Journey through
    (around) Moab and Moabite Toponymy', JBL 108 (1989),
    pp. 577–95.

Miller, J. W., 'Depatriarchalizing God in Biblical Interpretation: A Critique', *CBQ* 48 (1986), pp. 609–16.

Miller, P. D., 'The Blessing of God: An Interpretation of Numbers 6:22–27', *Int* 29 (1975), pp. 240–51.

Mitchell, T. C., 'The Meaning of the Noun *ḤTN* in the Old Testament', *VT* 19 (1969), pp. 93–112.

Mittmann, S., 'Num 20, 14–21 – Eine redaktionelle Kompilation', *Wort und Geschichte. Festschrift für K. Elliger, AOAT* 18, Neukirchen-Vluyn, 1973, pp. 143–9. *Deuteronomium 1:1–6:3. Literarkritisch und Traditionsgeschichtlich Untersucht, BZAW* 139, Berlin and New York, 1975.

Möhlenbrink, K., 'Die levitischen Überlieferungen des Alten Testaments', *ZAW*, N.F., 11 (1934), pp. 184–231.

Moore, M. S., 'Jesus Christ: "Superstar" (Revelation xxii 16*b*)', *NovT* 24 (1982), pp. 82–91; *The Balaam Traditions: Their Character and Development, SBLDS* 113, Atlanta, Georgia, 1990.

Morgan, D. F., *The So-Called Cultic Calendars in the Pentateuch: A Morphological and Typological Study*, unpublished dissertation, Claremont, 1974.

Morgenstern, J., 'Trial by Ordeal among the Semites and in Ancient Israel', *HUCA* Jub. Vol. (1925), pp. 113–43; 'The Book of the Covenant, Part II', *HUCA* 7 (1930), pp. 19–258.

Mowinckel, S., 'Der Ursprung der Bil'āmsage', *ZAW*, N.F., 7 (1930), pp. 233–71; ' "Rahelstämme" und "Leastämme" ', *Von Ugarit nach Qumran* (O. Eissfeldt *Festschrift*), ed. J. Hempel and L. Rost, *BZAW* 77, Berlin, 1958, pp. 129–50; *He That Cometh* (ET by G. W. Anderson), Oxford, 1959.

Muffs, Y., *Studies in the Aramaic Legal Papyri from Elephantine*, Leiden, 1969.

Müller, H.-P., 'Einige alttestamentliche Probleme zur aramäischen Inschrift von *Dēr 'Allā*', *ZDPV* 94 (1978), pp. 56–67; 'Die aramäische Inschrift von Deir 'Allā und die älteren Bileamsprüche', *ZAW* 94 (1982), pp. 214–44.

Murtonen, A., 'The Use and Meaning of the Words *l^ebârek* and *b^erâkâh* in the Old Testament', *VT* 9 (1959), pp. 158–77.

Na'aman, N., ' "Hebron was built seven years before Zoan in Egypt" (Numbers XIII 22)', *VT* 31 (1981), pp. 488–92.

Naveh, J., 'The Date of the Deir 'Allā Inscription in Aramaic Script', *IEJ* 17 (1967), pp. 256–8.

Neufeld, E., *Ancient Hebrew Marriage Laws*, London, 1944.

Neve, Ll., *The Spirit of God in the Old Testament*, Tokyo, 1972.

Newing, E. G., 'The Rhetoric of Altercation in Numbers 14', *Perspectives on Language and Text* (F. I. Andersen *Festschrift*), ed. E. W. Conrad and E. G. Newing, Winona Lake, Indiana, 1987, pp. 211–28.

Nicolsky, N. M., 'Das Asylrecht in Israel', *ZAW*, N.F., 7 (1930), pp. 146–75.

Noack, B., 'The Day of Pentecost in Jubilees, Qumran, and Acts', *ASTI* 1 (1962), pp. 73–95.

North, F. S., 'Four-Month Seasons of the Hebrew Bible', *VT* 11 (1961), pp. 446–8.

North, R., *Sociology of the Biblical Jubilee*, AnBib 4, Rome, 1954.

Noth, M., *Die israelitischen Personennamen im Rahmen der gemeinsemitischen Namengebung*, BWANT III/10, Stuttgart, 1928; *Das System der Zwölf Stämme Israels*, BWANT IV/I, Stuttgart, 1930; 'Der Wallfahrtsweg zum Sinai (Nu 33)', *PJB* 36 (1940), pp. 5–28 (reprinted in *Aufsätze zur biblischen Landes- und Altertumskunde*, i, Neukirchen-Vluyn, 1971, pp. 55–74); 'Num. 21 als Glied der "Hexateuch" – Erzählung', *ZAW*, N.F., 17 (1940–1), pp. 161–89; 'Israelitische Stämme zwischen Ammon und Moab', *ZAW*, N.F. 19 (1944), pp. 11–57; *Das Buch Josua*, HAT I/7, Tübingen, 1953; *The History of Israel* (ET rev. by P. R. Ackroyd), London, 1960²; *Leviticus* (ET by J. E. Anderson), *OTL*, London, 1965; *Exodus* (ET by J. S. Bowden), *OTL*, London, 1966²; *A History of Pentateuchal Traditions* (ET by B. W. Anderson), Chico, California, 1981.

Oded, B., 'Jogbehah and Rujm el-Jebēha', *PEQ* 103 (1971), pp. 33–4.

Olávarri, E., 'Sondages à 'Arô'er sur l'Arnon', *RB* 72 (1965), pp. 77–94; 'Fouilles à 'Arô'er sur l'Arnon', *RB* 76 (1969), pp. 230–59; 'Aroer', *EAEHL*, i, ed. M. Avi-Yonah, 1975, pp. 98–100.

Olson, D. T., *The Death of the Old and the Birth of the New: The Framework of the Book of Numbers and the Pentateuch*, BJS 71, Chico, California, 1985.

Oppenheim, A. L., 'Idiomatic Accadian', *JAOS* 61 (1941), pp. 251–71.

Orlinsky, H. M., '*Ḥāṣēr* in the Old Testament', *JAOS* 59 (1939), pp. 22–37; 'Numbers XXVIII 9, 12, 13', *VT* 20 (1970), p. 500.

Ovadiah, A., 'The Relief of the Spies from Carthage', *IEJ* 24 (1974), pp. 210–3.

Pace, J. H., *The Caleb Traditions and the Role of the Calebites in the History of Israel*, unpublished doctoral dissertation submitted to the Faculty of the Graduate School of Emory University, 1976.

Paradise, J., 'A Daughter and her Father's Property at Nuzi', *JCS* 32 (1980), pp. 189–207.

Pardee, D., *'Mārîm* in Numbers V', *VT* 35 (1985), pp. 112–15.

Parker, S. B., 'Possession Trance and Prophecy in Pre-exilic Israel', *VT* 28 (1978), pp. 271–85; 'The Vow in Ugaritic and Israelite Narrative Literature', *UF* 11 (1979), pp. 693–700.

Parpola, S., *Neo-Assyrian Toponyms*, *AOAT* 6, Neukirchen-Vluyn, 1970.

Paul, Sh. M., *Studies in the Book of the Covenant in the Light of Cuneiform and Biblical Law*, Leiden, 1970.

Perlitt, L., 'Mose als Prophet', *EvTh* 31 (1971), pp. 588–608.

Péter, R., 'L'imposition des mains dans l'Ancien Testament', *VT* 27 (1977), pp. 48–55.

Phillips, A., 'The Case of the Woodgatherer Reconsidered', *VT* 19 (1969), pp. 125–8; *Ancient Israel's Criminal Law*, Oxford, 1970; *Deuteronomy*, Cambridge, 1973; 'Another Look at Murder', *JJS* 28 (1977), pp. 105–26.

Ploeg, J. van der, 'Les Anciens dans l'Ancien Testament', *Lex Tua Veritas* (H. Junker *Festschrift*), ed. H. Gross and F. Mussner, Trier, 1961, pp. 175–91.

Pope, M. H., 'Seven, Seventh, Seventy', *IDB*, iv, pp. 234–5.

Porter, J. R., 'The Role of Kadesh-barnea in the Narrative of the Exodus', *JTS* 44 (1943), pp. 139–43; 'The Background of Joshua III-V', *SEÅ* 36 (1971), pp. 5–23.

Polzin, R., *'HWQY* and Covenantal Institutions in Early Israel', *HTR* 62 (1969), pp. 227–40.

Press, R., 'Das Ordal im alten Israel', *ZAW*, N.F., 10 (1933), pp. 121–40, 227–55.

Propp, W. H., *Water in the Wilderness: A Biblical Motif and its Mythological Background*, HSSMS 40, Atlanta, Georgia, 1987; 'On Hebrew *śāde(h)*, "Highland"', *VT* 37 (1987), pp. 230–6; 'The Rod of Aaron and the Sin of Moses', *JBL* 107 (1988), pp. 19–26.

von Rad, G., 'Die falschen Propheten', *ZAW*, N.F., 10 (1933), pp. 109–20. *Die Priesterschrift im Hexateuch*, BWANT IV 13, Stuttgart and Berlin, 1934. *Old Testament Theology* (ET by

D. M. G. Stalker), 2 vols., Edinburgh, 1962; 'The Tent and the Ark', *The Problem of the Hexateuch and Other Essays* (ET by E. W. Trueman Dicken), London, 1966, pp. 103–24; *Deuteronomy* (ET by D. Barton), *OTL*, London, 1966.

Rainey, A. F., 'The Order of Sacrifices in Old Testament Ritual Texts', *Bib* 51 (1970), pp. 485–98.

Ramsey, G. W., *The Quest for the Historical Israel*, London, 1982.

Redford, D. B., 'Exodus I 11', *VT* 13 (1963), pp. 401–18.

Reif, S. C., 'What enraged Phinehas? – A Study of Numbers 25:8', *JBL* 90 (1971), pp. 200–6. 'Dedicated to ḥnk', *VT* 22 (1972), pp. 495–501.

Rendtorff, R., 'Zur Lage von Jaser', *ZDPV* 76 (1960), pp. 124–35; *Die Gesetze in der Priesterschrift*, Göttingen, 1963²; 'The "Yahwist" as Theologian? The Dilemma of Pentateuchal Criticism', *JSOT* 3 (1977), pp. 2–10; *The Old Testament: An Introduction* (ET by J. Bowden), London, 1985; *The Problem of the Process of Transmission in the Pentateuch* (ET by J. J. Scullion), *JSOTS* 89, Sheffield, 1990 .

Reviv, H., 'The Traditions concerning the Inception of the Legal System in Israel: Significance and Dating', *ZAW* 94 (1982), pp. 566–75.

Richter, G., 'Zwei alttestamentliche Studien', *ZAW* 39 (1921), pp. 123–37.

Richter, W., *Traditionsgeschichtliche Untersuchungen zum Richterbuch*, *BBB* 18, Bonn, 1963.

Ringgren, H., 'Gā'al', *TDOT*, ii, 1975, pp. 350–5.

Robertson, D. A., *Linguistic Evidence in Dating Early Hebrew Poetry*, *SBLDS* 3, Missoula, Montana, 1972.

Robertson, E., 'The 'Urīm and Tummīm; what were they?', *VT* 14 (1964), pp. 67–74.

Robinson, B. P., 'The Jealousy of Miriam: A Note on Num 12', *ZAW* 101 (1989), pp. 428–32.

Robinson, G., 'The Prohibition of Strange Fire in Ancient Israel', *VT* 28 (1978), pp. 301–17.

Rofé, A., *Spr Bl'm. The Book of Balaam (Numbers 22:2–24:25): A Study in Methods of Criticism and the History of Biblical Literature and Religion* (Heb.), *JBS* 1, Jerusalem, 1979.

Rogers, C., 'Moses: Meek or Miserable?', *JETS* 29 (1986), pp. 257–63.

Romanoff, P., *Jewish Symbols on Ancient Jewish Coins*, Philadelphia, 1944.

Rose, M., *Deuteronomist und Jahwist*, *AThANT* 67, Zürich, 1981.

Rost, L., 'Zu den Festopfervorschriften von Numeri 28 und 29', *TLZ* 83 (1958), pp. 330–4.

Rouillard, H., 'L'anesse de Balaam', *RB* 87 (1980), pp. 5–37, 211–41; *La Péricope de Balaam (Nombres 22–24)*, Paris, 1985.

Rowley, H. H., 'Zadok and Nehushtan', *JBL* 58 (1939), pp. 113–41; *From Joseph to Joshua: Biblical Traditions in the Light of Archaeology*, London, 1950.

Rüger, H. P., 'Some Remarks on the Priestly Blessing', *BT* 28 (1977), pp. 332–5.

Runnalls, D., 'Moses' Ethiopian Campaign', *JSJ* 14 (1983), pp. 135–56.

Russell, D. S., *The Method and Message of Jewish Apocalyptic*, London, 1964.

Safren, J. D., 'Balaam and Abraham', *VT* 38 (1988), pp. 105–13.

Sakenfeld, K. D., 'The Problem of Divine Forgiveness in Numbers 14', *CBQ* 37 (1975), pp. 317–30; 'Theological and Redactional Problems in Numbers 20:2–13', *Understanding the Word: Essays in Honor of Bernhard W. Anderson* (ed. J. T. Butler, E. W. Conrad, and B. C. Ollenburger), *JSOTS* 37, Sheffield, 1985, pp. 133–54; 'In the Wilderness, Awaiting the Land: The Daughters of Zelophehad and Feminist Interpretation', *PSB* 9 (1988), pp. 179–96.

Sandys-Wunsch, J., *The Purpose of the Book of Numbers in Relation to the Rest of the Pentateuch and Post-Exilic Judaism*, unpublished doctoral dissertation, Oxford, 1961.

Sansom, M. C., 'Laying on of Hands in the Old Testament', *ExpT* 94 (1982–3), pp. 323–6.

Sasson, J. M., 'Numbers 5 and the "Waters of Judgement"', *BZ* 16 (1972), pp. 249–51; 'A Genealogical Convention in Biblical Chronography?', *ZAW* 90 (1978), pp. 171–85.

Sasson, V., 'The Meaning of *whsbt* in the Arad Inscription', *ZAW* 94 (1982), pp. 105–11.

Sawyer, J. F. A., 'A Note on the Etymology of Ṣāra'at', *VT* 26 (1976), pp. 241–5.

Sayce, A. H., 'Recent Biblical Archaeology', *ExpT* 13 (1901–2), pp. 64–6; 'Who was Balaam?', *ExpT* 15 (1903–4), pp. 405–6.

Scharbert, J., '"Fluchen" und "Segnen" im Alten Testament', *Bib*

39 (1958), pp. 1–26; *Heilsmittler im Alten Testament und im Alten Orient*, Freiburg, 1964.

Schenker, A., '*kōper* et expiation', *Bib* 63 (1982), pp. 32–46.

Scheiber, A., 'Ihr sollt kein bein Dran zerbrechen', *VT* 13 (1963), pp. 95–7.

Schmitt, H. C., *Die nichtpriesterliche Josephsgeschichte: Ein Beitrage zur neuesten Pentateuchkritik*, *BZAW* 154, Berlin, 1980.

Scott, R. B. Y., 'Weights and Measures of the Bible', *BA* 22 (1959), pp. 22–40; 'Weights, Measures, Money and Time', *NPC*, pp. 37–41.

Seale, M. S., 'Numbers xiii 32', *ExpT* 68 (1956–7), p. 28.

Seebass, H., 'Zu Num. X 33f.', *VT* 14 (1964), pp. 111–3; 'Num XI, XII und die Hypothese des Jahwisten', *VT* 28 (1978), pp. 214–23; 'Machir im Ostjordanland', *VT* 32 (1982), pp. 496–503.

Segal, J. B., 'The Hebrew Festivals and the Calendar', *JSS* 6 (1961), pp. 74–94; *The Hebrew Passover*, Oxford, 1963.

Segal, M. H., 'The Settlement of Manasseh East of the Jordan', *PEFQS* 50 (1918), pp. 124–31.

van Seters, J., *The Hyksos: A New Investigation*, New Haven and London, 1966; 'The Terms "Amorite" and "Hittite" in the Old Testament', *VT* 22 (1972), pp. 64–81; 'The Conquest of Sihon's Kingdom: A Literary Examination', *JBL* 91 (1972), pp. 182–97; *Abraham in History and Tradition*, New Haven and London, 1975; 'Oral Patterns or Literary Conventions in Biblical Narrative', *Semeia* 5 (1976), pp. 139–54; 'Once Again – The Conquest of Sihon's Kingdom', *JBL* 99 (1980), pp. 117–9.

Seybold, K., *Der aaronitische Segen: Studien zu Numeri 6, 22–27*, Neukirchen, 1977.

Shinan, A., 'Moses and the Ethiopian Woman', *Studies in Hebrew Narrative Art* (ed. J. Heinemann and S. Werses), *ScrHier* 27, Jerusalem, 1978, pp. 66–78.

Simons, J., *The Geographical and Topographical Texts of the Old Testament*, Leiden, 1959.

Simpson, C. A., *The Early Traditions of Israel: A Critical Analysis of the Pre-deuteronomic Narrative of the Hexateuch*, Oxford, 1948.

Skaist, A., 'Inheritance Laws and their Social Background', *JAOS* 95 (1975), pp. 242–7.

Smelik, K. A. D., *Writings from Ancient Israel* (ET by G. I. Davies), Edinburgh, 1991.

Smick, E. B., 'A Study of the Structure of the Third Balaam Oracle', *The Law and the Prophets: Old Testament Studies Prepared in Honor of Oswald Thompson Allis* (ed. J. H. Skilton), Nutley, New Jersey, 1974, pp. 242–52.

Smith, H. P., 'Notes on the Red Heifer', *JBL* 27 (1908), pp. 153–6.

Smith, W. R., *Lectures on the Religion of the Semites*, London, 1927³.

Snaith, N. H., 'The Meaning of "The Paraclete"', *ExpT* 57 (1945–6), pp. 47–50; 'Sacrifices in the Old Testament', *VT* 7 (1957), pp. 308–17; 'The Wave Offering', *ExpT* 74 (1962–3), p. 127; 'Genesis XXXI 50', *VT* 14 (1964), p. 373; 'The Sin-Offering and the Guilt-Offering', *VT* 15 (1965), pp. 73–80; 'The Daughters of Zelophehad', *VT* 16 (1966), pp. 124–7; 'Numbers XXVIII 9, 11, 13 in the Ancient Versions', *VT* 19 (1969), p. 374. 'A Note on Numbers XVIII 9', *VT* 23 (1973), pp. 373–5.

Snijders, L. A., 'The Meaning of *zār* in the Old Testament: An Exegetical Study', *OTS* 10 (1954), pp. 1–154.

Soggin, J. A., 'The Davidic-Solomonic Kingdom', *IJH*, pp. 332–80.

Speiser, E. A., 'Census and Ritual Expiation in Mari and Israel', *BASOR* 149 (1958), pp. 17–25; 'An Angelic "Curse": Exodus 14:20', *JAOS* 80 (1960), pp. 198–200; 'Unrecognized Dedication', *IEJ* 13 (1963), pp. 69–73; 'Background and Function of the Biblical Nāśī', *CBQ* 25 (1963), pp. 111–7.

Spencer, J. R., *The Levitical Cities: A Study of the Role and Function of the Levites in the History of Israel*, unpublished PhD dissertation, Chicago, Illinois, 1980.

Stade, B., 'Beiträge zur Pentateuchkritik', *ZAW* 15 (1895), pp. 157–78.

Stephens, F. J., 'The Ancient Significance of Ṣîṣîth', *JBL* 50 (1931), pp. 59–70.

Sumner, W. A., 'Israel's Encounters with Edom, Moab, Ammon, Sihon, and Og according to the Deuteronomist', *VT* 18 (1968), pp. 216–28.

Sutcliffe, E. F., 'A Note on Num 22', *Bib* 18 (1937), pp. 439–42.

Temerev, A., 'Social Organizations in Egyptian Military Settlements of the Sixth-Fourth Centuries B.C.E.: *dgl* and *m't*', *The Word of the Lord Shall go Forth* (D. N. Freedman

Festschrift), *ASOR* (ed. C. L. Meyers and M. O'Connor),
Winona Lake, Indiana, 1983, pp. 523–5.

Thom, A., 'Balaam's Prayer', *ExpT* 16 (1904–5), p. 334.

Thomas, D. Winton, 'The Word *rôḇaʿ* in Numbers xxiii. 10', *ExpT*
46 (1934–5), p. 285; 'Some Further Remarks on Unusual Ways
of Expressing the Superlative in Hebrew', *VT* 18 (1968),
pp. 120–4.

Thompson, R. J., *Moses and the Law in a Century of Criticism since
Graf*, *VTS* 19, Leiden, 1970.

Toombs, L. E., 'Scepter', *IDB*, iv, pp. 234–5.

Toorn, K. van der, 'Did Jeremiah see Aaron's Staff?', *JSOT* 43
(1989), pp. 83–94.

Tosato, A., 'The Literary Structure of the First Two Poems of
Balaam (Num. xxiii 7–10, 18–24)', *VT* 29 (1979), pp. 98–106.

Tov, E., 'Some Sequence Differences between the MT and LXX and
their Ramifications for the Literary Criticism of the Bible',
JNWSL 13 (1987), pp. 151–60.

Trible, P., 'Depatriarchalizing in Biblical Interpretation', *JAAR*
41 (1973), pp. 30–48; 'God, Nature of, in the OT', *IDBSup*,
1976, pp. 368–9.

Tucker, G. M., 'Covenant Forms and Contract Forms', *VT* 15
(1965), pp. 487–503.

Tur-Sinai, N. H., 'Was there an Ancient Book of the Wars of the
Lord?' (Heb.), *BIES* 24 (1959–60), pp. 146–8.

Tushingham, A. D., 'Excavations at Dibon in Moab, 1952–53',
BASOR 133 (1954), pp. 6–26; *The Excavations at Dibon (Dhībân)
in Moab: The Third Campaign 1952–53*, *AASOR* 40, 1972.

Uphill, E. P., 'Pithom and Raamses: Their Location and
Significance', *JNES* 27 (1968), pp. 291–316; 28 (1969), pp. 15–
39.

Valentin, H., *Aaron: Eine Studie zur vor-priesterschriftlichen Aaron-
Überlieferung*, Göttingen, 1978.

Vaughan, P. H., *The Meaning of 'bama' in the Old Testament. A Study
of Etymological, Textual and Archaeological Evidence*, Cambridge,
1974.

de Vaux, R., *Studies in Old Testament Sacrifice*, Cardiff, 1964; 'Notes
d'Histoire et de Topographie Transjordaniennes', *Vivre et
Penser* 1 (1941), pp. 16–47 (= *Bible et Orient*, Paris, 1967,
pp. 115–49); 'Le pays de Canaan', *JAOS* 88 (1968), pp. 23–
30; 'The Settlement of the Israelites in Southern Palestine

and the Origins of the Tribe of Judah', *Translating and Understanding the Old Testament: Essays in Honor of H. G. May*, ed. H. T. Frank and W. L. Reed, New York and Nashville, 1970, pp. 108–34; *The Early History of Israel* (ET by D. Smith), 2 vols, London, 1978.

Vermes, G., *Scripture and Tradition in Judaism*, Leiden, 1961; *The Dead Sea Scrolls in English*, Harmondsworth, 1962.

Vetter, D., *Seherspruch und Segensschilderung*, Calwer Theologische Monographien 4, Stuttgart, 1974.

Victor, P., 'A Note on *ḥôq* in the Old Testament', *VT* 16 (1966), pp. 358–61.

Vink, J. G., 'The Date and Origin of the Priestly Code in the Old Testament', *The Priestly Code and Seven Other Studies*, ed. P. A. H. de Boer (*OTS* 15), Leiden, 1969, pp. 1–144.

Vörlander, H., *Die Entstehungszeit des jehowistischen Geschichtswerkes*, Frankfurt, 1978.

de Vries, S. J., 'The Origin of the Murmuring Tradition', *JBL* 87 (1968), pp. 51–8.

Wagner, N., 'Pentateuchal Criticism: No Clear Future', *CJT* 13 (1967), pp. 225–32; 'Abraham and David?', *Studies on the Ancient Palestinian World*, ed. J. W. Wevers and D. B. Redford, Toronto, 1972, pp. 117–40.

Wagner, S., 'Die Kundschaftergeschichten im Alten Testament', *ZAW*, N.F., 35 (1964), pp. 255–69.

Wallis, G., 'Hand Füllen', *Henoch* 3 (1981), pp. 340–7.

Walsh, J. T., 'From Egypt to Moab: A Source Critical Analysis of the Wilderness Itinerary', *CBQ* 39 (1977), pp. 20–33.

de Ward, E. F., 'Superstition and Judgment: Archaic Methods of Finding a Verdict', *ZAW* 89 (1977), pp. 1–19.

Wefing, S., 'Beobachtungen zum Ritual mit der roten Kuh (Num 19:1–10a)', *ZAW* 93 (1981), pp. 341–64.

Weingreen, J., 'The Case of the Woodgatherer (Numbers XV 32–36)', *VT* 16 (1966), pp. 361–4; 'The Case of the Daughters of Zelophchad', *VT* 16 (1966), pp. 518–22.

Weippert, H., 'Das geographische System der Stämme Israels', *VT* 23 (1973), pp. 76–89; 'Canaan, Conquest and Settlement of', *IDBSup*, pp. 125–30; 'Die "Bileam" – Inschrift von Tell Deir 'Allā', *ZDPV* 97 (1981), pp. 77–103 (with M. Weippert).

Weippert, M., 'Erwägungen zur Etymologie des Gottesnamens 'Ēl
    Šaddaj', *ZDMG*, N.F., 36 (1961), pp. 42–62.
Weisman, Z., 'The Nature and Background of *bāḥūr* in the Old
    Testament', *VT* 31 (1981), pp. 441–50; 'The Personal Spirit as
    Imparting Authority', *ZAW* 93 (1981), pp. 225–34.
Wenham, G. J., 'Aaron's Rod (Numbers 17, 16–28)', *ZAW* 93
    (1981), pp. 280–1.
Wellhausen, J., *Prolegomena to the History of Israel* (ET by J. S. Black
    and A. Menzies), Edinburgh, 1885; *Die Composition des Hexateuchs
    und der historischen Bücher des Alten Testaments*, Berlin, 1889.
Westbrook, R., *Property and the Family in Biblical Law*, *JSOTS* 113,
    Sheffield, 1991.
Wharton, J. A., 'The Command to Bless: An Exposition of Numbers
    22:41–23:25', *Int* 13 (1959), pp. 37–48.
White, M., 'The Elohistic Depiction of Aaron: A Study in the Levite-
    Zadokite Controversy', *Studies in the Pentateuch*, ed. J. A. Emerton,
    VTS 41, Leiden, 1990, pp. 149–59.
Whitelam, K. W., *The Just King*, *JSOTS* 12, Sheffield, 1979.
Wifall, W., 'Asshur and Eber, or Asher and Ḥeber?', *ZAW* 82 (1970),
    pp. 110–4.
Wilkinson, J., 'Leprosy and Leviticus: A Problem of Semantics and
    Translation', *SJT* 31 (1978), pp. 153–66.
Wilson, R. R., 'Early Israelite Prophecy', *Int* 32 (1978), pp. 3–16;
    'Prophecy and Ecstasy: A Reexamination', *JBL* 98 (1979),
    pp. 321–37.
Winnett, F. V., 'Excavations at Dibon in Moab, 1950–51', *BASOR*
    125 (1952), pp. 7–20; 'Re-examining the Foundations', *JBL*
    84 (1965), pp. 1–19.
Wolff, H. W., *Anthropology of the Old Testament* (ET by M. Kohl),
    London, 1981².
Wolters, A., 'The Balaamites of Deir 'Alla as Aramean Deportees',
    HUCA 59 (1988), pp. 101–13.
Wright, D. P., 'Purification from Corpse-contamination in Numbers
    XXXI 19–24', *VT* 35 (1985), pp. 213–23.
Wright, G. E., *The Old Testament against its Environment*, *SBT* 2,
    London, 1950; 'The Lawsuit of God: A Form-Critical Study of
    Deuteronomy 32', *Israel's Prophetic Heritage: Essays in Honor of
    James Muilenberg* (ed. B. W. Anderson and W. Harrelson),
    London, 1962, pp. 26–67.

Wüst, M., *Untersuchungen zu den siedlungsgeographischen Texten des Alten Testaments I. Ostjordanland*, Wiesbaden, 1975.

Yadin, Y., *The Scroll of the War of the Sons of Light against the Sons of Darkness* (ET by B and Ch. Rabin), Oxford, 1962; *The Art of Warfare in Biblical Lands* (ET by M. Pearlman), London, 1963.

Yahuda, A. S., 'The Name of Balaam's Homeland', *JBL* 64 (1945), pp. 547–51.

Yardeni, A., 'Remarks on the Priestly Blessing on Two Ancient Amulets from Jerusalem', *VT* 41 (1991), pp. 176–85.

Zimmerli, W., and Jeremias, J., *The Servant of God*, SBT 20, London, 1957.

Zobel, H.-J., '*ḥesed*', *TDOT*, v, Grand Rapids, Michigan, 1986, pp. 44–64.

Zuber, B., 'Der Wallfahrtsweg zum Sinai', *Vier Studien zu den Ursprüngen Israels*, Orbis Biblicus et Orientalis 9, Freiburg, 1976, pp. 62–72.

Zuckschwerdt, E., 'Zur literarischen Vorgeschichte des priesterlichen Nazir-Gesetzes', *ZAW* 88 (1976), pp. 191–205.

Zvi, E. Ben, 'The List of the Levitical Cities', *JSOT* 54 (1992), pp. 77–106.

INTRODUCTION

to

Numbers

A. TITLE

The fourth book of the Pentateuch, Numbers, derives its name from
the title given to it in the LXX ('*Arithmoi*); the Greek name was
rendered *Numeri* in Jerome's Latin Vulgate, and 'Numbers' was
adopted as a title for the book in all subsequent English translations.
This title was obviously given to it on account of the many numbers
and numerical lists which it contains, such as the census of the
Israelite tribes (1:20ff.; 26:5ff.), the census of the various Levitical
groups (3:21ff.; 26:57ff.), the list of gifts (with precise amounts)
brought by the tribal leaders for the dedication of the altar (7:12ff.),
and the list of offerings (again, with exact amounts) to be brought
on the feast days and festivals throughout the year (28f.). However,
since this material constitutes only a relatively small portion of the
book, the name 'Numbers' can hardly be regarded as a particularly
appropriate title for the work as a whole. On the other hand, the
Heb. title, *bammidbār* ('in the wilderness'), taken from the fourth
word of the first verse, is a far more accurate reflection of the nature
of its contents, for the primary concern of the book is with the years
spent by the Israelite tribes 'in the wilderness', as they journeyed
from Sinai to the plains of Moab.

B. SOURCES

The traditional literary source criticism of the Pentateuch has been
the subject of much scholarly discussion and debate in recent years,
especially since the publication in 1977 of R. Rendtorff's seminal
work, *Das überlieferungsgeschichtliche Problem des Pentateuch* (= *The Problem of the Process of Transmission in the Pentateuch*). Disquiet concerning
the criteria traditionally employed to determine the various literary
strands had already been expressed by Martin Noth in his *Überlieferungsgeschichte des Pentateuch*, which was published in 1948 (=
Pentateuchal Traditions). Noth was generally opposed to the excessive
fragmentation of the individual narratives in order to distinguish
between the J and E strands of the Tetrateuch, and he argued that
the only criterion which could confidently be used to demonstrate
the presence of both these sources was the occurrence of doublets.
Despite his misgivings, however, Noth steadfastly adhered to the
Documentary Hypothesis associated with the name of Wellhausen,
although he went far beyond the literary-critical analysis of the

Tetrateuch by attempting to trace the growth of the present narrative tradition through the long course of its history. Noth concluded that the material contained in the Tetrateuch consisted originally of short, narrative units, which subsequently developed into larger complexes, and which eventually coalesced into five major themes, which he identified as the promise to the patriarchs, the deliverance from Egypt, the revelation at Sinai, the sojourn in the wilderness, and the occupation of the land. According to Noth, these five themes initially existed independently of one another, but, by the time of the Yahwist, they had been combined and embellished by means of a variety of local traditions; thus, the basic shape of the Tetrateuch was formed at a comparatively early period in Israel's history.

The work of Rendtorff, in many respects, carries the ideas of Noth to their logical conclusion. Rendtorff observed that most scholars since Noth had accepted the validity of both the standard source criticism of the Pentateuch (albeit in some modified form) and the traditio-historical approach; however, his own research led him to the conclusion that the two methods were fundamentally incompatible (cf. *JSOT* 3 [1977], pp. 2–10). Rendtorff argued that the Documentary Hypothesis was essentially flawed, and he believed that the only solution to the problem of the composition of the Pentateuch was to be found in the traditio-historical approach. This meant, of course, that the entire thesis associated with the name of Wellhausen had to be abandoned. According to Rendtorff, the Pentateuch developed over a long period of time, and its growth could best be explained on the assumption that several blocks of tradition had originally existed as more or less self-contained entities. These blocks of tradition coincided to some extent with Noth's five principal themes, viz., the primeval history, the patriarchal stories, the exodus narrative, the Sinai narrative, the sojourn in the wilderness, and the entry into the land. That these larger units once had an independent existence of their own was evident from the fact that no substantive connection could be posited between the various blocks of tradition.

For example, Gen. 1–11 had a literary character quite distinct from Gen. 12–50, and the two sections had no intrinsic connection with one another; similarly, the promise of land, progeny, blessing and guidance in the patriarchal stories hardly figured at all in the narratives contained in Exodus and Numbers (or, at least, not in the passages traditionally ascribed to one of the older sources). Rendtorff maintained that this lack of continuity was incompatible with the notion that individual sources could be traced from Genesis to Numbers; thus, he was led to the inevitable conclusion that there never was a 'Yahwist' in the sense in which the term was used by Wellhausen and his followers, and that all attempts (such as those made by von Rad) to expound the 'theology' of the individual sources were futile. The challenge which faced *OT* scholars, according to Rendtorff, was to free themselves from the shackles of the traditional documentary analysis, and confine their attention to the large, independent complexes of tradition that can be discerned in the Pentateuch. He believed that the joining together of these complexes of tradition was primarily the work of the Deuteronomic or Deuteronomistic redactor, and this task was achieved by introducing the promise to the patriarchs into the other traditions by means of strategically placed cross-references (e.g., Gen. 50:24; Exod. 33:1–3). Rendtorff also accepted a post-exilic Priestly editorial strand which, in the patriarchal stories in Genesis, could be discerned in a small group of 'theological' texts (e.g., Gen. 27:46–28:5; 35:9–13) and in a series of chronological notices (e.g., Gen. 47:9, 28).

Rendtorff has undoubtedly made a significant contribution to a difficult and contentious area of *OT* scholarship, but it is questionable whether he has succeeded in breaking the mould of traditional Pentateuchal criticism. In the first place, doubts must be raised concerning his view that the 'larger units' of the Pentateuch were originally independent, self-contained entities, which had little or no connection with each other. While there may be a clear distinction between the primeval history in Gen. 1–11 and the patriarchal stories in Gen. 12–50, the distinction between the other complexes of tradition is by no means so clear-cut. Thus, e.g., the murmuring traditions (which form a part of the 'wilderness' complex) contain references to the time spent by the Israelites in Egypt (which forms part of the 'exodus' complex; cf. 11:5, 18, 20; 14:2–4; 20:5); similarly, the narrative of Israel's encounter with Edom in 20:14ff. contains a historical reminiscence of the descent into Egypt, the oppression suffered in captivity, and the subsequent exodus of the people (20:14–16). Moreover, much of Rendtorff's case rests on the assumption that the short passages which connect the longer units together can be shown to be Deuteronom(ist)ic in character, but the fact is that the references to the patriarchal promise of land in such passages as 10:29; 14:23 probably belong to the oldest levels of tradition and do not represent the work of later redactors. If some of these connecting elements can be demonstrated to be pre-exilic in origin, then it seems entirely reasonable to postulate a Yahwistic framework for the various complexes of tradition.

Indeed, it must be regarded as questionable whether these larger complexes of tradition could have survived in splendid isolation for so long prior to the Deuteronom(ist)ic redaction without some kind of framework to hold them together. The exodus story would, from the outset, have demanded an explanation of how the Israelites had come to be in Egypt, and an account of their subsequent fortunes as they wandered through the wilderness. It is therefore not surprising that elements of interdependency should exist between the exodus, wilderness and occupation stories, and it is quite feasible that these formed a connected narrative at a relatively early date – at any rate, earlier than Deuteronomy. Exigencies of space preclude a more detailed discussion of Rendtorff's contribution, but it is clear that his thesis raises questions which have yet to be answered satisfactorily. There are, admittedly, deficiencies and weaknesses in various aspects of the traditional source critical analysis of the Pentateuch, but it seems prudent, for the time being, to retain it as a working hypothesis, and to admit that, despite its limitations, it still provides the most plausible explanation for the way in which the Pentateuch developed into its present form.

I. THE PRIESTLY SOURCE

It has been estimated that over three-quarters of the material in Numbers derives from the Priestly source (cf. Gray, p. xxxiii). The term 'Priestly' (= P) is particularly apposite to describe this strand of tradition, for it exhibits an intense interest in cultic and ritual institutions and in the rules and regulations governing the activities of the priests and Levites. This interest in cultic matters is one of the features that distinguishes this source from the other sources of the Pentateuch, but P's individuality is also apparent from its stereotyped and repetitive language, its measured, prosaic style, and its distinctive theological outlook. But while P represents a distinct tradition within the Pentateuch, it is by no means a literary unity, for it is marked by too many repetitions and contradictions for it to be considered as a unified, homogeneous composition. Von Rad (*Priesterschrift*), on the basis of a detailed examination of the structure of P, concluded that the material should be dissected into two separate, parallel strands, which he labelled P^a and P^b, but the basis of this approach was criticized by Humbert (*ZAW*, N.F., 17 [1940–1], pp. 30ff.), and the hypothesis won few supporters and was later abandoned by von Rad himself. It has now become customary to explain the duplications and discrepancies within P on the assumption that a basic P source (= P^g, from the German *Grundschrift*) has subsequently received a series of supplementary additions (= P^s), which were appended at various times until the final redaction of the Pentateuch was complete. These additions are couched in a style similar to P^g, but they often betray a distinctive slant of their own. The amount of P^s material in Numbers is quite considerable, and, according to Gray (p. xxxviii), consists of 7:1ff.; 8:1–4, 5–22; 9:1–14, 15–23; 10:12–28; 16:8–11, 16f., 36–40; 26:1ff.; 28–31; 35:1–8; 36:1ff.

On grounds of vocabulary alone it is not always easy to distinguish between P^g and P^s, and it must be conceded that the divisions often proposed by scholars involve a considerable degree of subjective judgment. Indeed, the line of demarcation is often so finely balanced that one recent commentator on Numbers has rejected the traditional distinction, preferring instead to think in terms of one Priestly author who provided the book of Numbers with a distinctive theological structure (cf. Budd, p. xxii). In the present commentary the P^g/P^s distinction will be retained, at least to some extent, for this provides the most plausible explanation of some of the contradictory elements within the Priestly material (e.g., the age of Levitical service in 4:3, 23, 30 and 8:23–26); on the other hand, in many passages the line of demarcation between P^g and P^s is by no means clear, and the symbol P will be used to indicate the fact that the material is clearly Priestly, but that it is uncertain to which strata of the tradition the material belongs.

It seems most probable that P originated in Babylon during the early post-exilic period. The view advanced by Kaufmann (*Conquest*, pp. 175ff.), namely, that P ante-dates Deuteronomy and that it belongs to the late pre-exilic period, has gained few adherents, and the linguistic arguments marshalled by Hurvitz (*HTR* 60 [1967], pp. 117ff.; *RB* 81 [1974], pp. 24ff.) for a pre-exilic date have generally been regarded as unconvincing (cf. Thompson, *Moses*, pp. 126, n. 3, 164). It is true, as Kaufmann pointed out, that P may well contain much early material, but the presence of such material does not prove anything concerning the date of the final redaction of the source. Indeed, scholars who date P in the exilic or post-exilic period, readily acknowledge that many of the traditions contained in this source have a long and complex pre-history, the origin of which may well be traced to pre-exilic times.

The use of the term 'source' in connection with P requires some justification, for some scholars have argued that P should be viewed not as a distinct narrative source but, rather, as a stage in the redaction of an existing narrative corpus. F. M. Cross (*Canaanite Myth*, pp. 293ff.), e.g., argued that P assumed a prior knowledge of JE and functioned in a redactional role to frame and systematise the JE material. In a similar vein, Rendtorff (*Transmission*, pp. 156ff.) maintained that P was not a continuous strand within the Pentateuch but consisted of isolated theological passages which basically served to join together various complexes of tradition. The probability is, however, that P consists both of indigenous Priestly material and a revision of earlier traditions, i.e., P was both an independent source and served a redactional role, and the two alternatives need not be regarded as mutually exclusive. P certainly appears at times to interpret earlier tradition, but the Priestly texts are also intelligible in themselves (despite their varying degree of fullness) and they do exhibit a certain logical coherence and continuity.

II. NON-PRIESTLY MATERIAL

The amount of non-Priestly material in Numbers is fairly small, and is found most clearly in 10:29–12:15; 20:14–21; 21:12–32; 22:2–25:5. In 13f.; 16; 20:1–13; 21:1–11, the non-Priestly material has been interwoven with extracts from P, but even in these sections the non-Priestly material can be separated with relative ease. Some scholars view the non-Priestly material in Numbers as a combination of the 'J' and 'E' sources, and argue that these passages formed part of an extended composite JE document. Within Numbers, however, it has proved particularly difficult to distinguish between J and E, and it seems preferable to refer the earlier material to J, while recognizing that various independent traditions have, in the course of time, become attached to this source.

The date of J remains a bone of contention among *OT* scholars. It has sometimes been dated in the period of David and Solomon, but its association with a tenth-century Israelite 'enlightenment' has been strongly disputed by scholars such as Winnet (*JBL* 84 [1965], pp. 1ff.) and Wagner (*CJT* 13 [1967], pp. 225ff.; *Studies*, pp. 117ff.). Van Seters (*Abraham*, pp. 148ff.) argued that the Yahwistic theology reflected, e.g., in the patriarchal stories, should rather be dated to the period of the exile, at a time when the promise and possession of land were significant issues, and the trend towards dating J in the exilic or post-exilic period may also be seen in the recent monographs of Vörlander (*Entstehungszeit*) and Schmitt (*Josephsgeschichte*). Such a late dating for the J material, however, is not without its problems, not the least of which is the fact that a vacuum is thereby left in the pre-exilic period, and it remains for advocates of an exilic or post-exilic date to provide a satisfactory alternative account of the development of the tradition, whether in oral or written form (cf. Blenkinsopp, *Pentateuch*, p. 26). Budd (p. xxiv) suggests dating J in the late pre-exilic period (the seventh century BC), and argues that its presentation of Israel's history readily fits the circumstances of Josiah's time. On the whole, however, the strong sense of national unity which pervades this source favours a date prior to the fall of the northern kingdom, though how long before the disaster of 721 is almost impossible to determine.

C. STRUCTURE

The structure of the book of Numbers has proved notoriously difficult to determine, for it appears to consist of a collection of unrelated fragments devoid of any unifying purpose or meaning. Laws are juxtaposed with narratives in a seemingly random fashion, confirming the impression that the various units were compiled without any logical or coherent plan. Moreover, the wide variety of material contained in Numbers (poetry, tribal lists, census lists, itineraries etc.) merely adds to the difficulty of finding the book's inner cohesion.

It is therefore not surprising that different approaches have been adopted by commentators in an attempt to discover the principles which govern its overall structure. Some scholars have sought a unifying framework for the book in its chronology, for Numbers contains several chronological indicators (1:1; 7:1; 9:1, 5; 10:11; 20:1; 33:3, 38) which occasionally appear to mark a decisive break in the narrative (cf., e.g., 10:11). However, it is doubtful whether temporal considerations were paramount in the arrangement of the material, for chs. 7 and 9 are set a month earlier than the census of ch. 1 (see on 7:1; 9:1), and there is a distinct lack of chronological information for the period of the forty years' wanderings which supposedly elapse between 10:11 and 20:22. A more plausible suggestion is that the structure of the book is based on its geographical references. Scholars who adopt this approach frequently divide the book into three sections, and the following may be regarded as one possible division: 1:1–10:10 (the wilderness of Sinai); 10:11–20:13 (the vicinity of Kadesh, where the bulk of the forty years are spent); 20:14–36:13 (from Kadesh to the plains of Moab, where preparations are made for the settlement in Canaan). But the difficulty with dividing the book on the basis of its topographical data is that it is not entirely clear where the major divisions begin and end. Noth, e.g., finds the end of the second section at 20:13, while Gray favours 21:9 and de Vaulx opts for 22:1. The subjective nature of this approach was criticized by Olson (*Death*, p. 35), who noted that of thirty-three commentators who based their suggested outlines of Numbers on its geographical notations, no fewer than eighteen different proposals were advanced.

Dissatisfaction with attempts to divide the book on the basis of its chronological or geographical references led Olson himself to divide the work into two parts, each beginning with a census of the people. Olson argued that the two census lists in chs. 1 and 26 may be regarded as providing a unifying literary and theological framework for the book, and he noted a number of formal and thematic indicators which suggested that the book should be divided at the point at which the new census of the people occurs. Such a division, according to Olson, has significant theological implications, for it suggests that Numbers was basically concerned to contrast two generations of Israelites – the old generation which had experienced the exodus from Egypt and the revelation at Sinai but which had rebelled against God, and had therefore been condemned to die in the wilderness (chs. 1–25), and the new generation which had trusted in Yahweh, and which was therefore being led by him to the brink of the promised land (chs. 26–36). But while Olson's work contains many illuminating insights, it must be regarded as questionable whether such a decisive break occurs at ch. 26, for the radical distinction which Olson posits between 'the old rebellious generation of death' and 'the new generation of hope' (p. 180) is by no means as clear-cut as he suggests. Thus, an element of hope can be discerned in the victories achieved by the 'old generation' against the king of Arad (21:1–3) and against Sihon (21:21–32) and Og (21:33–35), and this hope is reaffirmed in the blessings pronounced in the oracles of Balaam (cf. 23:7ff., 18ff.; 24:3ff., 15ff.); conversely, the prospect of 'death in the wilderness' remains a real possibility for the 'new generation' of Israelites (cf. 32:14f.), just as it did for the old (14:28–30).

Despite the criticisms noted by Olson, a division of Numbers according to its geographical references must be regarded as the most satisfactory way of outlining the book's overall structure. Since there is a large measure of agreement among commentators that a clear break comes at 10:10, with the departure from Sinai, the only contentious issue is at what point the second division of the book ends and the third begins. The view taken in the present commentary is that the second section concludes at 22:1, for the Israelites are here represented as having arrived at the plains of Moab, and there appears at this point to be a decisive break in continuity with the wilderness wandering recounted hitherto. The book will therefore be divided into three parts: 1:1–10:10 (the sojourn at Sinai), 10:11–22:1 (from Sinai to the plains of Moab), and 22:2–36:13 (preparations for entry into the land).

Any attempt to trace a coherent plan in Numbers is inevitably frustrated by the presence of a large number of disconnected units. Nevertheless, it is possible to discern in the book an overarching theme, which may be described as 'Israel's journey to the promised land' (cf. Clines, *Theme*, pp. 53ff.). Chs. 1:1–10:10 are primarily concerned with the preparations for the journey from Sinai to Canaan. This section, which derives exclusively from the Priestly source, begins with an account of a census of all the Israelites over twenty years old who were able 'to go forth to war' (1:3), and the scene is thus set for a military occupation of the land. The Levites were not to be included in this census, for they were to take no part in the battles ahead; rather, their responsibility was to guard the tabernacle from any approach by unauthorized persons (1:53; 3:21ff.), and to transport it through the wilderness (1:50; 4:1ff.). Chs. 1–4 may be regarded as constituting a self-contained complex of tradition, which has a fairly unified basic form; however, there follows in chs. 5f. a disparate collection of laws, only the first of which (5:1–4) is clearly related to the situation depicted in the previous chapters. Ch. 7 continues with a list of the gifts brought for the tabernacle by the tribal leaders, and, significantly, these included wagons and oxen (7:3ff.) to facilitate the transportation of the tabernacle through the wilderness. With the consecration of the Levites, and their official dedication to their various tasks (8:5ff.), the people were ready to depart. An account is given of the way in which the cloud served to indicate when the Israelites were to encamp and when they were to proceed on their journey (9:15ff.), and the section closes with a reference to the silver trumpets (10:1–10), which were to be used to assemble the people in an orderly manner and to give them the signal to depart.

At 10:11, the journey to the promised land begins in earnest. The need is soon recognized for a guide to lead the Israelites on their way, and Hobab is invited by Moses to function in this capacity (10:29ff.). By ch. 13, the Israelites are already poised on the brink of Canaan, and spies are dispatched to make a reconnaissance of the land. The intervening chapters (11–12) function to create an element of suspense in the narrative, for the people are here depicted as developing a craving for the food they had eaten in Egypt (11:4–6) and, rather ominously, a rebellion is instigated against the leadership of Moses (ch. 12). The suspense continues in chs. 13f., as the negative report brought back by the spies raises doubts among the people concerning the entire enterprise of the exodus (14:1–3), and the suspense is heightened as the Israelites determine to choose a new leader and return to Egypt (14:4). When the people, on their own initiative, attempt to take possession of the land of Canaan, they suffer an ignominious defeat, for they had acted without Yahweh's blessing (14:39ff.).

The theme of rebellion continues in chs. 16f., as Korah and his followers rise up against Moses and Aaron (16:1–11), and Dathan and Abiram refuse to go up into the land (16:12, 14). Again, an element of suspense is introduced into the account of the journey. Would the people ever succeed in occupying the land of Canaan? Would the promise which Yahweh had made to the patriarchs (cf. 10:29; 14:16, 23) ever be fulfilled? Some cultic regulations follow in chs. 18f., and in ch. 20 the land once again comes back into focus as the goal of Israel's journey. Moses and Aaron learn that, because of their unbelief, they would not be permitted to enter the promised land, but were to die in the wilderness (20:12, 24). Thus, an element of tension is once again introduced into the narrative: could the people possibly enter Canaan without a leader to guide them?

The suspense continues as the Israelites face a series of obstacles on the journey. Clashes occur with the kings of Edom (20:14ff.) and Arad (21:1ff.), and with Sihon, king of the Amorites (21:21ff.) and Og, the king of Bashan (21:33ff.). Dangers of a different kind are presented by a plague of fiery serpents (21:4ff.) and by the appointment of a foreign seer to curse the Israelites (chs. 22–24). All the obstacles, however, are overcome, and the oracles uttered by Balaam serve to reassure Israel of Yahweh's benevolent purpose. But just when the people had been given a foretaste of the glorious future which awaited them in the promised land (cf. 24:5ff.), and when it might be expected that they would embrace this hope with a renewed sense of destiny and purpose, the suspense is raised once more, as the people turn away from Yahweh and begin to worship other gods (25:1ff.). As a result of their apostasy at Baal-Peor, Yahweh sends a plague which destroys the last remnants of the sinful generation (25:9), and in 26:64f. it is formally established that the entire generation which had been numbered in the census at Sinai (ch. 1) had now died, the only exceptions being Caleb and Joshua, the faithful spies. A new census of the people is thus taken in the plains of Moab (26:1ff.) in order to determine the size of the various tribes so that the land of Canaan could be distributed between them on an equitable basis (26:52–56).

27:1–11 follows on quite naturally from ch. 26, for the thought moves from the allocation of the land between the tribes to a problem concerning the inheritance of the land by certain individuals, and the link between the two chapters is strengthened by the fact that it is the daughters of Zelophehad, mentioned in the census (26:33), who are represented as demanding to inherit the property of their deceased father. The prospect of Moses' death before entry into the land (20:12) necessitated the appointment of a new leader, and Joshua is duly installed as his successor (27:12–23). Further ordinances in chs. 28–30 are followed in ch. 31 by an account of a war of vengeance against the Midianites, from which the Israelites emerge victorious. Surely, Israel must now enter upon her inheritance! But, once again, an element of suspense is generated as Reuben and Gad demand an inheritance in Transjordan (32:1–5), and the possibility is envisaged that the other tribes might follow their example and decide to settle on the eastern side of the Jordan

(32:6ff.). However, a compromise is reached, and the threat is diplomatically averted.

As if to emphasize that Israel's goal was now in sight, ch. 33 recapitulates the stages of the journey from Egypt to the plains of Moab. The occupation of the promised land is now regarded almost as something of a formality, and final instructions are given concerning the removal of the Canaanites and the remnants of their religion (33:50ff.). Directions are given concerning the boundaries of the land, which were to be redrawn to accommodate the victorious Israelites (34:1–15), thus indicating again that the conquest was all but a foregone conclusion. Having made provisions for the allocation of the land between the secular tribes, it was natural that attention should turn to the special arrangements to be made for the tribe of Levi, and this issue is addressed in ch. 35. Here, it is decreed that the Levites were to possess forty-eight cities with their surrounding pasture lands (35:1–8), of which six were to function also as 'cities of refuge', i.e., as places of asylum to which a person who had killed another by accident could retreat (35:9–34). The book of Numbers closes with a ruling concerning the inheritance of property: daughters wishing to inherit must marry within their own tribe, thus ensuring that each tribe's original heritage was preserved for future generations (36:1ff.).

This broad outline of the contents of Numbers should not be allowed to disguise the fact that the book contains several passages which interrupt the flow of the narrative and which seem to bear little or no relation to the surrounding context. For example, a satisfactory explanation of the occurrence of the priestly blessing (6:22–27) in its present context has yet to be found; similarly, the connection between 8:1–4 and the material which precedes and follows it is by no means obvious. Attempts have been made (with varying degrees of success) to find associative terms or themes which bind the various units together into a coherent framework (cf. de Vaulx, Budd, Wenham), but such attempts inevitably court the risk of imposing a pattern of coherence where no such pattern exists. Scholars have argued, e.g., that the seemingly disparate laws contained in chs. 5f. *do* have a common thread that binds them together, namely, the theme of 'purity' (cf. Rendtorff, *Introduction*, p. 147), and it is suggested that these laws are quite in keeping with their present context, which is basically concerned with the purity and holiness of the camp (cf. Childs, *Introduction*, pp. 196f.). The difficulty with this line of argument, however, is that not all the laws contained in chs. 5f. are concerned with the theme of purity. 5:5–10, e.g., is concerned with restitution for wrongs committed, and the notion of 'purity' does not figure at all in this section; moreover, while the problem of uncleanness may be at issue in the description of the 'ordeal of jealousy' in 5:11ff., this is hardly made clear in the narrative itself. Attempts have similarly been made to justify the present location of the miscellaneous laws contained in ch. 15. These laws, it is argued, were framed from the perspective of life in the land after the conquest (cf. 15:2, 18); after the description of Israel's rejection of the land in chs. 13f., these regulations affirm that Yahweh would nevertheless bring his people into Canaan (cf. Wenham, p. 127; Budd, p. 167). But the difficulty with this interpretation is precisely the same as that encountered in connection with chs. 5f. The fact is that not all the laws contained in ch. 15 presuppose settled conditions in the land; 15:32–36, e.g., concerns a case which arose 'while the people of Israel were in the wilderness' (v. 32), and the regulation concerning the wearing of tassels in 15:37–41 contains no reference at all to Israel's settlement in Canaan. Moreover, even if the editors of Numbers *had* intended ch. 15 to be understood as a reaffirmation of God's commitment to the land, it is still unexplained why the chapter was placed at this particular juncture, rather than, e.g., after the rebellion recorded in chs. 16f., or after the last reported incident of rebellion on the part of the people (21:4–9). The fact is that several chapters in Numbers do not cohere at all well with the context in which they have been placed (cf. chs. 19, 28f., 30), and, on the whole, there is little to be gained from attempting to fit the disparate material contained in the book into a mould of our own making. The present location of several passages in Numbers remains an enigma which has yet to be satisfactorily resolved; it may be, however, that the final editors of the book were far less concerned with matters of structure and cohesion than modern commentators would like to suppose.

D. RELIGIOUS CONTRIBUTION

The book of Numbers makes a significant contribution to the religious thought of the *OT* in several areas. Three of these will here

be examined in greater detail, namely, its theology of the land, its
delineation of the status and duties of the priests and Levites, and
its emphasis on holiness and the need to maintain ritual cleanness.

I. THE LAND

It is already clear from the above outline of the structure of Numbers
that the land is a theme of central importance in the book. The
Israelites are depicted as marching from Sinai to the borders of the
promised land; yet, at the end of the book, the actual occupation of
Canaan remains a goal that is never quite reached. The reason for
the failure of the Israelites to enter upon their inheritance is
explained in the so-called 'murmuring' stories (cf. 11:1–3, 4–34;
16f.; 20:1–13; 21:4–9) which depict the journey to the promised
land as one which was continually interrupted and delayed by the
sins of the people. Despite the fact that they had experienced the
deliverance from Egypt, their behaviour was characterized by a
blatant ingratitude and contempt for Yahweh's purpose. The series
of crises with which they had to contend in the wilderness evoked
in the people a sense of annoyance and exasperation. At times, their
anger was directed against Moses (cf. 14:4), and they accuse him
of having led them out of captivity with the villainous intent of
letting them die in the wilderness; he had deluded them with visions
of a land of beauty, but his real purpose was to satisfy his own
insatiable lust for power (16:12–15; cf. 20:5). At other times, their
indignation was directed against Yahweh (cf. 14:3, 23), and it is he
who is blamed for the perils of the journey and for the 'miserable
food' which they were being given to eat in the wilderness (11:1–3,
4–6). From the point of view of the people, the entire enterprise of
the exodus had turned out to be a great disappointment; consequently, instead of looking forward to occupying Canaan, they
looked back nostalgically to the time they had spent in captivity
(11:5, 18, 20), and, somewhat perversely, they even came to regard
the land of Egypt rather than Canaan as the one flowing 'with milk
and honey' (16:13).

Such sins of unbelief and wanton disobedience on the part of the
people amounted to nothing less than a blatant repudiation of the
beneficent acts of Yahweh in redeeming them from bondage. As a
punishment, Yahweh determines to destroy the entire nation
(14:11f.) and he decrees that they would suffer the very fate which
they had wished upon themselves – death in the wilderness (14:2,

29). Having doubted Yahweh's promise of land, the people were deemed unfit to enjoy its fulfilment. Moses, however, seeks to deter Yahweh from carrying out his intended judgment, and does so by appealing to his reputation among the nations and to his own character as a gracious and merciful God (14:13ff.). He reasons that if Israel were to be completely destroyed, this would be interpreted by the surrounding nations as a sign of Yahweh's failure to bring his people into 'the land which he swore to give to them' (14:16). As a result of Moses' importunate intercession, Yahweh's initial judgment – the complete annihilation of Israel – was modified: the people as a whole would not be abolished, but nor would the transgressors be permitted to enter the promised land; instead, they would be condemned to wander in the wilderness for forty years. During this period, the constituency of the community would be completely changed, and a second generation of Israelites would emerge who, chastened by the wilderness experience, *would* be permitted to enter Canaan. The tragic failures of one generation would thus be retrieved in the experiences of the next, and so Yahweh's purpose for his people would not ultimately be defeated. The mercy shown by Yahweh was due not to any merit on the part of the Israelites, but to the oath which he himself had sworn to their ancestors (14:23). Yahweh had determined to remain faithful to his promise, despite the fact that the people had deliberately contrived to hinder its fulfilment.

It is made clear, however, that certain basic principles must govern the life of the community once it had settled in Canaan. In the first place, there could be no thought of fraternizing with the native inhabitants and cohabiting with them on a peaceful basis; on the contrary, the Israelites were expected to drive out the Canaanites and destroy all the appurtenances of their worship. If Israel failed in this duty, the Canaanites would remain a constant snare and hindrance for them, and a serious threat to their well-being (33:50ff.). Secondly, the land would have to be distributed on an equitable basis in order to forestall the possibility of dissension and inter-tribal jealousy. The allocation of land was therefore to be made by lot and in such a way that the size of the territory would be proportionate to the size of the tribe (26:52ff.). Thirdly, the purity of the land had to be maintained, for Yahweh, the holy God, would be dwelling in the midst of his people (35:34). Responsibility therefore rested upon the community to ensure that the land would not be defiled, e.g., by the shedding of innocent blood. Consequently, whenever murder or manslaughter was committed, monetary compensation for the loss of life must not be accepted, for only the execution of the murderer (or, in the case of manslaughter, the death of the high priest) could rid the land of blood guilt (35:31ff.).

In view of the interest in the land which permeates the book of Numbers, it is hardly surprising that some attention should be given to the property rights of individual citizens. This issue is raised in 27:1–11, where daughters demand the same rights of inheritance as those which applied to the male members of the tribe. In deference to their request, a new addition was made to the existing corpus of law concerning the inheritance of property: in cases where a man had died leaving no sons, special dispensation was given to the daughters to inherit their father's estate. But this new arrangement involved a potential hazard: the daughters might marry into another tribe, in which case the land which they had come to possess would permanently be alienated from the tribe to which it had originally belonged. It is thus stipulated that daughters who inherit land may marry only within their own tribe (36:1ff.), thus ensuring that the integrity of the tribal boundaries was preserved, and that the God-given allocation of land (34:1ff.) was maintained unaltered.

The story of a people preparing to settle in the land would have had obvious relevance for those in Babylon contemplating a return to Palestine. In the description of the Israelites on the threshold of Canaan, the exiles could see a reflection of their own position, alienated from their land and from the place which could give them a sense of security and identity. The Priestly editors undoubtedly intended the account of Israel's journey through the wilderness to provide a paradigm from the past which would give the Babylonian exiles encouragement, guidance and warning for their own particular situation. On no account must the factors which had prevented the generation of the exodus from entering Canaan be allowed to hinder them from returning to their native land. They must avoid the dangers of faithlessness and apostasy, and must not be seduced by the fleshpots of an alien country. Access to land and its resources was contingent upon a whole-hearted commitment by the people, and only by demonstrating complete and unwavering loyalty to Yahweh could the goal of political and economic security be reached. The challenge which faced the exiles, therefore, was to return to

Palestine and to re-establish their identity in the land, and for these people the ancient traditions of Israel were intended to take on a new meaning and arouse a new hope.

II. THE PRIESTS AND THE LEVITES

The book of Numbers deals at some length with the status and duties of the priests and Levites. It is clear from the opening chapter (1:47ff.) that the Levites were regarded as a body set apart from the secular tribes on account of the special responsibilities which they had been given in relation to the tabernacle. As a token of their privileged position, they were to be exempt from military service, and were to be numbered separately from the other tribes (cf. 4:1ff.; 26:57ff.). Within the priestly hierarchy, however, the Levites were to occupy a subordinate position to the 'sons of Aaron', and this basic distinction between the priests and Levites is a theme which recurs several times in Numbers. The primacy of the priesthood is evident, first of all, from the position which the priests occupied in the camp, for the most favoured location, on the eastern side, facing the entrance of the tent of meeting, was reserved for Moses and the 'sons of Aaron' (3:38). The inferior status of the Levites is also apparent from the service which they rendered in connection with the tabernacle. Their duties included the burdensome task of dismantling the structure of the tabernacle whenever the tribes were about to move camp, and reassembling it whenever they arrived at a new site (1:51f.). In performing this work, however, they were forbidden to touch (4:15), or even to look upon (4:20), any of the sacred objects of the tabernacle, lest they die; consequently, the task of dismantling and covering these had to be entrusted to the priests (4:5ff.). The Levites were also responsible for transporting the tabernacle furniture during the march through the wilderness (1:50), but even this duty was to be performed under priestly supervision (4:16, 28, 33). The priests, on the other hand, were in sole charge of all the rituals in connection with the sanctuary and the altar (18:5); the Levites were permitted to assist them, but only in such a way that they did not come into direct contact with the sacred objects (18:3). It is clear, therefore, that, with regard to the tabernacle, the Levites functioned merely as auxiliary personnel; their task was to serve the priests, and all the duties which they performed were under priestly control. That the Levites themselves were expected to recognize their subordination to the priests is evident from the fact that they had to contribute to the support of the latter by giving them a tithe of the tithe which they had received from the congregation (18:26).

It was, perhaps, inevitable that not all Levites would be content to serve in this ancillary capacity, and one of the narrative strands contained in chs. 16f. suggests that there was a certain amount of rebellion against the status which they had been accorded. At issue here was the right of a Levitical group, led by Korah, to share in the responsibilities and privileges of the 'sons of Aaron' (16:8–11). The purpose of the narrative was to emphasize that such overweening ambition on the part of the Levites was misplaced, and the account serves to reaffirm the distinctiveness and supremacy of the priesthood. Indeed, such a rebellion as that instigated by Korah and his followers was tantamount to a rebellion against Yahweh himself (cf. 16:11), for it was he who had elected Aaron and his sons to their priestly office.

In order to assuage such feelings of discontent, the Priestly writers were at pains to emphasize that, although the Levites were, indeed, subordinate to the priests, their role was nevertheless one of immense honour and privilege. They were accredited substitutes for the first-born males in Israel, and in this capacity they assumed a special obligation of service to Yahweh (cf. 3:11–13; 8:14–19). Moreover, as custodians of the tabernacle, they had been given an important duty, for their task was to prevent any unauthorized person from approaching it, thus preserving the tabernacle from the possibility of defilement. Since any such defilement would certainly have incurred Yahweh's wrath (cf. 1:53; 17:12f.), the duty of the Levites was absolutely vital to the well-being of the entire community. In recognition of the fact that they were performing a crucial – and potentially dangerous – ministry on behalf of the people, the Levites were to be duly rewarded, and the congregation was called upon to support them by giving them a tithe of their produce (18:21–4). Such a reward, however, was not merely an acknowledgement of the hazards inherent in their occupation; it was also a form of recompense for the fact that the Levites were to be given 'no inheritance among the people of Israel' (18:24).

The priests, too, were entitled to receive certain emoluments in recognition of their service, for they, like the Levites, were prohibited from possessing landed property in Canaan, and were thus denied their own means of support. The priestly remuneration was primarily derived from the system of sacrifices and offerings (cf. 6:10; 18:8ff.); these offerings belonged, in the first instance, to Yahweh, but in practice they would have become the possession of the priests, and would have provided an important means of support for them and their families. Additional remuneration for the clergy was to be derived from the tax which was levied on war booty, for 1/500th of the soldiers' share was to be allocated to the priests, and 1/50th of the congregation's share was to be allotted for the support of the Levites (31:25ff.). Further, when a person who had been defrauded had died leaving no kin, the reparation repaid by the embezzler was to be duly credited to the priesthood (5:8).

These various forms of recompense served to underline the fact that an effective priestly ministry had to be properly supported, and the Priestly writers emphasize that this was a responsibility which devolved upon the community at large. This is well illustrated in ch. 7, which depicts the twelve tribal leaders contributing gifts for the consecrated tabernacle; that each tribe should be represented as presenting offerings was a clear indication of the fact that the upkeep of the ecclesiastical establishment was the responsibility of the community as a whole. That the Priestly writers should have felt the need to urge generous support for the priests and Levites is understandable, for there is evidence to suggest that, in the post-exilic period, there was much slackness in the matter of the maintenance of the priesthood, and it is evident that this had a potentially damaging effect on priestly practice and morale (cf. de Vaux, *AI*, pp. 403ff.). The message of the Priestly writers was therefore quite clear and unequivocal: if the new, restored community, organized around the Second Temple, was to prosper and flourish, there must be a disciplined and generous giving by the people, just as there had been during the period of the wilderness wanderings.

III. PURITY AND HOLINESS

For the Priestly writers, the life of Israel was bounded by a great tension between the clean and the unclean, the holy and the profane. Since Yahweh was a God of ineffable holiness, to approach him in a state of uncleanness was regarded as dangerous, and could even lead to the death of the individual concerned. It was for this reason that the tabernacle had to be surrounded by a protective cordon of priests and Levites, whose task it was to prevent any unauthorized person from entering the domain of the sacred and having contact with the holy vessels (3:21ff.). Illicit contact with the tabernacle would inevitably provoke an outburst of divine wrath which was liable to engulf the entire community (17:12f.). Even the priests were in danger of defiling the tabernacle if they entered in an unclean state; hence, they were obliged to monitor their own members carefully and to ensure that the service of the tabernacle was confined to properly consecrated personnel (18:3). The Levites, who occupied a subservient position to the priests (see above), were excluded from the realm of the holy, and they are warned of the dire consequences that would ensue if they were to touch or even to look upon any of the sacred objects of the tabernacle (4:15, 20). Thus, when the time came to dismantle the tabernacle, the priests had to place various cloths and coverings over the ark and the other sacred objects to ensure that they would not be seen or touched by the Levites (4:5ff.).

Just as the sanctity of the tabernacle had to be protected so, too, the purity of the camp had to be preserved. Individuals who were deemed to be unclean had to be excluded from the camp, since they were a potential source of defilement. 5:1–4 lists three separate categories of unclean persons: those who had become afflicted with a skin disease, those who suffered from an abnormal sexual discharge, and those who had had contact with a corpse. Of these three categories, the third was regarded as by far the most serious, and the Priestly writers repeatedly emphasize the danger of contamination which would result from contact with the dead. In 19:14ff. it is emphasized that touching a corpse, or even entering the tent of a dead person, could render an individual unclean. Ch. 31 records that Israelite warriors who had killed in battle were deemed unclean, and had to remain so for a period of seven days (cf. 31:24). Contact with the dead rendered the Nazarite's vow null and void (6:6f.), and a Nazirite who had allowed himself to become defiled in this way was obliged to begin the period of his consecration anew (6:9ff.). Uncleanness occasioned by contact with the dead is one of two valid reasons given in 9:1ff. for not celebrating the Passover festival at its appointed time; thus, a supplementary Passover had to be implemented, which was to be observed precisely one month later, thereby giving ample time for those who had touched a corpse to be cleansed of their defilement.

Those who had contracted uncleanness by contact with the dead were able to rid themselves of all impurity by following certain prescribed procedures. In the case of the Nazirite who had defiled himself, various offerings were to be presented before Yahweh (6:10ff.). Such offerings were not required of ordinary Israelites who had become unclean, but they had to subject themselves to a ritual whereby they were sprinkled with the 'water for impurity' which had been prepared from the ashes of a red heifer (19:9). Those who deliberately remained unclean and refused to be cleansed in the appropriate manner would be 'cut off from the midst of the assembly' (19:20), i.e., they would place themselves outside the community of God's people.

One interesting aspect of the Priestly concept of holiness is its contagious quality. The reason for removing the unclean from the camp was in order to prevent the spread of uncleanness throughout the community (5:1–4). Similarly, the death of a person in the camp could pollute all those in it, and could even defile the tabernacle itself unless proper preventative measures were taken (cf. 19:13, 20). The contagious nature of uncleanness is well illustrated in the ritual concerning the red heifer described in ch. 19, for both the priest and those responsible for burning the animal and gathering its ashes were deemed to have become ceremonially unclean because they had had contact with something that was most holy or taboo (19:7–10). Defilement was capable of affecting material objects as well as living beings, and one could become unclean merely by touching the bone of a dead man or his grave (19:14–16). The account contained in 16:36–40 is particularly significant in this regard, for the censers offered before Yahweh by Korah and his followers were thought to have absorbed something of the divine holiness, and in order to ensure that they were not put to profane use, Eleazar was instructed to make of them a bronze covering for the altar. Even the coals which had been burned in the censers had to be scattered far and wide in order to prevent them from being used in an unworthy way.

Another significant aspect of the Priestly concept of holiness is the notion that there existed, within the sphere of the sacred, varying degrees of sanctity. Thus, a distinction is drawn between that which was considered to be 'holy' (cf. 18:17) and that which was regarded as 'most holy' (18:9f.). Yahweh was regarded as dwelling in the 'most holy' place, enthroned above the ark and the mercy seat, and flanked by two cherubim (cf. 7:89), and his presence made this area of the tabernacle qualitatively different from all the other areas. One token of the special sanctity attaching to the 'most holy' place was the fact that only the high priest was permitted to enter, and even he could only do so on the day of atonement after performing certain rituals and dressing in special vestments. The remaining areas of the tabernacle were considered to be 'holy', and were therefore confined to ritually clean and properly attired priests, while the Levites and the laity were permitted only into the outer court. The narrative concerning the rebellion of Korah and his followers, referred to above, suggests that opposition may have arisen in Israel from time to time to the principle that various degrees of holiness existed. Korah and his companions argue that Moses and Aaron had no right to elevate themselves above the assembly of the people and to regard themselves as the sole depository of holiness; rather, the entire congregation was 'holy' by virtue of the sanctifying presence of God in its midst (16:3). However, a decision is given in favour of a specifically sacerdotal holiness; only those who had been detached from the sphere of the secular and who had been consecrated by special rites were to be permitted to approach God. The people must therefore recognize that the priests possessed a special degree of ritual holiness, which enabled them, on behalf of the community, to perform the various rituals that took place within the tabernacle.

The emphasis in Numbers on the importance of purity and holiness may have been due to an awareness, on the part of the Priestly writers, that the Babylonian exiles had neglected the observance of Israel's laws of purity, perhaps because the distinction between the secular and the profane was not always clear to them, or because they felt that, in an alien land, such regulations were no longer binding. The exiles were therefore encouraged to safeguard, as far as possible, their condition of ritual purity, for this was a vital aspect of the preservation of Israel's identity as the people of God. Moreover, in the reconstituted community after the exile, the people must continue to be scrupulous in their avoidance of ritual defilement, since their only hope for the future lay in recovering a way of life in which Yahweh, the holy God of Israel, would be central to the people's life and worship.

E. HISTORICAL VALUE

The book of Numbers purports to be a record of the period spent by the Israelites in the wilderness prior to the settlement of the tribes in the land of Canaan. But to what extent this record may be regarded as preserving genuine reminiscences of the fortunes which befell Israel in the desert is by no means easy to determine. The matter is considerably complicated by the fact that the material relating to the exodus and the wilderness wanderings is the product of a long and complex history of literary development, and each unit of tradition had its own pre-history before it attained its present form.

There can be little doubt that the final, canonical presentation (Num.–Jos.) of an orderly, disciplined march of all twelve tribes through the wilderness, culminating in a successful invasion of the land of Canaan from the east by a unified Israel under the leadership of Moses and Joshua is a gross oversimplification of what actually happened. Almost certainly, sporadic attempts were made by individual tribes to gain a foothold in Canaan, and attacks against the land were not all mounted from across the Jordan. Thus, e.g., the narrative contained in 14:39ff., in its original form, probably recounted the settlement of the Hebron area of Canaan by a group of Calebites, who achieved their victory, quite independently of the other tribes, as a result of a direct assault from the south. It is true that the narrative, in its present form, tells of an attempt to conquer Canaan by all the Israelite tribes, which resulted in their defeat at Hormah (14:45); however, the tradition preserved in 21:1–3, which records a victorious attack mounted by the Israelites at Hormah, suggests that 14:39ff. may originally have described a successful campaign waged against the Canaanites. Moreover, the notion that Hebron was occupied by the Calebites as a direct result of an incursion from the south seems more credible than the idea that Caleb was made to wander in the desert for forty years, that he then accompanied Joshua in an invasion of Canaan from the east, and thence proceeded south to capture Hebron and its fertile surroundings (cf. Noth, *History*, p. 76; Mayes, *Israel*, pp. 100f.). The reason why an account of a successful incursion into Canaan was transformed into a story of an ignominious defeat suffered by Israel was partly, no doubt, to demonstrate the inevitable consequence of disobedience to Yahweh's will; it is probable that the main purpose, however, was to avoid the impression that the ultimate conquest of Canaan was anything other than a victory achieved by a united Israel. In a similar vein, Num. 32 incorporates early traditions which seem to presuppose attempts by individual tribes to gain territory in Transjordan (cf. 32:39, 41f.) which were quite distinct from any campaign mounted by 'all Israel'. The essential unity of Israel is further expressed by the fact that every tribe was obliged to send a spy to survey the land of Canaan in anticipation of its conquest (cf. 13:2), and every tribe was expected to supply a thousand men for the war against Midian (31:4). When two and a half tribes declared that they wished to settle in Transjordan, this was regarded as a most serious crisis, for it suggested an indifference to the need to preserve the unity of the nation. Significantly, it was only when the tribes of Reuben, Gad and half-Manasseh agreed to send their warriors across the Jordan along with the other tribes that they were given permission to settle in Transjordan (32:1ff.). It is clear, therefore, that any assessment of the historical value of the accounts of Israel's conquests in Numbers must make due allowance for the fact that the events have been narrated from a pan-Israelite perspective, which emphasized that the conquest of Canaan was the result of a concerted effort on the part of all the Israelite tribes.

Problems of historicity also arise in connection with the accounts of the wilderness wanderings. One of the recurring motifs in these narratives is that of the 'murmuring' or 'rebellion' of the people, which resulted from the various crises which they had to face during their desert sojourn. Many scholars are of the view that this 'murmuring' motif is only loosely connected with the stories themselves, and that it represents a later interpretation of the wilderness period (cf. Coats, *Rebellion*; de Vries, *JBL* 87 [1968], pp. 51ff.); however, the possibility should not be discounted that these traditions may occasionally reflect something of the actual experiences of Israel in the pre-settlement period. The reality of a harsh life in the arid desert may well have caused the people to rebel against their plight and to express a wish to return to Egypt. Similarly, the opposition levelled against Moses may reflect actual struggles for leadership during the period before the conquest. On the other hand, there can be little doubt that the stories are, for the most part, simply typical or paradigmatic examples of the ways in which the people who had been redeemed from Egypt had rebelled against Yahweh and his elected representatives during the journey towards the promised land. Moreover, the manner in which the stories are formulated clearly indicates that apologetic interests were at work, for the fortunes which befell Israel in the desert were clearly intended to provide a warning, for future generations of Israelites, of the dire consequences of rejecting Yahweh's plan of salvation. Thus, any attempt to determine the historical value of these narratives must make due allowance for the fact that they were intended to serve a didactic purpose, and that the events of the past were reinterpreted in such a way as to afford instruction for the present and guidance for the future.

Finally, the historicity of the Priestly material in Numbers calls for some comment. As has already been indicated (see above, pp. xlixf.), the Priestly source undoubtedly preserved some older traditions, and it is quite probable that ancient beliefs and practices are reflected, e.g., in the description of the 'ordeal of jealousy' in 5:11ff., in the regulations concerning the Nazirite in 6:1ff., and in the directions for purification from corpse contamination in 19:1ff. Yet the Priestly writers were not primarily interested in historiographical questions; rather, their concern was to legitimate the religious practices and institutions of their own day by projecting them back to the time of Moses. Thus, the whole sacrificial system and the constitution of the priesthood and the Levites are regarded as having originated in the pre-settlement period; similarly, the tent of meeting was a projection of the Jerusalem temple back into the period of the wilderness in the form of the portable tabernacle. Even when the Priestly writers turn to depict specific events in Israel's past, the accounts are highly idealistic, as is apparent, e.g., in the incredibly high numbers of Israelites who are represented as having come out of Egypt (ch. 1), from the depiction of the war against the Midianites (in which not a single member of the Israelite army was lost; cf. 31:49), and from the description of the boundaries of the land, which may be compared with the idealized conception in Ezek. 48 (cf. 34:1ff.). Thus, considerable caution must be exercised when drawing any conclusions about the pre-settlement period on the basis of the data provided by the Priestly writers, for they were more concerned with contemporary issues of community organization than with presenting an 'objective' account of Israel's past.

Clearly, then, it would be impossible, on the basis of the information provided by Numbers, to reconstruct a coherent picture of Israel's history in the pre-settlement period. Yet, it would certainly be wrong to assume that the book is devoid of any historical value. The possibility must remain open that some, at least, of the narratives do contain some historical reminiscences from the time before the settlement; on the other hand, allowances must be made for the

character of the texts themselves and the purpose they were intended
to serve by the biblical writers. But whatever one's judgment concerning the overall historical worth of the book, its abiding value as
a witness to the developing consciousness of Israel as a community
of faith during the first millennium BC cannot be denied.

F. CONTENTS

I. THE SOJOURN AT SINAI
(1:1–10:10)

COMMENTARY

on

Numbers

I. THE SOJOURN AT SINAI
1:1–10:10

All the events narrated in 1:1–10:10 take place between the first and twentieth day of the second month of the second year after the Israelites came from Egypt. The scene is set for the entry of the people into the promised land, but first Moses must number them and assign to each tribe its position in the camp relative to the sanctuary, and its appropriate place in the order of the march. It is generally agreed that this section in its entirety is to be attributed to the Priestly source, although it is most unlikely that it is the product of a single hand, and there is every indication that it has been modified, amplified and supplemented by later editors.

(A) THE CENSUS AND ORGANIZATION OF THE COMMUNITY
1:1–4:49
(a) THE FIRST CENSUS
1:1–46

According to P, the Israelites were numbered twice during the wilderness wanderings: the first census, recorded here, took place at Sinai during the second year after the exodus from Egypt, while the second census (26:1ff.) occurred thirty-eight years later in the plains of Moab, towards the end of the period of Israel's sojourn in the desert. On each occasion, Moses was instructed to number all males above twenty years old who were 'able to go forth to war' (v. 3; 26:2). In the present passage, Moses is assisted in this undertaking by Aaron and a representative from each of the twelve tribes, whose names are given at some length in vv. 5–15. The tribe of Levi, however, was to be counted separately (1:47), since this tribe was viewed by P as responsible for the tabernacle (cf. 4:1ff.), and was therefore deemed to be exempt from military service; the number twelve was nevertheless maintained for the purpose of the census by dividing the tribe of Joseph into two tribes, namely, those of his sons, Ephraim and Manasseh (v. 10). The section concludes with a detailed account of the numbers in each tribe (vv. 20–43), and a statement containing the grand total (vv. 44–46).

The form of the passage has been discussed at length by commentators. Kellermann (pp. 4ff.) traces its traditio-historical growth as follows: the basic form of the passage consisted of: (i) a command to Moses to number the people in the wilderness of Sinai (vv. 1a, 2f., with the verbs originally in the singular, and without the reference to 'you and Aaron' in v. 3b); (ii) a brief note indicating that the command was duly executed (v. 19b); (iii) a statement containing the number of men in each tribe (vv. 21b, 23b, 25b etc.); (iv) the final total (v. 46). To this basic narrative was added, at a later stage, information concerning the date of the census in v. 1b, the list of assistants in vv. 4–15, the recapitulation in vv. 17–19a, the recurring formula 'by their families . . . war' in vv. 20–43, and the concluding statement in v. 45. Finally, a later editor added vv. 16, 44 and 47, together with the phrases 'from the sons of Joseph' in v. 10, 'of the people of Joseph' in v. 32, 'Israel's first-born' in v. 20, 'their generations' in vv. 20, 22, 24 etc., and 'head by head, every male' in vv. 20 and 22.

Kellermann's view of the traditio-historical development of vv. 1–46 may, in broad outline, be regarded as reasonably tenable, although there is no need to assume that the passage has been so heavily edited as he supposes. For example, his argument that the recurring formula in vv. 20ff. originally consisted simply of the word *bᵉnê* ('the people of') followed by the name of the tribe and the sum total of its members does not seem particularly compelling, for there is no substantive reason to suppose that the words 'their generations, by their families, by their fathers' houses, according to the number of names, from twenty years old and upward, all who were able to go forth to war' are a later addition based on vv. 2f. On the contrary, the rather cumbersome repetition of the formula in vv. 20–46 may be viewed as a device deliberately deployed by the narrator to emphasize the fact that the command of vv. 2f. was carried out to the letter. Even the more modest proposal of other scholars – that only the term *tôlᵉḏōṯām* ('their generations') need be regarded as a later addition in these verses – cannot be regarded as convincing, for the word is found in all twelve occurrences of the formula in vv. 20–46 and it is presupposed throughout by the Vsns (albeit prefixed with the preposition *lamed*). On the other hand, the words 'head by head, every male' in vv. 20, 22 have every appearance of being a later accretion, since they are conspicuously absent in the following verses, though retained throughout in LXX. Similarly, the words 'those of them that were numbered' in v. 22 are probably to be regarded as an intrusion into the text, since they break the pattern of the formula, and are omitted in some of the Vsns (LXX; Syr.) and in some MSS of MT. Since the census results in vv. 20–46 are largely composed of a repetition of the formula contained in vv. 2f., it seems entirely natural to connect vv. 1–3 with vv. 20–46, and to regard them as deriving from the same author. Kellermann may well be correct in connecting v. 19*b* with these verses, for the singular verb *pāqad* ('numbered') in v. 19*b* ill accords with the reference to Moses, Aaron and the tribal representatives in v. 17, and it must be conceded that v. 19*a* (with its concluding formula, 'as the LORD commanded Moses') would form a more appropriate climax to vv. 17f. In fact, there is much to be said for regarding v. 19*b* as the original continuation of vv. 1–3: the verb *pāqad* in the singular would then refer simply to Moses ('you and Aaron' in v. 3 being regarded as a secondary insertion), and the reference to the 'wilderness of Sinai' in v. 19*b* would connect well with the same phrase in v. 1. That the list of tribal leaders in vv. 5–15 was derived from a separate source seems very probable in view of the awkward transition between vv. 4 and 5 (cf. Noth), and this seems to be confirmed by the fact that the tribes are listed here in a different order to that encountered in vv. 20–46. Vv. 4 and 16 may well have been inserted to provide a framework for the tribal leaders list in vv. 5–15, and vv. 17–19*a* were probably a subsequent addition intended to emphasize that Yahweh's command (vv. 1–3) was obeyed, without delay, on the same day that it was given.

(i) *Arrangements for the census count:* **1:1–19**
1. The LORD spoke to Moses: In all strata of P this is the favourite expression to introduce a speech by Yahweh. The phrase is often supplemented by one of two possible locations, viz., 'in the wilderness of Sinai' or 'in the tent of meeting'; only here in P are both locations mentioned together. **in the wilderness of Sinai**: This is the scene of all the events recorded between Exod. 19:1 and Num. 10:10. The 'wilderness of Sinai' is a general description of the desert region in the vicinity of Mount Sinai. Unfortunately, however, it is no longer possible to ascertain with certainty the exact location of Sinai, and it is therefore difficult to identify the geographical position of the Israelite encampment. Mount Sinai has traditionally been located at Jebel Musa, which is in the southern part of the modern

Sinai peninsula. This tradition goes back to the fourth century AD
(possibly even earlier), and this location has the advantage of being
consistent with the data contained in Dt. 1:2 and with the account
of the route taken by the Israelites as depicted in some of the OT
itineraries (e.g., Num. 33:1ff.). Some scholars, however, have proposed a different location for Sinai, viz., east of the Gulf of Akaba
in the north-western part of what is now Saudi Arabia. In favour
of this hypothesis is the fact that, according to Exod. 3:1; 18:1,
Midianites were to be found in the vicinity of Sinai, and it is thought
that they inhabited an area on the eastern side of the Gulf of Akaba
designated, since Roman times, by the name 'Midian'. Moreover,
the narrative contained in Exod. 19:16ff. (cf. Dt. 4:11) has been
taken to suggest that volcanic eruptions must have been witnessed
on Mount Sinai, and extinct volcanoes have, indeed, been found in
the region east of the Gulf of Akaba. However, this hypothesis is
weakened by the fact that Midianites are encountered in places
other than this region (cf. 22:1ff.; 31:1ff.; Jg. 6–8), and, in any case,
doubts have been expressed as to whether the references to the
Midianites in the exodus narrative can be regarded as an original
component of the Sinai tradition (cf. Noth, *History*, p. 131). Moreover, the description in Exod. 19:16ff. need not be taken to suggest
a volcanic eruption, for the phenomenon depicted here may have
been due to other factors, such as a violent storm (cf. Bright, *History*,
p. 122). A third hypothesis, favoured by some scholars (e.g., Herrmann, *History*, pp. 69ff.), is that Mount Sinai was situated in the
northern part of the Sinai peninsula, in the vicinity of Kadesh.
Support for this is found in Exod. 17:8ff., which states that Israel
fought a battle against the Amalekites near Hebron (i.e., Sinai), and
there are some indications in the OT that the Amalekites were
located in the Negeb and in the desert of Shur, west of Kadesh (cf.
14:43ff.; 1 Sam. 15:7; 27:8). Further, such a location for Sinai would
be quite in keeping with the biblical passages which suggest that
Israel moved directly from Egypt to Kadesh (cf. Exod. 15:22; Jg.
11:16), a journey which would represent the most direct route from
Egypt to Canaan. But the problem with this hypothesis is that it is
difficult to reconcile with those references in the OT which suggest
that Sinai stood at a considerable distance from Kadesh ('eleven
days' journey', according to Dt. 1:2). Other possible locations for
Sinai which have been suggested by scholars cannot be discussed
here. It must suffice to note that, while there is no consensus on the

subject, the traditional location at Jebel Musa seems to present the fewest difficulties. For a detailed discussion and a bibliography of relevant literature, see Davies, *VT* 22 (1972), pp. 152ff.; *The Way, passim*. **in the tent of meeting**: Heb. *'ōhel mōʿēḏ*; *AV*, 'tabernacle', following Vulg. *tabernaculum*. This is the expression most frequently employed by P to refer to the divine dwelling in the wilderness. The tent was viewed as a kind of moveable sanctuary which housed the ark of the covenant, the golden candlestick, the table for the shewbread, and the altar of incense. Its construction is described in detail in Exod. 25–31; 35–39. According to P, it was located in the middle of the camp (cf. 2:2, 17), and was carefully guarded by the Levites, who ensured that its holiness was at all times protected. Earlier tradition, however, located the tent outside the camp and implied that it was guarded by Joshua, who was a non-Levite (cf. Exod. 33:7ff.). Sometimes the tent is designated by the term *miškān* (lit., 'dwelling place'), and in a few passages the two expressions, *miškān* and *'ōhel mōʿēḏ*, appear to be used interchangeably (e.g., 1:50; Exod. 40:2, 6, 29). Some scholars, however, have suggested that a fine line of distinction should be drawn between them, the term *miškān* being taken to refer to God's permanent abode, and the expression *'ōhel mōʿēḏ* being understood to designate the place to which he came at an 'appointed' (Heb. *hōʿēḏ*) time (cf. Haran, *JSS* 5 [1960], p. 58). In a similar vein, Budd (p. 9) conjectures that the two terms reflect different aspects of P's understanding of the sanctuary, *miškān* emphasizing the element of divine *presence*, and *'ōhel mōʿēḏ* the element of divine *communication*. The incident recorded in this chapter is said to have taken place **on the first day of the second month, in the second year after they had come out of the land of Egypt**, i.e., a month had elapsed since the erection of the tabernacle recorded in Exod. 40:17.

2. Take a census: The Heb. expression *śᵉʾû ʾeṯ-rōʾš* (lit., 'lift the head') was evidently a technical expression for 'calculating the total' (cf. v. 49; 4:2, 22; 26:2). The occurrence of the verb in the plural form here is unexpected, since Moses alone is addressed in v. 1, and he alone is depicted as implementing the divine command in v. 19. It is probable that the original text read the singular form of the verb (cf. Syr.) but that this was later changed to the plural to accommodate the reference to 'you and Aaron' in v. 3, which has every appearance of being a later addition (cf. Baentsch, Gray, Kellermann). **of all the congregation**: The word 'congregation'

(Heb. *'ēḏāh*; LXX, *sunagōgē*) is frequently used to refer to the whole body of Israelites, including the Levites (cf. 14:7; 25:6); here, however, the latter would seem to be excluded (cf. 8:9, 20), since they were not to be numbered along with the secular tribes (cf. v. 47). **by families, by fathers' houses**: The probable meaning is that the census was to be taken clan by clan (Heb. *l'mišp'ḥōṯām*) and family by family (Heb. *l'ḇêṯ 'aḇōṯām*; cf. *NIV*, 'by their clans and families'). The precise meaning of the expressions used here to designate the sub-divisions within the tribal organization must remain uncertain, since the various traditions are by no means consistent in their use of these terms. However, their basic meaning is elucidated in Jos. 7:14 (*NIV*), where it appears that each tribe was composed of several clans, each clan of several families, and each family of several individuals (cf. de Vaux, *AI*, pp. 7f.). **head by head**: MT has *l'gulg'lōṯām*, lit., 'by their skulls' (cf. vv. 18, 20, 22). This term, which appears both in P and in the writings of the Chronicler (1 Chr. 23:3, 24), emphasizes the fact that each male was to be registered individually in order to ensure a complete count; thus, the census was one which had to be carried out with the utmost thoroughness.

3. The census was to include **all in Israel who are able to go forth to war**: The root *yāṣā'* ('to go forth') is sometimes used of going out to battle (cf. 31:36; Jg. 2:15; Isa. 41:12), and the presence here of the noun *ṣāḇā'* ('army, war') clearly indicates that this is its meaning in the present context (cf. Num. 31:14, 36; 1 Chr. 5:18; 7:11). The census, therefore, had a military purpose (cf. *REB*, 'fit for military service') and, as such, was limited to every male **from twenty years old and upward**, i.e., those who were old enough to bear arms. No upper age limit is indicated, but Josephus (*Ant.* III.12.4) maintained that in Israel military service ceased at the age of fifty. Noth (p. 20) comments that in the continuation of P's narrative, there was no question of any military activity on the part of the Israelite tribes, but this is to deny to P the account of the Midianite war recorded in ch. 31.

4. A new thought enters the narrative here. Moses (and Aaron) could not reasonably be expected to count all the Israelites unaided, so they are instructed to enlist the help of assistants, one man from each tribe, **each man being the head of the house of his fathers**. The term 'head' (*rō's*) is often used in the *OT* of men who had attained positions of authority or pre-eminence within the tribe, clan or family. Sometimes such positions were inherited by accident of birth, but occasionally men were selected by virtue of their innate ability and their inherent qualities of wisdom and leadership (Exod. 18:25; Dt. 1:12ff.; cf. Bartlett, *VT* 19 [1969], pp. 9f.).

5–15. These verses contain a list of the representatives of the twelve secular tribes. The names reappear in 2:3ff.; 7:12ff. and 10:14ff., but, with the exception of Nahshon and Amminadab (cf. Ru. 4:20), they are not mentioned anywhere else in the *OT*. The date of the list has been the subject of much scholarly debate, and is discussed below (Excursus I). The representatives were: **Elizur** ('God is a rock'), son of **Shedeur** ('Shaddai is a light'); **Shelumiel** (possibly, 'at peace with God'; cf. Gray) son of **Zurishaddai** ('Shaddai is a rock'); **Nahshon** ('serpent'), son of **Amminadab** ('the [divine] kinsman is generous'); **Nethanel** ('God has given'), son of **Zuar** ('little one'); **Eliab** ('God is father'), son of **Helon** (meaning uncertain); **Elishama** ('God has heard'), son of **Ammihud** ('the kinsman is glorious'); **Gamaliel** ('God is my reward'), son of **Pedahzur** ('the rock has redeemed'); **Abidan** ('the [divine] father has judged'), son of **Gideoni** (perhaps a variant of Gideon, 'the destroyer'; cf. Levine); **Ahiezer** ('the [divine] brother is a help'), son of **Ammishaddai** ('Shaddai is my kinsman'); **Pagiel** (meaning uncertain, perhaps 'fate [given by] God'; cf. Gray), son of **Ochran** (meaning uncertain); **Eliasaph** ('God has added'), son of **Deuel** ('God is a friend'); **Ahira** (meaning uncertain), son of **Enan** (meaning uncertain). The name Deuel is probably an error for 'Reuel' (cf. LXX, Syr.), the letters *r* and *d* being easily confused in Heb.

16. The individuals listed in vv. 5*b*–15 were **the ones chosen from the congregation**: MT here has the *Qᵉrê* form *qᵉrŷʾê*; this is more unusual than (and therefore probably preferable to) the *Kᵉṯîb* form *qᵉrîʾê*, which occurs in 26:9. Irwin (*AJSL* 57 [1940], pp. 95ff.) translates the phrase as 'announcers of the festivals', but this is hardly meaningful in the present context. **the leaders of their ancestral tribes**: This phrase is found only here in the *OT*. The *nāśîʾ* was the established leader of the clan or tribe; for a discussion of the term, which occurs predominantly in late texts, see Speiser, *CBQ* 25 (1963), pp. 111ff. **the heads of the clans of Israel**: *AV* reads 'heads of thousands in Israel', understanding the term *ʾelep* in its literal sense; however, the term is sometimes used in the *OT* to refer to a tribal division, irrespective of its exact number, and it should probably be understood in this way in the present passage.

18. on the first day of the second month: The repetition of
these words (cf. v. 1) emphasizes the fact that Yahweh's command
was implemented on the same day that it was given. **registered
themselves by families, by fathers' houses**: Better, 'by their clans
and families' (*NIV*). Noth (p. 20) suggests that the Hithpael form
of the root *yālaḏ*, which occurs only here in the *OT*, means 'entered
in the register of births'. Evidently, the thought here (contrast v. 2)
is not so much the numbering of the Israelites as the establishing
of their pedigree or descent (cf. *REB*; Johnson, *Genealogies*, pp. 14f.).
In the post-exilic period, the ancestry of the tribes and the purity
of each clan's pedigree came to be regarded as a matter of great
importance (cf. Ezr. 2:1ff. = Neh. 7:6ff.).

(ii) *The census results* **1:20–46**
This section contains the results of the census, and, apart from
some minor deviations in vv. 20 and 22 (cf. Gray), these results are
presented in a stereotyped formula. The order in which the tribes
are listed in these verses differs from that found in vv. 5–15 in that
the tribe of Gad (vv. 24f.) is here placed after Reuben and Simeon
but before Judah. The order in LXX differs slightly from MT, for Gad
is there placed towards the end of the list, between Benjamin and
Dan; the reason for this change was no doubt so that Gad would be
listed together with the other tribes descended from the concubines,
Bilhah and Zilpah. It is worth noting that the order of the tribal
names in vv. 20–46 is identical to that found in the other census
recorded in ch. 26 (except that Ephraim and Manasseh have
exchanged places), and in both cases a grand total for all twelve
tribes is given at the end of the census list. The numbers given per
tribe and the total in each census is as follows:

	Numbers 1	Numbers 26
Reuben	46,500	43,730
Simeon	59,300	22,200
Gad	45,650	40,500
Judah	74,600	76,500
Issachar	54,400	64,300
Zebulun	57,400	60,500
Ephraim	40,500	32,500
Manasseh	32,200	52,700
Benjamin	35,400	45,600

Dan	62,700	64,400
Asher	41,500	53,400
Naphtali	53,400	45,400
Total	603,550	601,730

For a discussion of the numbers in the two census lists, see Excursus II, pp. 14–18.

(b) THE DUTIES OF THE LEVITES
1:47–54

This section states that the tribe of Levi was not to be included in the census taken of the other tribes, for that census was concerned to establish the number of fighting men among the Israelites (cf. v. 3), whereas the role of the Levites was confined to matters concerning the tabernacle. Their duties included: (i) carrying the tabernacle during the march; (ii) dismantling the tabernacle whenever the Israelites began their march, and setting it up again when the people were stationary; (iii) pitching their own tents immediately around the tabernacle in order to prevent any unauthorized person from approaching it. The section belongs to the Priestly source, but it is widely regarded as redactional, since it anticipates the theme elaborately developed in chs. 2f.

47–49. But the Levites were not numbered: It is strange that the command not to number the Levites in v. 49 should appear *after* the statement in v. 47 to the effect that they were not, in fact, numbered with the other Israelite tribes. *RSV* seeks to surmount the difficulty by rendering *wayᵉdabbēr yhwh* in v. 48, 'For the LORD said . . .', but it is doubtful whether the *waw* consecutive can be construed as stating a reason. It seems preferable to suppose that either v. 47 is a gloss or that some transposition has taken place in the text.

50. but appoint the Levites: The verb *pāqaḏ* (here rendered 'appoint') has a wide range of meanings in the *OT* (cf. Grossfeld, *ZAW* 96 [1984], pp. 83ff.); for its use in connection with Levitical service, see Spencer, *Levitical Cities*, pp. 79ff. **over the tabernacle of the testimony**: This expression is rare in P, occurring only in this passage (cf. v. 53) and in 10:11 and Exod. 38:21; the 'testimony', of course, refers to the tablets of the decalogue which were kept, according to P, in the ark of the covenant.

51. The Levites were to guard the tabernacle, **and if any one**

else comes near, he shall be put to death: The Heb. *zār* ('any one else'; *NEB*, 'any unqualified person') usually means an 'outsider', but here, as is usual in P, it refers to anyone who was neither a Levite nor a priest (cf. 3:10; 16:40).

Excursus I: The date of the tribal list (1:5–15)

The date of the tribal list contained in 1:5–15 has been the subject of much scholarly debate. Noth (pp. 18f.; *Personennamen*, pp. 15ff.) argued that the twenty-four names were derived from a very early list, probably dating from the period after the conquest of Canaan but before the formation of the state under David. That the list cannot have been composed by P is evident, according to Noth, from the following considerations: (i) vv. 5–15 are joined somewhat awkwardly to v. 4, and this suggests that the list must have been derived by the Priestly writer from a separate source and inserted into the narrative at a point which seemed to him most appropriate; (ii) a detailed examination of the names contained in the list indicates that this tradition must have antedated P, since the name-formations give the list 'a definite impression of antiquity' (p. 18).

Since an early date for the tribal list has been accepted by several recent commentators (e.g., Milgrom, Maarsingh), it is, perhaps, in order to subject Noth's arguments to more detailed scrutiny. Firstly, while it is entirely probable that vv. 5–15 derive from a separate source from that of vv. 1–4, this in itself proves nothing about the actual date of the list. Secondly, Noth's assertion that the names themselves give 'a definite impression of antiquity' must be viewed with considerable reserve, since names alone are a notoriously unreliable means of deciding the age of the literary context in which they occur. It may well be that some of the names in vv. 5–15 can be shown to be ancient, but it does not necessarily follow that the list itself is early, since a late author may have composed a fictitious list, and consciously selected ancient names in order to give it an air of verisimilitude. Moreover, names of undoubtedly ancient origin may well have been current at a later period, and may have been included in a list dating from exilic or post-exilic times.

Since much of Noth's thesis revolves around the formation of the names in the list, it is worth examining this aspect of his argument in more detail. Noth makes the following observations concerning the formation of the names: (i) There is not a single instance in the list of a name formed from the divine appellation 'Yahweh', and this is significant, for such names were rare in the pre-monarchic period, and became relatively common only in post-exilic times (cf. Ezr. 10:18–43). (ii) Names including the components ṣûr ('rock') and 'ammî ('my kinsman') – of which there are six examples in the list – are probably ancient, since they have parallels in second millennium Mari. (iii) At least eight (and possibly ten) out of the twenty-four names in the list are noun-clause names (viz., Elizur, Shedeur, Shelumiel, Zurishaddai, Eliab, Ammihud, Ahiezer, Ammi-shaddai, and possibly Pagiel and Ahira), and such names tend to be more frequent in earlier than in later times. (iv) There are four examples in the list of verb-clause names which follow the order 'noun-verb' (viz., Amminadab, Elishama, Eliasaph and Abidan), and such names were more common in Israel in the early pre-exilic period than they were after the exile; on the other hand, the verb-clause names of the order 'verb-noun' were comparatively rare in early times and, significantly, only two examples of such names are found in vv. 5–15, viz., Nethanel and Pedahzur.

None of these arguments, however, can be regarded as conclusive, for the following reasons: (i) While it is true that personal names containing the divine appellation 'Yahweh' are conspicuously absent from the list, this (as Noth himself concedes) may have been deliberately contrived by the Priestly author who was aware that until the time of the revelation to Moses (Exod. 6:2ff.) the name Yahweh was unknown to the Hebrews (cf. Gray, *Proper Names*, pp. 190f.). (ii) While names containing the component 'ammî were clearly in use in early times (cf. Gray, *op. cit.*, pp. 41ff.), such names also occur as late as the Chronicler (1 Chr. 2:10; 6:22 [MT 6:7]; 15:10f.), and, as Kellermann (p. 157) has demonstrated, the parallels from Mari cited by Noth must be regarded as very dubious. Further, names containing the component ṣûr need not necessarily be early, and it is surely significant that in the *OT* such names are entirely confined to the late P source (cf. Gray, *op. cit.*, p. 194). (iii) The evidence presented by Noth concerning the use of noun-clause names is very ambiguous, for noun-clause names are common in post-exilic as well as early pre-exilic times (cf. Ezr. 10:18–43, which contains eleven names of this type), and the same is true of the verb-clause names which occur in the list (cf. 1 Chr. 2:41; 2 Chr. 17:8).

In fact, far from supporting an early pre-exilic origin for the list, it is arguable that the formation of the names suggests a late, post-exilic date. It is significant, for example, that a large proportion of the names included in the list (nine out of a total of twenty-four) contain the divine appellation 'El' as a theophoric element, and, as Gray (pp. 6f.) has demonstrated, this is more typical of later rather than earlier lists (cf. Ezr. 10:18–22; Enoch 6). Moreover, the proportion of compounded to uncompounded names is large (eighteen out of twenty-four), and this again is more typical of lists dating from a later period. Further, names such as Nethanel (v. 8) and Gamaliel (v. 10) are unknown in pre-exilic times, but the former is frequent in late *OT* texts (cf. 1 Chr. 2:14; 2 Chr. 17:7; Ezr. 10:22) and both are common in post-biblical literature. Finally, Kellermann (pp. 157f.) makes the pertinent observation that, although sixteen of the names in the list do not occur anywhere else in the *OT*, the remaining eight are predominantly found in later rather than earlier texts: Eliab (1 Chr. 15:18, 20; 16:5); Elishama (2 Chr. 17:8); Nethanel (1 Chr. 24:6); Ammihud (1 Chr. 9:4); Amminadab (Ru. 4:20; 1 Chr. 15:10f.); Ahiezer (1 Chr. 12:3); Nahshon (1 Chr. 2:10f.; Ru. 4:20); Eliasaph (3:24).

It is clear from the above discussion that the formation of the names contained in vv. 5–15 cannot be claimed to support an early date for the list, since the evidence is, at best, ambiguous, and, if anything, must be regarded as favouring a late post-exilic date. Moreover, Noth makes no attempt to explain how it was that a document from the pre-monarchic period survived the centuries until its inclusion in the Priestly narrative; indeed, it is not clear why such a bland list of names, unrelated to any specific context (and therefore seemingly devoid of any purpose or meaning), should have been preserved and transmitted at all. It is far more reasonable to suppose that the list of tribal dignitaries contained in vv. 5–15 is a comparatively late compilation, probably dating from exilic or post-exilic times.

Excursus II: The census numbers

It has long been recognized by *OT* scholars that the numbers recorded in the census lists contained in chs. 1 and 26 cannot be regarded as an accurate representation of the size of Israel's population during the time of the sojourn in the wilderness of Sinai. The vast population presupposed in these two lists (603,550 fighting men in the first census and 601,730 in the second) could hardly have found subsistence in the desert for any length of time, nor could they have encamped around the tabernacle in the neat formation implied in ch. 2. The following suggestions have therefore been made to explain the impossibly large numbers of those among the

Israelites in the wilderness who were able to 'go forth to war' (1:3).

(i) The most ingenious attempt to explain the phenomenon was undoubtedly that offered by Holzinger (pp. 5f.), who argued that the total number recorded in the first census should be interpreted on the basis of the principle of *gematria*, a system by which each letter of the Heb. alphabet was given a specific numerical value. Thus, the first ten letters of the alphabet represented the numbers 1–10, the next ten letters represented the number of tens, and the remaining letters represented the number of hundreds. On the basis of this system, Holzinger calculated that the numerical value of the letters in the Heb. phrase *bᵉnê-yiśrā 'ēl* ('people of Israel'; 1:45), when added together (2 + 50 + 10 + 10 + 300 + 200 + 1 + 30), yielded the sum of 603, which represents the total, in thousands, of those counted in the first census (603, 550; cf. 1:46). With regard to the remaining 550, Holzinger suggested two possibilities: (a) the letters in the phrase *kol-zāḵār lᵉkol-yōṣē'ṣābā'* ('every male, all who were able to go forth to war'; vv. 2, 45) yield a numerical value of 551, which could easily be reduced to the requisite 550 if Moses were discounted; (b) Sam. suggests reading *lᵉṣib'ᵒ ōtām* ('by their companies') in v. 45 (instead of *lᵉḇêt 'ᵃḇōtām*, 'by their fathers' houses'), and this word yields the sum of 563, or 550 if Moses and his twelve assistants are discounted. But although Holzinger's suggestion has been accepted by some recent scholars (cf. Fohrer, *Introduction*, p. 184), his theory is not without its difficulties. In the first place, it is by no means certain that the system known as *gematria* was known in Israel prior to the Hellenistic period, and there is certainly no clear example of the system at work in the *OT*. Secondly, Holzinger was unable to offer a similar explanation for the total number calculated in the census of ch. 26, nor was he able to explain how the figures had been calculated for the individual tribes in either census. Thirdly, the method used by Holzinger to obtain the number 550 seems contrived and unconvincing, and the fact that Heinisch (p. 17) was able to conjure up the number 550 from a different Heb. phrase merely emphasizes the arbitrary nature of such attempts to explain the large numbers involved.

(ii) G. E. Mendenhall (*JBL* 77 [1958], pp. 52ff.) argued that the term *'elep* (rendered 'thousand' in *RSV*) should be understood as a military term, designating a contingent of troops under its own leader. Thus, the census lists of chs. 1 and 26, in their original form, would have given for each tribe the number of troops or fighting units, followed by the number of individuals in each unit who were capable of bearing arms. On this view, the tribe of Reuben, e.g., would have consisted of forty-six units, comprising a total of 500 fighting men, and there would therefore have been an average of ten or eleven men in each unit (1:21). The twelve tribes together would have provided 598 units consisting of a total of 5,550 men (according to the first census) or 596 units consisting of a total of 5,730 men (according to the second census). According to Mendenhall, later scribes, unfamiliar with the terminology of Israel's ancient military organization, misunderstood the term *'elep* to mean 'a thousand', and thus calibrated the incredible totals recorded in 1:46 and 26:51. But this theory encounters two difficulties. In the first place, it is by no means clear why the size of the units should diverge so widely between the two census lists. According to the first census, e.g., the tribe of Simeon would have had five men in each unit (1:23), but according to the second census it would have had nine men in each unit (26:14); if both lists are early, it is difficult to explain why the size of Simeon's troops should have varied so much in such a relatively short space of time. Secondly, the high numbers are equally problematic in the census of the Levites recorded in 3:21ff. and 26:62, but *'elep* can hardly be understood in the sense of a 'fighting unit' here, since the Levites were exempt from military service (cf. 1:47ff.).

(iii) W. F. Albright (*JPOS* 5 [1925], pp. 17ff.) argued that the census figures contained in chs. 1 and 26 were basically accurate but represented a census, not of Israel's fighting men at the time of the exodus, but of the entire population of the land in the time of David (cf. 2 Sam. 24:1ff.). This theory, however, is usually rejected on the ground that the figures given in the two census lists are far too large, even for the period of the united monarchy (cf. de Vaux, *AI*, pp. 65ff.). Also, both census lists presuppose that Simeon was an independent tribe, whereas by the time of the monarchy it was in the process of being merged with the tribe of Judah.

(iv) A different approach to the problem was advocated by M. Barnouin (*VT* 27 [1977], pp. 280ff.; cf. *RB* 76 [1969], pp. 351ff.), who argued that some striking affinities exist between the census figures recorded in chs. 1 and 26 and the Babylonian lunar calendar. According to this theory, the census figures, when divided by 100, can be related to various planetary periods found in Babylonian texts. The clearest example of such a correlation is found in the case of the Benjaminites, whose total comprised 35,400 (1:37), i.e. 100 x a short lunar year (354 days). Other cases are more complicated, and involve adding together various numbers in the census list. For example, in the first census, the combined totals of Issachar (54,400 ÷ 100 = 544) and Ephraim (40,500 ÷ 100 = 405) is 949, which corresponds to the Babylonian solar year (365) + the Period of Venus (584). By making the tribal figures correspond to celestial movements, Israel could be represented as Yahweh's terrestrial army, just as the astral bodies were regarded as his celestial host (cf. Gen. 2:1; Dt. 17:3). The difficulty with Barnouin's theory, however, is that the supposed calendrical association with the census figures is, at times, very obscure, and the complexity of the mathematical calculations must raise doubts concerning the plausibility of the thesis. Moreover, it must be regarded as questionable whether the contemporaries of the Priestly writer would have realized that a correlation existed between these numbers and the Babylonian astronomical periods.

None of the above attempts to resolve the problem of the large numbers in the two census lists can be regarded as satisfactory, and it seems far preferable to view the numbers as a purely fictitious and idealized construction by the Priestly writer. It is most improbable that the numbers were intended to communicate information concerning the actual size of the various tribes; their purpose was, rather, to convey a sense of the grandeur of Yahweh's army. Thus, no special significance should be discerned in the totals given in 1:46 and 26:51, nor in the numbers given for the individual tribes, for the figures were probably merely the invention of the Priestly author. Some commentators (e.g., Noth, p. 21) have objected to such an approach on the ground that the numbers calibrated for each tribe give a very realistic impression; but the precision of some of the figures was probably merely a device deployed by the Priestly writer to give the census an air of verisimilitude. In fact, a close examination of the numbers given for the various tribes reveals them to be contrived and carefully manipulated. For example, the approximate total for the twelve tribes in each census (600,000) means that each tribe would have produced, on average, 50,000 fighting men. It is therefore striking that in both lists precisely six tribes have a number above, and six tribes have a number below 50,000. Moreover, it is noticeable that the totals for the individual tribes are nearly always rounded off to the nearest hundred; only twice (once in each census) does the author go beyond the 'hundreds' to indicate how many 'tens' there were (Gad in the first census and Reuben in the second). While a certain logic may underlie some of the numbers given (e.g., in both census lists Judah is given the highest number, as might befit the pre-eminent position of this tribe), for the most part no significance should be attached either to the numbers of the individual tribes or to the variations recorded between the first and second census. Rather, the numbers in both lists must be viewed as a purely idealistic construction, devoid of any historical basis.

(c) THE ARRANGEMENT OF THE CAMP
2:1–34

This chapter contains detailed information regarding the positions in which the twelve secular tribes were to encamp around the tent of meeting, and the order in which they were to march through the wilderness. The Israelites were to camp in a square (or rectangular) formation, with the tabernacle in the middle, and three tribes on each side. The twelve secular tribes were thus arranged in four separate groups, and each group bore the name of its leading tribe. It emerges from 3:21ff., however, that these tribes were not located in the immediate proximity of the tabernacle, but were rather separated from it by a protective cordon of priests and Levites. The camp arrangement envisaged in 2:1ff. and 3:21ff. may be represented diagramatically as follows:

The origin of such an arrangement is uncertain. Some scholars (cf. Noth) have suggested that the idea was inspired by an ancient Israelite cultic festival, during which pilgrims would pitch their tents around a central shrine (cf. Kraus, *Worship*, pp. 128ff.); others (e.g., Milgrom, Wenham) have argued that the arrangement was based on an Egyptian prototype, in which armies camped in a square formation, with the tent of the king and his officers at the centre (cf. Yadin, *Warfare*, pp. 236f.). It seems more probable, however, that the camp arrangement presupposed in these two chapters was based on the pattern of the new temple envisaged in Ezek. 40–48: in both cases the primacy of the eastern side is evident (cf. Ezek. 47:1), and the centrality of the divine presence is emphasized (Ezek. 48:8ff.); moreover, the Levites and priests in 3:21ff. may be regarded as fulfilling something of the function of the walls of the interior court of Ezekiel's temple, while the secular tribes in the present chapter may be viewed as fulfilling the function of the walls of the outer court of the temple (Ezek. 40:1ff.; cf. Budd, p. 24; Sandys-Wunsch, *Numbers*, pp. 11f.). But whatever the immediate background of the camp arrangement depicted in the present chapter, its object was clearly to emphasize the sacred presence of God in Israel's midst.

Ch. 2 is basically composed of a recurring formula which states (i) the position of each camp in relation to the tent of meeting; (ii) the names of the tribal chiefs; and (iii) statistics concerning the size of each tribe and the sum total of each group of three tribes. Judah and the two tribes in its group are mentioned first, and they were located on the eastern side of the tabernacle; together, these three tribes contained 186,400 fighting men, and these were the first in the order of the march. Next, Reuben and the two tribes in its group are mentioned, and these were positioned on the southern side of the tabernacle; together, these tribes consisted of 151,450 fighting men, and they occupied the second position in the order of the march. Ephraim and the two tribes in its group were situated on the western side; these tribes comprised 108,100 fighting men, and they occupied the third place in the order of the march. Finally, situated on the northern side of the tent, were Dan and the two tribes in its group; these three tribes numbered 157,600 fighting men, and they occupied the last position in the order of the march.

It is clear from the arrangement of the tribes, both in camp and on the march, that there was a distinct order of precedence among them, although it is by no means clear on what basis this precedence was established. Some commentators favour the view that the order was predicated on the basis of the rank of the ancestress from whom the various tribes were descended (so, e.g., Maarsingh, Budd). Thus, the descendants of Leah had priority over those of Rachel, since Leah was the elder of the two sisters, and the descendants of both had priority over those of their concubines, Zilpah and Bilhah. The difficulty with this view, however, is that it fails to explain why Gad (one of the sons of Leah's concubine, Zilpah) here appears to have priority over the sons of Rachel. A far simpler solution is that the author mentioned Judah and its associate tribes first, since they were the strongest contingent numerically, and that he located them on the eastern side of the tent as a token of their pre-eminence (see on v. 3, below); he then simply followed the points of the compass in a clockwise direction, listing the remaining tribes in the order in which they occur in 1:20ff. It is perhaps worth adding that the position of the tribes around the tent does not correspond to the geographical location of the tribes after the settlement, for while it is true that the tribe of Dan occupies a position to the north of the tent and later settled in northern Israel (Jg. 17f.), the same coincidence can hardly be said to obtain with regard to the other tribes (e.g., Gad eventually settled in the east of the land, although it was positioned to the south of the tent).

Commentators agree that the basic substance of the chapter may be attributed to P^g although, in its present form, there are indications which betray the work of a later hand. V. 17, in particular, is widely regarded as secondary, since the thought here seems to switch abruptly from the arrangement of the camp to the order of the march. Moreover, the reference in this verse to the 'camp of the Levites' seems to anticipate the detailed organization described in chs. 3f., and the positioning of the Levites between the tribes of Reuben and Ephraim appears to be at variance with 10:17ff., which presupposes a different order of march. The inclusion of v. 17 at this point was probably due to an editor who wished to make clear that the tent occupied a central position during the march as well as during the encampment. As regards the remainder of the chapter, Kellermann (pp. 17ff.) observes that the detailed statistical information contained here concerning the numbers in each tribe seems somewhat strange in the context of a Yahweh-speech, and he sug-

gests that this may well be the work of a redactor who gleaned
the information from 1:20ff. The same redactor, according to
Kellermann, was probably responsible for the computation of the
sum totals in each division in vv. 9, 16, 24, 31, and for inserting the
names of the tribal leaders in vv. 3*b*, 5*b*, 7*b*, 10*b*, 12*b*, 14*b*, 18*b*, 20*b*,
22*b* (cf. 1:5ff.). Kellermann also suggests that v. 32, which contains
the grand total of all the secular tribes, and v. 33, which anticipates
the Levitical census of ch. 3, may be regarded as supplementary,
since they appear to be little more than a mechanical repetition of
1:46f. (cf. Baentsch). Kellermann further argues that the references
to the march in vv. 9*b*, 16*b*, 24*b* and 31*b* are also later accretions,
probably inserted by the same editor who was responsible for the
inclusion of v. 17. Thus, on Kellermann's analysis, the original form
of the chapter consisted only of the introduction in vv. 1f. and the
instructions concerning the order in which the various tribes were
to encamp around the tent of meeting in vv. 3*a*, 5*a*, 7*a*, 10*a*, 12*a*,
14*a*, 18*a*, 20*a*, 22*a*, 25*a*, 27*a*, 29*a*, 34. Even these verses, however,
received secondary additions in the process of transmission, and
Kellermann suggests that the words 'and Aaron' in v. 1, 'those to
encamp' in vv. 3*a*, 5*a*, 12*a*, 27*a*, 'and so they set out' in v. 34, were
subsequently inserted at a later stage.

Whether the chapter has been quite so heavily edited as
Kellermann supposes seems questionable, although there can be no
doubt that in its present form it cannot be regarded as a literary
unity. On the whole, apart from some minor accretions noted
below, it seems preferable to confine the work of the later redactor
to v. 17 and to the calculation of the numbers in each tribe and
the total numbers in each division. See, further, von Rad, *Priesterschrift*, p. 89.

1. The LORD said to Moses and Aaron: The reference to Aaron
is probably secondary (cf. 1:3), since Moses alone is mentioned in
v. 34.

2. The Israelites were to encamp **each by his own standard**:
BDB (p. 186*a*) gives the Heb. *degel* the meaning 'standard' or
'banner', and takes the word to refer to the military flag of the
separate tribes (cf. *NEB*, *NIV*). The etymology of the word is uncertain, but Delitzsch (*Hebrew Language*, pp. 39f.) connected the word
with the Akkad. *dagālu* = 'to look, behold', *diglu* = 'that which is
looked at', hence 'banner'. Gray (p. 20; cf. *JQR* 11 [1898–9],
pp. 92ff.), however, objects that this meaning can hardly apply to

the word in v. 3, since the notion of an inanimate object such as a
banner 'encamping' makes little sense, and he suggests that throughout this chapter (cf. vv. 10, 17, 18, 25, 31, 34) the word should be
understood as referring to a military unit, and that it should be
translated as 'company'. V. 3 would then be rendered, 'those to
encamp on the east side . . . shall be the company of the camp of
Judah', and the meaning of the present verse is that the army of the
Israelites was to be divided into four groups or divisions, 'each with
his own company'. Gray concedes that there is little etymological
support for translating the word *degel* in this way, but he observes
that the ancient Vsns (LXX, Syr., Targ.) seem to support such a
meaning of the word in the present context. It may be added that
the term is used to designate a garrison sub-unit in Aram. documents
of the fifth and fourth centuries BC from Upper Egypt, Memphis
and Arad (cf. Temerev, *Fest. Freedman*, pp. 523f.; Levine, pp. 147f.),
and a similar meaning is also attested in the War Scroll found at
Qumran (cf. Yadin, *Scroll*, pp. 49ff.; Milgrom, pp. 38ff.). It is possible that the word had a double meaning, originally denoting the
banner around which the tribe was gathered, and subsequently
denoting the tribe itself (cf. Cheyne, *JQR* 11 [1898–9], pp. 232ff.;
Maarsingh, Noth). **with the ensigns of their fathers' houses**: The
Heb. *'ôṯ* has a wide range of meanings in the *OT* (cf. 17:10 [MT
17:25]; Gen. 9:12; Exod. 31:13, 17), but only here (and possibly Ps.
74:4) does it signify 'ensign'. The most probable meaning of MT is
that each group of tribes had its own 'standard' (*degel*), and each
family had its own 'ensign' or 'emblem' (*'ôṯ*; cf. *NEB*). It is not
known what form these emblems took, but, according to later rabbinic tradition (*Num.R.* 2:7), the ensign of each tribe was identified
by a piece of cloth attached to it, which was the same colour as
that tribe's particular stone in the high priest's breastplate (cf.
Exod. 28:21; 39:14). The people were to encamp **facing the tent of
meeting**: The Heb. term *minneged*, can mean 'opposite' or 'facing'
(cf. *BDB*, p. 617*b*), and this is how the word is understood in this
verse in LXX and some modern translations (*RSV*; *NEB*). However,
the word can also mean 'at a distance' (cf. Dt. 32:52; 2 Kg. 2:15),
and this meaning seems preferable in the present context (cf. *AV*,
'far off'; *NIV*, 'some distance from it'), since the Priestly writer
evidently envisaged a space between the secular tribes and the tent
of meeting, where the Levites were to set up camp (cf. 1:52f.; 3:21ff.).
It is in this latter sense that the word *minneged* was understood here

by ancient Jewish exegetes, who visualized the secular tribes as being stationed some 2,000 cubits (approx. 1,000 yards) from the tent, an interpretation probably based on Jos. 3:4, which implied that this was the distance separating the ark of the covenant from the secular tribes (cf. *Num.R.* 2:1).

3. Judah and its associate tribes were to encamp **on the east side toward the sunrise**: The expression is tautologous, but there is no need to emend MT, since such expressions are not untypical of the Priestly writer (cf. 34:15; Exod. 27:13; 38:13). LXX^B reads *kata noton* ('on the south side') here, but this is obviously an error. The eastern side was regarded as the most honoured position, since the entrance of the tent faced in this direction.

5. next to him: MT implies that Judah occupied a central position among the three tribes in its group, being flanked on either side by Issachar and Zebulun; the reading of LXX, however, implies that Issachar was positioned by the side of Judah, and Zebulun by the side of Issachar.

10. Reuben and its associate tribes were to encamp **on the south side**: Lit., 'on the right hand'. The rendering 'on the south side' is justified on the ground that the points of the compass would be named from the perspective of one facing east (cf. Dt. 3:27; Ezek. 20:46 [MT 21:2]; 48:28).

14. son of Reuel: MT elsewhere reads Deuel (cf. 1:14; 7:42, 47; 10:20), and some suggest that this is the correct reading here (e.g., Wenham; cf. *NIV*). However, it is generally assumed that Reuel is the correct form of the name. The letters *r* and *d* are very similar in Heb., and are easily confused.

17. each in position: Lit., 'upon his hand' (cf. 13:29; Dt. 23:12 [MT 23:13]; Jer. 6:3). As noted above, this verse is probably a later addition.

(d) THE ORGANIZATION OF THE PRIESTLY HIERARCHY
3:1-51

This chapter opens with a record of Aaron's genealogy (vv. 1-3) and an account of the fate which befell his two eldest sons (v. 4). The details recorded in these opening verses were readily available in tradition (cf. Exod. 6:23; Lev. 10:1f.), and the only new information presented here is that both Nadab and Abihu had died childless, a fact also reported in 1 Chr. 24:2. Vv. 5-10 describe the appointment of the Levites as servants of the priests, and vv. 11-

13 reveal that they were to function as representatives of the first-born among the Israelite tribes, a point further elaborated in vv. 40–51. In vv. 14–20 the three Levitical groups and their sub-divisions are identified, and in vv. 21–39 the number in each group is noted, together with the names of their leaders, their position in the camp, and their special responsibilities with regard to the tabernacle.

Most commentators agree that this chapter, in its present form, cannot be regarded as a literary unity, for (i) vv. 1–4 appear as an isolated section, and bear little relationship to what follows; (ii) the point of view expressed in vv. 11–13 (where the Levites belong to Yahweh) seems at variance with that implied in vv. 5–10 (where they are given over to Aaron and his sons); (iii) the division of the tribe of Levi into three groups (with additional sub-groups) is described in two different ways within the chapter: in vv. 17–20 it is presented in the form of a genealogy, and the names given are the *personal* names of the eponymous ancestors of the clans, but in vv. 21, 27, 33, the names are *collective* (as the definite article which precedes them indicates), and there is only a very tentative assimilation to the scheme presupposed in vv. 17–20; (iv) vv. 21–39 is clearly a composite section, containing details regarding the sub-divisions of the families (vv. 21, 27, 33), their census number (vv. 22, 28, 34), the position of the Levites around the tabernacle (vv. 23, 29, 35), and the specific responsibilities of each group (vv. 25, 31, 36); the disparate nature of these elements suggests that the section only gradually attained its present form; (v) vv. 40–51 appear to be a continuation of vv. 11–13, but whereas in the latter passage Yahweh's acceptance of the Levites as compensation for his right to the first-born is merely mentioned as a general principle, in vv. 40–51 the idea is elaborated at some length, and the compensation is calculated with great precision.

While there is general agreement regarding the composite nature of the chapter, there is no consensus regarding the way in which the tradition developed. Noth suggests that the basic core of the chapter comprised details concerning the status of the Levites in relation to the priests (vv. 5–10), their classification according to their families (vv. 21, 27, 33), and information regarding the responsibilities of the different groups (vv. 25f., 31, 36f.). Such details as the census figures, the position of the Levites vis à vis the tabernacle (vv. 23, 29, 35*b*, 38), the names of the Levitical leaders (vv. 24, 30, 35*a*), and the redemption of the first-born by the Levites (vv. 11–

13, 40–51) were added at a later stage. On the other hand, Kellermann (pp. 32ff.) argues that the census of the Levites contained in vv. 14–16, 21f., 27, 28*aba*, 33f., 39 formed the basic core (*Grundschrift*) of the chapter; into this census scheme were inserted details regarding the location of the Levites around the tabernacle and the names of the leaders of each group (vv. 23f., 29f., 35); later still, details regarding the duties of the Levites were added (vv. 25f., 31, 36f.), based on information contained in ch. 4. The next stage in the development of the tradition, according to Kellermann, was the inclusion of vv. 17–20, which merely reproduces information already contained in the *Grundschrift* (cf. vv. 21, 27, 33). A framework was then constructed for vv. 14–29, and this is found in vv. 11–13, 40, 42f., 44, 45*aaβb*, 46–51. The penultimate stage in the formation of the chapter was the inclusion of the references to the cattle of the Levites as substitutes for the cattle of the Israelites in vv. 41 and 45*aγ* . After all these elements had been merged into a single entity, an editor inserted vv. 5–8, 9f., 38; finally, vv. 1–4 were appended as an introduction to the chapter.

Clearly, any attempt to trace the literary growth of the chapter will involve a certain degree of subjective judgment. Even so, some conclusions may be regarded as reasonably probable. For example, there seems little doubt that vv. 1–4 is an isolated tradition which has been secondarily inserted into the present chapter. Further, vv. 40–51 may be regarded as a separate unit of tradition which was originally closely connected with vv. 11–13; if, as seems probable, vv. 11–13 are a later addition to the chapter, then vv. 40–51 must be later still, since the latter passage is probably secondary even to the former. As regards the remainder of the chapter, however, it seems virtually impossible to decide whether it developed along the lines suggested by Noth or those suggested by Kellermann, for the tradition is far too complex for us to trace its literary development, and the relative chronologies of its individual parts can no longer be gauged with any certainty.

(i) *Nadab and Abihu:* **3:1–4**

1. These are the generations of: This is a formula characteristic of P (Gen. 6:9; 10:1; 11:10, 27; cf. Johnson, *Genealogies*, pp. 15f.), and it is used here to mark a new beginning in the narrative. **Aaron and Moses**: *BHS* proposes deleting Moses, presumably because only the descendants of Aaron are mentioned in the following verses

(vv. 2–4). But while the reference to Moses is certainly unexpected in a Levitical genealogy (cf. 26:57ff.; Exod. 6:16ff.), it is unlikely that the name should be regarded as a gloss here, for it is present in all the Vsns, and it is improbable that an interpolator would have taken the liberty of reversing the usual order of names by placing Moses second. Von Rad (*Priesterschrift*, p. 90), suggests, rather improbably, that the genealogy of Moses was accidentally omitted at this point; Galil (*VT* 35 [1985], pp. 489f.), on the other hand, argues that the omission of Moses' descendants was a device deliberately deployed in biblical genealogies in order to underline the abiding significance of the house of Aaron. The simplest solution, however, is to assume that Moses' name was included because of the frequent association of him and Aaron elsewhere, but that the latter's name was given precedence in this case because the passage was concerned only with *his* descendants.

2–3. Aaron's four sons, Nadab, Abihu, Eleazar and Ithamar are here designated as **the anointed priests**: Some passages in P suggest that only the high priest was 'anointed' to his office (cf. Exod. 29:7; Lev. 8:12); consequently, the reference here to the anointing of priests is often regarded as a later development (cf. McNeile). In pre-exilic times, it appears that only the king in Israel was 'anointed' (cf. 1 Sam. 10:1; 16:13); it is probable, however, that after the end of the period of the monarchy, the royal prerogative was transferred to the high priest as head of the people, and that it was, later still, extended to all priests (cf. Noth, *Exodus*, p. 230). It is worth noting that, apart from the P passages in the Pentateuch, there is no certain evidence that priests were anointed prior to the Hellenistic period, and it is known that the custom had ceased altogether by the time of the Roman occupation (cf. de Vaux, *AI*, p. 105). **whom he ordained to minister**: MT reads, lit., 'whose hand was filled' (Heb. *'ăšer-millē' yāḏām*), and this appears to have been a technical expression used to refer to the installation of a priest to his office (cf. Exod. 28:41; Lev. 16:32; 21:10), although in one case it refers to the consecration of an altar (Ezek. 43:26). The original meaning of the Heb. idiom is uncertain. Burney (*Judges*, pp. 421f.) refers to a parallel phrase, *umalli kāta*, well-attested in Mesopotamian inscriptions, which is used in the sense of 'entrusting authority' to someone (e.g., it is said of Adadnirari that the god Ašur 'filled his hand' with an unrivalled kingdom; cf., also, Gray, p. 21). Other scholars (e.g., Noth, *Exodus*, pp. 230f.) suggest that the idiom was derived from the custom of placing money in the hands of the priest as payment for the performance of his priestly duties. This may find some support in Jg. 17:5, 12, which contains the oldest use of the idiom in the *OT*, and which records that a Levite had 'his hand filled' by Micah, i.e., he was 'hired' (*RSV*, 'installed') by him for the sum of ten pieces of silver per annum (Jg. 17:10). The most likely explanation of the idiom, however, is that it originally referred to the offerings placed in the priests' hands during the consecration ceremony which conferred upon them the authority to discharge their priestly functions (Exod. 29:22ff.; cf. Lev. 8:25ff.); the sacrifice received by the priest was referred to as the 'ram of ordination', lit., 'the ram of filling' (*millu'îm*; cf. Exod. 29:22, 26f., 31). For a discussion of the idiom *millē' yāḏām* see, further, Wallis, *Henoch* 3 (1981), pp. 340ff.

4. But Nadab and Abihu died before the LORD: The words 'before the Lord' are lacking in Sam., Vulg. and one MT manuscript; since the same phrase (*lip̄nê yhwh*) occurs later in the verse, its presence here may be due to dittography (cf. Paterson). **when they offered unholy fire before the LORD in the wilderness of Sinai**: The incident referred to here is recounted in Lev. 10:1ff. and recalled in Lev. 16:1. The precise nature of the sin committed by Nadab and Abihu is unclear, for there is no consensus as to the meaning of the phrase here rendered 'unholy fire' (Heb. *'ēš zārāh*). The term *zārāh* in this verse is sometimes rendered 'illicit' (cf. *NEB*, *NRSV*), and the word is taken to mean that the fire which Aaron's two sons offered 'before the LORD' was not in accordance with the regular ritual. Thus, Haran (*VT* 10 [1960], p. 115) suggests that Nadab and Abihu must have taken the fire for their censers from outside the altar-area, and in doing so they were in breach of the command contained in Lev. 16:12; others suggest that the ritual error lay not in the fire but in the incense (Lev. 10:1), which had presumably not been compounded according to the instructions given by God to Moses in Exod. 30:34ff. (cf. Levine, pp. 155f.). See, also, Snijders, *OTS* 10 (1954), pp. 116ff., 146. These suggestions, however, appear to be highly speculative, and on the whole it is preferable to assume that the severe punishment meted out to Nadab and Abihu was on account of the fact that they had become involved, in some way, in idolatrous worship and were therefore guilty of apostasy (cf. Aberbach and Smolar, *JBL* 86 [1967], pp. 139f.; Robinson, *VT* 28 [1978], p. 309). For the root *zûr* used with reference to foreign deities, cf. Dt. 32:16; Isa. 43:12; Ps. 44:20 (MT 44:21); 81:9 (MT 81:10), and for a discussion of the expression '*ēš zārāh*, see, further, Laughlin, *JBL* 95 (1976), pp. 559ff.; Gradwohl, *ZAW*, N.F., 34 (1963), pp. 288ff. Since Nadab and Abihu had died, it was left to Eleazar and Ithamar to serve as priests during **the lifetime of Aaron**: The Heb. phrase '*al-p̄enê* often means 'in the presence of', and it is so understood in this context by some commentators (e.g., Noth), who discern here a reference to Aaron's supervision over his two sons as they performed their priestly functions. However, the Heb. idiom can mean 'in the lifetime of' (cf. Gen. 11:28, *NIV*), and this yields a better sense here: the point is that Aaron's two younger sons continued to act as priests while their father was alive (cf. *REB, NIV, NJPS; BDB*, p. 818*b*).

(ii) *The subordination of the Levites to the priests:* **3:5–10**
7. The Levites were to be brought before Aaron the priest and were to **perform duties for him and for the whole congregation before the tent of meeting**. Milgrom (p. 16; *Studies*, pp. 8ff.; cf. Wenham, p. 70) has argued that the Heb. expression *šāmerû mišmeret* ('they shall perform duties'), used in connection with the tabernacle, has the technical connotation of 'guard duty', and that the reference here (already anticipated in 1:53) is to the Levites' role in protecting the tabernacle from any incursions by the laity. But it is doubtful whether the Heb. expression was intended to convey such a precise meaning, and it seems preferable to understand it in the more general sense of fulfilling various functions in connection with the tabernacle, such as helping the congregation with the offering of sacrifices (cf. 2 Chr. 29:34). For the various connotations of the expression *šāmar mišmeret* in Numbers, see Levine, pp. 141f., 156.
   9. The Levites were to be **wholly given to him** (i.e., to Aaron). LXX and Sam. read 'to me' (i.e., to Yahweh); however, the reading of MT should here be retained, and the rendering of the Vsns is probably an attempt to assimilate this verse to references elsewhere in which the Levites are said to have been given first to Yahweh, and then given by him to the priests (8:16–19). It has been suggested that the words rendered in *RSV* as 'wholly given' (*nᵉtûnîm nᵉtûnîm*) contain an allusion to the Nethinim, a low order of temple personnel (*RSV*, 'temple servants') mentioned in late, post-exilic texts (Ezr. 2:43; Neh. 10:28; cf. Batten, *Ezra and Nehemiah*, pp. 87f.). Their names, as recorded in Ezr. 2:43ff. = Neh. 7:46ff., suggest that they were of foreign extraction, and they may have been descendants of

Solomon's Canaanite slaves who had been given over to the service
of the temple (Haran, *VT* 11 [1961], pp. 159ff.; but cf. Levine, *JBL*
82 [1963], pp. 207ff.). Although their status improved somewhat in
the post-exilic period, their tasks vis à vis the temple remained
comparatively menial; thus, it is regarded as entirely appropriate
that the author here (and in 18:6) should think of the Levites as
'Nethinim' to Aaron, since the Levites were to occupy a subordinate
position to the priests (cf. Budd, p. 34). It is unlikely, however, that
a direct reference to the Nethinim was here intended, for the form
of the Heb. word *nᵉṯûnîm* is morphologically quite distinct from the
Aram. *nᵉṯînîm*, and, in any case, the latter is always preceded by
the definite article. Moreover, the fact that the *nᵉṯînîm* elsewhere
appear as quite distinct from the Levites (Ezr. 7:7; Neh. 10:28; 11:3)
speaks against the blurring of the distinction between them here.
Speiser (*IEJ* 13 [1963], p. 72) suggests that while the term *nᵉṯînîm*
refers to a distinctive occupation, the word *nᵉṯûnîm* in this verse (and
in 18:6) is less specific and refers to 'devotees'; however, this must be
rejected on the ground that such a meaning for *nᵉṯûnîm* is unattested
elsewhere. The simplest solution is to regard the reduplication as
emphatic (G–K § 123*e*), in which case 'wholly given' (*RSV*; cf. *NIV*)
correctly represents the meaning of MT.

10. And you shall appoint Aaron and his sons (LXX adds 'over
the tent of meeting'), **and they shall attend to their priesthood**
(LXX adds 'for all that concerns the altar and that is within the
veil'; cf. 18:7). **if any one else comes near** (i.e., approaches the
sanctuary, with a view to usurping the priest's role), **he shall be
put to death** (cf. v. 38). The point made here is that only Aaron
and his descendants were permitted to perform priestly duties.
The words 'any one else' are rendered by *NEB* as 'any unqualified person' (cf. *REB*, 'any lay person'); the phrase no doubt
included the Levites, and was, perhaps, especially directed at
them (cf. Sturdy).

(iii) *The Levites as Yahweh's possession:* **3:11–13**
The idea expressed here is that the Levites were to be regarded as
Yahweh's possession, and were to be consecrated to him as a substitute for the first-born among the people of Israel. Noth (pp. 33f.)
suggests that the privileged position accorded the Levites in these
verses was intended as a corrective to the rather disparaging view
of them in the previous section (vv. 5– 10), where they are regarded

as entirely subservient to the Aaronite priesthood. However, it is by no means obvious that such a view of the Levites was intended in vv. 5–10, and it seems altogether more probable that both sections, while recognizing the subordinate role of the Levites, nevertheless emphasize that their position was ultimately one of great honour and dignity (cf. Budd). The notion expressed in these verses, namely that the redemption of the human first-born was achieved by placing the Levites at Yahweh's disposal, seems to contradict statements elsewhere in P, which imply that such redemption was to be secured by the payment of money (cf. vv. 46ff.; 18:15f.). Binns' attempt (p. 15) to explain the discrepancy by supposing that the Levites were here intended to function as substitutes only for existing first-born, while redemption by payment was to be made for those born subsequently, must be rejected as having no basis in the text. The most probable explanation is that vv. 11–13 represent the view of a later redactor who used the idea of the substitution of the first-born (found in such texts as Exod. 13:13) to highlight the special position of the Levites. (For the dependence of vv. 11–13 on certain passages in Exod. 12f., see Kellermann, p. 44.)

13. all the first-born are mine: That the first-born of man and beast belonged to Yahweh was recognized at an early stage in Israel's history, and the principle is clearly enunciated in Exod. 13:2; 22:29. In the case of animals, Yahweh's right was duly recognized by the sacrifice of the first-born male (Exod. 34:19f.); it is unlikely, however, that the sacrifice of a human first-born was ever practised by the Israelites (*contra* McNeile, p. 14), and the *OT* texts usually cited in support of such a view (Gen. 22:2; 2 Kg. 3:27; Mic. 6:7) are capable of a different explanation (cf. de Vaux, *AI*, pp. 442f.; *Sacrifice*, pp. 63ff.). **I am the LORD**: This self-identification formula is occasionally found in P (cf. v. 41; Exod. 6:8; 12:12), but is especially characteristic of the Holiness Code (Lev. 17–26), where it lends a particular solemnity to the words uttered by Yahweh.

(iv) *The command to number the Levites:* **3:14–16**
15. Moses was commanded to number the Levites **by fathers' houses and by families**: These words occur regularly in ch. 1, although their order is there reversed (cf. 1:2, 18, 20ff.). The formula is not used with any consistency in the present chapter, for sometimes 'by (their) families' occurs without the reference to 'fathers' houses' (e.g., vv. 18–20), while in v. 24 the reverse is true. **every**

male from a month old and upward: Since the Levites were substitutes for the first-born, and the latter were not redeemed until
they were a month old (v. 40), only Levites a month old and upward
were to be numbered by Moses. Clearly, this census functioned
on a different basis to that recorded in ch. 1 (where all males
over twenty years old were numbered) and to that found in ch. 4
(where all male Levites between thirty and fifty years old were
counted).

16. So Moses numbered them: LXX adds 'and Aaron' after
Moses, possibly under the influence of v. 39. **as he was commanded**: The passive form of the verb *ṣawāh* is unusual, and *BHS*
suggests emending the text to read *ṣiwwāhû yhwh*, 'as the LORD commanded Moses' (cf. v. 51*b*), the absence of 'Yahweh' being explained
on the assumption that it was wrongly written as *wayyihᵉyû* at the
beginning of v. 17. However, the Pual form of the verb *ṣawāh* ('command'), though rare, does occur in P (cf. 36:2; Lev. 8:35; 10:13),
and MT may therefore be retained here.

(v) *The Levitical genealogy:* **3:17–20**
These verses contain the genealogical details of the Levitical
families. Num. 26:58 lists five families of Levi, but the tradition
reflected here (which refers only to the three sons, Gershon, Kohath
and Merari) represents the usual genealogy of the Levitical tribes
(cf. Möhlenbrink, *ZAW*, N.F., 11 [1934], p. 191). Gershon and
Merari are each represented as having two descendants, while
Kohath has four. The details contained here were probably drawn
from Exod. 6:16–19, although the author evidently also had at his
disposal the names of the three Levitical leaders (vv. 24, 30, 35)
which may have derived from actual Levite heads of families in the
post-exilic period (cf. Sturdy). Noth (p. 36) seeks to connect some
of the names with towns or regions on the assumption that geographical considerations played a part in the division of the Levites.
Thus, he suggests that the Libnites may have been associated with
the town of Libna in the west Judaean hill country, and the Hebronites may have resided, at one time, in the southern city of Hebron.
However, Noth's failure to associate the remaining names (Shimei,
Amram, Izhar etc.) with particular towns casts doubt on his theory,
and it seems more probable that the names contained in vv. 17–20

were all originally personal names, unconnected with any specific locality.

(vi) *The census of the Levites:* **3:21–39**

Vv. 21–39 contain details regarding the census taken of the three Levitical clans, their location in relation to the tabernacle, the names of their leaders, and the furnishings which were in their charge. The number of male Levites who were a month old, or over, is given as follows: 7,500 Gershonites (v. 22), 8,600 Kohathites (v. 28), and 6,200 Merarites (v. 34). It is assumed – though not explicitly stated – that the families of the Levites formed an inner circle around the tabernacle, while the secular tribes were camped some distance away. That there was a distinct order of precedence among the Levitical families is clear both from the positions which they occupied in relation to the tabernacle, and from the items entrusted to their care. The place of honour, on the eastern side, was reserved for the priests, who had overall charge of the rites performed within the sanctuary (v. 38). It is not entirely clear why the Kohathites should have been allocated the second most important position, on the southern side, but it may have been due to the fact that they were the largest of the three Levitical clans (v. 28; cf. Kellermann), or because they were entrusted to carry the most sacred objects connected with the tabernacle (v. 31; 4:2ff.; cf. Noth). Another reason for the privileged position of the Kohathites may have been because Moses and Aaron – and thus all the priestly groups – were descended, via Amram, from this family (Exod. 6:18, 20; see on v. 32, below). It was noted in ch. 2 that the secular tribes were located around the tabernacle by following the points of the compass in a clockwise direction, starting with the eastern side. However, this scheme (which also appears in ch. 4) is abandoned in the present chapter, for the order in vv. 21ff. seems to be: west, south, north, east. This order appears to be quite arbitrary, but it is noticeable that in both schemes the primacy of the eastern position is recognized, by being placed first in chs. 2 and 4, and last in ch. 3.

23. The Gershonites were to encamp **behind the tabernacle on the west**: Since the tabernacle was regarded as facing east, 'behind the tabernacle' would obviously refer to the west. The tautology here is quite characteristic of the Priestly style (cf. v. 38; see on 2:3).

25. The Gershonites were in charge of **the tabernacle**: Since the Merarites were responsible for the framework of the tabernacle (cf.

v. 36), it is probable that only the curtains and hangings are referred to here, and this is, in fact, made clear in 4:25. The Gershonites were also responsible for **the tent with its covering**: According to Exod. 26:7ff. the tent was raised over the tabernacle to protect it, and it was made from goats' hair; the 'covering' was made of tanned rams' skins and porpoise-hides (Exod. 26:14; *NEB*).

26. and its cords: The cords are assigned to Gershon here, but in v. 37 they are assigned to Merari. Some commentators suggest that this is simply an oversight on the part of the narrator; others seek to reconcile the apparent contradiction by suggesting that the cords mentioned here were used to fasten the hangings of the tabernacle, whereas those mentioned in v. 37 were used in connection with the framework.

28. The number of male Kohathites a month old or over is here given as 8,600, but if this figure is added to the 7,500 of v. 22 and the 6,200 of v. 34, the sum total is 22,300 instead of the 22,000 given in v. 39; thus the number in this verse is widely regarded as a textual error for 8,300, which presupposes the accidental omission by a scribe of a single consonant in the Heb. text.

31. The Kohathites were responsible for the most sacred objects of the tabernacle: **the ark** (cf. Exod. 25:10ff.), **the table** (cf. Exod. 25:23ff.), **the lampstand** (cf. Exod. 25:31ff.), **the altars** (cf. Exod. 27:1ff.; 30:1ff.), **the vessels of the sanctuary** (cf. Exod. 37:16) **and the screen** (Exod. 26:31–3; 35:12). The reference to the 'altars' in the plural is problematical, since originally there was only one altar, viz., the altar of burnt offerings mentioned in Exod. 27:1ff. It must be supposed, therefore, that either this was an error on the part of the narrator, or else MT originally read the singular noun here (cf. Syr.) and that this was changed to the plural form by a later editor in order to accommodate the golden altar of burnt incense, described in Exod. 30:1ff. (a passage which is generally regarded as a secondary insertion in Exod. 25ff.). The 'screen' mentioned here was probably the curtain which separated the holy place from the holy of holies, and it is to be distinguished from the 'screen for the door of the tent of meeting' which was entrusted to the care of the Gershonites (v. 25). Elsewhere, this curtain is referred to either simply as the 'veil' (Exod. 26:31), or as the 'veil of the sanctuary' (Lev. 4:6), the 'veil of the testimony' (Lev. 24:3), or the 'veil of the screen' (Exod. 35:12). Syr. reads 'veil of the screen' in the present verse, and this is preferred by some commentators, since nowhere else is the curtain referred to simply as 'the screen' (cf. Gray, McNeile, Marsh); however, MT should probably here be retained, and the reading of Syr. may be explained as an attempt to assimilate this verse to 4:5. Sam. adds 'the laver and its base' after the word 'screen' (cf. Exod. 30:18), and the same addition is made in 4:14 by both Sam. and LXX.

32. The Levitical leaders were to be under the supervision of Eleazar, Aaron's oldest surviving son. The verse is generally regarded as a later addition, based on 4:16 (so, e.g., Dillmann, Noth; but cf. Budd), and it was probably inserted at this point because Eleazar, through his father, Aaron, and grandfather, Amram, belonged to the family of Kohath (cf. Exod. 6:18, 20). The editor clearly wished to emphasize that the Levites were under priestly control.

36–37. The Merarites were responsible for the least important parts of the tabernacle, viz., **the frames** (cf. Exod. 26:15ff.), **the bars** (cf. Exod. 26:26ff.), **the pillars, the bases, and all their accessories** (cf. Exod. 27:10ff.), **the pegs** (cf. Exod. 27:19) **and cords** (Exod. 35:18).

38–39. Moses, Aaron and Aaron's sons were accorded the most important position, on the eastern side of the tabernacle. Moreover, only they were allowed to perform priestly duties inside the tabernacle, and anyone else (*NEB*, 'any unqualified person') who drew near was to be put to death. **whom Moses and Aaron numbered**: Several Heb. MSS and some of the Vsns (cf. Sam., Syr.) omit 'and Aaron' here (cf. *NEB*) and this reading is supported by the use of the verb *pāqaḏ* in the singular, and by the absence of Aaron in vv. 14, 16. The supralinear points (*puncta extraordinaria*) over the name in the Heb. text indicate that the Massoretes suspected some textual irregularity here.

(vii) *The Levites as substitutes for Israel's first-born:* **3:40–51**
41. Just as the Levites were a substitute for the first-born of the Israelites, so the **cattle of the Levites** were to be a substitute for **all the firstlings among the cattle of the people of Israel**. This extension of the substitutionary principle to include cattle, however, seems strange in the present context, and it is clearly at variance with 18:17, which states that the first-born of cattle were to be sacrificed to Yahweh, and were not redeemable. Dillmann (pp. 19ff.) accounted for the apparent contradiction by suggesting that the

reference in the present verse was to unclean cattle, and these, according to 18:15 (cf. Lev. 27:27), *were* to be redeemed, since they were unsuitable to be offered as a sacrifice; however, this explanation must be rejected on the ground that there is no indication in v. 41 that the injunction was intended to refer only to unclean beasts. Gray (p. 31) proposes a different solution to the problem. He points to an ambiguity present in the command in v. 45 to 'take the Levites instead of all the first-born among the people of Israel, and the cattle of the Levites instead of their cattle', and argues that 'their cattle' here refers not to the cattle of the Israelites (as is generally assumed) but to those of the first-born. He then seeks to assimilate v. 41 to this verse by rearranging the word-order (transposing *bᵉhēmāh* before *kol-bᵉk̲ôr*) so that the reference is not to the first-born of cattle but to cattle of the first-born (cf. Maarsingh). But this suggestion must be rejected on the ground that it finds no Versional support and it involves the dubious removal of the preposition *bet̲* before the word *bᵉhēmāh* ('cattle'). The most probable explanation is that the present verse dates from a period later than that of 18:17, when the demand to sacrifice the first-born of all (clean) cattle was found to be impracticable (McNeile; cf. Sturdy).

43. The number of first-born males a month old and over among the Israelites is here given as 22,273, but this figure cannot be reconciled with the number of male Israelites over the age of twenty given in 1:46 (603,550).

46–47. The aim of the census commanded in v. 15 was to ensure that the number of Levites over a month old corresponded to the number of first-born children among the secular tribes. In fact, the numbers did not tally, for the number of male Levites (v. 39) was 273 fewer than the number of first-born Israelites (v. 43); consequently, the surplus Israelites had to be redeemed by the payment of money, amounting to **five shekels a piece**. These shekels had to be reckoned according to **the shekel of the sanctuary**. At the time of the Priestly writer the shekel was not a coin but a unit of weight, equivalent to approx. 11.5 grams of silver. The 'shekel of the sanctuary' (*NEB*, 'sacred shekel') was so-called in order to distinguish it from the commercial shekel 'current among the merchants' (Gen. 23:16), which was marginally heavier. See, further, Scott, *NPC*, p. 38; *BA* 22 (1959), pp. 33f.

(e) THE MINISTRY OF THE LEVITES
4:1–49

In the previous chapter, the status and duties of the three Levitical families, Gershon, Kohath and Merari, were discussed in general terms; here, their specific functions are described in more detail. Their primary responsibility was the transport of the tabernacle furniture when Israel was on the march, and this duty was to be performed under priestly supervision (vv. 16, 28, 33). The Kohathites were responsible for the most sacred items, and since they were not permitted to handle 'the most holy things' (v. 4), the task of dismantling and covering these had to be entrusted to Aaron and his sons (vv. 5–15). The duties assigned to the families of Gershon and Merari were more humble: the former were responsible for the curtains and hangings of the tabernacle (vv. 24–26), while the latter were responsible for its structure and framework (vv. 31–33). This outline of Levitical duties appears in the context of a command to number all the male Levites aged between thirty and fifty who were eligible for the service of the tabernacle (vv. 1–3, 21–23, 29f.), and the chapter concludes with the results of the Levitical census (vv. 34–49).

There is no doubt that the chapter belongs to the Priestly source, but the general unevenness of the material has led many commentators to deny that vv. 1–49 form a literary unity. Kellermann (pp. 49ff.) argues that the chapter consists of two independent layers of tradition, one concerning the census of the Levitical families and the other containing a description of the Levitical duties in relation to the tabernacle. Of the two traditions, the older was the account of the census found in vv. 1–3, and in its original version this would have been followed directly by a report of the carrying out of the census in vv. 34–49. Kellermann finds no reason to deny most of this material to P^g. On linguistic grounds, he argues that the list of Levitical duties contained in vv. 21–33, and the corresponding material in vv. 4–15, must stem from a different author, and since much of the information here is dependent on various secondary passages in Exod. 25ff.; 35ff., this tradition must derive from a later stratum of P.

Kellermann's arguments in favour of viewing the chapter as the conflation of two independent units of tradition must be regarded as persuasive, although again, it is unlikely that the passage has been so heavily edited as he supposes. Thus, e.g., vv. 5–15 (which Kellermann argues is replete with secondary expansions) may be regarded as essentially a literary unity, for there is nothing particularly incongruous in the presence of explanatory clauses (such as those found in vv. 9, 12, 14) within the context of a Yahweh-speech. Similarly, it seems overly pedantic to argue that, because v. 21 reports that Moses alone was commanded to take the census, and v. 49 concurs that the task was duly carried out by him, the references to 'Aaron' in vv. 34, 37, 41, 45f., and to the 'leaders of the congregation/Israel' in vv. 34 and 46, must be secondary additions to the basic text. Moreover, there is little reason to doubt that, originally, vv. 21–23, 29f., were of a piece with vv. 1–3, 34–49, and it seems not improbable that much of the remainder of the chapter may be viewed as a separate literary unity. V. 16, however, appears to deviate somewhat from the main theme of the chapter, by noting the items in the tabernacle which were the special responsibility of Eleazar, and this verse may well be a later addition; moreover, the allusion in this verse to the supervisory role exercised by Eleazar may well have precipitated the references to the similar role exercised by Ithamar in vv. 28b, 33b (cf. Noth). Finally, vv. 17–20 may well be a secondary addition, designed to explicate further the dire warning contained in v. 15a.

(i) *The duties of the Kohathites:* 4:1–20

A census was to be taken of the Kohathites, and they were to be responsible for transporting the most sacred parts of the tabernacle. Since direct contact with these objects was the exclusive preserve of the priests, the task of dismantling them was to be given to Aaron and his sons, who were to take the added precaution of covering the holy objects, lest the Kohathites should accidentally touch them (v. 15) or even see them (v. 20). These objects were to be transported by the Kohathites on poles (v. 6), and the task was to be performed under the supervision of Eleazar, Aaron's son (v. 16).

1. The LORD said to Moses and Aaron: Some regard the reference to Aaron as a gloss (cf. Kellermann), partly because the name is lacking in a few Heb. mss, and partly because Moses alone is commanded to number the Gershonites (v. 21) and the Merarites (v. 29). On the other hand, Aaron's name is present here in the Vsns, and in the record of the census contained in vv. 34, 41, 45;

thus, it is possible that the name should here be retained as part of the text.

2. Take a census by their families and their fathers' houses: See on 1:2.

3. from thirty years old up to fifty years old: The *OT* contains no fewer than three different statements concerning the period of Levitical service. The references in this chapter (vv. 3, 23, 30, 39, 43, 47) state that it was to begin at thirty and end at fifty; in 8:24, however, the lower age limit is reduced to twenty-five, while in 1 Chr. 23:24, 27; 2 Chr. 31:17 and Ezr. 3:8 the minimum age is further reduced to twenty, and no upper limit is mentioned. LXX seeks to harmonize the statements in Numbers by substituting twenty-five for thirty in the present chapter, thus assimilating the references here to that found in 8:24. It is uncertain how the differences in the lower age limit in MT are to be explained. Snaith (p. 194) argues that the age was gradually lowered over a period of time, but this explanation is based on the unwarranted assumption that the relative dates of the passages in question can be ascertained with some confidence. The simplest way to account for the inconsistency is to assume that the various passages reflect the age of Levitical service at the period when they were written, the lower limit being lowered or raised depending on the shortage or abundance of qualified persons who were able to perform the Levitical duties. **all who can enter the service**: The word here translated 'service' (Heb. ṣābā') is the same as that rendered 'war' in 1:3. The use of the word to refer to the service of the tabernacle is comparatively rare, and is confined to this chapter (vv. 23, 30, 35, 39 and 43) and 8:24f., although it is used in two texts to refer to the work of the women who served at the door of the tent of meeting (Exod. 38:8; 1 Sam. 2:22). It is generally agreed that the military connotation of the term is the more original, and that its application to the service of the tabernacle is a later development (cf. Gray).

4. The Kohathites were to be in charge of **the most holy things**: The phrase, in Heb., is the same as that used elsewhere for the innermost part of the tabernacle, i.e., the most holy place (cf. Exod. 26:33). The precise significance of the expression in the present context, however, is not entirely clear. *NEB* assumes that the words refer to the special sanctity pertaining to the Kohathites' service ('it is most sacred'); on the other hand, *RSV* (cf. *NIV*, *NJPS*) takes the words to refer to the sacred objects of the tabernacle for

which the Kohathites were responsible. The use of the Heb.
expression in such passages as Exod. 29:37 and 30:10, 29 favours
the second alternative.

5–6. When the camp was about to set out, Aaron and his sons
had to dismantle **the veil of the screen**: The screen was evidently
the innermost curtain of the tabernacle, which separated the holy
place from the most holy (cf. Exod. 26:31ff.). This curtain was used
to cover **the ark of the testimony**, and it was itself then overlaid
with a **covering of goatskin**: The Heb. word translated here as
'goatskin' is *taḥaš*, and its precise meaning is uncertain, as is evident
from the different renderings found in the translations (*AV*, 'badgers'
skins'; *RV*, 'sealskin'; *JB*, *NRSV*, 'fine leather'; *NIV*, 'hides of sea
cows'; *NEB*, 'porpoise-hide'; *REB*, 'dugong-hide'). Some of the
ancient Vsns (LXX, Vulg.) understood the word to refer to a colour
('hyacinth'), but Jewish exegetes, from the time of the Talmud
onwards, interpreted *taḥaš* as referring to some kind of animal. That
a sea creature of some sort was intended by the term is suggested
on the basis of a similar Arab. word, *tuḥas*, which means 'dolphin'
(cf. *NJPS*). The translation of *NRSV*, 'fine leather', is based on the
supposition that the Heb. *taḥaš* is derived from the Egyptian *tḥs* =
'leather', but while such a translation may be suitable in Ezek. 16:10
(cf. *RSV*), where the word seems to refer to material used as foot-
wear, some such rendering as 'porpoise-hide' seems preferable in
the present context. The translation of *RSV*, 'goatskin', must be
regarded as dubious, for it is difficult to justify on philological
grounds. Apart from the ark, the furniture and vessels of the tabernacle were first covered in **a cloth all of blue** (cf. vv. 7, 9, 11f.) or
purple (v. 13), and were then overlaid with the protective covering
of porpoise-hide; in the case of the ark, however, the cloth of blue
formed the outer covering, thus clearly distinguishing it from all the
other holy objects, and marking it out as the most important of
the tabernacle furnishings. After ensuring that the ark was suitably
covered, Aaron and his sons were to **put in its poles**. This seems
to imply that the poles had been removed and had to be replaced
before the ark was transported; if so, then this clearly contradicts
the command of Exod. 25:15, which states that the poles were to
be left permanently in place. Gray (pp. 34f.) seeks to resolve the
discrepancy by tentatively suggesting that the verb translated 'put'
(*śîm*) may here mean 'adjust', but it is simpler to assume that the
two passages are the products of two different authors. The purpose

of the poles, of course, was to facilitate the transport of the ark, and to prevent the Kohathites from having to touch it as it was carried through the wilderness.

7–8. the table of the bread of the Presence: MT reads, lit., 'the table of Presence' (cf. *NEB; NIV*), but this phrase is without parallel in the *OT*. *RSV* (cf. *REB*) assumes that it is an abbreviated form of the expression regularly used elsewhere to refer to this piece of tabernacle furniture, which is described in some detail in Exod. 25:23ff. The table was to be covered with a blue cloth, and on the cloth was to be placed **the plates, the dishes for incense** (the reference to incense is due to LXX), **the bowls**, and **the flagons** which were used for pouring **the drink offering**. Also on the table was the **continual bread** (Heb. *leḥem hattāmîḏ*), a phrase which is found only here in the *OT*. Snaith (p. 195; cf. McNeile, Riggans) suggests that *tāmîḏ* might here more accurately be rendered 'regular' (cf. *NEB*, 'the Bread regularly presented'), since the reference is to the loaves which the high priest placed in the sanctuary each Sabbath as a gift to Yahweh (cf. Lev. 24:5–9). This custom was quite ancient (cf. 1 Sam. 21:4) and, according to some scholars, it was a relic of the heathen notion that the gods actually partook of the bread that was offered to them (cf. Noth, *Exodus*, p. 206). The bread, and all the other items on the table, were then overlaid with **a cloth of scarlet**; it is not known whether any special significance was attached to the various colours mentioned in this passage (cf. 'blue', v. 6; 'purple', v. 13), but some (cf. Milgrom, p. 25) suggest that they may originally have designated various degrees of holiness.

9–10. A blue cloth was also used to cover **the lampstand for the light**: The Heb. expression *mᵉnōraṯ hammā'ôr* is found only here and in Exod. 35:14 in the *OT*. The lampstand and its accessories (**its lamps, its snuffers, its trays, and all the vessels for oil with which it is supplied**) were to be overlaid with a covering of porpoise-hide (*taḥaš*; see on v. 6) and placed **upon the carrying frame**: The Heb. term *môṭ* usually refers to a 'bar' or 'pole' used to carry objects (cf. 13:23), and this is the probable meaning of the word here (*BDB*, p. 557a); the various objects were evidently thought of as being wrapped in their coverings, and the packages suspended from a pole (cf. *NEB*). *RSV*'s 'carrying frame' suggests a flat surface on which the various objects could be placed (cf. *NIV*), but the translation of *NEB* is to be preferred, and is supported by LXX and Syr., which use the same word to translate *môṭ* here as *baddāyw* ('its poles') in v. 6.

11. A cloth of blue was also spread over **the golden altar**: This was the 'altar of fragrant incense' referred to in Lev. 4:7, and described in great detail in Exod. 30:1ff.; it is, of course, to be distinguished from the altar for burnt offerings referred to in vv. 13f.

14. A purple cloth was to be used to cover the altar of burnt offerings (v. 13), and all the utensils of the altar were to be placed upon it. These included **the firepans**, which were probably used to remove the ashes from the altar after the sacrifice had been burned (cf. Lev. 6:8ff.); **the forks**, i.e., types of hooks used to turn the limbs of the sacrificial animal over in the fire in order to ensure that they were properly consumed (cf. Snaith); and **the basins**, used for throwing the blood of the sacrificial victim against the altar (cf. *NEB*, 'tossing-bowls'). At the end of this verse, LXX and Sam. have an extensive addition, noting the provision for the transport of the laver and its base; the addition was no doubt intended to complete the catalogue of utensils listed in Exod. 30:26–29. Some scholars suggest that LXX may here have been following an independent MS tradition (cf. Harrison, p. 96), but it seems more probable that the additional material testifies to a midrashic tendency in LXX similar to that exhibited by the later rabbis (cf. Gooding, *JTS*, N.S., 25 [1974], pp. 1ff.).

15. The Kohathites were forbidden to touch or even to look upon (v. 20) any of the sacred objects of the tabernacle, **lest they die**. For the disastrous consequences that might attend the touching of a sacred object, see 2 Sam. 6:6f.

16. Eleazar, Aaron's son, had general oversight of the **tabernacle and all that is in it**, and he was personally responsible for four items, namely, **oil for the light** (i.e., for the lamps; cf. Exod. 27:20), **the fragrant incense** (cf. Exod. 25:6; 30:34ff.), **the continual** (better, 'regular'; cf. *NEB*, *NIV*) **cereal offering** (probably a reference to the daily offering of the priest described in Lev. 6:19ff.), and **the anointing oil** (cf. Exod. 30:22ff.).

17–20. These verses are probably a later interpolation, amplifying the command given in v. 15b. Only the priests were to have access to the holy objects; if the Kohathites were to 'look upon the holy things even for a moment' (v. 20), they would die.

18. the tribe of the families of the Kohathites: The word for 'tribe', *šēbeṭ*, is regularly used in the *OT* to designate one of the main tribes of Israel (cf. Gen. 49:16; Exod. 24:4); its use here, to refer to a subdivision of a tribe, appears to be unique. The only other passages which might imply such a usage are Jg. 20:12 and 1 Sam. 9:21, where reference is made to the 'tribes' of Benjamin, but in both passages the construct plural form (*šiḇṭê*) is probably due to textual corruption (cf. Gray).

(ii) *The duties of the Gershonites and Merarites:* **4:21-33**

A census was to be taken of the Gershonites, and they were to be entrusted with the task of transporting (possibly in wagons; cf. 7:7) all the hangings and coverings of the tabernacle (cf. Exod. 26:1ff.). They were under the supervision of Ithamar (v. 28), the younger of Aaron's surviving sons. A census was also to be taken of the Merarites, and they were to be given the responsibility of carrying the wooden framework of the tabernacle and all its accessories (cf. Exod. 26:15ff.); they, too, were under the supervision of Ithamar (v. 33).

27. and you shall assign to their charge: The plural subject here refers to Moses and Aaron (cf. v. 1); LXX reads the singular, presumably because only Moses is addressed in v. 21.

(iii) *The results of the Levitical census:* **4:34-49**

This section contains the results of the census of the Levites between thirty and fifty years old who were eligible for the service of the tabernacle. The Kohathites numbered 2,750 (v. 36), the Gershonites numbered 2,630 (v. 40), and the Merarites numbered 3,200 (v. 44). The grand total of 8,580 is given in v. 48. The figures are not incompatible with those given in the previous chapter (cf. 3:22, 28, 34), where the sum total of all the Levites over the age of one month is calculated as 22,000 (3:39).

34. the leaders of the congregation: LXX has 'leaders of Israel' (cf. v. 46); see on 1:16.

49. MT is corrupt (cf. Gray), but *RSV* probably correctly represents what was originally intended by the author.

(B) VARIOUS DIVINE ORDINANCES
5:1–6:27

(a) PURITY, RESTITUTION AND THE ORDEAL OF JEALOUSY
5:1–31

The description of the ordering of the camp in chs. 1–4 and the
preparation for departure in chs. 7–10 is interrupted in chs. 5f. by
a miscellaneous collection of laws and rituals which appear to bear
little relation to each other or, indeed, to the immediate context
in which they occur. The content of these two chapters may be
summarized briefly as follows: the exclusion of unclean persons from
the camp (5:1–4); restitution for wrongs committed (5:5–10); the
ordeal of jealousy (5:11–31); laws regarding the Nazirite (6:1–21);
and the Aaronic blessing (6:22–7). It is generally agreed that these
sections, although introduced by the same formula, belong to different strata of the Priestly tradition, and it is probable that their
substance dates from widely different periods in Israel's history (cf.
de Vaulx). Some commentators have sought to trace in these two
chapters a common theme, and have suggested that the thread that
binds the various sections together is the notion of the 'ceremonial
purity of the camp' (cf. Sturdy; Wenham). But the difficulty with
this view is that there is a clear shift in 5:5–10 from cultic to ethical
concerns. Budd (pp. 54, 58) attempts to obviate this difficulty by
suggesting that even this section is 'essentially ceremonial', and he
seeks to justify the inclusion of chs. 5f. at this point by arguing that
it was entirely appropriate for the issue of cleanliness to be raised
after the description of the camp's organization but before the march
through the wilderness begins. However, this view seems difficult
to sustain, for the march does not, in fact, commence until 10:11,
and, in any case, there seems no obvious reason why the issue of
cleanliness should not have been included within the description of
the camp's organization, especially since the object of the elaborate
arrangement was to protect the sacredness of Yahweh's dwelling in
the midst of his people. The fact remains that, although 5:1–4 may
be regarded as a suitable conclusion to the description of the
ordering of the camp (cf. Gray), it is difficult to discern any logic
behind the inclusion at this point in Numbers of the remaining
material contained in chs. 5f.

(i) *The purity of the camp:* **5:1-4**

This section is concerned with the preservation of the camp from cultic defilement, a demand which was necessitated by the presence of Yahweh in the midst of his people (v. 3*b*). In order to ensure that the purity of the camp was maintained, certain unclean persons were expressly excluded from within its boundaries, namely, those with a skin disease, those with a bodily discharge, and those who had had contact with a corpse. Some scholars have suggested that this section may originally have referred to the conditions that were expected to prevail in a military camp, since a particularly high standard of purity was demanded of those who engaged in a holy war (cf. Dt. 23:9ff.; cf. Dillmann, p. 25; Kuschke, *ZAW*, N.F., 22 [1951], p. 76); however, it is difficult to envisage how the prohibition against touching a corpse could effectively have been enforced during a war, and thus the balance of probability must favour the view that the section was concerned, rather, to exclude unclean persons from the sanctuary, and to prevent them from participating in the offering of sacrifices.

Despite the brevity of this section, it cannot, in its present form, be regarded as a unity, for v. 3*a* almost certainly betrays the work of a later hand (cf. Kellermann, pp. 63ff.). This is confirmed by the fact that (i) the command to exclude the unclean from the camp is issued twice (vv. 2, 3*a*); (ii) the verb in v. 3*a* appears in the *second* person plural form, whereas the verbs in the rest of the section are in the *third* person plural; (iii) the reference to 'male and female' in v. 3*a* appears redundant after the three-fold repetition of 'every' in the previous verse. It would seem, therefore, that the original passage consisted of vv. 1-2, 3*b*-4.

2. The Israelites were commanded to exclude from the camp **every leper**: *RSV* 'leper' is based on the Gk word *lepros* (cf. Vulg.), which is used in LXX to render the Heb. term *ṣārûʿa*. However, it is generally agreed that the word 'leper' is an inappropriate translation of *ṣārûʿa*, for it is clear from Lev. 13f., where the noun *ṣaraʿat* (*RSV*, 'leprous disease') occurs twenty-nine times, that the term is used to refer to a wide variety of skin complaints, and that it should therefore be understood in a generic rather than a specific sense (cf. Wilkinson, *SJT* 31 [1978], pp. 154f.). Moreover, it is improbable that any of the skin diseases described in Lev. 13f. can be identified with 'leprosy' as this word is understood today (Hansen's disease; cf. Cochrane, *Leprosy*, pp. 6ff.), for the characteristic clinical symptoms of this affliction do not appear in the passage in Leviticus, and, in any case, 'leprosy' could not have infected material such as textiles (Lev. 13:47ff.) and buildings (Lev. 14:33ff.) in the way that *ṣāra'aṯ* clearly could. Indeed, there is some doubt as to whether 'leprosy' as such was known at all in the ancient Near East in *OT* times (Hulse, *PEQ* 107 [1975], p. 91). In order to overcome these difficulties, *NEB* has adopted the translation 'malignant skin-disease' in the present passage (although the terms 'leper' and 'leprosy' reappear in 2 Kg. 5:1; 15:5; 2 Chr. 26:19ff.); but this rendering, too, is unsatisfactory, since the term 'malignant' makes an unwarranted assumption about the nature of the disease in question. In view of the difficulties of finding an appropriate English word to translate *ṣārû'a*, it is perhaps best to translate it as 'one afflicted by skin disease'; such a rendering, although somewhat cumbersome, has the merit of keeping the reference as broad as possible, and seeks to do justice to the fact that the Heb. term encompassed a wide variety of skin abnormalities. On the etymology of the Heb. term *ṣāra'aṯ*, see Sawyer, *VT* 26 (1976), pp. 241ff. It is not specified in the present text how long the 'leper' was to be excluded from the camp, but Lev. 13:4, 21, 26, 31 states that the period of exclusion was to last for seven days or, in exceptional cases, fourteen days (Lev. 13:5, 33). The exclusion of the *ṣārû'a* from the camp was not based on hygienic considerations, for the notion of compulsory seclusion was not in any way related to modern concepts concerning the control of infectious diseases. Rather, the overriding concern of the provision was to protect the camp, and the Israelites within it, from cultic defilement (cf. Noth). Thus, such regulations did not apply to non-Israelites, such as Namaan, who, although similarly afflicted by *ṣāra'aṯ*, could nevertheless lead an active life in the community as the commander of an army (2 Kg. 5:1). **every one having a discharge**: This expression refers to emissions or discharges from the sexual organs, a subject discussed at some length in Lev. 15. Such a 'discharge' (Heb. *zāḇ*) not only rendered the individual concerned ritually unclean, but also had the effect of contaminating other persons or objects that came into direct or indirect contact with him. It is clear from Lev. 15, however, that such discharges were regarded as far less serious than the skin ailments described in Lev. 13f., for exclusion from the camp was not required of those suffering from this affliction; rather, they were merely expected to wait for a period of seven days after the condition had cleared, wash

their clothes and their bodies, and present (inexpensive) offerings
to God, in return for which they would regain their previous state
of cultic cleanness. The requirement of the present passage that
those with a discharge should also be excluded from the camp therefore represents a clear departure from the prescription contained in
Lev. 15. **every one that is unclean through contact with the
dead**: This is dealt with in detail in ch. 19. According to 19:11,
those who had had contact with a corpse were regarded as unclean
for a limited period of seven days; only in the present passage does
this form of defilement necessitate exclusion from the camp.

(ii) *Restitution for wrongs committed:* **5:5-10**

There is general agreement among commentators that these verses
are to be regarded as a supplement to Lev. 6:1-7 (MT 5:20-26), a
section which deals with the misappropriation of goods, and the
procedure to be followed when they are returned to their rightful
owner. The unusual formulation in v. 6 ('any of the sins that men
commit') may be explained as a contraction of Lev. 6:3*b* ('in any of
all the things which men do and sin therein'), and the words 'by
breaking faith with the LORD' in v. 6*b* are probably based on the
phrase 'a breach of faith against the LORD' in Lev. 6:2*a*; moreover,
the demand that the property must be returned to the original owner
in 'full', together with one-fifth of its value (v. 7), corresponds to
the ruling of Lev. 6:5, and the reference in the present passage to
the 'priest' (rather than 'Aaron and his sons') appears to be further
confirmation of the dependence of these verses on Lev. 6:1-7. The
only new element in the present law is found in v. 8*a*, which envis-
ages the possibility that the wronged person had, in the meantime,
died, and that he had no kinsman (*gōʾēl*) to whom the property could
be returned; in this case, restitution was to be made to the priest as
Yahweh's representative.

Budd (p. 57) maintains that vv. 5-10 may be regarded as essentially a literary unity; however, vv. 9f. seem to be only loosely connected to the preceding verses, for the subject discussed here appears
to be the right and dues of the priest rather than compensation
for wrongs committed. Kellermann (pp. 68f.) is therefore probably
correct in regarding these verses as later additions, possibly inspired
by the priestly interest expressed in v. 8.

6. any of the sins that men commit: The reference here is somewhat vague and must be understood against the background of Lev. 6:2f., where the offences in question are expressly itemized. The phraseology of the Heb. (lit., 'any sins of men') is ambivalent, for it may mean 'any sins committed *by* men', assuming a subjective genitive (so *RSV*; cf. LXX), or 'any sins committed *against* men', assuming an objective genitive (cf. *NEB*). Some commentators (e.g., Maarsingh, Levine) prefer the latter alternative, since the context is concerned with offences committed by an individual against his fellow-men. However, Lev. 6:3*b* (upon which this clause is probably based) favours the former alternative, and this is confirmed by the fact that the genitive following the word *ḥaṭṭā'ṯ* is usually subjective (cf. Gen. 31:36; 50:17); hence, *RSV* has probably interpreted the Heb. correctly. In committing wrong against his neighbour, the offender is also guilty of **breaking faith with the LORD**; thus, in addition to restoring the property to its rightful owner, the culprit was also obliged to offer to Yahweh a 'ram of atonement' (v. 8), and only when both reparations had been made would his relationship with God and with his fellow-men be restored.

7. he shall confess: In cases where evidence against the embezzler was lacking, and his detection therefore improbable, restitution could only be made if the guilty person came forth of his own volition and confessed his misdeeds. For other occasions when some kind of public confession was required, cf. Lev. 5:5; 16:21. **and he shall make full restitution for his wrong, adding a fifth to it**: The guilty person was required not only to restore the stolen property to the original owner but also to compensate him for the loss by adding to it a fifth of its value; this provision was no doubt intended to deter the embezzler from perpetrating such an offence again. The same amount (an additional one-fifth) was enjoined in other cases, too, where some form of recompense was required (cf. Lev. 22:14; 27:13, 15, 27, 31).

8. But if the man (i.e., the victim) **has no kinsman**: The reference here to the kinsman (Heb. *gō'ēl*) to whom restitution was to be made is usually taken to imply that the wronged person was no longer alive. Noth (p. 47), however, suggests that it may indicate nothing more than that the victim had lost his legal and economic independence (possibly owing to debts which he had been unable to repay), in which case he would no longer have been entitled to receive the restitution money. The duties of the *gō'ēl* normally involved buying back property which had been temporarily lost to the family (Lev. 25:25; Ru. 4:1ff.; cf. Davies, *VT* 33 [1983], pp. 231ff.) or buying back a relative who had been forced, through poverty, to sell himself into slavery (Lev. 25:47ff.). Num. 35:9ff. implies that he was also obliged to avenge the death of a murdered relative. The kinsman was usually the man's brother, or, failing him, an uncle, cousin or the nearest relative on the father's side. Since there was no shortage of people who could act as the *gōʾēl*, the situation envisaged in the present verse, where the victim had no kinsman to whom reparation could be made, must have been comparatively rare. In so far as such cases did arise, however, **the restitution for wrong shall go to the LORD for the priest**: The phraseology here is rather awkward, but the meaning is clear: compensation, in such cases, was to be made in principle to Yahweh, but in practice to the priest. The offender should not, however, deceive himself into thinking that the restitution he had made rendered sacrifice to Yahweh unnecessary, for such recompense was to be **in addition to the ram of atonement**: The expression 'ram of atonement' (*NEB*, 'ram of expiation') occurs only here in the *OT*, and it appears to refer to the ram mentioned in Lev. 6:6, which was presented as a 'guilt offering'.

9–10. The general principle enunciated in these verses is that **every offering** (*tᵉrûmāh*; see on 6:20) and all the holy gifts that were Yahweh's due should go to the priest, as his representative. Gray (p. 42) suggests that the point at issue here is that every gift which was made to a particular priest should belong to that priest and should not become the property of the priestly community at large (cf. Lev. 7:7–9, 14). However, it is more probable that the term *kōhēn* in these verses should be understood collectively, and that the gifts rendered to the officiating priest became, in effect, the possession of the priesthood in general (cf. Lev. 7:6, 10).

(iii) *The ordeal of jealousy:* **5:11–31**
This section describes a situation in which a husband suspects his wife of adultery, but has no definite proof of her guilt. In such cases, the normal judicial procedures were deemed to be inadequate, and the husband was permitted to submit his wife to a 'trial by ordeal'. This involved him in bringing his wife (and an appropriate cereal offering) to the priest who, in turn, would bring her 'before the LORD' and make her swear an oath; the priest would then give her a potion to drink consisting of 'holy water' mixed with dust from

the floor of the tabernacle and into which the written words of the
oath had been washed. If the woman was guilty, the potion would
have an injurious effect on her body, but if she was innocent, it
would prove to be harmless.

The form of vv. 11–31 has been the subject of much scholarly
debate, for the section, as it stands, is replete with repetitions and
inconsistencies. Stade (*ZAW* 15 [1895], pp. 166ff.) drew attention
to the fact that the woman is twice brought before Yahweh (vv. 16,
18), twice made to swear an oath (vv. 19, 21), and twice (if not
three times!) made to drink a potion of water (vv. 24, 26, 27).
Since it was inherently improbable that such duplication would
have occurred in the actual ritual, Stade concluded that the section
represents the conflation of two separate sources, reflecting two different rituals, one involving the 'cereal offering of remembrance'
(consisting of most of vv. 11–13, 15–20, 22*a*, 23f., 26*a*, 31), and the
other involving the 'cereal offering of jealousy' (consisting, in the
main, of vv. 14, 21, 22*b*, 25, 27–30). These two rituals, according
to Stade, were originally applied to two quite distinct cases: in one,
the wife was regarded as undoubtedly guilty and the procedure was
designed to ensure that she was suitably punished for her misdemeanour; in the other, the husband merely harboured suspicions
concerning his wife's infidelity, and the procedure was intended to
establish, beyond any doubt, her guilt or innocence. A broadly similar approach was advocated by Noth (p. 49), but he saw the confusion in the present text as due to the combination of different
forms of divine judgment, brought about, in one case, by the 'holy
water' mixed with dust from the floor of the tabernacle (v. 17), in
another case, by an oath in the form of a curse uttered by the woman
(vv. 19, 21), and in yet another by the drinking of a potion in which
the words of the curse had been washed into the water (v. 23).
Noth concedes, however, that in the present form of the text these
procedures are so closely interwoven that they can no longer be
separated.

A different view of the literary pre-history of vv. 11–31 has been
advanced by Kellermann (pp. 70ff.), who argues that this section,
in its present form, is due to the expansion and modification of a
single source rather than the conflation of two originally separate
sources. The basic core of the section consisted of a simple statement
concerning the circumstances during which the ordeal was to be
used (viz., when a husband was overcome with jealousy on account

of his wife's suspected adultery; v. 14a), and a description of the ordeal procedure itself. Kellermann outlines the ordeal procedure as follows: the husband brings his wife to the priest (v. 15aα), who then takes some water and mixes it with the dust from the floor of the sanctuary (v. 17); the priest then unbinds the woman's hair (v. 18aβ), and she, in turn, utters the oath of the curse (v. 21aα); the priest then solemnly proclaims the consequences of drinking it (vv. 21aβ, 22a), and the woman subjects herself to the ordeal (v. 22b); finally, the priest writes down the oath and washes its words into the water (v. 23), and gives the drink to the woman (v. 24). This narrative, in its original form, possessed a quasi-magical character, for the potion was believed to be automatically effective; it was left to a later editor to bring the ritual under the aegis of the Yahwistic faith by emphasizing that the procedure took place 'before the LORD' (vv. 16, 18a), and that it was he who was ultimately responsible for effecting the curse (v. 21a). The references to the 'offerings' in vv. 15a, 18a, 25, 26, were inserted at a still later stage, for these presuppose specific references in Lev. 2.

A third approach to the structure of the passage is to set aside questions concerning its literary pre-history and to view the section as a unified and coherent whole (cf. Frymer-Kensky, *VT* 34 [1984], pp. 11ff.; Fishbane, *HUCA* 45 [1974], pp. 25ff.; Brichto, *HUCA* 46 [1975], pp. 55ff.; Milgrom, *Sacred Literature*, pp. 69ff.). Scholars who adopt this approach emphasize that the repetitions and inconsistencies in the text are not necessarily indicative of a multiplicity of authors, but should be regarded, rather, as a literary device deliberately deployed to ensure that each detail of each stage in the complex ritual was described in full. According to Frymer-Kensky's analysis of the passage, the description of the ritual procedure is framed by an introduction (vv. 12–14) and a recapitulation (vv. 29f.), and the ritual itself can be represented in the following summary outline: (i) *initiation* by the husband, who brings his wife and an offering to the priest (v. 15); (ii) *preparation* by the priest, involving the woman and the potion (vv. 16–18); (iii) *adjuration* by the priest, and the woman's acceptance (vv. 19–23); (iv) *execution* by the priest, who makes the woman drink the water, and accepts the offering (vv. 24–28). The action in each of these sub-sections is complex and involved, but this is only because the narrator wished to indicate, for the benefit of the priest, the precise procedure that was to be followed.

That the text of vv. 11–31 can be read as a logical and unified composition must be regarded as doubtful, and the view that it represents a 'coherent unit untouched by [an] editor's pen' (Brichto, *op. cit.*, p. 55) does less than justice to the numerous repetitions and inconsistencies within this section. Whether the text should be viewed as a single ritual, subsequently interpolated and modified, or as a combination of two originally distinct rituals, is more difficult to decide. Certainly, accidental dislocation and editorial glossing may account for some of the inconcinnities present in vv. 11–31, but, on balance, the general confusion within this section must favour the view that it represents the combination of two distinct (yet closely allied) ordeal procedures: one probably involved the use of the 'water of bitterness' (vv. 15*a*, 16f., 19f., 22*a*, 23f.) and was intended to render a judicial decision in a reasonably definite case of adultery (vv. 12f., 29, 31), while the other involved a solemn, imprecatory oath (vv. 14*a*, 18*a*, 21, 22*b*, 25f.) and was intended to allay the suspicions of a husband who harboured doubts concerning his wife's fidelity (vv. 14, 30; cf. de Vaulx).

This section represents the only explicit illustration in the *OT* of a 'trial by ordeal'; whether the ordeal was more common in Israel than this isolated instance suggests, and whether it was originally resorted to in cases other than adultery must remain uncertain. Although no exact parallel to the ritual described in 5:11ff. has been discovered among Israel's neighbours, such ordeals were not uncommon in the ancient Near East, and examples are found in Sumer (cf. Kramer, *Or*, N.S., 23 [1954], p. 48), Mari (cf. Milgrom, p. 346; Frymer, *IDBSup*, p. 640), Nuzi (cf. Driver and Miles, *Iraq* 7 [1940], pp. 132ff.), Assyria (Driver and Miles, *Assyrian Laws*, pp. 86ff.) and Babylonia (Driver and Miles, *Babylonian Laws*, ii, p. 53). For the phenomenon of the 'ordeal' in Israel, see Press, *ZAW*, N.F., 10 (1933), pp. 121ff., 227ff.; Morgenstern, *HUCA Jub. Vol.* (1925), pp. 113ff.; de Ward, *ZAW* 89 (1977), pp. 1ff.; McKane, *VT* 30 (1980), pp. 474ff.

12. If any man's wife goes astray: The verb *śāṭah* ('go astray') occurs only in this chapter (cf., also, vv. 19, 20, 29) and in Prov. 4:15 and 7:25 in the *OT*; in the latter passage, as here, the verb appears to refer to marital infidelity. **acts unfaithfully against him**: The Heb. verb used here (*mā'al*) is the same as that used in v. 6 for 'breaking faith' with Yahweh.

13. and there is no witness against her: According to Dt. 17:6;

19:15 an offender could only be convicted on the evidence of at least two witnesses. However, in a case of suspected adultery, it must have been particularly difficult for a husband to produce witnesses who could testify to his wife's infidelity, and hence the 'ordeal' would often have been seen as the only method of ascertaining her guilt or innocence. There can be little doubt that if witnesses could have been produced, the normal judicial proceedings would have been instigated, and the wife, if found guilty, may have been put to death (cf. Lev. 20:10; Dt. 22:22–7).

14–15. If the husband harboured any suspicions concerning his wife's fidelity, but could not prove the case against her, he was required to bring her before the priest and present the necessary offering, in this case **a tenth of an ephah of barley meal**: The size of the ephah is uncertain, but the quantity here required would have been relatively small, equivalent to approx. 3 or 4 litres. The 'barley meal' (Heb. *qemaḥ śᵉʿōrîm*) is nowhere else mentioned in connection with sacrifice, and the term occurs only here in P; elsewhere it is used of animal fodder (1 Kg. 4:28 [MT 5:8]) and the food consumed by the poorer classes (Ru. 2:17; Jg. 7:13). Normally, 'fine flour' (Heb. *sōleṯ*) was required in connection with cereal offerings (cf. 6:15), but the present verse may be a relic of ancient times, when barley meal was regarded as an acceptable accompaniment of sacrifice (cf. Snaith). **he shall pour no oil upon it and put no frankincense on it**: Oil and frankincense were often regarded as symbols of joy and festivity (cf. Ps. 45:7), and some commentators (following Philo) explain the absence of these accompaniments here as due to the solemn nature of the occasion (cf. Sturdy). The only other example of a 'dry' cereal offering in the *OT* is the poor man's sin offering in Lev. 5:11. **a cereal offering of jealousy**: i.e., a cereal offering presented to Yahweh, occasioned by the husband's jealousy. **a cereal offering of remembrance**: The object of the offering was not to remind the wife (if guilty) of her misdemeanour but rather to draw Yahweh's attention to the supposed offence in order that he might render a just verdict.

16. The priest was to bring the woman forward **and set her before the LORD**: In Priestly terminology, this may mean 'before the tent of meeting', or, more precisely, 'before the altar' (cf. de Ward, *op. cit.*, p. 16); this was no doubt deemed the most appropriate place for the woman to take her oath (vv. 19–22). For a similar instance of oath-taking before the altar, cf. 1 Kg. 8:31f. The reference to the 'LORD' here clearly brings the ritual (whatever its origin) within the orbit of *OT* faith.

17–18. The priest was then to take an earthen vessel which contained some **holy water:** The Heb. expression *mayim q^edōšîm* is unique in the *OT*. Some commentators (following LXX *hudōr katharon zōn*) prefer to read 'running water' (*mayim ḥayyîm*) here, and point to the use of this expression in connection with similar rituals described in 19:17; Lev. 14:5f. (Gray, McNeile; cf. Paterson). *NEB*'s 'clean water' is similarly influenced by LXX. However, Vulg. and Sam. suggest that the reading of MT should here be retained. It is not entirely clear, however, why the water should be designated as 'holy'. W. R. Smith (*Religion*, p. 181) surmised that the water in question may have been taken from a holy spring, a suggestion accepted by some recent commentators (cf. Marsh). Others contend that it was called 'holy' in anticipation of its being mixed with the sacred dust from the floor of the tabernacle (cf. Kennedy). But the most probable solution is that it was 'holy' simply by virtue of its being kept in the sanctuary, and this is supported by the Mishnah (*Soṭah*, ii. 2), which suggests that the water was sacred because it was taken from the bronze laver which contained the pure water used by the priests in their ablutions (cf. Exod. 30:28f.; 38:8). The holy water was to be mixed with **the dust that is on the floor of the tabernacle**, presumably in order to increase the sacredness and potency of the potion. The priest was then to **unbind the hair of the woman's head**: Some commentators (e.g., Sturdy, Maarsingh) interpret this as a sign of mourning for the woman's shame and disgrace (cf. Lev. 10:6), whereas others (e.g., Wenham, Snaith) view it as an indication of her uncleanness (cf. Lev. 13:45). Having placed in the woman's hands the **cereal offering of remembrance, which is the cereal offering of jealousy** (see on v. 15), the priest was to take in his hand the **water of bitterness that brings the curse**: The expression 'water of bitterness' (Heb. *mê hammārîm*), which recurs in vv. 19, 24, has proved difficult for translators and commentators alike. Driver (*Syria* 33 [1956], pp. 73ff.) has argued that *hammārîm* is derived from the Heb. root *mārāh*, 'to be rebellious, contentious' (cf. *BDB*, p. 598a), and he postulates the existence in Heb. of a form *mareh* (= 'disputed, doubted matter') with an abstract plural *mārîm* (= 'contention, dispute, doubt'). Thus, the expression *mê hammārîm* would mean 'water(s) of contention, dispute' (cf. *NEB*), and Driver contends that such a meaning is supported by LXX (*to hudōr tou* *ĕlegmou*, 'water of disputation'), and makes admirable sense in the context of a trial by ordeal. The difficulty with this explanation of *mārîm*, however, is that it fails to account for all the occurrences of the word in the present chapter, for in vv. 24, 27, the water enters the woman's body *l*ʿ*mārîm*, but what could have been meant by stating that the action of the water in the woman was 'for contention' or 'for dispute' is by no means clear. The rendering of *RSV* (cf. *NIV*; *JB*) assumes that the word *hammārîm* is derived from the root *mārar*, 'to be bitter' (so Vulg., Targ.). Objections have been raised concerning this rendering on the following grounds: (i) the construct state before an abstract plural adjective would be quite exceptional in Heb., and 'waters of bitterness' would more naturally have been rendered as *mayim mārîm* (cf. *mayim qᵉḏōšîm* in v. 17); (ii) it is difficult to comprehend how the addition of a handful of dust from the floor of the tabernacle (v. 17) could have made the holy water 'bitter'. Neither of these objections, however, is insuperable, for (i) the phraseology of the Heb., although unusual, is grammatically justifiable (cf. G–K § 128*w*); and (ii) the term 'bitter' in this context may refer not to the taste of the water but to the effect it was deemed to have on the woman, i.e., it was water that caused bitterness or pain (cf. Jer. 2:19; 4:18), and the term *l*ʿ*mārîm* in vv. 24, 27 may support this interpretation. For other possible explanations of the expression *mê hammārîm* in this verse, see Sasson, *BZ* 16 (1972), pp. 249ff.; Brichto, *HUCA* 46 (1975), p. 59; Pardee, *VT* 35 (1985), pp. 112ff.

19–22. The next stage in the ritual was that the priest was to make the woman **take an oath:** No such oath on her part appears in the subsequent narrative, but it is possible that the simple affirmation 'Amen, Amen' in v. 22*b* was regarded as tantamount to uttering an oath (cf. Jer. 11:5; Tucker, *VT* 15 [1965], p. 493). The words of the priest that follow in vv. 19–22 refer to the two-fold effect of the potion: if the woman was innocent she would suffer no adverse consequence from drinking the substance, but if she was guilty the water would have a devastating effect on her body. **your thigh fall away:** *RSV* represents a literal translation of the Heb., but the expression is sometimes understood as a euphemism for a miscarriage (*NEB*; cf. Ps. 58:9; Job 3:16; Sir. 6:3). That the fertility of the guilty woman was at stake is clear from the fact that, if she was deemed to be innocent, she would be able to 'conceive children' (v. 28), but whether this means that she was condemned to suffer a miscarriage or to become sterile is difficult to determine. The most that can be said with any degree of certainty is that consumption of the water would cause in the guilty some bodily deformity that would prevent child-bearing. **and your body swell**: This translation of the Heb. *biṭnēk ṣāḇāh* is based on the ancient Vsns, for the verb *ṣāḇāh* in the sense of 'to swell' is not found elsewhere in the *OT*, and finds no support in the cognate languages. Driver (*Syria* 33 [1956], p. 75) therefore prefers to connect the verb with the Syr. *ṣḇâ*, 'to be dry, hot', and claims that the allusion here is to the ancient belief that a woman whose uterus was too dry would not conceive, since the seed would perish for lack of nourishment. Driver believes that two distinct alternatives are contemplated in the ordeal, and that two different punishments are alluded to in the expressions 'your thigh fall away' and 'your body swell': the former expression was concerned with the case of a woman who had experienced sexual relations with another man and had conceived a child in the process, and her punishment was that she would miscarry; the latter was concerned with the case of a woman who had experienced sexual relations with another man, but who had not conceived, and her punishment was that she would 'dry up', i.e., become sterile. However, Driver's exposition cannot be regarded as satisfactory, for there is nothing in the Heb. to suggest that the phrase 'your thigh fall away and your body swell' was intended to refer to two alternative forms of punishment, and his interpretation of the verb *ṣāḇāh* fails to explain why the Vsns unanimously understood the verb to mean 'to swell'. An alternative explanation of the verb *ṣāḇāh* has been proposed by Frymer-Kensky (*op. cit.*, pp. 20f.), who connects the word with the Akkad. root *ṣabû/ṣapû* = 'to soak', or 'to flood', and claims that the meaning here is that the woman's uterus would be 'flooded' by the curse-bearing waters, thus making her unable to conceive; such an affliction (commonly known as a 'prolapsed uterus') would have caused a distention of the abdomen, which may account for the rendering found in the Vsns. But whether the translators of the Vsns would have had sufficient medical knowledge of this particular affliction to have understood that it would have caused a swelling of the body must be regarded as doubtful; moreover, it remains to be explained why they did not simply use a verb that would have conveyed the sense of 'to soak' or 'to flood'. In general, attempts to diagnose the precise condition presupposed by the words 'your thigh fall away and your body swell' have not proved to be successful, and the fact that such a variety of diseases have been suggested – ranging from 'dropsy' (Josephus, *Ant.* III.11.6) to 'thrombophlebitis' (Sasson) and 'false pregnancy' (Brichto) – merely underlines the speculative nature of the inquiry. **(let the priest make the woman take the oath of the curse)**: This rubric in v. 21*a* interrupts the priest's words in vv. 19–22, and is rightly placed in brackets by *RSV* (cf. *NEB*).

23. The priest was instructed to write the words of the curse **in a book** (better, perhaps, 'parchment' or 'scroll'; cf. *NEB, NIV*) and **wash them off into the water of bitterness**: By this action it was believed that the words were symbolically transferred to the water, and the potion thus became imbued with the efficacy of a curse. Commentators on this verse frequently refer to parallel customs prevalent in Egypt, India and Tibet, where charms were written down and then swallowed (cf. Gray, McNeile, Sturdy), but since such charms were normally consumed in order to effect a cure for various diseases, it is difficult to see what relevance such parallels have for the present context.

26. as its memorial portion: The Heb. term *'azkārāh* is peculiar to P, and occurs only here outside the book of Leviticus (cf. Lev. 2:2, 9, 16; 5:12; 6:15 [MT 6:8]; 24:7). The term is traditionally rendered 'memorial' (*AV*; cf. LXX; Vulg. *memoriale*), but its precise meaning is obscure. The word is consistently used in connection with that part of the cereal offering that was burned on the altar, and Driver (*JSS* I [1956], pp. 99f.) suggests that it may originally have referred to a 'token portion' (cf. *NEB*) of the sacrifice which was presented to Yahweh, the remainder being the perquisite of the priests.

28. If the woman had not defiled herself, then **she shall be free**. Some commentators (McNeile, Binns) understand this to mean 'free from guilt', i.e., she was, in effect, formally declared innocent and acquitted of the charge against her (cf. Jer. 2:35). But it is improbable that the word was intended to have such a technical, forensic connotation in the present context, and it probably implied no more than that she was free of any harm which the water may have caused.

29–31. These verses form a concluding summary of the passage, recounting the purpose of the ritual and the manner in which it was to be put into effect.

29. This is the law: This expression is characteristic of the Priestly writer, who uses it both as an introductory (e.g., Lev. 6:9 [MT 6:2]) and concluding formula (e.g., Lev. 11:46; 12:7).

31. the man shall be free from iniquity: No blame was to be attached to the husband for submitting his wife to the ordeal, even if his suspicions proved to be entirely unfounded. It was otherwise in Mari, for a husband making such a false accusation would have been burned (cf. Cardascia, *Fest. Eilers*, p. 22). Brichto (*op. cit.*, p. 63) suggests that this verse refers not to the woman's husband but rather to her adulterous consort, and that the point is that he was to remain unpunished and that no steps were to be taken to identify him. However, this seems most unlikely, for Heb. law prescribed the death penalty for both the man and the woman found guilty of adultery (cf. Lev. 20:10; Dt. 22:22). The chapter concludes by stating that the woman, if found guilty, must **bear her iniquity**, i.e., she must suffer the consequences of her guilt. On the technical term employed here, *nāśā' ʿawōn*, see von Rad, *OT Theology*, i, pp. 268f.

(b) THE NAZIRITE
6:1–21

A substantial part of this chapter is devoted to the Nazirite, i.e., the man (or woman) who had taken a vow to consecrate himself (or herself) to Yahweh. The passage is usually divided by commentators into three parts. The first section (vv. 1–8) deals with the general conditions which the Nazirite had to observe during the period of his vow: he was to abstain from all intoxicating liquors and all products of the vine (vv. 3f.), refrain from cutting his hair (v. 5), and avoid becoming defiled through contact with the dead (vv. 6f.). The second section (vv. 9–12) depicts a situation in which the third of these taboos had been accidentally broken; should the Nazirite become defiled by unwittingly touching a corpse, he had to perform certain rituals and begin the period of his consecration anew. The third section (vv. 13–21) describes the ceremony to be observed on completion of the vow: the Nazirite was to offer a sacrifice (vv. 13–17), and then shave his head and throw the hair into the fire on the altar (v. 18); the priest was then entitled to take part of the offering as his own perquisite (vv. 19f.). When this ritual had been duly performed, the Nazirite was free to drink wine again and resume his normal life.

Etymologically, the term 'Nazirite' (Heb. *nāzîr*) is derived from the verbal root *nzr*, 'to separate'; the Nazirites were thus lay persons who had 'separated' themselves from the realm of things profane and who had dedicated themselves to the service of God. The institution seems to have existed from very early days (cf. Jg. 13–16; Am. 2:11) down to the final destruction of the temple (cf. Josephus, *Ant.* XIX.6.1; Eusebius, *H.E.* II.xxiii.4; see, also, the tractate *Nāzîr* in the Mishnah). Some scholars have sought its origin in traditions connected with the 'holy war' (cf. de Vaux, *AI*, p. 467), while others have suggested that it originated in a strict desire to conform to ancient custom and avoid contact with anything even remotely connected with Canaanite religion. The earliest recorded example of a Nazirite in the *OT* is Samson, who is explicitly described as a 'Nazirite to God' (Jg. 13:5); yet, the case of Samson presents certain peculiarities when compared with the regulations concerning the Nazirite contained in the present chapter. It is implied in the present chapter that any Israelite could, of his own accord, take a vow to become a Nazirite, but in the case of Samson there is no mention of a 'vow', and the service was evidently undertaken in response to a divine command which had been given even before Samson's birth (cf. Jg. 13:4f.). Moreover, Num. 6:1ff. presupposes that a person remained a Nazirite for a limited period only; on the other hand, Samson's dedication was no temporary measure, but a lifelong service (cf. Jg. 13:7). Further, although the regulation concerning the cutting of the hair (v. 5) was observed by Samson (cf. Jg. 13:5; 16:17), there is no indication that he deliberately abstained from wine (cf. Jg. 14:10) or that he had any scruples regarding contact with the dead (cf. Jg. 14:8, 19). The existence of these discrepancies has led some scholars to suppose that two types of Nazirite are envisaged in the *OT*, namely, those who were bound for life and those who took the vow for a fixed period only; the two types, it is argued, were bound by different regulations, and this accounts for the differences between the account of Samson in the book of Judges and the regulations governing the Nazirite encountered in the present chapter (cf. Kennedy, p. 220). However, there seems no substantive reason to suppose that two types of Nazirite co-existed in Israel, and it is preferable to view the temporary Naziriteship presupposed in this chapter as a later development of the earlier concept of 'lifelong' Nazirites. This seems to be confirmed by the fact that there are no references to 'temporary' Nazirites in the pre-exilic period, although they appear to have been numerous in later times (cf. I Mac. 3:49ff.); on the other hand, there are hardly any references to permanent Nazirites in the period after the exile, although they appear to have been the norm in pre-exilic times (cf. Gray, *JTS* I [1899–1900], pp. 202ff.).

Although the passage concerning the Nazirite reads coherently in its present form, its unity is generally disputed by commentators. Kellermann (pp. 83ff.) finds in vv. 1–21 two distinct components, one comprising vv. 2b–8, 9abα, 12aαb, and the other comprising vv. 1, 2a, 9bβ–11, 12aβ, 13–21. The first component, according to Kellermann, already had its own pre-history before it appeared in its present form. He finds the original nucleus of the law in v. 5aβ (the command to refrain from cutting the hair, which seems to have been a distinguishing feature of the Nazirite from earliest times; cf. Jg. 13:5). At a later stage the prohibition concerning the drinking of alcohol was added in v. 3a (possibly under the influence of the Rechabites), and this prohibition subsequently attracted to it the more detailed ruling concerning the consumption of the grape and its juice in v. 3b. The command to refrain from touching a corpse (which appears to have been unknown in ancient times; cf. Jg. 15:8, 16) was added at a still later stage (v. 6b). Thus, Kellermann argues that vv. 3, 5aβ, 6b once formed a single unit, and the regulations contained in these verses were originally concerned with the case of the life-long Nazirite. A later editor expanded this into a far more detailed ruling by the addition of vv. 2b, 4, 5aαb, 6a, 7f.; in doing so, however, the law was transformed into one which was concerned only with the case of the temporary Nazirite (cf. the reference to 'all the days of his separation' in vv. 4a, 5a, 6a, 8a). The prohibition against touching a corpse (v. 6b) provided an opportunity to include regulations concerning cases of accidental defilement, and these are included in vv. 9abα, 12aαb. The second component of the present section, according to Kellermann, consists mainly of vv. 13–21, which may be regarded as essentially a literary unity (with the possible exception of v. 21aγ). This section, which begins and concludes with the same formula ('And this is the law for the Nazirite; vv. 13, 21) probably derives from the same author as vv. 9bβ–11, 12aβ, for similar expressions occur in both passages (e.g., 'the door of the tent of meeting'; vv. 10b, 13b, 18a), and in both the priest plays a significant role in the ritual. Finally, this author was responsible for the inclusion of the introduction in vv. 1, 2a.

Clearly, much of Kellermann's literary-critical analysis must remain hypothetical, and some of the individual details of his reconstruction of the development of the passage will no doubt remain open to question. Nevertheless, there is much to be said for taking the command to abstain from cutting the hair in v. 5 as the starting-point, for this was undoubtedly the most marked feature of the Nazirite, and it is a feature which is almost invariably alluded to whenever the Nazirite is mentioned. It also seems likely that the command to refrain from wine and strong drink was originally expressed in the form of a simple prohibition (v. 3a), but that this was later expanded to include the grape out of which the wine was made (v. 3b), and even its seeds and skins (v. 4); similarly, the command to refrain from touching a corpse (v. 6b) was probably later elaborated by reference to the immediate family of the Nazirite (v. 7). The allusion to contamination by contact with the dead may well have led to the incorporation of a rite to deal with cases of accidental defilement, though the case for regarding vv. 9–12 as the product of two different authors cannot be regarded as conclusive. The fact that the Nazirite vow was of limited duration (cf. v. 4a) probably led to the later inclusion of vv. 13–21, which describes the ritual necessary to terminate the Nazirite's period of separation. For a further discussion of the literary development of the Nazirite law contained in 6:1–21, see Jastrow, *JBL* 33 (1914), pp. 266ff.; Zuckschwerdt, *ZAW* 88 (1976), pp. 191ff.

Commentators have generally recognized that vv. 1–21 derive from P, but since the passage appears to betray a dependence on the rituals contained in Lev. 1–7, it is generally assigned to one of the later strata within the Priestly corpus.

2. makes a special vow: This is the only place in the *OT* where a vow to become a Nazirite is expressly mentioned. The Heb. verb *pālā'* (rendered 'make' by *RSV*) usually means 'to be marvellous, wonderful', and, according to Noth (p. 55), its use here suggests that the vow of the Nazirite was something quite exceptional and extraordinary (cf. Budd, Maarsingh; Ibn Ezra, 'makes a remarkable vow'); however, the verb can also mean 'to accomplish something difficult' (cf. *BDB*, p. 810b), and if this is the sense in which it is used in the present context, it suggests that the vow of the Nazirite was not something to be undertaken lightly. For the use of the verb *pālā'* elsewhere in connection with vows, cf. 15:3, 8; Lev. 22:21; 27:2. It has been suggested that the vow of the Nazirite was not, as is often supposed, a pious pledge selflessly undertaken to demonstrate his (or her) personal piety and unwavering devotion to God, but was, rather, a conditional promise undertaken on the understanding that God would grant the Nazirite's petitions and answer his prayers (cf. Cartledge, *CBQ* 51 [1989], pp. 409ff.; *Vows*, pp. 18ff.). However, although this type of Nazirite vow is encountered in later Jewish tradition (cf. *Nāzîr* 2:7–10; Josephus, *War* II.15.1), it does not follow that it existed in *OT* times, and the lack of any specific statement in the *OT* concerning the circumstances in which such vows were taken, or the motives underlying the decision to become a Nazirite, must make such a conclusion uncertain.

3. he shall separate himself from wine and strong drink: The word rendered 'strong drink' here, *šēkār*, was a general term covering all sorts of intoxicating liquors. The first condition of the Nazirite vow, then, was total abstinence from alcoholic beverages and the products of the vine. Such abstemiousness may have been regarded by the Nazirite as a protest against the decadence, luxury and degeneracy of the age in which he lived. Wine and strong drink were also forbidden to priests before ministering in the tent of meeting (Lev. 10:9), and abstinence from such intoxicants was one of the distinguishing features of the Rechabites (Jer. 35:2ff.). The only other clear indication in the *OT* that the Nazirite abstained from wine is found in Am. 2:12. It is interesting to observe that Samson's mother was bidden to abstain from all intoxicants (Jg. 13:4, 7, 14), although whether her son was subject to the same restriction is not recorded.

4. During the entire period of his (or her) vow, the Nazirite was to eat **nothing that is produced by the grapevine**: This is preferable to *RV*'s 'nothing that is made of the grape-vine', which represents an over-literal translation of the Heb. *'āśah*; for this verb in the sense of 'produce, yield', cf. Gen. 1:11f.; Isa. 5:2, 4, 10 (*BDB*, p. 794*b*). **not even the seeds or the skins**: The Heb. words translated here as 'seeds' and 'skins' are *hapax legomena*, and their meanings can no longer be ascertained with any certainty (cf. *NEB*, 'shoot or berry'). However, the gist of the phrase is clear: the Nazirite was prohibited from eating anything connected with the vine, even the most unpalatable and unappetizing parts of the plant.

5. he shall let the locks of hair of his head grow long: The second condition of the Nazirite's vow was that he was to remain, like Samson, unshaven and unshorn (cf. Jg. 13:5; 16:17). Hair was regarded as taboo by many primitive peoples, and it was a common belief that the hair of sacred people was not to be touched; hence, in some ancient cultures, it remained completely shorn, whereas in others it was never shorn at all. The Nazirite's long hair was a visible sign of his consecration, and it was evidently regarded as such a characteristic feature that the term 'Nazirite' was used, metaphorically, of an unpruned vine (Lev. 25:5, 11).

6–8. he shall not go near a dead body: The third condition of the Nazirite's vow was that he was to avoid defilement occasioned by contact with a corpse. Since this regulation was not observed by Samson (cf. Jg. 14:19; 15:8), it is possible that this particular rule only became operative at a later period. By the time of P, however, this condition was absolutely binding, and could not be broken even for one's closest relative: **Neither for his father nor for his mother, nor for brother or sister, if they die, shall he make himself unclean**. In this regard, the restriction placed upon the Nazirite was as stringent as that placed upon the high priest (cf. Lev. 21:11), and was even more stringent than that which pertained to ordinary priests, for whom close relatives were excepted (cf. Lev. 21:1f.).

9–12. These verses state the procedure to be followed if the regulation noted in vv. 6–8 was accidentally infringed. No such procedure is prescribed for a breach of the first two conditions of the vow, presumably because these were regarded as within the individual's own control; however, a situation could conceivably arise where a death suddenly occurred in the Nazirite's presence, and he unintentionally touched the dead person's body. Since he had defiled himself in this way, his vow was automatically rendered null and void, and certain rites had to be observed before he could be declared clean again and begin the period of his consecration anew. He was to be regarded as unclean for seven days, at the end of which period he was to shave his head; then, on the eighth day, he was to bring an appropriate offering to the priest. There is no indication here as to what was to be done with the hair that was shorn. The Mishnah (*Temurah* 7:4) suggests that, because it was regarded as utterly unclean, it had to be buried; whether this was so or not must remain uncertain, but since it was no longer sacred, it could clearly not be burned on the altar and offered to God, as was the case when the Nazirite normally ended the period of his vow (cf. v. 18). The offerings which the Nazirite was to bring before God on the eighth day

consisted of **two turtledoves or two young pigeons**: These offerings were often prescribed for the poor who could not normally
afford more expensive forms of sacrifice (cf. Lev. 5:7; 14:21f.). It is
not clear why these particular offerings should be mentioned here,
since there is no suggestion that the Nazirite was necessarily a person
of modest means. However, since these sacrifices appear elsewhere
in the context of ceremonial uncleanness (cf. Lev. 12:8; 15:14, 29),
their presence here is not entirely inappropriate. The Nazirite was
required to offer one bird as a **sin offering**, and the other as a
burnt offering. The sin offering was presented at the consecration
of priests (Lev. 8:14ff.) and Levites (8:8, 12), but was also offered,
as here, to make atonement for inadvertent transgressions (cf. 15:24,
27). Milgrom (*VT* 21 [1971], pp. 237ff.) suggests that the term 'sin
offering' should rather be rendered 'purification offering' (cf. *REB*),
since its object was to restore a person who had broken a taboo to
his former state of ritual purity. The 'burnt offering' (*NEB*, 'whole-
offering'; cf. Snaith, *VT* 7 [1957], p. 309) was a sacrifice in which
the victim was completely burned on the altar and no part of it was
eaten by the worshipper or by the priest. In addition to the sin
offering and burnt offering, the Nazirite was required to present a
male lamb as a **guilt offering** (Heb. *'āšām*). It is not clear why a
guilt offering was demanded, for this was usually offered in cases of
reparation for some wrong or damage which had been inflicted, and,
as such, it was occasionally accompanied by the payment of a fine
(cf. Lev. 6:2ff.; Snaith, *VT* 15 [1965], pp. 73ff.). Dillmann (p. 36)
interprets the accidental defilement of the Nazirite as a punishment
from God for some inadvertent offence which he had committed,
and he suggests that the guilt offering was required as some form
of recompense. However, it seems more probable that the *'āšām* was
offered as a form of reparation to God for the Nazirite's delay in
fulfilling his vow. When all these offerings had been duly made, the
reconsecration of the Nazirite was complete, and he was in a position
to renew his vow for the same period as before.

13–20. These verses are concerned with the rites to be performed
when the Nazirite had completed the term of his vow. The first
stage in the procedure was that the Nazirite had to be **brought to
the door of the tent of meeting**: The element of compulsion
implied by the word 'brought' is not easy to explain, for it may be
supposed that the Nazirite would have come to the door of the tent
of his own volition, anxious to participate in the ceremony denoting

the completion of the period of his vow. Some scholars have therefore resorted to textual emendation here (cf. Paterson), but perhaps the Hiphil form of the verb was used in this instance merely to suggest an element of formality in the proceedings. Having reached the door of the tent, the Nazirite was to **offer his gift to the LORD**, and this was to include all the regular forms of sacrifice: a male lamb, a year old and without blemish, as a burnt offering; an unblemished ewe lamb, a year old, as a sin offering; and an unblemished ram as a peace offering. The Nazirite was also required to offer the cereal and drink offerings which traditionally accompanied these sacrifices. The fact that the burnt offering is mentioned before the sin offering is strange, since the latter would normally have been offered first; however, it should be noted that the present order is not without parallel in the *OT* (cf. Lev. 12:6, 8). The characteristic feature of the **peace offering** (the Heb. *šᵉlāmîm* is nearly always found in the plural in the *OT*) was that only a part of it was burned on the altar, and the rest was consumed by the priest and the worshipper; thus, a close bond was established between the deity and those who presented the offering, since all were regarded as partaking of a common meal (cf. *NEB*, 'shared-offering'; *NIV*, 'fellowship offering').

18. After presenting the appropriate offerings, the Nazirite was instructed to **shave his consecrated head at the door of the tent of meeting**, and place the hair **on the fire which is under the sacrifice of the peace offering**. Gray (pp. 68f.; *JTS* 1 [1899–1900], pp. 204f.) suggests that this rite had its origin in the primitive and widespread custom of 'hair offerings', in which the hair (believed to be imbued with divine life-giving power and thus symbolizing a person's vital being) was shaved and offered as a sacrifice to the deity (cf. Smith, *Religion*, pp. 331f.). However, it is improbable that the ritual described here was understood as merely another form of sacrifice (*contra* McNeile); rather, the burning of the hair was probably the most convenient way of disposing of something which had been consecrated to Yahweh, thus ensuring that it could not be defiled or misused in superstitious practices (cf. Noth).

19–20. A share of the sacrifice was placed in the hands of the Nazirite so that he could formally present it to the priest; the priest, in turn, would then offer it to Yahweh. On this occasion, the priest's perquisite consisted of the shoulder of the ram, an unleavened cake and an unleavened wafer, in addition to the statutory offerings which were regarded as his due, viz., **the breast that is waved and the thigh that is offered** (cf. Lev. 7:34). The Heb. here contains two technical terms, namely, *tᵉnûpāh* and *tᵉrûmāh*. The word *tᵉnûpāh* has traditionally been rendered 'wave offering' (*AV*; *RV*) and understood to mean that the priest 'waved' (*hēnîp*) the offering back and forth in the direction of the altar as a symbolic gesture that it was being presented to Yahweh. Driver (*JSS* 1 [1956], pp. 100ff.), however, has drawn attention to some of the difficulties inherent in this interpretation of the term, not the least of which is that it is difficult to envisage how the whole body of Levites could have been waved in the manner described in 8:11, 13, 15. He therefore suggests that the word *tᵉnûpāh* should be derived not from the root *nûp* I = 'to move to and fro', but from a root *nûp* II = 'to be high', which, on the basis of a parallel in Arab., may be rendered 'set apart'; the noun *tᵉnûpāh* would thus designate an offering which had been 'set apart', and the word should be rendered as 'special contribution' (cf. *NEB*). The term *tᵉrûmāh* has traditionally been rendered 'heave offering', and this term, too, has been taken to imply that a symbolic gesture (in this case 'heaving') was required by the priest as the offering was presented to Yahweh. However, an examination of the passages in which the Heb. term occurs indicates that the word denotes, rather, that which was 'lifted off' (Heb. *rûm*) or 'separated' (cf. LXX, *aphairema*, 'that which is taken away'; Vulg., *separatio*) from the rest of the offering in order that it may be presented to Yahweh as a 'reserved portion'. It is not clear whether any substantive difference is to be discerned between the two terms. Snaith (*ExpT* 74 [1962–3], p. 127) suggests that *tᵉnûpāh* referred to gifts allocated for the maintenance of the priesthood as a whole, while *tᵉrûmāh* referred to the gifts which were regarded as the perquisite of the officiating priest himself; however, it is doubtful whether the evidence available can justify the drawing of such a fine line of distinction between the two terms, and it seems preferable to regard them as virtually identical in every respect. Once these offerings had been duly presented, the Nazirite's period of consecration was complete, and he was free to **drink wine** and to resume his normal life.

21. His offering to the LORD shall be according to his vow as a Nazirite, apart from what else he can afford: The offerings demanded in the present passage were clearly regarded as the minimum amount that were to be presented; if the Nazirite could afford to present larger offerings, he was entitled (and no doubt encouraged) to do so. But if, at the time of his consecration, he had promised to give more offerings than the law required, then it was essential that these, too, be presented before he could be released from his vow.

(c) THE PRIESTLY BLESSING
6:22–27

Moses is here commanded to convey to Aaron and his sons the form of blessing which they were to pronounce upon the people. The introduction (vv. 22f.) is couched in the characteristic style of the Priestly writer (cf. Lev. 6:24f.), but commentators are agreed that the three-fold petition of the blessing which follows must have originated from a different source, for it is replete with words and idioms that are completely alien to the vocabulary of P (cf. Kellermann, p. 95; Rüger, *BT* 28 [1977], p. 332). Moreover, the sudden transition from second person plural verbs in v. 23 to second person singular verbs in vv. 24–26 confirms the view that vv. 24–26 originally formed an independent unit which was only later incorporated into its present context. The style of the concluding verse of the section (v. 27) differs from both the blessing and the introduction, and is probably to be regarded as a later insertion (cf. Kellermann, p. 97).

It is impossible to determine, even approximately, the date of the blessing, but its simplicity of expression may suggest that it derives from a very early period (cf. Noth), and it may well have been used by the priests who officiated at the Jerusalem temple in pre-exilic times. The antiquity of the blessing has recently been verified by the discovery of two inscribed silver plaques at Ketef Hinnom, in the environs of Jerusalem. The plaques were dated by the excavator, Gabriel Barkay (*Ketef Hinnom*, p. 29) to the mid-seventh century BC, though others (e.g., Yardeni, *VT* 41 [1991], p. 180) preferred a slightly later date, in the early sixth century BC. The task of deciphering the two plaques proved difficult, but it was discovered that both contained versions of the priestly blessing which were strikingly similar to that encountered in Num. 6:24–26. The blessing inscribed on the larger plaque proved almost identical to the biblical text, while that inscribed on the smaller plaque was an abbreviated version, the second and third blessings having been combined ('The LORD make his face shine upon you and give you peace'). For a brief account of the discovery, see Barkay, *BAR* 9/2 (1983), pp. 14ff.

It is by no means clear why the priestly blessing should have been placed in its present position, immediately after the section concerning the Nazirite (6:1–21) and before the list of offerings for the tabernacle (7:1ff.). Some commentators surmise that it was included at this point to indicate that a divine blessing would inevitably follow upon an act of voluntary devotion such as that exhibited by the Nazirite (cf. Sturdy). However, this suggestion seems rather forced, and it is more reasonable to suppose that vv. 24–26 are a misplaced fragment. The view that these verses originally stood after Lev. 9:22f. (cf. Dillmann, p. 38; Elliger, *Leviticus*, p. 130) has much to commend it, for here Aaron is represented as uttering a blessing, the words of which are not actually included in the ensuing narrative; however, since there is no Versional evidence to support such a dislocation, the suggestion must remain no more than a possibility.

The blessing itself contains just three lines, consisting, in Heb., of three, five and seven words respectively; each line consists of two jussive clauses (though cf. Jagersma, *Fest. van der Ploeg*, pp. 131ff.) with Yahweh as the explicit subject of the first clause and the implicit subject of the second. It is not clear whether the *waw* that joins the second clause of each line to the first is to be regarded as copulative (i.e., 'may Yahweh bless and protect'), in which case vv. 24–26 would consist of six separate blessings, or whether the *waw* was intended to indicate consequence (i.e., Yahweh's blessing would result in protection), in which case these verses would contain only three blessings (so Noth); the way in which the verbs of the blessing are rearranged in Ps. 67:1 (which appears to cite the blessing of vv. 24–26 in summary form) may favour the former alternative (cf. Fishbane, *JAOS* 103 [1983], pp. 115f.). For attempts to reconstruct the text of the blessing in order to give it a more symmetrical structure, see Loretz, *UF* 10 (1978), pp. 115ff.; Freedman, *Fest. McKenzie*, pp. 35ff.; and for a detailed discussion of various aspects of the blessing itself, see Seybold, *Segen, passim*.

23. Thus you shall bless the people of Israel: The act of blessing is here regarded as an intrinsic part of the duties of the priests, represented by **Aaron and his sons** (cf. Dt. 21:5). There is evidence, however, that the king could on rare occasions usurp the priestly prerogative, and himself bless the people (cf. 2 Sam. 6:18; 1 Kg. 8:14, 55). Blessings were uttered on different occasions, but were normally pronounced in the sanctuary, either when the worshippers entered (cf. Ps. 118:26) or, more commonly, when they were dismissed at the end of the service (cf. Lev. 9:22ff.; Murtonen, *VT* 9 [1959], pp. 166ff.). For the importance of the divine blessing in the theology of P, cf. Brueggemann, *ZAW* 84 (1972), pp. 397ff.; Miller, *Int* 29 (1975), pp. 240ff.

24. The LORD bless you: Although this supplication may appear to be somewhat vague and open-ended, it would no doubt have been understood by the Israelites in a specific, concrete way to mean that Yahweh would provide them with wealth and possessions (cf. Gen. 24:35), land and progeny (Gen. 35:9ff.), fertility, health, and success in battle (cf. Dt. 7:12ff.; 28:1ff.). **and keep you**: (*REB*, 'guard you') i.e., from all the misfortunes and calamities that might befall the worshipper. The meaning of this supplication is well illustrated by such passages as Ps. 121:3ff.; 140:4; 141:9.

25. The LORD make his face to shine upon you: This expression, which Noth (p. 59) characterizes as an 'unselfconscious anthropomorphism' occurs frequently in the Psalms (31:16; 67:1; 80:3, 7, 19; 119:135), where it appears as a metaphor for divine benevolence and favour. For a similar idiom in Mesopotamian literature, see Oppenheim *JAOS* 61 (1941), pp. 256ff.; Muffs, *Studies*, pp. 130ff.; Fishbane, *JAOS* 103 (1983), pp. 116f. The solemn, threefold repetition of the divine name in vv. 24–26 emphasizes the fact that Yahweh, and he alone, was the ultimate source of Israel's blessing, a point strongly reaffirmed in the concluding verse of the section (v. 27; cf. Miller, *op. cit.*, p. 249). According to the Mishnah (*Tamid* vii.2), the Jews, even when they had ceased to use the divine name 'Yahweh', retained it when this blessing was uttered daily in the temple in Jerusalem; when the blessing was pronounced in a synagogue, however, a substitute for the divine name was used.

26. The LORD lift up his countenance upon you: The idiom 'to lift up the face' (Heb. *nāśā' pānîm 'el*) has a variety of nuances in the *OT* (cf. Gruber, *ZAW* 95 [1983], pp. 252ff.), but here it means 'to look upon with favour or approval' (cf. *NEB*, 'look kindly on'). The converse expression, 'to hide one's face', indicates displeasure or disapproval (cf. Dt. 31:18; Ps. 30:7; Ezek. 39:23f.). **and give you peace**: The Heb. idiom *śîm śalôm* has no exact parallel in the *OT*, but a similar expression does occur in an Aram. letter dating from the fifth century BC (*ślm ysmū lk*; cf. Driver, *Aramaic Documents*, p. 37, letter XIII); however, the possibility that this expression is a direct quotation from Num. 6:26 cannot be ruled out. The Heb. word *śalôm* has a far wider range of meanings than its English equivalent 'peace', since it encompasses material benefits such as prosperity in addition to an inner sense of harmony, wholeness and well-being.

27. This verse is not, of course, a part of the blessing, and this is made clear in LXX, where it is placed after v. 23. **So shall they put my name upon the people of Israel, and I will bless them**: Many commentators have drawn attention to the awkwardness of the third person plural verb here, and the third plural suffix in the verb *'ᵃḇāreᵏem*, since the introduction in vv. 22f. would naturally lead one to expect the verb (and the suffix) to be in the second person plural. However, there is certainly no need to emend the text (*contra* de Vaulx), for a detailed comparison of vv. 23 and 27 indicates that they were composed by two different authors, and hence v. 27 should not be regarded as a continuation of the line of thought expressed in v. 23 (cf. Kellermann). The main interest of the verse has centred upon the words *weśāmû 'eṯ-šᵉmî 'al*, an expression which occurs only here in the *OT*. *NEB* renders it, 'they shall pronounce my name over', following Vulg. *invocare*, but de Boer (*VT* 32 [1982], pp. 3ff.) rejects this rendering on the ground that such a meaning would have been more idiomatically expressed in Heb. by *qārā' 'eṯ-šem 'al*. He therefore suggests that the preposition *'al* is a misreading of an original divine epithet *'ēl* (elsewhere, *'elyôn*) = the Most High, and he renders the verse, 'And when they shall name me The Most High of the Israelites, I, on my part, will bless them'. However, this suggestion seems most unlikely, for the expression 'the Most High of the Israelites' would be without parallel in the *OT*, and it would, in any case, be inherently improbable that a scribe would have had the temerity to alter the divine name in the text before him. It seems preferable to understand the verb *śîm* in this context in terms of the gesture normally adopted by the priest when he blessed the congregation; according to Sir. 50:20f., he would 'raise his hands over all the congregation of Israel' as he pronounced the blessing in the name of Yahweh (cf. Lev. 9:22). But however the verb *śîm* is understood, the thrust of the verse is clear: the priests were merely the agents or mediators of the divine blessing; it was Yahweh himself who caused the blessing to be effective.

(C) PREPARATIONS FOR THE DEPARTURE FROM SINAI
7:1–10:10
(a) THE GIFTS OF THE TRIBAL LEADERS
7:1–89

This chapter, the longest in the *OT* (apart from Ps. 119), lists the gifts for the tabernacle donated by the twelve tribal leaders. These gifts consisted, firstly, of six wagons and twelve oxen which were to be given to the Levites to facilitate the transportation of the various objects connected with the tabernacle (vv. 1–9). The Merarites, who had to transport the heaviest items (the wooden framework, etc.; cf. 3:36f.; 4:31f.) were given four wagons and eight oxen, while the Gershonites, who were responsible for carrying the lighter material (the curtains and hangings, etc.; cf. 3:25f.; 4:24ff.) received two wagons and four oxen. No wagons or oxen were given to the Kohathites, however, for the holy objects entrusted to their care (cf. 4:4ff.) had to be carried on their shoulders (v. 9). Other gifts brought by the leaders for the dedication of the altar are listed at length in vv. 10–83, and these were formally presented by them on successive days. The sum total of offerings presented is recorded in vv. 84–88. V. 89 is an isolated fragment, which describes how God spoke to Moses in the tent of meeting from between the two cherubim.

It has been suggested that the tedious, monotonous tone of much of this chapter is due to the fact that the author was here reproducing an archival record (Levine, pp. 259ff.; cf. *JAOS* 85 [1965], pp. 314ff.); whether this is so or not cannot be proved, but there can be little doubt that the object of its inclusion was to emphasize the unstinting generosity of the tribal leaders of old, a generosity which the author's own contemporaries would do well to emulate. In this way, support for the priestly ministry in post-exilic times was enjoined, and the fact that each of the twelve tribal leaders contributed offerings underlined the necessity for the entire community to be involved in the upkeep of the ecclesiastical establishment.

It is generally agreed by commentators that this chapter belongs to one of the latest strata of P (cf. Noth, p. 63), for it seems to presuppose not only chs. 1–4 but also some secondary P passages in Exodus and Leviticus. Dependence on chs. 1–4 is evident from the fact that the names of the tribal leaders in vv. 12ff. agree with those given in 1:5ff., and the order in which these leaders appear is the same as that encountered in 2:1ff. Moreover, the distribution of the wagons between the Gershonites and the Merarites is almost certainly to be understood against the background of chs. 3f., where the Merarites are depicted as having to transport the heaviest and most difficult parts of the tabernacle, while the Gershonites were responsible for the lighter and more manageable items. Further, the information that the Merarites were under the supervision of Ithamar, Aaron's son (v. 8), seems to be derived from 4:33. The references to the setting up and construction of the tabernacle, and the 'anointing' of the altar (vv. 10, 84) indicate a dependence on certain secondary passages in Exodus (e.g., Exod. 40:9f.), and the sacrifices and offerings which the leaders present in vv. 12ff. appear to presuppose such passages as Exod. 25:29; 27:3; Lev. 9:1ff.

The form of the chapter presents comparatively little difficulty. Kellermann (pp. 98ff.) regards vv. 2a, 3a (without 'and brought'), 4–9 as a literary unity, and maintains that the tradition contained in these verses concerning the gifts of wagons and oxen was subsequently used by the author of vv. 10–83 to supplement his own report concerning the gifts presented by the tribal leaders for the sacrificial worship of the tabernacle. The author of vv. 10–83 was probably responsible for the inclusion of v. 1 (thus giving the two reports a common introduction), and vv. 2b and 3b. The main section of the chapter (vv. 10–83) consists of an almost verbatim repetition of the formula encountered in vv. 12–17, the only substantive difference being the change in the name of the tribal leader. The similarity of style between this section and the concluding summary in vv. 84–88 suggests that the same author was responsible for both (but cf. Holzinger, p. 31, for a different view). V. 89 is clearly a later addition and is almost certainly a displaced fragment, the original context of which can no longer be determined.

1. On the day when Moses had finished setting up the tabernacle: According to Exod. 40:17, Moses finished setting up the tabernacle on the first day of the first month in the second year after the exodus; thus the date presupposed here is a month earlier than that mentioned in 1:1. Yet, curiously, the following verses presuppose that the events of chs. 1–4 had already taken place. Some scholars seek to account for the discrepancy by suggesting that the word translated 'day' (Heb. *yôm*) is here to be understood indefinitely in the sense of 'at the time when' (cf. Milgrom, *HAR* 9 [1985],

p. 224; *NIV*), a meaning attested elsewhere in the *OT* (e.g., Prov. 25:13). However, the most probable explanation is that the present chapter is the work of a later editor who had simply failed to notice the inconsistency.

2. the leaders of Israel: That these were the same leaders as those already referred to in 1:5–15 is clear from their names, as listed in vv. 12, 18, 24 etc. For the expression *nᵉśî'ê yiśrā'el*, cf. 1:44; 4:46; 7:84.

3. six covered wagons: The Heb. word *ṣāḇ* occurs only here and in Isa. 66:20 in the *OT*, and its meaning is unclear. Most modern translations agree with *RSV* in rendering it as 'covered' in the present context, and this reading is supported by some of the ancient Vsns (LXX, Vulg., Targ. Onk.). However, there is nothing in the etymology of the word to suggest such a meaning, and in Isa. 66:20 the word is rendered as 'wagons' in *NEB*, *NIV*, and as 'litters' in *RSV*, *JB* (so, too, Symm., Vulg.; cf. Akkad. *ṣumbu* = cart, wagon). In the present context, the singular form *ṣāḇ* following the plural noun *'eglōṯ* ('wagons') is certainly peculiar, and it is possible that the word *ṣāḇ* should here be regarded as an early gloss (cf. Gray).

9. But to the sons of Kohath he gave none: The ark and the various sacred objects entrusted to the care of the Kohathites (3:31f.; 4:4ff.) were evidently regarded as too sacrosanct to be loaded on wagons, although earlier writers saw nothing amiss in the ark being transported on a cart (cf. 1 Sam. 6:8, 11; 2 Sam. 6:3). **holy things**: *RV* renders Heb. *qōḏeš* here as 'sanctuary', but *RSV*'s 'holy things' is certainly to be preferred, despite the fact that the Heb. noun is singular, rather than plural.

10. The tribal leaders brought **offerings for the dedication of the altar**: The Heb. noun *ḥᵃnukkāh* is sometimes used in the concrete sense of a 'dedication offering' (cf. vv. 84, 88), and sometimes in the abstract sense of 'dedication' (cf. v. 11). The noun is only encountered in relatively late texts (cf. 2 Chr. 7:9; Neh. 12:27), but the verbal root (*ḥānak*) is ancient and may originally have meant 'to begin' or 'to initiate'; perhaps the most appropriate rendering in the present context would be 'initiation offerings for the altar' (cf. Reif, *VT* 22 [1972], pp. 497f.).

12–83. The twelve leaders are here represented as bringing identical offerings and presenting them on successive days. These offerings consisted of: **one silver plate** (*NEB*, 'dish') **whose weight**

was a hundred and thirty shekels (i.e., approx. 1,500 grams, the shekel being equivalent to 11.5 grams; cf. de Vaux, *AI*, p. 205); **one silver basin** (normally used to throw the blood of the sacrificial victim against the altar; cf. *NEB*, 'tossing bowl') weighing 70 shekels or approx. 800 grams; and **one golden dish**: The Heb. *kap*, lit., 'palm of the hand', possibly suggests a small dish shaped like the hollow of the hand (*NEB*, 'saucer'), but its light weight (10 shekels = 115 grams) may suggest that a 'spoon' (*AV*; *RV*) or 'ladle' (*NIV*) was intended. The first two vessels were used to carry the **cereal offering**, while the golden dish was used to carry the **incense**. The leaders then offered a bull, a ram and a male lamb as a **burnt offering**, a male goat as a **sin offering** and two oxen, five rams, five male goats and five male lambs as **peace offerings**. For the 'burnt offering' and 'sin offering', see on 6:11, and for the 'peace offering', see on 6:14.

89. This verse is clearly an isolated fragment bearing no obvious connection either with what precedes or with what follows. The words, 'and when Moses went into the tent of meeting to speak with him' (i.e., with the LORD; cf. *RSV*) clearly presuppose that Yahweh has already been mentioned in the immediate context of the passage, but since no such reference to the divine name is found, the words 'with him' lack an antecedent, and this has to be supplied by the various translations. Further, the end of the verse, **and it** (i.e., Yahweh's voice; cf. LXX) **spoke to him** suggests that a divine speech was to follow, but if such a speech existed, its content must have been either lost or displaced, for the verse ends most abruptly. Some of the Vsns (LXX, Targ.) try to overcome this difficulty by translating the verb in the last clause as imperfect, suggesting that the incident here recorded was a recurring practice, but the verb 'spoke' in Heb. is not frequentative, and there can be no doubt that the author intended to describe a specific incident. Suggestions concerning the original context of the verse vary considerably. Heinisch (p. 39) connects the verse with the priestly blessing in 6:22–27; Dillmann (p. 41) sees the continuation of v. 89 in Lev. 1, while Holzinger (p. 31) regards the verse as a bridge to 10:13; however, the multiplicity of suggestions in itself betokens the hypothetical nature of such theories. The content of the verse is obviously to be regarded as a fulfilment of Exod. 25:22, where Moses is promised that Yahweh will speak to him **from between the two cherubim**, which were above the **mercy seat** on the **ark of the testimony**. Why the fulfilment of this promise should have been placed at this particular juncture must remain a mystery unless, as Noth (p. 65) suggests, an editor inserted it here to express Yahweh's grateful acceptance of the gifts offered in the previous verses.

(b) THE LAMPSTAND

8:1-4

This section consists of a brief instruction to Aaron concerning the installation of the lamps in the sanctuary (vv. 1-3), followed by a description of the manufacture of the lampstand (v. 4). Since the information contained here basically corresponds to that found in Exod. 25:31-40 and 37:17-24, this section contains nothing new, save for the observation in v. 3a that Aaron did indeed position the lamps in the way that Yahweh had commanded.

With regard to the form of the section, Kellermann (pp. 111ff.) is probably correct in regarding vv. 1-3 as a unity, and v. 4 as a marginal gloss on the preceding verses, designed to emphasize once again (cf. v. 3) the importance of complete obedience to Yahweh's will. The description of the mounting of the lamps in vv. 1-3 finds a particularly close parallel in Exod. 25:37b, and most commentators assume that the present section is dependent on the Exodus passage. However, Kellermann has argued that the reverse was, in fact, the case, and that Exod. 25:37b was added at a later stage to Exod. 25:31-40 on the basis of Num. 8:1-3. The view that Exod. 25:37b is a later insertion into its present context has much to commend it, for the directions concerning the positioning of the lamps in this half-verse seem out of place in a passage that is otherwise concerned with the construction of the lampstand; but whether this half-verse was inserted into its present context on the basis of Num. 8:1-3, or whether the author of Num. 8:1-3 was familiar with the Exodus text in its final, edited form must remain an open question. V. 4, which describes the manufacture of the lampstand, finds its closest parallel in Exod. 25:40, and Kellermann concedes that this verse is probably dependent on the Exodus text. Analysts are generally agreed that the present passage is Priestly, and many view it as a relatively late accretion within the Priestly corpus.

2. in front of the lampstand: The expression *'el-mûl p^enê* (cf. v. 3; Exod. 26:9; 28:25, 37; Lev. 8:9; 2 Sam. 11:15) is difficult to translate, for it seems to mean 'in front of' and at the same time 'towards' or 'opposite' (*BDB*, p. 557; cf. *NEB*'s rather cumbersome 'forwards in front of'; *JB*, 'towards the front of'). The concern expressed here that the light should be cast in the proper direction is to be explained on the basis of Exod. 40:22–25 (cf. Exod. 25:37*b*), where it is implied that the lamps were intended to illuminate the table of the shew-bread, which stood opposite the lampstand. There was much discussion among the rabbis as to precisely how the lights of the *menorah* were aligned in the temple; see Romanoff, *Jewish Symbols*, pp. 33ff.

3. And Aaron did so: In the present passage, Aaron alone was entrusted with the responsibility of setting up the lampstand; this agrees with Exod. 30:8 (cf. Lev. 24:2f.), but in Exod. 27:20f., responsibility for the lampstand is shared between Aaron and his sons. **he set up its lamps to give light:** According to Exod. 30:7f. and Lev. 24:3 these lamps burned only at night, but there is evidence that in the sanctuary at Shiloh in the days of Samuel they burned during the day, and were extinguished at night (1 Sam. 3:3). Josephus (*Ant.* III.8.3) bears witness to a later custom whereby some of the lamps were kept burning continually. **in front of** (cf. v. 2) **the lampstand**: The lampstand (Heb. *menôrāh*) is described in considerable detail in Exod. 25:31–40; 37:17–24. Its exact representation is uncertain, but its general shape can be gleaned from the bas-relief on the Arch of Titus in Rome (supposedly an eye-witness reproduction), which portrays a lampstand taken from the temple of Herod in Jerusalem (cf. Eltester, *Fest. Jeremias*, pp. 62ff.). It consisted of a central shaft or stem, with three branches extending outwards on each side. Each of the six branches was decorated with three cups, shaped like the blossom of an almond tree, and the central stem was decorated with four cups. The original purpose of the lampstand was purely functional, viz., to light up the otherwise dark sanctuary; in later times, however, it was invested with a symbolic significance, its shape (which resembled that of a seven-branched tree) representing the fructifying and life-giving power of God (cf. Meyers, *Menorah*, pp. 133ff.).

4. from its base to its flowers: *RSV* renders the Heb. *yārēk* (lit., 'thigh', 'loin') as 'base' (cf. *NIV*; *BDB*, pp. 437f.), and the words 'from its base to its flowers' is taken to refer to the entire lampstand, from its lowest to its topmost part (cf. Noth); however, the term *yārēk* often means 'side' (cf. 3:29, 35), and the word here may well refer to the 'stem' of the lampstand (so *NEB*; *JB*; *AV*, 'shaft'; cf. LXX, Vulg.), in which case the reference would be to that part of

the lampstand from its stem to the flower-shaped cups at the end
of each branch. **according to the pattern which the LORD had
shown Moses**: Cf. Exod. 25:9, 40.

(c) THE PURIFICATION OF THE LEVITES
8:5–26

This section outlines the ritual by which the Levites were purified
and dedicated to Yahweh (vv. 5–22), and it concludes by stipulating
the age during which they were eligible for the service of the tabernacle (vv. 23–26). Much of the material contained here merely
repeats what has already been stated in 3:5–13, the only new information being the rules contained in vv. 6b–13 governing the purification of the Levites and their presentation to Yahweh. Several
commentators interpret the regulations concerning the Levites in
vv. 5–22 in terms of the rules relating to the consecration of priests
in Lev. 8, and the present section is generally regarded as implicitly
emphasizing the inferiority of the Levites to the priests. Thus,
whereas the Levites were merely 'sprinkled' with water (v. 7), the
priests were completely 'washed' (Lev. 8:6), and whereas the Levites
had their ordinary garments cleansed (v. 7), the priests were provided with new attire (Lev. 8:13). Moreover, whereas the Levitical
office required only that the Levites be ritually cleansed from ceremonial pollution, the priestly office demanded that its bearers
should be consecrated and brought into a special relationship with
Yahweh (Lev. 8:12; cf. Exod. 28:41). It is generally recognized by
commentators that vv. 5–26 derive from the Priestly tradition, and
some scholars assign the core of the passage to P^g (cf. Holzinger,
p. 33; von Rad, *Priesterschrift*, pp. 95ff.); however, certain idiosyncrasies of vocabulary and style make this conclusion improbable,
and the general familiarity which the passage displays with earlier
traditions favours, rather, its attribution to a later stratum of the P
tradition (cf. Kellermann, p. 123).

   The passage cannot, in its present form, be regarded as a literary
unity, for it contains too many repetitions and inconsistencies for it
to be considered as the work of a single author. Thus, e.g., the
command to cleanse the Levites appears twice (vv. 6, 15), and the
instruction to offer them as a 'wave offering' is given three times,
once to Aaron (v. 11), and twice to Moses (vv. 13, 15). Clearly, any
attempt to trace the literary development of the passage must be
regarded as very tentative, but the analysis offered by Kellermann

(pp. 115ff.) appears to account for most of the inconsistencies inherent in this section. He suggests that the nucleus of the chapter may be found in vv. 5–9a, 12–16a, 21 (reading 'Moses' instead of 'Aaron') and 22aαβ. A different author, who viewed the Levites as having been given to Yahweh by the community, subsequently added vv. 9b–11, 20, 22aγb. A further addition is represented by vv. 16b–19, and these verses are closely connected with 3:11–13 (though common authorship should not be assumed). In vv. 23–26, a different theme (viz., the period of service of the Levites) is introduced, and these verses probably represent the latest addition to the passage.

7. the water of expiation: The Heb. expression *mê ḥaṭṭā'ṯ* means, lit., 'water of sin', and it was presumably so designated in respect of its intended effect, i.e., the water was regarded as a means of 'washing' sins away (hence *RSV*; cf. *AV*, 'water of purifying', following LXX, Vulg.). Rashi claims that the water here referred to had been mixed with the ashes of the red heifer (cf. 19:1ff.), but this is merely a conjecture, and since the expression *mê ḥaṭṭā'ṯ* occurs only here in the *OT*, it is clearly impossible to determine whether the water was regarded as having been prepared in a special way. The purpose of this ritual cleansing is clear: it was to purify the Levites from ceremonial defilement, and to mark their dedication to Yahweh. **and let them go with a razor over all their body**: According to the Greek historian Herodotus (ii.37), Egyptian priests engaged in a similar practice, shaving their bodies every other day as a means of ritual purification. Shaving of the hair is also mentioned in the case of the Nazirite who had contracted uncleanness by contact with the dead (6:9); here, however, the hair of the whole body (and not just of the head) had to be removed.

10. the people of Israel shall lay their hands upon the Levites: Since it is difficult to envisage how all the Israelites could have been expected to perform this ritual, many commentators favour the view that it must have been enacted by representatives of the people, possibly the leaders of the various tribes (cf. Levine, p. 276); their action would have been understood as indicating that the whole community was offering the Levites as their gift. The ritual of the laying on of the hands here (cf. v. 12) has been explained in various ways. Some commentators (e.g., Riggans) suggest that the ritual was intended to confer a blessing upon the Levites, but this is most improbable, since in contexts where the 'laying of hands' indicates a blessing, the verb *śîm* or *śît* (rather than the verb *sāmak*) is regularly used with the noun *yād* (cf. Daube, *Rabbinic Judaism*, pp. 224ff.). Others favour the view that the ritual was here intended to express the idea of substitution, and claim that such an interpretation is confirmed by v. 16, which states that the Levites were appointed by the Israelites to serve instead of the first-born (so, e.g., Budd; cf. de Vaux, *AI*, p. 347; Péter, *VT* 27 [1977], p. 53). However, it is doubtful whether v. 16 should be used to illuminate the meaning of the present verse, since it is by no means certain that both verses originate from the same source (see above); moreover, if the idea of substitution *were* present it would be more natural for the hands of the first-born, rather than the hands of the people at large or their representatives, to be placed upon the Levites. It seems more probable that the gesture was here intended as a statement of ownership; the Israelites were, in effect, indicating that the Levites were *their* gift to Yahweh, and in so doing they were renouncing all claims which they might have upon them, thus allowing the Levites to fulfil effectively the tasks to which they had been appointed (cf. Sansom, *ExpT* 94 [1982–3], p. 325).

11. and Aaron shall offer the Levites before the LORD as a wave offering: *RSV* usually translates *hēnîp* (here rendered 'offer') as 'wave', but for obvious reasons, it assumes that in this instance the meaning is more figurative than literal (cf. *RV*). For a discussion of the verb, *hēnîp*, and the corresponding noun, *t^enûpāh*, see on 6:20.

12. At the dedication of the Levites, two bulls were to be sacrificed, **one for a sin offering and the other for a burnt offering**. For the 'sin offering' and 'burnt offering', see on 6:11.

16–18. These verses basically repeat the principle enunciated in 3:11–13, viz., that Yahweh was entitled to take the Levites as a substitute for the first-born among the people of Israel.

19. In return, Yahweh gives the Levites back to Aaron and his sons **as a gift** (Heb. *n^etunîm*; see on 3:9) so that they can serve in the **tent of meeting** and **make atonement for the people of Israel**: Since to 'make atonement' (*NEB*, 'make expiation'), is elsewhere regarded as a specifically priestly task, the Heb. *kippēr* should probably here be understood in its original, secular sense of 'cover'; the Levites were thus to act as a 'cover' or 'screen', protecting the people from the plague which would strike them if any lay person were to come too **near the sanctuary**.

24. from twenty-five years old and upward: The contradiction between these words and those in 4:3 (where the lower age limit is given as thirty) is probably to be explained on the assumption that the age of entry into Levitical service varied from one period to another, depending on the availability of suitably qualified persons to perform the Levitical duties. Thus the lowering of the age limit here probably reflects a lack of Levitical personnel at the time when this ruling was enacted. The problem of the shortage of Levites was further alleviated by the provision permitting those above the age of fifty (presumably the normal retirement age from active Levitical service; cf. 4:3) to continue to assist their younger fellow-Levites on a voluntary basis, if they so desired (vv. 25f.).

(d) THE SUPPLEMENTARY PASSOVER
9:1–14

This section records that some Israelites had been prevented from observing the Passover feast 'at its appointed time' (i.e., on the 14th of Nisan) because they had touched a corpse and were thereby deemed to be ceremonially unclean (vv. 6f.). Since there were no regulations governing such an eventuality, Yahweh's guidance was sought (v. 8), and the problem was duly resolved: Moses was to initiate a second, supplementary Passover, which was to be held exactly one month later (i.e., on the 14th day of the second month; v. 11). This supplementary Passover was to be celebrated not only by those who were ritually unclean but also by those who had been unable to celebrate the original Passover owing to their absence on a distant journey (v. 10). These two cases, however, were clearly regarded as quite exceptional, and anyone who failed to celebrate the original Passover without a legitimate reason would be severely punished (v. 13). The passage concludes by stating that the regulations concerning the Passover were to apply to the alien as well as to the native Israelite (v. 14).

The narrative is certainly Priestly and may well constitute a relatively late accretion within the Priestly corpus. Kellermann (pp. 124ff.) finds the nucleus of the present section in vv. 10b–12, which describe the institution of a second Passover for those who had been unable to celebrate the feast at the normal time owing to their absence on a distant journey. To this law was subsequently appended the narrative contained in vv. 1–10a (without the reference to Aaron in v. 6b), which provided an additional reason for the institution of the supplementary Passover, viz., to accommodate

those who could not observe the Passover proper owing to their
ritual defilement through contact with a corpse. V. 13, which takes
account of both possible reasons for failing to observe the Passover
at its appointed time, was added to vv. 1–12 at a later stage and,
later still, v. 14 was appended in order to clarify the position of the
resident alien with regard to the festival.

Whether this is the correct explanation of the origin and development of vv. 1–14, however, must be regarded as questionable. It
seems altogether more probable that the narrative contained in
vv. 1–8 was designed, from the outset, to place the law of vv. 9–
12 in its proper context by indicating that the supplementary Passover was an institution which could be traced back to the time of
Moses. The author of the section (no doubt with an eye to the
post-exilic situation, when merchant travellers were frequently
involved in journeys outside Israel) appended the case of those who
were unable to celebrate the Passover proper because of their
absence on a distant journey. The narrator may well have felt that
the exceptional cases mentioned in vv. 10–12 might have engendered a general sense of laxity or indifference among the Israelites
with regard to the Passover; hence, v. 13 was inserted to emphasize
that a severe penalty would be inflicted upon those who failed to
observe the Passover at the normal time, whenever possible. V. 14
is more loosely attached to the present section, and may possibly
constitute a later addition; however, as Budd (p. 97) observes, if the
author was intent upon explaining the position of the alien in regard
to the Passover, this was as appropriate a place as any for such
information to be included.

**1. in the first month of the second year after they had come
out of the land of Egypt**: The episode related in this section, like
that recorded in 7:1ff., is set a month before the census mentioned
in ch. 1 (cf. 1:1).

2. Let the people of Israel keep: MT reads 'and let' which, if
correct, might imply that some previous command or utterance has
been accidentally omitted from the text (cf. Gray). LXX prefixes the
verb 'let' by *eipon* ('speak and let the people'), which may suggest
that some verb such as *ʾemōr* stood in the original (cf. *BHS*). *RV*
supplies 'moreover' in order to fill the gap, but most modern translations tend simply to ignore the conjunction before the verb 'let'. **the
passover**: It is generally believed that the Passover (Heb. *pesaḥ*)
was originally a pagan festival involving apotropaic rites designed

to ward off evil powers, but that its significance was later transformed to serve as a commemoration of Israel's redemption from
Egypt. It is probable that the Passover festival, as described in
Exod. 12, represents the combination of two originally separate
events, namely the feast of Passover (celebrated by nomadic
shepherds in order to secure prosperity and fertility for their flocks),
and the feast of *maṣṣôṯ* or Unleavened Bread (celebrated by the
settled, agricultural community in Canaan to mark the beginning
of the new harvest). The combination of the two feasts may well
have been facilitated by their temporal proximity (both being held
in March/April), but it is impossible to determine precisely when
the two feasts were combined. Kraus (*EvTh* 18 [1958], pp. 47ff.)
argued that elements of Passover and *maṣṣôṯ* had already been assim-
ilated at a very early period, and that the resulting celebration took
place at an ancient festival held in Gilgal (cf. Jos. 5:10ff.). Kutsch, on
the other hand, argued that the Passover and *maṣṣôṯ* were observed
separately throughout the period of the monarchy and were not
combined until the time of Josiah, the assimilation of the two feasts
being the direct outcome of the Deuteronomic legislation (*ZTK* 55
[1958], pp. 1ff.). On the whole, the balance of probability favours
the view that the two festivals were combined at a fairly early date,
possibly soon after Israel's settlement in Canaan. For further discussion of the Passover and *maṣṣôṯ* festivals, see Auerbach, *VT* 8
(1958), pp. 1ff.; Halbe, *ZAW* 87 (1975), pp. 147ff.; May, *JBL* 55
(1936), pp. 65ff. A useful summary of the theories advocated by
various scholars is provided by Segal, *Passover*, pp. 78ff., and a
detailed bibliography of the relevant literature is given by Kraus,
Worship, p. 49, n. 64.

3. The Passover was to be observed on the 14th day of the first
month of the second year after the departure from Egypt, and was
to be celebrated **in the evening**: The meaning of the Heb.
expression *bên hā'arbayim*, lit., 'between the two evenings', is obscure,
and was much discussed by the rabbis. It was variously interpreted
to signify the period (i) between sunset and the appearance of the
first star; (ii) between the time when the sun started to decline
(shortly after noon) and sunset; (iii) between the time when the heat
of the day began to decrease (approx. 3 p.m.) and sunset. The third
explanation was favoured by the Pharisees, and finds support both
in the Mishnah (*Pes.* 5:1) and Josephus (*War* VI.9.3; *Ant.* XIV.4.3).
Most modern commentators take the expression to refer to the

period between sunset and complete darkness (cf. *NEB*, 'between dusk and dark'; *NIV*, 'twilight'). Cf. de Vaux, *Studies*, pp. 11f.; *AI*, p. 182; Böhl, *OLZ* 18 (1915), pp. 321ff. The Passover was to be observed **according to all its statutes and all its ordinances**: See Exod. 12:1–28, 43–49. For the legal terminology employed here, viz., 'statutes' (Heb. *ḥuqqôt*), and 'ordinances' (Heb. *mišpāṭîm*), see Liedke, *Gestalt*, pp. 180ff.

6. And there were certain men who were unclean through touching the dead body of a man: Participation in a sacrificial meal was prohibited to those who were regarded as 'unclean' (cf. Lev. 7:20f.), and one method of contracting cultic uncleanness was by contact with the dead (cf. 19:11). **and they came before Moses and Aaron**: 'Aaron' is almost certainly to be regarded as a later insertion here, since he is not mentioned elsewhere in this passage, and the words immediately following in v. 7a ('said to him') suggest that Moses alone was present.

7. why are we kept from offering the LORD's offering at its appointed time among the people of Israel?: The root *grʿ* (rendered 'kept from') is here used in the sense of 'restrain' (*BDB*, p. 175*b*; cf. *NEB*, 'debarred from'; *JB*, 'forbidden to'). The question here was obviously rhetorical, for those who made the inquiry would obviously have realized that it was on account of their uncleanness that they had been prevented from participating in the Passover. The words are probably to be understood as a petition for a modification in the law by those who felt that they had been unjustly denied a privilege freely granted to their fellow-men. The fact that the petition was successful (vv. 9–12) is interesting in that it shows that the law, so often regarded as rigid and unbending, could, on occasion, be seen to be flexible and accommodating.

8. Wait, that I may hear what the LORD will command concerning you: The case was, in effect, adjourned in order to give Moses the opportunity to seek further guidance from Yahweh. For other cases which required divine consultation before they could satisfactorily be resolved, cf. 15:32ff.; 27:1ff.; 36:1ff.; Lev. 24:10ff.

10. Yahweh's reply to Moses included a provision not only for those affected by cultic uncleanness but also for those **afar off on a journey** and unable, for that reason, to participate in the Passover feast. That the two cases mentioned here were intended to be exhaustive is clear from v. 13. Noth (p. 71; cf. Segal, *Passover*, p. 200) understands the words 'afar off on a journey' to mean 'abroad', and claims that this provision presupposes that the Passover had to be celebrated within Israel; others understand the words to be merely a recognition of the fact that the Passover was essentially a family festival, and was to be kept in the home (Exod. 12:3f., 46; but cf. Dt. 16:2, 5f.).

11–12. Those prevented from observing the Passover at the normal time for either of the two reasons mentioned in the previous verse were to be permitted to celebrate it precisely one month later, i.e., **in the second month on the fourteenth day in the evening**. Whoever took advantage of this provision, however, was obliged to observe the usual regulations governing the Passover, three of which are singled out for special mention in these verses. They were to eat the Passover meal **with unleavened bread** (Heb. *maṣṣôt*) **and bitter herbs**: Cf. Exod. 12:8. The consumption of 'unleavened bread' probably reflects a time when the feast of Passover had been combined with the feast of *maṣṣôt* (see above), though some scholars believe that unleavened bread was from the beginning eaten at the Passover, and that this was one of the factors which facilitated the assimilation of the two feasts. The 'bitter herbs' mentioned here are not identified (cf. Segal, *Passover*, p. 169), but they may have been a type of wild lettuce (Vulg.) or chicory (LXX); the eating of the bitter herbs was intended as a reminder of the bitterness of the sojourn in Egypt (cf. Dt. 16:3; Beer, *ZAW* 31 [1911], pp. 152f.). Further, the Israelites were to **leave none of it until the morning** lest it should spoil and become inedible (cf. Exod. 12:10); moreover, they were forbidden to **break a bone** of the sacrificial victim (cf. Exod. 12:46), thus ensuring that the Passover sacrifice was roasted whole and intact (cf. de Vaux, *Studies*, p. 10). For the significance of the prohibition against breaking the bones of the sacrificial animal, see Scheiber, *VT* 13 (1963), pp. 95ff.; Segal, *Passover*, pp. 170f.

13. Anyone who was able to keep the Passover at its appointed time, but who deliberately refrained from doing so, was to be punished by being **cut off from his people**: It is unclear whether this expression, which frequently occurs in the Priestly material (cf. Exod. 12:15; 30:33, 38; 31:14; Lev. 7:20, 25, 27) refers to death (cf. Gray, pp. 84f.) or excommunication (cf. Segal, *Passover*, p. 58; de Vaulx) and, if the former was intended, whether the death was to be inflicted by Yahweh, or at the hands of the community. It is clear that the expression could on occasion refer to the death penalty (cf. Exod. 31:14), but the inclusion of the words 'from his people'

perhaps favours the view that the milder penalty of excommunication was here intended. It may be, however, that from the point
of view of the offender, the difference between the two penalties
was largely immaterial, for, as von Rad observes, 'excommunication
from the community . . . virtually amounted to a sentence of death'
(*OT Theology*, i, p. 268). See, further, Phillips, *Law*, pp. 28ff.

14. The passage concludes with a provision enabling the 'stranger'
(*gēr*) who was sojourning in Israel to participate in the Passover
celebrations, but it is made clear that in availing himself of this
privilege he was bound by the same rules and regulations as those
pertaining to the native Israelite. The *gēr* was not an Israelite by
birth, but was rather a resident 'alien' (cf. *NEB*; *NIV*), i.e., one who
had placed himself under the care and protection of the Israelite
tribes. He was, to all intents and purposes, a member of the Israelite
community, and enjoyed rights and privileges similar to those
accorded to the widow and orphan (cf. de Vaux, *AI*, pp. 74f.). The
gēr was sharply distinguished from the 'sojourner' (*tôšāḇ*), i.e., the
'visitor' who was making only a temporary stay in the country, for
the latter was strictly forbidden to partake of the Passover meal
(Exod. 12:45). See, further, van Houten, *Alien*, pp. 124ff.

(e) THE FIERY CLOUD
9:15–23

This passage, which develops in some detail the brief statement in
Exod. 40:34–38, recounts how the cloud regulated the movement
of the Israelites during the march from Sinai and throughout the
wilderness wanderings. Whenever the cloud descended upon the
tabernacle, the people set up camp, and whenever the cloud was
lifted, they continued on their journey. At night the cloud assumed
a fiery appearance; thus, by night and day, it served as a visible
sign of Yahweh's presence in the midst of his people.

According to the J tradition, the Israelites were led by Yahweh
in the form of a pillar of cloud by day and a pillar of fire by night,
and the phenomenon first appeared at the time of the departure from
Egypt (14:14; Exod. 13:21f.). The Priestly tradition (represented in
the present passage) does not depict the cloud as a pillar, but it
agrees with J in describing its fiery appearance at night; in P, however, the cloud does not move ahead of the Israelites to guide them
on their way (contrast Exod. 13:21f.), but merely indicates when the

people should rest and when they should proceed on their journey (vv. 15ff.; Exod. 40:34–8).

The narrative clearly belongs to the Priestly tradition, though certain idiosyncrasies of vocabulary and style point to P^s rather than P^g (cf. Gray, p. 85). The literary unity of the passage has been disputed by Kellermann (pp. 133ff.), who argues that vv. 15–19 and vv. 20–23*a* stem from two different authors (v. 23*b* being a gloss added at a later stage). But, although the passage is rather repetitive and verbose, there is little reason to deny its basic unity. Vv. 20–23 may be regarded as a perfectly logical continuation of vv. 15–19: having explained the process of guidance in the wilderness and indicated that the period of encampment could last for several days (v. 19), it was natural enough for the narrator to explore further the theme of duration and to emphasize that, however long or short the interval of encampment, the people responded to Yahweh's instructions with the utmost diligence (vv. 22f.; cf. Budd, p. 102).

15. the tent of the testimony: The phrase is very rare, occurring only here and in 17:7f.; 18:2 in the Pentateuch (cf., also, 2 Chr. 24:6, which represents its only other occurrence in the *OT*). Elsewhere, the phrase used is either 'the tent of meeting' (cf. 1:1) or 'the tabernacle of the testimony' (cf. 1:50, 53; 10:11). The words are here regarded as a gloss by some commentators (cf. Paterson, Kellermann).

16. the cloud covered it by day: MT lacks 'by day', but it is probable that some word such as *yômām* has been accidentally omitted from the text (cf. *BHS*), for the sense of the passage clearly requires it, and it is presupposed by the ancient Vsns (LXX, Syr., Vulg.).

20. a few days: The Heb. *yāmîm mispār* is unusual; the final *mem* is probably due to dittography, and should be omitted (cf. Gray); the phrase would then read *y^{e}mê mispār* (cf. *BHS*).

22. The Israelites stayed in the camp irrespective of whether the cloud remained over the tabernacle for a couple of days, a month **or a longer time**: The word *yāmîm*, lit. 'days' (cf. LXX *hēmeras*), is here understood by *RSV* to indicate an indefinite period of time, though the context clearly implies that it was of longer duration than a month (cf. *REB*). Some commentators argue that *yāmîm* here means 'a year' (Snaith, Binns, Maarsingh; cf. *RV, JB, NEB, NIV, NJPS*), and in support of this interpretation reference may be made to such passages as Lev. 25:29; Jg. 17:10 and 2 Sam. 14:26. North

(*VT* 11 [1961], pp. 446ff.) suggests that *yāmîm* should here be translated 'season', and he argues that the word was sometimes used as
a technical term to designate a period of four months (cf. Jg. 19:2),
the length of an agricultural season in Israel. However, this
interpretation seems doubtful, for the Hebrew year was normally
divided into two seasons, not three, viz. seedtime (or 'ploughing
time') and harvest (Gen. 8:22; 45:6; Exod. 34:21), and the meaning
'season' for *yāmîm* would be particularly difficult to justify in such
passages as Gen. 24:55; Exod. 13:10 and 1 Sam. 27:7. On balance,
it seems preferable to accept the rendering of *RSV* here and to
assume that *yāmîm* in this instance refers to an undefined interval.

(f) THE SILVER TRUMPETS
10:1–10

In this section, Moses is commanded to make two silver trumpets,
and the passage specifies in some detail their various uses. These
were no fewer than five in number, three of which were connected
with the wilderness wanderings (vv. 2*b*–8), and the remaining two
with life after the settlement in Canaan (vv. 9f.). During the journey,
the instruments were to be used (i) to convene the whole congregation at the entrance of the tent of meeting (v. 3); (ii) to summon
the leaders of the people (v. 4); and (iii) to give the signal to begin
the march (vv. 5f.). In Canaan, the trumpets were to be blown as
an appeal to Yahweh to remember his people, whether they were
(iv) embroiled in war (v. 9) or (v) participating in joyful religious
festivals (v. 10). The use of the trumpets as a signal for departure
(vv. 5f.) is clearly at odds with the preceding section (9:15ff.), which
indicates that the movement of the Israelites through the wilderness
was determined by the position of the cloud above the tabernacle.
Some commentators play down the discrepancy, and even suggest
that the present passage complements the preceding section by demonstrating the need for a human response to the divine initiative
(cf. Budd, Wenham); however, it seems more probable that two
quite different traditions are here reflected concerning the signal for
Israel's departure.

It is generally agreed that the present section is from the Priestly
source, but its literary unity has been questioned by several commentators. Kellermann (pp. 140ff.) has argued that the nucleus of
the passage may be found in vv. 3f., which describe the use of the
trumpets for gathering together the congregation and the leaders of

the people. Vv. 5f., which indicate that the instruments were also used as a signal for the camps to set out on the march, were added to vv. 3f. at a later stage. A redactor subsequently inserted vv. 1f., 7f., and the final stage in the development of the passage was the inclusion of v. 9 and v. 10. Kellermann may well be correct in viewing vv. 9f. as later accretions, for the use of the trumpets here is markedly different from their use in the preceding verses, but whether the remainder of the passage developed precisely along the lines he suggests seems more questionable. The view taken here is that the nucleus of the passage consisted of vv. 1–4, 6b, 8, and that vv. 5, 6a, 7 (where the verbs appear in the second, as opposed to the third, person plural) represent redactional expansions of the original narrative.

2. Make two silver trumpets: The Heb. word here translated 'trumpet' (*BDB*, p. 384b, 'clarion'), $ḥ^aṣôṣ^erāh$, occurs twenty-nine times in the *OT*, almost always in the plural form, and is mostly confined to late texts (P, Chr.). The shape of this instrument is known from its representation on Jewish coins and on the arch of Titus, where it appears as a long, straight, slender metal tube, flared at one end (cf. Josephus, *Ant.* III.12.6); it was thus clearly distinguished from both the *yōḇēl* (cf. Exod. 19:13; Jos. 6:5) and the *šôpār* (cf. Exod. 19:16, 19), which were much smaller and shaped like a ram's horn. The $ḥ^aṣôṣ^erāh$ was normally used in connection with religious celebrations, and in only two passages in the *OT* is the instrument depicted as being used for secular purposes (2 Kg. 11:14 = 2 Chr. 23:13; Hos. 5:8). See, further, Finesinger, *HUCA* 3 (1926), pp. 61ff.; *HUCA* 8–9 (1931–2), pp. 193ff.

3–4. A blast on both trumpets was the signal for **all the congregation** to assemble together, but a blast on one trumpet was the cue for only **the leaders, the heads of the tribes of Israel** to congregate. The sound made with the trumpets to summon the congregation and the leaders, *tāqaʿ* (*RSV*, 'blow') was apparently different from that which gave the signal for breaking camp and beginning the journey, *tāqaʿ t^erûʿāh*, (*RSV*, 'blow an alarm'; vv. 5f.), though the nature of the distinction is by no means clear. According to Dillmann (p. 49), the former indicated a short, staccato tone, while the latter referred to a longer flourish; but quite the reverse is suggested by Jewish tradition (*Mish. RH* iv.9) which maintains that *tāqaʿ* referred to a single, sustained blast, while *tāqaʿ t^erûʿāh* designated a succession of three short, tremolo notes (cf. *BDB*, p. 348b).

If this tradition is correct, then a protracted sound on the trumpet
was the signal for the people (or their leaders) to assemble, whereas
a series of quick blasts was the signal for the camp to set out.

5—6. At the sound of the first alarm **the camps that are on the
east side** (i.e., Judah and its two associate tribes; cf. 2:3ff.) **shall
set out**; at the second alarm, **the camps that are on the south
side** (i.e., Reuben and its two associate tribes) **shall set out**. It is
unclear why MT refers only to the divisions encamped on the eastern
and southern sides of the tabernacle; LXX fills the lacuna with the
following extensive addition: 'and you shall blow a third alarm, and
the camp that is on the west side shall set out; and you shall blow
a fourth alarm, and the camp that is on the north side shall set out'.
Vulg. is more restrained, adding only a brief, explanatory note to
the effect that the remaining tribes (i.e., those on the western and
northern sides) set out likewise (*et iuxta hunc modum reliqui facient*).
But while MT admittedly gives the appearance of being 'strangely
incomplete' (Noth), there is certainly no reason to assume with
Kellermann (p. 140), that a part of the text has here been accidentally omitted; it is far more probable that the writer simply took for
granted that a separate alarm was blown for each of the four groups
of tribes, and regarded it as unnecessary and otiose to spell this out
in detail.

**8. And the sons of Aaron, the priests, shall blow the trum-
pets**: Here, for the first time in the passage, it is made clear that
the blowing of the trumpets was the prerogative of the priests. In
Chr., too, sounding the trumpets was the sole preserve of the priests
(cf. 1 Chr. 15:24; 16:6; 2 Chr. 5:12; 13:12, 14; 29:26), although
temple music in general was the responsibility of the Levites.

9—10. After the settlement in Canaan, the trumpets were to be
sounded when the Israelites went to war **against the adversary
who oppresses you**: For the use of trumpets in battle, cf. 2 Chr.
13:12ff.; 1 Mac. 4:40; 5:33. The trumpet blast at a time of war was
usually a signal to take up arms (cf. Hos. 5:8; Jl 2:1); here, however,
it was intended to bring Israel to Yahweh's remembrance. **that you
may be remembered before the LORD your God, and you shall
be saved from your enemies:** It is interesting to observe that the
War Scroll at Qumran refers to instruments known as the 'trumpets
of remembrance' (cf. 1QM XVI.2f.), an allusion possibly inspired
by this verse (cf. Baumgarten, *RevQ* 12 [1985–7], pp. 555f.). The
trumpets were also to be sounded on **the day of your gladness**

(i.e., either on the day of the victory celebration or, more generally, on the joyous occasion of a festival) and **at your appointed feasts** (such as those mentioned in chs. 28f.; Lev. 23) **and at the beginnings of your months** (cf. 29:1). Perhaps it was customary, at the time of the Priestly writer, to mark the beginning of religious festivals by sounding trumpet blasts throughout the land, just as the beginning of the new year (Lev. 23:24) and the commencement of the year of the Jubilee (Lev. 25:9) were marked by a blast on the trumpet. The trumpets were also to be sounded **over your burnt offerings and over the sacrifices of your peace offerings**: The reference to the blowing of the trumpets over the sacrifice may reflect a late custom, since it is mentioned only here and in 2 Chr. 29:26ff. in the *OT*. The War Scroll found in Cave 4 at Qumran contains a curious reference to 'the trumpets for the Sabbaths', which Baumgarten (*op. cit.*, pp. 556f.) suggests may have been sounded at the time the Sabbath sacrifices were offered; if this is so, then the Dead Sea Scrolls provide interesting parallels to the two uses of the trumpets mentioned in vv. 9f.

II. FROM SINAI TO THE PLAINS OF MOAB

10:11–22:1

The second main division of the book contains an account of the journey from Sinai to the wilderness of Paran (10:11–12:16), the reconnaissance of the land of Canaan and its sequel (chs. 13f.), the fate of Korah, Dathan and Abiram (chs. 16f.), and various incidents on the way to Moab (20:1–22:1). These narratives are interrupted by a series of miscellaneous laws in ch. 15, regulations concerning the duties and dues of the priests and Levites in ch. 18, and rules concerning cleansing from defilement occasioned by contact with the dead in ch. 19. The section is dominated by the theme of Israel's disobedience and rebellion, which provokes Yahweh's anger and leads to the postponement of entry into the promised land until all the rebellious generation had died. The period covered by this section was probably intended to be the full forty years of wandering (cf. 14:33), though the year of the final arrival at Kadesh has been omitted (20:1). The section contains a mixture of Priestly and non-Priestly material.

(A) FROM SINAI TO THE WILDERNESS OF PARAN
10:11–12:16
(a) THE DEPARTURE FROM SINAI
10:11–28

The Israelites were now ready to leave Sinai and travel as far as the wilderness of Paran, and they did so under the direction of the tribal leaders mentioned in 1:5–15. The tribes set out in the order described in 2:1–34, the only slight modification being in the place allotted to the Levitical families; contrary to the implication of 2:17, they did not travel together in a single contingent, occupying a central position in the order of the march, but were rather divided into two groups: the Gershonites and Merarites set out with the tabernacle immediately after the tribes of Judah, and the Kohathites followed on later, after the tribes of Reuben. The logic behind this arrangement is clear: it allowed an interval to elapse at each new place of encampment so that the tabernacle could be erected and made ready to receive the sacred objects (*RSV*, 'holy things') carried by the Kohathites (v. 21).

Various features in the present section (e.g., the date in v. 11; the concept of the cloud in v. 12; the names of the tribal leaders in vv. 14–18) clearly mark out the passage as a Priestly composition, but there are indications to suggest that it should be attributed to P^s rather than P^g (cf. Gray, p. 90).

11–12. In the second year, in the second month, on the twentieth day of the month: On P's reckoning, the Israelites had spent nearly a year in the wilderness of Sinai (cf. Exod. 19:1) before receiving the signal to depart. That signal was indicated by the lifting of the cloud **from over the tabernacle of the testimony**, in the manner explained in 9:17ff. After the cloud had been lifted, **the people of Israel set out by stages:** *RSV* here probably represents the correct interpretation of the Heb. expression *wayyisʿû lʿmasʿêhem*. The verb *nāsaʿ* means 'to pull up', and the term may originally have been related to nomadic travel, where journeys were begun and ended by 'pulling up' the tent pegs and implanting them in the new site (cf. Milgrom, p. 76; Delcor, *VT* 25 [1975], pp. 312f.); hence the verb came to mean 'to set out' and the noun *massaʿ* probably designated the various stations or stopping-places on the journey (cf. *BDB*, p. 652*b*). *RSV*'s 'set out by stages' is thus a perfectly satisfactory rendering of the idiom *wayyisʿû lʿmasʿêhem*, and the point is that the journey to **the wilderness of Paran** took several days and was not accomplished in a single march. The exact location of Paran is uncertain, but it is generally assumed to be in the northern part of the Sinai peninsula, south of the Negeb and west of the Arabah, i.e., its eastern border would roughly approximate to a line drawn from the Dead Sea to the Gulf of Aqaba.

17. And when the tabernacle was taken down: The verbs in this verse and in vv. 18, 21f., 25 are perfects with simple *waw*, and the writer probably intended them to be frequentative, indicating the general practice of the tribes throughout the period of the wilderness wanderings (cf. Baentsch, Gray).

21. The Kohathites had the duty of carrying **the holy things**: *AV* here reads 'sanctuary' (cf. *JB*), but although this is the usual meaning of the word *miqdāš*, it makes little sense to translate it as 'sanctuary' here, for it is clear from v. 17 (cf. 3:25, 36f.) that this was transported by the Merarites and Gershonites. Snaith (p. 224) tentatively suggests that the word $k^e lê$ has been accidentally omitted from MT, and that the original text referred to the 'vessels' or 'furniture' of the sanctuary, but this proposal is conjectural and lacks Versional support. Most commentators assume that *miqdāš* must here refer to the 'holy things' (cf. *NEB*; *NIV*) even though this meaning for the word would be quite exceptional.

(b) HOBAB AND THE ARK
10:29–36

In this brief narrative, Moses asks Hobab to accompany the Israelites to the land of Canaan, presumably in order to act as a guide on the journey (v. 29). Hobab, however, refuses, saying that he would prefer to return home to his own kindred (v. 30). Moses reacts to this negative response by urging him again to accompany them (v. 31), promising that, if he did so, he would share in the benefits which Yahweh had in store for his people (v. 32). The narrative continues by stating that the ark of the covenant preceded the Israelites on the journey (v. 33), and that the cloud formed a protective covering for them by day (v. 34). The section concludes with an account of what Moses is supposed to have uttered whenever the ark was removed from, and returned to, the camp (vv. 35f.).

Vv. 29–36 form a parallel to, rather than a continuation of, the preceding section (which contained P's account of the departure from Sinai), and commentators are generally agreed that here, for the first time in Numbers, the J source appears (cf. Baentsch, p. 500; Gray, pp. 92f.; Noth, p. 77). The passage is often regarded as fragmentary, for there is no account of Hobab's sudden arrival at Sinai, nor is there a record of the final response which he made to Moses' request. Moreover, there is general agreement that, despite its brevity, the story cannot be regarded as a unified whole. In the first place, v. 33*b* almost certainly comes from a different source, for the guiding role here attributed to the ark seems incongruous with the human guidance which Moses sought from Hobab (vv. 29, 31f.). The reference to the ark in v. 33*b* probably precipitated the subsequent addition of vv. 35f., although in these two verses the ark is no longer depicted as a means of guidance through the wilderness but as a means of ensuring Yahweh's presence at a time of war. The final stage in the development of the unit was probably the insertion of v. 34, which was no doubt intended to harmonize (albeit in a rather clumsy fashion) the tradition that the Israelites were guided by the ark (v. 33*b*) with the role assigned by the Priestly author to the cloud (vv. 11f.; cf. 9:15ff.). The fact that v. 34 breaks the logical sequence between v. 33*b* and vv. 35f., and that the verse is placed after v. 36 in the LXX (cf. Tov, *JNWSL* 13 [1987], pp. 155f.), tends to support the view that this verse was inserted at a relatively late stage in the composition of the passage.

The remainder of the narrative, vv. 29–32, may be regarded as a self-contained entity, and there is certainly no reason (*contra* Eissfeldt, *Hexateuch-Synopse*, pp. 59f.) to deny its unity on the basis of the repetition in vv. 29, 31f., for Moses' renewed appeal was merely intended to underline the urgency of his request, and may be regarded as a natural sequence in the development of the narrative (cf. Fritz, p. 14; Rudolph, pp. 63f.).

The background of the passage is difficult to discern, for it was probably intended to be more than a simple account of the acquisition by the Israelites of a temporary guide during their sojourn in the wilderness. De Vaulx (p. 145) suggests that the story reflects a pact of non-aggression which was entered into between the Israelites and the Midianites; the latter offered their services to Israel, permitting them to use their paths and stopping-places in return for which they received the protection of the Israelites (cf. Sturdy). However, since the relationship between these two peoples in the period after the settlement was not particularly amicable (cf. Jg. 6–8), it is difficult to explain why such a tradition should have been preserved. It seems preferable, therefore, to adopt the interpretation of the passage advanced by Fritz (pp. 65ff.) and Noth (p. 78). According to this view, the words 'whatever good the LORD will do to us, the same will we do to you' (v. 32), and 'come with us, and we will do you good' (v. 29), should be understood not in the general sense that Hobab (and, by implication, the Midianites) would partake of Israel's prosperity and good fortune, but in the more specific sense that he would have a share in the land which was to become Israel's possession. The tradition was therefore recorded and preserved in order to explain how it was that Midianite clans had come to dwell among the Israelites in the land of Canaan.

29. And Moses said to Hobab the son of Reuel (*AV*, 'Raguel'; cf. LXX) **the Midianite, Moses' father-in-law**: There are variant traditions in the *OT* concerning the name of Moses' father-in-law. In Exod. 3:1; 4:18; 18:1f. his name appears as Jethro; in Exod. 2:18 (J) he is called Reuel, whereas in the present passage (J) and in

Jg. 4:11 (and possibly in the original text of Jg. 1:16; cf. LXX), he is referred to as Hobab, Reuel's son. The name Jethro clearly derives from an independent tradition concerning Moses' father-in-law; the main problem, therefore, is why a single source, J, seems to attribute to him two different names, viz., Reuel and Hobab. Various attempts have been made to explain this apparent contradiction. Some scholars point to the ambiguity in the phrasing of the present verse and claim that the meaning of the text is that Reuel (not Hobab) was Moses' father-in-law, and that the verse is therefore in complete harmony with the statement in Exod. 2:18. Hobab would then have been Moses' brother-in-law, and this, it is argued, is the meaning of the term *ḥōṯēn* in Jg. 4:11 (cf. *RV, NEB, NIV*; Mitchell, *VT* 19 [1969], pp. 95f.). However, this interpretation seems doubtful, for *ḥōṯēn* in the *OT* regularly means 'father-in-law' (*BDB*, p. 368*b*), and although the Arab. cognate can mean 'brother-in-law', there is no evidence to suggest that the Heb. *ḥōṯēn* ever had this meaning. Moreover, this interpretation would be weakened even further if (as seems probable) Exod. 2:16 is taken to imply that Moses' father-in-law had no son. A different solution to the difficulty has been proposed by W. F. Albright (*CBQ* 25 [1963], pp. 1ff.). He takes up a suggestion by Gray that Reuel was the name not of an individual but of a clan, and argues that the name Jethro was accidentally omitted in the transmission of Exod. 2:18. He proceeds to argue that Jethro and Hobab should not be identified with one another; rather, Jethro was Moses' father-in-law, and Hobab was his son-in-law (reading *ḥāṯān* instead of *ḥōṯēn* in the present verse), and both belonged to the 'clan' of Reuel. However, there is no Versional support to favour Albright's reading of Exod. 2:18; nor is there any real evidence to suggest that *ḥōṯēn* should be pointed *ḥāṯān* in the present verse. A simpler way to resolve the difficulty is to assume that Hobab was the name of Moses' father-in-law in J, and that the name Reuel in Exod. 2:18 was a late gloss inserted by a redactor who, perhaps understandably, misunderstood the ambiguity in the present passage (cf. Rudolph, p. 5; Noth, *Pentateuchal Traditions*, p. 184, n. 516). A further complication is that Moses' father-in-law is here regarded as a Midianite (so, too, in Exod. 2:16ff.), but in Jg. 1:16 and 4:11 he is described as a Kenite; however, this discrepancy is usually resolved either by assuming that the Kenites were a branch or subdivision of the Midianites (so, e.g., Sturdy, Wenham; cf. Binns, *JTS* 31 [1930], p. 339) or by assuming that the words

'Moses' father-in-law' in Jg. 1:16 and 'the descendants of Hobab the father-in-law of Moses' in Jg. 4:11 are secondary insertions into the text (so, e.g., Richter, *Traditionsgeschichtliche*, p. 58). Another possibility is that 'Kenite' in Jg. 1:16; 4:11 means 'smith' and that these verses merely state that Hobab was a member of a group of metal-workers belonging to the Midianites (Albright, *op. cit.*, pp. 8f.; Gottwald, *Tribes*, pp. 578f.).

30. I will depart to my own land and to my kindred: Hobab declines Moses' request, preferring to return home instead. His words have been understood by some to imply that the route which the Israelites were to take to the land of Canaan lay in a different direction from that by which Hobab was to travel home to Midian, and it is argued that this has significant implications for the location of Sinai. McNeile (p. 55), e.g., suggests that the present verse undermines the traditional location of Sinai, for if the mountain were situated to the south of the peninsula, then the route of the Israelites would have coincided with that of Hobab, at least for some part of the journey, and there would have been no need for a parting of the ways. However, it is doubtful whether any definite conclusions as to the location of Sinai can be drawn on the basis of this verse (cf. Budd, p. 115); see, further, on 1:1.

31–32. Moses repeats his invitation and reiterates the promise which he had made previously (v. 29*b*). A nomad, such as Hobab, would have been familiar with the terrain through which the Israelites were passing and would have been well acquainted with the best places **to encamp in the wilderness**; consequently, if only he could be persuaded to accompany them he would no doubt prove to be a most valuable and efficient guide. **and you will serve as eyes for us**: Vulg. interprets the phrase to refer to Hobab's ability to serve as leader and guide (*ductor*; cf. *NEB*); LXX paraphrases, 'you will be our elder (*presbutês*)', i.e., to give wise counsel on the journey. The present form of the narrative gives no indication as to Hobab's response to this second entreaty, but there would seem to be little point to the account if he had refused; moreover, some scattered references in the *OT* suggest that he did eventually comply with Moses' request (cf. Jg. 1:16; 1 Sam. 15:6). A different tradition, however, has been preserved in Exod. 18:27, where Hobab is represented as leaving Moses and returning home.

33. So they set out from the mount of the LORD three days' journey: This is the only place where Sinai (or Horeb) is referred to as the 'mount of the LORD'; elsewhere in the *OT*, this phrase regularly refers to Mount Zion (cf. Ps. 24:3; Isa. 2:3; 30:29; Mic. 4:2). Some commentators (e.g., Baentsch, Gray) suggest that the present text originally contained a reference to the 'mount of God (Elohim)' (cf. Exod. 3:1; 4:27 etc.), but was altered by a later scribe to the less familiar 'mount of the LORD (Yahweh)'. **three days' journey**: For this expression, characteristic of J, cf. Gen. 30:36; Exod. 3:18; 5:3; 8:27. **and the ark of the covenant of the LORD went before them three days' journey**: The word 'covenant' in the expression 'ark of the covenant' is almost certainly a later Deuteronomistic addition, and reflects the belief that the words of the covenant (i.e., the decalogue) were contained inside the ark (cf. Dt. 10:8; 31:9, 25f.). It is difficult to comprehend why the ark should have travelled 'three days' journey' ahead of the Israelites, for it could hardly have functioned as an effective guide if it were moving this far in advance. In Jos. 3:4 it is more logically represented as moving a mere 2,000 cubits (i.e., approx. 1,000 yards) ahead of the people. In order to overcome this difficulty, Syr. here reads 'one day's journey ahead' (cf. *NEB*), but it is preferable to omit the expression altogether as a careless repetition by a scribe of the same phrase in the preceding clause (cf. Snaith, Noth, Paterson). Whether the author of the present passage conceived of the ark as moving of its own accord, like the pillar of cloud in P's account (so Baentsch, Gray) or as being transported upon a cart drawn by oxen, as in 1 Sam. 6:7ff.; 2 Sam. 6:3 (so Holzinger, Kennedy) must remain a matter of conjecture. **to seek out a resting place for them**: As was noted above, v. 33*b* is probably a later insertion in the present context, and this seems to be confirmed by the use here of the verb *tûr* (rendered 'seek out' in *RSV*), which occurs mainly in later literature, especially in the Priestly writings (cf. 13:2, 16f., 21, 25, 32; 14:6f., 34, 36, 38). It is possible that v. 33*b* was inserted by a redactor who considered it inappropriate that Hobab, a foreigner, should be honoured with the task of leading the Israelites through the wilderness, and who thought it more appropriate that Yahweh (represented by the ark) should be assigned this important role. The insertion of v. 33*b* may well account for the omission, in the present form of the text, of Hobab's final reply to Moses, for his response may have been deliberately excluded by an editor, who realized that the presence of the ark rendered unnecessary the human guidance provided by Hobab.

34. This verse, which is only loosely attached to the present context, probably derives from the Priestly source (cf. Gray, p. 93; McNeile, p. 56). The expression **the cloud of the LORD** occurs only here and in Exod. 40:38 in the *OT*, and LXX suggests that the original text may have read 'and the cloud was over them' (reading *yiḥ'yeh* instead of the divine name, *yhwh*), serving to protect the Israelites from the heat of the sun; however, in view of 14:14, a reference to the 'cloud of the LORD' does not seem inappropriate here. Seebass' suggestion (*VT* 14 [1964], pp. 111ff.) that the phrase 'the cloud of the LORD' (*'anan yhwh*) should be emended to read 'the ark of the LORD' (*'arôn yhwh*) is not compelling and lacks Versional support.

35–36. The two sayings preserved in these verses appear to be addressed directly to the ark as the visible manifestation of Yahweh's presence. The first saying was evidently uttered when the ark was carried before the Israelites into battle (cf. 1 Sam. 4:1ff.), and the second was pronounced when it returned to the sanctuary at the end of the campaign. The sayings were probably used regularly on such occasions (**whenever the ark set out**, v. 35) and they may well reflect ancient tradition (cf. Baentsch, p. 502, who regards them as belonging to the pre-Davidic period). As has often been observed by commentators, the two sayings seem strangely out of context here, and the second, in particular, ill-accords with the wilderness wanderings as described in v. 33 and seems, rather, to presuppose a time when the Israelites had settled in Canaan. In MT, vv. 35f. are enclosed by two critical marks (inverted *nuns*) which the rabbis understood to be an indication by an early scribe that the two sayings were an intrusion in their present setting. It is clearly no longer possible to determine the context to which these verses originally belonged, but the suggestions that they were derived from the 'Book of the Wars of the LORD' (21:14; cf. Kennedy), or from the apocryphal book of Eldad and Medad (as suggested in some mediaeval rabbinic sources; cf. Leiman, *JBL* 93 [1974], pp. 348ff.; Levine, *JBL* 95 [1976], pp. 122ff.) must be regarded as purely conjectural.

35. Arise, O LORD: Yahweh was conceived as sitting enthroned upon the ark, and the call for him to 'arise' may reflect the battle-cry used by the Israelites when they were engaged in a holy war (cf. von Rad, *Hexateuch*, pp. 109ff.). **and let thy enemies be scattered; and let them that hate thee flee before thee**: Embedded in the consciousness of the Israelites was the belief that Israel's enemies were Yahweh's enemies, and the hope expressed here is that Israel's foes would be vanquished and that Yahweh would emerge victorious from the battle. The words of this saying are quoted in Ps. 68:1 and referred to in Ps. 132:8.

36. Return, O LORD: Commentators have generally been much enamoured of Budde's proposal (*Transactions*, pp. 16ff.) that the verb *šûḇāh* ('return') should be pointed *š°ḇāh* ('rest'); cf. von Rad, *OT Theology*, i, p. 237; Sturdy, p. 79). But while this emendation (incorporated in *NEB*) certainly provides an effective counterpart to the opening words of the previous verse ('Arise, O LORD), the suggestion should probably be rejected, since it lacks Versional support. **to the ten thousand thousands of Israel**: MT seems to be defective, and the rendering of *RSV* assumes either that the preposition '*el* ('to') has been accidentally omitted from the text (cf. Vulg., Syr.) or else that the verb *šûḇāh* is here followed by an accusative of direction (G–K. § 118*d*, *f*). This is marginally preferable to *NEB*, which interprets the tetragrammaton as a construct form ('LORD of the countless thousands'), and is infinitely preferable to the further suggestion by Budde, namely that the verb *bēraḵ°tā* ('bless') has been accidentally omitted from the text (owing to its similarity to the following *riḇ°ḇôṯ*, and that the verse should be rendered, 'Rest, O LORD and bless the myriads of Israel's clans'. Gray (p. 97) follows Budde in understanding the Heb. '*elep* here in the sense of 'family, clan', as in 1:16, 46, and he translates, 'the ten thousand families of Israel'; however, the rendering of *RSV*, which presupposes that '*elep* here represents the numeral 'thousand' is perfectly acceptable and, indeed, preferable, since it heightens the poetic hyperbole of the utterance.

(c) TABERAH
11:1–3

This brief narrative recounts an occasion during the sojourn in the wilderness when the Israelites complained in Yahweh's hearing about their misfortunes. Angered by their behaviour, Yahweh punishes them by sending a fire which consumes the outskirts of the camp (v. 1). In their distress, the people appeal to Moses to intercede on their behalf and, as a result of his prayer, the danger is averted (v. 2). The story was evidently told to explain the meaning of the name Taberah (= 'burning'; cf. v. 3), and it exhibits the typical characteristics of the aetiological narrative. On this genre, see Childs, *VT* 24 (1974), pp. 387ff.; Fichtner, *VT* 6 (1956), pp. 372ff.; Golka, *VT* 26 (1976), pp. 410ff.; 27 (1977), pp. 36ff.; Long, *Etiological Narrative, passim.*

The unity of the passage is not in any doubt, and although some commentators have sought to link it with the following narrative (vv. 4–35; cf. Seebass, *VT* 28 [1978], p. 216), or with part of the preceding story (10:33*a*; cf. Fritz, pp. 68ff.), there is little evidence of any substantive connection, and it seems preferable to regard vv. 1–3 as a self-contained unit.

It has recently been suggested that the passage is the product of the Deuteronomistic school, partly because of the close similarity between the schema found here (disobedience-punishment-intercession-redemption), and that encountered repeatedly in Jg. 2–10 (cf. de Vaulx, p. 151), and partly because the words 'in the hearing of the LORD', and the reference to Yahweh's anger being 'kindled', are redolent of phrases in the Deuteronomistic history (cf. Aurelius, *Fürbitter*, p. 142). However, the parallel is more apparent than real, for the phrase characteristic of the Deuteronomistic history is 'in the sight of the LORD' (cf. Jg. 2:11; 3:7, 12; 4:1 etc.) and not, as here, 'in the hearing of the LORD', and the concept of Yahweh's anger being 'kindled' is by no means confined to the Deuteronomistic history, for it appears also in J (cf. 11:33; 12:9; 25:3). Moreover, in the Deuteronomistic passages in Judges the people cry to Yahweh, and are saved by the military activities of human agents; here, on the other hand, they appeal to Moses, and are saved as a direct result of divine intervention.

Older commentators tended to assign the passage to E (cf. Baentsch, Gray), primarily because Moses' role as intercessor is thought to have been especially characteristic of this source (cf. Gen. 20:7, 17; Jenks, *Elohist*, p. 54). However, there is little convincing evidence to posit the existence of an E source here, and it seems far preferable to attribute the section to J, since God is designated as 'Yahweh', and the passage betrays J's characteristic use of *hāʿām* to depict the people of Israel.

1. And the people complained in the hearing of the LORD about their misfortunes: The verb *ʾānan* ('to complain') is found only here and in Lam. 3:39 in the *OT*; its meaning is uncertain, but the usage of the root in various cognate languages, together with the fact that LXX here employs the word *gongudzôn* (elsewhere consistently used to translate *lûn* = to murmur), suggests that the rendering of *RSV* can be sustained (cf. Coats, *Rebellion*, pp. 125f.; *BDB*, p. 59*b*). The reason for the complaint in this instance is not stated, but the various privations of a desert march would no doubt have precipitated many such outbursts on the part of the people. Rabbinic tradition maintained that the people had complained of hunger (cf. vv. 4f.), and some commentators have even suggested emending *ra'* ('misfortune') to *rā'āḇ* ('hunger'; cf. *BHS*), but while the rabbinic tradition may well reflect what the author of the passage intended, such an emendation is not strictly necessary and, indeed, it has been regarded by Noth as 'linguistically quite unsatisfactory' (*Pentateuchal Traditions*, p. 123, n. 349). When Yahweh heard about the people's discontent, **the fire of the LORD burned among them**. The incident is frequently explained by commentators as due to lightning or some other electrical discharge (cf. Marsh), but for the author of the present passage the phenomenon was clearly understood as a supernatural occurrence. Fire in the *OT* is often regarded as the instrument of Yahweh's judgment (cf., e.g., Am. 1:4) or as a symbol of his anger (cf. Isa. 30:27ff.; Lam. 1:12f.); in this case, it was a visible manifestation of Yahweh's displeasure with his people, for it **consumed some outlying parts of the camp**, and threatened to destroy everything.

2–3. When the people became aware of the danger, they appealed to Moses, and he, in turn, interceded on their behalf before Yahweh, **and the fire abated**. To commemorate the event, the place was called **Taberah**, i.e., 'burning'. Noth (pp. 83f.) maintains that this explanation of the name was probably secondary, and he suggests that the word may originally have been derived from the root *b'r* = 'to remove' (or possibly 'to graze'), or that it was connected with Arab. *ba'r* = 'manure, dung, dirt'. According to the P source (which does not mention Taberah), Kibroth-hattaavah was the first halt which the Israelites made after their departure from Sinai (cf. 33:16). Keil (p. 238; cf. Milgrom, *Judaic Perspectives*, p. 50) suggests that Taberah and Kibroth-hattaavah refer to one and the same place, but since neither location can be identified with any certainty, this conclusion must be regarded as highly questionable. Taberah is mentioned only here and in Dt. 9:22 in the *OT*.

(d) THE COMPLAINTS AT KIBROTH-HATTAAVAH

11:4–35

The Israelites, incited by the 'rabble' who were among them, demand meat to eat (v. 4) and express their dissatisfaction with the monotonous diet of manna which they were being given in the wilderness (v. 6). Exacerbated by their continual complaining, Moses expresses to Yahweh his despair at the prospect of having to bear, alone, the burden of the people (vv. 11–15). Yahweh responds by instructing him to select seventy elders and gather them at the tent of meeting; there, Yahweh would take some of the spirit resting on Moses and confer it on those who had been assembled. Equipped by the spirit, they would be able to share with Moses the burden of caring for the people (vv. 16f.). The Israelites themselves are promised a plentiful supply of meat, but it is suggested, rather ominously, that this would be something of a mixed blessing, for it would be given in such abundance that it would make them feel nauseated (vv. 18–20). The narrative proceeds to record that the elders were endowed with some of Moses' spirit, and began to prophesy (vv. 24f.). Two of the elders, however, had remained in the camp, and yet they, too, were able to prophesy, much to the indignation of Moses' servant, Joshua. Joshua urges Moses to prevent them, but the latter merely expresses the wish that all the LORD's people would be prophets (vv. 26–30). The narrative concludes by describing the quails which Yahweh had provided in abundance for the Israelites (vv. 31f.); however, as soon as the people started eating them, they were smitten with a plague (v. 33). This was deemed condign punishment for the people's inordinate craving, and, in memory of the event, the place where it occurred was called Kibroth-hattaavah (= 'graves of craving'; v. 34). The Israelites then continued their journey to Hazeroth (v. 35).

This brief outline of the content of the passage clearly demonstrates that it cannot be regarded as a literary unity. It seems certain that at least two separate narratives have here been interwoven, one recounting the people's complaint concerning the lack of meat and how the grievance was answered by Yahweh (vv. 4–10, 13, 18–24a, 31–35), and the other recounting Moses' complaint regarding the 'burden of the people', and how he was given the assistance of the elders (vv. 11f., 14–17, 24b–30). The second narrative poses relatively few problems from the literary-critical point of view. The only uncertainty concerns vv. 11f., 14f., which Gray (p. 107) argues should be dislocated from their present context and transposed after Exod. 33:1–3; however, his arguments are not compelling, for the inclusion of these verses in the present chapter seems to be demanded by v. 17b (which Gray is compelled to regard as

editorial), and it could be claimed that they form a necessary pre-
amble to the story concerning the elders in vv. 24b–30. The first
narrative, on the other hand, has proved extremely difficult for analysts, since there is every indication that it has been heavily edited.
In the first place, vv. 7–9, which contain a detailed description of
the manna and the way it was prepared for use, are almost certainly
a later addition, probably precipitated by the reference to the manna
in v. 6 (cf. Noth, p. 86; Coats, *Rebellion*, p. 97); these verses are quite
unnecessary in the context, and they disturb the flow of the narrative. Secondly, it seems probable that, in the process of combining
the two narratives, some such phrase as 'and Moses said to Yahweh'
has been suppressed from the beginning of v. 13, and a corresponding phrase, such as 'and the LORD said to Moses', has been suppressed from the beginning of v. 18. Thirdly, the topographical note
in v. 35 is only loosely connected to the present context, and has
every appearance of being a later addition to the passage.

Even when these omissions and additions have been taken into
account, however, the narrative still poses a problem, for it appears
that two conflicting traditions concerning the divine provision of
meat in the wilderness have here been conflated, one regarding it
in a positive light, as a sign of God's benevolence, and the other
viewing it in a negative light, as a sign of his judgment. Hence, Fritz
(pp. 70ff.) has plausibly divided the narrative into two separate
strands, one consisting of vv. 4b, 10a, 13, 18–20aα, 21–24a, 31f.,
and the other comprising vv. 4a, 10b, 20b, 33f. The earlier tradition
recounted the desire of the people for meat (v. 4b) and recalled how
Moses overheard their complaint (v. 10a), and inquired of Yahweh
as to how such provision could be obtained in the wilderness (v. 13).
Yahweh assured him that meat would, indeed, be provided (vv. 18–
20aα), but Moses expressed his incredulity that such a promise could
be fulfilled (vv. 21f.). Yahweh again reassured Moses (v. 23), and
the narrative concludes by recounting how God ensured that the
people were given a plentiful supply of quails (vv. 31f.). In this
narrative, there is no hint that the desire for meat was regarded as
a sign of rebellion against Yahweh, and there is no indication of any
punishment or calamity befalling the people; on the contrary, the
emphasis is entirely upon Yahweh's helpful intervention in meeting
the people's need by means of his miraculous power. This tradition,
however, was subsequently connected with another which provided
an aetiology for the name Kibroth-hattaavah (vv. 4a, 10b, 20b, 33f.),

and this secondary insertion gave the final version of the narrative a decidedly negative slant by implying that the craving of the people had amounted to an outright rejection of Yahweh, and that such behaviour must be punished by the destruction of the rebellious from their midst. In this way, the story of a miraculous divine provision of food was transformed (probably by the Yahwist) into a didactic account which illustrated the dire consequences that inevitably resulted from an attitude of defiance and blatant ingratitude.

Within the narrative of the quails, a tradition was later inserted concerning the installation by Moses of the seventy elders (vv. 11f., 14–17, 24b–30). It is by no means clear why this story should have been inserted here, but it is possible that the exasperation expressed by Moses in v. 13 (which belongs to the quails story) attracted a tradition concerning a similar feeling of discontent on his part about the burden of leadership which he was forced to bear (vv. 11f., 14f.). The catchphrase 'this people' (vv. 11, 13) may also have served to link the two traditions together. There is no scholarly consensus concerning the attribution of vv. 11f., 14–17, 24b–30. Many commentators (e.g., Baentsch, Holzinger; cf. Jenks, *Elohist*, pp. 54f.) contend that these verses belong to the E source, primarily because some of the motifs which occur here reappear in other supposed Elohist passages. Such motifs include (i) the idea that the tent of meeting was located 'outside' the camp (vv. 26, 30); (ii) the concept of Joshua as Moses' 'minister' (v. 28); (iii) the interest in the prophetic activity of the seventy elders (v. 25) and of Eldad and Medad (vv. 26–30). However, the attribution of these verses to an E source must be regarded as very doubtful, for the term Elohim does not occur here, and consequently the argument is based entirely on the supposed connection between these verses and other passages, the origin of which must be regarded as equally uncertain. Noth is inclined to attribute vv. 11f., 14–17, 24b–30 to J (cf. *Pentateuchal Traditions*, p. 128, n. 361), but it is preferable to refrain from assigning them to any of the recognized Pentateuchal sources (so, e.g., Fritz).

The only other problem that remains to be discussed with regard to this passage is the significance of the episode concerning the bestowal of Moses' spirit upon seventy of the elders (cf. Weisman, *ZAW* 93 [1981], pp. 225ff.). Reviv (*ZAW* 94 [1982], pp. 571f.) draws attention to the lack of any specific reference in the passage to the duties which the elders were supposed to perform, and he therefore suggests that the task with which they were here entrusted was the familiar one of adjudication in legal disputes; hence, the passage is interpreted as reflecting the origin of the judicial system in Israel. But this is most unlikely, for while the elders do, admittedly, appear in a judicial role in Exod. 18, there is no hint at all in the present passage that they were destined to serve in this capacity. A more plausible explanation is that advanced by Noth (p. 89) and von Rad (*ZAW*, N.F., 10 [1933], pp. 115f.; cf. *OT Theology*, ii, pp. 8f.), namely, that the passage was designed to provide some legitimation for the phenomenon of 'ecstatic prophecy' in Israel by deriving it ultimately from the spirit of Moses. According to this view, the passage emanated from the circle of the 'ecstatics' who, no doubt conscious of the deprecatory way in which their frenzied behaviour was considered by some (cf. 1 Sam. 10:10–12; 19:23f.), wished their activity to be given the stamp of validity and to be viewed as something which was by no means incompatible with Yahwism. This explanation of the background of the narrative, however, encounters two difficulties. In the first place, it does less than justice to the general context of the passage, for if the activity of the elders was limited to 'prophesying', it is by no means clear how they could have been of any practical assistance to Moses in bearing the 'burden of the people' (v. 17; cf. vv. 11, 14). Secondly, if the object of the passage was merely to trace the phenomenon of 'ecstatic prophecy' to the activity of the elders of Moses' time, it is strange that the text should imply that such activity was manifested only on this one occasion, and thereafter ceased (v. 25*b*). Noth, aware of this difficulty, suggests emending MT's *weloʾ yāsāpû* ('and they did so no more') to read *weloʾ yāsûpû* ('and they did not cease'; cf. Targ. Onk., Vulg.), but it is methodologically unsound to effect an emendation of a text in order to sustain a preconceived theory about the nature and background of a particular passage. It seems preferable, therefore, to view the 'prophesying' of the elders in this instance as merely a visible sign of their authorization to a position of leadership in the community (cf. Milgrom, pp. 89, 383); it served, in effect, as a mark of their installation to a particular 'office'. Lindblom's suggestion (*Prophecy*, p. 101), that the text was intended to explain the origin of the office of 'eldership' in Israel, however, cannot be accepted, for the account clearly assumes that the 'elders' were already in existence (v. 16). Rather, it appears that the narrative was intended to distinguish a particular group of elders as having specific administrative functions in Israel, and their ecstatic behaviour was a token of their divine election to fulfil this role. Viewed in this way, the bestowal of the spirit upon the elders was an entirely appropriate response to Moses' request for help to bear the burden of caring for the people (vv. 11f., 14f.).

4. The discontent among the people had evidently originated not with the Israelites themselves but with **the rabble that was among them**: The word rendered 'rabble', *'asapsup*, is found only here in the *OT*; it may be a reduplicated form of *'āsap* = to gather, in which case the term was probably a general designation for a 'gathering' of people. Some scholars think that the term was a contemptuous one (cf. Vulg.'s *vulgus promiscuum*), here used to refer to people of various nationalities who had accompanied the Israelites during the exodus, and who had subsequently attached themselves to the Israelite camp (cf. Gottwald, *Tribes*, pp. 455f.; Albright, *BA* 36 [1973], p. 55). McNeile (p. 59) suggests that the word should be translated 'riff-raff' (cf. *NJPS*), a rendering which would encapsulate the disparaging nuance in the term and at the same time reproduce the alliteration present in the Heb. The discontent among the 'rabble' manifested itself in **a strong craving** for the rich and varied diet which they had enjoyed in Egypt. This craving evidently proved to be contagious, for it was soon shared by **the people of Israel** who **wept again** and began to long for more nourishing sustenance than that which the desert could provide. It is not entirely clear why the Israelites are represented as weeping 'again', for no previous weeping has been mentioned. LXX and Vulg. overcome the difficulty by reading 'and they sat down and wept' (i.e., emending *wayyāšubû* to read *wayyēšᵉbû*), a solution favoured by some recent scholars (cf. Beirne, *Bib* 44 [1963], pp. 201ff.; de Vaulx, pp. 148, 152). If MT is retained, however, it must be supposed that the word 'again' refers to an earlier, analogous incident, such as the 'murmuring' of the people at Taberah (vv. 1–3). **O that we had meat to eat!**: The complaint of the Israelites seems strange in view of the fact that, according to J, the people were richly endowed with flocks and herds throughout the wilderness wanderings (cf. 14:33; 32:1; Exod. 12:32, 38; 17:3; 34:3). It must be assumed, therefore, that either this tradition had been forgotten or overlooked in the present narrative (cf. Sturdy), or that the story contained here was independent of the main tradition concerning the wilderness wandering (cf. Snaith, *NPC*, p. 259).

5–6. Although the Israelites cry out for meat, the memory of their diet in Egypt was one of fish and fresh vegetables: **We remember the fish we ate in Egypt for nothing, the cucumbers, the melons, the leeks, the onions, and the garlic**. Fish seems to have been in plentiful supply in Egypt (cf. Exod. 7:21; Isa. 19:8), and it was evidently regarded as a staple diet of the lower classes. The historian Herodotus (ii.125) refers to 'radishes, onions and leeks' as being among the provisions supplied to the workmen on the pyramids. **but now our strength is dried up**: The Heb. word here translated 'strength' (*nepeš*) can mean 'throat' (cf. Ps. 42:1f.; Prov. 25:25), and Noth (p. 86) suggests reading 'now our throat is dry' (cf. *NEB*; Wolff, *Anthropology*, p. 12), thirst being one of the recurring hazards of travelling through arid areas. Snaith (p. 227) points out that *nepeš* can also mean 'appetite' (cf. *BDB*, p. 660*b*; *NIV*), and some prefer to translate the present phrase as 'there is nothing to whet our appetite' (cf. Riggans, p. 87). Noth's suggestion seems preferable, but either is an improvement on *RSV*.

7–9. The description of the manna in these verses is commonly regarded as a secondary insertion into the narrative (see above), and it betrays certain similarities to the description found in Exod. 16:13*b*–14, 31 (cf. Rudolph, pp. 66f.). Ever since ancient times, travellers have observed in parts of the Sinai peninsula a natural substance which bears a striking resemblance to the biblical description of the manna (cf. Josephus, *Ant.* III.1.6). This has been confirmed by modern travellers in Sinai who have noted the presence, in early summer, of a granular substance on a species of the tamarisk tree (*Tamarix gallica*). This substance was long thought to be a secretion of the tamarisk itself, but Bodenheimer (*BA* 10 [1947], pp. 2ff.) has suggested that it was, in fact, formed by small insects which suck the sap of the tree and then excrete what was superfluous to their needs. This excretion consists of sweet, edible globules which usually fall to the ground at night; if they are to be consumed, they must be gathered in the early morning, for they quickly melt in the heat of the sun. The annual crop of this substance in the Sinai peninsula, however, was usually very small (hardly more than a few kilograms), and consequently the Israelites must have been the beneficiaries of a spectacularly good season of manna production if they had managed to gather the huge quantities necessary to feed such a vast multitude (cf. v. 21) during the period of their desert sojourn. The probability is that the biblical writers conceived of the manna as a naturally occurring product of the desert (cf. Gray, p. 105), but that they discerned a miraculous element in the large and regular quantities available (cf. Exod. 16:4ff.). The manna was **like coriander seed**: The coriander was an umbelliferous plant whose seed (properly, 'fruit') had a pleasant, spicy flavour, and was regarded as particularly suitable for seasoning. The 'seed' was greyish-white in colour and was approximately the size of a peppercorn. **and its appearance** (lit., 'its eye'; for the idiom, see *BDB*, pp. 744f.) was **like that of bdellium**: The Heb. term *bᵉḏōlaḥ* occurs only here and in Gen. 2:12 in the *OT*; it is probably to be identified with the Gk *bdellion*, which was a transparent, resinous substance, valued both for its fragrance and for its soothing, medicinal properties. The LXX translators mistakenly thought that the word here referred to a stone, and rendered it *crustallon*, 'crystal'. On vv. 6–9, see, further, Malina, *Manna Tradition*, pp. 20–22.

10. This verse should be regarded as a continuation of v. 6. The words **and the anger of the LORD blazed hotly** are considered by Noth (p. 86) to be a later addition, since they break the sequence of thought between Moses' overhearing the people and the reference, at the end of the verse, to his displeasure at what he heard.

11–15. Far from rebuking the people for their complaints, Moses expostulates with Yahweh for placing upon him the duty of leading the Israelites, unaided, into the land of Canaan. In his despair, he vents his anger and frustration before the LORD, and levels against him a series of reproaches cast in the form of rhetorical questions. Why had Yahweh dealt with his dutiful servant in such a malevolent manner? Why had he placed upon him such an intolerable burden (v. 11)? Was it he, Moses, who was responsible for conceiving the people? Since he patently was not, why was he given the responsibility of carrying them in his bosom, as a nurse might carry a sucking child (v. 12)? Moreover, from where was Moses expected to obtain meat in the wilderness in order to satisfy the people's hunger (v. 13)? Moses' fierce outburst concludes with a simple confession: **I am not able to carry all this people alone, the burden is too heavy for me** (v. 14), and his exacerbation is dramatically underlined by his plea for Yahweh to kill him and have done with it, **that I may not see my wretchedness** (v. 15; cf. 1 Kg. 19:4; Jer. 20:14–18).

16. Gather for me seventy men of the elders of Israel: The 'elders' figure in almost every period of Israel's history, and they are mentioned in both early and late texts (cf. 1 Sam. 4:3; 8:4;

Ezr. 10:14). Sometimes they appear as official representatives of the people, and act on their behalf and in their interests (cf. Exod. 3:16, 18; Dt. 5:20; 27:1), while at other times they are regarded as the leading inhabitants of a particular town, who constitute the local judicial authority and through whom various matters were transacted and various disputes resolved (cf. 1 Sam. 11:3; 2 Sam. 19:11f.). Here, as in Exod. 12:21ff., they seem to be the heads of the various families, and to some extent they correspond to the 'leaders of the congregation' referred to in P. Nothing is mentioned here concerning the method by which they were selected, beyond the fact that those chosen were to be known by Moses to be **elders of the people**. For a discussion of the various occurrences of the word 'elder' (Heb. *zāqēn*) in the *OT*, see van der Ploeg, *Fest. Junker*, pp. 175ff., and on the role of the elders in general, see Davies, *Prophecy*, pp. 100ff.; de Vaux, *AI*, pp. 138, 152f.; McKenzie, *Bib* 40 (1959), pp. 522ff. **and officers over them**: The 'officers' (Heb. *šōṭᵉrîm*) are frequently mentioned in conjunction with the elders in the *OT* (cf. Dt. 31:28; Jos. 8:33; 23:2; 24:1). It is not entirely clear what the duties of these officials embraced. The root *šṭr* in Akkad. and other Semitic languages means 'to write', and LXX renders the term in the present context by *grammateus* ('scribe'). It is improbable, however, that the *šōṭᵉrîm* functioned solely in this capacity, for in 2 Chr. 34:13 they are mentioned alongside the scribes and, by implication, distinguished from them. The evidence of the *OT* would seem to suggest that their duties varied considerably, for in Exod. 5:6f. they appear as foremen in charge of forced labour, while in Dt. 20:5f. they are represented as military officials, and in Dt. 16:18 they appear to have a role in the administration of justice. They are often depicted in a subordinate position, for their task was usually to put in force decrees and directives issued by their superiors (cf. Driver, *Deuteronomy*, pp. 17f.). **and bring them to the tent of meeting**: This is the first reference to the tent in the non-Priestly material in Numbers; see, further, on 1:1.

17. and I will take some of the spirit which is upon you and put it upon them: The spirit (Heb. *rûaḥ*) is here conceived of as a quasi-material entity which comes upon a person from without, and which could almost be measured quantitatively. Moses evidently possessed the spirit in such abundant measure that some of it could be 'taken' (Heb. *'āṣal*; cf. LXX) from him and distributed between the seventy elders (cf. 2 Kg. 2:9; but see Neve, *Spirit*, p. 18, for a different, though somewhat over-subtle, interpretation of the rare verb *'āṣal* here). That the elders merely received a portion of the spirit that had been bestowed upon Moses was perhaps intended to suggest their subordination to him, a point further underlined by the fact that Moses remains the only person with whom Yahweh communicates directly (v. 17*a*). **and they shall bear the burden of the people with you, that you may not bear it yourself alone**: These words are sometimes regarded as an editorial insertion added by a later writer who wished to indicate that the inspiration of the elders was Yahweh's response to Moses' complaint in vv. 11–15 (so, e.g., Gray, McNeile), but the words need not be regarded as a gloss (cf. Budd, p. 128).

18. And say to the people: Syr. reads, 'and Moses said to the people', but this is clearly an inferior reading, designed to obviate the difficulty that in the remainder of the verse Yahweh is twice referred to in the third person within the context of a Yahweh-speech. **Consecrate yourselves for tomorrow, and you shall eat meat**: The people were to observe the necessary purificatory rituals before they could be deemed fit to receive the promised gift of God (cf. Exod. 19:10, 14f.).

19–20. The meat would be in such plentiful supply that the people would eat it for a whole month, by which time it would have become **loathsome** to them. The word rendered 'loathsome' (*zārā'*, perhaps a scribal error for *zārāh*) occurs only here in the *OT* (cf. Sir. 39:27); it probably derives from the root *zûr* = 'to become strange', hence 'repugnant', 'loathsome'. Vulg. takes the word to refer to 'nausea', an interpretation which is certainly in keeping with the phrase **until it comes out at your nostrils**, which may refer to 'violent vomiting' (so Gray).

23. Is the LORD's hand shortened?: *RSV* represents a literal translation of the Heb.; for the use of this idiom elsewhere to express powerlessness or impotence, cf. Isa. 50:2; 59:1. *NEB* paraphrases, 'Is there a limit to the power of the LORD?' (cf. *NRSV, NJPS*).

25. and when the spirit rested upon them, they prophesied: *NEB*'s 'fell into a prophetic ecstasy' probably more accurately conveys the meaning of MT. Once the spirit had been bestowed upon the elders, they were flung into a state of divine frenzy, similar to that which gripped the guilds of prophets in the days of Samuel and Saul (cf. 1 Sam. 10:5ff.; 19:20ff.). **but they did so no more**: *AV*'s 'and did not cease' (following Vulg., Targ. Onk.; cf. Noth) is quite

misleading and, in fact, conveys the very opposite of what is intended
by the Heb. text (cf. G–K § 120*d*; Sifre, Rashi, Ibn Ezra). The
point made here is that the prophetic frenzy was but a transient
phenomenon which affected the elders on this occasion, and on this
occasion only, as a confirmation of their position of leadership in
the community (cf. Parker *VT* 28 [1978], pp. 276f.; Weisman, *ZAW*
93 [1981], pp. 228ff.).

26. Now two men remained in the camp: It is not stated why
these two stayed in the camp while Moses and the other elders went
out to the tent; the suggestion that they were detained on account
of their ritual uncleanness (cf. Snaith, *NPC*, p. 259) is purely conjectural. **one named Eldad, and the other named Medad**: For the
assonance between the two names, Gray (p. 114) compares Jabal
and Jubal (Gen. 4:20f.), and Gog and Magog (Ezek. 38:2). Holzinger (p. 45) suggests that the original forms of the names were
Elidad (cf. 34:21) and Elmodad; the latter receives some indirect
support from LXX and Sam., both of which read Modad. Nothing
is known of these two men, but according to Jewish tradition, preserved in the Targums and Midrashim, they were half brothers, and
the gift of prophecy (cf. v. 27) was granted to them by God because
they were humble and deemed themselves unworthy to be numbered
among the seventy elders (cf. Russell, *Method and Message*, p. 68). In
the *Shepherd of Hermas* (ii.3), allusion is made to a book of Eldad and
Medad (or Modad), and its existence is also attested by several lists
of *OT* and *NT* apocryphal books, including the *Athanasian Synopsis*
and the *Stichometry of Nicephorus*. It may be presumed that this book
contained an account of the various prophecies which Eldad and
Medad were thought to have uttered in the wilderness. For an
account of their prophecies as recorded in Midrashic literature, see
Ginzberg, *Legends*, iii, pp. 251–3; vi, pp. 88f. **they were among
those registered**: This is sometimes understood to mean that Eldad
and Medad were two of the seventy elders mentioned in vv. 24f.,
but this is unlikely, since it is there stated that all seventy went out
to the tent, whereas it is here clearly indicated that Eldad and
Medad remained in the camp. The clause is regarded by some
commentators as a gloss (cf. Binns), a view which seems buttressed
by the fact that references to the 'registration' of individuals are
found predominantly in late *OT* texts (cf. 1 Chr. 4:41; 24:6; Neh.
12:22). If the clause is original, it must be assumed either that 'the
figure seventy is really to be understood as meaning seventy-two'

(Noth, p. 90), or that the 'registration' referred to was that of the whole body of elders from whom the seventy were chosen (v. 16; cf. Gray).

28–29. And Joshua the son of Nun, the minister of Moses: Joshua's presence at the tent of meeting is probably to be explained on the basis of Exod. 33:11, where he is depicted as permanently attached to the tent, serving there under the direction of Moses. **one of his chosen men**: *RV* mg. reads 'from his youth' (cf. *NEB*, *NIV*; Syr., Targ.), which may well represent the correct reading. The justification for the rendering of *RSV* (supported by LXX, Vulg., Sam.) is that if the present narrative was originally connected with the tradition of Exod. 33:7–11 (cf. Noth, p. 88, for the links between the two passages), Joshua would still have been a young man when this incident occurred (cf. Exod. 33:11), and so the words 'from his youth' here would be quite meaningless. **My lord Moses, forbid them**: When Joshua realized that Eldad and Medad were prophesying in the camp, he expressed his concern for his master's honour and authority by asking him to prohibit such irregular behaviour; his words, however, merely evoked a rebuke from Moses: **Are you jealous for my sake**? The Hebrew word *qānā'* can mean 'jealous' (cf. 5:14, 30) or 'zealous' (see on 25:11), and so it is not clear whether Joshua is here being reprimanded for his envy or for his misplaced zeal. **Would that all the LORD's people were prophets, that the LORD would put his spirit upon them!**: Moses here indicates his desire that all Yahweh's people should encounter the power of God's energizing spirit, a wish that also finds expression in the great prophecy contained in Jl 2:28f. Joshua was here no doubt intended to represent those who wished to subject the office of 'prophet' to institutional control, whereas Moses represents those who rejected such narrow exclusivism, insisting that the freedom and independence of the prophetic office should at all costs be preserved. The point made here is that prophecy was not a phenomenon to be confined rigidly to a favoured, privileged circle; it was a gift of God's spirit and, as such, should recognize no boundaries or limitations.

31–32. And there went forth a wind from the LORD: 'Wind' (Heb. *rûaḥ*), although an ostensibly natural phenomenon, is frequently viewed in the *OT* as the instrument of Yahweh's purpose; it was deployed, for example, to reduce the deluge (Gen. 8:1), to bring and disperse the locusts (Exod. 10:13, 19), and to drive back the Red Sea (Exod. 14:21). Here, it served to bring **quails from**

the sea: Quails are small birds of the partridge family which migrate northwards from Africa in the spring and return again in early autumn. The birds are so heavy that they are forced to fly in short stages; even so, they often fall to the ground, wearied by their flight, and are then easily netted in vast numbers (cf. Gray, *VT* 4 [1954], pp. 148f.). The description here of the quails falling in abundance **beside the camp** may well reflect a regularly recurring phenomenon in the Sinai peninsula; however, their arrival at the right place and at the right time inevitably led the author of the present passage to regard the event as a sign of a miraculous, divine provision. **about two cubits above the face of the earth**: *RSV* suggests that the quails lay approximately three feet deep on the ground; *NEB*, however, following Vulg., understands the text to mean that the birds were flying at a height of three feet from the ground. The rendering of *RSV* is consistent with the idea of an enormously large catch; on the other hand, the *NEB* translation accurately reflects the traditional method of netting these migrating birds. The quails were so numerous that the people spent two whole days and the intervening night collecting them, and so abundant was the supply that each individual gathered at least **ten homers**. The 'homer' was a dry measure of capacity which was equivalent to approx. 230 litres (cf. Scott, *NPC*, p. 38); ten homers would therefore have been a very large quantity indeed. After the quails had been gathered, the Israelites **spread them out for themselves all around the camp**: The object of this exercise was to cure the quails by drying them in the sun, a practice attested also in ancient Egypt (Herodotus, ii.77).

33. Yahweh's anger was kindled against the people even before the meat **was consumed**: MT reads, lit., 'was cut off' (Heb. *kārat*), but there is some evidence that the verb *kārat* in the Niphal can mean 'to fail' or 'to cease' (cf. Jos. 3:13, 16; Jl 1:16), and the meaning here may be that Yahweh's anger was kindled before the people's supply of meat failed, i.e., before it ran short, an interpretation favoured by several commentators (cf. Gray, McNeile, Riggans) and supported by LXX, Vulg., Targ. Onk. However, 'before it was consumed' (or, perhaps, better, 'before it was chewed'; cf. *RV*; *BDB*, p. 504*a*) forms a better parallel to the previous clause ('while the meat was yet between their teeth'), and may well reflect the meaning intended (cf. *NEB*, *NIV*). **and the LORD smote the people with a very great plague**: No further details regarding the nature of the plague are given, but it is clear from the next verse that it resulted in the annihilation of many Israelites in the wilderness. Jobling (*Biblical Narrative*, pp. 29f.; cf. Coats, *Rebellion*, p. 111) suggests that only the 'rabble' referred to in v. 4 died by the plague, and that the punishment was limited to them because they were the ones who had incited the Israelites to complain to Yahweh. But while this interpretation would provide the narrative with an appropriate ending, it is doubtful whether it can be sustained, for it is the people in general who complain in v. 10, and it would be reasonable to expect them to be included in the punishment (cf. vv. 19f.).

34. The place where the calamity occurred, **Kibroth-hattaavah**, can no longer be identified. The name is interpreted to mean 'graves of craving', for it was here that the **people who had the craving** were buried. Noth (p. 84) suggests that this explanation of the name is forced and artificial, and he maintains that Kibroth-hattaavah originally meant 'the graves at the boundary' or 'the graves of the Ta'awa tribe', but this is by no means certain.

35. The chapter concludes with a topographical note, indicating that the Israelites journeyed from Kibroth-hattaavah to **Hazeroth**. Hazeroth is mentioned elsewhere in the *OT* in 33:17f. and Dt. 1:1, but its location is uncertain. Attempts by older scholars (Baentsch, Holzinger) to identify it with 'Ain el-ḥadra, north of Jebel Musa in the Sinai peninsula, are now generally regarded as highly suspect.

(e) THE REBELLION OF MIRIAM AND AARON AGAINST MOSES
12:1–16

This chapter depicts the opposition of Miriam and Aaron to Moses because of his marriage to a Cushite woman (v. 1), and because of his claim to possess a unique relationship with Yahweh (v. 2). A divine oracle vindicates Moses' position (vv. 6–8), and Miriam is struck down with leprosy for daring to oppose him (v. 10). Moses, however, is persuaded by Aaron to intercede on her behalf (vv. 11f.), and, as a result of his intercession (v. 13), Miriam is cured of her affliction (v. 15).

The general unevenness of the chapter, together with the presence of various repetitions and inconsistencies, has led many commentators to question its literary unity. Indeed, the lack of cohesion is so marked that most analysts are of the view that either two separate narratives have here been interwoven (Rudolph, Fritz), or that one basic narrative has, to a greater or lesser degree, been subsequently modified, developed and supplemented (Baentsch). On the whole, it seems preferable to view the chapter as a fusion of two separate stories, and although the exact delimitation of each account must remain uncertain (cf. Noth, pp. 92f.), there is much to be said for Fritz's division (pp. 18f.) of the chapter into two strands, one consisting of vv. 1, 9a, 10aβ, 13–16, and the other comprising vv. 2–5a, 6–8, 9b, 10aα, 11 (vv. 5b, 10b, 12 being regarded as secondary). In the first strand, which was probably the earlier of the two, Miriam reproaches Moses on account of his Cushite wife; she is punished for reprimanding him by being afflicted with leprosy and excluded from the camp, but, as a result of Moses' intercession, she is healed, and her position in the camp is subsequently restored. The later narrative recounts the doubts raised by Aaron and Miriam concerning the exceptional position of Moses as Yahweh's intermediary, doubts which are finally dispelled by means of a divine oracle which confirms the uniqueness of Moses' position. The presence of Aaron in the later narrative may have led the compiler to introduce him into the earlier narrative also, no doubt in an effort to harmonize the two accounts; however, in the process of conflating the two traditions, several discrepancies emerged which are all too evident in the present form of the story. The two narratives were probably combined because Miriam was a protagonist in both, and because both reflected opposition to Moses, opposition which was rebuffed in one case by means of a divine judgment (v. 10aβ) and in the other by means of a divine oracle (vv. 6–8). By conflating the two accounts the narrative was infused with a gentle irony: Miriam and Aaron were forced to seek the mediation of the very one whose intimacy with Yahweh they had mistakenly called in question. For attempts to read the narrative as a unified whole, while recognizing that different traditions may here have been combined, see Coats, *Art and Meaning*, pp. 97ff.; Robinson, *ZAW* 101 (1989), pp. 428ff.; Milgrom, *Judaic Perspectives*, pp. 49ff.

The chapter is attributed to the E source by several commentators, partly because of its emphasis on the prophetic aspect of Moses' activity, partly on account of the interest exhibited in dreams and visions (elements thought to be especially characteristic of E), and partly because of certain idiosyncrasies of style and vocabulary (cf. Baentsch, p. 511; Snaith, pp. 234ff.). However, these arguments are far from compelling (cf. Budd, p. 134), and it seems preferable to attribute vv. 1, 9a, 10aβ, 13–16 to J, and to assign the remainder of the chapter to an indeterminate source, since it cannot confidently be identified with any of the recognized Pentateuchal sources (so, e.g., Fritz, p. 19).

The background of the present narrative has frequently been discussed by commentators but, as yet, no consensus has been reached. Some scholars claim that the chapter reflects a conflict between prophetic groups, while others maintain that it mirrors a dispute prevalent in priestly circles. However, neither view is entirely without its difficulties. If, on the one hand, the chapter is regarded as reflecting a prophetic conflict, then the presence of Aaron, the archetypal priest, is difficult to explain; if, on the other hand, the narrative is deemed to reflect a priestly dispute, then the presence of Miriam, regarded in tradition as a 'prophetess' (cf. Exod. 15:20), is difficult to justify. Since neither Aaron nor Miriam is characterized by any specific title or official designation in the present chapter, the significance of their role must be gleaned from the context, and it is here that scholars differ so markedly in their interpretation of the passage. Budd, for example, contends that there are no traces of priestly issues in the narrative, and that the concern of the chapter is primarily with the phenomenon of 'prophecy'. Miriam, regarded in tradition as a 'prophetess', represents, along with Aaron, the claims of prophetic inspiration, and the narrative merely establishes the principle that such forms of revelation must be regarded as subordinate to the ultimate authority of Mosaic religion (pp. 134f., 138f.). A very different view of the chapter, however, has been advanced by Burns (*Has the Lord Indeed Spoken?*, pp. 48ff.), who argues that the reference to Miriam as a 'prophetess' in Exod. 15:20 is anachronistic and should not, therefore, be used to interpret her role in the present chapter. Moreover, Burns contends that, although Moses is viewed in vv. 6–8 as superior to the prophets who received visions and dreams, there is no indication in these verses that he himself was here viewed in a 'prophetic' capacity; rather, he is portrayed as the oracular figure *par excellence*, and as the representative of the Levitical priesthood (cf., also, von Rad, *OT Theology*, i, p. 291; Coats, *Rebellion*, pp. 263f.; White, *VTS* 41 [1990], pp. 157f.). Within the context of the present chapter, these verses are thus seen as resolving a conflict concerning oracular authority which had arisen between a group of Aaronic priests (represented by Aaron and Miriam) on the one hand, and the Levites (represented by Moses) on the other; the divine pronouncement issued in vv. 6–8 makes it clear that only Moses (i.e., the Levite) had immediate access to

God, and that all rival claims to direct communion with him must
be rejected. Viewed in this light, Miriam is regarded as 'belonging
to Israel's priestly personnel' (Burns, p. 99), and in vaunting her
claim to equality with Moses she is depicted as representing 'a
priestly, not a prophetic group' (Burns, p. 78).

The argument advanced by Burns, although superficially attractive, must, however, be viewed with considerable reserve. In the first
place, the words 'if there is a prophet among you' (v. 6) addressed, as
they are, to Aaron and Miriam, strongly suggest that both are here
cast in a prophetic role, and even if these verses are regarded as an
independent unit of tradition which was only secondarily inserted
into its present context (cf. Burns, pp. 51ff.; Perlitt, *EvTh* 31 [1971],
p. 594; Seebass, *VT* 28 [1978], pp. 221f.), the fact remains that the
redactor of the passage must have viewed Aaron and Miriam here
as fulfilling a prophetic role. Secondly, there is no *a priori* reason
why Miriam should not be viewed as a 'prophetess' in the present
narrative, for it is by no means certain that the designation of
Miriam as a 'prophetess' in Exod. 15:20 should be regarded as
anachronistic; indeed, it could be argued that the title in Exod. 15:20
seems particularly appropriate in the context, since the activities
which she performs in this passage are redolent of those of the
ecstatic prophets of old. Thirdly, Burns' contention (p. 95) that
Miriam had Levitical connections stretching back to pre-exilic times
lacks conviction, for there is no evidence in the *OT* that *any* female
(let alone Miriam) was granted the privilege of exercising priestly
functions in Israel (cf. de Vaux, *AI*, pp. 383f.; Gray, *Sacrifice*,
pp. 190ff.). Burns does not, it is true, claim that Miriam was a
'priestess' *per se*, but even her more modest conclusion that 'at least
some layers of Hebrew tradition interpreted her role as containing
elements of a priestly character' (p. 100) must seriously be called
in question. Finally, if the conflict in this chapter was simply one
between the Aaronic and the Levitical priesthood, as Burns maintains, it is not at all clear why Miriam should have been introduced
into the narrative at all, for the point could just as easily (and,
indeed, more cogently) have been made by letting Aaron alone challenge the authority of Moses. This is not, of course, to deny that
conflicts and disputes did occasionally arise between rival priest-
hoods in Israel, but it seems most improbable that the present narrative was used to buttress the claims of any particular priestly group.

The inevitable conclusion, then, must be that Num. 12 reflects a conflict that arose in prophetic circles, and while it is not entirely clear why the figure of Aaron was introduced into the narrative, it must be conceded that it is considerably easier to envisage him in a 'prophetic' capacity (cf. Exod. 4:16; 7:1) than it is to envisage Miriam in a 'priestly' role. As representatives of Yahweh's prophets, their assertion that Yahweh had, indeed, spoken with them was not without justification; however, the point of the narrative is that such a privilege did not, of itself, justify their claim to possess equal status with Moses, for there was one factor which clearly distinguished them from him: Yahweh had spoken to prophets such as them only in dreams and visions, i.e., in enigmatic ways that needed interpretation, but with Moses he had communicated directly, 'mouth to mouth' (v. 8). This was not, of course, to deny or denigrate the legitimacy of the prophetic experience, but merely to emphasize that the 'ordinary' prophet's perception of the divine will was not as clear or coherent as the revelation received by Moses (cf. Wilson, *Int* 32 [1978], p. 12).

It has often been remarked that Num. 12 must be classified as a 'Moses story' rather than a 'wilderness story' (cf. Fritz, p. 76; Sturdy), and, this being so, it is by no means obvious why an editor should have included the present narrative as part of the account of the wilderness journey. However, the teaching encapsulated in vv. 6–8 concerning the unique relationship between Yahweh and Moses may well account for the present position of Num. 12. Num. 11:14–17, 24*b*–30, which depicted the sharing of Moses' spirit among the seventy elders, may have been erroneously interpreted to mean that Moses was merely first among equals; the present narrative, therefore, served to set the record straight by demonstrating that the bestowal of some of Moses' spirit upon the elders did not involve any diminution of his unique status, for his authority was still to be regarded as supreme and unassailable by virtue of his special relationship with God. For an exploration of this thematic link between chs. 11 and 12, see Jobling, *Biblical Narrative*, pp. 36f., 45f., 57f.

1. Miriam and Aaron spoke against Moses: The reference to 'Aaron' here is commonly regarded as a secondary insertion, for the verb 'spoke' is in the third feminine singular and, later in the narrative, it is Miriam alone who is punished for her outspokenness (v. 10). Moreover, if the reference to Aaron *were* original, it would be more natural for him to have been mentioned first, as in vv. 4f.

(cf. Rudolph, pp. 70f.). Miriam, who appears here for the first time in Numbers, is described in Exod. 15:20 as Aaron's sister, and in Num. 26:59 as the sister of both Aaron and Moses; however, this depiction of the three characters as members of a single family almost certainly represents a later tradition, and probably reflects the common literary fiction of relating characters in a story together (cf. Noth, *Exodus*, pp. 122f.; Sturdy, p. 89). There is certainly no indication in the present narrative of a familial relationship between Moses, Aaron and Miriam (cf. Noth, p. 94; Burns, p. 81). **because of the Cushite woman whom he had married**: The additional clause, **for he had married a Cushite woman**, is strictly redundant and is widely regarded as a gloss. The need for such an explanatory note (omitted in Vulg.) perhaps suggests that the tradition concerning Moses' marriage to a foreign woman was not widely known, even at this fairly late stage of redaction. The term 'Cush' in the *OT* usually refers to Ethiopia (cf. Gen. 10:6, 8; Isa. 11:11; 20:3, 5; 43:3 etc.), and it is so understood here by *AV* and some of the ancient Vsns (cf. LXX, Syr., Vulg.). However, it is improbable that 'Cushite' should be interpreted in this way in the present narrative, for there is no evidence elsewhere in the *OT* of Moses' marriage to an Ethiopian woman, and while it is true that later Jewish legends explored at some length Moses' connection with this country, including his marriage to an Ethiopian princess (cf. Shinan, *ScrHier* 27 [1978], pp. 66ff.; Runnalls, *JSJ* 14 [1983], pp. 135ff.), it appears that, in reality, Moses' sphere of activity would have been too far removed from this region for such a connection to have been at all feasible (cf. Noth, p. 94). Most commentators therefore prefer to identify Cush in this instance with Cushan, a region which is referred to in Hab. 3:7 as being in the vicinity of Midian, and suggest that the 'Cushite woman' here referred to was, in fact, Zipporah, whom Moses married in Midian (cf. Exod. 2:15ff.; 3:1; so, e.g., Sturdy, Rudolph). The difficulty with this view, however, is that the present verse tacitly assumes that Moses had only recently married his Cushite wife, whereas the tradition recorded in Exod. 2:21 suggests that he had long since been married to Zipporah. Moreover, since Cushan and Midian are not actually identified with one another in Hab. 3:7, but appear to refer to two separate regions, it seems preferable to distinguish the Cushite woman from Zipporah the Midianite. It must therefore be assumed either that Moses had taken a second wife, or that he had married the woman from Cushan after his separation from Zipporah (cf. Exod. 18:2) or after the latter's death (cf. Maarsingh). An alternative view, favoured by some commentators, is that 'Cushite' should be connected with the name Kusi, found on some Assyrian inscriptions in connection with a district or tribe in northern Arabia; if this identification is correct, then the statement that Moses had married a Cushite merely meant that he had taken a north Arabian wife, and this could be regarded as a variant form of the tradition that Moses' wife was a Midianite (10:29; Exod. 2:15ff.; 3:1) or a Kenite (Jg. 1:16; 4:11). Cf., further, Gray, pp. 121f. The grounds for Miriam's objection to Moses' marriage to the Cushite woman are not explained in the narrative. Ancient Jewish exegetes, who tended to identify the Cushite woman with Zipporah (no doubt in order to preserve Moses' monogamous status), interpreted the words 'sent her away' in Exod. 18:2 as an euphemism for 'divorce', and suggested that Miriam's anger in this instance was precipitated by Moses' intention to divorce his wife (cf. Targ. Onk.). Such a view, however, is highly conjectural, and finds no basis in the narrative under discussion. Dillmann (p. 64) suggests that Miriam was opposed to the principle of a foreign marriage on the grounds that it was inappropriate for a (black) foreigner to be the wife of the leader of the Israelites; but this view, too, may safely be dismissed, for the opprobrium attaching to such foreign marriages savours of a much later age than that to which this narrative belongs, and besides, no such qualms seem to have been registered at Moses' marriage to Zipporah, who was similarly of foreign extraction. Baentsch's view (p. 511) that Miriam wished to avoid a 'family scandal', and de Vaulx's contention (p. 161) that it was 'family jealousy' that precipitated her complaint, seem similarly misconceived, for, as was noted above, there is no indication in the present narrative that Miriam was regarded as Moses' sister. The most plausible conjecture is that Miriam's complaint had its roots in a motif which regarded relations with foreign women as precarious, since those of a vulnerable disposition might well be seduced into committing acts of apostasy. It is by no means clear why Miriam in particular should have been chosen as a vehicle to voice this complaint against Moses, but perhaps she was selected for no other reason than that she was revered as a leader in the community (cf. Mic. 6:4), and was thus regarded as an appropriate mouthpiece to voice a community concern (cf. Burns, p. 7).

2. Has the LORD indeed spoken only through Moses?: In

view of the statement in v. 1, it is strange that the complaint actually
voiced by Miriam was concerned not with Moses' marriage, but
with his claim to possess a special relationship with God. As was
noted above, this discrepancy has led some scholars to suspect that
two separate narratives have here been conflated. Those who defend
the unity of the chapter are inclined to argue that the complaint
regarding the Cushite wife was merely a smokescreen for the more
significant challenge to Moses' authority (cf. Wenham, pp. 110f.;
Harrison, p. 194; Budd, pp. 133f., 138), but it seems far more probable that two different sources have here been combined. This conclusion seems to be confirmed by the use of the verb *dibbēr* ('to
speak') followed by the preposition *bêṯ* in vv. 1 and 2, for in v. 1
the construction appears in a negative or hostile sense to indicate a
reproach or reprimand, while in v. 2 it is used in a positive sense
of a communication imparted by Yahweh to Moses (cf. Valentin,
Aaron, pp. 316f.). Miriam does not here deny Moses' prophetic
status, but merely wishes to claim equality with him in her capacity
as a recipient of the divine word. Her complaint is rendered in the
most emphatic terms, as is clear from the collocation of the two
words 'indeed' (Heb. *raq*) and 'only' (Heb. *'ak*), which occur in such
close proximity only here in the *OT*. The complaint was evidently
directed not to Moses himself, but to anyone within the Israelite
camp who was prepared to listen.

3. Now the man Moses was very meek: The term *'ānāw* (which
appears in the singular only here in the *OT*) often means 'poor',
'afflicted', but it also connotes the idea of meekness or humility
(*BDB*, p. 776b; cf. *NEB, NIV*), a virtue which Moses is said to have
exemplified more than all men that were on the face of the earth.
Coats (*Art and Meaning*, pp. 99f.) has argued strongly that *'ānāw*
should here be understood to mean 'honour' or 'integrity' (cf. 2 Sam.
22:36; Ps. 45:4 [MT 45:5]), for Moses is depicted in this passage not
as a passive, submissive figure which the term 'meek' might imply,
but as a man of honour who dutifully fulfils the responsibility
entrusted to him by God (v. 7). Rogers, on the other hand, contends
that the word here means 'miserable', for the basic meaning of the
root *'nh* means 'to be bowed down', and in the context of the preceding chapter, this must signify not 'bowed down' in submission (i.e.,
'humble') but 'bowed down' or 'burdened' with the responsibility of
caring for the people of Israel (*JETS* 29 [1986], pp. 257ff.). However,
neither suggestion is convincing or necessary, for the point of the

reference to Moses' meekness was to undermine any suggestion that Moses was guilty of a boastful arrogance in his supposed claim to be the sole recipient of Yahweh's word (cf. Robinson, *op. cit.*, p. 431). Moreover, within the context of the narrative, the modest reserve of Moses may be seen as standing in stark contrast to the ebullient self-assertiveness exhibited by Aaron and Miriam. Noth (p. 95) regards the reflection upon Moses' character in the present verse as a later addition which disrupts the connection between v. 2*b* and v. 4, but while v. 3 should certainly be read in parenthesis, there is no need to regard it as a gloss, since it is by no means inappropriate in the context (cf. Dillmann).

4–5. Yahweh requests Moses, Aaron and Miriam to **come out**, i.e., of the camp, **to the tent of meeting**, whereupon Yahweh descends in a **pillar of cloud** and addresses Aaron and Miriam at the door of the tent. **and they both came forward**: The verb in the Heb. is the same as that translated 'come out' in v. 4*b*. *RSV* assumes that the author intended the verb *yāṣā'* to be understood in a different sense here (cf. Rudolph, p. 71); if, on the other hand, it is deemed unlikely that a single author would use the same verb in a different sense twice in such close proximity, then there seems to be no alternative but to regard v. 5*b* as a gloss (so, e.g., Fritz).

6–8. The divine oracle contained in these verses is couched in poetic form (cf. *NEB*), and its metrical structure has recently been analyzed by D. N. Freedman (*Fest. McKenzie*, pp. 42–44). Albright (*Yahweh*, pp. 37f.; cf. *BA* 36 [1973], p. 72) has drawn attention to certain stylistic resemblances between this poem and passages in the Ugaritic Baal epic, and on this basis he argues that vv. 6–8 contain a piece of archaic poetry which can be dated as early as the time of Samuel. Noth, on the other hand, has more plausibly suggested that the oracle is comparatively late in origin, since it presupposes a fairly sophisticated and advanced reflection on the nature of 'prophecy', and represents an attempt to give a theological justification for the unique relationship that existed between Moses and God (*Pentateuchal Traditions*, p. 127; cf. Coats, *Rebellion*, p. 263).

6. If there is a prophet among you: MT reads, lit., 'if your prophet be Yahweh', which yields little sense, and is generally regarded as corrupt. The rendering of *RSV* (cf. Vulg.) presupposes a minor emendation of the text (*nābî' bākem* instead of *n'bî'ªkem*), which is widely accepted by commentators (cf. Dillmann, Baentsch, McNeile). The reference to Yahweh must either be omitted altogether (cf. *NEB*), or taken as the appositional subject of the following clause (cf. *RSV*) or, as *BHS* suggests, transposed with most of the ancient Vsns (LXX, Vulg., Sam., Targ.) to the beginning of the verse (cf. *REB*). Some scholars have attempted to make sense of the text as it stands, either by assuming that the clause is an example of a broken construct chain ('If there is among you a prophet of the LORD'; cf. Freedman, *op. cit.*, p. 43; Wenham, p. 112), or by interpreting MT to mean that a prophet, in delivering his message, could virtually be identified with Yahweh (cf. Johnson, *Cultic Prophet*, pp. 46f., n. 7); however, neither of these solutions has generally commended itself to scholars. **I the LORD make myself known to him in a vision, I speak with him in a dream**: It is here implied that visions and dreams were the normal methods of divine revelation; in later times, however, dreams were not regarded in such a favourable light and seem to have been linked, rather, with the false prophets of the day (cf. Jer. 23:23ff.).

7. Not so with my servant Moses: Kselman (*VT* 26 [1976], pp. 500ff.), on the basis of such passages as 2 Sam. 7:16; 23:1–5; Ps. 78:8, 37, has suggested that the Heb. *lō'-ḵēn*, rendered by *RSV* 'not so', should rather be understood as emphatic *lamed* ('surely') and Qal participle of *kûn* ('loyal'); the clause would then read, 'But my servant Moses is surely loyal', a rendering which Kselman claims would improve the parallelism with the next line. However, the rendering of *RSV* (cf. *NEB*, *NIV*) is perfectly intelligible and should be retained, *lō'-ḵēn* here being understood – as often elsewhere in the *OT* (cf. Dt. 18:14; 2 Sam. 20:21; Job 9:35; Ps. 1:4) – as indicating a situation different from the one that has previously been described or implied. Moses is called Yahweh's 'servant' some forty times in the *OT*, primarily in Deuteronomy and the Deuteronomistic history (Dt. 34:5; Jos. 1:1f., 7, 13, 15 etc.); the term was a title of honour bestowed upon several of God's intermediaries (cf. 14:24; Gen. 26:24; Job 1:8 etc.), and was usually conferred because of their particular devotion and loyalty to Yahweh (cf. Zimmerli and Jeremias, *Servant*, pp. 18ff.). The description of Moses as a 'servant' is particularly appropriate in the present context, for he is further depicted as having been **entrusted with all my house**, i.e., as a servant he had been assigned the responsibility of caring for the people of Israel. An alternative rendering, favoured by several commentators (cf. Snaith), is 'he is faithful in all my house' (cf. *NEB*, *NIV*), i.e., Moses had shown himself to be a loyal, trustworthy and responsible steward in God's household. For a detailed discussion, see Valentin, *op. cit.*, pp. 208–10.

8. With him I speak mouth to mouth: This expression occurs only here in the *OT*, and *RSV*'s rendering is to be preferred to *NRSV*'s 'face to face' (cf. *NEB, NIV*), which represents a different wording in the Heb. (cf. Exod. 33:11; Dt. 34:10). The point made here is that whereas God had communicated with other prophets through the refractory medium of visions and dreams (v. 6), he had revealed his will to Moses in a more direct and explicit fashion. Moses is thus portrayed here as more than *primus inter pares*, for no other prophet was accorded such an elevated status as the mediator of Yahweh's will. The notion that Moses enjoyed a unique and intimate relationship with God is a recurring motif in the Pentateuch, and is reflected in such passages as Exod. 33:7ff.; Dt. 5:4f. **clearly, and not in dark speech**: The word *mar'eh* usually means 'sight, vision', and the translation 'clearly' (cf. *NIV*) is largely based on the meaning that might be expected of the word here, appearing as it does in antithesis to 'dark speech'. But the difficulty with this rendering is that *mar'eh* (or, as LXX, Syr. and some Heb. MSS suggest, *b'mar'eh*) would be given a sense virtually opposite that which is accorded the same word (though pointed *mar'āh*) in v. 6, where 'in a vision' = dimly, obscurely. For this reason, some scholars suggest inserting *lō'* before *mar'eh* ('not in a vision'; cf. Paterson), and its omission is explained as due to the fact that there are two other occurrences of *lō'* preceding and following in two successive lines (cf. Albright, *Yahweh*, p. 37, n. 85). The difficulty with this proposal, however, is that such a statement would appear to be tautologous after vv. 6b, 7. *BDB* (p. 909b, accepting the reading *b'mar'eh*) suggests the rendering 'in personal presence', but such a translation hardly provides an effective antithesis to 'in dark speech' and, besides, a reference to Yahweh's presence here would anticipate unnecessarily the statement in the following line. It must be conceded that no satisfactory solution to the problem has yet been advanced; however, if it is accepted that *mar'eh* might be given two different (even opposite) meanings in vv. 6, 8 (and both the pointing of MT and the rendering of LXX suggest that they *should* be distinguished), then it is at least plausible that some such meaning as 'clearly' was intended by the author in the present verse. **and he beholds the form of the LORD**: Most of the Vsns, anxious to avoid such a bold anthropomorphism, render 'the glory of the LORD' (cf. LXX, Syr.). The 'form'

(Heb. *t͟emûnāh*) of the LORD was not the actual concrete image of Yahweh but, in a less tangible sense, the shape or semblance of that which the image represented. Other individuals might be allowed to perceive the 'form' of God in a dream or vision (cf. Job 4:16; Ps. 17:15), but none, except Moses, was permitted such a privilege in their regular communion with Yahweh. Some commentators regard the words 'and he beholds the form of the LORD' as a later addition to the text, partly because it disturbs the rhythm of the passage, and partly because a reference to the 'form of the LORD' appears strange within the context of a speech by Yahweh (cf. Noth); nevertheless, the gloss, if that is what it is, may be regarded as an entirely pertinent insertion after the preceding statements.

9–10. These verses (or, at least, vv. 9*a*, 10*a*β) are to be regarded as a continuation of v. 1. **And the anger of the LORD was kindled against them**: Although Yahweh's anger is here described as having been directed against both Miriam and Aaron, the original form of the narrative may well have read 'against her' (cf. Fritz, Rudolph), for it was probably Miriam (alone) who instigated the complaint concerning Moses' marriage (see on v. 1). **Miriam was leprous**: Since the Heb. term *ṣāra'at* covers a wide variety of skin infections, none of which strictly corresponds to 'leprosy' as it is known today (Hansen's disease), the *NEB*'s rather general rendering, 'there was Miriam, her skin diseased', is to be preferred. See, further, on 5:2. **as white as snow**: The epithet 'white' is not found in MT, which reads, simply, 'as snow' (cf. *NIV*); the adjective seems to have been first introduced by the Vulg. (cf. Isa. 1:18), and has found its way into most of the English translations. However, if, as is generally thought, biblical leprosy was a disorder which caused the skin to peel and flake, then the object of the comparison with 'snow' may not have been the whiteness of Miriam's appearance, but, rather, the flaking, desquamating character of the lesion which had inflicted her (cf. Hulse, *PEQ* 107 [1975], p. 93; Davies, *ExpT* 99 [1987–8], pp. 136ff.). Snaith (p. 236) takes the comparison to be with the 'moistness' of snow, and thinks that the reference was to an open, ulcerated wound.

11–12. These verses betray a certain inconsistency, for in v. 11 Aaron seems to share in Miriam's punishment, but in v. 12 he is introduced merely as a concerned observer of Miriam's predicament. The view of Gressmann (*Mose*, pp. 264, n. 1, 265f.; cf. Binns, p. 78) that in the original form of the narrative Aaron, too, was made leprous must be regarded as highly conjectural; rather, v. 11 gives the impression of being misplaced, since Aaron's plea makes little sense after Yahweh had already punished Miriam (cf. Rudolph, p. 70), and it seems more natural to assume that the verse originally belonged to the narrative contained in vv. 2–8. V. 12 would then be regarded as a later addition (cf. Fritz). Other commentators, however, prefer to explain the inconsistency by assuming that in v. 11 Aaron was expressing his solidarity with Miriam, as he appealed to Moses for the punishment to be rescinded. **Oh, my lord, do not punish us**: lit., 'do not lay sin upon us' (cf. *RSV* mg.), i.e., do not make us bear the consequence of our iniquity. V. 12 contains a graphic description of the baneful effect of the disease which had befallen Miriam: **Let her not be as one dead, of whom the flesh is half consumed when he comes out of his mother's womb**, i.e., let her not be as though she were a stillborn child whose body had already begun to putrefy *in utero*. Jewish commentators saw in these words an implied rebuke of Moses for allowing his 'sister' to remain in such a pitiful state instead of taking the initiative to intercede on her behalf (cf. Cooper, *JJS* 32 [1981], pp. 56ff.).

13. Heal her, O God, I beseech thee: The expression '*ēl nā*' is most unusual, and is regarded as suspect by many commentators because *nā*' is nowhere else connected with a noun (only with a verb or particle), and '*ēl* is nowhere else used in prose without some qualifying adjective or noun (cf. Paterson, Gray). *BHS* therefore suggests pointing '*al nā*' ('no, I pray'; cf. Gen. 19:18), an expression already encountered in vv. 11f., and the emendation is adopted by many commentators (cf. Dillmann, Baentsch, Holzinger). However, since it seems only right and proper that a reference to God should be made in an intercessory prayer, the rendering of *RSV* can be sustained.

14. If her father had but spit in her face: The phrase in MT begins, rather oddly, with a *waw*, 'and' (omitted in *RSV*), which perhaps implies that v. 14a has been preserved in a fragmentary and incomplete form. It is possible that the present construction is an example of a case where a clause preceding the *waw* has been suppressed (cf. *G–K* § 154b), and some commentators suggest that the original text may have read, 'If she had spoken against her father and mother, and her father had spat in her face' (cf. Kennedy). The action of spitting in the face is attested also in other *OT* passages (cf. Dt. 25:9; Isa. 50:6), where it seems to be regarded as a grave insult and a sign of utter contempt and disdain. **should she not be shamed seven days?**: It may be that when a daughter had been treated in this disdainful way as a punishment for some misdemeanour, she was expected to remain in disgrace for a week. The point here is: if such chastisement was meted out to a recalcitrant daughter, then surely no less could be inflicted upon Miriam, who had been put to shame by the divine infliction of 'leprosy'. **Let her be shut up outside the camp seven days**: Bechtel (*JSOT* 49 [1991], p. 59) notes that a person who had been spat upon would have been rendered unclean and socially unacceptable, and may well have found themselves temporarily excluded from the community. In the present instance, however, it is more probable that Miriam's exclusion from the camp is to be explained on the basis of such passages as Lev. 13:4ff.; 14:2ff., where it is stated that those who had been afflicted by leprosy had to be isolated for a period of seven days, while the usual rites of purification took place. If this is so, then the implication of the present verse is that Miriam had been cured of her affliction.

16. The Israelites were now ready to resume their journey, and so they **set out from Hazeroth** and encamped **in the wilderness of Paran**: For the 'wilderness of Paran', see on 10:12. This note concerning Israel's itinerary is probably redactional, and is only loosely connected to the preceding narrative. For this reason, the theory of Gressmann (*Mose*, p. 266) that the entire story of Miriam's 'leprosy' (Heb. *ṣāra'aṭ*) was constructed as an aetiology on the name Hazeroth, may safely be dismissed (see, further, Noth, *Pentateuchal Traditions*, p. 224, n. 595). The name Hazeroth may mean 'farm' or 'fixed settlement'; for a discussion of the etymology and meaning of the Heb. *ḥāṣēr*, see Orlinsky, *JAOS* 59 (1939), pp. 22ff. The location of Hazeroth is unknown, and attempts to identify it with 'Ain el-Ḥadra, north of Gebel Mūsa in the Sinai peninsula (cf. Baentsch, p. 510), must be regarded as very dubious.

(B) ISRAEL AT KADESH
13:1–20:13
(a) THE SPIES IN CANAAN
13:1–14:45

Before making an attempt to invade Canaan, the Israelites, in accordance with Yahweh's command, send out spies to report on the land and its inhabitants. On their return, the people are informed by the majority of spies that the inhabitants of Canaan would be formidable opponents and that the land itself would probably prove to be invincible. The people, as a result, lose heart and express a wish to return to Egypt, whereupon Yahweh determines to destroy them for their lack of faith. Moses, however, intercedes on their behalf, and Yahweh finally relents and indicates his willingness to forgive them. Yet, the people were not permitted to go entirely unpunished, and Yahweh announces that none of the present generation of Israelites (except Joshua and Caleb) would be allowed to enter the land. The people seek to defy the divine judgment, and they try (against Moses' advice) to enter Canaan from the south; however, the attempt proves fruitless, and the Israelites incur an ignominious defeat.

This brief outline of the content of chs. 13f. must not be allowed to disguise the fact that the narrative, in its present form, is by no means unified, for it is replete with inconsistencies, redundancies and duplications. Thus, e.g., according to 13:3, 26a the point of departure for the spies was the wilderness of Paran, but according to 13:26b they apparently departed from Kadesh (cf. 32:8; Dt. 1:19ff.); in 13:2, 17a, 21 it is suggested that the spies explored the whole of the land of Canaan, from north to south, but 13:22–24 implies a reconnaissance only of the southern region, around Hebron; in 13:32 the majority of the spies bring a negative report concerning the land, whereas in 13:27–29, the report is predominantly favourable, depicting the land as extremely productive, though it is conceded that it would probably be difficult to conquer; in 13:30, Caleb alone appears as the faithful spy who opposes the negative report of the majority, and he alone is exempted from punishment (14:24), but in 14:6–9, both Caleb and Joshua express their dissent, and both are preserved from Yahweh's judgment (14:38). In addition to these inconsistencies, the narrative contains several doublets (cf. 13:21 and 13:22ff.; 13:27f. and 13:32f.; 14:11f. and 14:26ff.) and the whole is marked by a distinct unevenness of style (cf. McEvenue, *Narrative Style*, pp. 101ff.).

Such factors have led most commentators to conclude that these chapters, in their present form, are composite, and earlier scholars sought to distinguish three (cf. Baentsch, pp. 514ff.; Holzinger, pp. 50ff.) or even four (cf. Eissfeldt, *Hexateuch-Synopse*, pp. 62f.) layers of tradition which had here been combined. However, attempts to distinguish between a J and an E source in these chapters have not proved persuasive (cf. Budd, pp. 142, 154), and Rudolph (pp. 74ff.) has convincingly demonstrated that these chapters can plausibly be viewed as containing two parallel narratives, which can be attributed to J and P.

The delimitation of the P version is fairly straightforward, and is based on the occurrence of specific words (e.g., 'leader', *nāśî*, 13:2; 'tribe', *maṭṭeh*, 13:2, 4–15; 'congregation', *ʿēdāh*, 13:26; 14:1, 2, 5, 7, 10, 27, 35f.; 'murmur', *lûn*, 14:2, 27, 29, 36) and phrases (e.g., 'Moses and Aaron', 13:26; 14:2, 5, 26; 'Joshua and Caleb', 14:6, 30, 38) which are generally regarded as characteristic of this source. Fritz (pp. 19ff.) concludes that the P source consisted of 13:1–17a, 21, 25, 26*abα*, 32f.; 14:1a, 2f., 5–7, 10, 26–38, although he concedes that these verses are not entirely devoid of later accretions and embellishments, and that 14:30, 34 are probably secondary additions. Apart from a few minor disagreements concerning individual verses, a similar source analysis of the P material in these chapters is offered by Noth, p. 101, and Rudolph, p. 74. Mittmann's division (*Deuteronomium 1:1–6:3*, pp. 42ff.) of the Priestly material in chs. 13f. into two layers, one of which broadly corresponds to the non-Priestly elements in these chs. and the other of which represents a much later tradition, does not appear to be particularly plausible or convincing (cf. Boorer, *Promise*, p. 333, n. 11). P's version of the spy story may be summarized as follows: Moses, at Yahweh's instigation, dispatches twelve men, one from each tribe, to spy out the land of Canaan (13:1–17a); they travel from the southernmost to the northernmost point of the land (13:21) and return, after forty days, to the wilderness of Paran (13:25, 26*abα*). The report rendered by the spies was unfavourable (13:32f.) and, as a result, the Israelites rebel and refuse to travel any further (14:1a, 2f.), much to the dismay of Moses and Aaron (14:5). Joshua and Caleb seek to encourage the people, emphasizing that the land was well worth conquering (14:6f.), but their words merely served to put their own lives in danger (14:10). Yahweh determines to punish the people for their rebellion, and announces that all who were over twenty years old would die in the wilderness, and that only their children would be permitted to see the promised land (14:26–29, 31–33). The narrative concludes by reporting that the spies who had been sent to reconnoitre the land died by a plague, but that Joshua and Caleb were both saved (14:36–38).

The J source, according to Fritz (pp. 22ff.) is found in 13:17*b*–20, 22–24, 26*b*β, 27–31; 14:1*b*, 4, 8f., 11–25, 39–45. As was the case with the P strand, this source, too, has subsequently attracted secondary additions (notably, 13:27*b*, 29; 14:8*b*, 25*a*, 44*b*). Moreover, 13:20, 23f., 26*b*β are probably later expansions of the original J narrative, and 14:12–21 may well represent an extensive Deuteronomistic digression within this core tradition (see below). J's version may be summarized as follows: Moses sends men to the Negeb to spy out the land (13:17*b*–20), and they travel as far as Hebron (13:22); on their return, the majority of spies report that the land appears impregnable (13:27*a*, 28), but Caleb dissociates himself from this negative appraisal and tries to convince the people that they were more than capable of conquering the inhabitants of Canaan (13:30). The people, however, remain unconvinced (13:21), and express a desire to return to Egypt (14:1*b*, 4), but Caleb reiterates his conviction that it would be possible, with Yahweh's help, to conquer the land (14:8*a*, 9). The people refuse to trust in Yahweh, and, as a punishment, an entire generation is excluded from entering the promised land, only Caleb being exempted from the judgment (14:11, 22–24). Despite Yahweh's pronouncement, the Israelites attempt to enter the land from the south, but the attempt proves abortive, and results in their defeat (14:39–44*a*, 45).

There are clear points of contact between the spy story as narrated in Num. 13f. and that recorded in Dt. 1:19–46. Indeed, even a cursory comparison of the two passages (cf. 13:17*b*, 23 and Dt. 1:24*a*; 13:20 and Dt. 1:25*a*; 13:28 and Dt. 1:28*b*; 14:23*a* and Dt. 1:35; 14:25*b* and Dt. 1:40; 14:42 and Dt. 1:42) indicates beyond any doubt that a literary connection of some kind exists between the two accounts. Since none of these parallels stems from P's version of the spy story, the literary link may be more closely defined as being between Dt. 1:19–46 and the J passages in Num. 13f., and most commentators favour the view that the J account is the older of the two and provided the *Vorlage* for the Deuteronomic version. Milgrom's contention (*Judaic Perspectives*, p. 58) that both the J and P strands of Num. 13f. were known to the Deuteronomist must be regarded as most improbable, for the Deuteronomic account does not, on the whole, reflect any of the peculiarities of P's style, and the fact that only Caleb is exempted from punishment in Dt. 1:36 suggests a complete lack of awareness of the P tradition, according to which both Caleb and Joshua were preserved from the divine judgment (cf. 14:30, 38).

The traditional view concerning the dependence of Dt. 1:19–46 upon the J strand of Num. 13f. has, however, recently been challenged by M. Rose (*Deuteronomist und Jahwist*, pp. 289ff.), who argues that the reverse was, in fact, the case, and that it is the non-Priestly elements in Num. 13f. which should be regarded as dependent upon the *Grundschicht* of Dt. 1:19–46. However, the arguments which he deploys are not altogether convincing. He observes, for example, that the land is described in Dt. 1:25 simply as 'good', whereas in the parallel account in Num. 13:27 it is depicted as 'flowing with milk and honey'; that such an expression, so characteristic of Deuteronomy (cf. Dt. 6:3; 11:9 etc.), should have been consciously avoided in Deuteronomy's retelling of the story seems to him quite inconceivable and favours the view that the J strand of Num. 13f. is the later of the two accounts. But this overlooks the fact that the reference to the land flowing with milk and honey in v. 27*b* is probably a later insertion into the J material (see above), and it can thus hardly be used as an argument against Deuteronomy's dependence on the J material in Num. 13f. Moreover, the fact remains that various facets of the Deuteronomic account can only be fully understood and appreciated if the earlier, J version, is presupposed. Thus, for example, there is no indication in Dt. 1:19ff. as to why Caleb should be exempted from the punishment which befell the rest of his generation (Dt. 1:36), and the motivation for treating Caleb differently can be understood only if Num. 13:30; 14:8f. is presupposed; also, the reference to the potential dangers of entering the land in Dt. 1:28 cannot be understood from the context of Dt. 1:19ff., and it clearly presupposes the report of the spies recorded in Num. 13:27–29, 31 (cf. Boorer, *Promise*, pp. 385f., 388f.). There can be little doubt, therefore, that it is the Deuteronomic account that is dependent upon the J version of the spy story, not vice versa, and, as several commentators have observed, it is probably quite legitimate to use the Deuteronomic narrative to clarify, at some points, the contents and wording of J, and even to reconstruct the original beginning of J's version, which was excised by a redactor in favour of the P variant (cf. Noth, p. 104; *Pentateuchal Traditions*, p. 132, n. 374; Fritz, p. 79).

The narrative contained in Num. 13f. has been subjected by Wagner (*ZAW*, N.F., 35 [1964], pp. 255ff.), to a detailed, form-critical study, and he has suggested, on the basis of a comparison with similar stories contained elsewhere in the *OT* (cf. Dt. 1:19ff.; Jos. 2:1ff.; 7:2–4; 14:7f.; Jg. 18:1ff.) that the 'spy story' constituted a traditional literary genre which comprised six basic elements: (i) the selection and naming of the spies; (ii) their dispatch, with specific instructions; (iii) an account of the execution of their mission; (iv) the return of the spies, and their report; (v) a statement, in the perfect tense, that Yahweh had effectively given the land into the hands of the Israelites; (vi) an account of the invasion of the land. The difficulty with this suggestion, however, is that these six elements do not recur with sufficient consistency in the narratives studied to warrant the conclusion that a specific literary *Gattung* is here represented. In Num. 13f., for example, there is no statement by the spies that Yahweh had given the land into the hands of the people; on the contrary, serious doubts are here entertained regarding the possibility of conquest (cf. 13:28, 31). Moreover, the present narrative does not conclude with a successful invasion of Canaan, but only with a tentative incursion into the south, which ended in Israel's ignominious defeat (14:39ff.). It is true that *some* similarities exist between the narrative recorded in Num. 13f. and other spy stories recounted in the *OT*, but this may well be coincidental and may merely reflect the way in which spy missions would, of necessity, have been executed, and subsequently recorded. Such considerations as these must render Wagner's hypothesis suspect, and the fact that his theory is predicated on comparatively few texts (only four different accounts, one of which is repeated three times), and that he himself concedes that the six elements need not always occur in the same order, must further undermine the validity of his arguments. Cf. McEvenue, *Narrative Style*, p. 96, n. 13; Olson, *Death*, pp. 133ff.

A more productive approach to Num. 13f. has undoubtedly been Noth's traditio-historical analysis of the material contained in these two chapters (pp. 102f.; *Pentateuchal Traditions*, pp. 130ff.). Noth suggests that the spy story owed its origin to the fact that, after the conquest of Canaan, Hebron and its surrounding territory apparently belonged to the Calebites (cf. Jos. 14:6ff.; Jg. 1:20). Noth therefore surmises that in the pre-literary form of the tradition, the narrative of 14:39ff. told of a successful invasion of the land from the south and the consequent settlement of the Hebron area by various tribal groups associated with Caleb. When this tradition was adapted by J, it became necessary to explain why the Calebites, of all people, who were not, after all, of pure Israelite stock (cf. 32:12; Jos. 14:6, 14) should have achieved the prize possession of the district of Hebron, renowned as it was for its fertile land and wealth of vineyards. The answer lay in the fact that Caleb, their ancestor, had, from the outset, shown immense courage and fortitude, and had trusted in God's ability to give the land to his people. In J's retelling of the story, the 'southern' purview of the tradition was retained by limiting the mission of the spies to the Hebron area (13:22–24), but the emphasis now was not so much on the fortitude shown by Caleb but on the pusillanimity and lack of faith demonstrated by the representatives of the other tribes. Their complete lack of trust in Yahweh's guidance inevitably incurred divine judgment, and it was decreed that the present generation of Israelites should remain in the wilderness for forty years and should all (apart from Caleb) be prevented from entering the promised land. This change of emphasis involved the transformation of the narrative of Caleb's conquest of Hebron (14:39ff.) into an account of an abortive attempt to occupy the land from the south. Naturally, the tradition could no longer retain its true character as an 'occupation story', and it had to be subsumed under the theme of 'guidance in the wilderness'. Nevertheless, by thus transforming the story, J was able not only to explain Israel's long sojourn in the wilderness, but also to accommodate the narrative to the already established tradition of a concerted effort by all the Israelite tribes to occupy the land of Canaan from the east. J's narrative was then further developed by P, who extended the mission of the spies to cover the whole country and who thus effectively reiterated J's view that the conquest of the entire land was a phenomenon achieved by an united Israel. On the development of the tradition, see, further, de Vaux, *Fest. May*, pp. 108ff.; Mayes, *Israel*, pp. 100f.; Pace, *Caleb Traditions*, pp. 34ff.

(i) *Reconnaissance of the land:* **13:1–33**
1–3. The LORD said to Moses: In the corresponding narrative in Dt. 1:19–46, it is the people who request Moses to send out spies to reconnoitre the land, and their action is viewed as a token of their lack of faith in Yahweh's leadership; here, on the other hand, the spies are sent out at the express command of Yahweh himself. Sam. seeks to combine the two accounts by appending the substance of Dt. 1:20–23*a* and Dt. 1:27–33, respectively, to the beginning and

the end of the present chapter. **Send men to spy out the land of Canaan**: Vv. 17*b*–20 explain that the object of the expedition was to gather intelligence about the land prior to a military assault. The 'land of Canaan' is P's regular designation for the promised land, but the expression rarely occurs outside the Hexateuch; for the extent of the territory covered by the term, see on 13:21, below. From each of the twelve tribes, the people were to select **a leader** (Heb. *nāśî'*); the task of exploring the land was clearly regarded as so important that only the deployment of men of standing, whose judgment could be relied upon, could be entertained. In response to the divine command, Moses sent out the spies from **the wilderness of Paran** (see on 10:12) to assess the land.

4–15. And these were their names: The formula is characteristic of P, although by no means confined to this source (cf. 2 Sam. 5:14; 23:8; 1 Kg. 4:8). Of the twenty-four names listed in vv. 4–15, eleven do not occur elsewhere in the *OT*; of the remaining thirteen names, some are found in early passages (e.g., Shaphat; cf. 1 Kg. 19:16) while others are confined to late texts (e.g., Zaccur; cf. Neh. 3:2). On the meaning of the names, many of which are very uncertain, see Marsh, pp. 204f. Although the evidence is by no means decisive, it is probable that the list is an artificial construction composed at a relatively late date, and this seems to be confirmed by the occurrence of a Persian name, Vophshi, in v. 14 (cf. Noth, *Personennamen*, pp. 34ff.; *Das System*, pp. 19f.) and by the presence of other names which betray a Persian influence (cf. Beltz, *Die Kaleb-Traditionen*, pp. 15f.). The list of spies in vv. 4–15, and the concluding note in v. 16, may well be a supplementary insertion into the Priestly narrative, since the unit seems reasonably self-contained, and since v. 17*a* takes up the thread of the narrative from v. 3*a* (cf. von Rad, *Priesterschrift*, p. 103; Noth, p. 103). It is noticeable that the names of the leaders, as listed in vv. 4–15, are different from those encountered in 1:5–15; this perhaps suggests the existence of a tradition according to which each tribe had more than one 'leader', from among whom a choice could be made. It is noticeable also that the tribes themselves are named in a different order from that encountered in 1:5–15, for Issachar is separated from Zebulun, and Ephraim from Manasseh; the arrangement found in the present chapter is so unusual that there is much to be said for Gray's contention (p. 136) that the text has here been disrupted and that, originally, vv. 10f. stood before vv. 8f. That no representative is mentioned

from the tribe of Levi is to be explained on the ground that the
mission of the spies had overt military overtones, and it is clear from
1:47ff. that Levi's tribe was exempt from military service; the sum
total of twelve tribes is nevertheless maintained by the division of
the tribe of Joseph into two, Ephraim and Manasseh.

16. And Moses called Hoshea the son of Nun Joshua: The
son of Nun is called Hoshea only in vv. 8 and 16 of the present
chapter and in Dt. 32:44, although in the latter case the name is
probably a textual error for Joshua (cf. LXX, Syr., Vulg.). The necessity for Moses to change Hoshea's name to Joshua (Heb. *yᵉhôšûaʿ*)
was no doubt due to P's view that the divine name 'Yahweh' had
not been revealed to Israel until after Joshua had been born
(Exod. 6:3), and so the latter could not originally have had a name
which contained a 'Yahweh' element.

17–20. Moses commanded the spies to go up **into the Negeb
yonder**: The Heb. word *negeb* is derived from a root (preserved in
Aram.) meaning 'to be dry, parched', and it is used here in its
technical, geographical sense to refer to the vast region which lay
on the southern border of Palestine, between the cultivated land
and the desert proper. After the settlement, however, the term
acquired the general sense of 'south' (just as 'the sea' acquired the
secondary sense of 'west'). *AV* unfortunately understood the word
in its secondary meaning in the present context, and rendered it
'southward', but this is quite misleading, since the spies were to
travel due north. The spies were instructed to ascertain the military
strength of the land (**whether the people who dwell in it are
strong or weak**), the number of its inhabitants (**whether they are
few or many**), its economic resources (**whether the land is rich
or poor**), and its fertility (**whether there is wood in it or not**).
The expedition is reported to have occurred during **the season of
the first ripe grapes**, i.e., towards the end of July or the beginning of
August (LXX's reference to the spring here is clearly misconceived).

21. The spies traversed the whole land of Canaan **from the wilderness of Zin to Rehob**: The wilderness of Zin (not to be confused
with the wilderness of Sin; cf. Exod. 16:1) was regarded as the
southernmost region of Canaan, while Rehob (sometimes called by
the fuller name Beth-rehob; cf. 2 Sam. 10:6) was in the far north,
near Mount Hermon and the city of Laish-Dan (cf. Jg. 18:27–9).
Rehob is further described as being **near the entrance of Hamath**,
a stock phrase used in the *OT* to describe the ideal northern boun-

dary of Israel (cf. 34:8; Jos. 13:5; Jg. 3:3; Am. 6:14). Some commentators (e.g., Budd, Sturdy) prefer to leave the Heb. untranslated, and assume that the reference is to Lebo-hamath (cf. *NEB*), a city situated near the source of the Orontes river in modern Lebanon (cf. Aharoni, *Land*, pp. 65f.). Those who favour reading 'the entrance of Hamath' take the reference to be the well-known pass which lay between Hermon and the Lebanon (cf. Binns, McNeile). But however the name is rendered, there can be no doubt that the phrase 'from the wilderness of Zin to Rehob, near the entrance of Hamath' was intended to describe the full extent of the land of Canaan, and, as such, it corresponds to the expressions 'from the entrance of Hamath (or Lebo-hamath) to the Brook of Egypt' in 1 Kg. 8:65, and 'from the entrance of Hamath (or Lebo-hamath) as far as the Sea of the Arabah' in 2 Kg. 14:25, which describe, respectively, the extreme limits of the land during the reigns of Solomon and Jeroboam II. A more familiar (and more realistic!) formula to describe the limits of the territory occupied by the Israelites was, of course, 'from Dan to Beersheba' (cf. 2 Sam. 3:10; 17:11; 1 Kg. 4:25 etc.).

22–24. These verses form a sequel to vv. 17*b*–20. According to J's version of the story, the expedition of the spies was limited to the Negeb, and they travelled northwards only as far as **Hebron**: Hebron (modern el-Khalil) was an ancient city, situated approx. 20 miles (32 km.) south of Jerusalem. It was here, according to tradition, that all three patriarchs were buried, and the city became David's capital during the early years of his reign. According to Jos. 14:15; Jg. 1:10, its original name was Kiriath-arba = 'four towns', or 'town of four (clans?)'. The names **Ahiman, Sheshai, and Talmai**, which recur in Jos. 15:14; Jg. 1:10, probably referred to individuals or clans which were thought to have once inhabited the Hebron area. The three are here described as being **the descendants of Anak** (cf. v. 28; 'sons of Anak' in v. 33). These are mentioned several times in the *OT*, though all the references are confined to four books, namely, Numbers, Deuteronomy, Joshua, and Judges (cf. Dt. 1:28; 2:10f., 21; 9:2; Jos. 11:21f.; 14:12, 15; 15:14; 21:11; Jg. 1:20). Noth (p. 105) connects the expression with the Hebrew word *ʿanāq* 'necklace, pendant' (cf. Jg. 8:26; Prov. 1:9), but since it is by no means obvious what the expression 'necklace descendants' or 'necklace people' was meant to signify, this suggestion has little to commend it. Another possibility is that the term *yālîḏ* in this context does not mean 'descendant' but, rather, 'dependent' or 'serf', and it is suggested that the term came to be applied to professional soldiers on account of the fact that they had given up their freedom to enter a military corps, such as the corps of Anak (Heb. *yᵉlîdê hāᶜᵃnāq*; cf. Jos. 15:14) or of Raphah (Heb. *yᵉlîdê hārāpāh*; cf. 2 Sam. 21:16, 18; de Vaux, *AI*, p. 219; L'Heureux, *BASOR* 221 [1976], pp. 83ff.). The difficulty with this suggestion, however, is that the *yᵉlîdê* are designated in v. 33 as 'the sons (*bᵉnê*) of Anak' (cf. Dt. 1:28; Jg. 1:20), which implies that *yᵉlîdê* in the present context does, indeed, mean 'descendants'. Maclaurin (*VT* 15 [1965], pp. 468ff.), noting that the term 'Anak' has no satisfactory Semitic etymology, has suggested that the term was originally a Philistine title of rank, and that it referred to hereditary rulers whose authority was largely based on succession and family position. This hypothesis, however, must remain conjectural, and, on balance, it seems preferable to connect 'Anak' with the Arab. word for 'neck', and to regard the phrase 'sons of neck' as an idiomatic expression for tall, long-necked, lanky people (cf. *BDB*, p. 778*b*). This would explain how the tradition originated that the Anakim were a race of giants (v. 33; cf. Dt. 2:21; 9:2). In the *OT* they are frequently associated with the neighbourhood of Hebron (cf. Jg. 1:20; Jos. 11:31; 14:12ff.; 15:13f.), which perhaps suggests that they were especially connected with this area; however, in one passage (Jos. 11:21f.), they are represented as being scattered all over the hill-country of Palestine, and remnants of them apparently still survived in the towns of the Philistines for a period after Joshua's time. A parenthetic note appended to v. 22 informs the reader that **Hebron was built seven years before Zoan in Egypt**: Zoan (mentioned also in Ps. 78:12, 43; Isa. 19:11, 13; Ezek. 30:14) was the Tanis of classical times, and it is commonly identified with the ancient Hyksos capital of Avaris in Egypt. A famous stele, discovered at Tanis, appears to establish the inauguration of the cult of Seth at Tanis and the settlement of the Hyksos there at approx. 1720 BC (*ANET*, pp. 252f.; cf. Gardiner, *Egypt*, p. 165). On this basis, Albright (*Stone Age*, p. 184) has interpreted the reference in the present verse to mean that Hebron was built seven years before the Hyksos established Avaris as their capital in 1720 BC. Other scholars have understood the chronological note to mean that Hebron was built seven years before the rebuilding of Avaris-Tanis by Israelite forced labour under Rameses II (cf. Rowley, *From Joseph*, p. 76). Both interpretations, however, must be regarded as highly questionable, for many scholars are now of the view that Tanis and Avaris represent two different sites, the former being identified with Şân el-Ḥagar in the north-east of the Delta, while the latter is located on the Pelusiac arm of the Nile, in the vicinity of Qantîr (cf. Na'aman, *VT* 31 [1981], pp. 488ff.; van Seters, *The Hyksos*, pp. 127ff.; Uphill, *JNES* 27 [1968], pp. 291ff.; 28 [1969], pp. 15ff.). That the reference in this verse reflects an ancient, authentic tradition concerning the establishment by the Hyksos of an Egyptian fortress in Hebron in the fourteenth century BC, as suggested by Mowinckel (*Donum Natalicium*, pp. 185ff.; cf. Clements, *Abraham and David*, pp. 40f.) cannot be proved on the basis of the evidence available, and it seems far more probable that the present note merely reflects a local tradition of Hebron which attributed to this city, David's first capital, the glory and honour of being older than Tanis, the erstwhile capital of Egypt (cf. Noth, p. 105; de Vaux, *History*, i, pp. 258f.; Pace, *Caleb Traditions*, pp. 203ff.). Having travelled as far as Hebron, the spies then came to the **Valley of Eshcol**, where they cut down **a branch with a single cluster of grapes**, and carried it back with them **on a pole** (Heb. *môṭ*; see on 4:10) as visible proof of the fertility of the land. The scene is depicted on a fragmentary marble relief from Carthage, probably dating from the fourth or fifth century AD (cf. Ovadiah, *IEJ* 24 [1974], pp. 210ff.). The Valley of Eshcol has not been identified with certainty, although many commentators believe that it is to be equated with the modern Beit Ishkahil, which was approx. 4 miles (6 km.) north-west of Hebron. This identification must, however, be regarded as highly conjectural, for in the other *OT* passages where the Valley of Eshcol is mentioned (32:9; Dt. 1:24), there is no connection with Hebron, and even the supposed connection between the two in the present passage may be editorial (cf. Gray, p. 142). The name 'Eshcol' means 'cluster', and the story recorded in vv. 23f. may originally have been aetiological, suggesting that it was the cluster of grapes found by the spies which gave the valley its name.

26. The spies returned to Moses, Aaron, and the congregation who had remained **in the wilderness of Paran, at Kadesh**: The reference to Kadesh here may well be a gloss, since this place is elsewhere located by P not in the wilderness of Paran but in the wilderness of Zin (20:1; 27:14; cf. Fritz, Noth). Kadesh, also known as Kadesh-barnea (32:8; 34:4) and Meribah of Kadesh (27:14; Dt. 32:51), is usually identified with the modern 'Ain Qadeis, on the southern border of the Negeb and some 50 miles (80 km.) south of Beersheba (so, e.g., Snaith), although some prefer to locate it at nearby 'Ain Qudeirat (cf. Meyers, *BA* 39 [1976], p. 149; Aharoni, *Land*, p. 65; see, further, Cohen, *BA* 44 [1981], pp. 93ff.). According to the J source, Kadesh was an important rallying-point for the Hebrew tribes during the period between the exodus from Egypt and the conquest of Palestine.

27. The report which the spies bring back begins in a positive vein, by drawing attention to the fertility of the land which they had explored: **it flows with milk and honey**. This is a common description of the land of Canaan, and is found especially in Deuteronomy (cf. Dt. 6:3; 11:9). Although the land referred to was not, in fact, particularly fertile, it must certainly have appeared so to the Israelites who had been accustomed to the barren, arid regions of the desert. It may seem strange that 'milk and honey' (rather than, e.g., 'corn and wine') should be regarded as the marks of a fertile country, but the phrase is probably traditional, since a similar expression recurs in Egyptian (*ANET*, pp. 18–25, lines 80–90) and in Ugaritic (*ANET*, p. 140) texts, and thus probably reflects a common literary motif in the ancient world.

29. The description contained in this verse of the nations who inhabited the Negeb, the hill-country of Palestine, and the Jordan valley, hardly seems appropriate in the context of the spies' report, and it is therefore widely regarded as a parenthetical statement inserted by a redactor (cf. Gray, Noth). For the view that such stereotyped lists are largely rhetorical and ideological, reflecting an archaizing tendency on the part of narrators to give their stories the appearance of antiquity, see van Seters, *VT* 22 (1972), pp. 64ff. The **Amalekites** were an aggressive nomadic tribe who occupied a region to the south of the Negeb. They are regarded in the *OT* as the traditional enemies of the Israelites (cf. Exod. 17:8ff.). Both Saul and David fought against them with some success (1 Sam. 15:1ff.; 30:1ff.), but a remnant survived which was only finally destroyed by 500 Simeonites during the reign of Hezekiah (1 Chr. 4:42f.). The **Hittites** were a powerful non-Semitic people who, in the latter part of the second millennium BC, established an extensive empire, based in southern Asia Minor. Their power declined from around 1200 BC, but reminiscences of their former glory are reflected in some *OT* passages (cf. Jos. 1:4; Ezek. 16:3). The Hittites whom the Israelites encountered in Canaan were probably the remnants of this once powerful nation. The **Jebusites** were the original inhabitants of Jerusalem before its capture by David, who made the city his capital (2 Sam. 5:6ff.). The **Amorites** were a West Semitic people who once inhabited large areas of Mesopotamia, where they furnished several important dynasties in the early part of the second millennium BC. King Hammurabi was an Amorite, and many of the early law codes were Amorite. In the *OT*, the term frequently refers to the pre-Israelite population of Palestine, and this usage can be traced back to Assyrian texts, dating from the time of Tiglath-Pileser I (1115–1070 BC) onwards, in which all the people of the west were regarded as belonging to the country of Amurru (cf. Dhorme, *RB* 40 [1931], pp. 172ff., and on the term 'Amurru', see van Seters, *Abraham*, pp. 43ff.). The Amorites are often associated with the **hill country** (cf. Dt. 1:7, 19f., 44; Jos. 10:5ff.; 11:3); only in Jg. 1:34f. are they depicted as being situated on the plain. The **Canaanites** sometimes appear in the *OT* as virtually synonymous with the Amorites (cf. Gen. 15:16), although they are here clearly distinguished from them, for they are said to have inhabited the coastal plain and the Jordan valley (cf. Dt. 1:7; 11:30).

30–31. Caleb's attempt to placate the people has appeared to some commentators as premature here, for it is not until 14:1 that the Israelites are represented as being unduly perturbed (cf. Gray, p. 150). However, there is no need to assume that 14:1 originally followed v. 29 (as suggested, e.g., by Coats, *Rebellion*, p. 145), for the narrative probably assumes that the reservations uttered by the spies in v. 28 had been overheard by the people, and that this was the cause of their agitation and alarm (cf. Noth). It is not clear whether Caleb's words in this verse were directed to the people in general or, as LXX and Sam. assume, to Moses alone, but in either case his confidence in the ability of the Israelites to conquer the land (**we are well able to overcome it**) is immediately rebuffed by the other spies, who were clearly disconcerted by the fact that its inhabitants were stronger than they and would probably prove to be invincible.

32. The spies bring before the people an **evil** (i.e., an unfavourable, but not necessarily false) **report** of the land, claiming that it **devours its inhabitants**. This is usually taken to mean that the land was barren and inhospitable, unable to support the people or to provide sufficient nourishment for their needs (so, e.g., Gray, McNeile). However, this interpretation must be regarded as questionable, for it ill accords with the following description of the inhabitants as **men of great stature**. Seale (*ExpT* 68 [1956–7], p. 28) seeks to resolve the problem by suggesting, on the basis of Arab. etymology, that 'devours' (Heb. *'ākal*) in this context means 'to conquer'; thus, the meaning of the present verse is that Canaan was a 'conquering land'. However, one of the difficulties of this proposal is the fact that the word 'inhabitants' has to be omitted as a late gloss. Binns (p. 88) suggests that 'devour' here is to be interpreted quite literally, and that the expression was intended to represent the inhabitants of Canaan as cannibals, but this seems entirely fanciful. A more plausible theory is that advanced by Coats (*Rebellion*, pp. 140ff.), who points to a similar expression in Ezek. 36:13, where the same verb, *'ākal*, has connotations of 'destruction', the reference being to the loss of inhabitants that had resulted from previous battles and skirmishes; the point of the spies' report, then, was that the land of Canaan was one which was geared for battle. A similar interpretation is suggested by Noth, who takes the expression to mean that the land was 'full of warlike dissensions' (p. 107).

33. And there we saw the Nephilim: *RSV* takes Nephilim to be a proper name; *AV* (cf. *JB*) translates it as 'giants' (cf. LXX, Vulg.). The Nephilim are referred to elsewhere in the *OT* only in Gen. 6:4, where the word refers to a race of quasi-divine beings, the offspring of an illicit union between the sons of the gods and the daughters of men. The derivation and meaning of the name are uncertain, but the word may be connected with the root *nāpal* = to fall, in which case the Nephilim would be 'the fallen ones', possibly a reference to the fallen gods who had been ejected from the celestial realm (cf. Levine). The words bracketed in *RSV*, which identify the Nephilim with **the sons of Anak**, are absent from LXX and are generally regarded as a scribal gloss, inserted on the basis of vv. 22, 28 (cf. Holzinger, Baentsch, Gray, Paterson). The spies claim that, in comparison with the inhabitants of the land, they had seemed to themselves **like grasshoppers**, i.e., small, weak and helpless (cf. Isa. 40:22), **and so we seemed to them**: Some commentators (e.g., Snaith, *NPC*, p. 260; cf. Maarsingh, p. 47) suggest reading *kēn* ('so') in the sense of 'gnats' here (cf. Isa. 51:6), i.e., in their own eyes the spies appeared no bigger than grasshoppers, but to the Nephilim they had seemed smaller still – no larger than gnats!

(ii) *The rebellion of the people:* **14:1-10**

These verses describe in detail the negative reaction of the people to the report of the spies, and the attempt by Joshua and Caleb to instil confidence in them to go forth and conquer the promised land.

2-3. Discouraged by the report of the spies, the people begin to complain against Moses and Aaron, expressing the thought that they would rather have died in Egypt or in the wilderness than face the prospect of perishing by the sword in an attempt to conquer Canaan. At the very least, they would prefer to return to their captivity, if only to protect their wives and children from the atrocities of war.

4. At the very moment of the fulfilment of the divine promise, when the people were on the verge of entering the promised land, they resolve to appoint a new **captain** (Heb. *rō'š*; on the term, see Bartlett, *VT* 19 [1969], pp. 1ff.) who would lead them back to Egypt.

5-7. Moses and Aaron, recognizing the affront to Yahweh that the people's rebellion entailed, **fell on their faces** in front of the congregation, as an act of contrition before God. Further, as a sign of sorrow at the behaviour of the people, Joshua and Caleb **rent their clothes**, the customary expression of grief in the ancient Near East (cf. Gen. 37:29, 34). In contrast to the 'evil report' of the land brought by the other spies (13:32), they give a favourable assessment, claiming that the land was **exceedingly good**.

8-9. There was no need to fear the inhabitants of Canaan, **for they are bread for us**, i.e., they could be annihilated just as easily as bread could be devoured (cf. 24:8; Ps. 14:4; Jer. 10:25). The difference between Israel and her adversaries was that Yahweh was present with his people, whereas the **protection** (lit., 'shadow') of the Canaanites would be **removed from them**, rendering them vulnerable and susceptible to defeat. 'Shadow' (Heb. *ṣēl*) is a common metaphor in the *OT* for 'protection'; the figure was drawn from the need to shelter under branches (Jg. 9:15) or under a rock (Isa. 32:2) from the excessive heat of the tropical sun; here, the reference is to the fact that the Canaanites would be denied the support usually afforded them by their gods.

10. The encouraging words of Joshua and Caleb merely served to aggravate the opposition against them, for the congregation decided **to stone them with stones**: This was not, as Wenham (p. 122) suggests, a case of the congregation exercising their judicial authority by seeking to exact the appropriate punishment for what they deemed was a false accusation of rebellion (cf. v. 9); rather, it must be viewed as a case of open mutiny, such as that described in 1 Sam. 30:6; 1 Kg. 12:18. The action of the people, however, was stayed by the appearance of **the glory of the LORD** (on which, see Budd, pp. 156f.) at the **tent of meeting**. According to P, Yahweh's glory manifested itself in a visible form and had the appearance of a devouring fire; it first appeared on Mount Sinai (Exod. 24:16f.), but was subsequently associated with the tent of meeting (cf. 9:15; Exod. 40:34).

(iii) *Moses' intercession and Yahweh's judgment:* **14:11–25**

Yahweh announces to Moses his intention to destroy the faithless Israelites and to create, from Moses' descendants, a greater and mightier nation (vv. 11f.); Moses, however, seeks to deter Yahweh from carrying out his intended judgment by appealing, firstly, to Yahweh's own reputation among the nations (vv. 13–16) and, secondly, to his character as a merciful and gracious God (vv. 17–19). As a result of Moses' importunate intercession, Yahweh relents and forgives the people (v. 20), but at the same time he avows that they will not go unpunished, for the rebels would die in the wilderness and none, save Caleb, would enter the promised land. For the tension here between Yahweh's readiness to forgive the people and his intention to punish them for their disobedience, see Sakenfeld, *CBQ* 37 (1975), pp. 317ff.

The precise delimitation of this passage is disputed, for it is variously regarded as consisting of vv. 11–24 (Gray), 12–20 (Holzinger), 11–21 (Rudolph), 11*b*–23*a* (Noth, Coats, Budd), 12–21 (Fritz); on the whole, it seems preferable to regard the unit as comprising vv. 11*b*–23*a*, for the reasons succinctly outlined by Boorer, *Promise*, pp. 334ff. It is generally agreed that the passage is permeated by Deuteronomistic ideas and phrases (for details, see Budd, pp. 152f.), and, in particular, there are clear points of contact with Dt. 1:34–40. It is uncertain, however, whether Num. 14:11–25 provided the prototype for the Deuteronomic version (so, e.g., Lohfink, *Bib* 41 [1960], p. 118, n. 1), or whether it represents a later amplification of the Deuteronomic passage (so, e.g., Aurelius, *Fürbitter*, p. 133). For a detailed 'rhetorical' analysis of the passage, see Newing, *Perspectives*, pp. 211ff.

11–12. Yahweh's response to the rebelliousness of the people takes the form of an indignant question: **How long will this people**

despise me? The use of the verb 'despise' (Heb. *nā'aṣ*) indicates the gravity of the situation, for at the very least it suggests that the people had 'spurned' Yahweh (*BDB*, pp. 610f.) and may even imply that they had rejected him completely (cf. Coats, *Rebellion*, p. 146; Sakenfeld, *op. cit.*, pp. 321f.). **And how long will they not believe in me:** The reference here is not to an intellectual assent to the existence of God, but to an expression of trust and confidence that Yahweh was, indeed, able to fulfil his promises. **in spite of all the signs which I have wrought among them:** The Heb. *'ōt*, 'sign', in the *OT* is often used of God's power, which could be exercised for good or ill; here it refers to Yahweh's miraculous interventions in Israel's history. The implication is that the wonders of the exodus and the wilderness journey should have led to an unconditional trust in Yahweh. **I will strike them with the pestilence**, i.e., with a disease that would prove fatal (cf. LXX, 'death') **and disinherit them:** Perhaps the exact meaning of the Heb. verb *yāraš* (in the Hiphil) should not be pressed, and that its connotation here (as in Exod. 15:9) is rather 'to annihilate, destroy' (cf. *NIV*; *BDB*, p. 440*a*). **and I will make of you** (LXX and Sam. add, 'and your father's house'; cf. *NEB*, 'and your descendants') **a nation greater and mightier than they**: The threat to make of Moses a new nation which would take Israel's place is found elsewhere only in the Deuteronomistic material (cf. Exod. 32:9ff.; Dt. 9:14), and the reference here may perhaps reflect a later tendency to magnify the role and office of Moses (Dt. 34:10ff.; cf. Coats, *Rebellion*, p. 147). Be that as it may, implicit in this verse is a threat to annul the promise made of old to Abraham (Gen. 12:2; 18:18), and there is a momentary glimpse of the outline of an entirely new plan of salvation.

13–19. The text of vv. 13f. is clearly corrupt, and the Vsns furnish little help to restore the original reading. Since vv. 15–17 contain the real point of Moses' appeal, some commentators (e.g., Gray) regard vv. 13f. as having been composed of a concretion of later additions; this is certainly possible, and would account for the awkwardness and unintelligibility of the text as it stands. Moses begins his intercession by appealing to Yahweh's honour and standing among the surrounding nations: if Yahweh were to carry out his threat to destroy Israel, the nations would inevitably regard it as a sign of his impotence and his inability to fulfil his promise to bring the people into the land of Canaan. Moses then appeals to Yahweh's gracious and forgiving nature, and does so in words taken from

Exod. 34:6f. (albeit in a slightly abbreviated form), a passage which is cited several times in the *OT* (cf. Neh. 9:17; Ps. 86:15; 103:8; 145:8; Jer. 32:18; Jl 2:13).

18. The LORD is slow to anger: The theme of Yahweh's forbearance is prominent in the *OT*, and is presented as an important element in his dealings with his people (cf. Neh. 9:19; Ps. 78:38f.). **and abounding in steadfast love:** The Heb. term *ḥeseḏ* is usually rendered 'mercy, loving kindness', but there is also implicit in the word an element of consistency and steadfastness; the term was therefore very apt to describe Yahweh's unchanging love for erring Israel. On the term in general, see Zobel, *TDOT*, v, pp. 44ff., and on its significance in the present context in particular, see Sakenfeld, *op. cit.*, pp. 323–26. **forgiving iniquity**: The word translated 'forgive' is from the root *nsˀ* = carry away, and the term rendered 'iniquity' *ʿāwōn*, can refer to the consequences of an offence; thus Budd (p. 158) is possibly correct in stating that the meaning of the expression here is 'the taking away of the punishment sin deserves'. **and transgression**: Exod. 34:6 adds 'and sin', and so LXX and Sam. here. The word translated by *RSV* as 'transgression', *pešaʿ*, would perhaps be better rendered 'rebellion' (cf. *NEB*; *NIV*; so, e.g., Snaith), since the word here denotes opposition to Yahweh rather than the infringement of specific rules. **but he will by no means clear the guilty**: i.e., the divine power can manifest itself in an ability to punish as well as to pardon. **visiting the iniquity of fathers upon children**: This was not intended as an assertion of divine vindictiveness, but was merely a recognition of the fact that in Hebrew thought the strength of family ties were such that both blessing and misfortune could be transferred from one generation to another. The reference to the **third** and **fourth generation** was intended to embrace all living members of a family; this was the maximum possible range of members that could be alive at any given time, and a fifth generation was evidently not contemplated (cf. Phillips, *Law*, p. 33).

21–24. truly, as I live: This is the usual form of an oath sworn by Yahweh (cf. Isa. 49:18; Jer. 22:24), although it occurs only here and in v. 28 in the Pentateuch; the corresponding oath sworn by humans was 'as the LORD lives' (cf. Jg. 8:19; 1 Sam. 14:39). The divine oath was intended to underline the certainty of the punishment which was to be meted out to the people, who had shown their utter contempt of Yahweh by putting him **to the proof these ten**

times: This rendering is preferable to *AV*'s 'tempted me', for the Heb. *nissāh* (like the Gk *peiradzô*) was a neutral term (as, indeed, was the English word 'tempt' originally; cf. Lat. *tentare*), meaning 'to put to the test', with either good or evil intent. The Talmud (*'Arakhin* 15a,b) understood the expression 'ten times' quite literally, and compiled a list of ten instances when Israel had put Yahweh to the test; however, it is more probable that the phrase was an idiomatic way of expressing the idea of 'often' or 'repeatedly' (cf. Gen. 31:7; Job 19:3). None of the generation who rebelled against Yahweh would be permitted to see **the land which I swore to give to their fathers:** LXX here has a lengthy insertion, based on Dt. 1:39, and anticipating v. 31. Caleb, however, would be exempted from this punishment, for he had shown complete confidence in Yahweh, and had clearly been motivated by a different spirit from that which had inspired the others. Consequently, he would be allowed to enter **the land**, and was promised that **his descendants shall possess it**. For the fulfilment of this promise, see Jos. 14:6ff.; Jg. 1:20.

25. Now, since the Amalekites and the Canaanites dwell in the valleys: These words are widely regarded as a gloss, partly because they are incompatible with the statements in 13:29; 14:45a, partly because they are omitted in Dt. 1:40 (which otherwise produces the substance of this verse), and partly because the words seem singularly inappropriate within the context of a divine speech (cf. Noth, pp. 109f.). As Paterson (p. 50) has observed, the gloss was probably inserted in order to explain why the Israelites were instructed to retrace their steps through the wilderness, making a lengthy detour to the south **by the way to the Red Sea:** The 'Red Sea' is the traditional translation of *yam-sŭp*, and is due to the rendering of LXX; the Heb., most probably, means 'sea of reeds'. The reference here (as in 21:4 and Dt. 1:40) is almost certainly to the Gulf of Akaba (cf. Davies, *Way*, p. 42), though the same term sometimes appears to refer to the Gulf of Suez (cf. 33:10f.; Exod. 10:19). For J, the 'Red Sea' was the place where the wilderness wanderings began (cf. Exod. 15:22), and so the point here is that the Israelites were being compelled to go back to the very beginning of their desert sojourn (cf. Fritz, p. 85).

(iv) *The punishment of the people:* **14:26–38**
The renewed introduction to Yahweh's words in v. 26 indicates that P now takes up the narrative, which continues until v. 38. Yahweh

avows that, as a punishment for their rebellion, all the people above twenty years old (except Caleb and Joshua) would be condemned to wander in the wilderness for forty years, and would die there because of their lack of faith. The spies who brought an evil report of the land, and who were thus ultimately responsible for the people's apostasy, would perish (presumably at once) by a plague (vv. 36f.). The passage is not without its bitter irony: those who had expressed a wish to die in the wilderness (v. 2) will indeed be granted their request (vv. 28ff.)! Conversely, the children, who had been expected to perish in Canaan (v. 3), will be given possession of the promised land (v. 31)!

The unity of this passage has been questioned by many analysts. In particular, vv. 30–34 are widely regarded, in whole or in part, as secondary, and designed to make explicit the exemption of Joshua, Caleb and the children of the rebellious Israelites from the punishment which was to be inflicted upon the people in general (cf. Baentsch, pp. 530f.; Holzinger, pp. 58f.; Rudolph, p. 79; Noth, pp. 110f.; Fritz, p. 21; Simpson, *Traditions*, p. 230). However, the arguments for regarding vv. 30–34 in their entirety as secondary are not altogether convincing (cf. Budd, p. 153), and the view taken here is that only v. 34, which offers a somewhat artificial explanation of the duration of Israel's punishment, need be regarded as a gloss (cf. McEvenue, *Bib* 50 [1969], p. 457; Coats, *Rebellion*, p. 139).

27. How long shall this wicked congregation murmur against me? MT, which reads, lit., 'how long for the complaints . . . ?' is obscure, and some commentators assume an ellipsis of a verb (possibly, *sālaḥ*; cf. v. 19) here: 'How long shall I forgive this evil generation?' It is simpler, however, to assume, with *BHS*, that the preposition *lamed* with first person singular suffix has been accidentally omitted (cf. Jer. 2:18), in which case the verse could be idiomatically rendered, with *NEB*, 'How long must I tolerate the complaints of this wicked community?'

28. As I live, says the LORD: For the divine oath, see on v. 21. The expression 'says the LORD' (Heb. *nᵉʾum yhwh*) is the one frequently used by the prophets to introduce a message from Yahweh; the phrase is rare outside the prophetic books, and occurs in the Pentateuch only here and in Gen. 22:16.

29–30. None of the rebellious Israelites **numbered from twenty years old and upward**, i.e., those registered in the census recorded in ch. 1, would be permitted to enter the land which **I swore** (lit.,

'lifted up my hand', the conventional gesture for an oath; cf. Gen.
14:22; Exod. 6:8) **that I would make you dwell**, the only exceptions
being **Caleb the son of Jephunneh and Joshua the son of Nun**.
It is probable that P tacitly assumed that the Levites, who were
not included in the census (cf. 1:47ff.) were exempted from this
punishment; certainly Eleazar, the priest, who was presumably over
twenty years old at this time (cf. 3:3f., 32; 4:16), was permitted to
enter Canaan (cf. Jos. 14:1; 17:4; 24:33). This verse provides one of
the links between the spy story of chs. 13f. and the census lists of
chs. 1 and 26, which Olson (*Death*, pp. 138ff.) regards as significant
for the framework of the book of Numbers as a whole. See, further,
above, pp. liif.

31. The very ones whom the people had thought would become
a prey (*NEB*, 'spoils of war') would be permitted to **know** (LXX,
'possess', presumably reading *wᵉyārᵉšû* for *wᵉyāḏᵉʿû*; cf. Dt. 1:39) **the
land which you have despised**.

**33. And your children shall be shepherds in the wilderness
forty years**: *RSV*'s 'shepherds' correctly represents the meaning of
MT, but Jewish exegetes, under the influence of 32:13, interpreted
the Heb. *rōʿîm* here to mean 'wanderers' (Targ. Ps. Jon.; cf. Vulg.),
and this reading is preferred by *NEB*. But 'shepherds' is perfectly
acceptable in the present context, the implication being that the
next generation, instead of settling down to a sedentary agricultural
life in Canaan, would be condemned to roam around with their
flocks in the wilderness for forty years. This was the punishment
that the children had to endure **for your faithlessness**: The Heb.
zᵉnûṯêkem means, lit., 'whoredoms' (cf. *AV*; *NEB*, 'wanton dis-
loyalty'), a metaphor frequently applied to Israel by the prophets,
who accused the nation of being unfaithful to Yahweh by worship-
ping foreign deities (cf. Hos. 2:7; 9:1) or by courting foreign alliances
(cf. Ezek. 16:26; 23:1ff.).

34. The people would have to bear their iniquity for forty years,
a year for each day (Heb. *yôm yôm laššānāh*; cf. *G–K* § 123*d*) the
spies had spent exploring the land. Maarsingh (p. 51) comments on
the curious connection between 'the forty days of preparation for an
entry that did not take place and forty years of awesome preparation
for an entry that would take place' – albeit for a new generation.
During this prolonged period, the people **shall know my displeasure**: The root *nûʾ* means 'to hinder, restrain, frustrate' (*BDB*,
p. 626*a*); consequently, 'you shall know my frustration' would be a

better translation than *RSV*'s rather anodyne rendering. The precise
meaning of the text is uncertain, for the first person possessive suffix
in the word *t^enū'ātî* can be construed subjectively or objectively; in
the former case, the reference would be to the frustration of
Yahweh's purpose *vis à vis* Israel, whereas in the latter case it would
be to his *being* frustrated *by* Israel. Either understanding produces
theological difficulties, as was realized by ancient translators and
mediaeval exegetes alike. On the one hand, the notion of a frustrator-
God is problematic, for it appears to impute to Yahweh a measure
of sheer obstructionism; on the other hand, the notion of Yahweh's
being frustrated or 'thwarted' (cf. *NEB* mg.) in his purpose is equally
difficult from the theological point of view, since it appears to
impugn the divine omnipotence. For a thorough discussion of past
attempts to circumvent this theological conundrum, or to meet its
challenge, see Loewe, *Fest. Thomas*, pp. 137ff.; *JJS* 21 (1970), pp. 65ff.

(v) *The defeat at Hormah:* **14:39–45**
Having heard the divine sentence imposed upon them by Yahweh
(vv. 20–25), the people express their remorse, and resolve to win
Yahweh's favour by marching up to the Negeb and attempting to
enter Canaan from the south. In doing so, however, they disregard
Moses' warning that Yahweh would not help them and, as a result,
they suffer a crushing defeat at the hands of the Amalekites and the
Canaanites. The story of this abortive attack is repeated, with minor
differences, in Dt. 1:41–45, and there may be a reminiscence of the
event in Exod. 17:8–16.

44. The people determine to go up into the hill country, but
**neither the ark of the covenant of the LORD, nor Moses,
departed out of the camp**: The qualifying phrase 'of the covenant'
is probably a gloss inserted under Deuteronomistic influence, since
there is no evidence in the J source that the tablets of the covenant
laws had been placed inside the ark. An important function of the
ark in Israel's early traditions was to lead the people into battle and
to ensure the success of the campaign (cf. 1 Sam. 4:1ff.); thus the
fact that the ark in this instance remained in the camp was an
ominous portent that the enterprise was doomed to failure.

45. The Israelites are attacked by the **Amalekites and the
Canaanites** (Dt. 1:44 represents the opposition as being the Amorites) who **pursued them** (or, perhaps, with *NIV*, 'beat them down';
for this meaning of the verb *kātat*, see *BDB*, p. 510) **even to**

Hormah: The location of Hormah is uncertain, but it may tentatively be identified with the modern Tell el-Meshash, some 10 miles (16 km.) east of Beersheba (cf. Noth, pp. 111, 154; Aharoni, *Land*, pp. 184f.; *BA* 31 [1968], p. 31). Other suggestions include Tell esh-Sheri'ah, about 12 miles (19 km.) northwest of Beersheba (Albright, *BASOR* 15 [1924], pp. 6f.) and Tell el-Milḥ, about 8 miles (13 km.) southwest of Tell Arad (Mazar, *JNES* 24 [1965], pp. 298f.).

(b) MISCELLANEOUS LAWS
15:1–41

This chapter contains a miscellaneous collection of laws relating to five different subjects: (i) the cereal offerings and drink offerings which were to accompany the sacrifices (vv. 1–16); (ii) the first coarse meal offering (vv. 17–21); (iii) offerings for inadvertent transgressions (vv. 22–31); (iv) breaking the Sabbath (vv. 32–36); (v) the tassels to be worn on garments (vv. 37–41). The first four are generally regarded as deriving from the Priestly tradition, while the fifth contains certain affinities with the Holiness Code (Lev. 17–26).

It is not at all clear why these laws should have been included at this particular point in Numbers, for there is no obvious connection either with the story of the spies in chs. 13f. or with the narrative concerning Korah's rebellion in chs. 16f. Nevertheless, it has been suggested by some commentators that the laws contained here may be regarded as a pertinent comment upon the incidents narrated in the previous chapters: despite the manifest unbelief of the people and their presumptuous attempt to take the land, the covenant promises had not been completely annulled, and if only the Israelites were prepared to indicate their repentance by offering the appropriate sacrifices, they would, indeed, be brought into the land of Canaan (cf. 15:1f., 18) and would experience once again the blessings of God. Viewed in this way, the present chapter, far from being an irrelevant insertion, is regarded as a bold reaffirmation of God's commitment to his people, and as 'a startling assertion of a practical and pragmatic faith' (Budd, p. 167; cf. Wenham, pp. 41f., 126f.). The difficulty with this explanation, however, is that it can, at best, explain only why certain sections within ch. 15 were incorporated in their present context; the fact is that some of the laws contained in this chapter contain no reference at all to Israel's life in the

promised land (cf. vv. 37–41), and vv. 32–36 clearly presuppose
the period of the wilderness wandering rather than that of the settlement in Canaan. The difficulty occasioned by the lack of connection
between the present chapter and its overall context is compounded
by the fact that the individual parts of this collection have no obvious
connection with each other, although a tenuous link may exist
between the laws contained in vv. 32–36, 37–41 and those which
immediately precede them (see below). But why an editor should
have grouped together the laws contained in vv. 1–16, 17–21, 22–
31, and why he should have included the legislation contained in
the present chapter at this particular point in Numbers, must remain
as much a mystery here as in the case of the similar collection of
laws contained in chs. 5f.

(i) *Offerings to accompany the sacrifices:* **15:1–16**
This passage stipulates the requisite amount of flour, oil and wine
that was to accompany the various animal sacrifices offered to
Yahweh. The quantity was determined in each case in accordance
with the type of animal that was sacrificed: the more valuable the
animal, the more costly were the cereal and drink offerings that were
to accompany it. These regulations may well have been regarded as
generally applicable when sacrifices were offered; however, three
specific cases are here singled out (v. 3), namely, the sacrifice offered
(i) at the fulfilment of a special vow; (ii) at the presentation of a
freewill offering, and (iii) at the appointed feasts.

Several commentators have drawn attention to the similarity
between the present passage and Lev. 2, which also contains regulations concerning the cereal offering, but which fails to prescribe
the amounts of oil and flour required. Kuenen (*Hexateuch*, p. 96; cf.
Holzinger, p. 61) described the present chapter as a 'novella' to
Lev. 2, which was intended to regulate by law what was once left to
the discretion of the individual worshipper. However, the connection
between the present passage and Lev. 2 is more tenuous than is
often supposed, for there is no mention here of the accompanying
frankincense (cf. Lev. 2:2) or salt (cf. Lev. 2:13), and, in any case,
the present section is concerned with the cereal offering as a supplement to the animal offerings, whereas Lev. 2 is concerned with
the cereal offering as an offering in its own right.

A closer parallel with the present passage can, perhaps, be discerned in Ezek. 46:5ff., which similarly stipulates the quantity of

cereal offering required in connection with the sacrifice (see Gray, p. 170, for a tabulated comparison). Here too, however, there are clear differences between the two passages which cannot be ignored. The amounts specified in Ezekiel are larger than those demanded in the present passage, and in Ezekiel the quantity of the cereal offering and oil remains the same, irrespective of the animal offered. Further, Ezekiel was concerned only with the public offerings of the prince (nāśî'), whereas the present passage is concerned with the public and private offerings of the people at large. Moreover, the prophet makes no mention of wine as a drink offering, and there is an optional element in Ezekiel which is lacking in the passage here under discussion. Some commentators explain these differences by regarding vv. 1-16 as a later elaboration and modification of the passage in Ezekiel (cf. Budd), but there is much to be said for regarding the two passages as independent of one another. There can certainly be no justification for tracing a chronological development between Lev. 2, Ezek. 46 and the present passage as suggested, e.g., by Marsh (p. 215); rather, the amounts of cereal offerings deemed necessary probably varied from one period to another, and these passages merely reflect the custom that happened to prevail at the time when they were written.

Several commentators have drawn attention to the lack of unity in the present section. V. 8, for example, seems to refer back to v. 3, but contains an unexpected reference to the 'peace offering'; v. 11 appears to refer to the regulations concerning the sacrifice of the bull, ram and lamb in vv. 4-10, but extends them, without explanation, to include 'kids'; the law governing the requisite amount of offerings seems at one point to be confined to the 'native' (v. 13), but it is suddenly extended in v. 14 to include the stranger who is 'sojourning with you'; moreover, v. 16 is little more than a reformulation of v. 15, and appears to be quite superfluous. Such inconsistencies, together with the fact that the section is expressed partly in an impersonal style (vv. 4, 9) and partly in the form of direct speech (vv. 1-3, 12-15) suggest a progressive reshaping and recasting of older traditions (cf. de Vaulx). It appears, however, that the original form of the passage can no longer be determined with any certainty.

2. When you come into the land you are to inhabit: It is here implied that the regulations mentioned in the following verses were to be valid only after the Israelites had occupied Canaan, a fact confirmed by the types of offering required (flour, oil, wine; cf.

vv. 4f.), which presuppose a settled agricultural community. The phrase translated 'into the land you are to inhabit' (Heb. *'el-'ereṣ môšʿbōṯêkem*; lit., 'into the land of your habitations') is not found elsewhere in the *OT*, although the notion that certain regulations applied only to Israel's life in the promised land is one that occurs in the introduction to various *OT* laws (cf. v. 18; Lev. 14:34; 19:23; 23:10; 25:2; Dt. 6:1, 10; 7:1 etc.).

3. an offering by fire: This type of sacrifice is mentioned, with rare exceptions (Dt. 18:1; Jos. 13:14; 1 Sam. 2:28), only in the Priestly writings, where it occurs some sixty-two times. The etymology and original meaning of the Heb. term *'iššeh* is obscure. *BDB* (pp. 77f.) derives it from the root *'ānaš* II = to establish friendly relations, i.e., with the deity, but although this would express well the propitiatory effect of the sacrifice, this proposed etymology of the word must be regarded as dubious, since there is no definite evidence for the existence of this verbal root in Heb. Cazelles (*Le Deutéronome*, p. 82) suggests that the word is related to the Sumerian *EŠ* (= 'food'), and that it referred to a 'food offering' (cf. *NEB*), but while there are certainly traces in the *OT* of the notion of sacrifice as 'food' for the deity, it is doubtful whether such an idea was still in vogue at the time of the Priestly writer. *RSV*'s 'offering by fire' assumes that the term *'iššeh* is related to the Heb. word for 'fire' (*'ēš*; cf. *G–K* § 86*i*), and although a connection between the two words is by no means certain, it is probable that the Priestly writer was aware of the association between them, and that he understood *'iššeh* as a general term to denote offerings which had been consumed either wholly or in part by fire (cf. Gray, *Sacrifice*, pp. 9ff.; de Vaux, *Studies*, pp. 30f.). The association of *'iššeh* with fire is also suggested by the LXX rendering, *holokautôma*, which suggests that the sacrifice in question was burned. **a burnt offering or a sacrifice**: The 'burnt offering' (Heb. *'ōlāh*) was one in which the whole sacrifice was presented to the deity (cf. *NEB*'s 'whole offering'), the flesh being entirely destroyed in the fire, with no part of it being retained to be eaten by the worshipper; by contrast, the 'sacrifice' (Heb. *zebaḥ*) was one in which the worshipper was permitted to partake of the offering. **to fulfil a vow or as a freewill offering**: Snaith (p. 250) considers the *neder* ('vow') and *nʿḏāḇāh* ('freewill') to refer to specific types of sacrifice (*zebaḥ*), but it is more probable that these terms referred to the occasion on which the sacrifice was offered (so, e.g., de Vaux, *Studies*, p. 33). **to make a pleasing odour to the LORD**:

The phrase is a survival of the primitive notion, common in the ancient Near East (cf. *DOTT*, p. 23) that the deity took delight in the smell of the burning sacrifice (cf. Gen. 8:21); in later usage, the crude, anthropomorphic origin of the idea was forgotten, and the phrase became a vivid metaphor for acceptable worship, as the Targum's paraphrase ('an offering which is received with pleasure before God') well illustrates (Gray, *Sacrifice*, p. 80).

4–5. When the sacrificial victim was a lamb, the accompanying cereal offering was to consist of **a tenth of an ephah of fine flour**: MT lacks 'ephah', but the word is tacitly assumed, and is correctly inserted into the text by *RSV* (cf. LXX). The ephah was a dry measure, and a tenth of an ephah would be equivalent to approx. 4.5 litres. The fine flour was to be mixed with **a fourth of a hin of oil**: Apart from Ezek. 4:11, the hin is mentioned only in ritual contexts, where it describes the quantity of wine or oil that was to accompany the sacrifice (de Vaux, *AI*, p. 200). In contrast to the ephah, it was a liquid measure, and a fourth of a hin would be equivalent to approx. 1.8 litres. On the measurements mentioned here, see Scott, *NPC*, p. 38. The wine was to be used **for the drink offering**: The *OT* contains no information regarding the method of presenting the drink offering, and it must remain uncertain whether it was poured over the sacrifice itself, in accordance with ancient Greek and Roman custom (so, e.g., Marsh), or whether it was poured out at the foot of the altar, as suggested by Josephus (*Ant.* III.9.4; cf. Sir. 50:15; so, e.g., Sturdy). That the custom of presenting a drink offering originated at an early date is clear from the allusions in 1 Sam. 1:24; 10:3; Hos. 9:4.

6–10. When the sacrificial victim was a ram, the accompanying offerings were to consist of approx. 9 litres of flour and 2.5 litres each of oil and wine. LXX adds in v. 6, 'when you prepare it for a burnt offering or for a sacrifice' (cf. v. 8), but while this helps to elucidate the meaning of the verse, the addition is superfluous. When the sacrificial victim was a bull, the accompanying offerings were to consist of approx. 13.5 litres of flour and 3.75 litres each of oil and wine.

12. so shall you do with every one according to their number: Should more animals be sacrificed than the law required, then the accompanying offerings had to be increased accordingly.

14. And if a stranger is sojourning with you, or any one is among you throughout your generations: For the 'stranger'

(Heb. *gēr*), see on 9:14. Gray (p. 176) suggests that two different classes of people are here alluded to, i.e., the 'stranger' and those who lacked the fixed status and recognized rights of either the stranger or the native (cf. McNeile; Budd). However, this distinction has little to commend it, and it is more probable that the reference here is to two types of *gērîm*, i.e., those who were temporarily resident in Israel and those whose families had lived for generations among the Israelites. Be that as it may, the general meaning of the verse is clear: the regulations concerning the cereal offerings and drink offerings were to be equally binding on the resident alien and the native-born Israelite, a principle reiterated in v. 15.

15. For the assembly: The Heb. *haqqāhāl* is omitted in Syr. and Vulg., and it should probably be regarded as a gloss (cf. Holzinger). LXX and Sam. connect it with the previous verse (the LXX adding a reference to Yahweh): 'as you do, so shall the assembly (of the LORD) do' (cf. *NJPS*), but this has little to commend it.

(ii) *The first coarse meal offering:* **15:17-21**

Moses is here directed to command the people to present an offering of the first part of their coarse meal to Yahweh. V. 18 provides a link with v. 2, although it does not necessarily follow (*contra* Kuenen, *Hexateuch*, p. 96) that both passages have a common origin. The section is certainly Priestly, and may well represent a relatively late accretion within the Priestly corpus.

18-19. The Israelites, once they had settled in Canaan, were to **present an offering to the LORD**: The 'offering' (Heb. *t'rûmāh*) was, in effect, to be presented to the sanctuary or to the priest; for the *t'rûmāh*, see on 6:20.

20. Of the first of your coarse meal you shall present a cake as an offering: The regulation is obscure, mainly because the meaning of the Heb. term *'ªrîsāh* (here rendered 'coarse meal') is uncertain. The word is encountered elsewhere in the *OT* only in Neh. 10:37 (MT 10:38) and Ezek. 44:30, where it also occurs in the plural and in connection with *rē'šît* ('the first of'). *RSV*'s 'coarse meal' (cf. *NIV*, 'ground meal') is based on the meaning of *'arsān* in post-biblical Heb., where it is used to refer to a kind of 'barley paste' (cf. Syr. *'arsānā'* = 'hulled barley'), which was regarded as particularly suitable for consumption by invalids and children. *NEB*, however, renders *'ªrîsāh* as 'dough' (cf. *AV*; *RV*), and this meaning, favoured by Eissfeldt (*Erstlinge*, pp. 61ff.), is supported by LXX *phurama* (cf. Rom.

11:16) and, indirectly, by Targ. Onk. and Syr., both of which understand it to refer to a 'kneading trough'. At any event, the fact that the offering was to be presented in the form of a **cake** (*ḥallāh*; cf. *BDB*, p. 319*b*) suggests that some product of household cookery was here intended (cf. Ezek. 44:30, where the offering is presented in order that 'a blessing may rest on your house'). The term *rē'šîṯ* in this context does not mean 'first-fruits' (*contra* Riggans) but rather the 'first part prepared' (cf. Gray); the meaning of the regulation, therefore, seems to be that at each new baking some, at least, of the first batch of cakes prepared had to be set aside as an offering. This rather speaks against the meaning 'dough' for *ʿarîsāh*, for bread would have been baked virtually on a daily basis, and the requirement to reserve a few loaves at each baking would have proved very onerous indeed (cf. Holzinger). On the other hand, cakes prepared from coarse meal would only have been baked periodically, and it is by no means improbable that the priesthood would have demanded a small but regular token of this kind.

(iii) *Offerings for inadvertent transgressions:* **15:22−31**
This section deals with the offerings to be made in the case of inadvertent transgressions. If such offences had been perpetrated by the community as a whole (vv. 22−26), a young bull was to be presented as a burnt offering (together with the appropriate cereal and drink offerings), and a male goat was to be presented as a sin offering; if such offences had been perpetrated by an individual (vv. 27−29), the only requirement was that a female goat be presented as a sin offering. The passage contains no specific example of the type of offence envisaged, nor does it indicate how the transgressions had come to light; its concern is only with the measures to be taken to remove the guilt which had been incurred. The section concludes with the observation that the offerings were required whether the offender was a native Israelite or a resident alien (*gēr*; v. 29), and that sacrificial expiation was not possible for sins which had been committed wilfully and defiantly (vv. 30f.).

The section lacks an introductory formula (cf. vv. 1f., 17f.), and this has led some commentators to view vv. 22−31 as a continuation of vv. 17−21 (cf. Snaith, p. 252; Kiuchi, *Purification Offering*, pp. 56ff.). Dillmann (p. 84), on the other hand, regards vv. 22−31 as a separate unit, but argues that vv. 17−18*a* originally formed the introduction to this section, vv. 18*b*−21 having been inserted at a later stage. Neither of these solutions, however, has generally commended itself to commentators, and a far more probable explanation for the lack of an introduction is that this section once belonged to an entirely different context, and was only later inserted into its present position (cf. Gray, Binns). It is, of course, no longer possible to identify its original context, but the reference to 'all these commandments' in v. 22 perhaps suggests that at one time it formed the conclusion to a series of legal prescriptions.

The provisions concerning inadvertent transgressions here are similar to those found in Lev. 4f., and this has led many commentators to suggest that a connection of some kind exists between the two passages. The nature of this connection has often been explored, but no consensus has yet been reached. Some scholars maintain that Num. 15:22ff. betrays a dependence on Lev. 4f. (de Vaulx, p. 185; Kellermann, *Fest. Elliger*, pp. 107ff.); others assert that Lev. 4f. is dependent upon Num. 15:22ff. (Baentsch, p. 536; Rendtorff, *Die Gesetze*, pp. 14ff.); while still others maintain that the differences between the two passages are sufficiently striking to warrant the assumption that neither is dependent upon the other, but that each represents an independent tradition (Kennedy, p. 274; Milgrom, *Fest. Freedman*, pp. 211ff.).

There can be little doubt that there are significant differences between the two sets of laws, and these may be summarized briefly as follows: (i) Num. 15:22ff. deals with only two types of offender (the congregation and the individual), but two further categories are mentioned in Lev. 4f., namely the high priest and the ruler (*nāśî'*). (ii) The type of sacrifice to be presented differs in the two passages: in Num. 15:22ff., the unwitting sin is to be expiated by the presentation of a bull as a burnt offering and a male goat as a sin offering; in Lev. 4f., on the other hand, the bull is demanded as a sin offering and no burnt offering is required. Moreover, in Num. 15:22ff., an individual's unwitting sin requires that a female goat a year old be presented as a sin offering, but Lev. 4 gives the offender the option of presenting either a female goat (4:28f.) or a female lamb (4:32), and the age of the animal is not specified. Further, Lev. 4f. makes no reference to the cereal and drink offerings mentioned in Num. 15:24. (iii) Special provisions are made for the poor in Lev. 5:7–13, but these are lacking in Num. 15:22ff.; on the other hand, Num. 15:22ff. extends the regulations to cover the *gērîm*, but these are not mentioned in Lev. 4f. (iv) The affirmation in Num.

15:30f. that no sacrifice could atone for sins committed deliberately finds no counterpart in Lev. 4f.

Clearly, then, there are differences between the two passages which cannot simply be glossed over or ignored. On the other hand, it can hardly be denied that there are striking similarities, both in content and vocabulary, which suggest that either one passage is directly dependent upon the other or that the respective authors made use of a common *Vorlage*. Thus, for example, the word *bišgāgāh* is used repeatedly in both passages of 'unwitting sins' (cf. vv. 24-29; Lev. 4:2, 22, 27; 5:15, 18); Num. 15:24a bears a striking resemblance to Lev. 4:13; Num. 15:25a has a clear parallel in Lev. 4:20b, 26b, 31b, 35b, and the Heb. text of Num. 15:27a agrees verbatim with Lev. 4:27a. The arguments concerning the relative antiquity of the two passages are complicated by the fact that neither Lev. 4f. nor Num. 15:22ff. may be regarded as a homogeneous unit; hence it is possible that each complex contains material which dates from different periods (cf. Kellermann). Thus the borrowing may not all be in one direction, and it could be argued, e.g., that Num. 15:22-26 exhibits a literary dependence on Lev. 4:13-21, while Lev. 4:27-31 betrays a dependence on Num. 15:27-29. Exigencies of space precludes a more detailed discussion of the problem here, but it must suffice to note that the nature of the literary relationship between the two passages is probably far more complex than has generally been supposed.

22. But if you err, and do not observe all these commandments which the LORD has spoken to Moses: In these words, some of the rabbis found a clue to the distinction between the present section and Lev. 4f.; the former, they argued, was concerned with 'sins of ommission' (i.e., neglecting to do what the law required) whereas Lev. 4f. was concerned with 'sins of commission' (i.e., acts of blatant disobedience). But while the phraseology of the present verse and that found in Lev. 4:2, 13, 22, 27; 5:17 may appear to support this conclusion, such a distinction cannot, upon closer inspection, be sustained, for Num. 15:24, 29 is clearly concerned with a positive violation of the law, not merely a failure to do what the law enjoined.

24. if it was done unwittingly: The Heb. expression *lišgāgāh* (normally *bišgāgāh*) is characteristic of P, and refers to sins committed inadvertently or unconsciously as opposed to those committed 'with a high hand' (v. 30), i.e., deliberately and intentionally.

without the knowledge of the congregation: Lit., 'from the eyes of', i.e., unnoticed, unseen by the congregation (cf. *G–K* § 119*w*).

26. The law was applicable to the Israelites and to **the stranger who sojourns among them**: For the status of the *gēr* ('sojourner'), see on 9:14. It is not entirely clear why the *gēr* should suddenly be introduced at this point, but the reasoning seems to be that the 'stranger', as a member of the nation, inevitably shared in the guilt which had been incurred by the people at large, and therefore had to be included in any act of atonement.

30. It is here made clear that the sacrificial system provided no means of expiation for anyone who had committed an offence **with a high hand** (*NEB*, 'presumptuously'), i.e., in deliberate defiance of God's will (cf. *NIV*). Such a person **reviles the LORD**: The verb *gādap*, here translated 'revile', is rare and occurs only here in the Pentateuch; *RSV*'s 'revile' or *NIV*'s 'blaspheme' is certainly to be preferred to the rather weaker 'insults' of *REB* (cf. BDB, p. 154*b*). Whoever behaved in such an abominable manner would have to bear the consequences of his action, for he would be **cut off from among his people**: It is not clear whether the penalty involved death or excommunication, but the words 'from among his people' perhaps favours the latter alternative. See, further, on 9:13.

(iv) *Breaking the Sabbath:* **15:32—36**
This short narrative, which describes the fate of a man found gathering wood on the Sabbath, was probably placed here as a concrete example of an offence committed 'with a high hand' (v. 30). The man is brought before Moses, Aaron and the whole congregation for trial, but since Moses did not know how to deal with the case, the accused had to be placed in custody while guidance was sought from Yahweh (cf. 9:6ff.). The penalty subsequently pronounced by divine decree was death by stoning (v. 35), and the sentence was then duly carried out (v. 36).

The difficulty occasioned by this passage is that it is by no means clear why a divine directive should have been sought in this instance, for the man's action was a manifest infringement of the Sabbath law, and the penalty for profaning the Sabbath had already been made abundantly clear (cf. Exod. 31:14f.; 35:2). The rabbis tried to resolve the difficulty by suggesting that the issue at stake here was not the type of penalty to be imposed (since it would have been taken for granted that the man deserved to die) but rather the method by which the penalty was to be carried out (*Sanh.* 78*b*; cf. Rashi). Thus the purpose of the present narrative was to make clear that a breach of the Sabbath law was to be punished by bringing the guilty person 'outside the camp' and stoning him to death. The difficulty with this explanation, however, is that the law frequently prescribes the death penalty without specifying the method of execution (cf. Exod. 21:12, 14–17), and it is by no means clear why a specific directive should have been sought in this particular instance.

A different solution to the problem has therefore been suggested by Weingreen (*VT* 16 [1966], pp. 361ff.). He rejects the traditional rabbinic explanation, but argues that the passage may nevertheless be regarded as illustrating, albeit in rudimentary fashion, a principle well established in rabbinic thought, namely, that of setting 'a fence around the Torah'. According to this dictum, certain acts, although quite innocuous in themselves, were forbidden on the ground that they might lead to a breach of particular religious prohibitions. While the motive behind the doctrine was to deter would-be offenders from breaking the law, Weingreen suggests that the rabbis may also have been concerned with the question of 'intent'. Thus, in the present case, the man's 'intent' in gathering wood on the Sabbath was clearly to light a fire, but this very act raised the question as to whether a premeditated intention to break the law was tantamount to an actual breach of the law itself, and, if so, whether it deserved the same penalty. It was this issue that the present narrative sought to resolve, and it did so by giving the question a clear and definitive answer: an intent to break the law was, indeed, just as reprehensible as a breach of the law itself, and was to be punished in like manner. This explanation of the narrative, however, is beset with difficulties. In the first place, it reads back into the *OT* a principle which only became established at a later period. Secondly, to raise the question of 'intentionality' in this instance is surely a red herring, for the act of gathering wood in itself constituted work and would, according to Exod. 31:14f., have been punishable by death. Moreover, even if Weingreen's assumption is allowed, it must be regarded as inherently improbable that such drastic punishment as that envisaged in vv. 35f. would be meted out to someone who merely expressed an intention to break the law.

A different explanation of the purpose of the narrative has been advanced by A. Phillips (*VT* 19 [1969], pp. 125ff.). He argues that the story was recorded in order to extend the scope of the Sabbath commandment. Earlier references to the Sabbath, according to Phillips, merely prohibited the performance of occupational activity (Exod. 23:12; 34:21), but the present narrative extended the enactment to embrace domestic work (cf. Exod. 16:23; 35:3). However, this explanation is equally unsatisfactory, for there is nothing in the texts of Exod. 23:12 and 34:21 to suggest that the prohibition was intended to be limited to one particular type of activity; rather, the performance of *any* kind of work on the Sabbath seems to be prohibited.

Dissatisfaction with these explanations led Robinson (*VT* 28 [1978], pp. 301ff.) to propose yet another explanation: the man was gathering wood not in order to kindle an ordinary domestic fire but, rather, to kindle a 'strange fire', i.e., a fire to strange gods, and the penalty imposed upon him (death by stoning) would have been regarded as condign punishment for committing what amounted to a blatant act of idolatry. But this solution, too, is not without its difficulties, for if the man's intention was to kindle a 'strange fire', as Robinson suggests, this would surely have been made clear in the narrative itself. Moreover, to deduce, as Robinson does, that because the procedure followed in this case has a parallel in Dt. 17:2ff., both narratives must be concerned with a similar offence (i.e., idolatry) involves a very dubious presupposition; on this premise, it could be claimed, just as cogently, that the offence in the present narrative was one of 'blasphemy', since it is arguable that Lev. 24:10ff. (which concerns the case of a blasphemer) affords a closer analogy to vv. 32-36 than Dt. 17:2-6. None of the above interpretations of the narrative can be regarded as entirely satisfactory, but perhaps the one that involves the least difficulty is the traditional Jewish interpretation, namely, that the man was placed in custody in order to ascertain the precise manner in which he was to be punished.

36. And all the congregation brought him outside the camp: The whole community was involved in ensuring that the transgressor was duly punished, and in this way responsibility for his death was shared by everyone equally. The punishment was inflicted 'outside the camp', thus ensuring that the holy place was not contaminated by ritual pollution (cf. Lev. 24:23; 1 Kg. 21:13). **and stoned him to death**: Stoning was also the penalty prescribed in the

OT for such offences as idolatry (Dt. 17:2ff.), divination (Lev. 20:27), blasphemy (Lev. 24:15f.) and adultery (Dt. 22:22ff.). This method of execution avoided the shedding of blood and any subsequent blood-guilt.

(v) *The tassels worn on garments:* **15:37–41**
In this section, the Israelites are instructed to attach tassels to the corners of their garments as a continual reminder of the need to obey Yahweh's commands. Perhaps the passage was incorporated at this point to emphasize that transgressions, whether inadvertent (cf. vv. 22–29) or intentional (vv. 32–36), could be avoided by taking this precautionary measure (de Vaulx, Sturdy). Commentators have frequently drawn attention to the similarity between this section and H (Lev. 17–26), especially its emphasis on God's holiness in v. 40*b* (cf. Lev. 19:2) and the expressions 'go after wantonly' in v. 39 (cf. 'play the harlot' in Lev. 17:7; 20:5f.) and 'I am the LORD your God, who brought you out of the land of Egypt' in v. 41 (cf. Lev. 19:36; 26:13). Gray's view (p. 183) of the possible origin of the present passage is fairly representative: 'Of all the scattered laws outside Lev. c. 17–26 which have been claimed for H, this has best made good its claim'. Whether the present section was originally a fragment of H or deliberately cast in the style of H is virtually impossible to determine.

38. Moses is instructed to command the people **to make tassels on the corners of their garments**: The term *ṣîṣīt* (here rendered 'tassels') occurs elsewhere in the *OT* only in Ezek. 8:3, where it means a 'lock of hair'. The precise significance of the word in the present passage is disputed. Some commentators take it to mean 'fringe' (cf. *RV*, *AV*, following LXX, Targ.), and assume that the garment in question was one with a continuous fringe around all four edges (cf. Snaith). However, *RSV* is probably correct in assuming that the text contemplates a garment with a tassel attached to each corner. This is supported by the fact that (i) in the parallel provision in Dt. 22:12, the word used for 'tassels', *gᵉdîlîm*, means 'twisted cords'; and (ii) the *ṣîṣīt* actually worn by Jews in later times consisted of cords twisted and knotted (Gray, p. 185). The custom of wearing tassels on garments appears to have been quite old and it is attested elsewhere in the ancient Near East, as is evident from Egyptian and Mesopotamian paintings, reliefs and sculptures (cf. Bertman, *BA* 24 [1961], pp. 119ff.; Stephens, *JBL* 50 [1931],

pp. 59ff.). It is possible that the tassels were worn by the Israelites
originally as magical charms, and that they were regarded as having
an apotropaic function (so Noth, pp. 117f.); however, such superstitious associations are clearly absent from the present passage, for
the custom is here imbued with a religious significance, serving as
a visible reminder of the need for continual allegiance to Yahweh
and obedience to his commands. Because of this religious motivation, the wearing of tassels remained important in *NT* times (cf.
Mt. 23:5; *NEB*, *NIV*), and the custom still survives today among
orthodox Jews. The tassels were to be attached to the garment by
a cord of blue (*NEB*, 'violet thread'), not mentioned in the parallel
provision of Dt. 22:12. In later Judaism, the blue coloration was
invested with deep symbolism (cf. Riggans, Maarsingh; Bokser, *Proceedings*, pp. 25ff.), but the colour in this instance was probably not
intended to have any special significance. According to the Mishnah,
the practice of using a blue thread later fell into desuetude (possibly
because of the difficulty in procuring the expensive dye required),
and a white thread came to be regarded as equally permissible
(*Menakh.*, iv.1).

39. The tassels were to serve as a reminder to obey Yahweh's
commands, and as a warning **not to follow after your own heart
and your own eyes**: The verb used here, *tûr*, usually means 'to
seek out, spy, explore' (*AV*, 'seek after'), and is used in 13:21 in
connection with those who spied out the promised land. The original
meaning of the verb, however, may have been 'to turn to' or 'to
turn about' (cf. Assyr. *târu* = turn about, back; *BDB* p. 1064*a*) and
LXX reads 'turn back' here, hence *RSV*'s 'follow after'. The people
were strictly forbidden to follow their own inclinations and desires
in preference to the requirements of the law.

(c) THE REBELLION OF KORAH, DATHAN AND ABIRAM
16:1–50 (MT 16:1–17:15)

Chapter 16 purports to give an account of a single rebellion against
the authority of Moses and Aaron by Korah, Dathan, Abiram and
250 'leaders of the congregation' (vv. 1f.). A detailed analysis of the
chapter, however, betrays its composite character, and although
attempts have been made to defend its unity (cf. Richter, *ZAW* 39
[1921], pp. 128ff.), and to read it as a single, connected narrative
(cf. Magonet, *JSOT* 24 [1982], pp. 16ff.), it is difficult to avoid
the conclusion that it originally contained (at least) two separate

accounts of rebellion instigated by two different groups – Korah and his followers on the one hand, and Dathan and Abiram on the other (cf. Gordon, *JSOT* 51 [1991], pp. 64ff.). That the story of Korah was initially quite distinct from that of Dathan and Abiram is suggested by the fact that in Dt. 11:6; Ps. 106:17, Dathan and Abiram are referred to, with no mention of Korah, whereas in 27:3 (cf. Jude 11) Korah is referred to, with no mention of Dathan and Abiram; moreover, within the present narrative, Korah alone is mentioned in vv. 5, 6, 8, 16, 19, while Dathan and Abiram alone are mentioned in vv. 12, 25, 27*b*. Since the two narratives have been rather clumsily combined by an editor, it has not proved too difficult to disentangle them. In fact, apart from associating Korah's name with that of Dathan and Abiram in vv. 1, 24*b*, 27*a*, and inserting a reference to the fate of Korah's company in v. 32*b*, it appears that the compiler has done very little to fuse the two narratives and to give them a sense of cohesion. The story of Dathan and Abiram is found (with some later accretions, discussed below) in vv. 1*b*, 2*a*, 12–15, 25, 27*b*–31, 33*ab*α, 34, and it is usually attributed to J. Earlier scholars (e.g., Baentsch, Holzinger) maintained that the non-Priestly narrative in this chapter should be divided into two separate strands, J and E, but their analysis of the components belonging to each proved so speculative that it was subsequently generally abandoned (cf. Eissfeldt, *Hexateuch-Synopse*, pp. 173–75). The rebellion of Korah is contained in vv. 1*a*, 2*b*, 3–11, 16–24, 27*a*, 35, and on the basis of style and vocabulary, these verses must be attributed to the Priestly source.

The main difficulty which emerges from a source analysis of the chapter is that the Priestly narrative itself is by no means homogeneous, but seems to consist of two distinct strands which have at times been almost inextricably woven together. While there is some disagreement as to precisely which verses belong to each of the Priestly strands (cf. Ahuis, *Autorität*, p. 73, n. 1), it may tentatively be suggested that (with various accretions discussed below) one strand consisted of vv. 1*a*, 2*b*-7*a*, 18, 23f., 27*a*, 35, while the other consisted of vv. 7*b*-11, 16f., 19–22. The former strand depicted Korah and his 250 followers disputing the priestly prerogatives of the tribe of Levi on the ground that the Levites were no more sacrosanct than any of the other Israelite tribes, while the latter represented Korah as a spokesman for a group of Levites who sought to arrogate to themselves the dignity and honour which pertained to the priestly office. The relation of the two Priestly versions to one another has proved problematic, but there is widespread agreement that the version contained in vv. 1*a*, 2*b*–7*a*, 18, 23f., 27*a*, 35 is the earlier of the two, and it is possible that vv. 7*b*–11, 16f., 19–22 never existed as an independent, self-contained narrative but was, from the outset, a secondary development of the earlier account (cf. Noth, p. 122). As for the remainder of the chapter, vv. 36–40, with its emphasis on Aaron's priestly prerogative, betrays certain affinities with the secondary level of Priestly material in vv. 1–35; vv. 41–50, on the other hand, seem to be connected with the primary Priestly material in vv. 1–35. But while both these sections clearly presuppose vv. 1–35, neither should be understood as a direct continuation of these verses; rather, it seems preferable to regard them as loosely attached appendices added at a later date. It is no longer possible to determine whether these sections were appended to the Priestly elements in vv. 1–35 before or after these verses were merged with the Dathan and Abiram story.

Many attempts have been made to uncover the roots of the Dathan and Abiram story, but its traditio-historical background has proved difficult to determine. Gressmann (*Mose*, pp. 255f.) argued that the narrative was originally aetiological, and that it was designed to explain the existence of a massive geological fissure located in Reubenite territory (cf. v. 32); at the same time, he sought to identify a local interest in the story by drawing attention to the word *blʿ* in v. 32, and connecting it with the place name Bela. However, this view is difficult to sustain, for the phrase 'and the earth opened its mouth' in v. 32 is capable of various explanations (see below), and the suggestion that *blʿ* referred to a specific location must remain very doubtful in view of the absence of an explicit name aetiology in the story (contrast 11:1–3). Other scholars find a clue to the traditio-historical background of the narrative in the fact that Dathan and Abiram are represented as Reubenites (v. 1), and it is argued that the story can only be understood properly in the light of the history of this particular tribe (cf. Coats, *Rebellion*, pp. 177f.; Liver, *Studies*, pp. 204f.; Milgrom, *SBL 1988 Seminar Papers*, p. 572). Originally, the Reubenites seem to have enjoyed a position of pre-eminence among the Israelite tribes (cf. Gen. 49:3; Dt. 33:6), but their superior status was evidently short-lived, for at some time early in the period of the conquest, its importance rapidly diminished, and it ceased to be regarded as a major force in Israel (cf.

Mauchline, *VT* 6 [1956], pp. 21f.). The story of the rebellion of Dathan and Abiram against Moses' leadership is thus taken to reflect the struggle of the Reubenites to regain their former position of supremacy among the tribes, and to retrieve their erstwhile status as leaders of the people. The difficulty with this interpretation, however, is that the story gives no indication that the rebellion in question extended beyond the immediate circle of Dathan and Abiram, and there is certainly no suggestion that the narrative was intended to refer to the fate of the tribe of Reuben as a whole. A third possibility is based on the assumption that the tribe of Reuben had, at some stage, engaged in priestly activity, and the story is taken to reflect the opposition of the Reubenites (represented by Dathan and Abiram) to the claims of the Levitical priesthood (cf. Gunneweg, *Leviten*, pp. 171f.). Support for this is found in the words, 'Do not respect their offering' in v. 15, which perhaps suggests that the narrative, in its original form, began with an account of Dathan and Abiram offering a sacrifice before Yahweh. But this interpretation is weakened by the fact that the word rendered 'offering' (*minḥāh*) in v. 15 need not necessarily be understood in a specifically cultic sense (cf. Rudolph, p. 83) and, besides, the remainder of the Dathan and Abiram narrative affords little ground for supposing that the story originally revolved around a controversy concerning the legitimacy of cultic personnel. The most plausible theory regarding the origin of the Dathan and Abiram story is that advanced by Fritz (pp. 86ff.). He finds the clue to its background in the contemptuous reply of Dathan and Abiram to the summons issued by Moses ('We will not come up'; vv. 12, 14), and he suggests that these words should be understood as a refusal on the part of the Reubenites to join the other tribes in their attempt to enter the promised land from the south. This theory is supported (i) by the similarity in phraseology between the words of Dathan and Abiram in vv. 12, 14, and the words of Caleb and the spies in 13:30f., where 'to come/go up' refers to entry into the promised land from the south; and (ii) by the statement in v. 30 that 'these men have despised the LORD', for the verb 'despise' (Heb. *nā'aṣ*) is used elsewhere in J (cf. 14:11, 23) to characterize the refusal of the people to occupy the land. The reason for the refusal of the Reubenites in this instance can no longer be determined, for the beginning of the story of their rebellion is missing from the extant text, but their reluctance to participate in the conquest would have served, in retrospect, to explain why the

Reubenites did not settle in the land of Canaan like the other tribes, but occupied territory to the east of the Jordan (cf. 32:1ff.). In the present form of the story, Dathan and Abiram are represented as opposing Moses, but the rather awkward transition between vv. 12 and 13f. suggests that this feature was inserted secondarily into the narrative. The effect of this insertion was to transform the focus of the entire story, for it no longer functioned as part of the 'land-conquest tradition' but became, instead, a part of the 'Moses tradition'.

The background of the earlier Priestly story, in which Korah and 250 laymen opposed the position of Aaron and Moses on the ground that every Israelite was holy and therefore equally entitled to approach Yahweh, is equally problematic. Ibn Ezra speculated that the laymen in this instance were among the first-born who had been displaced by the Levites (3:11ff.), and that their rebellion was due to the fact that they had been unjustly denied their cultic prerogatives; however, there is no justification in the text for such a far-fetched interpretation of the passage. An alternative approach is advocated by Milgrom (*Fest. Cazelles*, pp. 142f.), who draws attention to the fact that prominent lay leaders in Israel could occasionally function in a cultic role (cf. Jg. 6:26; 1 Sam. 7:9); since the $n^e\acute{s}\hat{\imath}\hat{\imath}m$ were the lay leaders *par excellence*, there was nothing improbable in the idea that a clash may have arisen between them and the Levites concerning the rights to the priesthood. But this is very much an argument from silence, for there is no record in the *OT* of any struggle for the priesthood by a group of lay representatives in Israel. It must be conceded, therefore, that it is no longer possible to determine the contemporary situation which gave rise to this version of the Priestly account.

The background of the later Priestly version is somewhat easier to ascertain, for it almost certainly reflects a challenge posed in the early post-exilic period by a group of Levites to the exclusive position enjoyed by the Zadokites *vis à vis* the cult (cf. Budd, pp. 189f.). The account of Josiah's reform in 2 Kg. 23:4ff. intimates that the Levites were not permitted to officiate at the temple in Jerusalem (cf. 2 Kg. 23:9), and it must be supposed that the privilege of performing priestly duties was limited to the Zadokites, who traced their lineage back to Aaron. In the event, the Levites had to be content with performing relatively menial tasks in relation to the cult, and it is clear from the superscription to some of the Psalms (e.g., 42–49, 84f.) and from the writings of the Chronicler (cf. 1 Chr. 6:31ff.; 9:19;

26:1, 19; 2 Chr. 20:19) that they functioned merely as temple singers and door-keepers. It is hardly surprising, therefore, that relations between the Levites and the Zadokites were often strained and antagonistic, and it is not at all improbable that the former should occasionally have rebelled against their subservient position, and claimed equal precedence with the latter in the hierarchy of the temple personnel. The narrative concerning the rebellion of Korah, however, clearly indicates the viewpoint of the Priestly writer on this matter: those who were Levites should remain within the limits of their own vocation and should not seek to exalt themselves by demanding priestly recognition. The hierarchical arrangement was one which Yahweh himself had ordained, and if any Levite wished to challenge it, he was reminded of the fate of Korah and his company, who had similarly claimed equality with Aaron, and who had suffered the most dire consequences as a result.

The literary history of the chapter is complicated. According to Lehming (*ZAW*, N.F., 33 [1962], pp. 291ff.), the earliest form of the Priestly tradition contained no reference to Korah or to the Levites, but simply reported a challenge issued by 250 laymen, representing the whole congregation, to be granted the right to offer incense (cf. Gunneweg, *Leviten*, pp. 176ff.). The reference to 'all the congregation, every one of them' in v. 3a is claimed to support this theory, for these words would be unintelligible if Korah and a limited group of his followers were merely making a claim for themselves. The difficulty with this view, however, is that, in the extant text, Korah's name seems to be so inextricably linked with the 250 leaders that it seems most unlikely that it could, at one time, have been quite separate. An alternative suggestion is that Korah *did* appear in the earliest level of tradition, but that both he and his followers were regarded as laymen; only as the tradition developed was Korah, the leader, 'converted' into a Levite. This view is favoured, e.g., by Gray (pp. 193f.), who notes that two different Korahs are mentioned in tradition, and maintains that the one referred to in the earliest form of the Priestly narrative was not the Levitical Korah, but rather the Korah who appears in 1 Chr. 2:43 as the son of Hebron, and as a descendant of Judah (cf. 1 Chr. 2:3); the genealogy now contained in v. 1, which represents Korah as a Levite, was a later insertion into the original account. But this suggestion, too, seems improbable, for Korah the Hebronite was such an insignificant figure in tradition that it appears most unlikely that he would have been represented as having instigated a rebellion of this kind. On the whole, it seems preferable to regard the Korah of the earlier Priestly version as a Levite who was prevailed upon to use his good offices to champion the claims of a group of laymen intent upon contesting the privileged position of the tribe of Levi.

A history of the development of the traditions contained in the present chapter must, of necessity, be tentative, but the following outline seems the most plausible: (i) the pre-Yahwistic tradition concerned the refusal of two Reubenites, Dathan and Abiram, to join the other tribes in entering the land of Canaan from the south (vv. 12, 14); (ii) this was taken up by the Yahwist and converted into an account of a rebellion against Mosaic leadership; (iii) the theme of 'rebellion' against a person in authority attracted to the narrative the account of a rebellion by Korah, the Levite, who claimed for his followers (the 250 laymen) the right to be given Levitical privileges; (iv) a later editor represented both Korah and his followers as Levites, and depicted them as claiming for themselves the privileges of priesthood; (v) an appendix (vv. 36–40) was added, providing a pertinent comment upon the secondary additions to the Priestly account, and, at the same time, explaining the origin of the bronze altar coverings; (vi) a further appendix (vv. 41–51) was added, possibly to justify the harsh treatment which Korah and his followers had received at the hands of Moses and Aaron.

(i) *The leaders of the rebellion:* **16:1–2**
Vv. 1f. were clearly designed to give the narrative, at the outset, a sense of cohesion by naming, together, the three protagonists, Korah, Dathan and Abiram. These verses are partly the work of the Priestly writer, as is indicated by such phrases as 'chosen from the assembly' (cf. 1:16; 26:9) and 'well-known men' (cf. Gen. 6:4), but the reference to Dathan and Abiram and their family connections in v. 1, together with the observation (in v. 2a) that they 'rose up before Moses' were probably taken from the J account.

1. Now Korah ... took men: MT is difficult, for the verb rendered 'took' (Heb. *lāqaḥ*) lacks an object, and some word such as 'men' (*RSV*, following Ibn Ezra) or 'offerings' (Binns) has to be supplied for the verse to make any sense. The difficulty would be obviated if the verb *wayyiqqaḥ*, 'he took', were emended to read *wayyāqom*, 'he rose' (cf. Dillmann, Paterson, McNeile), but such an emendation unfortunately lacks unambiguous textual support. The suggestion of Meek (*JBL* 48 [1929], pp. 167f.) that *wayyiqqaḥ* should be emended to *wayyāzed*, 'became rebellious', similarly lacks textual witness, and has not generally commended itself to scholars. The rendering of *NIV*, 'became insolent', is based on a suggestion by Eitan (*Contribution*, pp. 19f.), which was favoured by Driver (*WO* 1 [1947–52], pp. 235f.), namely, that a Heb. root, *yqḥ*, cognate with the Arab. *waqiḥa* = 'to be impudent, shameless' is found here (cf. Snaith, *VT* 14 [1964], p. 373). It is this root that is also presupposed in *NEB*'s 'challenged the authority of'. However, the evidence for the existence of such a Heb. root is by no means conclusive, and it seems preferable to assume that the verb used here is a form of the root *lqḥ* = to take, and that either its object was accidentally omitted when the various sources were combined (so *RSV*), or its original object has now been preserved in v. 2aβb (so *NRSV*; cf. Simpson, *Traditions*, p. 240; Coats, *Rebellion*, pp. 156f.). The renderings of LXX ('and he spoke'), Syr. ('and he separated') and Vulg. (*ecce autem*) suggest that the ancient translators were similarly perplexed by the meaning of MT. **and On the son of Peleth**: Since On is not mentioned in the subsequent narrative (or, indeed, anywhere else in the *OT*), many commentators favour the view that the name should here be omitted as a dittography of Eliab (so, e.g., McNeile); moreover, Peleth (a name which occurs elsewhere in the *OT* only in 1 Chr. 2:33) is widely regarded as a scribal error for Pallu. The text would then be rendered, 'And Dathan and Abiram, the sons of Eliab, the son of Pallu, the son (reading the singular with LXX; cf. Dt. 11:6) of Reuben', and this would correspond to the genealogy contained in 26:8f. Nothing is known of Dathan and Abiram, apart from the information contained in the present narrative; they are referred to elsewhere in the *OT* only in Dt. 11:6 and Ps. 106:17, but these two references are based on this chapter.

2. Korah was joined in his rebellion by **two hundred and fifty leaders of the congregation**, i.e., representatives of the non-Levitical tribes, who were **chosen from the assembly** (cf. the similar, but not identical, phrase in 1:16), and who were **well-known men** (Heb. *'anšê-šēm*), i.e., famous (cf. 1 Chr. 5:24) or, possibly, men of stature and repute (cf. Gen. 6:4).

(ii) *The test involving incense:* **16:3–7**
Korah and his followers assemble before Moses and Aaron, and claim equal privileges with the tribe of Levi on the ground that the

entire congregation was 'holy' by virtue of the sanctifying presence
of God in their midst (v. 3). Moses challenges them to put the matter
to the test by undertaking a specifically priestly task, namely, the
offering of incense (cf. Haran, *VT* 10 [1960], pp. 122f.). By the
manner in which Yahweh would receive the incense offering, it
would be made known who was holy and entitled to draw near him
(vv. 5–7). The section is clearly a part of the earlier of the two
Priestly accounts, and it may be regarded as essentially a literary
unity, although some uncertainty remains concerning the present
position of v. 7*b* (see below).

3. You have gone too far! The precise significance of the Heb.
raḇ-lāḵem is unclear; the phrase is here used elliptically, and has
been variously interpreted to mean, 'You take too much upon yourselves' (*NEB*; *JB*); 'you have gone too far' (*RSV*; *NIV*); 'we have
had enough of you (and your pretensions)' (Gray, Binns). The
phrase may have been a slogan adopted by the rebels, who rejected
the notion of the privileged position of the Levites (cf. de Vaulx,
p. 191). It has been suggested (cf. Paterson, Gray) that the phrase
'sons of Levi' should be transposed from v. 7*b* and inserted at this
point in the narrative, for these words appear far more appropriate
in an address by Korah's company to Moses and Aaron rather than
in an address by Moses to Korah's followers, who were laymen
rather than Levites. An alternative suggestion is that the whole
phrase, 'You have gone too far, sons of Levi!', should be transposed
from v. 7*b* to the end of v. 3 (cf. McNeile, p. 87); the defiant speech
of Korah's company would then begin and end with the same words,
as in the case of Dathan and Abiram's address in vv. 12–14.

4. When Moses heard it, he fell on his face: This rendering of
the Heb. is rather unfortunate; *NEB*'s 'he prostrated himself' is
altogether more dignified. *BHS* suggests reading *wayyippᵉlû*, 'and his
countenance fell', but in view of v. 22, MT here seems perfectly
acceptable and should be retained. Moses' action need not be interpreted as a prelude to an intercession on his part, but may merely
have been a token of his deference to Yahweh.

5. Moses claims that the matter would be resolved the following
morning, when Yahweh would decide who was holy: **him whom
he will choose he will cause to come near to him**. The verb
qāraḇ, 'come near', is often used in a technical sense in the *OT* to
refer to the right of priests to approach Yahweh at the altar (cf.
16:40 [MT 17:5]; Lev. 16:1; 21:17).

6. Do this: take censers: These were flat pans used for carrying burning material; the same word, *maḥtāh*, is rendered in *RSV* as 'tray' in 4:9 and 'firepan' in 4:14. Only in the present narrative and Lev. 10:1; 16:12 is the word used in the *OT* to refer to a receptacle for holding incense. **put fire in them and put incense upon them**: According to some, the test was, in effect, an 'ordeal by sacrifice' (cf. 1 Kg. 18:20ff.; so, e.g., Coats, *Rebellion*, p. 171; Ahuis, *Autorität*, pp. 59ff.); however, there is no evidence to suggest that an 'ordeal', as such, was here envisaged.

(iii) *Moses' response to Korah's demands:* **16:8–11**
This section cannot be reconciled with the preceding, for here Korah and his company are actually in possession of the privileges which they are represented as demanding in vv. 3–5. Moreover, the rather abrupt introduction in v. 8 tends to support the view that this unit is a secondary expansion of the 'core' narrative contained in vv. 3–7. Moses here responds to a demand made by Korah for a share in the prerogatives of priesthood. By being entrusted with the Levitical service in the tabernacle, Korah and his companions had already been given preferential treatment over the rest of the congregation, and with this they ought to be satisfied. In vaunting their claim to a share in the priestly office, it was not Aaron's authority that they were challenging, but the authority of God himself, the implication being that it was Yahweh who was ultimately responsible for the distinction between the priests and the Levites.

(iv) *The rebellion against Moses' leadership:* **16:12–15**
These verses report the civil rebellion of Dathan and Abiram against the leadership of Moses. When Moses summons them to appear before him, they take the opportunity to instigate a rebellion by ignoring his command and accusing him of misleading the people and arrogantly assuming the role of leader. This section derives from the Yahwist, and its literary unity can be sustained (cf. Budd, pp. 182f.), notwithstanding doubts raised by some scholars concerning the status of v. 15 (Fritz), or at least v. 15*b* (Simpson, *Traditions*, p. 239). Since the only details in the previous verses (vv. 1–11) which could conceivably have formed a part of the Dathan and Abiram story are the names of the two rebels in v. 1 and the observation that they 'rose up before Moses' in v. 2*a*, it must be supposed that the beginning of the narrative is missing from the extant text.

Coats (*Rebellion*, p. 158) suggests that it may have been deliberately omitted by a redactor because of its similarity to the Korah material, which he had decided to include.

12. We will not come up: The phrase is sometimes used in the *OT* of appearing before a superior (cf. Gen. 46:31; Dt. 25:7; Jg. 4:5), but Fritz (pp. 87f.) may well be correct in suggesting that the words in this instance reflect an earlier stage of the tradition which reported a refusal on the part of Dathan and Abiram to join the other tribes in entering the land of Canaan from the south (see above). Some scholars have divined in Dathan and Abiram's refusal to 'go up' a conscious irony on the part of the author, since their ultimate fate was to 'go down' to Sheol (v. 30; cf., e.g., Magonet, *JSOT* 24 [1982], pp. 18, 21).

13. Is it a small thing that you have brought us up out of a land flowing with milk and honey: The phrase 'land flowing with milk and honey' in the *OT* usually refers to Canaan (cf. 13:27; 14:8); that it should be used of Egypt, as here, is quite exceptional, and yet not inappropriate, if understood as an ironical comment by the rebels, who regarded the fertile country whence they came, rather than the unknown country to which they were being led, as the 'promised' land. Their words served to express not only their doubts concerning the whole enterprise of the exodus, but also their utter contempt for Yahweh's plan of salvation for his people. **to kill us in the wilderness**: The motif of death in the wilderness is a stock element within the wilderness stories (cf. 14:2; 20:4; 21:5; Exod. 14:11f.; 16:2f.; 17:3). See Coats, *Rebellion*, pp. 29ff.

14. Will you put out the eyes of these men?: This phrase, which occurs in a literal sense in Jg. 16:21, is here used metaphorically to mean 'to hoodwink' (*NEB*). Gray (p. 201) suggests that the nearest English equivalent would be 'to throw dust in the eyes' (cf. Snaith, Marsh). Some commentators (e.g., Budd, p. 187; cf. Coats, *Rebellion*, p. 165) refer to Dt. 16:19, where it is stated that the taking of a bribe 'blinds the eyes', and suggest that something similar was intended here: Moses is, in effect, accused of being a deceiver, beguiling the people with false promises.

15. Do not respect (i.e., pay no heed to) **their offering**: Since there is no reference to an offering or sacrifice in the narrative as it stands, some have suggested that, in the original version of the story, Dathan and Abiram were represented as offering a sacrifice, possibly before Moses at the sanctuary (cf. v. 2*a*; so, e.g., Coats, *Rebellion*,

p. 166). But although this would make the rebellion of Dathan and
Abiram similar to that of Korah, and may, indeed, have furnished
one of the reasons for combining the two narratives, the suggestion
must remain purely hypothetical. BHS suggests that *minḥātām*
('their offering') is a mistake for *tōḵaḥtām* ('their groaning') or
'anḥātām ('their sighing'); however, there is no need to emend the
text, and the expression, as it stands, is perfectly explicable within
the context of the Dathan and Abiram story, for it may be understood loosely as a plea for Yahweh to withhold his favour from them,
as in the analogous, though not identical, phrase in Gen. 4:4f. **I
have not taken one ass from them**: Moses' defence of himself
seems to bear little relationship to the accusation brought against
him by Dathan and Abiram in vv. 13f., and consequently some (e.g.,
Fritz) have regarded the present verse as a later accretion; however,
the phrase may simply have been a conventional way of asserting
one's honesty and integrity (cf. 1 Sam. 12:3). LXX here has *'epithu-
mēma*, 'anything desirable', which perhaps presupposes the Heb.
ḥāmûḏ instead of *ḥᵃmôr* ('ass'), but in view of 1 Sam. 12:3, MT seems
preferable, and should be retained.

(v) *The incense test at the tent of meeting:* **16:16–24**

This section should be regarded as a continuation of the Korah
narrative in vv. 3–11. Moses repeats his challenge to Korah (cf.
vv. 6f.), and the latter assembles the whole congregation at the door
of the tent of meeting to oppose Moses and Aaron. The glory of
Yahweh appears, and Moses and Aaron are bidden to separate
themselves from the rest of the people in order that they may be
saved from the impending destruction. Before doing so, however,
they prostrate themselves before Yahweh, and intercede on behalf
of the people, pleading that all should not perish because of the sin
of one man. Yahweh thereupon permits the congregation to withdraw, and exempts them from the punishment, leaving only Korah
and his confederates to be destroyed.

The unity of the section has proved problematic. Vv. 16f. (which
seem to reduplicate the instruction of vv. 6–7a) must be regarded
as a sequel to vv. 8–11. V. 19 appears redundant after v. 18, for
Korah and his company had already been assembled at the entrance
of the tent of meeting; consequently, this verse must be a later
addition (so, e.g., Fritz) or else v. 19a must be transposed to a
position before v. 18 (so, e.g., Simpson, *Traditions*, p. 241). Moreover,

vv. 20–22 have every appearance of being a secondary insertion. Thus, in this section, only vv. 18, 23f. can with any confidence be regarded as part of the 'core' narrative, and even here it seems likely that the reference to Moses and Aaron in v. 18 is secondary, as is the reference to Dathan and Abiram in v. 24.

22. O God, the God of the spirits of all flesh: This phrase, which occurs only here and in 27:16 in the *OT*, is very common in post-biblical literature, occurring in Enoch alone more than a hundred times (cf., also, Jub. 10:3; 2 Mac. 3:24; 14:46). The expression is generally regarded as reflecting the advanced theological standpoint of the Priestly writer (cf. Knierim, *Hauptbegriffe*, pp. 106ff.), for whom Yahweh was not merely the God of Israel, but the God of 'all mankind' (*NEB*). The implication behind the expression is that the God who creates and sustains the physical life of every human being, is equally capable of destroying it, if that is his wish (cf. Job 34:14f.; Ps. 104:29f.). **shall one man sin, and wilt thou be angry with all the congregation?**: This, too, reflects an advanced theological viewpoint, for the notion of collective guilt, characteristic of early Hebrew thought, is implicitly rejected in favour of the idea of individual responsibility. As many commentators have observed, the author's standpoint here is particularly redolent of Ezekiel's strong individualism (cf. Ezek. 18:1ff.; 33:1ff.). The 'one man' referred to here was, of course, Korah; that no mention is made of his followers perhaps reflects a belief that Korah was the primary culprit, responsible for leading the others astray.

23–24. Yahweh directs Moses to instruct the congregation to move away **from about the dwelling of Korah, Dathan, and Abiram**: This expression, which recurs in v. 27, is strange, for the term *miškān* is not used elsewhere in the *OT* of an ordinary human dwelling (except in the plural in one poetic passage; cf. 24:5); moreover, the singular here implies that Korah, Dathan and Abiram all inhabited the same tent, a fact which seems to be contradicted by v. 26. The peculiarity is almost certainly due to the combination of sources, and this seems to be confirmed by the fact that the verse occurs at the juncture between the Korah narrative and the Dathan and Abiram story, which resumes in v. 25. Budd (pp. 181, 183) suggests that the text originally referred to the 'tabernacle of Korah', and he conjectures that this may have been a disparaging reference to a rival Levitical shrine set up by Korah and his followers (cf. L'Heureux, p. 86), but while this is certainly possible, the suggestion is somewhat weakened by the fact that there is no allusion to such a shrine in the rest of the narrative. It seems preferable to assume that the original text referred to the 'tabernacle of the LORD' (cf. 17:13), since v. 19 states that the congregation had assembled at the tent of meeting (cf. Baentsch, p. 548; Gray, p. 204; Simpson, *Traditions*, p. 241). The same reading should probably be restored in v. 27. LXX resolves the difficulty in the present verse by omitting Dathan and Abiram, and reading 'congregation' instead of 'tabernacle', and the clause is interpreted to mean that the people were to separate themselves from the group which surrounded Korah; however, this seems to be no more than an attempt by the translator to make sense of a difficult verse.

(vi) *The punishment of the rebels:* **16:25–35**

This section forms a sequel to vv. 12–15, and provides the conclusion to the Dathan and Abiram story. Moses, accompanied by the elders of Israel, goes to the tents of Dathan and Abiram, and announces a test which would decide the question of his authority once and for all. If nothing unusual were to happen, and the rebels were to die a natural death, then it would be shown that they had been correct, and that Moses' leadership was, indeed, self-assumed; if, on the other hand, Yahweh was to intervene in a miraculous way and destroy the rebels, then it would be proved that Moses' authority was by divine appointment. In the event, Korah and his companions, together with all their possessions, are destroyed.

V. 26 is regarded by some as a later addition, primarily because the word 'congregation' (*'ēḏāh*) is a term characteristic of the Priestly writer, and seems ill-suited in the context of a J narrative; others prefer to retain the verse, on the grounds that it is mostly couched in terms characteristic of J, and the difficulty occasioned by the presence of *'ēḏāh* is obviated by emending it to read *'am*, 'people' (cf. Noth, Simpson). But there is no textual support for the change, and there is much to be said for regarding the entire verse as secondary, and taking v. 27*b* as the natural continuation of v. 25. However the problem of v. 26 is resolved, the presence of *'ēḏāh* here should certainly not be used as evidence of a Priestly version of the Dathan and Abiram story (*contra* Vink, *Priestly Code*, pp. 119f.). The reference to the 'dwelling of Korah, Dathan and Abiram' in v. 27*a* (cf. v. 24) is a blatant attempt to combine the two narratives, and is clearly

an editorial addition. There is no difficulty in attributing vv. 28–30
to J, since the vocabulary here employed is, on the whole, compatible
with this source (e.g., 'sheol', cf. Gen. 37:35; 42:38; the 'despising'
of Yahweh, cf. 14:11, 23; the ground 'opening its mouth', cf. Gen.
4:11), and it is quite characteristic of the Yahwist to propose tests
of the kind here envisaged (cf., e.g., Exod. 7:16f.). The unity of
vv. 31–35 is, however, more problematic. In its present form, this
section has appeared to some as repetitive and verbose, and consequently vv. 32a, 33ba, 34 are regarded as later elaborations of J (cf.
Budd, Ahuis). There are certainly grounds for regarding v. 32a as
a later parallel tradition, since it does little more than repeat the
content of v. 31, using different terminology ('ereṣ instead of 'ᵃḏāmāh,
and pātaḥ instead of bāqaʻ), and the words 'and they perished from
the midst of the assembly' in v. 33b have every appearance of being
a secondary addition to the Yahwist's account. The secondary status
of v. 34 is less certain, for the action of the Israelites, fleeing in
terror, seems perfectly natural in the circumstances, and, far from
repeating the contents of previous verses, serves to introduce a new
element into the story; nevertheless, the occurrence of the word
'earth' ('ereṣ) here, and the rather banal nature of the words uttered,
must tip the balance in favour of regarding this verse, too, as secondary. In addition to these later accretions, the reference to the destruction of Korah's followers and all their possessions in v. 32b must be
regarded as the contribution of the Priestly writer, as must the note
in v. 35 regarding the fate of the 250 men who offered incense.

25. Then Moses rose and went to Dathan and Abiram: Since
Dathan and Abiram had refused to go to Moses (vv. 12–14), he
was compelled to go to them.

26. Moses warns the congregation to depart from the tents of
Dathan and Abiram, and not to touch anything belonging to them
(cf. Jos. 7:1ff.) **lest you be swept away with all their sins**. The
verb used here, sāpāh, is the same as that employed in Gen. 18:23,
19:15 with reference to the men of Sodom. LXX appears to have read
some form of the verb sûp = 'come to an end', whereas Vulg.
paraphrases, 'lest you be involved'.

30. But if the LORD creates something new: The Heb. reads,
lit., 'creates a creation', i.e., if Yahweh were to intervene with a
miracle. Hanson (*VT* 22 [1972], pp. 353ff.) suggests that the clause
should be translated, 'if the LORD splits open a crevice' (cf. *NEB*),
since the primary meaning of the verb bārāʼ was 'to form by cutting'.

But although *bārā'* in the Piel means 'to cut, hew down' (used, e.g., with reference to a forest in Jos. 17:15, 18), and although cognates of the verb in other Semitic languages suggest the idea of 'cutting' or 'hewing' (*BDB*, p. 135a), the overwhelming evidence of the *OT* is that *bārā'* in the Qal (the form in which the verb occcurs here) means 'to shape, fashion, create'. It seems preferable, therefore, to interpret the expression to mean that the event which was about to occur was completely unexpected and unprecedented, comparable to the awesome act of creation (so, e.g., Snaith, p. 260; cf. Isa. 48:6f.; Jer. 31:22), or that the punishment which Yahweh would inflict upon the rebels would be deemed to be 'as wonderful as the work of creation' (Noth, p. 128). **and the ground opens its mouth**: Hort (*ABR* 7 [1959], pp. 2ff.) suggests that this event reflects a natural phenomenon of the wilderness, the *kewir*, which is formed from subsoil covered with a hard crust of salt; according to Hort, this can suddenly break up during a downpour of rain, and anyone having the misfortune to be standing upon it at the time could easily be swallowed up in the morass of mud. Whether this is the correct explanation of the event here described (so, e.g., Sturdy) cannot be proved, but it is equally possible that some form of earthquake was envisaged. **and they go down alive into Sheol**: Sheol was the abode of the dead, and was conceived as being located in the depths of the earth (Prov. 15:24). It was generally regarded as a place of gloom (Job 10:21f.) and decay (Isa. 14:11), from which there was no escape (Job. 7:9). Since it was also a place where man was denied all fellowship with God (Ps. 6:5; 28:1; 30:9), the notion of being swallowed up by Sheol (while still alive!) must have been particularly repugnant for the Israelite.

32. and all the men that belonged to Korah and all their goods: This clause, which anticipates the proper fate of Korah and his company noted in v. 35, was added somewhat clumsily at this point by an editor in an attempt to bring together the two divergent narratives within the chapter.

35. This verse is a continuation of vv. 18, 24, 27a, and forms a succinct conclusion to the Korah story. The sin of Korah's followers was similar to that of Nadab and Abihu as, indeed, was their punishment (cf. Lev. 10:1f.). It is not indicated here whether Korah himself perished along with the 250 rebels, but that he did so is implied in v. 40 and explicitly stated in 26:10.

(vii) *The disposal of the censers:* **16:36–40 (MT 17:1–5)**
In the Hebrew Bible, v. 36 forms the beginning of ch. 17. This
section describes the disposal of the censers used by Korah and
his company. The censers had been offered to Yahweh and were,
therefore, holy, despite the fact that the men who had offered them
were not authorized to do so. Eleazar is commanded to take the
bronze of the censers and hammer it out into a plate to form a
covering for the altar, thus giving it a legitimate cultic use. This
was to remain as a 'sign' (*'ôṯ*; v. 38) and a 'reminder' (*zikkāṛōn*;
v. 40) that none but an Aaronic priest was entitled to draw near to
Yahweh and to offer incense to him.

It is generally recognized that this section forms an appendix to
the narrative contained in vv. 7*b*-11, 16f., 19–21, for the test of the
censers is regarded as proving the superiority of the priests over the
Levites, and not the superiority of the Levites over the laymen
(v. 40). The essential unity of the section is not in doubt, although
Noth (p. 130) suggests that the words 'then scatter the fire far and
wide' in v. 37 may be secondary, since this command is not observed
in what follows.

**37. Tell Eleazar the son of Aaron the priest to take up the
censers out of the blaze**: Eleazar was no doubt selected for the
task of collecting and disposing of the censers because Aaron, the
high priest, was regarded as too holy to have any contact, even an
indirect one, with the dead (cf. Lev. 21:10f.). It was for a similar
reason that Eleazar was chosen to perform the rite of the red heifer
(19:3ff.). The words 'out of the blaze' suggest that Eleazar was to
extract the censers from the still burning mass, but the Vsns (LXX,
Syr., Vulg.) interpret the word *śᵉrēp̄āh* to mean 'that which is burnt',
and imply that Eleazar was to wait until the fire had been extinguished (cf. *NEB*; *JB*). **then scatter the fire far and wide**: Even
the coals burned in the censers (vv. 7, 18) had to be scattered in
order to ensure that no ordinary fire could be kindled from them.
The fire in the censers was 'holy fire, though irregularly holy'
(Snaith), and consequently could not be put to any profane use.

38. For they are holy, the censers of these men: Since the
censers had been presented before Yahweh, they had acquired a
degree of holiness which made the objects unsuitable (and, indeed,
dangerous) for future use. They therefore had to be converted
into **hammered plates** (the Heb. *paḥ* occurs elsewhere only in
Exod. 39:3) in order to provide **a covering for the altar**. A

divergent tradition is reflected in Exod. 38:2, where it is stated that Bezalel had overlaid the altar with bronze when it was first constructed at Sinai (cf. Exod. 27:2). In Exod. 38:22, LXX attempts to reconcile the two conflicting traditions by stating, anachronistically, that the covering made by Bezalel had actually been formed from the censers mentioned in the present chapter; the fact that the rebellion of Korah occurred a long time after the altar was originally constructed was evidently not taken into account. The altar covering was henceforth to serve as **a sign**, i.e., a warning, **to the people of Israel** of what would happen to anyone who followed Korah's example and sought to encroach upon the privileges and prerogatives of the legitimate priests.

(viii) *The outbreak of the plague:* **16:41–50 (MT 17:6–15)**
This section forms the continuation of the earlier of the two Priestly narratives. The people hold Moses and Aaron responsible for the slaughter of Korah and his companions, and for this they are punished by an outbreak of plague. Aaron, however, under Moses' direction, makes atonement for them, and the plague ceases, but not before 14,700 people had died. The incident was regarded as vindicating Aaron's priestly prerogative, and as demonstrating that, unlike the incense offered by the rebels, what was offered by a duly qualified person was regarded as acceptable to Yahweh.

41. The congregation's sympathy with the rebels, which had hitherto only been implied, is now given clear expression, for they begin to 'murmur' against Moses and Aaron, and accuse them of murder: **You** (the personal pronoun is emphatic in the Heb.) **have killed the people of the LORD**: Although only Korah's followers had died, Moses and Aaron seem to be accused of having killed the whole body of the Israelites. This may simply be a blatant exaggeration on the part of the accusers (so, e.g., Sturdy), or the idea may be that, in causing the death of the representatives of the people (the 'leaders of the congregation'; v. 2), Moses and Aaron had, in effect, slain the people themselves (so, e.g., Gray).

44–45. and the LORD said to Moses: LXX adds 'and Aaron', no doubt because the following words, **Get away from the midst of this congregation**, are addressed in the plural form. Yahweh had determined to destroy the rebellious people, and so he warns Moses and Aaron to stand apart from them, in order that they may be spared.

46. Moses commands Aaron to take his censer, light it with fire from the altar, fill it with incense, and **make atonement** for the congregation. The offering of incense as a means of effecting atonement was unusual, for normally the shedding of blood was required (cf. Lev. 17:11). The incident here described should not, however, be regarded as reflecting an otherwise unattested ritual for making atonement in Israel; rather, it was simply considered by the narrator to be an appropriate way of contrasting the unauthorized use of incense by the rebels (v. 18) with the offering of incense by a duly qualified person, the clear implication being that only the latter was acceptable to God. Atonement was regarded as necessary, **for wrath has gone forth from the LORD**: The divine anger is here almost personified as an independent agent with an existence of its own, once it had proceeded from Yahweh (cf. 2 Chr. 19:2); its power to inflict harm could be deflected only by the intervention of an authorized priest.

48–49. and the plague was stopped: The atonement proved efficacious, although for 14,700 people, it came too late.

(d) AARON'S ROD
17:1–13 (MT 17:16–28)

The challenge to Korah and his company to present incense before Yahweh (16:6, 17), and the dire consequences which followed (16:31–33, 35), should have proved beyond any doubt that their overweening ambition was misplaced. But the congregation had reacted merely by accusing Moses and Aaron of having killed 'the people of the LORD' (16:41). Now, Yahweh arranges a further demonstration of the privileged status of the Levites which was to be even more conclusive than the last. Moses is instructed to take a rod from each of the tribal leaders, and to inscribe on each rod the name of the tribe to which it belonged (vv. 1–3). He was then to place the rods in the tent of meeting in front of the ark (v. 4), and was told that the rod of the person whom Yahweh had chosen would sprout (v. 5). Moses did as he was commanded (vv. 6f.), and on the following day he found that the rod of Aaron, representing the tribe of Levi, had not only sprouted, but had blossomed and produced ripe almonds (v. 8). Yahweh then commands that Aaron's rod should be preserved in the sanctuary as a perpetual reminder of the elevated status of the Levites, and as a warning to those who, in future, might be tempted to rebel. The chapter concludes with a recognition on the part of the people of the mortal danger of approaching the presence of Yahweh (vv. 12f.).

Since the object of the story was clearly to indicate the superiority of the tribe of Levi over the other tribes, and to confirm Yahweh's choice of the Levites to perform the ministry of the sanctuary, it is natural to regard this narrative as a sequel to the primary Priestly version contained in ch. 16. Earlier commentators (e.g., Holzinger) sought to attribute the core of the present chapter to P^g, but although the story of Aaron's rod is couched in the characteristic style of the Priestly writer, it has every appearance of being an appendix attached at a later stage to the account contained in the previous chapter. The essential unity of the present narrative is not in question. Noth (p. 131) harbours doubts concerning the authenticity of v. 5a on the basis that Moses' words here unnecessarily anticipate the miracle described in v. 8, but since Moses is depicted elsewhere as knowing in advance what was about to happen (cf. 16:30), there seems little reason for regarding v. 5a as secondary. It must be conceded, however, that vv. 12f. are only loosely connected to the story of Aaron's rod, and these verses were probably inserted at a later stage and intended primarily as an introduction to ch. 18.

The background of the story is by no means clear. Gressmann (*Mose*, pp. 279ff.) suggests that the temple in Jerusalem housed a rod in the form of an almond branch, and that the present narrative was constructed as an aetiology to explain its origin. This view has recently been developed by van der Toorn (*JSOT* 43 [1989], pp. 83ff.), who suggests that the present chapter was composed at a time when the origin of the almond rod in the temple had been forgotten. The idea that it was, in fact, Aaron's rod, miraculously transformed overnight, was suggested by its association with the staff which was normally carried by the priest who was on duty in the temple. In support of his argument, van der Toorn points to archaeological evidence which indicates that priests serving at the temple carried a staff in order to distinguish them from the laity. Thus the rod in the temple, interpreted as Aaron's rod, became the prototype of the priestly staff, and was regarded as symbolizing the divinely endorsed privileges of the priestly élite. While this suggestion is certainly attractive, it must remain hypothetical, for there is no indication in the *OT* that priests in the temple regularly carried rods as a sign of their status, and since they presumably wore priestly vestments (cf. de Vaux, *AI*, pp. 349f.), it is unclear why a rod should have been needed to distinguish them from the laity. Moreover, apart from the present narrative, and references to it elsewhere in the Bible (cf. Heb. 9:4), there is no evidence to suggest that Aaron's rod was actually deposited in the temple. Indeed Noth (p. 131) expresses doubts as to whether such a rod ever existed! It seems preferable to suppose that the author of the present chapter was familiar with various stories concerning the budding and blossoming of dead wood (for the prevalence of such legends in Jewish, Christian and classical literature, see Gray, p. 217; Binns, p. 118), and one such story was applied by him to Aaron's rod (cf. Exod. 7:9f., 12, 19) as a memorable way of depicting the privileged position of Levi among the Hebrew tribes. At the same time, it furnished a positive test to corroborate the negative one depicted in the previous chapter.

2. and get from them rods: The reference is not to sticks freshly cut from trees, since these may conceivably have blossomed in the normal course of events, with no miracle having occurred; rather, the term *maṭṭeh* here designates the official staffs carried by the ancient tribal leaders as a symbol of their authority (cf. Coats, *Moses*, pp. 186ff.). The same Heb. word, *maṭṭeh*, means 'tribe', and there may well be a deliberate play on words in the story: the 'rod' (*maṭṭeh*) which blossomed would represent the 'tribe' (*maṭṭeh*) which was to be Yahweh's special choice. **one for each fathers' house**: The term 'fathers' house' (Heb. *bêṯ 'āḇ*) usually designates a subdivision of a tribe (see on 1:2), but here, exceptionally, it refers to a tribe proper; the usual word for tribe, *maṭṭeh*, was probably deliberately avoided at this point lest it should introduce an element of confusion into the narrative.

6. and the rod of Aaron was among their rods: The rod of Levi's tribe was inscribed with the name of its most important descendant, Aaron. It is not clear whether there was a total of twelve rods, with the tribes of Joseph (Ephraim and Manasseh) counting as one (cf. Dt. 27:12), or thirteen rods, one for each of the twelve secular tribes, and an extra one for the tribe of Levi. Budd (p. 195) suggests that only twelve rods in all was intended (cf. Maarsingh, Noth), but it seems more probable that Aaron's rod was regarded as the thirteenth, for it was the customary practice of the Priestly writer to regard the tribe of Levi as distinct from the twelve secular tribes (cf. Num. 1–3). This interpretation is confirmed by the Vulg.'s understanding of the present verse, which states that there were 'twelve rods besides the rod of Aaron'. The rabbis understood the present verse to mean that Aaron's rod was placed in the middle of the others, thus precluding any possibility that this rod could have had an unfair advantage by being placed nearest the testimony!

8. and it bore ripe almonds: It was by no means impossible for almonds to blossom overnight, but the miraculous element was that the fruit which it produced was already ripe (cf. Sturdy). The Heb. word for 'almond', *šāqēd*, means 'wakeful', and the tree was so named because it was the first to produce blossom in the spring, and the first to awake, so to speak, from its winter's sleep (*BDB*, p. 1052*a*). Wenham (p. 140; cf. *ZAW* 93 [1981], pp. 280f.) suggests that the white blossom of the almond was regarded by the narrator as symbolic of the purity and holiness personified by Aaron and the tribe of Levi, but since the colour of the blossom is not specifically mentioned in the story, this seems to read rather too much into the account.

9–10. each man took his rod: The rods of the other tribal leaders, being of no particular significance, were returned to them, but Moses was instructed to place Aaron's rod **before the testimony**, i.e., before the ark. According to Heb. 9:4 and later rabbinic tradition, Aaron's rod was actually placed inside the ark, but 1 Kg. 8:9 makes it clear that there was never anything in the ark apart from the two tablets of stone.

12–13. The people recognize that unrestricted access to **the tabernacle of the LORD** would prove fatal. **Behold, we perish, we are undone, we are all undone**: These verbs are all prophetic perfects, suggesting an outcome so certain that it may as well be depicted as having already occurred (cf. *G–K* § 106*n*). Vv. 12f. form an effective transition to the following chapter, which describes a renewed appointment of the tribe of Levi as guardian of the sanctuary; this was a necessary precaution, lest any layman should perish by approaching it, as Korah and his companions had attempted to do.

(e) THE DUTIES AND DUES OF THE PRIESTS AND LEVITES
18:1–32

The chapter opens with instructions concerning the duties of the priests and Levites, presented in the form of an address by God to Aaron (vv. 1–7). The priests were in sole charge of the sanctuary (v. 5), but they were to be assisted by the Levites, who were to ensure that no unauthorized person approached it (v. 4). The Levites were themselves forbidden, on pain of death, to come into direct contact with the sacred vessels or the altar (v. 3). Since the responsibilities of the priests and Levites *vis à vis* the sanctuary are referred to in 1:50–53; 3:5–10, vv. 1–7 merely repeat in summary form ideas which have already been expressed in previous chapters.

Vv. 8–32 are primarily concerned to establish the means of support for the clergy and, to this end, a list is given of the gifts which the priests (vv. 8–20, 25–32) and the Levites (vv. 21–24) were entitled to receive in return for the service rendered at the sanctuary. The priests were to receive those parts of the cereal offerings, sin offerings and guilt offerings which were not burned on the altar (v. 9), together with all the wave offerings (v. 11), and all the best of the oil, wine and grain (v. 12); they were also to be given the new produce of the year that was dedicated to God (the first fruits and the first ripe fruits; vv. 12*b*, 13*a*), and 'every devoted thing' (v. 14). Moreover, they were entitled to appropriate the redemption money paid for the human first-born and the first-born of unclean animals (v. 15); the firstlings of clean animals could not be redeemed, and had to be sacrificed, but their flesh then became the property of the priests (vv. 17f.). Some of the offerings could be eaten by any member of the priest's family, provided that they were ceremonially clean (vv. 11–13, 19). Of course, all the offerings mentioned were, in the first instance, the property of Yahweh, but they were given by him to the priests as compensation for the fact that they could possess no landed property in Canaan (v. 20). The Levites, who were similarly to be deprived of territorial inheritance, were to receive all the tithes presented by the people (vv. 21–24); however, they were obliged to give a tenth part of this to the priests (v. 26), thus furnishing the latter with an additional source of revenue.

(i) *The duties of the priests and Levites:* **18:1–7**
The chapter as a whole is couched in the Priestly style, although it probably belongs to a late stratum of P. It was perhaps inserted at this point because a discussion of the duties and dues of the priests and Levites was felt to be singularly appropriate after the dispute concerning priestly privileges in chs. 16f. Moreover, the fear of the people concerning the rights of access to the tabernacle, expressed in 17:12f., are here allayed by the assurance that the priests and

Levites had been given the duty of guarding the sanctuary, lest it should be approached by any unauthorized person.

1. So the LORD said to Aaron: That Aaron should be addressed directly by God is unusual, and apart from the present chapter (cf. vv. 8, 20), the only other instance of this is in Lev. 10:8; elsewhere, Yahweh's instructions to Aaron are regularly mediated through Moses (cf. 6:22f.; 8:1f.). **You and your sons**: The reference here is to Aaron, and the priests who traced their descent to him. **and your fathers' house with you** (*NEB*, 'members of your father's tribe'), i.e., the rest of the tribe of Levi. **shall bear iniquity in connection with the sanctuary**: The technical expression 'to bear iniquity' (Heb. *nāśā' 'eṯ-ʿᵃwōn*; *NEB*, 'be fully answerable for') occurs frequently in P and Ezekiel (e.g., Lev. 5:1; 7:18; 17:16; Ezek. 14:10; 18:19f.; cf. Kiuchi, *Purification Offering*, pp. 49ff.) and means, in effect, to face the consequences of, or bear the punishment for, one's guilt. The point at issue here is that the priests and Levites must pay the penalty for any faults committed in connection with the sanctuary, e.g., if anyone approached too near it (cf. 1:51; 17:12f.), or if there were any errors or defects in matters of ritual or worship.

2. that they may join you: The verb rendered 'join', *lāwāh*, contains a play on the name 'Levi' (cf. Gen. 29:34), but the pun probably has little etymological value. For suggested etymologies of the name, see Spencer, *Levitical Cities*, pp. 9ff. The verb in Heb. is properly passive ('that they may be joined') but in this context it is better rendered as reflexive, 'that they may join themselves to you'. The Levites were thus 'attached to' (*NEB*) the priesthood, and were to assist the priests whenever the latter performed their duties in the sanctuary (here referred to as the **tent of the testimony**, an expression which occurs elsewhere only in 9:15; 17:7f.).

3–4. The Levites were forbidden to come too near the altar or the holy vessels **lest they, and you, die**: i.e., the Levites would die for breaking the prohibition, and the priests would die for allowing it to be broken. For the prohibition against coming into contact with the sacred objects of the sanctuary, cf. 4:15. The Levites, and they alone, were permitted to assist the priests, **and no one else shall come near you**: The Heb. *zār* here, in effect, means a 'layman' (*NEB*, 'unqualified person'), i.e., anyone who was neither a priest nor a Levite; the same word in v. 7, however, refers to anyone (including the Levites) who was not a priest.

5. And you shall attend to the duties of the sanctuary and

the duties of the altar: Since the subject of the verb is not expressly indicated, it is not clear whether 'you' here refers to the priests only (so Noth; cf. *NEB*) or to the priests and Levites together (so Gray). The former alternative is preferable, but if the latter is accepted, then clearly the reference to 'the sanctuary' (*haqqōḏeš*) must be understood in its widest sense to embrace the tent of meeting, the outer court and everything contained in them, which were to be guarded from the approach of any lay person.

6. The Levites were especially chosen from among the Israelites and were presented as **a gift to you, given to the LORD, to do the service of the tent of meeting**. For the notion that the Levites were a gift from the people to Yahweh, and a gift from him, in turn, to the priests, see 3:9; 8:16, 19. The position of the Levites, though subordinate to that of the priests, was nevertheless one of immense privilege and honour.

7. The priests, and they alone, were permitted to discharge the duties in connection with the altar and all that was **within the veil**. The expression 'within the veil' in P normally refers to the most holy place, i.e., the innermost part of the sanctuary, where only the high priest could enter (Lev. 16:2–4). If this is the meaning of the expression here, then P must have contemplated the entrance of ordinary priests into the most holy place. However, this must be regarded as intrinsically improbable, and it is far more likely that the author here either tacitly assumed a reference to the 'high priest' (cf. Noth), or understood the expression 'within the veil' to mean 'within the screen', this being one example among many in the present chapter of cultic terms being rather loosely employed. It is emphasized that the priests themselves had done nothing to merit the special privilege which had been bestowed upon them, for it had been freely granted by Yahweh **as a gift**: MT reads, lit., 'service of gift' (cf. *AV*), idiomatically rendered by *NEB* as 'gift of priestly service'.

(ii) *The reward for services rendered:* **18:8–32**
8. I have given you whatever is kept of the offerings made to me: For the *tᵉrûmāh*, 'offering', see on 6:20. The word *mišmereṯ* (here rendered 'whatever is kept of') normally means 'care of, responsibility for', and is so understood here by *RV* ('I have given thee the charge of'; cf. *NIV*) and by some recent commentators (e.g., Budd). The meaning would then be that the priests were given charge

of, or responsibility for, the various contributions, presumably by ensuring that they were not profaned in any way by lay persons. However, such an interpretation of *mišmeret* in the present context is regarded by some as doubtful, for the following verses are concerned with the dues rather than the duties of the priests; consequently, the word is sometimes rendered 'reserved, kept back' (cf. *RSV*), a meaning which, although rare, is by no means impossible (cf. 19:9; Exod. 12:6; Gray). If this is how *mišmeret* is to be understood here, then the meaning is that the priests were entitled to those parts of the sacrifice which had been 'reserved' or 'kept back from' the altar. These sacrificial offerings were to be given to the priests **as a portion** and **a perpetual due**. *RSV*'s 'as a portion' is clearly preferable to *RV*'s 'by reason of the anointing', which mistakenly assumes that the Heb. *mošḥāh* is related to the root *māśaḥ* = to anoint. A different root, *māśaḥ*, 'to measure', is familiar from the Targums (cf. Akkad. *māśāḥu* = to measure) and provides ample justification for rendering *mošḥāh* here as 'share' or 'portion', a meaning clearly demanded by the following reference to 'perpetual due'. The expression 'perpetual due' (Heb. *ḥoq-ʿôlām*) occurs frequently in P (cf. Exod. 29:28; Lev. 7:34); for the meaning of the term *ḥoq* in the *OT*, see Victor (*VT* 16 [1966], pp. 358ff.).

9–10. In these and the following verses, the priests' dues of **the most holy things** are enumerated. Priestly legislation usually drew a sharp distinction between those dues which were 'most holy' (and which could be consumed only by the priests themselves within the precincts of the sanctuary), and those which were 'holy' (and which could be consumed in any place by the priests and their households, provided that they were ceremonially clean); however, this distinction is blurred in the present chapter, for the two expressions seem to be used indifferently. This is a further example (cf. v. 7) of the scant regard which the author of this passage paid to the precise use of cultic terminology. The offerings listed here as the priests' dues were naturally only those which were **reserved from the fire** (*min-hāʾēš*), i.e., those which were not burned on the altar (cf. *NEB*). *BHS* prefers to read *hāʾiššeh* ('of the offering made by fire') instead of *hāʾēš* (cf. LXX; so, too, Snaith, *VT* 23 [1973], p. 374), but MT, although tersely expressed, is perfectly intelligible and should be retained. The amount of the **cereal offering** which was burned on the altar and therefore did not fall to the priests was 'a handful', according to Lev. 2:2; 5:12; in the case of an animal sacrifice, the

part burned as a **sin offering** and **guilt offering** was merely 'all
its fat' (cf. Lev. 4:26; 7:3–5). The offerings were to be eaten by the
priests **in a most holy place**, an expression which usually refers to
the innermost part of the sanctuary (cf. Exod. 26:33). However,
since the priests were not permitted to enter 'the most holy place',
the expression must here refer, exceptionally, to the court of the tent
of meeting, i.e., the place elsewhere designated by the term 'holy
place' (cf. Lev. 6:16, 26). This is yet another example of the impre-
cise use of cultic language in the present chapter. *NEB*'s rendering,
'you shall eat it as befits most holy gifts' has little to commend it,
and is rightly abandoned in *REB*.

11–13. The priests were also to be given **the offering of their
gift**: This refers to the portions of the peace offering which were
given to the priest (usually the breast and the right thigh; cf.
Lev. 7:30ff.). It is unclear why the vague word *mattān*, 'gift', should
be used here instead of the usual term *dᵉlāmîm*, but, as Snaith
(pp. 266f.) observes, 'throughout this chapter the technical terms
for the types and parts of sacrifices are not used in the normal way'.
The priests were to be given **all the wave offerings** (Heb. *tᵉnûp̄ōt̠*)
of the people of Israel, and these were to consist of **all the best**
(lit., 'all the fat') **of the oil, and all the best of the wine and of
the grain**, although the exact quantities of these commodities are
not stated. Oil, wine and grain represented the three main products
of the soil of Israel, and are frequently mentioned together in the
OT (cf. Dt. 7:13; 11:14; Jer. 31:12; Hos. 2:8). It is uncertain how
the **first fruits** (Heb. *rē'šît̠*) **of what they give to the LORD** (v. 12*b*)
differed from the **first ripe fruits** (Heb. *bikkûrîm*) **of all that is in
their land** (v. 13*a*). Gray (pp. 225ff.; *Sacrifice*, pp. 28f.) suggests that
the former was a contribution given outright to the priest, with
little or no religious ceremony, whereas the latter only became the
property of the priest after it was presented at the temple with
the appropriate ritual (cf. Neh. 10:35ff.). However, in view of the
fact that cultic terms are loosely employed in this chapter, it seems
prudent not to draw any distinction between these two words in the
present context.

14. Every devoted thing in Israel shall be yours: The Heb.
word *ḥerem* ('devoted thing') was a technical term designating something that was to be entirely withdrawn from ordinary, secular use
and given over to the deity; it was henceforth regarded as his exclusive possession and could not, therefore, be redeemed or disposed

of in any way. The meaning of the term is perhaps most clearly seen
in the context of Israel's military practice: all booty taken in war
was *ḥerem*, and so all prisoners and cattle had to be destroyed (Jos.
6:21), and all inanimate objects had to be given over to the sanctuary
(Jos. 6:19). In the present context, the word appears to refer to the
voluntary offerings which the people had dedicated to God, and
which could not thereafter be redeemed (cf. Lev. 27:28f.). On the
term *ḥerem* see, further, de Vaux, *AI*, pp. 26of.; Lohfink, *TDOT*, v,
pp. 180ff.

15–18. These verses enunciate the principle that all the first-born
of man and beast belonged to the priest; however, the human first-
born and the first-born of unclean animals (i.e., those which were
not suitable for sacrifice) had to be redeemed by the payment of
money. In the case of the human first-born the redemption price
was fixed at five shekels, and the money was to be paid to the priest.
The first-born of clean animals could not be redeemed, for they were
holy; these were therefore to be sacrificed and their flesh became
the perquisite of the priest. Provisions concerning the first-born of
clean animals are also found in Dt. 12:17f.; 14:23; 15:19ff., but it is
there stated that these were to be eaten by the owner and his household at the central sanctuary. For attempts to explain the discrepancy between the Deuteronomic provisions and those of the present
passage, see Driver, *Deuteronomy*, p. 187.

15. The priests were to be given **everything that opens the
womb of all flesh, whether man or beast**: Earlier laws demanded
the sacrifice of only the *male* first-born (cf. Exod. 13:2, 12f., 15), and
some have understood the words 'everything' and 'of all flesh' here
as an extension of the older provision to include both male and
female first-born, a change which is thought to reflect the increasing
demands of the priesthood in the post-exilic period. However, it is
probable that these terms were intended to encompass 'man and
beast' as opposed to 'male and female', for the redemption price of
five shekels noted in v. 16 was the tariff prescribed elsewhere only
for the *male* child (the female being valued at three shekels; cf.
Lev. 27:6).

16. The **redemption price** for the human first-born was fixed at
five shekels in silver, according to the shekel of the sanctuary:
For the 'shekel of the sanctuary', see on 3:47. No such fixed price
is given for the redemption of the firstlings of unclean animals (cf.
Brin, *JQR* 68 [1977–8], pp. 6ff.), probably because this varied

according to the priest's valuation (cf. Lev. 27:11f., 27). This verse is generally regarded as a later addition, since it interrupts the connection between vv. 15 and 17 (Dillmann, Noth).

17. You shall sprinkle their blood upon the altar, and shall burn their fat as an offering by fire: It is unclear why *RSV* renders the verb *zāraq* as 'sprinkle' here, since elsewhere in similar contexts the verb is translated, more accurately, as 'throw' (cf. Exod. 24:6, 8; 29:16, 20; Lev. 1:5, 11 etc.); cf. *NEB*, 'fling their blood'. The ritual prescribed here is similar to that required in the case of peace offerings (cf. Lev. 3:2ff.), except that in this instance the flesh was not consumed by the offerer and his family (cf. Lev. 7:19ff.), but became the perquisite of the priest (v. 18*a*).

19. By means of the offerings which were presented to them, **a covenant of salt** was established between Yahweh and the priests. It is generally agreed that the phrase 'covenant of salt' denotes a covenant which was regarded as eternal and indissoluble, but the origin of the expression, which occurs only here and in 2 Chr. 13:5 in the *OT*, is obscure. It may derive from the common use of salt as a preservative in the ancient world, the commodity thus becoming a symbol of permanence and durability. Alternatively, it may be connected with the custom, well-attested in the ancient Near East, of sealing a covenant by means of a sacrificial meal (cf. Gen. 31:54) at which salt would no doubt have been used as a condiment. Snaith (p. 36; cf. Riggans) refers to an Arab. idiom, 'to eat a man's salt', which meant creating a firm and lasting bond of fellowship between host and guest. See, further, Gray, p. 232; Smith, *Religion*, p. 270; McCarthy, *Old Testament Covenant*, pp. 41f.

20. The priests (here represented only by **Aaron** instead of the more usual 'Aaron and his sons') were to receive all these dues on account of the fact that they were to possess no landed property in Canaan: **You shall have no inheritance in their land, neither shall you have any portion among them**. This emphasis upon the priests' lack of territorial inheritance was no doubt intended to instil in the people a spirit of generosity as they presented their offerings at the sanctuary. According to vv. 23f., the Levites were also excluded from possession of land in Canaan and, as compensation, they were to be allotted all the tithes paid by the people of Israel. The view expressed in vv. 20, 23f. is clearly at variance with that found in 35:1−8 (cf. Jos. 21:1ff.), which states that the priests and Levites were to be assigned forty-eight cities with their surrounding pasture lands after the settlement in Canaan. In the case of the priests (but not of the Levites), it is here stated that Yahweh himself was to be their **portion** and their **inheritance among the people of Israel**.

21-23. In return for the service which they rendered at the sanctuary, the Levites were to receive **every tithe in Israel for an inheritance**: The tithe (i.e., the exaction of a tenth of one's produce) was a phenomenon widely attested in the ancient Near East (cf. Anderson, *Sacrifices*, pp. 78ff.); in Israel, the custom may have originated as a royal tax before it came to be regarded as a sacral due payable to the temple and its personnel (cf. 1 Sam. 8:15, 17; cf. Levine, p. 450; Cazelles, *VT* 1 [1951], pp. 131ff.). That a tithe was required for the sustenance of the Levites is stated also in Dt. 14:22ff. (cf. Dt. 26:12ff.), but whereas in the present passage they were to receive the whole of the tithes themselves (apart from that which they gave to the priests, v. 26), in Deuteronomy they were expected to share it, in two years out of every three, with the offerer and his household, and in the third year with the sojourner, the widow and the orphan, i.e., those who generally possessed no property of their own (Dt. 14:29; 26:12; cf. Davies, *WAI*, pp. 362f.). The difference between the two laws probably reflects different stages in the development of the institution of the tithe in Israel. See, further, Driver, *Deuteronomy*, pp. 169ff.; McConville, *Law and Theology*, pp. 68ff. The present passage seems to limit the tithe to agricultural produce (cf. vv. 27, 30), but Lev. 27:30ff. contemplates a tithe on cattle and sheep as well as on crops; the extension of the tithe in Leviticus to include animals may be a later provision, reflecting the increasing demands of the Levitical priests in the post-exilic period. In any event, the payment of tithes to the Levites was an acknowledgement of the risks which they inevitably incurred in the discharge of their duties (vv. 22, 23a), and it was entirely appropriate, therefore, that the regulation concerning the tithes was to be a **perpetual statute throughout your generations**, thus ensuring that the position of the Levites was permanently secure.

25-30. Of the tithe paid by the people to the Levites, the latter were to pay a tenth part (**a tithe of the tithe**, v. 26) to the priests. As Noth (p. 137) observes, the Levites here occupy an intermediary position between priests and laymen, for on the one hand, as cultic officials, they were entitled to receive tithes, but on the other hand they were obliged, like the ordinary Israelite, to make a suitable

contribution to the priests as Yahweh's representatives. Once the
Levites had paid their dues, however, they and their families were
free to enjoy the remainder where and when they pleased. The
priest's entitlement to a tenth of the Levite's income is also presupposed in Neh. 10:37f., and it is there stated that the priest was
entitled to supervise the receipt of the Levitical tithe, no doubt
because he had a vested interest in checking that the proper amount
had been duly received.

29. The Levites' contributions to the priests were to consist of the
choicest part of the tithes which they themselves had received. This
is clearly the meaning of the verse, although it is rather awkwardly
expressed: **from all the best of them, giving the hallowed part
from them**. The punctuation of the word *miqd°šô* is peculiar, and
BHS suggests that MT may originally have read *miqdāšô*; but *miqdāš*
properly means 'sanctuary', which would make little sense in the
present context. *NEB* retains the consonantal text but revocalizes it
to read 'and the gift which you hallow (*REB*, 'consecrate') must be
taken from the choicest of them' (Brockington, *Text*, p. 20).

30. The verse is awkwardly constructed, but its general gist is
that once the Levites had contributed to the priests the best part of
the tithe which they themselves had received, the remainder was to
be enjoyed for their own use.

**32. And you shall not profane the holy things of the people
of Israel, lest you die**: The 'holy things' in this instance evidently
refers to the 'tithe of the tithe' which was to be given to the priests.
The danger here envisaged is that the Levites might be tempted to
misappropriate it and consume it themselves, thus profaning that
which, in essence, belonged to God.

(f) THE RED HEIFER
19:1−22

The Israelites are here commanded to bring an unblemished red
heifer to Eleazar the priest, and the animal was to be slaughtered
in his presence outside the camp (vv. 1−3). After sprinkling some
of its blood seven times towards the front of the tent of meeting
(v. 4), the animal was completely burned (v. 5), and from its ashes
a mixture was prepared ('the water for impurity', v. 9) which was
to be used for cleansing a person from any defilement occasioned
by contact with the dead (vv. 11−13). Vv. 14−22 contain further
detailed instructions concerning the use of the mixture in a variety

of specific instances, and it is here made clear that defilement could be caused without necessarily coming into direct, physical contact with the dead, for even those dwelling in a tent where a person had died were regarded as having been contaminated for a period of seven days (v. 14). Moreover, the defilement caused by the dead was considered to be so contagious that it was capable of affecting material objects as well as living beings (v. 15). The proper procedure to cleanse those who had been defiled in this way is described in detail in vv. 17-19, and anyone who had become contaminated but who refused to be cleansed would be duly punished by being excluded from the community of God's people (v. 20). Finally, it is stated that the person who had administered the cleansing was likewise to be regarded as unclean, albeit for a short period, for in the very act of sprinkling the 'water for impurity' he would inevitably have come into contact with a substance that was 'holy', and therefore taboo.

The belief that contact with the dead rendered a person ritually unclean was both ancient and widespread (cf. Dillmann, pp. 104f.; Gray, pp. 243f.); however, in the *OT* this notion is mainly reflected in later texts, especially those belonging to the Priestly corpus (cf. 5:2; 9:6-10; Lev. 22:4). The possibility of being purified from such contamination is alluded to in several passages (cf. 6:6-12; 31:19; Lev. 22:4-6), but only here in the *OT* is the ritual of the red heifer described, although the rite is evidently presupposed in 31:21-24. The ritual has no exact parallel in antiquity, but there is some evidence to suggest that the Romans used the ashes of a slaughtered calf in lustration ceremonies (Gray, p. 247). The particular method by which the 'water for impurity' was prepared (vv. 3-6, 9; cf. vv. 17f.) suggests that the ritual was magical in origin (Noth), but, as was the case with the ordeal involving the water of bitterness (5:11ff.), or the tassels worn on garments (15:37ff.), it is clear that an ancient rite has here been appropriated by the Priestly school and reinterpreted in the spirit of a later age. Whether this ritual was ever practised on a regular basis in Israel seems doubtful; indeed, it is not clear why this particular method of lustration should have been instigated at all, for provisions elsewhere in the *OT* indicate that washing in plain water was sufficient to remove any contamination incurred by contact with the dead (cf. Lev. 11:24ff.; 22:4ff.). Significantly, the Mishnah records that only seven or nine red heifers were slain in all – one by Moses, one by Ezra, and the others at a later period (*Parah*, iii.5). On the other hand, there is evidence to suggest that some such rite was performed by the Essenes at Qumran in an effort to uphold the proper standards of Levitical purity (cf. IQS 3:4–10; Bowman, *RevQ* 1 [1958], pp. 73ff.). The rite described in the present chapter is referred to in Heb. 9:13f., and the ritual was invested with considerable allegorical significance by the early Church Fathers (cf. de Vaulx, pp. 218f.; Gray, pp. 247f.). For a discussion of various aspects of the ritual described in this chapter, see Bewer, *JBL* 24 (1905), pp. 41ff.; Smith, *JBL* 27 (1908), pp. 153ff.

The present chapter appears to be an isolated fragment, bearing no obvious connection either with the preceding narratives concerning the rebellion of Korah and the privileges of the priests and Levites (chs. 16–18), or with the following narrative, which describes the arrival of the Israelites at Kadesh (20:1ff.). Attempts to justify the present location of the chapter on the ground that the wholesale slaughter which followed Korah's rebellion (cf. 16:35, 49) would inevitably have necessitated some such procedure as is here described in order to deal with the consequent defilement (cf. Budd, pp. 211f.) seem somewhat forced and contrived, for the chapter is essentially concerned with death in normal everyday circumstances (cf. vv. 14, 16), not with fatalities that were the direct result of divine punishment. Moreover, if the editor did have in mind the annihilation of Korah and his followers, it would be reasonable to expect the present section to have been placed immediately after ch. 17. It is difficult to avoid the conclusion that the present chapter would have been more appropriately placed in a different context, such as Lev. 11–15, where laws of purification from ceremonial uncleanness are set out in detail (Dillmann, p. 104; Gray, pp. 241f.).

Earlier commentators were inclined to divide the chapter into two sections, vv. 1–13 (which describe the preparation of the ingredients of the 'water for impurity'), and vv. 14–22 (which contain instructions for its use in specific cases). These two sections were commonly regarded as the product of two different authors, since there were significant differences between vv. 1–13 and 14–22 both in the phraseology employed (cf. Gray, p. 254) and in the procedure adopted during the ritual itself (e.g., the hyssop is used to sprinkle water in v. 18, but is burned along with the heifer in v. 6; the defiled person sprinkles *himself* with water in vv. 11f., but in v. 19 the water is sprinkled upon him by another; also, the priest, mentioned in

vv. 3f., 6f., does not figure at all in vv. 14–22). More recent analysts, however, have argued that the chapter is composed of three, rather than two, distinct sections, for vv. 10*b*–13 (which contain legal statements in participial form) appear to belong to a different literary genre to that of vv. 1–10*a*, and may well have been composed by a different author (cf., e.g., de Vaulx). This conclusion is buttressed by the observation that vv. 10*b*–13 do not refer to the red heifer, and, apart from v. 13*b* (which is probably a later addition; cf. Noth, p. 142), and the enigmatic 'with it' (*RSV*, 'with the water') in v. 12, they contain no reference to the 'water for impurity' as a means of lustration.

Within each of these three sections, there are ample indications that the original material has been considerably revised and expanded, and this inevitably makes any attempt to trace the literary history of the chapter a complicated and uncertain endeavour. The heart of the chapter is undoubtedly the description of the preparation of the 'water for impurity' in vv. 1–10*a*, but even this section cannot, in its present form, be regarded as a unity, as is evident from the fact that in vv. 2–4 the verbs oscillate between the second and the third person plural. Moreover, the various persons involved in the ritual (the priest, the man who burns the heifer, the man who gathers the ashes) seem to confirm the impression that different traditions have here been combined. While it is virtually impossible to distinguish with any degree of certainty between the primary and secondary material in this section, it may be suggested, tentatively, that its core consisted only of a very basic description of the preparation of the ingredients of the 'water for impurity' in vv. 2*b*, 3*b*, 5, 6 (without the reference to the priest), 9*a*. At a later stage in the development of the tradition, the priest was introduced into the description of the ritual, and he was subsequently identified with Eleazar (vv. 3*a*, 4*a*); in this way, an originally pagan rite was brought under the aegis of the legitimate cult of Yahweh (cf. de Vaux, *AI*, pp. 461f.). The cleansing of all the participants involved in the ritual (vv. 7, 8, 10*a*) was probably added at a still later stage and, finally, the entire section was placed within the framework of Israel's sojourn in the wilderness (vv. 1–2*a*, 9*b*). Vv. 10*b*–13 probably stem from a different author, but v. 13*b* (with its reference to the 'water for impurity') was probably added by a redactor to provide a connecting link with the preceding verses (de Vaulx). A third author was responsible for vv. 14–22, although this section, too, exhibits a

distinct lack of unity; vv. 14–16 constitute a kind of *torah* couched
in a juridical style (cf. v. 14, 'this is the law . . .') listing the persons
and things to be purified, but vv. 17f. revert to a description of the
ritual procedure similar to, though not altogether compatible with,
that described in vv. 1–10*a*. Vv. 19–22 are marked by an unevenness
of style, and were probably inserted by a redactor to provide a link
with the two preceding sections, v. 20 referring back to vv. 10*b*–13,
and vv. 21f. restating the regulations contained in vv. 7, 8, 10*a*. For
a detailed literary-critical analysis of the chapter, see Wefing, *ZAW*
93 (1981), pp. 341ff.

The chapter as a whole was probably incorporated into the Pentateuch at a fairly late stage (cf. Noth, p. 139; Grelot, *VT* 6 [1956],
pp. 174ff.). Although it cannot be attributed to P^g (cf. Dillmann,
p. 104; Holzinger, p. 78), it shows clear signs of having been edited
by the Priestly school (Gray, pp. 242f.).

1. Now the LORD said to Moses and to Aaron: The words 'and
to Aaron' are lacking in some Heb. MSS and should probably be
regarded as a later addition, for there is no particular reason why
Aaron should be mentioned here, and the regular formula used
elsewhere when such laws are adumbrated is simply, 'And the LORD
said to Moses'; cf. 5:1, 11; 6:1; 15:1, 17 etc. The singular 'you' in v. 2
confirms the impression that Moses alone was originally addressed,
though the verb in v. 3*a* reverts to the second person plural form.

2. This is the statute of the law: The phrase is unusual, and
BHS suggests reading *happārāh* ('the heifer') instead of *hattôrāh* ('the
law'), i.e., 'the statute (concerning) the heifer', an emendation
favoured by some commentators (cf. Maarsingh), and one which
has some indirect support from Vulg.'s *religio victimae*. However,
since the expression 'the statute of the law' recurs in 31:21, and
since similar phraseology is encountered in 27:11 and 35:29, it seems
preferable to retain the reading of MT here. **Tell the people of
Israel to bring you a red heifer**: The Heb. word *pārāh* normally
means 'cow', and is so rendered here by *NEB* (cf. Vulg.). The traditional translation 'heifer' (*RV, AV*) is no doubt due to the rendering of LXX, *damalis* (cf. Heb. 9:13), the Greek translators having
evidently assumed that since the animal had never been used for
ploughing (see below), it must have been relatively young. However,
this was a false inference, for the Heb. word is that usually used for
the full-grown animal (cf. Gen. 41:2–4; 1 Sam. 6:7), and according
to Jewish tradition its age might range from two to five years old

(*Parah*, i.1). It is impossible to determine whether any special significance attached to the animal's colour, but in view of the fact that red frequently figures in lustration ceremonies elsewhere in the ancient Near East (cf. Gray, pp. 248f.) there is some justification for Noth's conclusion that the colour in this case was 'obviously considered to be important for the intended effect' (p. 140). According to some commentators, the red coloration was symbolic of fire as a cathartic agent (so, e.g., Kennedy) but others more plausibly suggest that it was symbolic of blood as the instrument of purification (so, e.g., Sturdy). **without defect, in which there is no blemish**: The tautology emphasizes the fact that the animal must be totally free from all physical defects, such as lameness, blindness or malformation of limb. Further, the animal had to be one **upon which a yoke has never come**, i.e., like the heifer mentioned in Dt. 21:1ff., it had to be one which had not hitherto been used for ordinary, domestic purposes (cf. 1 Sam. 6:7), or, as Josephus puts it, one that was 'yet ignorant of the plough and of husbandry' (*Ant.* IV.4.6).

3. And you shall give her to Eleazar the priest: Eleazar was probably chosen to officiate at the ritual, partly in order to safeguard the purity of Aaron, the high priest, and partly because Aaron was confined to the sanctuary (cf. Lev. 21:10–12), whereas this rite had to be performed **outside the camp**. The Mishnah (*Parah*, iii.6) states that in the time of the Second Temple the ceremony here described actually took place on the Mount of Olives, i.e., at a suitably safe distance from the sanctuary. The fact that the animal was to be slaughtered outside the precincts of the sanctuary indicates that it could not have been regarded as a sacrifice to Yahweh (*contra* Milgrom, *VT* 31 [1981], pp. 62ff.), for while it is true that the flesh of animals offered in sacrifice was sometimes taken outside the camp to be burned, this was only *after* the sacrifice proper had been made (cf. Lev. 4:11f., 21; 8:17; 9:11); moreover, flesh was burned during sacrifice in order to avoid the danger of defilement and not, as here, to provide a means of restoring cultic purity.

4. Eleazar was then commanded to sprinkle **with his finger** some of the blood of the slaughtered animal **toward the front of the tent of meeting seven times**: This gesture was a visible demonstration of the fact that the blood (and, by implication, the animal as a whole) was sacred to Yahweh. 'Seven' frequently appears as a sacrosanct number in the *OT*, and this is no doubt why the blood had to be sprinkled seven times in order for the rite to be effective (cf. Lev. 4:6, 17).

5. The heifer was then completely burned in Eleazar's presence: **her skin, her flesh, and her blood, with her dung**. That the skin of the animal should be burned was unusual (cf. Lev. 4:11), but that its blood should be burned was quite unique. Normally, the blood of a sacrificial animal was drained off, either to be sprinkled upon the horns of the altar, or to be poured at its base, signifying the return of the blood to Yahweh, to whom it rightfully belonged. *NEB*'s 'offal' is preferable to *RSV*'s 'dung', since *pereš* properly refers to the contents of an animal's intestines rather than to its excrement (Paterson).

6. As the animal was burning, the priest was required to throw three items into the fire: **cedarwood and hyssop and scarlet stuff**. The only other instance in the *OT* where these three items are mentioned together is in the rite of the cleansing of the leper in Lev. 14, although there the cedarwood and hyssop are presumably tied together by means of the scarlet thread, and used to sprinkle blood upon the afflicted person and his house (Lev. 14:4, 6, 49, 51f.). Why these items in the present case should have been burned is not clear, but an analogy may perhaps be found in the Babylonian custom of adding aromatic woods such as cedar, cypress and tamarisk to holy water in order to enhance the efficacy of the mixture (cf. Snaith, p. 272). In accordance with Jewish tradition, *NEB* renders the Heb. *'ezôb* as 'marjoram' (Lat. *Origanum marjorana*), and perhaps this is preferable to *RSV*'s 'hyssop' (Lat. *Hyssopus officinalis*), since the hyssop was not native to Israel. But whatever the precise species of plant intended (cf. Harrison, *EvQ* 26 [1954], pp. 218ff.), it was doubtless used here for its cleansing and purifying properties (cf. Ps. 51:7). *RSV*'s 'scarlet stuff' is a suitably ambiguous translation of the rather vague Heb. expression *šnî tôlā'at*; *NIV* has 'scarlet wool', and *NEB* reads 'scarlet thread'. The colour of the material (like that of the heifer) is regarded by some commentators as symbolic of blood.

7−10. All three people who participated in the preparation of the mixture − the priest (v. 7), the man responsible for burning the heifer (v. 8), and the one who gathered the ashes (v. 10) − were regarded as unclean for the rest of the day (**until evening**), and had to undertake the appropriate ritual washing. The priest and the man who burned the heifer were required to wash their bodies and

their garments (vv. 7f.), but the man who collected and disposed of
the ashes was required only to wash his clothes (v. 10). Paradoxi-
cally, the very ashes which purified the unclean defiled the clean,
and this enigma caused considerable perplexity for the rabbis of a
later age, who claimed that it was beyond the wit even of Solomon
to resolve the apparent contradiction (cf. Milgrom, p. 438; Snaith,
NPC, p. 263). The ashes were collected by a ceremonially clean
man who subsequently deposited them in a clean place **outside the
camp**, where they would be ready for future use. By means of these
ashes it was possible to prepare, as the need arose, **water for
impurity, for the removal of sin**: The expression 'water for
impurity' (i.e., water for the removal of impurity; cf. *NEB*'s 'water
of ritual purification'; *NRSV*, 'water for cleansing') is peculiar to this
chapter (vv. 9, 13, 20f.) and 31:23. The Heb. term *niddāh* denotes
something loathsome or abhorrent (cf. *BDB*, p. 622*b*), and is used
to refer to various types of ceremonial impurity, including menstru-
ation (cf. Lev. 12:2; Ezek. 18:6); hence the rendering of *RSV*,
'impurity', is perfectly acceptable. *AV*'s 'water of separation' is
based on traditional, but incorrect, Jewish exegesis (Ibn Ezra), while
LXX's 'water for sprinkling' (cf. Syr., Vulg., Rashi) is based on the
false assumption that *niddāh* represents the Aram. form of the Heb.
nizzāh = to sprinkle. The Heb. phrase rendered by *RSV* 'for the
removal of sin' has caused difficulty for translators and commentators alike, because the precise meaning of the term *ḥaṭṭā'ṯ* in this
context is disputed. Milgrom (*VT* 31 [1981], pp. 62ff.; cf. Levine,
p. 464) argues that the word should here be regarded as a technical
term for 'sin offering' (cf. *NEB*) or, rather, 'purification offering' (cf.
Milgrom, *VT* 21 [1971], pp. 237ff.), a rendering adopted by both
REB and *NRSV*. However, this rendering must be rejected on two
counts. In the first place, it assumes that the expression *ḥaṭṭā'ṯ hî*
refers to the 'heifer' which had been slaughtered, but it is quite
possible that these words refer to the 'ashes' of the heifer (rendered
in Heb. by the singular *'ēper*) in which case it would make little
sense to render *ḥaṭṭā'ṯ* here as a 'purification offering' (cf. Baentsch,
p. 562). But even if it is conceded that the phrase refers to the heifer,
it is most improbable that the heifer would have been regarded as
a 'purification offering' or, indeed, as a sacrifice of any kind, for, as
already noted, the slaughter of the animal took place outside the
camp, not at the altar, and while the animal was admittedly burned,
the verb used (Heb. *śārap*) normally denotes a non-sacrificial burn-

ing (cf. Wenham). Even if the expression is regarded as a gloss (cf. Holzinger, Noth), it is inconceivable that a redactor would have understood the term to refer to an offering to Yahweh, despite the quasi-sacrificial character of the rite. Thus *RSV* is probably correct in understanding *ḥaṭṭā' ṯ hî'* in this context in the more general sense of something that removes sin (cf. *NIV*, 'for purification from sin'; lxx, *hagnisma*). The ritual was to become a **perpetual statute** which was to be binding not only upon **the people of Israel** but also upon **the stranger who sojourns among them** (for the 'stranger', see on 9:14).

11–13. Whoever touched a person's **dead body** (for this use of the word *nepeš*, see Wolff, *Anthropology*, p. 22) was to be regarded as **unclean seven days**. On the third and seventh day of his defilement, he was to cleanse himself with the 'water for impurity'; the contamination caused by the dead was regarded as so powerful that the appropriate ritual cleansing had to be performed both at the middle and at the end of the period of defilement. Failure to observe this rite would entail the most severe punishment (**that person shall be cut off from Israel**; see on 9:13), for such uncleanness was highly contagious and might contaminate **the tabernacle of the LORD** (cf. Lev. 15:31).

14–16. If a man died in a tent (lxx reads *oîkia*, 'house', reflecting the later circumstances of the Israelites), then both those who were living in the dwelling at the time and those who were merely visiting, would be **unclean seven days**. Indeed, even inanimate objects were affected when exposed to the miasma of impurity: **And every open vessel, which has no cover fastened upon it, is unclean** (cf. Lev. 6:27f.; 11:32ff.). Defilement also attached to those out in the open countryside who came into contact with anyone who had died, whether naturally or by violent means (**slain with a sword**); similarly, defilement would occur if someone were merely to touch the remains of a dead body, whether or not it was buried. It was in order to avoid accidental pollution of this kind that tombs in *NT* times were whitewashed or marked by chalk, thus providing a warning for the unwary, lest they walk on them without realizing that they were being defiled (cf. Mt. 23:37; Lk. 11:44).

17–22. Here, precise instructions are again given regarding the preparation of the 'water of impurity' and its application: some of the ashes of the red heifer were to be added to **running water** (lit., 'living water'; *NEB*, 'fresh water'), i.e., water from a spring or a running stream as opposed to water from a stagnant pool or cistern; a clean person was then required to take some hyssop, dip it into water, and sprinkle it upon the persons and objects which had been contaminated. This ritual was to be performed twice, **on the third day and on the seventh day**; the defiled person was then required to wash his body and his garments, **and at evening he shall be clean** (v. 19). The person who sprinkled the sacred water was also rendered unclean (vv. 21b, 22), but in his case the uncleanness persisted only **until evening** – the shortest possible period for ritual impurity to last (cf. Lev. 11:27f.) – and it could be removed simply by washing **his clothes**.

(g) WATER FROM THE ROCK
20:1–13

This section opens with a report of the death of Miriam (v. 1) and proceeds to record one final incident of rebellion on the part of the Israelites (vv. 2–13). This time, the people complain about the lack of water in the wilderness, and Moses remedies the deficiency by striking the rock with his rod. In doing so, however, both he and Aaron offend against God and, as a punishment, they are prevented from leading the people into the promised land (v. 12). The story clearly falls into the category of the 'aetiological narrative'; it concludes by reporting that the place at which the incident occurred was named Meribah (i.e., 'contention'), for it was here that the people had 'contended with the LORD' (v. 13).

The vocabulary employed in this section, and the ideas contained therein, indicate that it derives in the main from the Priestly writer (cf. Kohata, *AJBI* 3 [1977], pp. 3ff.), though some scholars have noted traces of the older Pentateuchal sources (e.g., in the reference to the death of Miriam in v. 1b; see below). Doubts have been raised, however, concerning the essential unity of the section. Noth (pp. 144ff.), e.g., observed that the narrative in its present form contains some doublets (cf. v. 4 and v. 5; v. 3a and vv. 2b, 3b), and he concluded that two distinct parallel strands could be discerned in vv. 1–13. The presence of two different strands was explained by Noth on the assumption that a later hand had subsequently inserted into the Priestly narrative (which comprised vv. 2, 3b, 4, 6, 7, 8aβbβ, 10, 11b, 12) certain elements of the story contained in Exod. 17:1–7 (cf. Rudolph, pp. 84ff.). Thus v. 3a was inserted into the Priestly account directly from Exod. 17:2aα, and the opening of v. 5 was inserted on the basis of Exod. 17:3*b*α; v. 8*a*α, according to Noth, is merely an abbreviated form of Exod. 17:5*b*, and v. 8*b*α has its origin in Exod. 17:6*a*β*b*. However, Noth's argument is not without its difficulties. In the first place, the presence of doublets in this passage has been seriously challenged, and the verses which have been considered to be doublets may well have formed an integral part of the tradition which P has inherited (cf. Coats, *Rebellion*, pp. 71ff.). Secondly, v. 11*a*, which records the twofold striking of the rock, is not part of the Priestly strand (on Noth's analysis) and yet it has no parallel in Exod. 17:1–7; thus Noth is forced to conclude that v. 11*a* is a redactional addition to the passage. Thirdly, if the 'rod' referred to in the present section was that of Aaron (see on v. 8, below), then this would weaken the thesis that the reference to the rod in v. 8*a*α is derived directly from Exod. 17:5*b* (where the rod in question is clearly that of Moses). On the whole, therefore, the argument that parts of Exod. 17:1–7 have been secondarily inserted into the present section does not appear to be very compelling, and it seems altogether more probable that the Priestly writer himself has amplified and modified the account contained in Exod. 17:1–7 with a view to explaining why Moses and Aaron had been denied the privilege of entering the promised land. *Some* explanation had to be given to account for Moses' failure to enter Canaan, and by introducing into the episode narrated in Exod. 17 the motif of Moses' distrust, the Priestly writer was able to offer just such an explanation: the leaders of the people, like the rest of their generation, had been guilty of the sin of unbelief, and their punishment, likewise, was to die in the wilderness.

1. The Israelites, who had previously been in the wilderness of Paran (10:12; 13:3) are now depicted as arriving at **the wilderness of Zin**. The brief itinerary note in v. 1*a* states that this happened **in the first month**, though the year, surprisingly, is not specified. There is every reason to suppose, however, that a reference to the precise year was included in the original text, for otherwise the words 'in the first month' would be quite meaningless. The year in question would probably have been the fortieth year of the wilderness wanderings, for, according to 33:36–39, the wilderness of Zin was the last stopping-place before Mount Hor, where Aaron died in the fortieth year after the exodus from Egypt. Thus, on P's chronology, it was at the close of the period of the wanderings that the Israelites **stayed in Kadesh**; according to J, on the other hand,

Kadesh had been reached at a very early period of Israel's sojourn in the wilderness (13:26; cf. Porter, *JTS* 44 [1943], pp. 139ff.). It was perhaps in order to avoid such a glaring inconsistency that the redactor of the present passage omitted a reference to the precise year at this point. The mention of the death and burial of Miriam in v. 1*b* is generally thought to derive either from a different source (Gray) or from a later redactor (Sturdy), since Miriam is not otherwise mentioned in P. Some have even suggested that the reference to Kadesh also derived from a non-Priestly source and that an intrinsic connection exists between v. 1*aβ* and v. 1*b*, reflecting a tradition that knew of a grave of Miriam at Kadesh (Noth, Fritz). The insertion of the reference to the death and burial of Miriam at this point may have been precipitated by the account of the death of Aaron in vv. 22ff. For a further discussion of this verse and its significance for the biblical portrait of Miriam, see Burns, *Has the Lord Indeed Spoken . . . ?*, pp. 116ff.

3. The people, distressed by the lack of water (v. 2), reproach Moses for having brought them into the wilderness. The verb used in the Heb., *rîḇ* (*RSV*, 'contended'; *NRSV*, 'quarreled') forms a play on the word Meribah, as is explained in the aetiology of the place name in v. 13. On the forensic background of the root *rîḇ*, see Limburg, *JBL* 88 (1969), pp. 301ff.; Wright, *Fest. Muilenburg*, pp. 26ff. The hardship endured by the people was such that they wished they had suffered the fate of their **brethren** who had **died before the LORD**, a clear reference to the destiny which befell some of the Israelites at the time of Korah's revolt (cf. 16:35, 49; 17:12f.).

6. Moses and Aaron withdraw to the **tent of meeting** to seek Yahweh's guidance, and there **the glory of the LORD** (often suggestive of the divine anger; cf. 14:10; 16:19) appears to them.

8. Take the rod: It is not clear whether the rod was that of Moses, which was used by him to strike the Nile, turning its water into blood (Exod. 7:20), and to divide the sea (Exod. 14:16), or whether the reference is to the rod of Aaron which was placed before the testimony (17:10). The reference to 'his rod' in v. 11 seems to favour the former alternative, whereas the reference in v. 9 to the rod which had been placed 'before the LORD' seems to favour the latter. Those who believe the rod in question was that of Moses are inclined to regard the words 'before the LORD' in v. 9 as an editorial addition to the narrative (so, e.g., Noth); on the other hand, those who believe that the rod was Aaron's are forced to concede that *maṭṭēhû*, 'his rod', in v. 11 is a textual error for *maṭṭeh*, 'rod' (so, e.g., Propp, *JBL* 107 [1988], p. 22). Clearly, much depends upon whether the references to the extraction of water from the rock have been secondarily inserted into P's narrative on the basis of Exod. 17:1–7 (in which case it would be natural to think of the rod as that of Moses) or whether, as seems more probable, the miracle here recorded represents P's own adaptation of the Exodus story (in which case the rod would be Aaron's, since, in P, the rod by which miracles are wrought, is almost always his; cf. Exod. 7:9, 12, 19f.; 8:5, 16). The present form of the narrative leaves the purpose of the rod unexplained, and this has led a few commentators to suggest that some clauses containing directions as to what Moses was to do with it have been accidentally omitted from the text of this verse (McNeile).

10. Hear now, you rebels: Some commentators have observed that these words are not particularly appropriate as an address by Moses and Aaron to the people, since they had not 'rebelled', as such, but had merely contended, or quarrelled, with Moses; consequently, these words are taken as having originally been addressed by Yahweh to Moses and Aaron, who are accused in v. 24 of having 'rebelled against my command at the waters of Meribah' (cf. 27:14; Simpson, *Traditions*, pp. 244f.). But the difficulty with this explanation is that its advocates have to assume that in the original form of the narrative Moses and Aaron had expressed incredulity at the notion that water could emerge from a rock, and that such scepticism on their part was tantamount to a rebellion against Yahweh's command (cf. Cornill, *ZAW* 11 [1891], pp. 20ff.). On the whole, therefore, it seems preferable to preserve these words as an address by Moses and Aaron to the people, and to understand the dissent expressed in vv. 3–5 as a form of rebellion.

12–13. The nature of the transgression committed by Moses and Aaron, which prevented them from entering the promised land, is by no means clear in the text as it stands, and it is, therefore, not surprising that the present episode has been regarded as 'perhaps the most enigmatic incident of the Pentateuch' (Arden, *JBL* 76 [1957], p. 50). Of the various suggestions proposed as to how the two leaders had incurred Yahweh's displeasure, two may briefly be noted here: (i) Moses had been instructed by God merely to speak to the rock (v. 8) but, instead, he had struck it with his rod (v. 11), an act which clearly constituted disobedience to the divine command

(Holzinger, Rudolph); indeed, Moses' insubordination was augmented by the fact that he struck the rock twice, evidently believing that a single stroke was insufficient (Rashi). In favour of this interpretation is the fact that no command to strike the rock is given in v. 8, and in view of the parallel in Exod. 17:6, this omission must have been deliberate, presumably to emphasize the fact that the spoken word was to suffice. On the other hand, the absence of a command to strike the rock in v. 8 may be taken as undermining this interpretation, for if no explicit directions were given as to the use Moses was to make of the rod, it is impossible to deduce whether, in striking the rock, he was obeying or disobeying the divine command. A further difficulty with this interpretation is that Aaron is not represented as striking the rock at all and yet he, too, was regarded as equally culpable and was similarly to be excluded from entering the land of Canaan. On this interpretation, Aaron's punishment has to be justified on the grounds that he was 'guilty by association', and that he had tacitly acquiesced in what Moses was doing (cf. Propp, *op. cit.*, p. 24). (ii) Moses' sin lay in the rhetorical question uttered by him in v. 10, which may be rendered either as 'Can we bring forth water . . . ?', indicating an element of doubt that Yahweh's command could be fulfilled (cf. Targ. Ps. Jon.; G–K § 150*d*), or 'Must we bring forth water . . . ?' (cf. *NEB, NIV*), indicating an element of unwillingness to comply with the divine decree. Alternatively, the phrase may be rendered, 'Shall *we* bring forth water . . . ?', and construed as a claim that it was *they* – Moses and Aaron – who had the power to provide water from the rock; in speaking in such terms, the leaders were effectively usurping Yahweh's prerogative and preventing the full power of the divine will from being manifested to the people (cf. Budd). This interpretation has the advantage of explaining Aaron's exclusion from the land of Canaan, for he would have been included in the 'we' of v. 10, and it is quite in keeping with the explanation of Moses' sin offered in Ps. 106:32f., which suggests that his culpability lay in the 'rash' words which he had uttered. Doubts have been expressed, however, concerning both the above interpretations, primarily because the sin of Moses and Aaron is described as 'unbelief' in v. 12 and as 'rebellion' in v. 24 but (unless a great deal is read between the lines) the narrative as it now stands does not properly bear out either charge. It is therefore supposed that either the author of the passage had been deliberately vague about the sin which had

been committed (cf. Kapelrud, *JBL* 76 [1957], p. 242), or else that
the offence had, indeed, been clearly defined in the original narrative
but had been deliberately obscured in the course of transmission
(cf. Snaith, *NPC*, p. 264); in either case the motivation was to avoid
incriminating Moses and Aaron unduly by dwelling on the precise
nature of their transgression. On the problem of Moses' offence, see,
further, Buis, *VT* 24 (1974), pp. 275ff.; Margaliot, *JQR* 74 (1983),
pp. 196ff.; Sakenfeld, *Fest. Anderson*, pp. 147ff.; Milgrom, *Fest. Mendenhall*, pp. 251ff. It is interesting to observe that in Dt. 1:37f.; 3:26;
4:21 a different reason is given for Moses' exclusion from Canaan,
for here it is the people who offend against Yahweh by refusing to
enter the promised land after hearing the report brought back by
the spies, and Moses is made to bear the guilt for their disobedience
by being refused entry into Canaan. For the theological distinctions
between the Priestly and Deuteronomic explanations of Moses' sin,
see Mann, *JBL* 98 (1979), pp. 481ff. **Because you did not believe
in me, to sanctify me in the eyes of the people of Israel**: Since
the miracle had not been performed in the divinely intended fashion,
Moses had, in effect, compromised the divine holiness, i.e., he had
failed to impress upon the people the holiness of God which mani-
fests itself in his mighty works. The word 'sanctify' (Heb. *qāḏaš*)
provides an intentional play on the name Kadesh just as, in v. 13,
Meribah provides a play on the verb 'contend' (Heb. *rîḇ*), thus
giving the narrative the form of an aetiology. For a discussion of the
OT texts relating to Massah and Meribah, see Propp, *Water*, pp. 51ff.

(C) FROM KADESH TO THE PLAINS OF MOAB
20:14–22:1
(a) ISRAEL'S ENCOUNTER WITH EDOM
20:14–21

Israel, having failed to enter Canaan from the south (cf. 14:45), now
seek permission to cross the territory of Edom so that an attack on
Canaan could be mounted from the east. If the Israelites could
have been granted safe passage through Edom, their journey to
the promised land would have been considerably shortened; in
the event, however, permission was refused (vv. 18, 20), and the
Israelites were forced to make a long circuitous detour round
the southern end of Edom (cf. 21:4) and then northwards along its
eastern border.

The unity of the passage has been questioned by Noth (pp. 149f.), who observes that the messengers sent by Moses speak initially in the singular on behalf of a collective Israel (vv. 14bα), but then speak in the plural on behalf of the Israelites (vv. 14bβff.); further, the address of the messengers seems at first to be directed specifically to the king of Edom (vv. 14–17), but it is evidently the people of Edom as a whole who respond (vv. 18–21). However, such oscillation with regard to the social unit is by no means uncommon in Hebrew narrative (cf. Gray, pp. 265f.; Johnson, *The One and the Many*, pp. 11f.), and Noth himself concedes that these differences could be due to a variation of style or even carelessness in the manner of expression. Of more significance, in Noth's view, is the repetition of the basic content of vv. 17f. in vv. 19f.; he argues that it is inherently improbable that a resumption of negotiations would be reported (vv. 19f.) after the initial request had been so definitively refused (v. 18) and, in any case, Israel's promise to pay for any water which they might consume (v. 19) is hardly consistent with the promise of the people in v. 17 that they would refrain from drinking any water. But, as Budd (p. 223) correctly notes, the differences between vv. 17f. and 19f. are not so sharp as Noth suggests, and there is little reason to regard these verses as doublets. The repetition of Israel's request to Edom, like that of Moses' request to Hobab (10:29–32), may rather be viewed as a natural sequence in the development of the narrative: the point is that the people are now prepared to make a concession by offering payment for any resources which they might use, in the hope that this will be a further inducement for the Edomites to grant them rights of passage (cf. Milgrom). Thus the essential unity of the narrative can be maintained.

Commentators who have regarded vv. 14–21 as a composite text have been inclined to divide the unit between J and E; however, the division of this passage into two different sources has proved far from conclusive, for it has been virtually impossible to decide which parts of the text can be attributed to which source. Thus Binns (p. xxxiii) attributes vv. 19f. to J, but Eissfeldt (*Hexateuch-Synopse*, pp. 178f.) assigns them to E; Baentsch (p. 571) attributes vv. 14–18 to E, while Eissfeldt assigns them to J. It is therefore not surprising that some recent analysts have expressed a reluctance to posit any link between this passage and the older Pentateuchal sources, preferring instead to view it as almost entirely Deuteronomistic in style and redactional in origin (cf. Fritz, pp. 28f.; Mittmann, *Fest. Elliger*, pp. 143ff.; Wüst, *Untersuchungen*, pp. 9ff.). In this regard, much attention has focused on the connection between the present passage and various passages in Deuteronomy, and the verbal correspondence is deemed to be so close that a literary dependence of some kind is often posited (though, cf. Sumner, *VT* 18 [1968], pp. 216ff.). The recapitulation of Israel's history in vv. 14-16 bears some striking similarities to the so-called 'historical credo' contained in Dt. 26:5-9, and Mittmann has argued that vv. 14*b*β-16 is an abbreviated version of the credo found in Deuteronomy. In a similar vein, van Seters (*JBL* 91 [1972], pp. 182ff.) drew attention to the similarity between vv. 17-19 and Dt. 2:27-29, and argued that the present passage should be viewed as the work of a very late redactor working on the text of Deuteronomy; the inconsistencies present in the Numbers account (cf. vv. 17f. and 19f.) arose when an editor tried to modify the narrative in conformity with the version found in Jg. 11:12ff. However, it is by no means certain that the present passage betrays a dependence on Deuteronomy. Carmichael (*VT* 19 [1969], pp. 273ff.), has marshalled arguments in favour of regarding Dt. 26:5-9 as dependent on Num. 20:14-16, and there is much to be said for regarding Dt. 2:27-29 as later than Num. 20:17-19, for all the elements humiliating to Israel (e.g., the ignominious rejection of their request for safe passage) have been removed in the Deuteronomic narrative (cf. Budd, p. 223). The similarities with Dt. may indicate nothing more than that the present passage is 'proto-Deuteronomic' (Budd), and there is no substantive reason why the passage as a whole should not be attributed to J.

Noth (p. 148; *Pentateuchal Traditions*, pp. 206f.) contends that the present passage marks a significant shift in the structure of the Pentateuch, for it is here that the transition is made from the 'wilderness theme' to the 'conquest theme'; however, there is much to be said for the view that the present unit remains a part of the wilderness theme, and that the conquest theme proper begins with the actual crossing of the Jordan (cf. Coats, *JBL* 95 [1976], pp. 177ff.)

14. In order to reach the border of the land of Canaan without undue delay, Moses dispatches messengers to **the king of Edom** requesting a peaceful passage through his territory. The reference to the 'king' of Edom is interesting, for Hebrew tradition recognized that Edom was well in advance of Israel in attaining monarchical government (cf. Gen. 36:31ff.); as a matter of fact, however, it is unlikely that there was any national unity in Edom before the mid-ninth century BC, and it is probable that, prior to the period of Saul and David, Edom's 'kings' were merely rulers who exercised control over various localities within Edom's territory (cf. Bartlett, *JTS*, N.S., 16 [1965], pp. 301ff.; *PEQ* 104 [1972], pp. 26ff.). According to some commentators (cf. Wenham, de Vaulx, Maarsingh), the diplomatic representation made by Moses to the king of Edom conforms closely to oriental scribal practice known from the archives of Mari, Babylon, Alalakh and El-Amarna (cf., e.g., *DOTT*, p. 43; *ANET*, pp. 488f.), for it comprises the following standard features: mention of the recipient (the 'king of Edom'; v. 14); the sender and his rank ('your brother Israel'); the reason for the request ('You know all the adversity etc.'; vv. 14b–16); and, finally, the request itself ('Now let us pass through your land etc.'; v. 17). However, since there are no obvious signs of antiquity in vv. 14–17 (cf. von Rad, *Deuteronomy*, p. 41), the parallels may be no more than a matter of coincidence, and it is quite improbable that the author deliberately intended to portray Moses as observing the niceties of ancient Near Eastern diplomatic protocol. The opening words of Moses' request (**'Thus says your brother Israel . . .'**) discloses the close connection which existed between the Edomites and the Israelites, a connection which also finds expression in the patriarchal traditions, where Edom is identified with Esau, the twin brother of Jacob (= Israel; cf. Gen. 25:23–26). For an examination of the *OT* references to Edom's 'brotherhood', cf. Bartlett, *JTS*, N.S., 20 (1969), pp. 12ff. Traditionally regarded as rivals from birth, relations between the two peoples reached a particularly low ebb during and after the exile, when Edom succeeded in gaining territory at the expense of Judah (cf. Obadiah). **You know all the adversity that has befallen us**: Given that Edom was Israel's 'brother', the recital of the sufferings and hardships endured by the embattled Israelites might be expected to engender in the Edomites a display of pity and sympathy; in the event, however, Moses' overtures proved futile, for his request was met with a brusque refusal (v. 18).

15–16. These verses recall, in summary form, how God had brought Israel out of the land of Egypt and as far as Kadesh; similar recapitulations of Israel's history are found in Dt. 26:5–9; Jos. 24:2–13. Kadesh is described as **a city on the edge of your territory**, which implies that the land occupied by the Edomites at this time extended to both sides of the Arabah. Noth (p. 151), however,

regards the statement concerning the geographical location of
Kadesh as of dubious historical value, for (i) Kadesh merely consisted of a cluster of wells, and to describe it as a 'city' would be
something of a misnomer; (ii) Edomite territory did not extend west
of the Arabah either during the period when the present passage
was composed or during the period to which it refers. Noth thus
concludes that the phrase was intended as an explanatory statement
to account for the unmotivated leap from Kadesh to Edom which
is presupposed in the story.

17. An assurance is given that the Israelites would not in any
way violate the land of the Edomites or even drink water from their
wells; rather, the people would keep to the **King's Highway** and
would not deviate **to the right hand or to the left**. The King's
Highway was the regular trade route through Edom which ran in
a north-south direction from Damascus to the Gulf of Akaba.

18. Edom clearly believed that to permit the Israelites to pass
through its territory could, militarily, have proved dangerous, since
they would be left vulnerable to attack; the request was therefore
refused, and the refusal was accompanied by a menacing threat to
repel the potential invaders with armed resistance.

21. so Israel turned away from him: The Israelites, anxious to
avoid direct military conflict, refrained from engaging in battle,
though it is not clear whether they did so for fear of being over-
powered by the Edomites, or out of deference to the kinship that
existed between them. Further, it is unclear why a similar threat
directed against Israel by the Amorites should have led to the commencement of hostilities between the two peoples (cf. 21:23f.).

(b) THE DEATH OF AARON
20:22–29

The Israelites arrive at Mount Hor, where Aaron dies and where
Eleazar, the elder of his two surviving sons, is installed as priest in
his place. The section is clearly linked to the story contained in
vv. 1–13 (cf. v. 24), which suggested that, on account of his com-
plicity in the sin at Meribah, Aaron would not be permitted to enter
the promised land.

The language and content of the passage suggest that it stems
from the Priestly source, and some commentators are prepared to
assign it to Pᵍ (cf. Gray, p. 269). The only doubt concerns v. 22a
which, owing to its reference to Kadesh, is sometimes attributed to

one of the older Pentateuchal sources (Noth, Rudolph). Noth regards vv. 23*aβb*, 24 as later insertions into the passage, but his arguments are not compelling (cf. Budd, p. 227), and the essential unity of the section can be maintained.

22. The Israelites travel from Kadesh and arrive at **Mount Hor**. This mountain has traditionally been identified with Jebel Nabî' Hārûn ('the Mount of the Prophet Aaron'), near Petra, but, although the tradition is as early as Josephus (*Ant.* IV.4.7), it is usually rejected by modern scholars on the grounds that the mountain would thus have been situated in the middle of the territory of Edom, whereas v. 23 specifically states that it was located 'on the border of the land of Edom' (cf. 33:37). Consequently, some have suggested identifying Mount Hor with Jebel Madurah, which was situated on the north-western border of the land of Edom, and this identification is certainly more compatible with the data contained in the present passage. A variant tradition as to the place of Aaron's death is recorded in Dt. 10:6, where it is stated that he died and was buried at Moserah. In 33:31 Moserah (or Moseroth) is located some seven stopping-places *before* Mount Hor (cf. 33:37).

24. gathered to his people: The word rendered 'people' is the plural of *'am* with a suffix, and here, perhaps, it preserves the sense of 'father's kin' (cf. *NEB*). The phrase 'gathered to his people' is used of Abraham (Gen. 25:8), Ishmael (Gen. 25:17), Isaac (Gen. 35:29), Jacob (Gen. 49:33) and Moses (Num. 27:13; 31:2; Dt. 32:50), and it may well at one time have been understood, quite literally, as a reference to the burial of the dead in the family tomb. Archaeological discoveries have shown that a family could continue using the same tomb for several centuries (cf. Smelik, *Writings*, pp. 160f.).

26. Moses is commanded to **strip Aaron of his garments, and put them upon Eleazar his son**. The vestments of the high priest are described in Lev. 8:7–9, and the regulations regarding their transfer from one person to another are contained in Exod. 29:29f. The formality of investing Eleazar with Aaron's robes was a mark of his succession to the high priestly office (cf. Dt. 10:6).

29. all the house of Israel wept for Aaron thirty days: Mourning for the dead in Israel usually lasted seven days (cf. Gen. 50:10), but as a token of special respect for the high priest, the Israelites mourned Aaron for thirty days, the same period as they were later to mourn Moses (Dt. 34:8).

(c) VICTORY AT HORMAH
21:1-3

This short section reports an attack mounted upon the Israelites by the Canaanites of the Negeb. The people of Israel, having lost some of their men as captives (v. 1), vow to Yahweh that if he were to grant them victory they, in turn, would utterly destroy the cities of the enemy (v. 2), placing them under the 'ban' (Heb. *ḥerem*). Israel thereupon fought a successful battle, and an aetiological note at the end of the narrative reports that the place where the victory was achieved was called Hormah (= 'destruction'; v. 3).

It is generally agreed by commentators that this narrative did not originally belong to its present context. In the first place, it breaks the literary connection between the previous chapter and vv. 4ff., for the reference to Mount Hor in v. 4*a* (though probably editorial) links up with the mention of this mountain in 20:22-29. Secondly, the section is geographically misplaced, for in ch. 20 the Israelites were moving south to skirt Edom in order to enter Canaan from the east, but here they are represented as fighting a victorious battle far to the north. It must be concluded, therefore, that the present story probably originally had nothing to do with the attempts (recorded in chs. 20f.) to enter Canaan from the east. The original location of the present unit cannot be ascertained with any certainty, though it is natural to suppose that at one time it was connected with the reports of an attack from the south, such as those reflected in Num. 13f. Whether the present section was originally placed before Num. 13f. (so, e.g., Rudolph, p. 79; Miller, *IJH*, pp. 224f.) or immediately after 14:45 (so, e.g., Baentsch, Holzinger) must remain a matter of conjecture. Why a later editor should have placed the present narrative at this particular juncture in Numbers is a problem which has yet to be satisfactorily resolved. The section is probably the work of the Yahwist, who was determined to preserve a tradition of the defeat of Hormah (cf. Jg. 1:17f.), notwithstanding the fact that it conflicted with his own account of the battle at Hormah as recorded in 14:39-45.

1. When the Canaanite, the king of Arad who dwelt in the Negeb, heard: The words, 'the king of Arad' are widely regarded as a gloss, for (i) the position of these words after the name of the nation is linguistically awkward (cf. Paterson); (ii) since Arad was situated in the Negeb, the words 'who dwelt in the Negeb' would be rendered redundant; (iii) the inclusion of the words 'the king of Arad' naturally leads to the inference that Arad was the place which the Israelites named Hormah (v. 3), but Jos. 12:14 indicates that Arad and Hormah cannot be identified with one another. It is possible that the close juxtaposition of 'the king of Hormah' with 'the king of Arad' in Jos. 12:14 led the redactor to insert 'the king of Arad' at this point (cf. Sturdy; Fritz, *ZDPV* 82 [1966], p. 341). The term *hakkᵉnaʿᵃnî* ('the Canaanite') should probably here be regarded as a collective noun, in which case the clause would originally have read, 'When the Canaanites who dwelt in the Negeb heard etc.' (cf. 14:25, 45). Arad is usually identified with Tell Arad, which was approx. 17 miles (27 km.) south of Hebron and 50 miles (80 km.) north of Kadesh. Excavations at Arad (cf. Aharoni and Amiran, *EAEHL*, i, pp. 74ff.) have shown that it was a city of some importance in the Early Bronze Age and during the period of the Israelite monarchy; indeed, in the days of Solomon, it appears to have been a well-fortified settlement which contained a sanctuary to Yahweh (cf. Aharoni, *IEJ* 17 [1967], pp. 247ff.). However, since no remains of the city have been found dating from the Middle and Late Bronze Ages, it has been suggested that Arad should either be regarded as a district, with Hormah as its capital (cf. Mazar, *JNES* 24 [1965], pp. 297ff.), or that it should be identified not with Tell Arad, but with Tell el-Milḥ, some 7 miles (11 km.) to the southwest, a location which *does* appear to have contained Middle Bronze Age fortifications (cf. Aharoni, *BA* 31 [1968], p. 31). The Canaanites heard that Israel was advancing **by the way of Atharim**; *AV* has 'the way of the spies', and this follows the interpretation of Atharim adopted by most of the early Vsns (except LXX), which understood the name to be an alternative spelling of *tārîm*, 'spies'. However, there is no philological connection between the two words, and it is therefore preferable to follow *RSV*, *NEB* in regarding Atharim as a place name. Snaith (p. 279) suggests that Atharim (a site not otherwise mentioned in the *OT*) is to be identified with Tamar or Hazazon-tamar in the Arabah, in which case the 'way of Atharim' would be a road which went up to Arad from south of the Dead Sea; Aharoni, on the other hand, traces a route from Kadesh to Arad, which was marked at a later stage by small forts during the Iron Age (*IEJ* 17 [1967], p. 11).

2–3. I will utterly destroy their cities: These words take the form of a vow, probably uttered during a military campaign, immediately before battle, and it was tacitly assumed that the vow would be fulfilled as soon as the condition had been met (cf. Parker, *UF* 11 [1979], pp. 696f.). The causative of the verb *ḥāram*, 'to utterly destroy', is linked in v. 3 to the place-name **Hormah**. The Heb. verb *ḥāram*, which means 'to exterminate, ban', refers to the ancient Israelite custom of destroying all the captives and all the booty taken in battle, and consecrating them to Yahweh, in recognition of the fact that he was the real victor of the war (cf. Dt. 7:2; 20:17; Jos. 10:28; see, also, on 18:14). In view of the reference to the destruction of 'their cities' in v. 2, Gray (pp. 273f.) suggests that Hormah was a name given to a district rather than a town; however, no such region is attested elsewhere, and it is thus preferable to regard Hormah as a reference to a specific town, as in other *OT* texts where the name occurs (cf. Jos. 12:14; 15:30; 19:4; Jg. 1:17; 1 Sam. 30:30; 1 Chr. 4:30). For the various possible identifications of Hormah, see on 14:45.

(d) THE BRONZE SERPENT
21:4–9

The Israelites once more complain to Moses (cf. 14:2f.; 20:3–5), this time on account of the lack of water in the wilderness and the 'worthless food' which they were being given to eat (v. 5). As a punishment for their ingratitude, Yahweh sends among them a plague of 'fiery serpents' and, infected by their poisonous bites, many of the people die (v. 6). The Israelites implore Moses to intercede on their behalf, and he complies with their request (v. 7). Yahweh thereupon instructs him to make a model of a serpent and set it up on a pole, so that those who gazed upon it could be healed of their affliction (v. 8). The narrative concludes by stating that Moses obeyed Yahweh's command, and constructed a serpent of bronze. The story was one which later readily lent itself to allegorical interpretation; cf. Wisd. 16:6f.; Jn 3:14; Philo, *de Alleg.*, ii.20; *de Agricul.*, 22. For a thorough discussion of the text and its exposition in Hellenistic Jewish literature, early rabbinic midrash, the Targumim and early Christian writers, see Maneschg, *Erzählung, passim*.

Apart from the itinerary note in v. 4a (which provides a redactional link with 20:22–29), the familiar features of P are entirely absent in the present narrative. Earlier analysts tended to assign the passage to E, partly because of its connection with 20:14–21 (which they attributed to the Elohist), and partly because of the occurrence of the word Elohim in v. 5 (cf. Holzinger, Baentsch). But the attribution of 20:14–21 to E is very questionable (see above, pp. 207f.) and, in any case, the connection of the present passage with 20:14–21 is tenuous and arises primarily from the redactional link in v. 4a (cf. Coats, *Rebellion*, p. 116). Moreover, although the term Elohim occurs in v. 5, this is outweighed by the more frequent references to Yahweh in the remainder of the passage. The designation of the people by the term *hā'ām*, and the reference to Moses functioning alone (i.e., without Aaron), suggest that the present passage should be attributed to J. This finds some confirmation in the similarity between the structure of the present passage and that encountered in 11:1–3 (= J; cf. Fritz, p. 93; Budd, pp. 233, 235). In both narratives, the people complain of their misfortune (11:1a; cf. 21:5) and are punished by Yahweh (11:1b; cf. 21:6); they turn, in desperation, to Moses, who prays to Yahweh on their behalf (11:2a; cf. 21:7), and, as a result of his intercession, the calamity ceases (11:2b; cf. 21:8f.). Although there is considerable alternation in the terminology deployed in the present section (cf. 'fiery serpents', v. 6; 'serpents', v. 7; 'fiery [serpent]', v. 8; 'bronze serpent', v. 9), there is no reason to suppose that more than one source is here in evidence (cf. Noth, p. 156; *ZAW* 58 [1940–1], p. 178).

The interpretation of this episode must take as its starting-point the account in 2 Kg. 18:1ff. of the bronze serpent (called Nehushtan) destroyed by Hezekiah, for in 2 Kg. 18:4 this cult object is expressly identified with the serpent made by Moses on this occasion. According to 2 Kg. 18:4, this serpent had become an object of idolatrous worship for the Israelites, and the emblem was demolished by Hezekiah, since he regarded it as incompatible with the true spirit of the Yahwistic faith. Rowley (*JBL* 58 [1939], pp. 113ff.) has plausibly argued that this bronze serpent was probably of Canaanite origin, and that it was part of the Jebusite cult which was in Jerusalem before David captured the city. The fact that this bronze serpent was (presumably) housed in the temple up to the time of Hezekiah obviously called for some explanation, and the present story functioned, in effect, as an aetiology designed to legitimate its presence there by associating its original construction with Moses.

The cult of the serpent appears to have been widespread in ancient times, not least in Palestine, for bronze serpent images have been discovered at various sites, including Gezer, Hazor, Megiddo and Beth-shemesh (cf. Joines, *JBL* 87 [1968], pp. 245ff.; *Serpent Symbolism*, pp. 62ff.; Jaroš, *Die Stellung*, p. 270). Moreover, an oblique reference to the notion that serpents were once regarded as sacred in Israel has been found in the allusion to the 'Serpent's Stone' in 1 Kg. 1:9 (cf. Rowley, *op. cit.*, p. 137). Joines (*Serpent Symbolism*, p. 91) argues that in ancient Egypt the emblem of the serpent had an apotropaic significance, designed to ward off evil spirits, while in Canaan and Mesopotamia it was primarily a symbol of fertility. In the present narrative, however, the serpent appears as a symbol of healing and protection, and some commentators have drawn attention to the connection between serpents and the preservation (or restoration) of life in pagan mythology, the most celebrated example being the Greek god Asklepios, who assumed the form of a serpent in healing dreams (cf. Binns, Gray).

4. The Israelites set out **by the way to the Red Sea** (see on 14:25) and, not for the first time, they **became impatient on the way**: Heb. reads, lit., 'the soul (*nepeš*) of the people was short', an idiom used elsewhere, too, in the *OT* to express 'impatience' (cf. Jg. 16:16; Zech. 11:8). Perhaps 'short-tempered' captures the meaning of the Heb. in the present context. For the use of the term *nepeš* to express various emotions, see Wolff, *Anthropology*, pp. 17f., and for a study of the idiom *qṣr nepeš* in the *OT*, see Haak, *JBL* 101 (1982), pp. 161ff. The reason for the peoples' impatience ostensibly appears to be the long, protracted detour which they were forced to make **around the land of Edom**; however, since v. 4*a* is probably a redactional addition, it is preferable to understand their impetuosity in connection with the complaint which they utter in v. 5 concerning the frugal life which they were forced to endure in the barren wilderness (cf. Coats, *Rebellion*, p. 119).

5. And the people spoke against God and against Moses: That the murmuring should be directed against both God and Moses is unusual; normally, the complaint is levelled specifically against one (14:27, 29, 35; 16:11; 17:17; 27:3; Exod. 16:7f.) or the other (cf. 14:36; Exod. 15:24; 17:3). LXX understands the present clause to mean that the people spoke to God against Moses, and it takes the verb in the accusation (**'Why have you brought us up out of Egypt?'**), to be singular (cf. Syr., Sam.), as does the consonantal text of the Heb.; in MT the verb is written defectively. **We loathe this worthless** (*NRSV*, 'miserable') **food**: This was clearly intended as a disparaging reference to the manna which Yahweh had provided for the sustenance of the people in the wilderness (cf. 11:6).

The adjective rendered 'worthless', *qᵉlōqēl*, occurs only here in the *OT*, but the root from which it probably derives, *qll* ('to be slight, swift, trifling') is common enough (*BDB*, p. 886). *qālal* may originally have meant 'to be light', hence *AV*'s rendering, 'this light bread'; but the reference to the manna in the present context was clearly intended to be critical, not complimentary, and since *qālal* is used in the *OT* of 'treating with contempt' (cf. 2 Sam. 19:43 [MT 19:44]; Isa. 23:9; Ezek. 22:7), such renderings as 'worthless', 'miserable' or 'contemptible' seem altogether more appropriate here. The term *nepeš* occurs here, too (cf. v. 4), this time as the subject of the verb *qûs*, 'to loathe' (lit., 'our *nepeš* loathes this worthless food'); for the *nepeš* as the organ which feels hunger and thirst and experiences taste, cf. Prov. 16:24; 25:25; 27:7; Wolff, *op. cit.*, pp. 12f.

6. Yahweh's response to the people's complaint is to dispatch among them a plague of **fiery serpents**. The adjective here rendered 'fiery' (*śᵉrāpîm*) is usually derived from the verb *śārap* 'to burn', and it is taken to refer to the burning sensation caused by the poisonous bite of the serpent (cf. *NIV*, 'venomous snakes'; *NEB*, 'poisonous snakes'; *NRSV*, 'poisonous serpents'). Some commentators object to this interpretation on the ground that the adjective 'fiery' here does not describe the bite of the serpent (much less the effect of the bite), but is rather illustrative of the serpent itself, which may have been conceived as 'fiery' in appearance (cf. Coats, *Rebellion*, p. 117, n. 51). But, although fire-breathing serpents appear to have been known in ancient Egypt (cf. Joines, *Serpent Symbolism*, pp. 44f.), it is improbable that the author of the present passage regarded the wilderness serpents as such, and LXX's rendering of *śᵉrāpîm* as 'deadly' supports the view that the word here refers to the baneful effect of the serpent's bite. Attention has frequently been drawn to the similarity between the adjective used here, *śᵉrāpîm*, and the 'seraphim' (Heb. *śᵉrāpîm*) which appeared in Isaiah's vision (cf. Isa. 6:2, 6), but the connection is by no means clear, for in Isaiah the seraphim are depicted as having 'hands' and 'feet', and appear to be human rather than serpentine in form. On the winged serpents of Isaiah's vision, see Joines, *JBL* 86 (1967), pp. 410ff.; *Serpent Symbolism*, pp. 42ff.

7. We have sinned: The confession by the people, reminiscent of that made by Aaron and Miriam in 12:11, paves the way for an intercession on the part of Moses. On Moses' role as intercessor, see Aurelius, *Fürbitter*; Scharbert, *Heilsmittler*, pp. 81ff.

9. So Moses made a bronze serpent: Bronze is an alloy of copper and tin, and is well-attested in ancient times; however, although *nᵉḥōšeṯ* undoubtedly means 'bronze' in some *OT* passages (cf. 1 Sam. 17:5f.; 1 Kg. 4:13), it has been suggested that in the present context the reference is to unalloyed copper (cf. Gray, Wenham). For the notion that the power of dangerous creatures could be annulled by making an image of them, cf. 1 Sam. 6:4f. Similar analogies from elsewhere are noted by Gray, p. 276.

(e) THE JOURNEY TO MOAB
21:10–20

The people continue their journey by stages until they reach 'the top of Pisgah which looks down upon the desert' (v. 20). The passage is constructed as an itinerary into which has been inserted, in vv. 14f., 17f., two fragments of archaic poetry, the first deriving from an otherwise unknown source referred to as the 'Book of the Wars of the LORD' (v. 14*a*). Several of the places mentioned in the itinerary can no longer be identified with any certainty, and the list of stopping-places contains certain geographical problems, though these are probably due to the fact that the section, in its present form, is composed of a variety of different sources. But precisely which sources are here in evidence is by no means clear. Most commentators tend to assign vv. 10–11*a* to P, since the names contained in these verses (Oboth and Iye-abarim) recur in the itinerary contained in ch. 33, which is generally regarded as deriving from the Priestly writer. As regards the rest of the passage, however, no consensus has emerged. Some earlier analysts viewed it as deriving predominantly from E (Baentsch, Holzinger), while more recent commentators, such as Budd, have contended that it should be attributed to J. Something of an intermediate position is represented by Gray, who derives vv. 11*b*–13 from E and vv. 16, 18*b*–20 from J. The itinerary contained in vv. 10–20 is by no means consistent in its literary form (cf. Walsh, *CBQ* 39 [1977], pp. 26f.), and the sequence of stations listed is not (as far as can be ascertained) geographically plausible; indeed, vv. 10–13 have been described as a 'geographical hodgepodge totally incomprehensible in terms of the geographical realities of southern Transjordan' (Miller, *JBL* 108 [1989], p. 587). Thus, there is much to be said for Noth's view (pp. 158f.; *ZAW* 58 [1940], pp. 170ff.) that the present passage is basically a compilation of diverse *OT* texts of mixed origin (vv. 10–12 based on 33:43*b*–44; Jg. 11:18; Dt. 2:13; and vv. 18*b*–20 based

on 22:41; 23:14, 28; Dt. 3:29; 34:6), and that it was given the form
of a fictitious itinerary. If this is so, then vv. 10–20 cannot be
regarded as a description of a real route taken by the Israelites;
rather, it is a very late composition, partly invented and partly
borrowed from various sources, and inserted here by an editor in
order to fill the gap left between the episode of the bronze serpent
(vv. 4–9) and the encounter with Sihon and Og (vv. 21–35).

10–11. For **Oboth** and **Iye-abarim**, see on 33:43f. Whether
vv. 10–11*a* have been borrowed from 33:43*b*–44 or whether the
editor of Num. 33 borrowed from 21:10–11*a* is disputed, but since
vv. 43f. are fairly well integrated in ch. 33 whereas vv. 10–11*a* are
geographically misplaced in the present section, the former possibility seems more likely. **in the wilderness which is opposite Moab,
toward the sunrise**: Davies (*VT* 33 [1983], pp. 10f.) suggests that
these words are a later addition, based on Jg. 11:18, and intended
to harmonize the conflicting traditions that represented Israel on
the one hand as passing straight through Edomite territory (vv. 10,
11*a*; cf. 33:45f.) and on the other as making a detour around these
lands (v. 13; cf. Jg. 11:18).

12. The Israelites proceed on their journey and encamp in the
Valley of Zered. This place is mentioned elsewhere only in Dt.
2:13f., and it is usually identified with the Wadi el-ḥesa, which flows
into the south-eastern end of the Dead Sea. If this identification is
correct, then the mention of the Valley of Zered is quite out of place
in the present context. Some commentators, aware that the allusions
to Oboth and Iye-abarim in vv. 10f. would demand for the Valley
of Zered a location further north, have suggested identifying it with
the Wadi el-Franji or the Seil Sʿaideh, a branch of the Arnon (cf.
Binns); but since the passage is probably merely an accumulation
of references culled from various *OT* sources (see above), it seems
invidious to try to locate Zered on the basis of the reference to Oboth
and Iye-abarim in the previous verses. It might be added that even
if the traditional source-critical analysis of the present passage
is adopted, it cannot automatically be assumed that the editor
was sufficiently familiar with the topography of the district to
place Oboth and Iye-abarim in their correct position in the
itinerary.

13. The Israelites set out from the Valley of Zered and encamp
on the other side of the Arnon: From the standpoint of the settled
Israelites, the 'other side' of the Arnon (modern Wadi el-Mojib)

would denote its southern side but, interpreted from the point of view of those engaged in the march (cf. Jg. 11:18), it would designate its northern side. **which is in the wilderness**: This clause was probably intended to define more precisely one of the many streams of the great wadi. In Dt. 2:26 the wilderness in question is named Kedemoth. **for the Arnon is the boundary of Moab**: The Arnon at this time formed the northern border of Moab; according to v. 26 (cf. Jg. 11:22) the Moabites, at the time of the Israelite invasion, had been forced south of the Arnon by the Amorites. According to the Mesha Inscription (cf. *DOTT*, pp. 195–8), the Arnon formed the northern boundary of Moab at the time of Omri, but the inscription also notes that, prior to Omri's reign, Moabite territory extended to the north of the Arnon, as it did again in the time of Mesha.

14–15. At this point in the itinerary, a fragment of poetry has been inserted, presumably in order to corroborate the statement that the Arnon was, indeed, the border of Moab. The fragment was evidently a quotation from **the Book of the Wars of the LORD**. This book is not referred to elsewhere, but its title suggests that it contained an anthology of war poems, presumably dealing with the conflict between the invading Israelites and the original inhabitants of Canaan. The date of the book cannot be determined, but there is a general consensus that it is early. A similar collection of songs was preserved in the Book of Jashar (cf. Jos. 10:13), which contained (among other poems) David's lament over Saul and Jonathan (2 Sam. 1:18). It is most regrettable that only a few damaged lines from the Book of the Wars of the LORD have survived, the words quoted here being a mere fragment without any beginning or ending. Tur-Sinai (*BIES* 24 [1959–60], pp. 146ff.) expressed doubts as to whether a book of this title ever existed, and he proposed reading v. 14a as 'Hence it is written in the book: there were wars of Yahweh . . .', but this rendering of the verse has not generally been followed by commentators. The variations in the renderings of vv. 14b, 15 found in the Vsns, both ancient and modern, attest to the difficulties inherent in the Heb. text. Albright (*Yahweh*, p. 44) regards the passage as hopelessely corrupt, and Noth (p. 160) claims that the text is so obscure as to defy all explanation. **Waheb in Suphah**: *AV* follows Vulg. (which is, in turn, dependent on the Targum), and reads, 'what he did in the Red sea, and in the brooks of Arnon'. This involves understanding *wāhēb* as the rare Heb. root *yḥb* (common in Aram., Syr., Arab.), and *bᵉsûpāh* as the equivalent of *bᵉ(yam)sûp*. LXX reads, 'he has set Zoob on fire and the torrents of the Arnon', which involves reading the root *zḥb* for *wḥb*, and taking *sûpāh* as deriving from the root *spp* (= 'to burn', Aram.). There is much to be said, however, for regarding Waheb and Suphah as two place names, the former, presumably, a town, and the latter the district in which it was located. Neither place is mentioned elsewhere in the *OT*, although some commentators suggest that Suphah may be identical with the obscure Suph mentioned in Dt. 1:1. In the original song, Waheb must have been governed by a verb, perhaps relating that the Israelites 'passed through' or 'captured' the town (cf. Gray). Christensen (*CBQ* 36 [1974], pp. 359f.) reconstructs the text in such a way as to make Yahweh the subject of the various clauses (e.g., *'eṯ-wāhēḇ* is emended to read *'āṯā yhwh*, 'the LORD came'), but such a reconstruction, though favoured by some recent commentators (e.g., Wenham, Budd, Milgrom), must remain hypothetical. *NEB* regards the two place names as part of the prose text, but it is preferable to regard them as (part of) the first line of the poem, with *RSV, NIV*. **and the slope of the valleys**: The Heb. *'ešeḏ* ('slope') occurs only here in the singular; the term (in the plural) is usually applied to the 'slopes of Pisgah', overlooking the Dead Sea (cf. Dt. 3:17; 4:49; Jos. 12:3; 13:20). The precise meaning of *'ešeḏ* is uncertain, for the root in Heb. occurs only in this one word. Snaith (p. 282) suggests it means 'watershed' (cf. *NEB*); Gray, on the other hand, prefers to render the word here as 'cliff' (p. 286; cf. McNeile). **that extends to the seat of Ar**: 'Seat' (Heb. *šeḇeṯ*) here is a poetical expression for 'site' (cf. *NIV*). Ar was an important city in Moab (cf. Isa. 15:1), and it may have been its capital; it was situated in the valley of the Arnon (see on 22:36), but its exact site is uncertain. For various suggestions as to its location, see Miller, *JBL* 108 (1989), pp. 592ff., and for the view that Ar was not, in fact, a town, but a region, see Simons, *Texts*, p. 435.

16. The itinerary resumes here by reporting that the Israelites continued on their journey to **Beer**. The name means 'well' (*RSV* mg.) or 'water-hole' (*NEB* mg.), and some commentators have suggested that the word may be an abbreviated form of a compound name (cf. Beer-sheba). A place named Beer-elim in Moab is mentioned in Isa. 15:8, although it is by no means certain whether it is to be identified with the Beer of the present verse. Be that as it may, the mention of Beer here provides the occasion for the citation of another poem (vv. 17*b*, 18), sometimes referred to as 'the song of the well'.

17–18. This short poem may originally have been a work-song, traditionally sung by workers during the digging of a well (cf. Eissfeldt, *Introduction*, p. 88). But if this was, indeed, its origin, the reference to the participation of the **princes** and **nobles** is, to say the least, unexpected, since it is most unlikely that the leaders of the nation would have been engaged in such a laborious activity; moreover, the instruments which they carried (the **sceptre** and **staves**) can hardly have been regarded as suitable implements for digging a well. It has therefore been suggested that the song contains a relic of an ancient custom whereby, when water was discovered in the desert, there was a formal opening of the well by certain dignitaries, who accomplished the duty by means of a symbolic gesture using a sceptre or stave (Budde, *New World* 4 [1895], pp. 136ff.). Certainly, the discovery in a parched land of an underground water-supply would have been a cause of great rejoicing, and may well have given rise to a song such as this. Noth (p. 160), on the other hand, takes the sceptre and stave here as symbols of authority, and suggests that the well was dug under the supervision of the chiefs and with their blessing. In a similar vein, Budd (p. 239) suggests that the leaders were present to indicate where the digging should be carried out, perhaps using the sceptre and stave in some divinatory procedure. But whatever the precise occasion which gave rise to the poem, it was probably of quite ancient origin, since it contains some characteristic features of early Heb. poetic style (cf. Freedman, *ZAW*, N.F., 31 [1960], pp. 105f.). **And from the wilderness they went on to Mattanah**: In MT these words are part of the song, and they are thus understood in *NEB*, which reads 'a gift [understanding *mattānāh* as a common noun; cf. Gen. 25:6] from the wilderness' (cf. Budde, Baentsch). The difficulty with this rendering, however, is that it involves omitting the *waw* before 'wilderness' and (following the hint of LXX^L) reading Beer instead of Mattanah in v. 19. Of course, the rendering of *RSV* is not entirely free of difficulty, for to state that the Israelites moved 'from the wilderness' to Mattanah seems odd at this point in the itinerary, given that the people had already left the wilderness (v. 13) when they moved to Beer (v. 16). It was this difficulty that no doubt led the translators of LXX to read 'And from Beer to Mattanah' at the end of v. 18. LXX is undoubtedly the easier reading, providing a smooth continuity in the itinerary, but MT should be retained on the principle of *lectio difficilior*. The location of Mattanah is unknown, but it has tentatively been identified with Khirbet el-Mudeiniyeh, about 11 miles (18 km.) northeast of Dibon; cf. Simons, *Texts*, p. 262; Glueck, *AASOR* 14 (1933–4), pp. 13ff. Targ. Onk. and Targ. Ps. Jon. at this point contain a legend according to which the well followed the itinerant Israelites on their journey over hill and dale; it is, perhaps, this legend that is referred to in 1 C. 10:4.

19. The next stopping-place on the journey was **Nahaliel**. The name means 'God's wadi', but its location is uncertain. One possibility is that it is to be identified with the Wadi Zerqa Main, which flows into the Dead Sea about mid-way between its northern end and the mouth of the Arnon (so Davies, *Way*, p. 92).

20. From Nahaliel the people journeyed to **Bamoth**. The name means 'high places', but these were so numerous in the hilly land of Moab that the exact location of this stopping-place cannot safely be identified. Bamoth may be an abbreviation of a compound name, in which case it may be the same place as Bamoth-baal (mentioned in 22:41; Jos. 13:17) and Beth-bamoth referred to in the Mesha Inscription. Snaith (p. 282) suggests that Bamoth may be identified with modern Khirbet el-Quweiqiyeh, 5 miles (8 km.) north of Dibon. From Bamoth, the route took the Israelites to **the valley lying in the region of Moab by the top of Pisgah**: The expressions 'in the region of Moab' and 'by the top of Pisgah' are placed rather awkwardly in apposition, and this perhaps justifies the suspicion that the latter is a scribal gloss, inserted to limit the rather wide definition of the district (cf. Gray). Certainly, the text as it stands seems somewhat ambiguous and overburdened. The 'valley' referred to may be the Wadi 'Ayûn Mûsā, which runs into the Jordan valley about 4 miles (6 km.) north of the northern end of the Dead Sea (cf. Simons, *Texts*, pp. 262f.). **Pisgah** seems to have been a collective term for the projections or promontories of the Moabite plateau which jut out towards the Dead Sea, giving a wide view of the land of Canaan across the water (cf. 23:14; Dt. 3:27; 34:1). Here, Pisgah is described as looking down **upon the desert**, i.e., the arid region to the northwest of the Dead Sea. The word here rendered 'desert', *yᵉšīmōn*, is often applied to the desolate country on the opposite side of the Dead Sea (cf. 1 Sam. 23:19, 24; 26:1, 3), but here (and in

23:28) it is used of the eastern side. With the article, the noun
sometimes appears virtually as a specific geographical location, and
it is thus understood here in *REB*.

(f) THE DEFEAT OF SIHON AND OG
21:21—22:1

The narrative contained in this section explains what happened
when the Israelites arrived at the border of the Amorite kingdom.
A message was sent to Sihon, king of the Amorites, requesting permission to march through his country. The message was similar in
content to that sent to the king of Edom (20:14ff.) and, as on that
occasion, the request was refused. This time, however, instead of
withdrawing and proceeding along another route, the Israelites
engaged in battle with the Amorites, and inflicted a crushing defeat
upon them at Jahaz. Having secured their victory, the Israelites
were able to occupy the land, including Heshbon, the chief city of
the Amorite kingdom. Further advance brought them into conflict
with Og, king of Bashan, and he, too, was defeated at Edrei (vv. 33–
35). Since the battles against Sihon and Og represented the last
serious obstacles Israel had to face before entering the promised
land, the recollection of these events was especially cherished by
later Hebrew writers, and the victory achieved was regarded as one
of the great feats accomplished in the days of old (cf. Jg. 11:19ff.;
Neh. 9:22; Ps. 135:8ff.; 136:19f.).

In discussing the composition of this passage, it will be convenient
to begin with vv. 33–35. Vv. 33f. are almost identical in wording
with Dt. 3:1f., the only difference being the substitution of the first
person of Moses' speech in Deuteronomy for the third person of the
narrative in Numbers. Commentators have generally recognized
that the present passage represents a secondary insertion derived
from Deuteronomy, for (i) several of the expressions common to the
two passages (e.g., 'Do not fear him; for I have given him into your
hand', v. 34) are characteristic of the Deuteronomist but quite alien
to the style of the older Pentateuchal sources; (ii) 22:2 refers to the
victory over the Amorites but omits any reference to the defeat of
Og; (iii) the final clause of v. 35, 'and they possessed his land', is
best understood as a summary of the account of the capture of the
cities and plunder recorded in Dt. 3:4ff. The material from
Deuteronomy was probably introduced at this point to supply what
was evidently regarded as an omission in the narrative. Sam. con-

tains many examples of the incorporation of material from Deuteronomy in Numbers, and the present passage may be viewed as an earlier instance of this tendency manifested in the Heb. text itself.

With regard to vv. 21–32, commentators have tended to assign them to one of the older Pentateuchal sources, although there has been no consensus as to which source is primarily in evidence. Some scholars (e.g., Noth) have argued that the base narrative was essentially E, while others (e.g., Rudolph) have contended that it was J. This uncertainty has served to fuel doubts among some recent scholars as to whether a source critical analysis along traditional lines is appropriate in this instance, and the acknowledged similarity between vv. 33–35 and Dt. 3:1ff. has led them to wonder whether the entire section (vv. 21–35) should not be viewed as the work of a redactor who made use of Deuteronomy (among other sources) in constructing his narrative. The original independence of the song contained in vv. 27–30 was, of course, regarded as axiomatic. As for the rest of the section, v. 32 was viewed as a redactional gloss, inserted in anticipation of the settlement of Reuben and Gad recorded in 32:1; vv. 26, 31 were regarded as transitional passages designed to incorporate the song of vv. 27–30 into its present context; the remainder of the unit (vv. 21–25) was considered to be a typically Deuteronomistic composition. Van Seters (*JBL* 91 [1972], pp. 182ff.), e.g., observed that virtually the whole of vv. 21–25 is found in Dt. 2:26–37, though the Numbers version was patently much shorter. Only the 'messenger speech' in v. 22 and the reference to Israel's settlement in v. 25 departed significantly from Deuteronomy; as for the remainder, the two versions were so close in content and wording that either one had to be dependent upon the other, or both must have been derived from a common literary tradition. Van Seters also brought Jg. 11:19–26 into the discussion, for this, too, exhibits many parallels with the present section and, significantly, on each point where the Judges account departs from Deuteronomy, Numbers departs from Deuteronomy in the same way. E.g., in Deuteronomy, Moses is the subject of the conquest story, but in Judges the subject is Israel, and it is the Judges version that is followed in Numbers. Since the Judges passage is characteristic of the Deuteronomistic editor's presentation elsewhere, it is improbable that the Judges account is dependent on Numbers; rather, Num. 21:21–35 appears to be the result of the accounts contained in Dt. 2:26–37 and Jg. 11:19–26.

Despite the arguments advanced by van Seters, however, the balance of probability must favour the priority of the present passage. The fact that 21:21–35 does not mention Moses, God or divine intervention suggests not that Numbers has removed common Deuteronomic traits, but that Deuteronomy has used the material from Numbers and imbued it with its own characteristic emphases. Moreover, van Seters' opinion that the use of 'Israel' in the Numbers passage represents a striking inconsistency with its context and must therefore have been derived from Jg. 11 has been successfully refuted by Bartlett (*JBL* 97 [1978], p. 348; though cf. van Seters' rejoinder in *JBL* 99 [1980], pp. 117ff.). Further, van Seters' contention that 21:23f. is similar to battle accounts found in Neo-Babylonian chronicles, and should therefore be regarded as a late composition, has been seriously challenged by Gunn (*JBL* 93 [1974], pp. 513ff.; though cf. van Seters' rejoinder in *Semeia* 5 [1976], pp. 139ff.). Thus it is probable that the Deuteronomic account is a development of that contained in Num. 21:21–32, and the Numbers passage probably also furnished the source of the account found in Jg. 11:19–26. The development of the tradition contained in 21:21–35 may be summarized as follows: the Deuteronomist took up the Sihon story from Num. 21:21–32; he then formulated his own account of the conquest of Og, following the same pattern; this latter story was then taken up and incorporated in Num. 21:33–35.

Any discussion of the literary source of the account contained in 21:21–32 must inevitably take into consideration the striking similarity between certain parts of this passage and the narrative contained in 20:14–21. Mittmann (*Fest. Elliger*, pp. 143ff.) argued that the latter was the work of a late redactor who based his composition partly on the Sihon story contained in 21:21–23 (which he attributed to E) and partly on the 'historical credo' contained in Dt. 26:5–9; the resulting composition became the starting point for the developing tradition found in Dt. 2:4–6, 8a and Jg. 11:17. However, there is much to be said for regarding 20:14–21 and 21:21–23 as the product of a single author (cf. Budd, p. 223), and in view of the probable attribution of the former passage to J (see above, pp. 207f.) it is natural to suppose that the present passage is also essentially the work of the Yahwist. V. 31 may be regarded as J's own summary of the preceding material, but v. 32 probably represents a later editorial addition, possibly prompted by the reference to Jazer in v. 24b (cf. Budd, pp. 244, 247).

The narrative was clearly intended to justify Israel's occupation of territory claimed at various times by Moab, and, in view of its apologetic intent, it is perhaps inevitable that the question of its historicity has been raised. Miller, e.g., suggests that the notion that Israel managed to gain full and immediate possession of central and northern Transjordan in the manner here described is probably entirely fanciful or, at least, a gross exaggeration of what actually occurred (*IJH*, p. 227). In a similar vein, van Seters contends that these accounts must be regarded 'with grave suspicion', and he argues that their highly ideological character renders them 'historically untrustworthy' (*JBL* 91 [1972], p. 197). Mendenhall, on the other hand, sought to defend the historicity of the account contained in vv. 21–32 by suggesting that the inhabitants of Sihon's kingdom consisted primarily of Hebrew farmers and shepherds who had migrated from western Palestine; having settled in the region, however, these people had scant regard for their king, and when the Israelites appeared in the neighbourhood, they had no compunction about deserting Sihon and defecting in vast numbers to the religious community of Moses (*BA* 25 [1962], pp. 81ff.). However, Mendenhall's 'peasants' revolt' theory has been subjected to considerable criticism, for the model appears to have been superimposed upon the biblical traditions and finds no real basis in the *OT* itself (cf. Miller, *IJH*, p. 279; Hauser, *JSOT* 7 [1978], pp. 2ff.; Ramsey, *Quest*, pp. 93ff.). A more judicious approach to the narrative was adopted by Noth. He observed that Moses is not mentioned in the account of the conquest recorded in the present passage, and that the implication of 32:39, 41f. is that the conquest of Transjordan was accomplished by individual tribal groups; on this basis, Noth (*History*, p. 149) suggested that, although the present passage implies a conquest by all Israel, it was, in fact, only the tribe of Gad that was involved. That the Gadites did eventually settle in this area of Transjordan is suggested not only by various references in the *OT* (cf. 32:34–36; Jos. 13:24–28), but also by an allusion in the Mesha Inscription which states that 'the men of Gad had always dwelt in the land of Ataroth' (l. 10). According to Noth, Gad, having initially settled in the district of Jazer, subsequently extended its territory southwards by taking land from Sihon. If this is correct, then the present passage may be regarded as containing at least a historical nucleus; it is merely the number of Israelites involved and the extent of Israel's success that has been somewhat overestimated.

The historicity of the account of the conquest of Og has also frequently been questioned because, as was suggested above, it does not seem to have been preserved in any tradition earlier than Deuteronomy. Noth, in particular, expressed doubts as to whether the narrative could be regarded as reflecting a historical event, and he argued that the intention of the story was simply to justify the claims made by the half-tribe of Manasseh to a region which the Israelites had never, in fact, possessed (*History*, pp. 159f.). However, while the issue is by no means easy to decide, there is nothing in the nature of the case to render such a conquest as is here described improbable. As Bartlett (*VT* 20 [1970], pp. 266f., 271) has observed, it is difficult to deny all historicity to the very concrete reference to a battle at Edrei (v. 33), and there is no *a priori* reason why an Israelite group should not have attempted to settle in this region. Edrei was probably singled out for special mention as being the furthest point reached by the Israelites in this area. Thus there is little reason to deny outright the historicity of the accounts contained in vv. 21–35, for the description of the victories achieved over Sihon and Og may well reflect at least a nucleus of historical truth.

21. The Israelites, having presumably reached the border of the land of the Amorites, send messengers to Sihon requesting safe passage through his territory. Sihon is here called **king of the Amorites** (cf. 32:33; 1 Kg. 4:19), though elsewhere in the *OT* he is designated 'king of Heshbon' (cf. Dt. 2:26, 30; 3:6; 29:7; Jos. 12:5); in Dt. 1:4; 3:2; Jos. 12:2; 13:10, 21, he is described as the king of the Amorites who 'lived' or 'reigned' in Heshbon.

22. For the contents of the message sent to Sihon, see on 20:14ff.

23. Sihon and his army fought against Israel at **Jahaz** (sometimes spelled Jahzah; cf. Jer. 48:21). Its exact location is unknown, though it presumably lay somewhere on the eastern border of Sihon's territory, since this was the most likely place for an encounter with the Israelites to have occurred. It may be inferred from the Mesha Inscription that Jahaz was a place of some military importance, located near Dibon, and some suggest that it is to be identified with the modern Khirbet Umm el-Idhâm, some 5 miles (8 km.) north of Dibon (cf. Snaith). Aharoni (*Land*, pp. 187, 308) tentatively suggests that it should be identified with Khirbet el-Medeiyineh, (cf. Dearman, *ZDPV* 100 [1984], pp. 122ff.). Another possibility is that Jahaz is to be identified with Khirbet libb on the King's Highway between Medeba and Dibon (cf. Simons, *Texts*, p. 118; de Vaux, *Bible et*

Orient, pp. 119f.). Jahaz was one of the four Levitical cities in the territory of Reuben, but it later came under Moabite control, and its capture by Mesha is referred to in the Mesha Inscription, l. 19f.

24. This verse describes the extent of the territory subdued by Israel: it stretched from the Arnon in the south to the Jabbok in the north, and from the border of Ammon in the east to the Jordan in the west. **for Jazer was the boundary of the Ammonites**: The rendering of *AV*, 'for the border of the children of Ammon was strong', represents the correct translation of MT; if this reading is accepted, then the point of the statement is that the Israelites did not at this time further their conquests because the Ammonite border was impregnable (so, e.g., Wenham; cf. *NEB, NIV, NRSV*). The difficulty with this, however, is that the Heb. word *ʿaz*, 'strong', must be given the sense of 'well-fortified', a meaning which Gray (p. 297) regards as 'unparalleled and questionable'. LXX read the word as Jazer (*yaʿzēr*), and this reading is followed by *RSV*, and may find some support in the ambiguous reference to Jazer in v. 32. The site of Jazer is unknown, and various suggestions have been made as to its identification. One possibility is that it is Khirbet Jazzir, some 12 miles (19 km.) south of the Jabbok (cf. Simons, *Texts*, p. 119); another possibility is that it is Tell ʿArēme (cf. Rendtorff, *ZDPV* 76 [1960], pp. 124ff.). During its chequered history, it passed through Amorite, Israelite, Moabite and Ammonite hands.

25. The statement that **Israel took all these cities** is strange, since no Ammonite cities have yet been mentioned. Commentators generally conclude that a portion of the narrative which contained a list of the captured cities has fallen out of the text, or been displaced (cf. de Vaux, *Vivre et Penser* 1 [1941], p. 21). The Israelites settled for some time (the duration is not specified) in **all the cities of the Amorites**, and the most famous of these cities, **Heshbon**, is singled out for special mention. It is thought that the name of this city has survived in the modern Ḥesbân, which is situated some 20 miles (32 km.) east of the northern end of the Dead Sea. The phrase **all its villages** (lit., 'all its daughters') refers to the small towns that were dependent on Heshbon.

27–30. The narrative of the defeat of the Amorites leads to the inclusion in vv. 27–30 of a song, almost certainly of independent origin, celebrating a victory over the king of Moab. The poem, however, is problematic, for it is unclear whether the conquest it depicts was achieved by the Amorites or by the Israelites themselves. Those who adopt the former interpretation (cf., e.g., Gottwald, *Tribes*, p. 215; Hanson, *HTR* 61 [1968], pp. 297ff.) view the poem as an Amorite victory song, possibly composed by one of Sihon's own followers; in favour of this is the fact that the poem would then be viewed as a logical continuation of the historical note contained in v. 26, according to which Sihon had succeeded in taking from the king of Moab the whole country as far as the Arnon. The difficulty with this interpretation, however, is that many scholars regard it as inherently improbable that the work of an Amorite poet should have found its way into the Heb. text, and it would certainly be easier to account for the preservation of the poem had it been written by a native Israelite. In view of this, most scholars prefer to regard the song as of Israelite origin, and the following are among the interpretations of its original significance that have been offered: (i) The poem is a satirical ode directed by Israel to the Amorites, whose capital, Heshbon, the Israelites had just destroyed. According to this view, vv. 27f. are an ironical address by the victorious Israelites to the vanquished Amorites, and their taunt is, in effect, 'You once conquered the Moabite capital; now it has been destroyed again, so come and rebuild it – if you can!' (cf. Ewald, *History*, ii, pp. 205ff.). If this interpretation is adopted, then v. 29 must be understood as an address by the Israelites to the Moabites who had been conquered, not by themselves, but by the Amorites, and v. 30 must be viewed as a reference to the Israelites exulting in their own victory over the Amorites. The basic thrust of the poem would thus be that the Amorites had destroyed Moab, but Israel had destroyed the Amorites, the implication being that the Israelites must, indeed, be quite invincible. But the problem with this interpretation is that it is regarded as too subtle and complicated for a poem of this kind; besides, it involves a considerable degree of reading between the lines, for there is nothing at all in the poem itself to indicate that vv. 27f. were intended as a taunt, nor is there the slightest hint that the conquerors of v. 30 were any different from those mentioned in vv. 27f. Some scholars have sought to defend the above interpretation of the song by arguing that the Heb. *mōšᵉlîm* in v. 27 should be rendered 'taunters' (cf. van Seters, *JBL* 91 [1972], p. 194) but this, surely, prejudices the interpretation of the text, for the term *māšāl* is capable of various connotations and, as Gray notes, 'satire is neither the original nor even the most frequent meaning of the word' (p. 300). (ii) The poem is regarded as a triumphal song composed to celebrate Israel's victory over Moab, possibly the victory achieved in the time of Omri (2 Kg. 3:4f.), described also in the Mesha Inscription, l. 4f. (cf. Meyer, *ZAW* 1 [1881], pp. 130ff.; Baentsch, pp. 584ff.); on this view, the last line of v. 29 ('to an Amorite king, Sihon') must be regarded as a gloss, and vv. 27f. represent an address to the Israelites in which they, having conquered Heshbon, urge themselves to set about the task of rebuilding it. The difficulty with this, however, is that the poem would then be an irrelevance in the present context, for nothing has been mentioned in the preceding narrative of any conquest of Moab by the Israelites. (iii) Noth (*ZAW* 58 [1940–1], pp. 166ff.) takes the poem to refer to a conquest achieved not by the Israelites in general, but by a specific Israelite tribe (possibly Gad); it celebrates a victory which this tribe had won over the king of Heshbon, who had exercised a tyrannical rule over the area north of the Arnon (vv. 28f.). This interpretation is attractive, and would be quite in keeping with Noth's interpretation of the event recorded in vv. 21ff.; however, much depends on Noth's hypothetical reconstruction of the difficult text of v. 30, and on his assumption that the verbs in v. 28 should be rendered as pluperfects, since the event described in this verse was previous in time to that described in v. 30 (cf. Bartlett, *PEQ* 101 [1969], pp. 96f.). The fact is that no explanation of the song which has hitherto been offered is entirely satisfactory, and perhaps, as Gray suggests, the only certain fact about the poem is that it celebrates a victory over Moab.

The date of the poem is a matter of conjecture and clearly depends, to some extent, on its interpretation. Van Seters (*JBL* 91 [1972], p. 194) suggests that the song may be quite late, possibly belonging to the early exilic period; at the other extreme, Freedman has suggested a date in the thirteenth century BC (*ZAW*, N.F., 31 [1960], p. 106; *No Famine*, p. 46). Bartlett (*op. cit.*, p. 100) sees in the song a reference to the campaign of David against Moab (2 Sam. 8:2, 12), and dates it in the tenth century BC, while those who regard it as celebrating Israel's victory over Omri naturally date it c. 900 BC. However, since the text, translation and interpretation of the poem are so uncertain, the question of its date – like that of the historical event to which it refers – is best left open.

27. Therefore the ballad singers say: This represents a distinct improvement on *AV*'s 'they that speak in proverbs', for the *mōšᵉlîm*

were possibly minstrels who wandered from place to place reciting
or singing ballads. The term *māšal* has a variety of meanings (see
on 23:7) but it can, as here, designate 'a short song or ode with
some special characteristic either in its contents or in its artistic
construction, such as a dirge, a taunt-song over a fallen foe, or more
generally a ballad' (McNeile, p. 120). The tense of the verb 'say'
here has a frequentative force, implying that the ballad was one
which was regularly recited by the *mōš°lîm*; moreover, the use of the
verb 'say' may suggest that the poem was derived from an oral
source (unlike the poem quoted in vv. 14*b*, 15). The song begins
with a call to rebuild Heshbon, so that **the city of Sihon** could be
re-established.

28. For fire went forth from Heshbon: Two interpretations are
possible here. The first is that Heshbon itself had been destroyed,
though this need not mean that the city had literally been razed to
the ground, for the ravages of war are often in the *OT* compared to
the devastation wrought by fire (cf. Am. 1:4). The second possibility
is that fire (or devastation) had spread *from* Heshbon, the unfortunate victims being 'Ar of Moab' and the 'heights of the Arnon' (so,
e.g., Noth). In view of the call to rebuild Heshbon in the previous
verse, the former alternative is to be preferred here, and the meaning
is that Heshbon and the country southwards to the Arnon had
suffered the same fate, i.e., utter ruin. Having destroyed Heshbon,
the conquest had proceeded in a southerly direction until **Ar of
Moab** (see on v. 15, above) had been devastated; Ar means 'city',
and some commentators believe that the parallelism within the present verse would be improved if this clause were rendered 'cities of
Moab' (cf. *BHS*; Noth, pp. 161, 165; Hanson, *op. cit.*, p. 301; van
Seters, *JBL* 91 [1972], p. 193), but this is hardly necessary. The fire
destroyed not only Ar but also **the lords of the heights of the
Arnon**: The term 'heights' (Heb. *bāmôṯ*) may conceivably mean
'high places' (so *AV*), in which case the reference would be to the
hill-shrines of Moab. This is the way in which the Targums interpreted the phrase, the expression 'lords of the heights' (Heb. *ba⁽a⁾lê
bāmôṯ*) being taken as a reference to the heathen priests who officiated at the cultic shrines. However, the text of MT is by no means
certain, and it is probable that the word rendered 'lords' should be
emended with LXX to read 'devoured, swallowed up' (i.e., *bāl°āh*
instead of *ba⁽a⁾lê*), thus considerably improving the parallelism of the
verse; cf. *NEB*, *NRSV*. Some commentators take the phrase rendered

'the heights of the Arnon' to be a reference to a specific geographical
location, Bamoth-Arnon (cf. de Vaulx; *NJPS*), but this seems
improbable.

29. This verse laments (perhaps in a mocking tone) the fate which
had befallen **the people of Chemosh**. Chemosh was the national
deity of the Moabites, and is referred to in the Mesha Inscription
and in several passages in the *OT* (cf. 1 Kg. 11:7, 33; 2 Kg. 23:13).
He has made his sons fugitives, and his daughters captives:
The thought here is that the Moabite god had been so angry with
his people that he had given them over to captivity (cf. MI, l. 5).
In the citation of this poem in Jer. 48:46, a passive verb is used,
thus denying the heathen god, Chemosh, any direct influence in the
shaping of history. **to an Amorite king, Sihon**: There is much to
be said for regarding these words as a gloss, for (i) the expression
in Heb. is rather unusual; (ii) the clause has no parallel in the poem
as it stands, and is metrically superfluous; (iii) the phrase does not
appear in the corresponding passage in Jer. 48:46. If the phrase
is omitted, then the possibility must be considered that the poem
originally had nothing to do with a victory achieved by Sihon. It is
true, of course, that Heshbon is called 'the city of Sihon' in v. 27,
but later generations could have described Heshbon in this way,
and there is no need to assume that Sihon was still its king at the
time of the events described in the poem (cf. Bartlett, *PEQ* 101
[1969], p. 95).

30. The text of this verse is hopelessly corrupt, and it is no longer
possible to reconstruct the original with any confidence. *AV*'s 'we
have shot at them' accurately reproduces the meaning of MT, but
the sudden introduction of the first person plural here is strange,
and the form of the Heb. verb is unusual. The rendering of *RSV*
follows LXX by reading *wᵉnînām* ('and their descendants') instead of
wannîrām ('we shot at them'), and restores 'from' before Heshbon,
with Vulg. and Targ. The second half of the verse is equally problematic. MT reads, lit., 'we have laid waste to Nophah which to
Medeba'; LXX and Sam. suggest that *ᵃšer*, 'which', should be read
as *'ēš*, 'fire', and it is possible that Nophah (which, as a town, would
otherwise be unknown) is to be read as the perfect Pual of the verb
nāpaḥ, 'to blow' (cf. *BDB*, p. 656a), i.e., until fire was blown as far
as Medeba; hence *RSV*'s **until fire spread to Medeba**. For another
possible reconstruction of the text, see Althann, *Bib* 66 (1985),
pp. 568ff. The restoration of *RSV* must be regarded as very tentative,

and perhaps nothing more can be said with certainty than that the verse describes the destruction of certain Moabite towns. These towns included **Dibon**, the modern Dhiban, some 5 miles (8 km.) north of the Arnon, and **Medeba** (which appears as Mehedeba in the Mesha Inscription), the modern Madeba, situated between Heshbon and Ma'in. For an account of the excavations carried out at Dibon, see Winnett, *BASOR* 125 (1952), pp. 7ff.; Tushingham, *BASOR* 133 (1954), pp. 6ff.; and for those at Medeba, see Avi-Yonah, *EAEHL*, iii, pp. 819ff.

31. This verse forms a sequel to v. 24a, and contains a statement which has a parallel in v. 25b.

32. The reference to Jazer and its dependent towns stands in a curiously isolated position after the general statement contained in the previous verse. Some commentators regard it as a detail derived from another source, but it may well be a later editorial addition precipitated by the reference to Jazer in v. 24.

33–35. These verses provide a summary account of the defeat of Og, king of Bashan, his family and his people, and the occupation of his land by the Israelites. With the victory over Sihon (vv. 21ff.), the southern part of the land east of the Jordan was conquered; now, with the battle against Og, Israel's sphere of action shifts to the north. Josephus states that Og was in alliance with Sihon but that he arrived too late to take part in the battle at Jahaz (*Ant.* IV.5.3). For the view that these verses are a supplementary addition to Numbers, based on the account in Dt. 3:1–3, see above.

33. The Israelites, after the conquest of Sihon, travelled in a northerly direction and **went up by the way to Bashan**. Bashan was the broad, fertile tract of country on the eastern side of the Jordan, noted for its rich pastures, forests and herds of cattle (cf. Am. 4:1; Isa. 2:13; Ezek. 27:6). The battle between the Israelites and Og took place at **Edrei**, probably the modern Der'ā, which is situated some 30 miles (48 km.) east of the Sea of Galilee.

35. In accordance with Yahweh's promise (v. 34), Og was defeated and his territory passed into the possession of the victorious Israelites.

22:1. This verse, which is generally recognized as deriving from the P source, indicates that the Israelites had finally arrived **in the plains of Moab**. This expression, which appears to be peculiar to P (cf. 26:3, 63; 31:12), designated the open, fertile area immediately to the north of the Dead Sea on the eastern side of the Jordan; it corresponds to the 'plains of Jericho' (cf. Jos. 4:13; 5:10) on the opposite side of the river. The location of the Israelites is further defined by the words **beyond the Jordan at Jericho**: These words seem to imply that the Israelites had crossed the Jordan to Jericho, but, of course, 'beyond the Jordan' represents the point of view of one already settled in Canaan, and therefore refers to the eastern side of the river. The phrase in Heb. is in the construct state, 'the Jordan of Jericho', but the expression clearly refers to that part of the river which flows in the vicinity of Jericho (cf. the reference to the 'waters of Megiddo' in Jg. 5:19). Jericho, modern Tell es-Sulṭân, is mentioned here for the first time in the *OT*.

III. PREPARATIONS FOR ENTRY INTO THE LAND
22:2–36:13

The final part of the book of Numbers contains a miscellaneous collection of narratives and laws, all of which are represented as having taken place, or having been formulated, during Israel's stay at Moab. The basic theme of this section is the preparations that were considered necessary for the occupation of the promised land. The opening chapters (chs. 22–24) describe the attempt of Balak, king of Moab, to defeat the Israelites by hiring a heathen seer, Balaam, to curse the people. This is followed by an account of Israel's apostasy at Baal-Peor (ch. 25), and by a second census of the Israelites, which was necessitated by the fact that all those who had been numbered in the first census (apart from Caleb and Joshua) had since died in the wilderness (ch. 26). The remaining chapters are primarily concerned with various rules and regulations, including the rights of daughters to inherit property (27:1–11; 36:1ff.); the public offerings due at the various cultic feasts throughout the year (chs. 28f.); the validity of vows taken by women (ch. 30); the appropriate attitude towards the Canaanites and their cult (33:50–56); Israel's boundaries on the west of the Jordan (ch. 34); the Levitical cities (35:1–8), the cities of refuge and the law of homicide (35:9–34). Interspersed with these regulations are accounts of the appointment of Joshua as Moses' successor (27:15–23), the war waged against Midian (ch. 31), the assignment of territory to tribes on the east of the Jordan (ch. 32), and the itinerary of the Israelites from Egypt to Moab (ch. 33). Both the J and P sources are in evidence in this section, though most of the material derives from P.

(A) THE STORY OF BALAAM
22:2–24:25

It has long been recognized by commentators that chs. 22–24 cannot be regarded as a homogeneous literary unit. Ch. 22, in particular, is clearly the product of more than one author, as is evident from (i) the presence of doublets (cf. v. 2*a* and v. 4*b*; v. 3*a* and v. 3*b*);

(ii) the fact that Balak's messengers appear to be 'elders' in v. 7 but 'princes' in vv. 8, 15, 21; (iii) the contradiction between v. 20 (where Balaam is depicted as having Yahweh's permission to proceed to Moab) and v. 22 (where the seer appears to have proceeded contrary to the divine will). Attempts have been made to harmonize these inconsistencies (cf., e.g., Sutcliffe, *Bib* 18 [1937], pp. 439ff.) but they have not, in general, proved to be very convincing. The composite nature of the narrative is not so evident in chs. 23f., but even here the repetition of 23:22, 24 in 24:8f., and the postponement of Balaam's introduction of himself to the third and fourth poems (24:3f., 15f.) confirm the impression that the Balaam cycle cannot have been the work of a single hand.

The presence of such repetitions and inconsistencies led many earlier commentators (Holzinger, Baentsch, Gray) to discern in the Balaam cycle traces of two different sources (usually identified as J and E) which had been combined and edited by a redactor. Attempts to disentangle these sources, however, have proved problematic, and even Noth was forced to concede that these chapters did not yield very easily to the traditional documentary analysis. Nevertheless, Noth himself (pp. 171ff.) offered a source-critical division of the narrative along the following lines: 22:2–21 belonged to E (with some traces of J); 22:22–40 belonged to J (with some traces of E); 22:41–23:27 was, for the most part, the work of E, while 23:28–24:19 could be attributed in the main to J, and 24:20–25 was a later interpolation. But as Noth rightly recognized, any analysis of the Balaam narrative along these lines has to be regarded as very tentative, for distinguishing marks of style are noticeably absent; moreover, attempts to analyze the sources on the basis of their use of the divine names, Yahweh and Elohim, are fraught with problems, for the names do not follow the expected source-critical pattern and, besides, the divine name criterion has to contend with the most intricate textual difficulties in this section (cf. Gray, pp. 310ff.). In view of these complications, some more recent scholars have expressed a reluctance to resolve the problem of the composition of the Balaam narrative along conventional source-critical lines (cf., e.g., Gross, *Bileam*), and it has even been suggested that the entire narrative (except, perhaps, 22:22–35) should be viewed as a connected, continuous whole. Such an approach is exemplified, e.g., by Sturdy (p. 157), who discerns an increasing confidence in the prophecies of Balaam, and a significant development in the seer's behaviour as the story unfolds; these features, he argues, are entirely lost if the narrative is divided up between two different Pentateuchal sources. A similar view is advocated by Wenham (pp. 165f.), who claims that the presence in these three chapters of interlocking literary patterns makes the usual source-critical analysis improbable and, indeed, unnecessary.

Attempts to view the Balaam cycle as a coherent whole, however, must be regarded as somewhat ill-judged, for, quite apart from the probable secondary interpolation of 22:22–35, it is by no means certain that all four of Balaam's oracles were originally of a piece with the narrative in which they are now embedded. In particular, the two oracles contained in ch. 24 probably circulated independently at one time, and were only subsequently incorporated in their present context (see below). Various other indications, noted in the course of the commentary, confirm the impression that the Balaam narrative cannot be regarded as a unified whole. Nevertheless, doubts must be raised concerning the division of these chapters between the J and E sources. The very fact that some scholars are able to attribute the entire Balaam narrative to the Yahwist, who combined two separate stories (cf. Rudolph, pp. 97 ff.), while others are equally convinced that the entire tradition developed in E circles (cf. Jenks, *The Elohist*, pp. 55ff.), merely underlines the unsatisfactory nature of the traditional documentary analysis of this material. It seems more probable that the story was drawn from an independent source, which may well have contained two parallel accounts of the Balaam story; at some stage, a redactor combined the two traditions into a single coherent account. This task was effected with considerable skill, but it was inevitable that, in the process, certain inconsistencies should be introduced and that, consequently, traces of unevenness remain. Other problems, peculiar to chs. 22–24, call for discussion at this point, namely, the date of the oracles contained in chs. 23f., the character of Balaam himself, and the purpose of the narrative. An excursus on the Deir 'Allā texts and their significance for the interpretation of these chapters is included on pp. 281–84.

(a) THE DATE OF THE ORACLES

Some early scholars tended to favour a comparatively late date for the oracles contained in 23:7–10, 18–24; 24:3–9, 15–19. Holzinger (p. 116), e.g., discerned in such passages as 23:9*b*, 10*a* the spirit of exclusiveness which was characteristic of post-exilic times, and the

confident tone which permeated the poems in general was interpreted in terms of the hopes and aspirations of the Messianic age.
Such views, however, were sharply criticized by Gray (pp. 313f.),
who argued that the oracles should rather be interpreted as giving
expression to the quickened consciousness of nationality which
emerged in Israel after the establishment of the monarchy. Mowinckel (*ZAW*, N.F., 7 [1930], pp. 268ff.) similarly argued that the
references in the poems to Israel's greatness, good fortune and power
were redolent of the early period of the monarchy, though he
believed that only the two oracles contained in 24:3–9, 15–17 should
be dated in the time of David and Solomon; the two oracles contained in ch. 23 (vv. 7–10, 18–24) belonged to the time of Josiah
(seventh century BC), while the narrative itself probably dated from
the middle of the ninth century BC. Responding to Mowinckel's
article, Albright (*JBL* 63 [1944], pp. 226f.) argued that the oracles
should be dated to a much earlier period, and on the basis of a
detailed text-critical and philological analysis of the poems, he suggested that they originated between the middle of the thirteenth and
end of the twelfth centuries BC. In support of his conclusion, he
noted several parallels to the grammar, lexicography and epigraphy
of other Northwest Semitic texts from approximately the same
period. An eleventh century BC date was subsequently defended by
Freedman (*JBL* 96 [1977], p. 18), and Vetter (*Seherspruch*, pp. 9f.,
61f.) similarly advocated a date in the pre-conquest period (cf., also,
Craigie, *TynB* 20 [1969], pp. 76ff.). However, some of the evidence
cited by Albright is textually suspect, and Robertson (*Linguistic
Evidence*, p. 145) has shown that the presence of primitive elements
in the oracles is more probably due to a deliberate archaizing on
the part of the writer than to a genuine late second millennium
origin.

On the whole, the balance of probability must favour the dating
of the oracles in the early monarchic period, for the allusions to
persons and events from this period are too clear and unambiguous
to be explained away. Thus, the reference to Agag in 24:7 suggests
an origin in the time of Saul (1 Sam. 15:8f., 32f.), while the allusion
in 24:17, 18f. to the demise of Moab and Edom fits well with David's
conquest of these countries. Moreover, the reference in 24:17 to the
appearance of the 'star' from Jacob and the 'sceptre' from Israel
suggests that the author probably had David in mind. The series of

oracles contained in 24:20–24, on the other hand, were appended to the Balaam narrative at a later stage and, owing to their brevity and vagueness, they are impossible to date with any certainty.

(b) THE CHARACTER OF BALAAM

The story of Balaam is undoubtedly one of the most intriguing in the *OT*. The representation of a heathen seer as an inspired prophet of Yahweh, the literary skill with which the entire episode has been composed, and the religious fervour and optimistic outlook enshrined in the oracles, have combined to invest this section of the book of Numbers with an unusual interest. In this regard much attention has focused upon the enigmatic figure of Balaam himself, for it is not clear whether he was regarded as a 'diviner' (*qôsēm*; cf. Jos. 13:22), revealing the typical characteristics of the Babylonian *bârû* (Daiches, *Fest. Hilprecht*, pp. 6off.; Wright, *Environment*, pp. 82f.) or the Arabic *kahin* (cf. Lindblom, *Prophecy*, pp. 9off.), or whether he was regarded as exemplifying the virtues of the true Israelite prophet (cf. Coats, *Semeia* 24 [1982], pp. 61f.). On the variety of separate, yet complementary, roles in which Balaam is cast in the *OT*, see Moore, *Balaam Traditions*, pp. 97ff.

The problem concerning Balaam is further complicated by the fact that there seems to be something of a dichotomy in the way in which his character is viewed in Scripture. In the present narrative (apart from 22:22–35) he is depicted in a favourable light. Although he was a seer of foreign extraction, he readily acknowledged Yahweh as his lord, and recognized that the divine will had to be obeyed (cf. 22:18, 20, 38; 23:3, 5, 12, 16, 26; 24:13f.). He is presented as a model of piety, who takes the precaution of inquiring of Yahweh as each new development unfolds, ensuring that the divine command is at all times implemented. Despite financial inducements to curse the Israelites (22:17f., 37), Balaam steadfastly insists on blessing them and, as the obedient seer, he himself implicitly receives the blessing of God (24:9*b*). Later biblical tradition, however, was not so favourably disposed to Balaam, presumably because the phenomenon of a heathen seer as the recipient of a genuine divine revelation would have offended Jewish sensibilities. Thus while chs. 22–24 suggest that Balaam was under a divine compulsion to bless Israel, the implication of Dt. 23:4f. is that he was vehemently opposed to the Israelites and would have cursed them had not Yahweh intervened and converted Balaam's evil intention to good (cf. Jos. 24:9f.;

Neh. 13:2). Moreover, according to the Priestly tradition reflected in 31:8, 16, Balaam's death during Israel's campaign against Midian was regarded as condign punishment for his nefarious involvement in the apostasy at Baal-Peor (25:1ff.; cf. Jos. 13:22). This negative appraisal of Balaam's character is also evident in the *NT*. In Rev. 2:14 he is accused of leading Israel astray, and in 2 Pet. 2:15f. (cf. Jude 11) his conduct is explained in terms of his insatiable greed and avarice, a charge which appears also in Philo's assessment of his character (*De Vit. Mos.* i.48).

Some scholars, anxious to discern a unified and coherent estimate of Balaam's character throughout Scripture, have argued that the seer is depicted in a predominantly negative light even in chs. 22–24 (Wenham, Harrison). The statements in these chapters to the effect that Balaam would only declare God's will merely indicate 'the inspiration of his oracles rather than the holiness of his character' (Wenham, p. 167). The fact that Balaam is described as having been inspired by the spirit of God does not necessarily mean that he was a good man or even that he was a true believer in Yahweh; it merely shows God's prerogative to use whoever he wished to be his spokesman and to mediate his will. That Balaam was basically a person of ill-repute is confirmed by the fact that he practised 'divination' (22:7) and resorted to 'omens' (24:1), customs which were regarded as utterly abominable and reprehensible in Israel (cf. 23:23; Dt. 18:10; 1 Sam. 15:23; 2 Kg. 17:17). Moreover, that Balak was forced to send a second envoy with even costlier gifts before Balaam could be persuaded to curse Israel (22:15ff.) may be understood as an indication of the seer's greed and rapaciousness. Other scholars (cf. Albright, *JBL* 63 [1944], p. 233) have sought to account for the change in the estimate of Balaam's character by suggesting that he was, in fact, a convert to Yahwism (hence the positive appraisal in chs. 22–24), but that he later abandoned Israel and joined the Midianites in opposing the Israelites (hence the predominantly negative appraisal in the rest of Scripture). However, such attempts at harmonization can hardly be regarded as satisfactory, for while later texts cannot be ignored in interpreting chs. 22–24, it is methodologically unsound to allow later reflections upon Balaam's character to dominate the exposition of the chapters here under consideration. As Coats (*BibR* 18 [1973], pp. 21f.) rightly points out, responsible interpretation should not seek a harmony between the various texts but, rather, a comparison that will allow the unique character of each text to appear. Viewed in this way, it must be conceded that either two alternative, parallel traditions existed about Balaam, or that the early positive estimation of his character was later replaced by a negative one.

The negative appraisal of Balaam was developed at considerable length in post-biblical tradition. In the Targumim, in particular, he is usually portrayed as a villain, and reviled on account of his immorality and apostasy. Although his prophetic powers and mantic skills are readily acknowledged by the rabbis, he is seldom referred to without a pejorative epithet (such as 'wicked' or 'evil') being appended to his name. Indeed, evidence of his malevolent intent was found in the very meaning of his name, which was rendered as 'corrupter' or 'devourer' of the people (*B. Sanh.* 105*a*). On account of his evil deeds, he died before his time (*B. Sanh.* 106*b*) and was denied a place in the world to come (*M. Sanh.* 10:2; *M. Aboth* 5:19). For the motivations which may account for the calumny heaped upon Balaam in Jewish literature, see Baskin, *Pharaoh's Counsellors*, pp. 91ff.

Balaam proved an important figure for early Christian exegetes, too, although the obloquy here aimed at him appears in a far milder form, no doubt because the prophecy contained in 24:17 was regarded as a prediction of the coming of Christ. Indeed, in the writings of the early Christian fathers, Balaam was sometimes regarded as a model of the Gentile prophet who guides the nations to true religion, and he became established in tradition as the founder of the magi, i.e., the first representatives of the nations to recognize and worship the infant Jesus. Yet, early Christian writers could not entirely ignore the biblical evidence concerning Balaam's wrongdoing, and they were therefore faced by the inevitable dilemma that a divinely inspired prophet, appointed to make Christ known to the Gentiles, could, at the same time, be a scoundrel who was quite unworthy to hold such a privileged office.

(c) THE PURPOSE OF THE BALAAM NARRATIVE

Such prominence has been given in studies of chs. 22–24 to the nature of Balaam's character that the purpose of the narrative and its religious import have all too often been eclipsed. Yet, the fact that this diviner of foreign extraction was subservient to the power and authority of the God of Israel clearly had important theological implications, for it demonstrated Yahweh's supremacy and his omnipotent control over human events. All attempts on the part of Balak, king of Moab, to foil the purpose of God were doomed to failure, for nothing could mar the glorious future which Yahweh had in store for his people, and nothing could deprive them of their destined reward. Thus the story illustrates the inevitability of Yahweh's plans and the folly of those who conspired to oppose them; the will of God was decisive, and however elaborate the stratagems devised by human adversaries they could not, in the end, succeed. At another level, the narrative indicates that Yahweh's will prevails against the sinister underworld of black magic and evil spirits (cf. Freedman, *Fest. Cross*, pp. 320f., 332ff.); such threats posed the 'acme of menace for the people of God' (von Rad, *OT Theology*, i, p. 288) and could have constituted a danger far greater than anything which they had faced hitherto on their journey. Thus the narrative illustrates that Yahweh was capable of protecting his people even from the baneful influence of a powerful spell; indeed, the story clearly demonstrates that to invoke extraneous elements in order to wreak destruction upon God's people was an enterprise which was both foolish and ineffectual. God, and he alone, was the ultimate source of all power, and such power as was possessed by humans could only be exercised in conformity with the divine will.

(d) BALAK SENDS FOR BALAAM
22:2–6

Balak, the king of Moab, aware that the Israelites had destroyed the Amorites, is concerned lest they should now encroach upon his territory. He therefore sends messengers to Balaam, a reputable seer, inviting him to curse the people of Israel, thus ensuring that they would pose him no threat.

2. The name **Balak** is derived from a root which means 'to lay waste', and hence the name may mean 'ravager', 'destroyer' or 'devastator'. **the son of Zippor**: This name, which is from the root *ṣpr* II, 'to twitter, cheep', probably designates a species of small bird, such as the sparrow. The masculine form of the name is not found elsewhere in the *OT*, but the feminine form, Zipporah, appears as the name of Moses' wife (cf. Exod. 2:21; 18:2).

3. Moab was overcome with fear: The verb *qûṣ* is used in the *OT* to express a feeling of 'loathing, abhorrence, sickening dread' (*BDB*, pp. 880f.), and the rendering of *RSV* (cf. *NEB*'s 'sick with fear') is certainly an improvement on the milder 'distressed' of *AV*,

RV. The extent of Balak's fear was played down by Josephus (*Ant.* IV.6.2), who states that the king was merely 'concerned' (*eŭlabeito*) at the prospect of Israel's growing numbers.

4. The **elders of Midian** are here (and in v. 7) represented as making common cause with the Moabites against Israel. As numerous commentators have pointed out, however, the reference to the 'elders of Midian' in these two verses seems strange, for in the remainder of the narrative contained in chs. 22–24, Balaam's dealings are with the Moabites only. Exegetes, from earliest times, have attempted to explain the unexpected intrusion of the Midianites at this point (cf. Josephus, *Ant.* IV.6.2), and one possibility considered was that Midian and Moab, former enemies (cf. Gen. 36:35), were in this instance united by their mutual fear of a formidable enemy (*Sif. Num.*, 157; cf. Vermes, *Scripture*, p. 128). Recent analysts, however, are inclined to regard the reference to the 'elders of Midian' in vv. 4, 7 as a gloss, probably based on the connection of Balaam with the Midianites in 31:8, 16 (cf. Noth).

5. Balak sends messengers to **Balaam the son of Beor**: Reference is made in Gen. 36:32 to Bela, the son of Beor, who was the king of Edom, and since the names Balaam and Bela are almost identical in Heb., some have ventured to suggest that the two persons were one and the same (cf. Lods, *Israel*, p. 185; Gray, p. 324), and that an Edomite connection may be posited for Balaam (cf. Sayce, *ExpT* 15 [1903–4], pp. 405f.). However, there is no firm evidence to support the identification of the two characters (cf. Driver, *Genesis*, p. 317; Albright, *JBL* 63 [1944], p. 231), and the view that the name Balaam in Heb. is simply Bela with an afformative -*am* seems most unlikely. The etymology of the name Balaam is uncertain, but the suggestion (found, e.g., in Targ. Ps. Jon.) that it means 'swallower (i.e., destroyer) of the people' (from the root *bl'* 'to swallow') is without philological basis, and merely reflects the antipathy felt by the rabbis towards the heathen seer. For other ancient explanations of the name, which similarly reflect the animosity of tradition towards Balaam, see Milgrom, p. 186. Balaam evidently resided at **Pethor, which is near the River**: Since the 'river' in question is almost certainly the Euphrates (*NRSV*; *NEB*; cf. Gen. 31:21; Exod. 23:31; Jos. 24:2; 2 Sam. 10:16), scholars have generally identified Pethor with Pitru (mentioned in Assyrian and Egyptian sources; Parpola, *Toponyms*, p. 279), which was situated a few miles from the river, a little to the south of Carchemish, in the most northerly part of Syria. This identification would be in basic agreement with the statement in 23:7, according to which Balaam was brought 'from Aram' (= Syria), and it would also be consistent with Dt. 23:4, which locates Pethor in Mesopotamia. Pethor is further described as being situated **in the land of Amaw**: MT reads, lit., 'the land of the children of his people' (so, too, LXX; cf. *AV*), but if this expression was intended as a paraphrase for 'homeland' or 'native land', it must be conceded that it is quite meaningless in the present context, and it can hardly be regarded as an informative addition to the previous clause. In any case, the Heb. text, as it stands, hardly represents an idiomatic way of expressing one's native country (cf. Gen. 11:28; 24:7; 31:13 for the more usual terminology to express one's 'homeland'). The suspicion, therefore, inevitably arises that the present text is corrupt, and the rendering of *RSV* (cf. *NEB*) presupposes that the enigmatic *'ammô* ('his people') should be emended to read *'ammaw*, which involves only a slight change of the Heb. (cf. Yahuda, *JBL* 64 [1945], pp. 547ff.). No other reference to Amaw is found in the *OT*, but in a fifteenth century BC inscription found at Alalakh in north Syria, reference is made to a place called 'Amau in the land of Alalakh, which Albright (*BASOR* 118 [1950], p. 15, n. 13) locates somewhere between Aleppo and Carchemish. If this is correct, then it fits in admirably with the above-mentioned location of Pethor. Some scholars, however, have doubted whether the phrase *'ereṣ bᵉnê-'ammô* should be taken as a reference to the land of the people of 'Amau, and similar reservations have been expressed concerning the identification of Pethor with Pitru (cf. Delcor, *VTS* 32 [1980], pp. 68ff.), for Balaam would be represented as living some 400 miles (640 km.) from Moab, and this distance is regarded as too far in view of the number of journeys required by the subsequent narrative. Accordingly, it is sometimes suggested that Pethor in northern Syria was mistaken for another place of the same name (otherwise unknown) in the vicinity of Moab, or the name is emended to provide a location which would be more consonant with the facts required by the remainder of the narrative (so, e.g., Cheyne, *ExpT* 10 [1898–9], pp. 401f.). Moreover, the 'land of the children of his people' is interpreted (by the addition of a single letter to the word *'ammô*) to mean 'the land of the children of Ammon' (a reading found in some Heb. MSS and supported by Vulg., Syr., Sam.; cf., e.g., Delcor, *op. cit.*, pp. 65, 71), Ammon being only a short distance from Moab. If this explanation is correct, then the 'River' cannot, of course, refer to the Euphrates, and it has been suggested that the words 'in the land of Ammon' were added precisely in order to make clear that the river referred to was in the land of the Ammonites and was not to be confused with the Euphrates, *the* river *par excellence* (cf. Lust, *ETL* 54 [1978], pp. 6of.). The advantage of this alternative theory is that Balaam would have been resident within easy travelling distance of Moab, and this, it is argued, is in keeping not only with the frequent journeys which Balaam, and Balak's messengers, make in the course of the narrative, but also with the (independent) tradition reflected in vv. 22–35, which implies that Balaam's journey consisted of only a short distance on an ass through fields and walled vineyards rather than the long desert trek from northern Syria, for which a more appropriate means of transport (e.g., a camel; cf. Gen. 24:10) would have been required (cf. Maarsingh, p. 79; Gray, p. 333). But if Ammon is the correct reading, it is by no means clear where Pethor is to be located, and some scholars who support this reading are forced to conclude that v. 5 represents the conflation of two distinct traditions, one regarding Balaam as an Ammonite, and the other regarding him as a Syrian (so, e.g., Gray, p. 315). On the whole, therefore, it seems preferable to assume that the 'River' here, as elsewhere, refers to the Euphrates, and that Pethor is to be identified with Pitru in northern Syria; moreover, since other sources connect Amaw with this area, it seems reasonable to retain the rendering of *RSV*. It is true that, according to this interpretation, Balaam would have resided at some distance from Moab, and that the four journeys required by the story may well have taken a considerable time (three months, according to Gray's estimate), but such pedantic details were probably not uppermost in the narrator's mind, and they should not, therefore, be pressed too rigidly. Moreover, if the fable recorded in vv. 22–35 was originally a distinct unit of tradition which was only secondarily transferred to Balaam (see below), then details from this section cannot plausibly be regarded as furnishing evidence concerning Balaam's homeland. On the vexed question of Balaam's homeland, see, further, Albright, *JAOS* 35 (1915), pp. 386ff.; Rouillard, *Balaam*, pp. 43ff.

6. Come now, curse this people for me: The custom of cursing an enemy before engaging in battle in order to ensure victory was both ancient and widespread (cf. Binns, p. 151). Thus, the hiring of a specialist such as Balaam may well have been the natural instinct of a military leader, who would often have viewed the opposing army in terms of the supernatural forces which empowered it (cf. Moore, *Balaam Traditions*, pp. 97f.). Balak, aware of the superior power of the Israelites (**since they are too mighty for me**) wished to have the enemy placed under a powerful spell so that the dreaded invaders might be defeated. The efficacy of the curse (and, of course, of the blessing) is presupposed throughout the *OT* (cf. 5:23f.) and elsewhere in the ancient world (cf. Gray, pp. 327f.), although whether its effectiveness depended on the power of the spoken word or on the authority of the person who pronounced it is unclear.

(e) THE FIRST EMISSARIES ARE SENT
22:7–14

Balak sends messengers to Balaam offering him a reward if he consented to return with them and curse the people of Israel. Balaam invites the emissaries to stay overnight while he consults Yahweh; in the event, God forbids Balaam to accede to Balak's request, and the messengers, in turn, convey the discouraging tidings to Balak.

7. The elders of Moab and Midian approach Balaam with **the fees for divination** in their hand. MT reads, simply, 'divinations' (*q^esāmîm*), and the word was interpreted by Rashi (following some of the early rabbis; cf. *Num. R.* 20:8; *Tanḥ. B. Num.* iv.135) as a reference to the paraphernalia necessary for Balaam to practise his augury; however, *RSV*'s 'fees for divination' (cf. *AV*'s 'rewards of divination') probably accurately reflects the meaning of the original (cf. Vulg.). Later tradition regarded this offer of a reward as a sign of avarice on Balaam's part (cf. 2 Pet. 2:15; Jude 11), but, in fact, the presentation of a gift or honorarium to a seer for services rendered was a well-established custom in Israel (cf. 1 Sam. 9:8; 1 Kg. 14:3; 2 Kg. 8:8f.). Moreover, it was quite in accord with oriental practice that such fees should be offered in advance.

8. Balaam indicates that he must first obtain a decision from Yahweh, and since he evidently expected this to be given in a nocturnal vision (cf. v. 20), the messengers are invited to remain overnight. Balaam promises to give them an answer in the morning which would be in accordance with the word which **the LORD** would grant him. The fact that the divine name is uttered by Balaam has been taken by some to indicate that he must have been a Yahweh-worshipper, but it is more probable that this simply reflects the pious narrator's conviction that the God of Israel was speaking through the heathen seer. The name Yahweh ('LORD') appears here and in v. 13, while the term *'elōhîm* ('God') is used in vv. 9–12; on the perplexing interchange of divine names in the Balaam narrative generally, and on the many variants found in the Vsns, see Gray, pp. 310ff.

12. you shall not curse the people, for they are blessed: Since it was necessary to inform Balaam that Israel was blessed, he is presumed to be ignorant of the Israelites and of their special relationship to Yahweh.

13. So Balaam rose in the morning: Cf. Comb. I.3f. of the Deir 'Allā text: 'And Balaam arose on the morrow'. As in the Deir 'Allā text, Balaam is depicted as relaying the divine response to the previous night's inquiry: **Go to your own land; for the LORD has refused to let me go with you**. Binns (p. 154) suggests that oriental methods of bargaining may have led Balaam to refuse the offer of the first delegation, in anticipation that a fresh effort would then be made to open negotiations, and that a more generous reward would be forthcoming; however, there is no hint at all of such a mercenary motivation on Balaam's part in the present narrative (cf. v. 18).

(f) THE SECOND EMISSARIES ARE SENT
22:15–21

Undeterred by the fact that his first invitation to Balaam had been declined (vv. 7–14), Balak now issues a second invitation, and this time, in an effort to impress the seer, he dispatches a larger and more prestigious deputation (v. 15). Balaam insists that he must obey God's command (v. 18), and the emissaries are once more requested to tarry overnight while the divine will is ascertained (v. 19; cf. v. 8). This time the seer is permitted to go to Balak, but he is constrained to say and do only what Yahweh bids him (v. 20).

17. for I will surely do you great honour: As v. 18 indicates, 'honour' in this context implies a monetary payment or 'honorarium'. Thus, the meaning here is not that Balak would show great respect towards the seer, but that he would reward him liberally for his services.

18. Balaam here conceives of himself as a submissive instrument in the hand of Yahweh, for no matter how great the financial inducement that would be offered him, he could not go against God's will **to do less or more**, i.e., to do anything at all (for the idiom, cf. 1 Sam. 20:2; 22:15).

19. Pray now, tarry here this night also: The position of the word *gam* ('also') in MT suggests that the emphasis is not on a second overnight stay, as *RSV* implies, but on the second group of dignitaries, as is rightly recognized in *NRSV* ('You remain here, as the others did'). The primary meaning of the verb *yāšaḇ* ('tarry') is 'to sit down', and if the verb were thus rendered here, an interesting parallel could be noted with the Deir 'Allā text, I.5 ('Sit down . . . I will tell', *šbw* . . . *'ḥwkm*. See excursus, pp. 281–84.

20. And God came to Balaam at night: Nocturnal visions are often regarded as a source of divine revelation in the *OT* (cf. Job 4:12ff.; Zech. 1:8). It is interesting to note that in the Deir 'Allā text (I.1–3), Balaam received his message at night, while he was lying down, asleep (cf. Hackett, *Balaam*, p. 36).

(g) BALAAM'S ASS
22:22–35

Balaam is here depicted as proceeding on a journey which was contrary to the will of Yahweh, and the 'angel of the LORD' makes three attempts to hinder his progress; on each occasion, Balaam's ass is aware of the angel's presence, while Balaam himself remains oblivious to the divine intervention. The story contained in these verses is not without an element of comic irony: Balaam, the renowned seer, is depicted as less perceptive than his ass, and more recalcitrant than an animal renowned for its sheer obstinacy (cf. Milgrom, p. 469). In these verses, Balaam appears in a decidedly less favourable light than in the remainder of the Balaam narrative contained in chs. 22–24, and this has led many commentators to suggest that this section either contains a variant tradition of the Balaam story (cf. Noth), or that it represents an originally independent folktale, which was only subsequently transferred to Balaam in order to heighten the element of tension in the narrative (cf. Sturdy). Certainly, the present section cannot be regarded as a sequel to the preceding verses, for here Balaam is accompanied by only two servants, whereas in v. 21 he is escorted by a retinue of Moabite princes, and here Balaam undertakes his journey contrary to Yahweh's wish (v. 22), whereas in v. 20 God expressly grants permission for the seer to go to Balak. For the view that the present section is a later interpolation in the Balaam cycle, see Rouillard, *RB* 87 (1980), pp. 19ff.; Gross, *op. cit.*, pp. 333ff., and for attempts to view it as an integral part of the Balaam story, see Clark, *Literary Interpretations*, pp. 137ff.; Margaliot, *Proceedings*, pp. 79f. The episode, described by Noth (p. 178) as 'a masterpiece of ancient Israelite narrative art' has been variously classified as a 'folk tale' (Milgrom, p. 468), 'legend' (Bewer, *AJT* 9 [1905], p. 258), 'fable' (Coats, *Semeia* 24 [1982], pp. 57f.) and 'burlesque' (Rofé, *Balaam*, p. 51).

22. But God's anger was kindled: According to D. Winton Thomas (*VT* 18 [1968], p. 121), the use of the divine name, *'elōhîm*, here is an example of one of the unusual ways of expressing the superlative in Heb.; he therefore suggests that 'God's anger' would more appropriately be rendered, 'a divine, terrible anger'. **the angel of the LORD**: Usually in the *OT*, the 'angel of the LORD' (*mal'ak yhwh*) is distinguished from Yahweh himself; here, however, the angel is regarded as a special manifestation of the deity, 'a temporary appearance of Yahweh in human form' (Gray, p. 333). In v. 35 the angel utters Yahweh's own words, just as if Yahweh himself were speaking. The angel appears as Balaam's **adversary**: The Heb. word *śāṭān*, here used in its simple sense of 'opposer, adversary' (as, e.g., in 1 Sam. 29:4; 2 Sam. 19:22 [MT 19:23]; 1 Kg. 5:4 [MT 5:18]; 11:25) is also used in the *OT* (with the definite article) to denote *the* adversary *par excellence* who appears as the public prosecutor in the heavenly court to challenge the ways of men (Job 1–2; Zech. 3:1). Balaam was accompanied on his journey by his **two servants**: These play no further role in the story, and may only have been introduced at this point to demonstrate that the seer was travelling like a man of superior status (cf. Noth). The Talmud identified the two servants as Jannes and Jambres, two of Pharaoh's magicians (Exod. 7:11, 22) who 'opposed Moses' (2 Tim. 3:8).

23–27. The angel of the LORD tried to halt Balaam's journey by standing in the road with **a drawn sword in his hand**. The ass, who was evidently the only one to see the phenomenon, turned off the track and entered a field, but was beaten by Balaam and forced back onto the road. The angel then sought to stop the ass by standing in front of her as she passed along **a narrow path**, enclosed on either side by the walls of two adjacent vineyards. This time, the animal had no open country to turn into and was therefore compelled to try to pass the angel by pushing against the wall (and hurting Balaam's foot in the process!), at which point the ass was beaten for a second time by her owner. The ass then stood in a narrow passage, **where there was no way to turn either to the right or to the left**, so that the animal was forced to crouch down; she was then beaten by Balaam, for a third time, **with his staff**.

28. Then the LORD opened the mouth of the ass, thus enabling
it to speak. The only other parallel to this phenomenon in the *OT*
is the serpent who converses with Eve (Gen. 3:1, 4f.), but examples
of animals speaking with a human voice are not uncommon in
ancient folklore (Gray, p. 334).

30. In reply to Balaam's accusation that she had made sport of
him (v. 29), the ass defends herself by asking whether he had ever
known her to do such a thing during all the years he had owned
her. Balaam was forced to concede that she had not.

31. Only when Yahweh had **opened the eyes of Balaam** was
he able to see the angel standing in the way, sword in hand, and,
realizing that he was in the presence of the supernatural, he **fell on
his face** in obeisance.

32. because your way is perverse before me: The meaning of
the Heb. is uncertain. The verb *yāraṭ* occurs only here and in Job
16:11 in the *OT*, and according to *BDB* (p. 437*b*) it means 'to
precipitate' or 'to be precipitate'. Snaith (p. 290) considers the possibility that the phrase may mean 'because the way is precipitous
before me', i.e., because the sides of the road were steep, but this
seems unlikely, for Balaam's answer in v. 34 suggests that the phrase
was intended to express divine disapproval of his journey. Dillmann
(p. 147) suggests reading *yāraṭtā*, 'you have precipitated (the journey
in front of me)', i.e., you have rushed recklessly in front of me, and
this reading is favoured by some modern versions (cf. *NEB*, 'you
made straight for me'). The most probable solution is that the words
were intended to express the angel's censure of Balaam for
embarking upon a reckless, foolhardy mission.

34–35. Balaam concedes that he had made a grave error (**I have
sinned**) and offers to return home. An editorial note in v. 35 states
that Balaam was nevertheless permitted to proceed on his journey,
though he was constrained to speak only the words which Yahweh
had commanded him.

(h) BALAK MEETS BALAAM
22:36–40

Balak goes to meet Balaam at the border of his territory (v. 36) and
upbraids the seer for his delay in coming. Was this the appropriate
way to respond to the summons of a king? Or did the seer think
that Balak would be unable to reward him adequately (v. 37)? In
reply, Balaam merely tells the king that, although he had now come,

he was nevertheless able to utter only the words which Yahweh had commanded him to speak (v. 38). A sacrificial meal was then held, and this was served to Balaam and the dignitaries who were with him (v. 40).

36. Balak went to meet Balaam **at the city of Moab**. *NEB* reads 'Ar of Moab', which involves a slight emendation of the Heb. ('*ār* instead of '*îr*). Although this reading cannot claim the support of the ancient Vsns, the emendation is probably justified, since a city by this name is mentioned in 21:15 and there, too, it is described as being situated on Moab's border. *NRSV* similarly understands the reference here to be to a specific city, but takes it to be Ir-moab. The exact location of Ar of Moab (or Ir-moab) is unknown, but it was evidently situated **on the boundary formed by the Arnon**. The Arnon is here regarded as forming Moab's northern frontier; thus Moab at this time presumably possessed no land to the north of the river (cf., also, 21:14). The following clause defines the locality further: **at the extremity of the boundary**, i.e., presumably, the eastern end of the frontier, since it was from the east that Balaam was coming. That Balak was prepared to go so far to meet Balaam would have been understood as a mark of the high esteem in which the king held the seer (cf. Sturdy).

39. Balaam accompanies Balak to **Kiriath-huzoth**: This place, which means 'the city of streets', is mentioned only here in the *OT*, and its location is unknown.

40. In honour of Balaam's arrival, **Balak sacrificed oxen and sheep**: Snaith (*NPC*, p. 265) argues that the root *zbḥ* is here used in its primary sense of 'slaughtering' animals for food (cf. *NEB*); thus the action here described was not a religious ritual, as the rendering of *RSV* implies, but simply a demonstration of hospitality on the part of Balak. However, the Heb. verb *zābaḥ* usually means 'to slaughter for sacrifice' (*BDB*, pp. 256f.), and such a meaning would suit the present context admirably, since sacrificial meals were a regular means of fêting holy men (1 Sam. 9:12ff.; 16:2ff.), and were often regarded as a way of strengthening mutual ties. The phrase **and sent to Balaam** has proved difficult, for it implies that Balak was sending to fetch Balaam from a distance, whereas according to vv. 38f. they had already met, and, indeed, were in each other's company. It is therefore usually assumed either that the object of the verb 'sent' has been accidentally omitted from the text, or that it was deliberately left unexpressed and was intended to be supplied on the basis of the preceding clause, in which case the meaning may be that Balak sent 'portions of flesh' to Balaam and the Moabite princes who had accompanied him (cf. McNeile, p. 130). Alternatively, it may be that the sacrificial meal was eaten a short distance away from the spot where the animals themselves had been sacrificed, and so Balaam and the Moabite princes had to be 'sent for', and brought to the appropriate place (so, e.g., Noth).

(i) BALAAM'S FIRST ORACLE
22:41–23:12

Balak takes Balaam to a vantage point from where he can see the Israelites (v. 41) and, at the seer's request (23:1), Balak builds for him seven altars, upon each of which are sacrificed a bull and a ram (v. 2). The king was then told to remain by the sacrifice while Balaam went off to a bare height (v. 3), hoping to receive a revelation from Yahweh. Balaam receives an oracle from God (v. 5) which he then proceeds to declare (vv. 7*b*–10), but instead of cursing the Israelites, as Balak had demanded, he announces that no curse can harm them, and, as if to emphasize the point, the oracle concludes with a description of the magnitude of Israel's numbers. Balak reproaches Balaam for delivering such an oracle (v. 11), but the seer responds by stating that he had no choice but to speak the words that Yahweh had put in his mouth (v. 12).

41. On the morning after his arrival, Balaam is taken by Balak to **Bamoth-baal**: The Heb. reads, lit., 'the high places of Baal' (cf. *RV*; *NEB*, 'the Heights of Baal'), and some commentators believe that the expression here should not be construed as a place-name, but that it was, rather, a descriptive term of the general area, which consisted of several hill-tops, some of which were dedicated to various deities, such as Baal, Nebo, Peor etc. Nevertheless, many modern versions (cf. *NIV*, *NRSV*, *REB*, *JB*) concur with *RSV* in rendering the expression as 'Bamoth-baal' (cf. Jos. 13:17); its site is unknown, but it is perhaps to be identified with the Bamoth mentioned in 21:19. Noth (p. 182) points to a widespread belief in the ancient world that, for a curse to be effective, it was essential to be able to see the person or object that was to be execrated, and it was presumably for this reason that Balaam was taken to a vantage point from which he could see **the nearest of the people**. *BDB* (p. 892) gives *qāṣeh* the meaning 'end, extremity', but the correct rendering of the word in the present context depends upon which

'end' of the people is here intended. *RSV* assumes that the nearest
end was meant (so, too, Gray), and that, therefore, only a section
of the Israelites would have been visible to Balaam, the rest being
obscured from his view, possibly because they were too numerous
to be seen all at once. *NEB*, on the other hand, understands the
word to refer to the furthest end and assumes that Balaam was
therefore able to see 'the full extent of the Israelite host'. The former
alternative can claim the support of LXX, while the latter can claim
the support of the Vulg. Perhaps the narrator intended to imply
that Balaam was able to see only the outer fringe of the Israelites
in the valley below him, and that the point of his being conducted
subsequently to other vantage points (cf. 23:13*a*, 28) was that he
would then be able to obtain a clearer view of the Israelite camp.

23:1. Before Balaam could utter his oracle, it was necessary for
the appropriate ritual preparations to be made, and so Balak is
instructed to build **seven altars** and to provide **seven bulls and
seven rams** for the sacrifice. The sacredness of the number 'seven'
goes back to very ancient times, and its significance has frequently
been investigated (cf. König, *HDB*, iii, p. 565; Pope, *IDB*, iv,
pp. 294f.); for other examples of the use of seven sacrificial victims,
see 28:19, 27; Gen. 21:28ff.; Job 42:8. Wenham (p. 172) suggests
that the choice of bulls and rams may have been intended to enhance
the prestige of Balaam's offering, since these were the most valued
of Israel's sacrificial animals (cf. Lev. 4:1ff.; 5:14–6:7); Balaam and
Balak are thus represented as doing their utmost to ensure a favourable response from Yahweh.

2. and Balak and Balaam offered: The verb 'offered' is in the
singular, and this may suggest that, originally, Balak alone was the
intended subject; this is confirmed by the reference to 'your (singular)/his burnt offering' in vv. 3, 6, 15, 17, and by the fact that
Balaam plays no part in the offering of the sacrifice in vv. 14, 30.
The reference to Balaam here is therefore probably a gloss (cf. LXX;
NEB); the seer's role was not to offer sacrifice but merely to make
contact with Yahweh once the necessary ritual had been accomplished. The gloss was no doubt precipitated by Balaam's statement
in v. 4*b*, but, in fact, v. 4*b* is probably misplaced in its present
context, and there is much to be said for transferring the words,
'and he [*RSV*, 'Balaam'] said to him, "I have prepared the seven
altars, and I have offered upon each altar a bull and a ram"' to the
end of v. 2, and regarding it as part of Balak's speech informing

Balaam that he had done according to his request. In this case, v. 5*a* would follow on from v. 4*a*; cf. v. 16 (so, e.g., Gray, Paterson; cf. *NEB*).

3. After inviting Balak to stand beside his burnt offering, Balaam went off to a **bare height**. The rendering of *RSV* presupposes that *šepî* is the singular form of *š^epāyîm*, which occurs in Isa. 49:9; Jer. 3:2, 21; 4:11; 7:29; 12:12; 14:6; 49:9. But the word has appeared to many as suspect because (i) apart from the doubtful exception of Job 33:21, the word occurs only in the singular in the *OT*; (ii) none of the ancient Vsns appears to have understood the word in the sense of 'bare height'; (iii) if 'bare height' were the intended meaning, it is surprising that a verb such as *'ālāh*, 'to ascend', was not used instead of *hālak*, 'to go'; (iv) it is unclear why Balaam should want to go to a 'bare height', since he was already on an elevated position at Bamoth-baal (22:41). In view of these difficulties, several alternative renderings have been suggested. *NEB*, on the basis of LXX, Vulg., reads 'he went forthwith'; Targ. Onk. suggests that he went 'alone' (cf. *AV* mg.; *NJPS*); Targ. Neofiti has 'quietly, calmly'. However, none of these alternative proposals appears to be particularly convincing, and, as Gray (p. 344) notes, it is by no means clear that the Vsns had anything other than the present Heb. text before them. On the whole, it seems preferable to retain the reading of *RSV* (cf. *NIV*, *REB*, *JB*), and to regard Balaam's departure to a 'bare height' as a reflection of his desire to be alone in order to receive a communication from God.

7–10. These verses contain the first of Balaam's four oracles. The seer begins by stating, in summary form, how he, a Mesopotamian seer, had come to prophesy against Israel (v. 7), but he concedes that he was unable to curse the Israelites (v. 8), since they stood apart from other nations (v. 9). Balaam refers to the vast number of Israelites (v. 10*a*), and concludes the oracle by expressing the hope that his own fate may be like theirs (v. 10*b*). The oracle reveals complete rhythmic uniformity (3:3) and displays the synonymous parallelism which is so characteristic of Hebrew poetry. Noth (p. 184) regards v. 10*b* (with its distinctly personal note) as a later addition, and argues that the structure of the oracle is thereby improved (cf., also, Paterson). On the literary structure of vv. 7–10, see, further, Tosato *VT* 29 (1979), pp. 98ff. The relationship between this oracle and the surrounding narrative is disputed. According to some, the oracle presupposes the Balaam saga and is, in fact, quite unintelligible without it (cf. Mowinckel, *ZAW*, N.F., 7 [1930], p. 264; Noth, p. 183; Milgrom, pp. 196, 467f.); others argue that the oracle did not originate with the narrative but, rather, circulated independently as a brief summary of the saga in rhythmic form (cf. Mauchline, *Fest. Stevenson*, p. 79).

7. And Balaam took up his discourse: The Heb. word here rendered 'discourse', *māšāl*, is used in the *OT* of many different types of utterances, including aphorisms (1 Sam. 10:12; 24:13 [MT 24:14]; Ezek. 12:22), taunts (Isa. 14:4; Hab. 2:6), parables and allegories (Ezek. 17:2; 24:3), popular proverbs and didactic sayings (Prov. 1:1; 10:1). The underlying idea seems to be the use of figurative or representative language (cf. Johnson, *VTS* 3 [1955], pp. 162ff.) and, as Gray (p. 344) notes, the word could be used of 'any suggestive saying that implied more than it actually said'. *RSV*'s 'discourse' is certainly preferable to *AV*'s 'parable', but it is not an entirely satisfactory rendering of the term in the present context. *NRSV*'s 'oracle' (cf. *NIV*, *NEB*) represents a distinct improvement, although it must be remembered that the word *māšāl* is never used in the *OT* of the speeches uttered by the prophets. Balaam states that he had been brought by Balak **from Aram**, i.e., from Syria, and had been summoned from **the eastern mountains**, i.e., from the high ranges of the Syrian desert. This location of Balaam's homeland agrees with the reference in 22:5, which states that Balaam came from Pethor, i.e. (in all probability) the Pitru of the Assyrian and Egyptian inscriptions, which was near the Euphrates. The suggestion that the word Aram should here be emended to read Edom (e.g., Holzinger, p. 116, and, initially, Albright, *JAOS* 35 [1915], p. 387; but cf. his later view in *JBL* 63 [1944], p. 211, n. 15) has little to commend it, for although the two names are practically identical in Heb. and are occasionally confused in the *OT* (cf. 2 Sam. 8:12f.; 1 Chr. 18:11), such an emendation in the present passage has no support either in the Heb. manuscripts or in the Vsns. **Come, curse Jacob for me**: Here, as in the other oracles of Balaam (vv. 21, 23; 24:5, 17, 18f.), 'Jacob' is used as an alternative name for 'Israel'; this usage is found elsewhere in the Pentateuch only in Exod. 19:3 and in the Blessing of Moses (Dt. 33:4, 10, 28).

8. How can I curse whom God has not cursed? Balaam here gives expression to the thought that a curse could not be efficacious if it was contrary to the will of Yahweh. In this and the previous verse no fewer than three different (but synonymous) verbs for 'curse' are employed.

9. lo, a people dwelling alone: *BDB* (pp. 94f.) gives *bāḏāḏ* (here rendered 'alone') the meaning 'isolation, separation', but its precise nuance in the present context is disputed. Some commentators see here a reference to Israel's strength: the nation dwells 'alone', i.e., securely, peacefully, unmolested by other nations (cf. Gray, Milgrom); others discern a reference to Israel's exclusiveness: the nation stands 'alone', i.e., aloof from other peoples, either by virtue of its special relationship with God (cf. Wenham, Maarsingh), or by virtue of the fact that it had remained independent and had not aligned itself to other nations (cf. Malamat, *JQR* 76 [1985], pp. 47ff.). The parallelism between this clause and the following line might be regarded as supporting the latter alternative, but the fact that isolation is elsewhere in the *OT* coupled with the idea of security (cf. Dt. 33:28; Jer. 49:31; Mic. 7:14), and that reference is made in the next verse to the numerical strength of Israel, tends to favour the former (cf. Mauchline, *op. cit.*, p. 78). If the allusion *is* to Israel's exclusiveness, however, this should certainly not in itself be regarded as an indication that the oracle is late (*contra* Holzinger, Mowinckel), for the notion of Israel's privileged status was current in pre-exilic times (cf. Am. 3:2; von Rad, *Deuteronomy*, p. 205; Rudolph, p. 116). **and not reckoning itself among the nations**: This is the only occurrence of the root *ḥšḇ* in the Hithpael in the *OT*. Hertz (*ExpT* 45 [1933–4], p. 524) refers to the view of M. Jastrow that the verb here, as in Neo-Hebrew, means 'to conspire', and that the implication is that Israel does not conspire against the nations, and thus posed no threat which might call for a curse. But the traditional rendering is better suited to the context: the Mesopotamian seer is made to confess that the people of Israel occupied a position of special privilege, and, as such, were to be distinguished from the nations that surrounded them.

10. That the Israelite people had been blessed was evident from its huge population, which was so immense that it could not even be numbered: **Who can count the dust of Jacob . . . ?** Gevirtz's suggestion (*Patterns*, pp. 64f.) that this and the following clause contain an oblique reference to Mesopotamian magical practices seems somewhat fanciful, especially since 'dust of the earth' is a familiar enough image in the *OT* to express the notion of abundance beyond measure (cf. Gen. 13:16; 28:14; 2 Sam. 22:43; Isa. 40:12). Guillaume, however, finds the notion of counting particles of dust absurd, and he prefers to connect *'āpār* ('dust') with Arab. *'ifirrīn* = a bold, resolute, strong man, and he translates the clause as follows: 'Who can count the warriors of Jacob?' (*VT* 12 [1962], pp. 335ff.); he concedes, though, that there may here be a deliberate play on the word *'āpār* = dust, used with reference to Gen. 13:16. But whether the author of the present oracle consciously intended such a *double entendre* must be regarded as very doubtful. **or number the fourth part of Israel?:** MT here contains an impossible construction, and the rendering of *RSV* involves a necessary emendation of the text (*mî sāpar 'et-rōḇaʻ* instead of *mispār 'et-rōḇaʻ*). *RSV* follows *RV* in retaining the word *rōḇaʻ* = the fourth part, the idea presumably being that even a quarter of Israel's army would be impossible to number, much less the people as a whole. But while this interpretation has commended itself to some commentators (e.g., Maarsingh), others have expressed doubts as to whether *rōḇaʻ* represents the original reading for, as Paterson (p. 57) observes, to state that the fourth part of Israel is impossible to number seems to be something of a contradiction in terms. Albright (*JBL* 63 [1944], p. 213, n. 28) refers to the Akkad. *turbuʼtu* = 'dust cloud', and suggests emending the Heb. to read *tarbaʼat*, 'dust'; the parallelism with the preceding line would thus be considerably improved, and this reading has been adopted by *NRSV* (cf. *JB*) and accepted by several recent scholars (Snaith, de Vaulx). Others (Dillmann, Gray, Marsh) prefer to emend the Heb. to read *riḇʻḇōt*, 'myriads' (cf. LXX), and this reading is adopted by *NEB*, *REB* (cf. 10:36). Hertz's suggestion (*op. cit.*, p. 524) that *rbʻ* here means 'ashes' ('Who can number the ashes of Israel?') has not generally been accepted (though cf. Thomas, *ExpT* 46 [1934–5], p. 285). **Let me die the death of the righteous:** The plural *yᵉšārîm* ('righteous') is unexpected, since the word *kāmōhû* ('like him') at the end of the verse properly requires a singular antecedent. Albright (*op. cit.*, p. 213, n. 28a) overcomes the difficulty by suggesting that the *mem* in *yᵉšārîm* is enclitic and not the sign of the plural (so, too, Freedman, *ZAW*, N.F., 31 [1960], p. 104). *BHS*, on the other hand, on the basis of the Vsns, suggests reading the plural *kāhēm* ('like them'). If MT is retained, the plural adjective must be taken as referring to the Israelites, while the singular pronoun in *kāmōhû* must refer to the 'nation', understood as a single entity. **and let my end be like his:** Some suggest, on the basis of LXX, that 'my end' (Heb. *'aḥᵃrîtî*) here means 'my posterity' (cf.

Thom, *ExpT* 16 [1904–5], p. 334), and that Balaam's wish is that his descendants might share in the blessings of Israel (cf. Binns); others argue, on the basis of Talmudic tradition and such passages as Job 8:7; Prov. 24:20, that Balaam was referring to his death, and that his words even contain a vague hint of the world to come (cf. Loewenstamm, *JJS* 16 [1965], pp. 183ff.). But by far the most probable interpretation is that Balaam was here invoking upon himself a blessing that the closing years of his natural life might be spent in the manner enjoyed by all righteous people, 'not premature or violent' but 'peaceful and in a good old age' (Gray, p. 347).

11–12. Balaam is here rebuked by Balak for having blessed Israel; yet, curiously, no such blessing is invoked in the preceding oracle. It is quite possible, however, that Balaam's refusal to curse the Israelites was construed by Balak as tantamount to an endorsement of their blessing. Balaam's defence is merely that he was constrained to utter only the words which **the LORD puts in my mouth**, a fact which he had made clear from the very beginning (cf. 22:18f., 38).

(j) BALAAM'S SECOND ORACLE
23:13–26

Undeterred by this initial setback, Balak still hopes that a curse might be pronounced against Israel, and so he chooses another site and builds seven new altars, upon which seven bulls and seven rams are again sacrificed (vv. 13f.). Balaam then leaves Balak beside his offering and confers with Yahweh some distance away (v. 15). When he receives a further revelation (v. 16), Balaam returns to Balak (v. 17) and utters another oracle, in which he emphasizes Yahweh's unchanging purpose towards Israel (vv. 19f.); he also announces that, because of God's presence in their midst, it would be impossible to interrupt Israel's triumphant march of conquest (vv. 21–24). On the literary structure of the oracle, see Tosato, *op. cit.*, pp. 101ff., and on its relationship, both to the surrounding narrative and to the third oracle contained in 24:3–9, see Noth, pp. 185f.

13. Come with me to another place, from which you may see them: In the ancient world, soothsayers who were unable to obtain an omen upon their first attempt often persisted until the outcome proved more successful (cf. Milgrom, p. 189); occasionally, this involved moving to a more propitious location (cf. Gray, McNeile). It may be, however, that Balak is here deliberately depicted as a quasi-comic figure, convinced that it was simply the wrong vantage point which had caused the curse to backfire (cf. Wharton, *Int* 13 [1959], p. 44). The implication of v. 13*a* is that from this new vantage-point Balaam would be able to see the Israelites in their entirety, but the qualification which follows in v. 13*b* appears to suggest that the seer's view this time, too, would be restricted (cf. 22:41). This inconsistency has led many commentators to view the words **you shall see only the nearest of them, and shall not see them all** as an editorial addition; as has often been observed, if they were authentic, Balaam would have been in no better position to curse Israel than before. The motivation for inserting this additional clause is not difficult to discern: if Balaam had been able from this vantage-point to see the whole of Israel, then there would have been little point in his later being taken to yet another site, viz., the top of Peor (v. 28). By suggesting that even on this second occasion only some of the Israelites were visible to Balaam, the editor effectively reserved the full, unimpeded view of the people for Balaam's third and final attempt. Commentators who defend the authenticity of the qualifying phrase tacitly assume that from this second vantage point Balaam was able to see a larger portion of the people than had been visible from Bamoth-baal (22:41; cf., e.g., Maarsingh), but there is nothing in the text to suggest that this is what the writer intended.

14. And he took him to the field of Zophim: The word 'Zophim' means 'watchers', and it is by no means certain that the word is to be understood here as a place name (cf. *NEB*, 'Field of the Watchers'; *JB*, 'Field of Spies'). If it *was* so intended, then it must be conceded that its location is quite unknown, though it was probably situated on an elevated position, since the name clearly implies that it afforded an extensive outlook. This may be confirmed by the use of the term *śāḏeh* (rendered 'field' in *RSV*), which in some *OT* texts (cf. Jg. 5:18; 2 Sam. 1:21; Jer. 13:27; 17:3; 18:14) appears to carry the sense of 'mountain' (cf. Akkad. *śāḏū* = mountain). See, further, Burney, *Judges*, pp. 111f.; Propp, *VT* 37 (1987), pp. 230ff. For **Pisgah**, see on 21:20.

18. hearken to me: MT's *'aḏay* is difficult, and the rendering of *RSV* ('to me'), presupposes that the word is a mistake for *'ālay* or *'ēlay* (cf. Paterson); Albright (*op. cit.*, p. 214, n. 31), however, prefers to read *'ēḏî*, 'my testimony', an emendation which can claim the support of LXX and Syr. (cf., also, Vetter, *Seherspruch*, p. 17; L'Heureux, p. 89).

19. God is not man, that he should lie: Attempts to discern in passages such as this a 'depatriarchalizing' principle at work in Scripture (cf. Trible, *JAAR* 41 [1973], pp. 30ff.; *idem*, *IDB Sup*, pp. 368f.) are clearly wide of the mark, for it was certainly not the author's purpose to challenge the belief that Yahweh was a male deity (cf. Miller, *CBQ* 48 [1986], pp. 609ff.); the intention, rather, was to give expression to a belief in the consistency of God's activity and the immutability of the divine character. The same thought is expressed in similar terms, albeit in prose, in 1 Sam. 15:29, though there is no reason to suppose a literary connection between the two passages (cf. Mauchline, *op. cit.*, p. 80). **or a son of man**: *NRSV*'s 'mortal' must be considered an improvement, since it avoids the later theological connotations implicit in the expression 'son of man'. **that he should repent**: As Snaith (*ExpT* 57 [1945-6], pp. 48f.) observes, the meaning of 'repent' (Heb. *niḥam*) in this clause is 'to change one's mind' and the idea here, as in the parallel line, is that God is not subject to the caprice of human behaviour, and cannot be induced to alter his disposition arbitrarily. This statement concerning the unchangeability of the divine purpose is especially apposite in the context of the Balaam narrative, for Balak had entertained the possibility that, after blessing Israel (vv. 7-10), Yahweh could still be persuaded to effect the desired curse (v. 13). Some *OT* texts suggest (in apparent contradiction to the present passage) that God could, in certain circumstances, be persuaded to 'relent' (cf. Am. 7:1ff.).

20. The implication of the steadfastness of the divine purpose is here spelled out: Israel had been blessed by Yahweh and that blessing could not in any way be retracted or revoked. **he has blessed**: Many commentators (Paterson, Gray, Marsh) prefer to follow LXX and Sam. here, which read the first person singular, 'I will bless' (cf. *NEB*; *JB*); this, it is argued, conforms better with the following words ('I cannot revoke it') and with the preceding line ('Behold, I received a command to bless'). But while it is true that this reading would involve only the slightest emendation of the Heb., and would have the advantage of making Balaam the subject throughout, the text of MT is by no means indefensible: the meaning may simply be that Yahweh had decreed that Israel would be blessed (cf. 22:12), and no attempt on Balaam's part could negate the effects of that blessing.

21. He has not beheld ... nor has he seen: The rendering of *RSV* presumes that God is the subject of both verbs, but it is preferable to regard the subject here as impersonal (cf. *NEB* mg.). Gray (p. 352) and others (McNeile, Marsh, Vetter) follow Syr., Targ. Onk. here and read the first person singular (cf. *JB*), thus continuing the first persons of the previous verse, but this is hardly necessary. **misfortune in Jacob ... trouble in Israel**: *NEB* renders *'āwen* ('misfortune') as 'iniquity', and *'āmāl* ('trouble') as 'mischief' (cf. *AV*, *RV*), thus interpreting Balaam's words as a statement of the ethical superiority of Israel over other nations, an idea which finds expression elsewhere in such passages as Isa. 26:2; Hab. 1:13. But this interpretation, which is based on Syr. and rabbinic commentators, is not entirely in harmony with the present context, and the rendering of *RSV*, which implies that Israel was free, not from moral blemishes, but from material disasters (cf. LXX) is to be preferred. The word *'āmāl* is regularly used in the *OT* in the sense of 'trouble', 'calamity' (*BDB*, p. 765*b*), and *'āwen* is used in this sense in such passages as Prov. 12:21; 22:8. Having depicted Israel's bliss in negative terms in the first half of the verse, the poet now turns to its positive aspect: Yahweh is with his people, **and the shout** (LXX 'glory'; cf. Cheyne, *ExpT* 10 [1898–9], p. 401) **of a king is among them**. The Heb. *t˘rû'āh* ('shout') is used in the *OT* of the blast of the trumpet, the victory shout of the battle-field, and the acclamation of the people at the crowning of the king; the reference to the triumphant exodus from Egypt in the next verse suggests that the word here refers to the shout of victory with which the Israelites were accustomed to greet their king (cf. 1 Sam. 4:5; 2 Sam. 6:15). Mowinckel (*op. cit.*, p. 267; *He That Cometh*, pp. 63f.) takes the reference here to be to an earthly king, and interprets the 'shout' as the cultic acclamation uttered during the New Year Festival's re-enactment of Yahweh's ascension to his throne; however, the parallelism in the present verse strongly suggests that the word *melek* ('king') should be understood as a reference to Yahweh. For the notion of Yahweh as a divine king, cf. Dt. 33:5; 1 Sam. 8:7; 12:12; Eissfeldt, *ZAW*, N.F., 5 (1928), pp. 81ff.; Maag, *VTS* 7 (1959), pp. 129ff. The idea probably originated in the early years of the monarchy (if not before), and was no doubt intended as a reminder to the monarch that there was a heavenly king to whom he was ultimately responsible (cf. Johnson, *Sacral Kingship*, pp. 38f.). See, further, Brettler, *God is King, passim*.

22. they have as it were the horns of the wild ox: The predicate is ambiguous, for it is not clear whether the horns are an attribute of Israel (so *RSV*; cf. Albright, *op. cit.*, p. 215, n. 47) or of God (so *NRSV*; *NEB*; cf. von Rad, *OT Theology*, i, p. 24). In favour of the former alternative is the fact that Israel is compared to a lion and lioness in v. 24, and so a comparison with an ox would certainly not be out of place here; in favour of the latter alternative is the fact that in the ancient Near East the horns of an ox were recognized symbols of divine power, as is evident from the sculptured representations of Babylonian deities. Perhaps, however, the distinction is more apparent than real, for the writer would clearly have understood Yahweh's strength and indomitable power to be manifest in the military prowess of Israel. The meaning of the word rendered 'horns' in *RSV* (Heb. *tô'ăpōṭ*) is obscure. In Ps. 95:4 it refers to the peaks of mountains, and in the present context it is probably to be understood as a poetic metaphor for the towering horns of the ox. It is generally recognized that the 'wild ox' (Heb. *r'ēm*) is to be identified with the *rîmu* of the Assyrian inscriptions, which is represented as an enormous species (now extinct) of bison. *AV*'s 'unicorn' is based on LXX, but is clearly erroneous, since the *r'ēm* was regarded as having more than one horn (Ps. 22:21). Among the Hebrews, the *r'ēm* was believed to be untamable (cf. Job 39:9–12) and, with its formidable horns, it was regarded as a particularly dangerous animal; it was thus a suitable metaphor to characterize the fierce, irresistible advance of an army with a divine king at its head.

23. This verse has proved difficult, partly because its translation is problematic and partly because the connection between the two halves of the verse, and between the verse as a whole and its surrounding context, is by no means clear. The lack of connection between v. 23*a* and 23*b* is sometimes resolved by regarding v. 23*a* as a mistaken gloss on v. 21*a*, and interpreting v. 23*b* as a comment upon God's action in delivering Israel from Egypt in v. 22*a* (cf. McNeile). Noth (p. 187), on the other hand, regards v. 23*b* as secondary, and takes v. 23*a* to mean that since Israel was immune to spells wrought by magic and divination, Balak's machinations would inevitably prove to be ineffectual. But whichever half of the verse is retained, it still appears intrusive, and there can be little doubt that the connection between v. 22 (with its reference to the 'wild ox') and v. 24 (with its reference to the 'lion' and 'lioness') is considerably improved if the entire verse is regarded as a secondary insertion (so, e.g., Gray, Marsh). Attempts to rearrange the sequence of the verses in order to improve the composition of the oracle (Vetter) are inevitably subjective and, for that reason, unconvincing. The problem regarding the translation of the verse arises from the fact that it is uncertain whether the poet was stating that there was no enchantment or divination 'against' Jacob/Israel (*NRSV*; *NIV*; *JB*) or 'in' Jacob/Israel (*NEB*; *REB*). If the former rendering is adopted then the sense seems to be that since Yahweh was Israel's God, no magical practice could possibly have any baneful effect upon the people; if the latter rendering is adopted then the sense seems to be that Yahweh's very presence in Israel rendered divination and enchantments as a means of perceiving the future wholly unnecessary. Although neither translation is without its difficulty, the balance of probability tends to favour the rendering 'in Jacob/in Israel', for, as Gray (p. 355) observes, 'against' involves an improbable use of the preposition *bēṯ* (though cf. Albright, *op. cit.*, p. 215, n. 49), and the words used here, *naḥaš* ('enchantment') and *qesem* ('divination'), refer merely to methods of divining the future and do not, of themselves, suggest magical practices which might prove injurious to others. The term *naḥaš* is usually taken to refer to divination from natural omens, of which the most familiar example was the observation of the flight of birds (so LXX; cf. Driver, *Deuteronomy*, p. 225); the word *qesem* refers to the casting of lots, e.g., by arrows (Ezek. 21:21; cf. Davies, *Bib* 61 [1980], pp. 554ff.), though the word probably also included other kinds of divinatory practices.

24. Israel's terrifying strength is compared to that of a lion, about to spring upon its prey (cf. Gen. 49:9, 27; Dt. 33:20; Mic. 5:8). The metaphor forms an appropriate climax to the oracle, suggesting that Israel was invincible and had the ability to inflict a crushing defeat upon Moab.

25–26. In his anger and disillusionment, Balak refuses to allow Balaam to make any further utterances regarding Israel, and implores him to remain neutral towards his avowed enemy. Balaam replies by reminding Balak that he could say only what Yahweh had commanded him (cf. 22:38; 23:3, 12). These two verses read like the close of the narrative, and the insertion of further oracles in ch. 24 comes as something of an anti-climax. Many commentators are thus of the view that one version of the Balaam story ended at this point, possibly with the note now contained in 24:25 to the effect that Balaam then returned home.

(k) BALAAM'S THIRD ORACLE
23:27–24:9

Vv. 27–30 are basically editorial and serve to link the two separate versions of the Balaam story. These verses simply repeat the content of 23:13f., and in this way the editor was able to assimilate the third oracle uttered by Balaam to the first two. Balaam is taken to yet another location in the hope that this time he would be able to curse Israel, and the same preparations are made as before (23:29f.). But Balak was to be disappointed once more, for the oracle which Balaam was to utter merely described, in glowing terms, the vast expanse of Israel's encampment (24:5f.), the fertility of its land (v. 7*a*), the greatness of its rulers (v. 7*b*), and the awe and terror which it inspired in its enemies (vv. 8f.). Far from cursing the people, Balaam is led to bless them 'with accolades and promises which are unsurpassed in the entire Pentateuch' (Olson, *Death*, p. 159). Unlike the oracles contained in the previous chapter, Balaam's utterance in vv. 3*b*–9 (and in vv. 15*b*–19) appears to be quite unconnected with the narrative framework in which it has now been incorporated. The seer is here introduced as if nothing were previously known about him, and in the introduction to both oracles (vv. 3*b*f., 15*b*f.) Balaam is referred to in the third person, although according to the surrounding narrative, he himself is the speaker. It is possible, therefore, that the two oracles contained in ch. 24 were, at one time, independent entities, which were originally unconnected with the narrative contained in chs. 22–24 (cf. de Vaulx). For an analysis of the structure of Balaam's third utterance, see Smick, *Fest. Allis*, pp. 242ff.

28. Balak takes Balaam **to the top of Peor, that overlooks the desert**: These words bear a striking similarity to those found in 21:20, except that Pisgah is read there instead of Peor. On this basis, some suggest that the word Pisgah originally stood in the present context, too, but that it was subsequently changed by a redactor in order to provide Balaam with a different location to that in which he had uttered his second oracle (cf. 23:13f.; so, e.g., Paterson, Marsh). However, there is no reason to doubt that 'Peor' represents the original reading here, and although no reference to Mt. Peor is found in the *OT*, it is quite possible that a mountain of this name existed, and that it overlooked the plains of Moab. Noth (p. 188) suggests that it may have been in the vicinity of Beth-peor (cf. Dt. 3:29; 4:46; 34:6; Jos. 13:20), which was situated a little to the north of Mount Nebo (cf. Henke, *ZDPV* 75 [1959], pp. 155ff.). The word *yᵉšîmōn*, rendered 'desert' in *RSV* (*NRSV*, *NIV*, 'wasteland') refers to particular regions of the desert (cf. 1 Sam. 23:19), in this case the east bank of the lower Jordan valley. *NEB* interprets the word here as a proper noun, Jeshimon, although, surprisingly, it translates it as 'desert' in 21:20; the inconsistency is remedied in *REB*, which reads Jeshimon in both passages.

24:1. When Balaam realized that it was Yahweh's intention to bless Israel, he did not attempt, **as at other times**, to seek omens, but resolved, rather, to pronounce his oracle forthwith. The words rendered 'as at other times' are ambiguous, for it is unclear whether they were intended to refer to Balaam's customary habit on similar occasions, or to the practice which he had deployed during his previous encounter with Balak (cf. *NEB*, 'as before'). In either case, the words cannot be from the same source as ch. 23, for if the meaning is that Balaam did not follow his usual custom, the observation would have been better placed at the beginning of that chapter and not after he had already uttered two of his oracles; on the other hand, if the words refer specifically to Balaam's encounter with Balak, then their import is difficult to explain, for there is no indication in the previous chapter that Balaam had sought omens of any kind.

2. Previous divine communications to Balaam had been effected by Yahweh's putting his words in Balaam's mouth (23:5, 16), but now **the Spirit of God came upon him**, and Balaam presumably fell into a trance (cf. vv. 3f.) in the manner of Israel's ecstatic prophets (cf. 1 Sam. 10:5f., 10f.; 19:18ff.; 1 Kg. 22:24). In the *OT*, the spirit of God was regarded not as a permanent abiding presence but rather as a temporary endowment empowering mighty men (Jg. 14:6), kings (1 Sam. 11:6) and prophets (1 Sam. 10:10) to perform specific tasks.

3. The oracle of Balaam the son of Beor: The fact that Balaam deems it necessary to introduce himself at this point (cf. v. 15) suggests that this oracle, and the one contained in vv. 15–19, are derived from a source separate from those encountered in ch. 23. The Heb. *nᵉʾum* ('oracle of') is almost always in the *OT* followed by a divine name; 2 Sam. 23:1; Prov. 30:1 and, possibly, Ps. 36:1 (MT 36:2) appear to be the only exceptions. The word is the same as that frequently employed in prophetic utterances where, with rare exceptions (cf. Isa. 1:24), it occurs in the middle or at the end of the prophet's speech. Its use here may suggest that the author regarded Balaam as the bearer of an authentic word from God, and that, in this capacity, he functioned in a role similar to that occupied by the prophets of Israel (cf. Freedman, *JBL* 96 [1977], pp. 21f.). The oracle in this case was uttered by a man **whose eye is opened**: This is a noted *crux interpretum*, for the meaning of the Heb. *š^etum*, which occurs only here and in v. 15 in the *OT*, is by no means certain. Commentators who defend the rendering of *RSV* (cf. Syr.) point to a root *štm* = 'to open', found in the Mishna and Talmud, where it is used of opening a vessel or a cask of wine (cf. *'Abodah Zarah* 5:4). *RV*, on the other hand (cf. *RSV* mg.), presupposes that Balaam's eye was 'closed' (cf. Vulg.), and scholars who favour this interpretation observe that a similar (though not identical) root, *stm*, occurs in some *OT* passages, where it means 'to close' (cf. 2 Kg. 3:19; Lam. 3:8; Dan. 8:26). If the former alternative is preferred, the meaning would be that the seer's 'inward eye' was open to receive a vision, but the difficulty with this interpretation is that the statement in v. 4 to the effect that 'his eyes were uncovered' would then be rendered unnecessary and tautologous. If, on the other hand, the latter alternative is accepted, the meaning would be that Balaam's bodily eye was closed, presumably in the posture of a trance, but it has been objected that this would be 'inappropriate in a general description of the seer in his visionary capacity' (cf. Lindblom, *Prophecy*, p. 91, n. 66). A third alternative (cf. *RSV* mg.) presupposes the same consonantal text but a different division of the words, i.e., *š^ettammāh 'ayin* ('whose eye is perfect'); this reading, suggested by Wellhausen (*Die Composition*, p. 350) can claim some Versional support (cf. LXX; Targ. Onk.), and is favoured by some recent scholars (cf. Albright, *op. cit.*, p. 216, n. 56, and, tentatively, Vetter, *op. cit.*, p. 27). An early suggestion by Ehrlich, recently revived by Allegro (*VT* 3 [1953], pp. 78f.), claims that the Heb. root *štm* should be connected with Arab. *šatama*, 'reviled', and that the meaning here is that Balaam looked upon Israel with a 'malicious eye', annoyed at their good fortune. Clearly, no translation is without its difficulty, and it would be hazardous, on the basis of the present text, to reach any conclusion concerning the precise manner in which Balaam received the divine communication.

4. Before uttering the contents of his message, Balaam emphasizes the divine authority of his words: **the oracle of him who hears the words of God**. The parallelism of this verse with v. 16 requires that the words 'and knows the knowledge of the Most High' should be inserted after 'God' (cf. Paterson); the verse would then consist of two distichs (as opposed to one tristich), and its structure would thereby conform to the rest of the oracle (apart, possibly, from v. 8). Other scholars seek to achieve a symmetry by omitting the last clause of the verse as a gloss (so, e.g., Budd). The divine revelation granted to Balaam entailed not only an auditory experience, but a visual one, too: **who sees the vision of the Almighty**: The tense of the verb in Heb. may imply that this was a privilege which Balaam was accustomed to enjoy (cf. Gray). The origin and meaning of the Heb. *šadday* is much disputed (cf. Driver, *Genesis*, pp. 404ff.; Weippert, *ZDMG*, N.F., 36 [1961], pp. 42ff.), and the English term 'Almighty' is based on the renderings of LXX (*pantokrator*) and Vulg. (*omnipotens*). Sometimes, the fuller form El Shadday ('God Almighty') is used (Gen. 43:14; 49:25; Ezek. 10:5), but Shadday alone is found some forty times in the *OT*, of which thirty-one occur in the book of Job. The use of the word in the present context is given added significance by the fact that a group of gods called *šdyn*, is alluded to in the Deir 'Allā text (cf. Hackett, *Balaam*, pp. 85ff.), where they appear to Balaam in a dream and inform him of the coming disaster, and the reasons for it. See excursus, pp. 281–84. Balaam's comportment while receiving the revelation is described in graphic terms: **falling down**, i.e., in an ecstatic trance (though LXX interprets it to mean 'fall asleep', suggesting that Balaam received the vision in a dream; cf. 12:6), **but having his eyes uncovered**, i.e., his eyes were opened to perceive what was hidden from normal sight.

6. Like valleys that stretch afar: Heb. *naḥal* means 'valley, wadi', but *NEB* is probably correct in interpreting the word here, on the basis of Arab. *naḫl*, to mean 'palm-tree' (cf. *NRSV*); this certainly coheres better with the reference to 'gardens' in the next line and with the allusion to 'aloes' and 'cedar trees' in v. 6*b* (cf. Snaith, de Vaux). It is not entirely clear whether Balaam was here comparing the sight of Israel's tents pitched below him to strong, flourishing trees stretching into the distance (Milgrom), or was intent upon describing the fertility of the land which the people were destined to possess (Wenham). **like aloes**: Some commentators are inclined to emend the Heb. *'ªhālîm* to read *'ēlîm* 'palms' (cf. Dillmann), since the aloe was not indigenous to Israel and would, therefore, not have been familiar to the Hebrews; others, however, prefer to retain MT on the ground that, in deploying such a rich metaphor, the author may deliberately have contrived to refer to an exotic tree that flourished only in distant lands (cf. Snaith, Sturdy, Budd). McNeile (p. 137) doubts whether *'ªhālîm* can be interpreted to denote a tree *per se*, since elsewhere (Prov. 7:17; Ps. 45:8 [MT 45:9]) the word appears to refer to an aromatic perfume, and is mentioned along with other fragrant substances such as myrrh, cinnamon and cassia (cf. Gray); however, there is surely nothing to prevent the supposition that in a poetic passage such as this the word may be taken to refer to the tree which produced the aromatic substance. Most of the Vsns (apart from Targ. Onk.) read 'tents' instead of 'aloes', which is interesting in so far as they bear witness to the consonantal text of MT. **like cedar trees beside the waters**: As has often been noted, cedars do not normally grow beside rivers, preferring instead the dry slopes of the mountain-side; it has therefore been suggested (Cheyne, *ExpT* 10 [1898–9], p. 401) that the trees mentioned in this and the previous line should be interchanged: 'like cedar trees that the LORD has planted/like aloes (Cheyne, 'poplars') beside the waters'. This proposal, favoured by several scholars (Gray, Albright, Vetter, de Vaulx), gains some support from the fact that cedars are elsewhere in the *OT* described as trees which Yahweh had 'planted' (Ps. 104:16). But the author of the present passage was almost certainly not as pedantic as modern critics would like to suppose, and, assuming that the language here is figurative rather than literal, MT should be retained.

7. This verse marks a transition from the second to the third person form of address, a phenomenon which is by no means unusual in ancient poetic texts (cf. Dt. 33:18f.; Jg. 5:4f.; Gilbert and Pisano, *Bib* 61 [1980], pp. 343ff.). **Water shall flow from his buckets**: The metaphor seems to be that of a man returning from his springs with an abundant supply of water for the irrigation of his crops; it here serves as a most appropriate description of Israel's overflowing prosperity. **and his seed shall be in many waters**: The text is somewhat obscure, and many commentators regard MT as corrupt. Gray (p. 365) claims that the line, as it stands, 'defies

explanation', and he therefore accepts an emendation originally proposed by Cheyne (*op. cit.*, p. 401), namely, that *mayim*, 'water',
should be read as '*ammîm*, 'peoples' (the repetition of *mayim* in two
parallel lines being regarded as highly suspicious), and that *zarᵉˁô*,
'his seed', be punctuated as *zᵉrōˁô*, 'his arm'; the line would thus be
rendered, 'his arm shall be upon many peoples', and the idea would
be that Israel's might would be felt by many nations. But the difficulty with this is that it provides a very poor parallel with the
preceding line, and consequently Cheyne and Gray are forced to
resort to further emendation of the text in order to make that line
read, 'Peoples shall tremble at his might'. The text, thus restored,
would admittedly provide an appropriate introduction to the lines
which follow, but the fact is that the proposed emendations do too
much violence to the text of MT for them to be considered even
remotely satisfactory. Some commentators try to overcome the difficulty inherent in the text by suggesting that *zeraˁ*, 'seed', here refers
to Israel's offspring (so, e.g., Wenham; cf. L'Heureux, p. 90) and
that the idea expressed is that Israel's progeny would be numerous,
its vast population resembling 'a flooding wadi in appearance'
(Harrison, p. 318). But this explanation does not seem to be particularly in harmony with the context. On the whole, it seems preferable
to interpret the clause to mean that Israel's crops ('seed') will grow
in well-watered ground (cf. Ps. 65:9f.). It is true that this thought
is somewhat strangely expressed, but it is probably the explanation
which does most justice to the text as it stands. LXX interprets the
entire verse messianically and renders the first two lines: 'A man
shall issue from his seed/and he shall have dominion over many
peoples'. For the messianic interpretation of the verse in other Vsns,
see Vermes, *Scripture*, pp. 159f. **his king shall be higher than Agag**:
Agag was the Amalekite king captured by Saul and slain by Samuel
(1 Sam. 15:8f., 32f.). If the text of MT is correct, then this clause
must provide a *terminus a quo* for the date of the poem, for it cannot
belong to a period prior to the institution of the monarchy. But
many regard MT here as suspect, partly because the ancient Vsns
(apart from the Vulg.) read 'Gog' (cf. Ezek. 38f.), and partly because
the power of Amalek does not seem to have been sufficiently formidable to make a comparison with Israel's king particularly meaningful
(cf. Gray). However, it is most improbable that 'Gog' represents
the original reading, for this would necessitate a very late date for
the oracle. On the whole, it seems preferable to retain the reading

'Agag', and the comparison with Israel's king might conceivably have some force if the oracle derived from a period prior to the destruction of the Amalekites by Saul. As Noth (p. 191) observes, if the oracle belonged to a much later period, then far more impressive proofs of Israel's political supremacy could have been adduced.

8. The first two lines are virtually identical with 23:22; of the remaining three lines, some commentators omit either the second (Gray) or the third (Noth), so that the verse would comprise two couplets. **and pierce them through with his arrows**: Some suggest emending the text here because *māḥaṣ* (rendered 'pierce' in *RSV*) usually means 'to shatter, smash', and such a verb could not very suitably be predicated of 'arrows' (Paterson, Gray). Syr. seems to have read *ḥᵃlāṣayw*, 'his loins', instead of *ḥiṣṣāyw*, 'his arrows', and it must be admitted that this would provide an excellent parallel with the preceding line (assuming it to be part of the original text; cf. Dt. 33:11); this is adopted by *NEB* ('crunch their bones, and smash their limbs in pieces'), and is favoured by some modern commentators (cf. Snaith, *NPC*, p. 265). *BHS* favours emending *ḥiṣṣāyw* to read *lôḥᵃṣāyw*, 'his oppressors', which would also give good sense, especially if the preceding line is deemed to be a gloss ('he shall eat up the nations, his adversaries/and shatter his oppressors'); cf. Gray. Other possible emendations, too, have been suggested (cf. Gaster, *ExpT* 78 [1966–7], p. 267), but none is strictly necessary, since a good case can be made out for retaining MT. *BDB* (p. 563*b*) gives *māḥaṣ* the meaning 'smite through' or 'wound severely' in addition to 'shatter', and if this meaning is attributed to the verb in the present clause, it is by no means impossible that it could have been used in connection with 'arrows'.

9. He couched, he lay down like a lion: The metaphor here and in the following line recalls that found in 23:24. **Blessed be every one who blesses you, and cursed be every one who curses you**: The concluding words of the oracle express the thought that the solidarity of Yahweh and Israel was such that whoever blessed Israel would himself be blessed, and whoever cursed Israel would himself be cursed (cf. Gen. 12:3). A similar idea occurs in Gen. 27:29, and it has been suggested that one passage served as a model for the other (Beentjes, *Bib* 63 [1982], pp. 509f.); it seems more probable, however, that the saying reflected in these two texts was one which was current in Israel (Gray). Whether or not these words were part of Balaam's original utterance (cf. Coppens, *Mélanges Eugène Tisserant*, i, p. 70) they certainly form a most effective climax to the oracle as a whole.

(1) BALAAM'S FOURTH ORACLE
24:10–19

Balaam is dismissed by Balak with anger and contempt and is advised to flee back to his land (vv. 10f.); Balaam, however, defends himself by emphasizing that he was bound to utter the message which Yahweh had given him (vv. 12f.). Before parting finally from the Moabite king, Balaam announces his intention of revealing what the future holds in store for Moab at the hands of Israel (v. 14). Balaam thus proceeds to utter his fourth oracle, which depicts Israel's success and Moab's demise (v. 17) and predicts Israel's conquest of Edom (vv. 18f.).

10. Angered by the fact that Balaam's oracle had been so unfavourable, Balak **struck his hands together**, a recognized gesture of derision and contempt (cf. Job 27:23; Lam. 2:15). The words **you have blessed them these three times** are clearly an editorial addition to cover all the previous attempts mentioned in the two versions of the Balaam story.

11–13. Balak insists that the promised honorarium would be withheld from Balaam, owing to the failure of the latter to comply with his wishes. Balaam replies that he had been faithful to his word, for he had told Balak's messengers at the outset that he was merely a vehicle to transmit the word which Yahweh had given him to pronounce (cf. 22:18).

14. Before departing, Balaam utters a final, unsolicited oracle, indicating what Israel would do to Moab **in the latter days** (or, better, with *NRSV*, 'in days to come'; cf. *NEB*, *NIV*). Ancient Jewish interpreters, ever anxious to besmirch Balaam's character, represent him here as advising the king how to outwit the Israelites by inducing them to sin against God (cf. Targ. Ps. Jon.; *Sanh.* 106*a*); Jewish tradition proceeds to record that Balak followed Balaam's advice, and in this way a direct link was established with 25:1ff. and 31:16. See Vermes, *Scripture*, pp. 162ff.

15*b*–16. The opening words of this oracle are virtually identical with those of the preceding discourse (vv. 3*b*–4), although the phrase **and knows the knowledge of the Most High** is there lacking. The title 'Most High' (Heb. *'elyôn*) occurs elsewhere in the Pentateuch only in Gen. 14:18ff. and Dt. 32:8. The inclusion in v. 16 of three early names of Israel's deity – ʾēl ('God'), ʿelyôn ('Most High') and šadday ('Almighty') – is especially noteworthy. That a pagan seer should enjoy the privilege of discerning the divine will in such a fashion naturally caused considerable consternation among the rabbis, one of whom asked, sardonically, 'How can he know the knowledge of the Most High, when he cannot even read the mind of his ass?' (*Sanh.*, 105b, cited by Vermes, *Scripture*, p. 165).

17. I see him . . . I behold him: Gray (p. 369) takes the personal pronoun 'him' to be a reference to Israel, but Noth (p. 192) discerns here an allusion to a vague, indeterminate figure, whose identity is partially clarified by the description which follows of a rising star and a sceptre, implying that the figure was, in fact, a king, possibly David (cf. Rashi, Ibn Ezra). The vision of Balaam clearly relates to the distant future, for the figure which he sees is visible, but **not now . . . not nigh. a star shall come forth**: The use of the verb *dārak* here is unexpected, for it usually means 'to tread, march' (*BDB*, pp. 201f.). Many commentators, following Wellhausen (*Die Composition*, p. 351), emend the text to read *zāraḥ*, 'arise' (cf. LXX). The 'star' was a common metaphor for a king in the ancient Near East, though such a metaphorical use of *kôkāb* is rare in the *OT* (cf. Isa. 14:12; Ezek. 32:7). But that the word *was* here intended to have royal associations is clear from the reference in the next line to the **sceptre** (unless *šēbeṭ* here means 'comet'; cf. Gemser, *ZAW*, N.F., 2 [1925], p. 301; *NEB*), which was a recognized item of the king's insignia (cf. Ps. 45:6; Am. 1:5, 8; Toombs, *IDB*, iv, 234f.). As Noth (p. 192) observes, it seems probable that the author of the present passage had in view the future glory of king David, and it may well be that the historical emergence of David formed the background to the present oracle. Early Jewish interpretation, found in the Targum, attests to the fact that this verse was understood as a prediction of the coming Messiah (cf. Targ. Onk.; Targ. Ps. Jon.), and the messianic interpretation is already found at Qumran (IQM 11:6f.; cf. Allegro, *JBL* 75 [1956], pp. 182ff.) and in the *NT*, where the allusion to the 'bright morning star' (Rev. 22:16) was doubtless inspired by the present passage (though cf. Moore, *NovT* 24 [1982], pp. 82ff.). In the second century AD a messianic pretender appeared who, significantly, had his name changed from Bar Cozeba to Bar Cochba ('Son of the Star') as a sign of his messianic claims (cf.

Eusebius, *H.E.* IV.6). **it shall crush the forehead of Moab**: Heb.
pēʾāh means, lit., 'side' or 'corner' (*BDB*, p. 802*a*), and the rendering
of *RSV* assumes that the word here refers to the side of the head (cf.
Lev. 13:41; 19:27). The Vsns (LXX, Vulg.; cf. Targ. Onk.) interpret
the word metaphorically of the 'leaders' or 'chiefs' of Moab (cf.
NEB, 'squadrons'; *REB*, 'warriors'), but there is no evidence of such
a metaphorical use of the term elsewhere in the *OT*. Heb. *pēʾāh*
sometimes designates 'region, district, border', hence *NRSV*'s
'borderlands of Moab', but whether this is entirely suitable as an
object of the verb *māḥaṣ* is questionable. The rendering of *RSV*,
however, is perfectly acceptable (cf. Jer. 48:45), although, given that
pēʾāh here appears in its construct dual form, Gray's rendering 'the
temples of Moab' appears preferable (cf. Dillmann, p. 160), the
temple being the part of the head where a blow might prove to be
especially dangerous. The reference is clearly to the conquest and
subjugation of Moab by David (2 Sam. 8:2); an event here regarded
as having been preordained by Yahweh and in complete accordance
with his will. **and break down all the sons of Sheth**: *RSV*'s 'break
down' may be rendered, with only the slightest change in the Heb.
(*qodqod* instead of *qarqar*), 'skull' (cf. Sam.), and this would give
an admirable couplet; cf. *NIV*, 'He will crush the foreheads of Moab/
the skulls of all the sons of Sheth'. This emendation is attractive,
especially in view of the similar phraseology deployed in Jer. 48:45,
and the fact that *qodqod* also appears in Ps. 68:21 (MT 68:22) as a
direct object of the verb *māḥaṣ*. The reference to the 'sons of Sheth'
has proved problematic. Sheth or, rather, Seth was the third son of
Adam (Gen. 4:25); thus, it might be expected that the expression
'sons of Sheth' would be equivalent to the 'descendants of Adam',
i.e., all mankind (so Targ. Onk.; Rashi); however, a threat directed
at such a broad constituency seems distinctly at odds with the more
specific references in the present context to Moab, Edom and Seir,
and, in any case, the 'sons of Sheth' interpreted in this way would
presumably have included the Israelites themselves! It is therefore
sometimes suggested that the Heb. *šēt* should be emended to read
šēʾt, 'tumult' (*RV*, 'sons of tumult'; cf. Lam. 3:47) or *sˀēt*, 'pride' (so,
e.g., Wellhausen, *Die Composition*, p. 351, followed, among others, by
Gray); the former reading may be justified on the basis of Jer. 48:45,
while the latter may be defended on the ground that 'pride' was a
well-known characteristic of Moab (cf. Isa. 16:6; 25:11; Zeph. 2:10).
The difficulty with these two suggestions, however, is that the

present context appears to require a tribal name (cf. Sturdy), and there can be little doubt that the Vsns (LXX, Syr., Vulg.) understood *šēt* here to be a proper name. Consequently, an early suggestion by Sayce (*ExpT* 13 [1901–2], p. 64), that the reference here is to the Sutu, a nomadic tribe which lived in Palestine and which is mentioned in Egyptian execration texts from the second millennium BC, has commended itself to several recent commentators (cf. Wenham, Budd, Milgrom); perhaps a later poet, who no longer understood the archaic allusion, reinterpreted it as 'the sons of Sheth' (cf. L'Heureux, p. 90; Albright, *op. cit.*, p. 220, n. 89). But if this solution is accepted, it must be conceded that nothing whatsoever is known about the ethnic relationship which may have existed between the Sutu and the Moabites of later times.

18–19. On stylistic and thematic grounds, some commentators contend that these verses may not have formed an original part of the preceding oracle (cf. Gray), but the evidence for this is by no means conclusive, and it seems preferable to regard vv. 18–19 as the climax of the final oracle uttered by Balaam. The text of both verses has been seriously disturbed in the course of transmission, but its general purport is clear. Edom would be subjugated by the Israelites, and the victorious campaign of the latter would continue unimpeded. The position of *'ōyᵉḇāyw*, 'his enemies', seems awkward, even in English translation, and in MT the word is, moreover, metrically superfluous. Some commentators view it as a gloss, while others regard it as the remnant of a lost line (cf. McNeile). Albright (*op. cit.*, p. 221, n. 94), however, has plausibly suggested transferring it to v. 19*a*, and attaching the *mem* prefixed to 'Jacob' to the preceding word as an enclitic (cf. de Vaulx, Vetter). The restored text may be translated as follows: 'And Edom shall be dispossessed/ And Seir shall be dispossessed;/ while Israel does valiantly/ Jacob shall rule over his enemies'. **Seir** probably appears here (cf. Jg. 5:4) as a synonym for Edom (though, cf. Bartlett, *JTS*, N.S., 20 [1969], pp. 8f.). *RSV*'s **survivors of cities** seems obscure, since no specific cities are mentioned; Paterson (p. 59) suggests emending the text to read 'survivors of Seir' (i.e., reading *miśśēʿîr* instead of *mēʿîr*). A simpler solution, however, would be to revocalize the Heb. text, and to understand the word rendered 'cities' in *RSV* as a proper noun, Ar (so *NEB*; cf. *NRSV*, 'Ir'), the reference being to Ar of Moab, referred to already in 21:28 (cf. Snaith, Budd). Since vv. 20ff. are

universally regarded as a later addition to Balaam's oracle (see
below), a reference to Moab's defeat would form a fitting climax to
Balaam's utterance.

(m) ORACLES AGAINST THE NATIONS
24:20–24

These verses contain three brief, cryptic oracles dealing with the
fate of the Amalekites (v. 20), the Kenites (vv. 21f.), Asshur and
Eber (vv. 23f.). These sayings were almost certainly added to
Balaam's utterance at a later date, for they contain no reference at
all to Moab, and have no apparent connection with the preceding
verses (vv. 15*b*–19). Their independent status is further confirmed
by the fact that they are prefixed by new introductory formulae
(vv. 20, 21, 23). Why these oracles should have been included at
this point is by no means clear, but, as several commentators have
observed, their inclusion brings the total number of oracles in the
Balaam cycle to seven, the symbol of wholeness and completeness.
Unfortunately, the text of these concluding verses has been badly
preserved, and consequently their interpretation has proved very
problematic; this difficulty is compounded by the brevity and vagueness of the utterances themselves, and by the uncertainty regarding
their probable date and origin.

   20. This oracle announces the impending destruction of **Amalek**.
The Amalekites were a confederacy of nomadic tribes who occupied
the desert to the southeast of Palestine, though it is possible that
there was also a northern Amalekite enclave in the hills of western
Samaria (cf. Exod. 17; Jg. 6–7; 2 Sam. 1:2–26; Edelman, *JSOT* 35
[1986], pp. 71ff.). The Amalekites were implacably opposed to Israel
and, not surprisingly, they consistently appear in the *OT* in a negative light. Since there are very few references to the Amalekites after
the reign of David, it seems not unlikely that the present oracle
belongs to the early period of the monarchy, or shortly thereafter.
The precise significance of the description of Amalek as **the first**
(Heb. *rē'šîṯ*) **of the nations** is not entirely clear. *OT* usage (cf. Am.
6:1; Job 40:19) suggests that the phrase ought to refer to Amalek's
might and pre-eminence, but there is no historical evidence to indicate that the Amalekites were ever a particularly powerful race.
Edelman (*op. cit.*, p. 74) suggests that they were 'pre-eminent' in
the sense that they were the predominant group in the long-standing
rivalry with Israel for control of the Ephraimite hills, but the

uncertainty regarding the occasion of the oracle must make this
conclusion somewhat tentative. The phrase 'the first of the nations'
could conceivably be taken to indicate that the Amalekites were the
oldest of all the nations, but the difficulty with this is that the *OT*
knows of no tradition which acknowledges them as such (cf. Gen.
36:12). The Targums, on the basis of Exod. 17:8ff., understood the
phrase to refer to the fact that the Amalekites were the first to oppose
Israel on the wilderness journey (cf. Vermes, *Scripture*, p. 167). Perhaps the expression was one which the Amalekites were known to
have used of themselves with reference to their origin or status;
alternatively, in a poetic passage such as this, the phrase may have
been used for no other reason than that it provided an appropriate
antithesis to the ominous words which follow: **but in the end he
shall come to destruction**. The Amalekites were, in fact, almost
annihilated during the period of the early monarchy (1 Sam. 15;
30), and, according to 1 Chr. 4:42f., they were finally destroyed in
the time of Hezekiah.

21-22. And he looked on the Kenite: That some connection
existed between the Amalekites and the Kenites is suggested elsewhere in the *OT* (cf. 1 Sam. 15:6), and this seems to be confirmed
by the location of the present oracle, appearing as it does immediately after the oracle against Amalek (v. 20). The Kenites occupied
a position in the south-eastern part of Judah, and in the *OT* they
appear to be on friendly terms with Israel (cf. Jg. 5:24; 1 Sam.
30:29); indeed, according to Jg. 4:11, Moses' father-in-law was a
Kenite. Why this race should here be singled out for condemnation
and included in this prophecy of destruction has remained largely
an unsolved problem. Mauchline (*op. cit.*, p. 91) emends the text so
that it reads as a blessing rather than a curse upon the Kenites
('For even if it be burned/ For ever blessed will be thy dwelling'),
but his proposed emendation is very dubious, and it would still
remain to be explained why an oracle of blessing should have been
placed among others which pronounce doom. **Enduring is your
dwelling place**: Note that in contrast to the preceding oracle, the
direct form of address is here employed. *BDB* (pp. 450f.) gives the
Heb. *'êṭān* the meaning 'perennial, ever-flowing' (cf. Exod. 14:27;
Dt. 21:4; Ps. 74:15), but the word is here used figuratively in the
sense of 'strong' (*AV*; cf. LXX, Syr.), 'secure' (*NEB, NIV*), 'enduring'
(*RSV*); for the figurative use of the word elsewhere in the *OT*, cf.
Job 33:19; Jer. 5:15; Mic. 6:2. See, further, Driver, *Deuteronomy*,

pp. 241f. **and your nest is set in the rock**: The Heb. word for 'nest', *qên*, contains an obvious play on the word 'Kenite', *qênî*, and the allusion to the 'rock' is sometimes taken as an oblique reference to their mountainous place of origin (cf. Budd, Maarsingh). The point here seems to be that, although the people were apparently secure and their habitation ostensibly inaccessible (cf. Jer. 49:16; Ob. 4; Hab. 2:9), they would, for all that, be destroyed: **nevertheless Kain** (the reputed ancestor of the Kenites) **shall be wasted**. The Heb. expression *lᵉḇāᶜēr qāyin* seems to have confused the translators of LXX, who rendered the clause, 'he shall be to Beor a nest of corruption' (cf. *JB*); instead of *qāyin*, Kain, they evidently read *qên*, nest, and interpreted *bāᶜēr* as a personal name, Beor, the reference presumably being to Balak, son of Beor, king of Moab, mentioned in Gen. 36:32. The agent of the Kenites' misfortune was to be Asshur, who would take them into captivity; this idea, however, is rather awkwardly expressed in the Heb. **How long shall Asshur take you away captive?**: An alternative rendering is found in *NEB*, 'How long must you dwell there in my sight?' This presupposes that *tišbekā* is derived from the root *yāšaḇ*, 'to dwell' (rather than *šāḇāh*, 'to take captive') and that *'aššûr* be pointed as first person singular of the verb *šûr*, 'behold, regard'; however, in view of the context, this does not seem a particularly attractive alternative, and has rightly been abandoned in *REB*. The text of MT, however, does not yield a good sense, and it may well be corrupt, though none of the proposed emendations seems entirely satisfactory. Some commentators have tentatively suggested that the words *'aḏ-māh* ('how long') may be a corruption of the name of the place to which Asshur was expected to carry away the captives (cf. Binns, McNeile), but this seems to be clutching at straws. The text would certainly run more smoothly if *'aḏ-māh* could be rendered 'until' (*AV*) or 'when' (*REB*, *NIV*), but the difficulty is that *'aḏ-māh* in the *OT* generally means 'how long?' (cf. Ps. 4:2 [MT 4:3]; 74:9f.) and translations such as 'when' or 'while' can plausibly be adumbrated only by emending the text (so, e.g., Albright, *op. cit.*, p. 222, n. 103, followed by de Vaulx, Vetter). A much more drastic emendation was proposed by Cheyne (*op. cit.*, p. 399), who managed to make the text read, 'Edom shall beat in pieces his dwelling', but this rendering is purely conjectural and lacks Versional support. The difficulty is further compounded by the reference to Asshur. Asshur in the *OT* usually refers to the mighty Assyrian empire (cf. Gen. 10:22; Isa. 10:5; Hos. 14:3),

and is so understood here by some commentators (e.g., Marsh); if
this is so then the oracle could hardly have originated in a period
prior to the emergence of neo-Assyrian power in the eighth (or
possibly ninth) century BC (cf. Noth, p. 193). Others, however, seek
to avoid the anachronistic mention of Assyria on the lips of Balaam,
and assume that the reference is to the Asshurim, a small tribe
which lived in northern Syria and which is mentioned in Gen. 25:3
(cf. Milgrom, de Vaulx). None of these solutions is entirely free from
difficulty, for if, on the one hand, the reference is to Assyria, then
it must be conceded that there is no historical record which suggests
that this country ever deported the Kenites; on the other hand, if
the reference is to the Asshurim, then it is by no means clear why
such an obscure and relatively unimportant tribe should have been
singled out for special mention in this oracle.

23–24. This is the most obscure and problematic of all the poems,
for the text is obviously corrupt, and no historical event is known
to which the words (in so far as they can be reconstructed) could
refer. The rendering of *RSV* may be regarded as a reasonable attempt
to make sense of the text as it stands. Vv. 23*b* and 24*a* are particularly difficult, and Snaith (p. 301) has attempted the following tentative reconstruction based, to some extent, on the renderings of the
Vsns: 'Alas, who shall come to be (cf. Sam.) from the north, and is
coming forth to war (cf. LXX) from the direction of Kittim?'; cf.
NEB. Several other emendations have been proposed but they are
all highly conjectural; indeed, Gray (p. 377) has conceded that there
is 'little probability that any interpretation of the text as it stands,
or as it has been variously emended, reaches the original meaning'.
And he took up his discourse: MT gives no indication as to whom
this oracle was addressed (contrast vv. 20, 21); LXX suggests that it
was directed at Og (cf. *JB*) or Gog (LXX[L]), but this may be based
on 21:33–35, which is itself a late editorial insertion. Some scholars,
noting that Gog appears in LXX in 24:7 as a rendering of MT's Agag,
suggest that Agag may also have stood originally in this introductory
formula (cf. Albright, *op. cit.*, p. 222, n. 106; Vetter, *op. cit.*, p. 54),
but this is by no means certain. **But ships shall come from Kittim**:
There is no verb in the Heb., and the rendering of *RSV* assumes
that some word such as *yāḇō'ô* ('shall come') has been accidentally
omitted from the text in the process of transmission. If the text
of MT is correct, then 'ships from Kittim' must be regarded as
the subject of the verb 'afflict' in the next line, in which case the

intervening 'and' of *RSV* should be discarded. Further, 'from Kittim' should properly be rendered, 'from the direction of Kittim' (cf. *NEB*, 'from the region of'; *NIV*, 'from the shores of'; *JB*, 'from the coasts of'); for this figurative use of the Heb. *yād*, see *BDB*, p. 390. Kittim (or Kition, as the Greeks called it) was a town in Cyprus; the name later came to be used of Cyprus itself and, by extension, of western maritime nations generally (cf. Jer. 2:10; Ezek. 27:6). In Dan. 11:30, the word clearly refers to the Romans (cf. LXX), and a similar identification is made in the Qumran scrolls (cf. Vermes, *Scrolls*, pp. 65f.). **and shall afflict Asshur**: Asshur has here been variously interpreted as referring to the Asshurim of Gen. 25:3 (Milgrom), to Assyria (Budd; cf. *NEB*), or, if the oracle is deemed very late, to the Seleucid empire of Syria (cf. Noth). **and Eber**: In Gen. 10:21; 11:14, Eber refers to the eponymous ancestor of the Hebrews, but it can hardly have been used in this sense here (despite LXX), for the oracle would thus constitute an oblique threat to Israel itself. One suggestion, based on the fact that Heb. *'eber* means 'across', is that the reference is to the land 'beyond the Euphrates' (so, e.g., Marsh; cf. Targ. Onk.), but this is very uncertain. Wifall (*ZAW* 82 [1970], pp. 110ff.) suggests that Asshur should be pointed to read 'Asher' and that Eber should be emended to read Heber; on this basis, he suggests that the reference here is to the tribe of Asher, mentioned in Jg. 5:17, and to Heber, an important clan within this tribe (cf. 26:45; Gen. 46:17). The point of the oracle, according to Wifall, is that both Asher and Heber would be afflicted by ships coming from the direction of Cyprus, and he suggests that the allusion may be to the event recorded in 1 Kg. 9:10-14. But this is most unlikely, for if the whole tribe of Asher was to be afflicted, what was the point of singling out a specific clan? Moreover, the fact that the orthography of both names in MT has to be altered in order to sustain the theory must raise serious doubts concerning its plausibility. It must be conceded that the reference to Eber in this oracle is a complete enigma, and the mystery has yet to be resolved satisfactorily. The interpretation of the oracle as a whole will depend upon the date which is assigned to it: those who favour an early date are inclined to see here a reference to the invasion of the Sea Peoples (possibly the Philistines) in the thirteenth and twelfth centuries BC (cf. Wenham; Mauchline, *op. cit.*, p. 91), while those who advocate a much later date regard Asshur as a reference to the Persian empire (as in Ezr. 6:22), and discern in the poem a reference to the overthrow of that empire by Alexander the Great (cf. 1 Mac. 1:1).

Excursus III: The Deir 'Allā Texts

In 1960 an expedition was made from the University of Leiden to Deir 'Allā in the Jordan Valley under the direction of H. J. Franken, and in the spring of 1967 a text was discovered which casts interesting light on the person of Balaam. The text, entitled 'The Document about Balaam, the son of Beor', was inscribed on white plaster walls in red and black ink, and it is usually dated, on paleographical grounds, to the late eighth century or early seventh century BC (though a mid-eighth century date was advocated by Naveh, *IEJ* 17 [1967], p. 258, and Lemaire, *BAR* 11 [1985], p. 30). According to Franken, the excavator, the text may have been publicly displayed in a sanctuary before the building was eventually devastated by an earthquake (*VT* 17 [1967], pp. 48of.). Unfortunately, the text itself is fragmentary, and parts of it are no longer legible; moreover, its interpretation is complicated by the fact that the script is a consonantal one, and several words are open to more than one meaning, depending on which vowels are inserted. The actual process of distinguishing the characters, however, was greatly facilitated by the fact that the script strongly resembled biblical Aramaic, though it exhibited several characteristics which were otherwise either very unusual or completely unknown in standard Aramaic cursive (cf. Hoftijzer, *BA* 39 [1976], p. 12). Indeed, some features of the Deir 'Allā text appeared to align it with the Canaanite dialect, and scholars are still undecided as to whether the language of the inscription is a form of Aramaic fused with an admixture of Canaanisms (so, e.g., McCarter, *BASOR* 239 [1980], pp. 5of.), or a form of Canaanite laced with Aramaisms (so, e.g., Hackett, *Or* 53 [1984], pp. 57ff.; *Balaam*, pp. 109ff.).

The fragments are usually distributed into several groups or 'Combinations'; of these, the first two are by far the most important, since they contain the greatest quantity of text. The lavish volume published by Hoftijzer and van der Kooij (*Aramaic Texts*) provides a transcription and translation of the texts, together with a philological commentary, although it should be noted that some of the readings and interpretations contained in this volume have subsequently been modified by other scholars who have studied these texts in

detail (cf. Caquot and Lemaire, *Syria* 44 [1977], pp. 189ff.;
McCarter, *op. cit.*, pp. 49ff.; Hackett, *Balaam*, pp. 21ff.; see, now,
Hoftijzer and van der Kooij, *The Balaam Text from Deir 'Alla Re-
evaluated*).

As has been indicated, the fragmentary nature of the text allows
for a great deal of subjectivity in its interpretation, and there are
some quite significant differences in the reconstructions proposed
by such scholars as Hoftijzer, Caquot–Lemaire and McCarter.
Nevertheless, the general thrust of the story contained in Combination I may be outlined as follows: Balaam, son of Beor, receives
a visit one night from the gods, who convey to him an ominous
message. The content of the message can no longer be reconstructed,
but it clearly devastated Balaam, for the next day he was found
weeping and fasting, and his unusual behaviour aroused the curi-
osity of the people. Balaam informs them that he had received from
the 'gods' (*šdyn*) a message of impending doom. In his vision he had
seen the divine council sitting in assembly, and he had heard them
decree that a catastrophe of cosmic proportions was to afflict the
earth. A goddess, who has been variously identified as Shagar
(Hoftijzer), Shamash (Caquot–Lemaire) and Sheol (McCarter), is
instructed by the assembly to close the heavens with a dense cloud
and to seal up the sky forever, and the time of catastrophe is vividly
portrayed by a series of pictures which depict the reversal of the
normal order.

The precise nature of the relationship between the first two 'Combinations' is by no means clear, for they were found at a distance
of several meters from each other, and Balaam is not mentioned at
all by name in the extant portions of Combination II. Nevertheless,
many scholars believe that the second Combination is essentially a
continuation of the story begun in the first, and that Balaam is
the unifying factor linking both together. Problems of interpretation
abound in this Combination, for only a few scattered words and
phrases within it are intelligible, but the following represents the
reconstruction proposed by Levine (*JAOS* 101 [1981], pp. 220ff.).
An unnamed person (probably Balaam) is addressed and told that
his counsel will no longer be sought and that his powers of execration
will no longer function. Balaam's punishment for interfering in the
affairs of the gods is that he is condemned and consigned to Sheol.
For alternative interpretations of this Combination, see Hoftijzer
and van der Kooij, *Texts*, pp. 270, 280ff.; Hackett, *Balaam*, pp. 56ff.

The Deir ʿAllā text represents a very significant discovery, for there can be no doubt that the Balaam mentioned here is the same as Balaam, son of Beor, whose oracles are preserved in Num. 22–24. Clearly, then, the story contained in Num. 22–24 was not an isolated account confined to the literature of Israel but was rather part of a more broadly disseminated tradition in the ancient Near East. It was perhaps inevitable that parallels and similarities should be noted between the biblical account of Balaam and the Deir ʿAllā text (cf. Levine, *Proceedings*, pp. 335ff.; Lemaire, *op. cit.*, pp. 37f.; Müller, *ZAW* 94 [1982], pp. 238ff.), and it has even been suggested that the author(s) of Num. 22–24 may have been familiar with some form of the Transjordanian Balaam tradition (cf. McCarter, *op. cit.*, p. 57). Of particular interest to biblical scholars is the light that the recently discovered text throws upon the character of Balaam as portrayed in the chapters here under discussion. The fact that Balaam is designated in the Deir ʿAllā text as a 'seer of the gods', for example, is particularly suggestive, for Balaam is never explicitly given the title *ḥōzeh* in the *OT*, although it is clear that the biblical authors regarded him as a 'seer', for he was capable of receiving visionary experiences (cf. 24:3f., 15f.). Hackett (*BA* 49 [1986], p. 220) has concluded from the Deir ʿAllā text that Balaam was a religious leader of a cult which recognized the existence of several gods. If this is so, then the seer would have been regarded as one of Israel's most powerful religious rivals, and the portrayal of him in Num. 22–24 as one who had to call upon Yahweh to determine his every movement, and one who had no choice but to bless Israel, would clearly have delighted an early Hebrew audience. The very person who was held in such high esteem by Israel's neighbours had been revealed to be completely impotent and ineffective! Further, the description in the Deir ʿAllā text of the world of nature behaving in a way contrary to its natural inclination gives added significance to Philo's description of Balaam's powers of prophecy: 'For he foretold to some people heavy rain in high summer, to others, drought and even burning heat in mid-winter, and to still others barrenness after a good season, and, conversely, a yield after famine' (*The Life of Moses*, i, 264f., quoted by Hackett, *Fest. Cross*, p. 128). But the most suggestive reference in the entire Deir ʿAllā text is undoubtedly the allusion to a group of gods known as the *šdyn*, a term reminiscent of the Heb. designation Šadday, which appears as an epithet of God in the *OT*. It has been suggested that traces of the *šdyn* may be found in such passages as Dt. 32:17 and Ps. 106:37 (cf. Hackett, *Balaam*, pp. 88f.); be that as it may, it is surely not without significance that Balaam in 24:4, 16 describes himself as one who 'hears the words of God (El), who sees the vision of the Almighty (Šadday)'.

An extensive literature has arisen on the subject of the Deir 'Allā text; in addition to the works cited above, reference may be made to Müller, *ZDPV* 94 (1978), pp. 56ff.; Smelik, *Writings*, pp. 79ff.; H. and M. Weippert, *ZDPV* 97 (1981), pp. 77ff.

(B) MISCELLANEOUS LAWS AND NARRATIVES
25:1–36:13

(a) THE APOSTASY OF ISRAEL AND THE ZEAL OF PHINEHAS
25:1–18

The present chapter contains two unconnected stories, the first (vv. 1–5) forming part of the old Pentateuchal narrative tradition, and the second (vv. 6–18) deriving from the Priestly writer. The two stories were probably combined because they shared a common theme, viz., the danger of consorting with foreign women. In the first narrative, sexual promiscuity with the 'daughters of Moab' leads to the idolatrous worship of their gods, and this constituted an act of apostasy that had to be severely punished; in the second, a relationship is recorded between an Israelite man and a Midianite woman, and both are killed by Phinehas in a rage that mirrored the divine anger. But despite the similarity of theme, the main interest of the two accounts is markedly different. The focus of the first is upon the struggle between the pure worship of Yahweh and the false worship of the native local cults, while the primary interest of the latter is in the establishment of a perpetual priesthood for Phinehas and his descendants. Both stories, in their present form, are fragmentary: the first lacks an ending (for no account is given of the judicial execution commanded in vv. 4f.), and the second presupposes circumstances (the reason for the plague of vv. 8f.) which are not related in the narrative itself.

Several commentators have regarded vv. 1–5 as composite, for the section, brief as it is, is thought to contain some basic inconsistencies. Thus, in v. 2 the Moabite gods to whom the people offer sacrifices are not named, but in vv. 3, 5 'Baal of Peor' is explicitly mentioned. Moreover, the instructions given in v. 4 regarding the punishment to be meted out seem strangely unconnected with those given in v. 5. On this basis, scholars have often posited the existence of two parallel sources in this section, and vv. 3 and 5 are commonly attributed to E (cf., e.g., Jaroš, *Die Stellung*, pp. 390ff.), while vv. 1, 2 and 4 (or substantial parts thereof) are attributed to J (cf. Baentsch, Holzinger). However, the inconsistencies within the present section are more apparent than real. It is quite possible that a single narrator may have wished to describe Israel's apostasy in general terms in vv. 1*b*, 2 before focusing upon the particular act (v. 3) which had precipitated the divine wrath. Further, Moses may well initially have been instructed to execute the chiefs of the people (v. 4) before ordering the judges to punish other individuals who had also participated in the pagan sacrifices (v. 5). Thus there is no substantive reason to deny the unity of the passage, and since even some firm advocates of the E source hesitate to find any traces of it in the present section (cf. Jenks, *Elohist*, p. 58), it seems reasonable to attribute the passage to J. The essential unity of vv. 6–13 is not in question, though vv. 14f. and vv. 16–18 are probably later additions to the original narrative.

(i) *Israel's apostasy:* **25:1–5**
1. While Israel dwelt in Shittim: The name (which appears with the article in Heb.) means 'the acacia trees'. The fuller form, Abel-shittim, appears in 33:49, where it is represented as the last stopping-place of the Israelites before crossing the Jordan. According to Jos. 2:1; 3:1, it was from here that Joshua later dispatched his spies, and led Israel across the Jordan. For the location of Shittim, see on 33:49, and for the view that it was an ancient pre-Israelite sanctuary where worship was marked by strongly Canaanite features, see Porter, *SEÅ* 36 (1971), pp. 10ff. **the people began to play the harlot with the daughters of Moab**: Some commentators (e.g., Wenham) suggest that the Israelites are here depicted as participating in some form of sacred prostitution, but, as Noth (p. 196) observes, there is no indication in the text that the relations entered into had a specifically cultic background, though they did clearly have cultic consequences (cf. v. 2).

2. Having entered into illicit sexual relations with the Moabite women (v. 1), the Israelites were then encouraged to participate in their sacred feasts, at which sacrifices were offered to **their gods**. Some suggest that the plural *'elōhêhen*, should here be rendered as singular, 'their god', and that the reference is to Chemosh, the national god of the Moabites (cf. Gray, Snaith). Be that as it may, there is no doubt that, by joining in the sacrificial feast, the Israelites were, to all intents and purposes, indulging in idolatrous worship.

3. So Israel yoked himself to Baal of Peor: The verb rendered 'yoked himself', *ṣāmaḍ*, is rare in the *OT* (cf. Ps. 106:28), and its precise meaning is uncertain. It is obviously related to the common cognate noun, *ṣemeḍ*, 'yoke', but what precisely 'yoking oneself' to a god entailed is by no means clear. *NEB* (cf. *NIV*) takes the word to mean simply 'joining in the worship of', but the verb may also imply participation in sexual rites (cf. Sturdy, p. 184; L'Heureux, p. 90; Mendenhall, *Tenth Generation*, pp. 110ff.; Jaroš, *op. cit.*, pp. 394f.). Given that Baal was the god of fertility, it is quite possible that the verb does have this connotation in the present context. Various towns or regions were supposed by the Semites to have a local deity, or a local manifestation of the national deity, hence there were many Baals in different parts of the country; the one referred to here was evidently the local god of Peor. The illicit worship of Baal-Peor is often alluded to in the *OT* (cf. 31:16; Dt. 4:3; Jos. 22:17; Ps. 106:28; Hos. 9:10).

4. Indignant at such a flagrant act of apostasy, Yahweh instructs Moses to take **all the chiefs of the people, and hang them in the sun before the LORD**. Why the chiefs of the people, rather than the offenders, should be punished is not clear. The reading of Sam. suggests that only those who actively participated in the offence were condemned, but since this is patently an attempt to reconcile the present verse with v. 5, it can hardly be regarded as representing the original text. Some favour the view that something has fallen out of the text at this point, causing 'them' (*'ôṯām*) to refer to the chiefs, whereas in the original it would have referred to the offenders (Paterson). But it is preferable to leave the text as it stands, and to assume that the chiefs are here singled out for punishment as representatives of the people (cf. Marsh, Maarsingh; also, Mendenhall, *op. cit.*, p. 114), or because they had neglected their duty of vigilance in permitting the Israelites to act in such a fashion (Harrison). The mode of punishment indicated by the verb *yāqaʿ* is unclear, for the causative form of the verb occurs only here and in 2 Sam. 21:6, 9 in the *OT*, though the verb occurs in the Qal form in Gen. 32:25 (MT 32:26) to refer to the dislocating of Jacob's thigh. Polzin (*HTR* 62 [1969], pp. 227ff.) argues that the verb *yāqaʿ* (in the Hiphil) signifies a ritual act of execution imposed for breach of covenant, and he suggests that it means 'to dismember', but the evidence for this is far from convincing, for *yāqaʿ* is not the verb used in other texts where dismemberment is implied (cf. Jg. 19:29; 1 Sam. 11:7). Smith (*Religion*, p. 419, n. 2) connects the Heb. root with the Arab. *wakaʿa*, 'to fall down', and suggests that the meaning here may be 'to throw down', as from a cliff or high rock (cf. *NEB*). Snaith (p. 302), supporting this interpretation, refers to 2 Chr. 25:12 as evidence that being thrown over a cliff did constitute one form of execution in Israel (cf. Lk. 4:29); however, his argument is considerably weakened by the fact that the verb *yāqaʿ* does not occur in the passage in 2 Chr. Syr. suggests that the meaning of the verb in the present context is 'to expose' (cf. Dillmann; *NIV*), but, as Gray (p. 383) notes, this meaning hardly corresponds to the established usages of the root. Aquila took the verb to mean 'to impale', and this has been accepted by some scholars (cf. Paterson), and is reflected in the rendering of *JB*. The translation of *RSV*, 'hang', based on the Vulg. (cf. Rashi), may be somewhat misleading, since there is no evidence that hanging was a recognized method of execution in Israel (cf. Phillips, *Law*, p. 25). If the rendering of *RSV* is accepted, then it must be interpreted to mean that, after execution, the corpses of the condemned were to be hung up, perhaps as an example to others (cf. de Vaux, *AI*, p. 159). The bodies were to be hung up **in the sun**, which may be understood literally (i.e., in broad daylight) or metaphorically (i.e., openly, publicly); in either case, the action was evidently intended to have a propitiatory significance: **that the fierce anger of the LORD may turn away from Israel**.

5. Each section of each tribe had its own chieftains who functioned also as judges (cf. Exod. 18:25f.); here, these judges are commanded to put to death the offenders that belonged to the particular divisions over which they exercised authority. No record is preserved of the carrying out of this sentence, but the story may well originally have concluded with a report of the implementation of Moses' command.

(ii) *The zeal of Phinehas:* **25:6–18**
The narrative recorded here tells how Phinehas' zeal for Yahweh's honour was rewarded by the promise that the priesthood would remain perpetually in his family. The incident has only a very loose connection with that recorded in vv. 1–5, and the reference to Peor in v. 18 is clearly a harmonizing addition intended to bind the two

stories together. The point of the story seems to have been to legitimize the position of the descendants of Phinehas within the priestly hierarchy, and to uphold their privileged status in the face of any possible opposition. At the same time, by portraying Phinehas as the enforcer of ritual purity, the narrative serves to highlight the importance of the priestly duty of protecting the community from contamination. In this regard, Phinehas is seen to function much like the Levites in Exod. 32:24ff., who similarly owed their clerical office to a zealous act of retribution in the face of cultic apostasy.

6. An unnamed Israelite (identified by a later editor in v. 14 as Zimri, the son of Salu) **brought a Midianite woman to his family**, i.e., presumably, took her as his wife. This was done while the rest of the congregation were **weeping at the door of the tent of meeting**. The weeping is probably to be understood as a cultic lament, though the explanation for this display of remorse is not given until vv. 8*b*, 9, which state that a plague had been sent to afflict the Israelites. The reason for the plague is not at all clear from the present form of the narrative, but it would no doubt have been elucidated in the original introduction to the story, which appears to have been suppressed by an editor in favour of vv. 1–5.

7–9. At this point, Phinehas, the son of Eleazar and grandson of Aaron, is introduced into the narrative. His name appears to be of Egyptian origin and means 'the Negro'. With spear in hand, he followed the Israelite into the **inner room**. The Heb. word rendered 'inner room', *qubbāh*, occurs only here in the *OT*, and its meaning is uncertain. One possibility is that it refers to the rear area of the man's tent (Paterson); another suggestion is that it designates the innermost part of the tent of meeting (Sturdy), or the interior of a separate 'tent shrine' (Reif, *JBL* 90 [1971], pp. 200ff.). The English word 'alcove' (cf. *JB*) is derived from the cognate Arab. word with the article *al* prefixed. Phinehas pierced the Israelite and his consort **through her body**. The word here rendered 'body', *qobātāh*, is very similar to the word for 'inner room', *qubbāh*, and Reif suggests that *qobātāh* here means 'in her shrine' (cf. Budd, p. 280); however, in view of the usage of this word in Dt. 18:3, where it appears to designate the 'stomach' of an ox or sheep, the rendering 'body' (or, perhaps, more specifically, 'belly', with *NRSV*; cf. *JB*, 'groin'), seems preferable. According to Jewish tradition, Phinehas struck the man and the woman through their private parts (cf. Bab. Tal. *Sanh.* 87*b*), and Targ. Ps. Jon. almost delights in filling in the gruesome details. Phinehas' action brought to an end **the plague**, which had already claimed 24,000 lives. The story is alluded to in 1 C. 10:8 as a warning to Christians, though the number of deaths is there given as 23,000.

11. By his action, Phinehas had shown himself to be **jealous with my jealousy**, i.e., his 'jealous anger' (*NEB*) was so real and deeply felt that it adequately expressed Yahweh's own jealousy, rendering unnecessary any further recriminations on Yahweh's part. The word 'jealous' (*qin'āh*) here could equally well be rendered 'zealous' (see on 11:29); by his pious zeal for Yahweh's honour, Phinehas had, as it were, already anticipated the divine resentment, and had mitigated the full force of the divine punishment. The zeal which Phinehas displayed on this occasion was to become proverbial in later times (cf. Ps. 106:30; 1 Mac. 2:24ff., 54), and his resolute and uncompromising behaviour came to be regarded as a model to be followed by the Zealots (4 Mac. 18:12).

12. As a reward for his action, Yahweh granted Phinehas his **covenant of peace**. Snaith (pp. 303f.) suggests revocalizing the word *šālôm* ('peace') as *šillûm* (cf. *BHS*), and reads 'my covenant (of the priesthood) as a reward', but since the expression 'covenant of peace' occurs elsewhere in the *OT* (Isa. 54:10; Ezek. 34:25; 37:26; Mal. 2:5; cf. Batto, *CBQ* 49 [1987], pp. 187ff.) the revocalization seems quite unnecessary in this instance.

13. The covenant of peace is here further defined as **the covenant of a perpetual priesthood**: The clear implication is that, owing to Phinehas' action, the priesthood would always remain in his family (cf. 1 Chr. 6:4ff.).

14–15. The identity of the two offenders (**Zimri** and **Cozbi**) appears at a very late stage in the story, and gives every impression of being a subsequent addition (cf. Noth). **Zur** (Cozbi's father) is mentioned in 31:8 as one of the five 'kings' of Midian; in v. 18 he is represented as a 'prince' (*nāśî*); cf. Jos. 13:21.

16–18. These verses are widely regarded as a later addition; they combine the two stories (vv. 1–5, 6–13) together by suggesting that it was, in fact, the Midianites who were responsible for tempting Israel in both cases. The direction to take vengeance on the Midianites anticipates the command given to Moses in 31:1, and was probably inserted here to pave the way for that chapter. The negative attitude exhibited towards the Midianites in chs. 25, 31 stands in

sharp contrast to the more positive appraisal of them encountered
elsewhere in the *OT* (cf. Exod. 2; 18); see, further, Coats, *Moses*,
pp. 55f.

(b) THE SECOND CENSUS
26:1-65

This chapter reports the results of a second census of the Israelites
taken by Moses and Eleazar in the plains of Moab (v. 3), almost
forty years after the census recorded in ch. 1. This second census
was necessitated by the fact that those who had orginally come out
of Egypt had since died in the wilderness, the only exceptions being
Caleb and Joshua (cf. vv. 63-65). In the present form of the chapter,
the census serves a two-fold purpose, viz., to establish the strength
of the Israelite army in preparation for the imminent invasion of
Canaan (v. 2; cf. 1:3), and to ascertain the total number in every
tribe in order to ensure that each would be allotted a portion of
land relative to its size (vv. 52-56). The census list in vv. 5-50
follows a stereotyped pattern: first, the names of the subdivisions of
the tribe are given, and these are identified with the sons (and
sometimes with the grandsons; cf. vv. 21, 40) of the tribal ancestor;
then, the number of males over the age of twenty who belong to
each tribe is recorded. The sum total of adult males is given in v. 51
as 601,730, which represents 1,820 fewer than the total number in
the first census (cf. 1:46; see Excursus II, pp. 14-18, for a discussion
of the numbers involved). The order in which the tribes are listed
in MT follows that already encountered in 1:20-43 (except that Ephraim and Manasseh have exchanged places); a different order, however, is presupposed in LXX, which basically follows that found in
Gen. 46. As in the case of the first census, the Levites were counted
separately (vv. 57-62), since they were not to participate in the
occupation of Canaan, and were not entitled to receive a portion of
its territory.

There can be little doubt that the basic form of the chapter belongs
to the Priestly source, but it has every appearance of having been
compiled from various components which probably originally
existed as independent units. With regard to the main body of the
chapter (vv. 5-51), it seems probable that two quite distinct
elements of tradition have been combined, viz., a list of the clans
which made up each of the twelve tribes, and a set of census figures
denoting the number in each tribe. The secondary character of the

census figures is suggested by the fact that, in each case, they follow the concluding formula 'these are the families of . . .', and the numbers given do not relate to the individual clans enumerated in the list, but to the totality of each tribe (cf. Noth). Moreover, that these two traditions originally had little connection with one another is clearly demonstrated in the case of Dan (vv. 42f.) which, although consisting of a single clan, is given the remarkably high number of 64,400. Even the clan list itself, however, can hardly be regarded as a unified composition in its present form, for it has clearly been supplemented in various ways (see, e.g., on vv. 8–11, below). Further, it seems almost certain that the reference to the division of the land in vv. 52–56 is a later addition, for the original purpose of the census was to ascertain Israel's military capability (cf. v. 2) and no mention is made prior to these verses of land distribution. On the literary unity of vv. 52–56 and vv. 57–62, see below. Vv. 63–65 constitute an editorial conclusion, possibly inserted to correct the impression given in v. 4*b* that the census involved an enumeration of the Israelites who had come out of the land of Egypt. It is here clarified that this was not the case, for the Israelites who had taken part in the exodus had all perished in the wilderness, the only exceptions being Caleb and Joshua.

(i) *Directions for taking the census:* **26:1–4**

1. After the plague (referred to in 25:8f., 18) **the LORD said to Moses and to Eleazar the son of Aaron**: Since Aaron was now dead (cf. 20:22ff.), the task of assisting Moses with the second census was to be entrusted to Eleazar, Aaron's son (LXX omits 'the son of Aaron').

2. Take a census of all the congregation of the people of Israel, from twenty years old and upward, by their fathers' houses, all in Israel who are able to go forth to war: The command is similar to that given to Moses alone in 1:2f., though it is here more succinctly expressed. The reference to 'war' is probably an allusion to the forthcoming advance against Midian (ch. 31) and the imminent invasion of the land of Canaan.

3–4. MT is here clearly defective, for it appears that the beginning of the speech following the word *lē'mōr* ('saying') at the end of v. 3 is missing. *BHS* tries to make sense of the passage by emending *wayᵉdabbēr* ('and he spoke') to read *wayyipqōḏ* ('and he numbered') at the beginning of v. 3, and deleting the word *lē'mōr* at the end of the verse (cf. Syr.); the passage would then read: 'And Moses and Eleazar the priest numbered them in the plains of Moab by the Jordan at Jericho, from twenty years old and upward, as the LORD commanded Moses' (cf. Noth; Paterson). However, a simpler solution is to assume (on the basis of similar phraseology in v. 2), that the words 'Take a census of the people' have been accidentally omitted by a scribe at the beginning of v. 4 (cf. *RSV, NIV*).

4. The people of Israel, who came forth out of the land of Egypt, were: *RV* understands this clause as the second object of the verb 'commanded' in v. 4*a*, and renders, 'as the LORD commanded Moses and the children of Israel etc.'; however, this phrase would be unparalleled in the *OT*, and such a construction would properly require the particle *'eṯ* before *bʰnê yiśrāʾēl* ('the people of Israel') to correspond to the same particle before the word 'Moses'. It is far preferable, therefore, to follow *RSV* and to regard this clause as the subject of the following verses (cf. Gen. 46:8). If this is the correct reading, however, it must be conceded that the writer's thought here has been rather carelessly expressed, for the census contained in vv. 5ff. could not possibly have been an enumeration of the Israelites 'who came forth out of the land of Egypt', since they had nearly all died during the wilderness wanderings, a fact rightly recognized in v. 64.

(ii) *The census results:* **26:5–51**
Noth (*Das System*, pp. 126ff.) has argued that, while the census figures given in vv. 5–50 may well be late, the list of tribal names contained here derives from an early and authentic document, which may be dated in the second half of the period of the judges. The fact that Manasseh is mentioned in the list suggested to Noth that it came from a time later than the Song of Deborah (for in Jg. 5 Manasseh was not, as yet, regarded as an independent tribe); on the other hand, Noth argued that the details concerning the clans of the various tribes could only be satisfactorily explained if the list was dated to a time when these sub-divisions were still significant, i.e., a period before the establishment of the monarchy and its new administrative organization. But whether the list dates from pre-monarchic times must be regarded as very doubtful (cf. Mowinckel, *Fest. Eissfeldt*, pp. 139ff.), and it is by no means clear why such a list should have been preserved until the time of the Priestly writer,

considering that (on Noth's own admission) it would no longer have had any practical value.

A comparison of the list of tribes in vv. 5–50 with that contained in Gen. 46:8–27 has led most commentators to conclude that a literary connection of some kind exists between the two passages, for the names which appear in the two lists are virtually identical, and the few divergences between them can readily be explained as due to scribal errors. Noth (pp. 202f.) gives priority to the list in the present chapter, and argues that it has directly influenced the genealogy found in Gen. 46; however, for reasons succinctly outlined by Budd (pp. 288ff.), it seems far more reasonable to suppose that the reverse was, in fact, the case, and that vv. 5–50 represent an elaboration of the material in Gen. 46.

5–7. The clans of Reuben consisted of **Hanoch, Pallu, Hezron** and **Carmi** (cf. Gen. 46:9; Exod. 6:14; 1 Chr. 5:3).

8–11. It is generally agreed by commentators that the section on Reuben originally consisted only of vv. 5–7, and that vv. 8–11 are a later interpolation, since (i) they interrupt the stereotyped formula which recurs in vv. 5–50, and (ii) their content seems to presuppose the narrative of ch. 16 in its present, composite form. The purpose of the addition, which recalls that Dathan, Abiram and Korah were completely annihilated, was evidently to provide a warning of the dire consequences of disobedience (cf. v. 10*b*).

8. the sons of Pallu: The plural form 'sons' is used in spite of the fact that only one son, **Eliab**, is listed; this phenomenon, however, is by no means uncommon in genealogies (cf. Gen. 46:23; 1 Chr. 1:41).

9. Eliab is here represented as having three sons, **Nemuel, Dathan** and **Abiram**, though elsewhere only the latter two are named (cf. 16:1, 12; Dt. 11:6); it seems probable, therefore, that the name Nemuel has accidentally slipped into v. 9 on the basis of its occurrence in v. 12, where it appears as the name of the first Simeonite clan.

10. and they became a warning: The word here translated as 'warning' (Heb. *nēs*) is regularly used elsewhere in the *OT* to refer to a 'standard', 'ensign' or 'signal' (cf. Isa. 11:10; 30:17; Ezek. 27:7); however, since the signal was occasionally one of impending catastrophe (cf. Isa. 13:2; 18:3; Jer. 4:6, 21), the word no doubt came to have the derived meaning of 'warning' (*BDB*, pp. 651f.; cf. *NIV*, 'warning sign'). The reference here is clearly to the incident recorded in 16:1ff., although in that passage it is the holy censers rather than

Korah, Dathan and Abiram which are to serve as a 'sign' ('*ôt*; cf. 16:38 [MT 17:3]).

11. the sons of Korah did not die: These words were no doubt intended to correct a possible misunderstanding of 16:32, which might be taken to mean that Korah's sons had also perished in the rebellion. The interpolator was aware that this could not possibly have been the case, since descendants of Korah were still alive in his own day (cf. 1 Chr. 9:19; 26:1ff.). Targ. Ps. Jon. suggests that Korah's sons had been preserved from the catastrophe because they had followed Moses' guidance and had not consented to their father's plan. The term 'sons of Korah' appears in the superscription of several psalms (42–49, 84, 85, 87, 88), and it appears that they functioned as a guild of temple singers in the post-exilic period (cf. 2 Chr. 20:19).

12–14. The clan of Simeon consisted of **Nemuel** (a variant of Jemuel; cf. Gen. 46:10; Exod. 6:15), **Jamin, Jachin** (who appears, mistakenly, as Jarib in 1 Chr. 4:24), **Zerah** (a variant of Zohar; cf. Gen. 46:10; Exod. 6:15) and **Shaul**. A sixth clan, Ohad, is mentioned after Jamin in Gen. 46:10 and Exod. 6:15, but is omitted both here and in 1 Chr. 4:24.

15–18. The clan of Gad consisted of **Zephon** (who appears, mistakenly, as Ziphion in MT of Gen. 46:16; but cf. LXX), **Haggi, Shuni, Ozni** (who appears as Ezbon in Gen. 46:16 and 1 Chr. 7:7), **Eri, Arod** (Arodi in Gen. 46:16), and **Areli**.

19–22. V. 19 interrupts the usual stereotyped formula, and is regarded by some as a later addition (cf. Noth). **and Er and Onan died in the land of Canaan:** See Gen. 38:7–10. The clans of Judah (vv. 20f.) are listed according to his sons (**Shelah, Perez, Zerah**), and his grandsons (**Hezron, Hamul**); cf. Gen. 46:12; 1 Chr. 2:3f.

23–25. The clans of Issachar consisted of **Tola, Puvah, Jashub** (who appears, mistakenly, as Iob in MT of Gen. 46:13; but cf. LXX) and **Shimron**.

26–27. The clans of Zebulun consisted of **Sered, Elon** and **Jahleel** (cf. Gen. 46:14).

28–34. These verses provide a description of the clans of Manasseh that is much more detailed than that of the other tribes. These clans consisted of **Machir**, Manasseh's son, **Gilead**, Manasseh's grandson, and six of Manasseh's great grandsons, **Iezer** (an abbreviated form of Abiezer; cf. Jos. 17:2; 1 Chr. 7:18f.), **Helek, Asriel, Shechem, Shemida** and **Hepher**. Different genealogical schemes are presupposed in Jos. 17:1f.; 1 Chr. 2:21–23; 7:14–19. Cf. Seebass, *VT* 32 (1982), pp. 496ff. V. 33, which mentions the daughters of Zelophehad, may well be a later addition, inserted in anticipation of 27:1ff.; 36:1ff. Noth (p. 207) suggests that their names (**Mahlah, Noah, Hoglah, Milcah**, and **Tirzah**) originally had a topographical significance (cf. Gray, *Proper Names*, p. 116), and this finds confirmation in the fact that Tirzah was a well-known town, and two of the other names (Noah and Hoglah) occur as districts in the Samaria ostraca. The point evidently made here is that the inhabitants of these places had become incorporated into the tribe of Manasseh. The place-names may have been represented as 'daughters' in later tradition on account of the fact that each had a feminine ending.

35–36. The clans of Ephraim are listed according to his sons, **Shuthelah, Becher** and **Tahan** (LXX, Tanach), and his grandson, **Eran**. Some commentators are of the view that the name Becher (omitted in LXX) is here misplaced and should be transferred to v. 38, since elsewhere this clan is represented as belonging to the tribe of Benjamin (Gen. 46:21; cf. 2 Sam. 20:1).

38–41. The clans of Benjamin are listed according to his sons, **Bela, Ashbel, Ahiram, Shephupham** (Shuppim in 1 Chr. 7:12) and **Hupham** (Huppim in 1 Chr. 7:12; cf. Gen. 46:21), and his grandsons, **Ard** and **Naaman**. In Gen. 46:21, Ard and Naaman are regarded as Benjamin's sons rather than his grandsons. Further, Gen. 46:21 lists some names not included in the present passage, viz., Becher (see on vv. 35–36) and Gera; the names Ehi, Rosh and Muppim in the Genesis text are suspect, for they do not occur in any of the other Benjamite genealogies, and Gray (p. 393; cf. *Proper Names*, p. 35, n. 1) suggests that they may be due to a faulty reading of a consonantal text which contained the names Ahiram and Shephupham, correctly read here.

42–43. Dan is represented as having only one clan, **Shuham** (Hushim in Gen. 46:23), which perhaps suggests that at one time this tribe was regarded as comparatively small (cf. Jg. 18:2). The incongruously high census figure for this tribe (64,400) confirms the suspicion that the clan list originally existed independently of the census results (see above).

44–47. The clans of Asher are listed according to his sons **Imnah, Ishvi** and **Beriah**, and his grandsons, **Heber** and **Malchiel**. It is

no longer clear why the name of Asher's daughter, **Serah**, appears
in v. 46.

48–50. The clans of Naphtali consisted of **Jahzeel, Guni, Jezer**
and **Shillem** (Shallum in 1 Chr. 7:13).

(iii) *The division of the land:* **26:52–56**
This section, which concerns the distribution of the land between
the tribes, is problematic, for two different – and seemingly irreconc-
ilable – principles of division are here enjoined: on the one hand,
the land was to be apportioned between the various tribes according
to their size (vv. 53f.); on the other hand, it appears that the land
was to be divided by lot (vv. 55f.). One way of explaining these
conflicting principles has been to assume that the *location* of the tribal
territory was to be determined by lot, while the *size* of the territory
was to correspond to the size of the tribe (cf. Snaith; Milgrom). The
difficulty with this solution, however, is that the text itself gives no
hint whatsoever that this was what was intended. The most probable
explanation of the inconsistency is that the passage, as it stands, is
the product of more than one author (cf. Auld, *Joshua*, p. 73). The
core of the passage is probably to be found in vv. 52–54, which
establishes the principle of land-division according to the numerical
strength of the tribe; this was no doubt why the account of the
procedure of land-allotment was placed immediately after the computation of the numbers in each tribe (vv. 5–51). A later editor
subsequently appended v. 55, in deference to the well-established
tradition that the land to the west of the Jordan was divided by lot
(Jos. 15:1; 18:6, 8, 10). The inclusion of v. 55, however, meant that
two theoretically incompatible principles of distribution existed side
by side; thus, a rather forced attempt was made to reconcile the two
conflicting principles by the addition of v. 56, which suggested that
the lot would in any case fall in such a way that the inheritance
would correspond to the relative size of the tribe.

54. To a large tribe you shall give a large inheritance: Since
this command is issued to Moses (cf. v. 52), it is here presupposed
that the distribution of land would take place before his death, i.e.,
while the people were still in the land of Moab (cf. Jg. 1:1–3); other
passages, however, suggest that the allotment of land was made by
Eleazar and Joshua *after* the conquest of Canaan had been accomplished (cf. Jos. 14:1ff.).

55. But the land shall be divided by lot: The lot seems to have been used for a variety of purposes in Israel, such as deciding contentious cases (Prov. 18:18), distributing spoil (Jl 3:3) and selecting specific persons (1 Sam. 10:20f.). The seemingly haphazard decision rendered by the lot was thought to reflect God's will (Prov. 16:33); thus, lot-casting was regarded as a religious act and was frequently performed by the priest at the sanctuary. The custom was widely practised in the ancient Near East, and it survived in Israel down to *NT* times (cf. Ac. 1:26). See, further, Lindblom, *VT* 12 (1962), pp. 164ff.

(iv) *The second Levitical census:* **26:57–62**

At the first census, the Levites were numbered separately from the secular tribes because they were exempt from military duties (cf. 1:47ff.; 3:14ff.); here, they are numbered separately because they were not entitled to any share of the land after the settlement (v. 62). This section, despite its brevity, cannot be regarded as a literary unity, for vv. 57 and 58*a* contain different traditions of the genealogy of the Levites, and these two verses could hardly have stood together in the original composition. It seems probable, therefore, that v. 58*a* derives from an older source, which was secondarily incorporated into the present context. Vv. 58*b*–61, which appear to be based on a variety of sources (Exod. 2:1; 6:18–20; Lev. 10:1f.) may well represent a further addition to the passage, the reference to Kohath in v. 58*b* presumably providing a link with v. 57.

58a. While v. 57 presents the usual grouping of the Levites into three families, Gershon, Kohath and Merari (cf. 3:17ff.), v. 58*a* disregards this three-fold division and notes, instead, five Levitical families, namely, the **Libnites**, the **Hebronites**, the **Mahlites**, the **Mushites** and the **Korahites**. Noth (p. 209) suggests that these names may well represent early regional or local groupings of Levites; thus, e.g., the Libnites and Hebronites would have inhabited the towns of Libnah and Hebron in the south of Judah. However, the uncertainty regarding the locality of the remaining Levitical families makes this conclusion uncertain (see on 3:17–20).

58b–60. The Kohathites receive more detailed treatment than the others since it was to this family that Moses and Aaron belonged. Their line is traced to Aaron's sons, two of whom (Nadab and Abihu) **died when they offered unholy fire before the LORD** (see on 3:4).

62. The Levites, in the second census, numbered 23,000; at the first census they numbered 22,000 (3:39).

(c) THE DAUGHTERS OF ZELOPHEHAD
27:1–11

The present section is concerned with the right of daughters to inherit the property of their father when he had died without leaving any sons. The issue is presented in the form of a narrative concerning the daughters of Zelophehad, who belonged to the tribe of Manasseh (v. 1). They appealed to Moses, Eleazar, the leaders and the congregation stating that, since their father had died without male progeny, they should be accorded the legal right to inherit his estate (vv. 2–4). The case was so exceptional that Moses had to seek Yahweh's guidance in the matter (v. 5), and a divine decision was rendered acknowledging the legitimacy of their claim (vv. 6f.). A formal law was then drafted which established a specific order of precedence in the inheritance of property: upon the death of a father, the estate was to pass to his son, and in the absence of a son, to his daughter; in default of any daughters, the inheritance passed to the brother(s) of the deceased; failing any brothers, it passed to the deceased's uncles and, failing them, to the nearest male relative (vv. 8*b*–11). The intention of the law was clearly to keep the family inheritance within the tribe and to prevent it from passing into alien hands, and, to this extent, it enshrined the same principle as that which undergirded the custom of levirate marriage (Dt. 25:5–10) and the laws concerning the jubilee year (Lev. 25:8ff.) and the redemption of land by a relative (Lev. 25:25–28; cf. Jer. 32:6–15). Permitting daughters to inherit property, however, involved a potential hazard which the present legislator had evidently not foreseen: a daughter might be tempted to marry outside her own tribe, and since she would have taken the family property with her, the land would have been permanently alienated from the tribe to which it had originally belonged, and the purpose of the legislation here enacted would have been completely negated (cf. Mace, *Hebrew Marriage*, p. 112). In order to safeguard against such a contingency, a supplement had to be appended to the present law, requiring that daughters who inherited their father's estate should marry within their own tribe (36:1ff.).

The present law marked a new departure in Israel in the rights and privileges accorded to women. Earlier legislation permitted only sons to inherit the property of their deceased father (Dt. 21:15–17; cf. Davies, *VT* 36 [1986], pp. 341ff.), and, if the father had left no

sons, the institution of levirate marriage would have provided his
widow with male heirs (Dt. 25:5–10). It is not entirely clear why
no allowance for the levirate custom was made in the present section,
since this institution would have served the same ends (viz., reten-
tion of land within the family) as the new legislation permitting
daughters to inherit. Some commentators (e.g., Binns, p. 187) suggest that the levirate law may have been unknown to the author,
but this is most improbable, since the levirate custom was quite
ancient and was deeply rooted in Israelite tradition (cf. Gen. 38:1ff.;
Ru. 3:1ff.). Others suggest, on the basis of such passages as
Lev. 18:16; 20:21, that the Priestly author may have disapproved of
the levirate custom (cf. Gray, p. 398), and may even have intended
to abrogate it completely, or at least to hasten its demise (cf.
Morgenstern, *HUCA* 7 [1930], p. 183, n. 235); however, this explanation is equally unsatisfactory, for although Lev. 20:21 seems to
prohibit marriage with a brother's wife, and Lev. 18:16 appears to
forbid any sexual relations between them, it is probable that these
laws applied only during the lifetime of the brother, whereas levirate
marriage was operative after his death. The most probable explanation for the lack of any reference to the levirate custom in the
present narrative is that the narrator had assumed that the brother-
in-law's obligation could not, in this particular instance, have been
discharged, either because Zelophehad himself had no brother, or
because Zelophehad's wife had also died, thus leaving no opportunity for her to be provided with male heirs.

N. H. Snaith (pp. 21, 309f.; *VT* 16 [1966], pp. 124ff.) has argued
that the present narrative has nothing to do with rules regarding
the inheritance of property, but was merely a story designed to
explain how the tribe of Manasseh came to occupy territory to the
west of the Jordan (Jos. 17:1–6), although it had been allotted land
on the eastern side of the river. The fact that the daughters received
an inheritance 'among their father's brethren' (v. 7) is taken by
Snaith to mean that they received territory among the tribes on the
western side of the Jordan, and the allocation to Manasseh of 'ten
portions' (Jos. 17:5) is regarded as significant, for each of
Zelophehad's five daughters, in effect, received the 'double portion'
normally granted to the heir (Dt. 21:15–17). However, this
interpretation is not without its difficulties. In the first place, the
'double portion' was not given to the heirs in general, as Snaith
seems to imply, but only to the eldest (cf. Davies, *JSS* 38 [1993],

pp. 175ff.), and since the legislation of Dt. 21:15−17 refers explicitly to the eldest *son*, there seems little justification for interpreting the reference to 'ten portions' in Jos. 17:5 in the light of this provision. Moreover, as Budd (p. 301) has rightly recognized, Snaith's interpretation fails to explain why the present narrative is concerned specifically with *daughters*, for the account of Manasseh's occupation of territory to the west of the Jordan could equally well have been composed in terms of sons. It thus seems preferable to interpret the present passage, with most commentators, as an attempt to clarify the legal position of women with regard to the inheritance of land. The case depicted was one which led to the filling of a gap in the law, and, as such, it may be viewed in the same light as other narratives designed for the same purpose, e.g., that concerning the man who gathered wood on the Sabbath (15:32ff.).

That the present passage is derived from the Priestly source is not in doubt (cf. Baentsch, p. 636). However, it is improbable that it should be attributed to P^g, for, as de Vaulx (pp. 318f.) has observed, the form of the narrative bears striking similarities to other passages where cases of a difficult or unprecedented nature are considered (9:6ff.; 15:32ff.; 36:1ff.; Lev. 24:10ff.) and these almost certainly stem from a very late stage in the Priestly redaction of the Pentateuch (cf. Grelot, *VT* 6 [1956], pp. 174ff.). The passage under discussion, therefore, probably belongs to a late stratum of P (cf. Holzinger, pp. 136f.), although the possibility must remain open that vv. 8b−11, which present a formal statement of the law of inheritance in Israel, are based on older, traditional legal material (Noth, p. 211). For a structuralist interpretation of the narrative, see Jobling, *SBL 1980 Seminar Papers*, pp. 203ff., and for an analysis of the narrative from a feminist perspective, see Sakenfeld, *PSB* 9 (1988), pp. 179ff.

1. the daughters of Zelophehad: Their names (**Mahlah, Noah, Hoglah, Milcah and Tirzah**) appear in 26:33 as towns or clans in the northern kingdom (cf. Gray, p. 392; *Proper Names*, p. 116). Since the Hebrew names all had feminine endings, the author of the present passage was able to reinterpret them to refer to daughters and to relate the story as an historical occurrence in the lives of particular individuals. In a similar fashion, Gilead and Machir are here treated as persons, although they were, in fact, divisions within the tribe of Manasseh (cf. Lemaire, *VT* 31 [1981], pp. 39ff.).

2. And they stood before Moses, and before Eleazar the

priest: Eleazar is here associated with Moses, as in 26:1, but in the supplement to this law in 36:1, Moses alone is mentioned. Ironically, according to 1 Chr. 23:22, Eleazar himself died without male issue, leaving only daughters.

3. In stating their case before Moses, Eleazar and the leaders of the congregation, the daughters emphasize that their father had died **for his own sin**, like the rest of his generation who perished during the wilderness sojourn (cf. 14:26ff.), and his death had not been a punishment for any flagrant act of apostasy, such as that committed by Korah and his followers, who had **gathered themselves together against the LORD** (cf. 16:1ff.). The plea of Zelophehad's daughters seems to presuppose that, had their father been involved in Korah's rebellion they, as his heirs, would automatically have been deprived of a right to his inheritance (cf. de Vaulx, pp. 319f.; Maarsingh, Wenham). Weingreen (*VT* 16 [1966], pp. 518ff.) has deduced from this that anyone in Israel found guilty of treason would have been punished by having his property forfeited to the crown. Thus, by emphasizing that Zelophehad had taken no part in the abortive insurrection instigated by Korah, the daughters were affirming that, apart from the unprecedented nature of the case, there was no obvious legal impediment to their taking possession of their father's property. As many commentators have observed (cf. Gray, McNeile, Binns), the reference here to Korah's rebellion, if original to the narrative (cf. Noth), is interesting in that it implies that Korah's followers were not composed exclusively of Levites, for the possibility is here entertained that Zelophehad, a Manassite, could have been numbered among them; thus, the tradition reflected here accords with the earlier of the two Priestly versions of Korah's rebellion contained in ch. 16 (see above, pp. 162ff.).

4. Why should the name of our father be taken away from his family, because he had no son? Since the family name was indissolubly linked with the family patrimony (cf. Davies, *VT* 31 [1981], pp. 141f.; Neufeld, *Marriage Laws*, p. 47), it was important that Zelophehad's daughters be granted their father's property in order that his name and reputation could be perpetuated.

7. The daughters of Zelophehad are right: The decision rendered was favourable, and the daughters' plea was accepted; they were entitled to receive their father's inheritance, and Jos. 17:3–6 records that they were, in fact, given possession of it. The ruling is presented as a special dispensation from Yahweh, and in this

way the legal innovation was invested with a divine and definitive
authority. The right of a daughter to inherit her father's property
was recognized elsewhere in the ancient Near East (cf. Gordon, *RB*
44 [1935], p. 38; Driver and Miles, *Babylonian Laws*, i, pp. 335ff.;
Paradise, *JCS* 32 [1980], pp. 189ff.; Skaist, *JAOS* 95 [1975],
pp. 245f.; Ben-Barak, *JSS* 25 [1980], pp. 22ff.), although it was often
(as here) restricted to cases where there were no male heirs at the
time of the father's death.

8–11. The divine judgment rendered in the case of Zelophehad's
daughters was to be transformed into a general ruling that was
henceforth to be valid and binding in Israel. The ruling given in
these verses, however, goes well beyond the case envisaged in vv. 1–
7, for it covers not only the plight of a man who had died without
any sons, but also that of a man who had died childless. This dispar-
ity led Noth (pp. 211f.) to conclude that vv. 8*b*–11 were probably
based on an already existing tradition which, apart from the
additional enactment concerning daughters, probably reflected the
inheritance scheme that was operative at a much earlier stage in
Israel's history.

**11. And it shall be to the people of Israel a statute and ordi-
nance**: The expression *ḥuqqaṯ mišpāṯ*, rendered 'statute and ordinance', occurs only here and in 35:29 in the *OT*; *NEB* renders it as
'legal precedent', while Weingreen (*op. cit.*, p. 522) suggests 'rule
of law'.

(d) THE APPOINTMENT OF MOSES' SUCCESSOR
27:12–23

Two distinct, but related, events are recorded in this section. In
vv. 12–14, Moses is instructed to view the promised land from the
'mountain of Abarim', and he receives an intimation of his impending death; in vv. 15–23, Joshua is appointed as his successor. The
Priestly origin of the passage is evident from its style and phraseology, its allusion to Eleazar the priest (vv. 19, 21), and the fact
that it is closely connected with the Priestly account of Aaron's
death in 20:22–29. The main problem of the present section is the
nature of the relation of vv. 12–14 to the prediction of the death of
Moses recorded in Dt. 32:48–52 (cf. Mittmann, *Deuteronomium 1:1–
6:3*, pp. 111f.). Von Rad (*Deuteronomy*, p. 201) suggested that the
Deuteronomic passage was a variant of Num. 27:12–14, but the
agreement between them seems too close to render this solution

probable. Rather, Dt. 32:48–52 is to be viewed as a secondary repetition (in slightly expanded form) of Num. 27:12–14, and its purpose was evidently to bridge the gap between the announcement of Moses' death in Num. 27:12–14 and the actual account of his death preserved in the Priestly portions of Dt. 34. Vv. 15–23 may have been added to vv. 12–14 after the Pentateuch had been linked with the Deuteronomistic historical work, for it is in the Deuteronomistic literature (Dt. 3:23–29; 31:1–8; Jos. 1:1f.) that Moses' death was connected with the installation of Joshua as his successor (cf. Noth, p. 213).

12–14. Go up into this mountain of Abarim: This phrase, in the Heb., agrees verbatim with Dt. 32:49. *RSV* (cf. *NEB*) erroneously gives the impression that Abarim was a specific mountain, but in fact the name refers to an extensive chain of mountains (cf. the plural in 33:47f.) which extended round about the northern end of the Dead Sea; the rendering of *NRSV*, 'this mountain of the Abarim range' is therefore to be preferred (cf. *NIV*). LXX here clarifies the rather vague reference of MT by specifying Mount Nebo, and in so doing it brings the text in line with Dt. 32:49; 34:1. From the mountain-top Moses would be granted a view of **the land which I have given to the people of Israel**. The fact that Moses was to die (on the expression **you also shall be gathered to your people**, see on 20:24) before he himself could enter the land is explained as the result of his rebellion against God's command **during the strife of the congregation**, when he failed to **sanctify me at the waters before their eyes**. These words contain the same play on the words **Meribah** ('strife') and **Kadesh** ('sanctify') as in 20:12f. The Priestly view that Moses' untimely death was due to sin on his part contrasts with the Deuteronomic tradition that Moses was to die because he was to suffer vicariously for the sins of the people (cf. Dt. 1:37f.).

15–17. Moses is here depicted as taking the initiative and asking Yahweh, **the God of the spirits of all flesh** (see on 16:22), to appoint a successor so that the people would not be bereft of a leader after his death. Moses requests the appointment of one **who shall go out before them and come in before them, who shall lead them out and bring them in**: These expressions were no doubt intended as a comprehensive summary of the duties which the chosen leader would be expected to perform, though they may have had special reference to the task of military leadership (cf. 1 Sam. 18:13, 16; 29:6). Without such an able commander, the people would

be **as sheep which have no shepherd**. For the metaphor of a
shepherdless flock, see 1 Kg. 22:17; Ezek. 34:5.

18–21. Yahweh grants Moses' request by commanding him to
install as his successor Joshua, the son of Nun, **a man in whom is
the spirit**. The 'spirit' with which Joshua had been endowed is not
described in precise terms here, but it is defined in Dt. 34:9 as the
spirit of wisdom and sagacity. As part of the official investiture of
Joshua, Moses is instructed to **lay your hand upon him**. The
'laying on of the hand' (or 'hands'; cf. Gray, p. 402; Péter, *VT* 27
[1977], pp. 48ff.) is an expression which occurs in a wide variety of
contexts in the *OT*, and it appears to have had more than one
significance; see on 8:10. Here, it signifies the transfer of Moses'
office to Joshua, symbolically indicating that the burden of leadership had formally been placed upon him. Noth (p. 215; cf. *Leviticus*,
p. 22) suggests that a magical efficacy was originally attributed to
the act, and that it had its roots in the sacrificial cult (cf. Lev. 16:31).
During the commissioning ceremony Moses was to confer upon his
successor some of his own **authority**. The word rendered 'authority'
(*hôd*) occurs only here in the Pentateuch; elsewhere, it refers to the
honour, glory and majesty of the king (cf. Ps. 21:5 [MT 21:6]; 45:3
[MT 45:4]; Jer. 22:18) or of God himself (Ps. 104:1). It is noticeable
that Joshua was to be invested with only **some** (on the significance
of the partitive *min* here, see Coats, *CBQ* 39 [1977], pp. 36f.) of
Moses' authority; clearly, no-one could be deemed worthy enough
to receive the whole of Moses' authority, but Joshua was to receive
enough of it to make the people respect and obey him. The basic
difference between Moses and his successor is indicated by the fact
that Moses could commune directly with God and needed no intermediary (cf. Exod. 33:11), but Joshua would have to seek Yahweh's
will through **Eleazar the priest**, who would obtain the divine oracle
by casting the sacred lot. The lot is here referred to by the term
Urim, an appurtenance which, in the *OT*, nearly always appears
in association with the Thummim. The etymology of these words,
and the type of objects which they designated, is by no means clear.
It has been suggested that they were stones, discs, sticks or dice of
different shapes or colours. They were apparently placed in a box
or pouch in such a way that a priest could put his hand in and
withdraw one or other, thus securing a 'yes' or 'no' answer; sometimes an answer was withheld. Examples of their use are probably
preserved in 1 Sam. 14:18f., 41f. (LXX); 23:9ff. As Noth (p. 215)

observes, the reference to the sacred lot in this instance is deliberately archaistic, for the custom of using this oracular procedure had almost certainly fallen into desuetude long before the time of the Priestly writer. Indeed, there is some evidence to suggest that the Urim and Thummim ceased to be used after the time of David, and that thenceforth the kind of question which had hitherto been addressed to these oracular devices was increasingly addressed to the prophet (1 Kg. 22:7; 2 Kg. 3:11; cf. de Vaux, *AI*, pp. 352f.; Long, *JBL* 92 [1973], pp. 490f.; Cody, *History*, p. 47). It is true that the Urim and Thummim are mentioned as the hallmarks of the priest as late as the time of Ezra (Ezr. 2:63 = Neh. 7:65), but they are probably here referred to as vestigial remnants of an ancient custom. On the Urim and Thummim, see Lindblom, *VT* 12 (1962), pp. 170ff.; Lipiński, *VT* 20 (1970), pp. 495f.; Robertson, *VT* 14 (1964), pp. 67ff.

(e) THE LIST OF OFFERINGS
28:1–29:40 (MT 28:1–30:1)

Chs. 28f. contain an elaborate list of offerings to be presented on behalf of the people of Israel at various festivals throughout the year. The list is arranged according to the frequency of the sacrifices to be offered, beginning with the statutory daily offerings (28:3–8), and continuing with the weekly Sabbath offerings (28:9f.), the monthly new moon offerings (28:11–15) and, finally, the annual offerings to be presented at the five great feasts, here enumerated in chronological order, viz., the feast of Unleavened Bread (28:16–25), the feast of Weeks (28:26–31), the New Year Feast (29:1–6), the Day of Atonement (29:7–11), and the feast of Tabernacles (29:12–38). The list contains only the public offerings required on these occasions and takes no account of the private offerings which the individual Israelite could present of his own volition (29:39). The requisite offerings for each occasion may be represented in tabular form as follows:

| OCCASION | BURNT OFFERINGS | | | SIN OFFERING |
	bulls	*rams*	*lambs*	*goats*
1. Daily offerings (28:3–8)	---	---	2	---
2. Sabbath offerings (28:9f.)	---	---	2	---
3. New Moon (28:11–15)	2	1	7	1

4. Feast of Unleavened
   Bread (each day;
   28:16–25)   2   1   7   1
5. Feast of Weeks
   (28:26–31)   2   1   7   1
6. New Year (29:1–6)   1   1   7   1
7. Day of Atonement
   (29:7–11)   1   1   7   1
8. Feast of Tabernacles
   (29:12–38)

   1st day   13   2   14   1
   2nd day   12   2   14   1
   3rd day   11   2   14   1
   4th day   10   2   14   1
   5th day   9   2   14   1
   6th day   8   2   14   1
   7th day   7   2   14   1
   8th day   1   1   7   1

The sacrifices required on each occasion were to be accompanied by the appropriate cereal offerings and drink offerings, calculated according to the scale found in 15:1ff.

As many commentators have observed, chs. 28f. may be regarded as constituting, in effect, a festal calendar, indicating the date, duration and names of the various feasts which were celebrated during the course of the Jewish liturgical year. Similar 'calendars' have been discerned in Exod. 23:14–17; 34:18–24; Lev. 23; Dt. 16:1–17; Ezek. 45:18–46:15, although in these texts the lists of appointed feasts are less complete and less systematic than those encountered in the two chapters here under discussion. (On the 'festal calendars' of the Old Testament, see Kraus, *Worship*, pp. 26ff.; Segal, *JSS* 6 [1961], pp. 74ff.; van Goudoever, *Biblical Calendars*, pp. 3ff.; Morgan, *Cultic Calendars, passim*.)

It is generally conceded that, apart from a few minor additions (noted below), chs. 28f. may be regarded as essentially a literary unity. These chapters clearly derive from the Priestly source, although they probably represent a relatively late accretion within the Priestly corpus (cf. Baentsch, p. 641; Gray, pp. 402ff.). The reasons usually given for positing a late origin for these two chapters may be summarized briefly as follows: (i) Num. 28f. require a fixed amount of offerings, whereas earlier legislation left the quantity to the discretion of the individual worshipper, exhorting him merely to give 'according to the blessing of the LORD your God which he has given you' (Dt. 16:17). (ii) These chapters state that the offerings were to be presented at set times ('in its due season', v. 2), whereas prior to Deuteronomy the dates of the feasts appear to have varied, depending on the agricultural season. (iii) The sacrifices required in Num. 28f. are limited to burnt offerings and sin offerings, and these were to be entirely given over to Yahweh, with no provisions enabling the worshipper to partake of the offering himself; earlier legislation, however, never mentions the burnt offering or sin offering in connection with these feasts, but stipulates that the appropriate sacrifice to be presented on such occasions was the 'peace offering', and that this was to be shared by priests and laity alike. (iv) The reference to the eighth day of the feast of Tabernacles (29:35) points to a post-exilic date (cf. Dt. 16:13–15), and the fact that the Day of Atonement was celebrated on the tenth day of the seventh month possibly suggests a period after the time of Ezra (cf. Neh. 9:1). (v) These chapters appear to presuppose passages which themselves did not originate until the exilic or post-exilic age (e.g., 15:1–6; Lev. 1–7; 23), and, as Noth (p. 219) observes, the present text gives the impression of being a 'final, definitive and systematic treatment of its subject'. These points, taken together, strongly suggest that Num. 28f. constitute a late supplement to P, and although some scholars have suggested, on the basis of Ugaritic parallels (cf. Fisher, *HTR* 63 [1970], pp. 498ff.) or parallels in early archival documents from Mesopotamia (cf. Levine, *JAOS* 85 [1965], pp. 317f.), that the ritual contemplated in these texts may be early, the balance of probability must favour the view that these chapters reflect, rather, the established practice of Jewish worship in the post-exilic period when the texts themselves were composed.

(i) *Directions concerning the offerings:* **28:1–2**

1. The LORD said to Moses: The entire content of chs. 28f. is encased within the framework of a speech by Yahweh, and the offerings required are thereby given a divine sanction. God's command to Moses (v. 2a) is fulfilled in 29:40, and this serves to give the two chapters a sense of unity and cohesion (cf. Morgan, *op. cit.*, pp. 189ff.).

2. My offering: The Heb. *qorbān*, lit., 'what is brought near' (i.e., to God, as a gift), is a comprehensive term frequently used by the

Priestly writer to denote the sacrifices which were Yahweh's due
(cf. 7:17, 23, 29, 35; Lev. 1:2, 14; 2:1, 4, 12). The term is confined
to P and Ezekiel in the *OT*. **my food for my offerings by fire, my
pleasing odour**: For a discussion of the use of the term *leḥem* (here
rendered 'food') in cultic contexts, see Rost, *TLZ* 83 (1958),
pp. 330ff. The belief that the gods actually ate the sacrifices offered
to them was both primitive and widespread (cf. Smith, *Religion*,
p. 224), and although such ideas had long fallen into desuetude by
the time of the Priestly writer, a vestige of the notion has clearly
survived in the archaic language here employed (cf. Lev. 21:6ff.; Jg.
9:13). See, further, Gray, *Sacrifice*, pp. 21f., 78; de Vaux, *Studies*,
pp. 39ff. For the expressions **offerings by fire** (*NEB*, 'food offering')
and **my pleasing** (*NEB*, 'soothing') **odour**, see on 15:3.

(ii) *Daily offerings:* **28:3–8**
As a **continual** (Heb. *tāmîd*; *NEB, NRSV*, 'regular'; cf. Ezek. 39:14)
offering, two yearling male lambs without blemish were to be sacrificed, one in the morning and the other in the evening (lit., 'between
two evenings'; see on 9:3), and they were to be offered as a burnt
offering, together with the appropriate cereal offering (**a tenth of
an ephah of fine flour**, v. 5) and drink offering (**a fourth of a
hin of beaten oil**). This sacrifice, which was to be offered daily
throughout the year, constituted the basis of the whole sacrificial
system in Israel (Snaith, pp. 312f.; cf. Wellhausen, *Prolegomena*,
p. 80), and was regarded as so important that its cessation at the
time of the persecution of Antiochus IV was seen as a decisive
turning-point in Israel's history (cf. Dan. 8:11ff.; 11:31; 12:11). The
regulation concerning the 'continual offering' prescribed in these
verses concurs with that found in Exod. 29:38–42, but differs from
that which was evidently in force during the monarchy, when the
daily sacrifice consisted of a burnt offering in the morning and a
cereal offering in the evening (2 Kg. 16:15). Yet another variation is
represented by Ezekiel, who mentions only a morning burnt offering,
accompanied by the appropriate cereal offering (Ezek. 46:13–15; cf.
Neh. 10:33). The precise regulation no doubt varied from one period
to another. On the measurements 'ephah' and 'hin' used here in
connection with the cereal offerings and drink offerings, see on 15:4.
V. 6, with its reference to the promulgation of the law at Sinai (cf.
Exod. 29:38ff.), interrupts the train of thought between vv. 5 and
7, and is widely regarded as a later insertion (so, e.g., Baentsch,

Gray, de Vaulx). Similarly, v. 7*b*, which states that the drink offering was to be poured **in the holy place**, is frequently regarded as an explanatory gloss (Paterson, Dillmann, Noth). The **holy place** must here, exceptionally, be taken to refer to the inner court of the sanctuary, where the altar of burnt offering stood, since it was at the base of this altar that the drink offerings were usually poured (cf. Sir. 50:15; Josephus, *Ant.* III.9.4). Since the drink offering regularly consisted of wine, it is curious that it is here stated to consist of **strong drink** (Heb. *šēkār*), a general term which is normally used in the *OT* to denote various types of alcoholic liquors *excluding* wine (cf. 6:3; Lev. 10:9; Dt. 29:6). Commentators assume either that this is an exceptional use of the term *šēkār* (so, e.g., Gray; cf. Vulg.), or that the word should here be related to the Akkad. *šikaru*, which appears in Babylonian ritual texts as a technical term in connection with drink offerings (so, e.g., Snaith, Sturdy, Budd).

(iii) *Offerings for the Sabbath:* **28:9–10**
The Sabbath was distinguished from other days by special offerings which were to be presented over and above the daily sacrifices. In effect, the daily offerings were to be doubled on the Sabbath, for the worshipper had to offer, as an extra, **two male lambs a year old without blemish, and two tenths of an ephah of fine flour for a cereal offering, mixed with oil, and its drink offering**. Although it is not entirely clear from the rendering of *RSV*, it is, of course, the flour rather than the cereal offering that was to be mixed with oil (cf. *NEB*; Snaith, *VT* 19 [1969], p. 374; Orlinsky, *VT* 20 [1970], p. 500). This is the only law relating to a special Sabbath offering in the Pentateuch, and its observance is not explicitly attested before the time of Ezekiel, who states that the 'prince' (Heb. *nāśî*) was to present a Sabbath offering consisting of six lambs and a ram, with their accompanying cereal offerings and drink offerings (Ezek. 46:4f.). Whether this law was actually enforced in Ezekiel's time, however, must remain uncertain, and the lack of any other explicit reference to its observance in the pre-exilic period (though cf. Isa. 1:13; Hos. 2:11) perhaps suggests that it was only observed on a regular basis in post-exilic times (cf. Neh. 10:33; 2 Chr. 8:13; 31:3).

(iv) *Offerings for the feast of New Moon:* **28:11–15**
Vv. 11–15 stipulate the offerings to be presented on the first day of each month. This festival (usually referred to as 'new moon') was

known in Israel from early times (cf. 1 Sam. 20:5; 2 Kg. 4:23; Isa. 1:13; Am. 8:5; Hos. 2:11), although this is the only law in the Pentateuch legislating for its observance. Some scholars suggest that this feast may have been ignored by earlier legislators owing to its association with the widespread worship of the moon among the Semites (so, e.g., Kennedy; but cf. Binns), and Gray (p. 410) opines that its presence here was due partly to the importance of the new moon in fixing the liturgical calendar, and partly because of the prevailing tendency of the Priestly writers to invest ancient folk customs with a new significance. The importance here attached to the feast of New Moon is suggested by the sharp increase in the quantity of sacrifices to be offered, which effectively placed it on a par with the great feast of Unleavened Bread (vv. 16–25) and the feast of Weeks (vv. 26–31). As was the case with the Sabbath offerings, the sacrifices required on the feast of New Moon (two bulls, one ram and seven lambs) were to be in addition to the regular daily offerings (v. 15b). Moreover, during the New Moon, as on all subsequent feasts mentioned in this and the following chapter, a male goat was to be sacrificed as a **sin offering to the LORD** (v. 15a). Noth (p. 219) regards the references to the presentation of a goat as a sin offering in these two chapters (cf. vv. 22, 30; 29:5, 11a, 16a, 19a, 22a, 25a, 28a, 31a, 34a, 38a) as later additions, partly because they appear to conflict with the normal ritual procedure (the sin offering being usually presented *before* the burnt offering; cf. 6:16; 7:87; Lev. 15:15, 30), and partly because they reflect a cultic practice that did not emerge until later (cf. Holzinger, p. 142). However, neither of these arguments seems conclusive. In the first place, the order in which the sacrifices are mentioned in these two chapters need not necessarily reflect the actual order of the ritual procedure, for it is quite possible that a distinction was drawn between the administrative order in which materials allocated for sacrifice were listed, and the operative order in which the materials were actually presented as a sacrifice (cf. Rainey, *Bib* 51 [1970], pp. 495f.; Levine, *IDB Sup*, p. 634); secondly, the custom here described need not reflect later practice, for the presentation of a goat as sin-offering already has an integral place in Ezekiel's list of offerings for the feast of Unleavened Bread (Ezek. 45:23b). There seems no justification, therefore, for regarding these references as later additions to the text (cf. Budd, p. 315).

(v) *The feast of Passover and Unleavened Bread:* **28:16–25**

Vv. 16–25 (especially vv. 16–19*a*, 25) bear a striking similarity to
Lev. 23:5–8, but it is uncertain whether the present section is based
on Lev. 23:5–8 (cf. Binns, de Vaulx) or whether both passages are
mutually dependent on a common source (cf. Gray, Marsh). V. 16
merely reports that **on the fourteenth day of the first month** there
was to be a Passover celebration. No sacrifices are prescribed for
this occasion because it was regarded by the Priestly legislators as
essentially a family observance to be celebrated in the home rather
than a public festival with its attendant sacrificial offerings. In Ezek.
45:21f. the Passover seems to be regarded as the first of the seven
days of the feast of Unleavened Bread, and its earlier independent
existence is totally obscured; here, on the other hand, a clear distinction is drawn between the two festivals. As has already been noted
above, the sacrifices to be offered on each day of the feast of
Unleavened Bread were the same as those required on the New
Moon, i.e., two bulls, one ram and seven lambs (cf. vv. 11–15); this
differs from the more onerous requirement of Ezekiel for the same
occasion, where a total of seven bulls and seven rams (though no
lambs) were to be offered during each day of the feast. Ezekiel
concurs with the present legislation, however, in demanding that a
male goat be offered each day as a sin offering (cf. Ezek. 45:23).
The feast of Unleavened Bread was to begin and end with a **holy
convocation** (Heb. *miqrā'-qōdeš*; *NIV*, *NEB*, 'sacred assembly'; cf.
Noth, *Leviticus*, pp. 168f.), i.e., a meeting summoned for public worship, during which the people were to refrain from performing any
laborious work. The reference to 'laborious' work (somewhat mis-
leadingly rendered as 'servile' work in *RV*) perhaps suggests that
this prohibition (cf. 29:12, 35) was not as absolute as that which
pertained to the Day of Atonement, when no work of any kind was
permitted (29:7).

(vi) *Offerings for the feast of Weeks:* **28:26–31**

This section stipulates the sacrifices to be offered **on the day of the
first fruits** (v. 26), a unique designation for the feast elsewhere
called the 'feast of harvest' (Exod. 23:16) or the 'feast of weeks'
(Exod. 34:22). The latter term does, however, appear in v. 26, albeit
in an abbreviated form in the Heb. (lit., 'at your weeks'). In contrast
to the other feasts mentioned in chs. 28f., the date of this feast is
not precisely fixed, but is defined in rather vague and general terms:

when you offer a cereal offering of new grain to the LORD.
The offerings required for this occasion differ somewhat from those
prescribed for this feast in Lev. 23:18, where one bull, rather than
two, was deemed sufficient, but where two rams, rather than one,
were required. No comparison can be made in this instance with
Ezekiel, for this festival does not appear at all in his calendar of
liturgical feasts. The feast of Weeks originally marked the completion of the grain harvest, and, according to Dt. 16:9–12, it was
reckoned to commence seven weeks after the sickle was first put to
the standing corn, i.e., seven weeks after the beginning of harvest
(but cf. Lev. 23:15f. for a different reckoning). No special historical
significance was attached to this festival in the *OT*, although later
Jewish tradition regarded it as commemorating the giving of the
covenant and the law in the third month after the departure from
Egypt (cf. Exod. 19:1; 2 Chr. 15:10ff.; Jubilees). At Qumran, too,
the renewal of the covenant was probably celebrated during the
feast of Weeks, and this feast was regarded as the most important
in the Qumran calendar (cf. Noack, *ASTI* 1 [1962], pp. 89f.). The
phrase **see that they are without blemish** seems misplaced in v. 31,
and it should probably be transposed to the end of v. 27 (cf. v. 19);
Sam. includes the words in both verses. Cf. Dillmann, p. 183.

(vii) *Offerings for the first day of the seventh month:* **29:1–6**
The seventh month of the year (later known as Tishri) was marked
by three distinctive festivals, the first being held on the first day of
the month and designated as a **day for you to blow the trumpets**
(v. 1*b*). The word 'trumpets' does not appear in the Heb., which
reads simply 'a day of *t'rû'āh*', i.e., 'of shouting' (cf. *NEB*'s 'day of
acclamation'); however, since the corresponding verb is explicitly
used in the context of trumpet-blowing in 10:1–10, and since that
passage states that trumpets were blown at the beginning of every
month (10:10), there is ample justification for the rendering of *RSV*
here (cf. *NIV*). The first day of the seventh month is not mentioned
as a special feast in Ezekiel, but it is referred to in H (Lev. 23:23–
25), where it is described as a 'day of solemn rest, a memorial
proclaimed with blast of trumpets, a holy convocation'. In pre-exilic
times, before the native Hebrew calendar was replaced by a Babylonian one, the year began in the autumn, and some scholars have
argued that the feast held on the first day of the seventh month was
actually a New Year Festival, at which the king played a prominent

part, and at which the divine kingship of Yahweh, as lord of all
creation, was celebrated (cf. Mowinckel, *He That Cometh*, pp. 8off.).
But it may be that the first day of the seventh month was singled
out as a special day for no other reason than that the seventh month
was regarded as especially sacred, being the month during which
the Day of Atonement was celebrated. Thus the feast on the first
day of the seventh month was, in all probability, nothing more than
'an unusually solemn new moon' (de Vaux, *AI*, p. 503). The offerings prescribed for this day were quite considerable, for in addition
to the regular daily offerings of two lambs (cf. 28:3) and the special
New Moon offerings of two bulls, one ram and seven lambs (28:11–
15), a further sacrifice was required, consisting of a bull, a ram and
seven yearling lambs, together with their appropriate cereal offerings
and drink offerings, and the customary goat **for a sin offering**.

(viii) *Offerings for the day of atonement:* **29:7–11**
The second celebration of the seventh month was held on the tenth
day, and is usually known as the Day of Atonement, although the
technical term *yôm hakkippûrîm* does not appear in these verses (or,
for that matter, anywhere else in the *OT* except Lev. 23:27f.; 25:9).
The complicated ritual to be performed on this day is described in
detail in Lev. 16. According to the present passage, the people were
required to observe the occasion by holding a **holy convocation**
and by refraining from all manner of work. They were also instructed
to **afflict** themselves (*w⁽ᵉ⁾innîtem 'et-napšōtêkem*), although the precise meaning of this expression (which also occurs in Lev. 23:27,
32 in connection with the Day of Atonement) is unclear. The self-
affliction is traditionally interpreted in terms of fasting (cf. Isa. 58:3;
NRSV mg.); however, since the verb *'ānāh* in the Piel can mean 'to
lower or humble (oneself)' (cf. *BDB*, p. 776a), the expression may
refer to any form of self-abnegation, such as the wearing of sackcloth.
Targ. Ps. Jon. suggests that it involved various forms of abstentions,
such as refraining from food and drink, bathing, wearing sandals
and having sexual intercourse. The primary interest of the present
passage, however, is not in the rites that were to be performed on
this day, but rather in the sacrifices that were to be offered, and
these were the same as those required for the first day of the seventh
month.

(ix) *Offerings for the feast of Tabernacles:* **29:12–38**

The third great celebration of the seventh month was the feast of Tabernacles, which extended over a period of seven days, from the 15th to the 21st of the month, with a supernumerary eighth day, marked by a solemn assembly (v. 35), being observed on the 22nd. This eighth day appears to have been an addition to the original festival, and may have been regarded as a day of transition, before the people returned to their daily chores. The name of the feast, 'Tabernacles' or 'Booths' (Heb. *sukkôṯ*), originally referred to the temporary dwellings in which the farmers lived while the harvest was being gathered, but later tradition invested the name with a different significance, and regarded it as a graphic reminder of the time when the Israelites lived in tents during their sojourn in the wilderness (Lev. 23:43). This feast was one of the most popular and most important in the Israelite calendar, and it was a time of great rejoicing, celebrating as it did the harvest of the fruit (especially the olives and grapes) in early autumn. Like the Day of Atonement (vv. 7–11), the feast was to be marked by a **holy convocation**, by refraining from work (here, **laborious work**; vv. 12, 35) and by presenting offerings to Yahweh. The number of offerings required for each day was exceptionally high, and was considerably in excess of those demanded by Ezekiel (45:25) for the same feast. According to the present passage, the total number of sacrifices to be offered during the entire feast (including the eighth day, not mentioned in Ezekiel) was 71 bulls, 15 rams, 105 lambs, and 8 goats, together with the accompanying cereal offerings and drink offerings. In addition to these, the regular daily offerings were to be presented as usual. One curious feature of this passage is that the number of bulls declined by one each day, from thirteen on the first day of the feast to eight on the last, while the number of other animals remained the same throughout. The reason for this has never been satisfactorily explained, and suggestions that the dwindling number symbolized the waning moon or the gradual decline in the people's joy as the feast drew to its close (cf. Dillmann) have little to commend them and may safely be discarded. On the eighth day, the number of sacrifices reverted to the amount offered on the first and the tenth day of the seventh month (29:2, 8), i.e., one bull, one ram and seven lambs, with their accompanying cereal offerings and drink offerings. Moreover, on this day, the Israelites were to continue to refrain from performing **laborious work**, and were to gather together in

solemn assembly (29:35). There is nothing in the Heb. term *ⁿṣeret*
to indicate that the assembly was necessarily of a solemn nature;
the basic sense of the verb *'āṣar* is, rather, 'to hold back, restrain'
(cf. *BDB*, p. 783*b*), and hence the term probably indicated a day
when special abstinences or restraints were required, although what
these were (apart from the obvious abstinence from work) can no
longer be determined (cf. Noth, *Leviticus*, pp. 174f.).

(x) *Freewill offerings:* **29:39**
The offerings listed in this and the preceding chapter were only the
public, obligatory sacrifices which were to be presented to Yahweh,
and they were by no means intended to preclude the possibility
that private, voluntary sacrifices (**your votive offerings and your
freewill offerings**) could be presented by individual worshippers
or their families, if they so desired (cf. Lev. 23:38).

(f) WOMEN'S VOWS
30:1–16 (MT 30:2–17)

Apart from the opening command in v. 2, which states that a man
must always keep a vow which he has made, the rest of the chapter
(vv. 3–16) is concerned exclusively with vows made by women, and,
in particular, the validity of vows uttered by women who were under
the authority of a man. This chapter, in fact, contains the only law
in the *OT* that deals specifically with women's vows, although other,
more general, aspects of the vow are considered elsewhere, e.g.,
Lev. 5:4f. (vows uttered precipitately), Lev. 27:1ff. (the redemption
of persons and property vowed to Yahweh), Dt. 23:21–23 (the
importance of keeping vows), and Num. 6:1ff. (the Nazirite vow).

In the present chapter, the following general principles are laid
down: (i) An unmarried woman living in her father's house (vv. 3–
5), or a married woman living with her husband (vv. 6–8, 10–13)
was obliged to keep her vow only if the father or husband raised no
objection when he first heard of the vow having been made; if the
father or husband objects immediately, then the vow is automatically annulled. (ii) If the husband raised no objection to his wife's
vow at the time it was made, but subsequently sought to prevent
her from discharging it, then he himself would have to bear the
punishment for its non-fulfilment (vv. 14f.). (iii) Vows uttered by
widows or divorced women (i.e., those who were not under the
authority of a man, and who were thus responsible at law for their

own actions), were regarded as valid and binding, and were not subject to any veto (v. 9). The position of older, unmarried women (i.e., those who were not under the authority of a father or a husband) is not considered, perhaps because such persons would have been comparatively rare in Israel, where marriage was effectively regarded as a religious duty (cf. Mace, *Hebrew Marriage*, p. 144); however, it may be assumed that they would have been subject to the same rules as those which pertained to a widow or divorcee.

There can be no doubt that the passage derives from the Priestly source, although the introductory formula in v. 2, and certain peculiarities of style and phraseology encountered in the course of the chapter, suggest that it should be attributed to a relatively late stage of P (cf. Holzinger, p. 146; Baentsch, p. 648; Gray, p. 413). The fact that the passage has no obvious connection with either the preceding or the following chapters is usually regarded as further evidence of the supplementary nature of this material (cf. Dillmann, p. 185). Some scholars have sought to establish a link with the surrounding context, e.g., by suggesting that vows were often made in connection with sacrifices (Num. 28f.; cf. de Vaulx, Sturdy) or prior to a war (Num. 31; cf. Wenham), but on the whole such arguments seem contrived and unconvincing. The chapter may be regarded as essentially a literary unity, apart from a few minor additions and alterations (cf. de Vaulx, p. 347).

1. Moses said to the heads of the tribes of the people of Israel: The expression 'heads of the tribes' is unusual, and occurs elsewhere only in 1 Kg. 8:1 (= 2 Chr. 5:2), but it is clearly synonymous with the phrase 'the heads of their fathers' houses' in 7:2 (cf. 1:4). **This is what the LORD has commanded**: P's familiar formula, 'The LORD said to Moses, "Say to the people of Israel . . ."' (cf. 5:11f.; 6:1f. etc.) has here been replaced by a direct statement from Moses to the effect that the command had come from Yahweh; this, too, is unusual, although not entirely without parallel (cf. Lev. 8:5; 9:6).

2. When a man vows a vow to the LORD, or swears an oath to bind himself by a pledge: Commentators are generally agreed that the term 'vow' (Heb. *neḏer*) is used in this chapter of a positive commitment to give or consecrate something to God (cf. Gen. 28:20–22), whereas the term 'pledge' (*'issār*; cf. vv. 5, 7, 13) is used in a negative sense to refer to some form of abstinence or self-denial. Outside of this chapter, however, the general term *neḏer* embraces both kinds of commitment, and is applied equally, for example, to the vow of Hannah (which involved a promise to *give* her son to the service of God; cf. 1 Sam. 1:11) and to the vow of the Nazirite (which involved an undertaking to *abstain* from wine; cf. 6:2–4). For a discussion of the root *ndr* in the *OT*, see Cartledge, *Vows*, pp. 138ff. **he shall not break** (lit., 'profane') **his word**: It is here regarded as self-evident that if a man makes a vow, he must keep it 'without exception and without concession' (Snaith, p. 321). **he shall do according to all that proceeds out of his mouth**: The emphasis here upon the utterance of the vow reflects the belief that once a vow had been expressed in words it had to be fulfilled (cf. Jg. 11:35f.). The same was deemed to be true of blessings and curses, which were regarded in Israel as binding even if they did not correctly represent the speaker's intention (cf. Gen. 27:33–35). Later Jewish thought opposed such a view, at least in so far as vows were concerned, and declared that 'no utterance is binding unless the mouth and the heart agree' (*Terûmot* iii.8), i.e., unless the words expressed accurately reflected the speaker's mind.

3–5. The first case envisaged was that of a young woman who still lived in her father's house. The word *bin'urehā*, rendered by *RSV* 'in her youth', is somewhat vague, for it is used in the *OT* to designate a person of any age from infancy (cf. Job 31:18) to the first stages of womanhood (Jg. 19:3); here, however, it probably refers to a woman of marriageable age but who was not, as yet, married. If her father disapproved when he heard **of her vow and of her pledge**, and wished them to be annulled, he had to register his objection forthwith (**on the day that he hears of it**); silence on his part would be construed as tacit approval, and would mean that the vow would be regarded as valid and binding. It appears, however, that even if a father decided to veto his daughter's vow, the vow itself was not thereby simply abrogated; it had been uttered and thus, technically, it had to be fulfilled. But since a daughter could hardly be regarded as blameworthy if she failed to discharge a vow which her own father had overruled, she would, in such circumstances, be pardoned for its non-fulfilment: **and the LORD will forgive her, because her father opposed her**. The chapter gives no indication as to the motive which might induce a father to repudiate his daughter's vow; the matter was evidently left to his own discretion, and no reason or justification for his decision had to be given.

6–8. These verses have traditionally been understood to refer to vows made by a married woman, and they have been interpreted to mean that her husband could exercise his right to veto her vow or pledge, just as her father had been entitled to do previously. The difficulty with this interpretation, however, is that vv. 10–12 would thereby be rendered redundant, since the same principle is there repeated without adding anything essentially new. Moreover, if vv. 6–8 and 10–12 are both concerned with married women who were under the authority of their husbands, then it is difficult to account for the present location of v. 9, for this verse seems to interrupt the sequence of thought by introducing the case of women who were widowed or divorced. In order to overcome these difficulties, some commentators (e.g., Snaith, p. 322) suggest that, contrary to the impression given by *RSV* and most modern translations, vv. 6–8 refer to a woman who was betrothed, but not, as yet, married, and the beginning of v. 6 should therefore be rendered, 'if a woman belongs to a man', i.e., if she is engaged to him (cf. Rashi). The situation depicted in vv. 6–8, therefore, was that of a betrothed woman who uttered a vow without her father hearing it, and the point of the provision was to clarify the husband's prerogative when he hears of her vow after she had married and had gone to live with him. Thus, a woman who was about to enter into marriage while under a vow constituted a special case, which was quite distinct from that of the married woman envisaged in vv. 10–12. The advantage of this interpretation is that v. 9, far from being awkwardly placed, could be viewed as representing the second of three separate categories, and the sequence of thought would move progressively from the case of a betrothed woman (vv. 6–8), to a woman who was widowed or divorced (v. 9) and, finally, to a woman who was married (vv. 10–12). Not surprisingly, perhaps, this interpretation has commended itself to several recent commentators (cf. Sturdy, Wenham, Budd), but it must be conceded that it is not without its difficulties. In the first place, the idiom here employed (*wᵉ'im-hāyô ṭihyeh*) is one encountered elsewhere in the context of a *marriage* between a man and woman (cf. Lev. 21:3; Dt. 21:13). Further, if the present legislation had been concerned merely with the case of a betrothed woman, this would surely have been made clear, as it is, e.g., in Dt. 20:7; 28:30. It seems far preferable to suppose that vv. 6–8 refer to the case of a woman who, at the time of her marriage, was still bound by a vow which she had previously taken with her father's approval; when her husband hears of it, he may exercise his prerogative to annul it or allow it to stand. This situation differs from that envisaged in vv. 10–12 in that there the woman's vow is not made until *after* her marriage ('if she vowed in her husband's house', v. 10), in which case the husband could similarly approve of the vow or annul it, as he saw fit (cf. Baentsch, pp. 647, 649). This interpretation does not, of course, obviate the difficulty that v. 9 intrudes awkwardly between two cases relating to married women, but this verse may either be read in parenthesis, or regarded as a later addition to the chapter, designed to fill an obvious gap in the discussion (cf. Holzinger, Noth, Marsh).

13–15. Vv. 13f. merely recapitulate the rules concerning the sanctioning or the annulment of a woman's vows. If a husband wishes to annul his wife's vow, he must do so as soon as he hears of it, and his decision must not be delayed by lengthy prevarication. If he says nothing **from day to day**, then his silence will be construed as tacit consent, and his wife's vows will stand, for **he has established them, because he said nothing to her on the day that he heard of them**. By urging the husband to resolve the matter expeditiously, the law discouraged him from pondering interminably on the matter and perhaps thereby introducing irrelevant considerations into his decision. Moreover, a prompt response on his part would have prevented an ambivalent situation from arising, and would have allowed the person to whom the vow had been made to act with some measure of assurance and security. The point of v. 15 is that if the husband had given his tacit approval to the vow at the time he heard it being made, but later compelled his wife to break it, he himself would incur any guilt for her default: **he shall bear her** (LXX, Syr., Sam., 'his') **iniquity**, i.e., he would face the consequences, just as if he had broken a vow which he himself had made.

(g) THE DEFEAT OF MIDIAN AND THE DIVISION OF
THE SPOILS

31:1–54

In this chapter, Moses is commanded to organise an expedition, the purpose of which was to 'execute the LORD's vengeance on Midian' (v. 3). An army of 12,000 Israelites (1,000 from each tribe) is sent to battle accompanied by Phinehas, the priest, and the result is that all the Midianite warriors are annihilated but, miraculously, not a single member of the Israelite army is lost (vv. 1–12, 49). The

Israelites return triumphantly from the battle with their spoil, but when Moses sees them he commands the immediate execution of all the Midianite women (with the exception of the virgins) and all the male children (vv. 13–18). Two legal enactments follow from this account. The first prescribes the ceremonial purification which was deemed necessary after battle (vv. 19–24), while the second deals with the principle which was to govern the division of the spoils of war (vv. 25–54).

Although some scholars have argued that the chapter contains some archaic features, and may preserve an authentic historical memory of a battle against Midian (cf. Eissfeldt, *JBL* 87 [1968], pp. 383ff.; Albright, *Translating*, pp. 197ff.; Wenham, pp. 209f.), it seems most unlikely that the story can be regarded as historical. Its fictional character is suggested by the following considerations: (i) the lack of details concerning the site of the battle or the date at which it occurred; (ii) the exaggerated numbers involved (the Midianite virgins alone numbering 32,000, the animals taken as booty numbering in excess of 800,000, and the gold ornaments captured being valued at a staggering 16,750 shekels); (iii) the complete annihilation of all the Midianites (v. 7) is incompatible with their reappearance as a powerful tribe in the period of the judges (Jg. 6–8); (iv) the intrinsic improbability of the reported outcome of the battle, viz., that not a single Israelite was killed (v. 49) whereas all the Midianite males were slaughtered (v. 7). It is, of course, possible that the narrative contains some traditional elements, such as the names of the five 'kings' in v. 8 (cf. Gray, pp. 419, 421), but, as has been noted by several commentators, the chapter as a whole displays the distinctive character of a midrash, i.e., a story recorded to illustrate a specific theme, law or custom. According to de Vaulx (pp. 355ff.), the particular theme here developed was that of the 'day of Midian' (cf. Isa. 9:4; Ps. 83:9), a tradition which originated in Gideon's defeat of the Midianites as recounted in Jg. 6–8. In both battle accounts the same enemy is in view, and in both reference is made to the use of the trumpet in battle (v. 6; cf. Jg. 7:18), and the surrender of the gold objects taken as booty (vv. 50–54; cf. Jg. 8:24–27). According to de Vaulx, the author of the present passage, in effect, projected the victory of Gideon back to the time of Moses, and in so doing he created an imaginative and idealized version of the story which was no longer concerned with historical events but, rather, with the eschatological victory of God over his enemies. But whether the intention of the narrator was, indeed, to provide a theological reflection upon the tradition of the 'day of Midian' must be regarded as speculative, for the story bears similarities not only to Jg. 6–8 but also to other battles recorded in the *OT*, notably the account of the defeat of Amalek in 1 Sam. 15 and the battle narratives recorded by the Chronicler (cf. 2 Chr. 13:12; 20:13–30). In fact, it seems more probable that the story of the actual battle against Midian was subsidiary to the author's purpose (cf. Budd, p. 330; Sturdy, pp. 214f.), and that his primary aim was rather to explain how uncleanness contracted by contact with the dead was to be removed (vv. 19–24) and how booty gained in battle was to be distributed equitably (vv. 25–54).

It is generally recognized that the present narrative belongs to a relatively late stage of the Priestly tradition, for it presupposes many of the details previously recorded in P^g, e.g., that Aaron is now dead and has been succeeded by Eleazar (cf. 20:22–29), and that the death of Moses was imminent (v. 2; cf. 27:12–23). Moreover, the reference to the trumpets in v. 6 and the rites of purification in vv. 19–24 recall earlier legislation recorded in 10:9; 19:11–22. The possibility that the present chapter might itself be ascribed to P^g is, however, precluded by the significant departures from the usual style and vocabulary of that source, and by the fact that P^g does not normally deploy the midrashic method of instruction (cf. Gray, pp. 419f.). Further, the chapter appears to presuppose ch. 25 in its final, edited form, and this seems to support the supposition that it must belong to a period much later than P^g; indeed, Noth (p. 229) is of the view that this chapter should be regarded as a supplement to a completed form of the Pentateuch.

(i) *The defeat of Midian:* **31:1–18**
2. Yahweh instructs Moses to organize a campaign against the Midianites in retaliation for their part in the Baal-Peor episode (25:16ff.). This is represented as one of the last acts which Moses was to perform before his death: **afterward you shall be gathered to your people** (cf. 20:24; 27:13). Several mss of MT read the conjunctive *waw* ('and') before the adverb *'aḥar* ('afterward'), and this reading is reflected in the renditions of LXX, Vulg., Sam. According to an old rabbinic tradition (*Bab. Tal. Ned.* 37*b*) this was one of the five *'iṭṭûrê sōperîm* ('omissions of the scribes') found in Scripture (the others being in Gen. 18:5; 24:55; Ps. 36:7; 68:26); in each of these

cases the conjunctive *waw* appears to have been deliberately removed by a scribe in order to restore a reading preserved among the scribes themselves (see, further, Esh, *Textus* 5 [1966], p. 87; Fishbane, *Biblical Interpretation*, p. 82).

3. Arm men from among you for the war: *BDB* (pp. 322f.) records two roots for the verb *ḥālaṣ*: (i) to draw out, withdraw; (ii) to equip for war. The rendering of *RSV* assumes that the verb in this context is derived from the second root. Snaith (pp. 324f.), however, argues that there was only one root, *ḥālaṣ*, and that its meaning was 'to withdraw'; when used (as here) in connection with *ṣābā'* ('war') it meant 'release for the campaign'. The idea would then be that certain men were to be 'withdrawn' from their normal social life in order to take part in the forthcoming battle (cf. *NEB*'s 'drafted for active service'). The verb *ḥālaṣ* here should probably be pointed as a Hiphil (cf. LXX, Vulg., Syr., Sam.), since the Niphal has a reflexive meaning, which would make little sense in the present context.

4. You shall send a thousand from each of the tribes of Israel to the war: The selection of exactly 1,000 men from each tribe underlines the purely schematic and artificial character of the narrative, for no account is taken of the relative strength of the individual tribes. A more equitable arrangement is presupposed in Jg. 20:8–11, where a tenth of the fighting men of each tribe is sent to battle against Benjamin. The important factor in the present context, however, was not the precise number sent from each tribe, but the mere fact that each tribe was represented in the war; in this way, the eventual victory could be seen as a result of the concerted action of the entire people, accomplished under Yahweh's guidance and protection (cf. Weisman, *VT* 31 [1981], pp. 446f.).

5. So there were provided: The verb *māsar*, 'to provide', appears frequently in post-biblical Heb. and in Aram., but occurs only here and in v. 16 (but see below) in the *OT*. Some scholars (cf. Paterson, McNeile, Binns) are of the view that *wayyimmāsᵉrû* in this verse is a scribal error for *wayyissāpᵉrû*, 'and they numbered', an emendation which can claim the support of LXX (*exêrithmêsan*). However, in view of the lateness of the passage (see above), there seems no substantive reason why the post-biblical meaning of *māsar* cannot be applied to the verb in this instance, and *RSV*'s 'provided' or *NRSV*'s 'conscripted' makes excellent sense in the context.

6. Phinehas the son of Eleazar (LXX adds 'the son of Aaron')

the priest: The fact that the Israelite army is accompanied not by Moses or Joshua but by Phinehas, the priest, clearly indicates that the campaign in which the Israelites were engaged was a 'holy war' (on this phenomenon, see Jones, *WAI*, pp. 299ff.). Phinehas was presumably chosen in preference to his father, Eleazar, since the latter, as high priest, had to be preserved from contact with the dead, which would have been impossible had he taken part in the battle (see on 16:37). The selection of Phinehas was also no doubt justified on the basis of the zeal which he had previously displayed against the Midianites (cf. 25:6–8). The fact that Phinehas was to take with him to the battle-field the **vessels of the sanctuary** is a further indication of the religious character of the war which was to be fought. It is not entirely clear what was intended here by the phrase 'the vessels of the sanctuary'. The word $k^e l\hat{\imath}$ (rendered 'vessels') can have a very general sense, and in Dt. 22:5 it means 'garment'. A similar nuance is sometimes ascribed to the word here, and the verse is understood to mean that Phinehas was to go to war clothed 'with the holy (i.e., priestly) vestments' (cf. Dillmann). However, this meaning of $k^e l\hat{e}\ haqq\bar{o}de\check{s}$ is rather contrived and has received little support among commentators. In 3:31; 4:15; 18:3 the phrase $k^e l\hat{e}\ haqq\bar{o}de\check{s}$ appears to refer to the furnishings of the tabernacle or to the sacred objects housed in its precincts, and there is much to be said for understanding the expression in this sense in the present context. But, assuming this to be the meaning of the phrase, which of the furnishings or objects of the tabernacle did the author have in mind? The most obvious solution (favoured, e.g., by Snaith) is that the reference is to the ark of the covenant, which was regularly carried into battle to ensure Israel's victory (cf. 10:35f.; 14:44; 1 Sam. 4:4); however, Noth (p. 229) objects that a specific command to take the ark would not have been given, since this would have been taken to battle as a matter of course. The most probable solution is to take the expression $k^e l\hat{e}\ haqq\bar{o}de\check{s}$ in apposition to the following clause, and to understand the conjunction before $h^a\d{s}\bar{o}\d{s}^e r\hat{o}\d{t}$ as a *waw explicativum*; the phrase would then be rendered 'the holy instruments, specifically, the trumpets for the alarm'. For the use of these trumpets to assemble the community in time of war, see on 10:9.

8. All the Midianite male warriors were killed in battle, including five tribal chiefs, here rather grandiosely called **kings**. The royal title may well have been given to them in this instance to underline the magnitude of the victory. The names of the defeated 'kings' were: **Evi, Rekem, Zur, Hur, and Reba**. Zur appears in 25:15 as the head of a Midianite family, but nothing is known of the other chiefs mentioned. Their names recur, in the same order, in Jos. 13:21f., where, as here, they are associated with Balaam. It is sometimes suggested that there is a literary connection between the two passages (cf. Noth, p. 230; Budd, pp. 330, 333); however, the fact that in Jos. 13:21 the five individuals are designated not as 'kings' but as 'leaders of Midian' and 'princes of Sihon' suggests, rather, that the passage in Joshua represents a different tradition. In contrast to chs. 22-24, where Balaam appears (by and large) in a favourable light, he is viewed in the present narrative as the villain who was responsible for leading Israel astray in the incident at Baal-Peor (v. 16; cf. ch. 25); it was thus regarded as condign punishment that he should die along with the five tribal chiefs.

13-18. Moses is indignant that the Midianite women had been spared, since it was they who were responsible for leading Israel astray (cf. 25:6ff.). He therefore commands that all the male children and all the women, apart from the virgins, be slain forthwith. The virgins were to be spared presumably because they were innocent of any involvement in the sin of Baal-Peor. Why the male children should be killed is not explained, but such an action may have been sanctioned in order to ensure that a new generation of Midianites would not be permitted to arise. In the context of the 'holy war', the extermination of the women and male children is to be explained on the basis of the 'ban' (*ḥērem*), which demanded the complete destruction of all peoples and objects which were offensive to Yahweh. Normally, the ban was applied with the utmost rigour, and admitted of no exceptions whatsoever (cf. Jos. 6:18ff.; 1 Sam. 15:1ff.); here, however, it appears in a more moderate and restricted form, since the lives of the virgins were to be spared (cf. Dt. 2:34f.; 3:6f.; Jg. 21:11).

13. Moses, Eleazar and the leaders of the congregation go out to meet the army **outside the camp**. This action was no doubt intended to keep the camp free from contamination, for the returning warriors would have been deemed unclean through contact with the dead (cf. on v. 6, above).

16. The reason given for the extermination of the women is that they had conspired to **act treacherously against the LORD**: The rendering of *RSV* presupposes that *limsār*, from the root *māsar* (rendered 'to provide' in v. 5), is a scribal error for *limʿōl*, an emendation which is widely accepted (cf. 5:6; 2 Chr. 36:14; Ezek. 14:13). The Midianite women had seduced Israel away from Yahweh and had caused them to be disloyal to him, and in so doing they had acted upon the **counsel of Balaam** (*NRSV*, 'on Balaam's advice'). Since the original story, as recorded in 25:1ff., appears to know nothing of any such counsel or advice proffered by Balaam, *NEB* rather boldy renders the phrase *biḏᵉḇar bilʿām* as 'on Balaam's departure'. However, this is a somewhat forced and arcane interpretation of the common Heb. word *dāḇār*, and it ill accords with the use of the word in the expression *ʿal-dᵉḇar-pᵉʿôr* (*NEB*, 'that day at Peor') which occurs later in the present verse. Moreover, the rendering of *NEB*, in effect, absolves Balaam from any guilt in the Baal-Peor incident, but it appears almost certain that the author of the present passage intended to implicate Balaam in Israel's sin, for there would otherwise be no obvious motive for having him exterminated with the five Midianite chiefs in v. 8. Why the author of the present passage should have involved Balaam in the incident at Baal-Peor (25:1ff.) is not clear. McNeile (pp. 144, 166) suggests that a part of the extant narrative in ch. 25 may have been lost, and that in the original account Balaam was instrumental in persuading the Midianite women to seduce the Israelites into marrying them in order to provoke Yahweh's anger. But this is very speculative, and it seems most improbable that such a late narrative as that recorded here should have preserved an original variant of the old Balaam tradition. A more plausible solution is that advanced by Noth (p. 231; cf. Sturdy, p. 216), who suggests that the mere juxtaposition of the Balaam stories in chs. 22-24 and the Baal-Peor story in ch. 25 may have led the author of the present passage to suppose that Balaam had, in some way, been responsible for the Midianites' plan. But however Balaam's involvement in the Baal-Peor incident is explained, his collusion with the Midianites to lead Israel astray was undoubtedly one of the reasons for the bad reputation which Balaam was to gain in later Judaism (cf. de Vaulx, pp. 263f.; Baskin, *Pharaoh's Counsellors*, pp. 77ff.; Vermes, *Scripture*, pp. 127ff.).

18. The Israelites, having been instructed to exterminate the Midianite women and the male children, are commanded to keep the virgins **alive for yourselves**. This is sometimes interpreted to mean that the virgins were to become the wives of the Israelites (cf. Marsh,

Wenham), but the text may merely imply that they were to become their slaves or concubines. For the verb *hāyāh* in the Hiphil in the sense 'to preserve, keep alive', cf. 22:33; Gen. 6:19f.; 45:7.

(ii) *The purification of the warriors and the booty:* **31:19−24**

Vv. 19f. contain the regulations concerning the purification of the warriors, their garments and belongings, a custom which has several analogies elsewhere among primitive peoples (cf. Gray, pp. 243f.). All those who had been defiled by contact with the dead were instructed to remain outside the camp for seven days and to perform the requisite ritual purification as set out in 19:12, 16−19. In vv. 21−24, further instructions are given concerning the purification of the booty gained in battle; here, a distinction is drawn between objects which could withstand fire and those which could not, and provisions are made for the latter to be purified by means of water (v. 23*b*). Vv. 21−24 are widely regarded as secondary because the instructions are here given by Eleazar, not by Moses (as in vv. 19f.), and, apart from the implication in v. 24 that the people were outside the camp, these verses appear to have little connection with what precedes.

23. Everything that could withstand fire (e.g., metal objects) was to be passed through fire and then purified by the **water of impurity** (*NEB*, 'water of ritual purification'). It is sometimes suggested that the passing of objects through the water of impurity would have been an unnecessary procedure, given that they had already been purified by means of the fire; consequently, the words **nevertheless it shall also be purified with the water of impurity** are sometimes regarded as a gloss (so, e.g., Baentsch, Noth). But this is hardly necessary, for there is nothing intrinsically improbable in the idea that the process of purification by fire should be completed by the application of the specially prepared mixture described in ch. 19. Objects that could not withstand fire were to be passed **through the water**: This is not a reference to the 'water of impurity', as the *RSV* translation implies, but to ordinary water (cf. Lev. 14:5), the article in *bammāyim* being generic (*G–K* § 126*n*; cf. Wright, *VT* 35 [1985], pp. 218f.).

(iii) *The distribution of the spoils:* **31:25−47**

A principle is here established concerning the division of the spoils of war. These were to be divided into two equal halves, one of which was to be given to those who had taken part in the battle, and the other to the congregation who had remained in the camp. In this way, both the combatants and non-combatants were able to share in the material benefits of the victory. This may well be an ancient custom, since the ruling can be traced back to the time of David's defeat of the Amalekites recorded in 1 Sam. 30:24f. (but cf. Whitelam, *The Just King*, pp. 96f., 213, for the authenticity of the attribution of this custom to David). The author of the present passage provides the custom with a Mosaic precedent, thus giving it a more authoritative sanction. At the same time, a new element is here introduced, namely, the stipulation that a tax (Heb. *mekes*) was to be levied from each group for the benefit of the clergy: one five-hundredth of the soldiers' share was to be set aside for the maintenance of the priests, while one fiftieth of the congregation's share was to be given over for the support of the Levites. Some commentators (e.g., Snaith and, more tentatively, Gray, McNeile) suggest that the payment of this due was an old and well-established custom in Israel, but this cannot be proved, for there is no mention of such a tax on war booty anywhere else in the *OT*. Given the Priestly writer's preoccupation elsewhere with the proper support of the priests and Levites (cf. chs. 7, 18, 28f.), and the fact that the proportion of the Levites' share to that of the priests was ten to one (i.e., approximately the same as the proportion of tithes stipulated in 18:25ff.), there is much to be said for the view that the notion of such a tax originated with the Priestly writer himself and reflected the increasing demands made by the post-exilic priesthood (cf. Budd, pp. 331, 334).

32. Now the booty remaining of the spoil: The meaning is unclear, but the reference may be to the booty left over after the massacre ordered in v. 17 had been carried out; alternatively (but less probably) the author may have intended to refer to the booty that was left after discounting the animals that had died on the homeward journey and those that had been slaughtered to provide food for the returning army.

(iv) *Offerings to the LORD:* **31:48–54**

48–49. The idealistic character of the battle against Midian is clearly seen in the report of the officers (*śārîm*) to Moses to the effect that every single Israelite soldier had returned safely from the campaign: **there is not a man missing from us**. No hint of failure was allowed to mar the miraculous victory which the Israelites, under Yahweh's guidance, had achieved.

50. The officers present an **offering** (*qorbān*) to Yahweh, consisting of various gold ornaments which had been stripped from the bodies of the slain. Ornaments of this kind were frequently worn by roving nomads, and Jg. 8:24–26 records that gold ornaments were taken from the Midianites when Gideon won his famous victory. The precise meaning of some of the individual articles mentioned in the present passage is uncertain, but they seem to have included **armlets** (*RV* has 'ankle chains', but it is clear from 2 Sam. 1:10 that the *'es'ādāh* were worn on the arm), **bracelets** (*sāmîd*), **signet rings** (*tabba'at*), **earrings** (*'āgîl*) and **beads** (*kûmāz*). These costly gifts were given over to Yahweh by the officers **to make atonement for ourselves before the LORD**. If the rendering of *RSV* is accepted, then it must be presumed that such atonement (*kipper*) was deemed necessary because the census which had been conducted by the officers (v. 49) was regarded as sinful (cf. Exod. 30:11f.); *NEB*'s rendering, 'as a ransom for our lives', understands the gifts as a payment given to Yahweh by way of thanks for the fact that not a single life, on Israel's side, had been lost in battle.

53. The point of this verse (which may be a gloss; cf. Paterson) is obscure. Some commentators take it to mean that the offering presented to Yahweh was made only by the officers, while the rank and file of soldiers kept the booty for themselves. But the expression *'anšê hassābā'* most naturally refers to all who had taken part in the battle (cf. vv. 28, 32, 42); consequently, it seems preferable to understand the verse as a note, in parenthesis, indicating that the offering received by Moses and Eleazar on behalf of Yahweh was from the booty taken by every man who had participated in the campaign (cf. Budd).

54. Moses and Eleazar received the gold offerings from the leaders and deposited them in the tent of meeting **as a memorial for the people of Israel before the LORD**: On the term *zikkārôn*, 'memorial', see von Rad, *OT Theology*, i, pp. 242f. The rendering of *RSV* suggests that the object of this action was to provide the people with a permanent reminder of the incident which had occurred. *NEB*, on the other hand, understands the presentation of the offerings as a means by which Yahweh might be reminded of his people ('that the LORD might remember Israel'). Perhaps the two alternatives are not mutually exclusive, for the offerings may have been designed to ensure both that Yahweh would constantly remember his people (cf. 10:10), and that the Israelites would continually direct their thoughts to him.

(h) THE SETTLEMENT OF REUBEN AND GAD
32:1-42

In this chapter, the tribes of Reuben and Gad approach Moses with a request that they be allowed to settle in the territory on the east of the Jordan, since they saw this area as providing fertile terrain which would be well suited for their numerous flocks (vv. 1-5). Moses is indignant when he first hears of their proposal, for he is convinced that their action would weaken the solidarity of the tribes, and may have the effect of discouraging others from entering the land, as their fathers had been discouraged when they heard the reports of the spies (vv. 6-15; cf. chs. 13f.). Reuben and Gad seek to allay Moses' fears by reassuring him that they would participate fully in the military conquest of Canaan, provided they could first ensure the safety of their families and flocks in Transjordan; they themselves would only return after the foe had been defeated and after the conquest of Canaan had been successfully accomplished (vv. 16-19). Moses accepts their proposition (vv. 20-27), and conveys the terms of the agreement to Eleazar, Joshua and the tribal leaders, charging them to see to it that the promise was kept (vv. 28-30). Reuben and Gad reaffirm the terms of the agreement (vv. 31f.) and proceed to rebuild some of the newly conquered cities in order to provide refuge for their wives, children and livestock (vv. 34-38). The chapter concludes with Moses officially granting lands to Reuben, Gad, and the (hitherto unmentioned) half-tribe of Manasseh in Transjordan (vv. 33, 39-42).

The aim of the narrative is to explain how it came about that certain Israelite tribes occupied land to the east of the Jordan, separate from the main body of the nation; at the same time, the account affirms that, in their desire to conquer the promised land, the Israelites were imbued with a sense of cohesion and common purpose.

Most commentators have recognized that the present chapter poses acute source-critical problems, for it contains numerous discrepancies and inconsistencies which suggest that various elements, belonging to different periods, have here been combined. That the chapter cannot be regarded as a literary unity is suggested by the

following considerations: (i) the list of cities in v. 3 recurs (in fuller
form) in vv. 34–38; (ii) in v. 19, it is implied that the allocation of
land east of the Jordan had already been made to the tribes of
Reuben and Gad, whereas in vv. 20–27 the negotiations are still in
progress; (iii) in vv. 28–30, Eleazar, Joshua and the leaders of the
tribes are instructed by Moses to give the land to the Gadites and
Reubenites only when they had fulfilled their promise to participate
in the conquest of Canaan, but in v. 33 it is Moses who assigns the
land to them, and he appears to do so unconditionally; (iv) the
half-tribe of Manasseh is mentioned most abruptly in v. 33, for
hitherto in the chapter only the tribes of Reuben and Gad are represented as wishing to remain in Transjordan. In addition to these
incongruities, an analysis of the style and vocabulary of the chapter
confirms its lack of homogeneity, for it appears to contain material
characteristic of J, D and P. Earlier commentators sought to distinguish between these various strands, and were content to view the
present form of the chapter as the result of the fusion of different
sources. Typical of this approach is the analysis of Baentsch
(pp. 659ff.), who assigns elements in vv. 1–4, 5–6, 20–23, 25–27,
33 to J; vv. 1b, 3, 16, 17, 24, 34–38 to E; vv. 1a, 2b, 4a, 18–19, 28–
30 to P, while vv. 7–15 were a later addition composed in the style
of the Deuteronomistic and Priestly writers. Later commentators,
however, expressed doubts as to whether such a division of the
chapter into sources was tenable, for the account as a whole
appeared to be so replete with revisions and additions that a detailed
literary-critical analysis seemed all but impossible. Even Gray, who
generally had no qualms about applying detailed source-critical
analysis to other chapters in Numbers, was forced to concede that,
in this case, 'a strict analysis of the chapter as between J/E and P
cannot be satisfactorily carried through' (p. 426). Gray preferred to
view the chapter (or at least vv. 1–38) as having been freely
composed by a late writer who worked on materials derived from
J/E and P, and who had at his disposal some narratives (such as
that of the spies in chs. 13f.) in their present, composite form. More
recent analysts, however, have been inclined to trace in the chapter
a basic 'core' element which has subsequently been expanded by
secondary additions. Mittmann, e.g., finds the oldest literary 'core'
of the chapter (which may be the work of either J or E) in vv. 1,
16–17a, 34, 35, 37–38 (*Deuteronomium 1:1–6:3*, pp. 95ff.). Even this
'core', however, represents an expanded tradition, for the original

account was probably concerned only with Reuben's settlement in the land of Jazer, and the reference to the 'land of Gilead' and the 'sons of Gad' in v. 1 may well be a later addition to the *Grundschicht*. This core was later developed by the inclusion of the note about Machir in v. 39, and the reference to Jair and Nobah in vv. 41f. Fundamental to the later traditio-historical growth of the chapter, according to Mittmann, was the speech of Reuben and Gad in vv. 16–17*a*, for this monologue was subsequently developed into a dialogue between the two tribes and Moses, now contained in vv. 2 (without the reference to Eleazar the priest and the leaders of the congregation), 4*b*, 6–11, 16*aα* ('then they came near to him'), 17*b*– 18, 20*aα*, 24, 33*aα* ('and Moses gave to them'), 33*b*, the reference to Jazer in v. 35, and v. 36. To this was added a second dialogue (vv. 5, 12–15, 20*a* β–23) which served to give precision and emphasis to the first; thus, what was merely a mild warning and reprimand by Moses in vv. 6–11 was later transformed into a sharp rebuke and an undisguised threat (vv. 12–15). A third stratum of dialogue is preserved in vv. 19, 25–29, in which Reuben and Gad's promise of assistance to conquer Canaan is solemnly reaffirmed, and a fourth dialogue was finally incorporated in vv. 30–32.

There can be little doubt that Mittmann is correct in regarding the basic tradition contained in the chapter as the product of one of the old Pentateuchal sources, and it seems entirely feasible that this source was the Yahwist, although the chapter may well contain a more substantial element of J than Mittmann was prepared to allow. But whether the chapter actually developed precisely along the lines he proposes, i.e., by the gradual accumulation of different 'dialogues', must remain hypothetical. The view taken here is that the list of cities built by Reuben and Gad in Transjordan contained in vv. 34–38 probably represents the nucleus out of which the present chapter evolved (for the early date of the list, cf. Wüst, *Untersuchungen*, pp. 152f., 182). This nucleus was developed by J into a full-blown account of a request by Reuben and Gad to be allowed to settle in the land to the east of the Jordan, and this narrative is contained in vv. 2 and 4 (in part), 16*a*, 17, 20–23, 25–27, 33*a* (without the reference to the half-tribe of Manasseh). To this was added, at a later stage, vv. 39, 41f., which contain an independent tradition concerning the settlement of the half-tribe of Manasseh in Transjordan. The account was subsequently enlarged by the addition of vv. 5–15, which is couched in the Deuteronomistic-Priestly style, and additions by the Priestly editor can be discerned in vv. 18f., 28–32, 33*b*. At a later stage, v. 3 was added, as a gloss, based on vv. 34–38, and v. 40 was inserted in order to provide Mosaic authority for the occupation of Transjordan by the clans of Manasseh.

The historicity of this account of the settlement of the tribes to the east of the Jordan has been much discussed by scholars but, as yet, no consensus has been reached. R. de Vaux (*History*, p. 584) takes the view that the request of Reuben and Gad to remain east of the Jordan is historically authentic, but that the idea that this was conditional upon their participation in the conquest of Canaan is probably the result of the Deuteronomistic historian's concept of a conquest of the promised land by all the Israelite tribes (cf. Jos. 1:12ff.; 22:1ff.). In support of this conclusion, de Vaux notes that, apart from these late passages, no part at all is played by the tribes of Reuben and Gad in the accounts in Jos. 1–11 and Jg. 1 of the settlement of Israel in the land to the west of the Jordan. A different view of the historicity of the present narrative, however, is represented by Herrmann (*History*, pp. 101ff.). He argues that neither Reuben nor Gad settled in Transjordan prior to the conquest of Canaan, and that their occupation of this area was only gradually achieved over a relatively long period, after Israel had already gained a firm foothold to the west of the Jordan. Thus, what is described in the present chapter as virtually a direct movement of the tribes from south to north was, in fact, a movement from west to east, and the conquest of Sihon and Og (v. 33) was only achieved when the Israelites had become so strong and numerous in Canaan that they were forced to move to Transjordan. A mediating position is taken by Noth (*History*, pp. 63ff.). He argues that the tribe of Gad probably made a permanent settlement in the land east of the Jordan prior to the conquest of Canaan, but that other tribes (including Reuben) only migrated later into this area from their original home to the west of the Jordan. That Reuben resided for some time to the west of the Jordan is confirmed, according to Noth, by the Song of Deborah, which mentions the tribe of Reuben in connection with an early Israelite victory in this region (Jg. 5:15*b*–16). Moreover, Reuben's erstwhile residence in this area is confirmed by the reference in Jos. 15:6; 18:17 to the 'stone of Bohan, the son of Reuben', which was located near Jericho, on the west side of the Jordan. Of course, these references to Reuben's settlement to the west of the

Jordan are capable of a different explanation, viz., that Reuben originally settled east of the Jordan (as the present chapter implies), but that this tribe (or some families thereof) later migrated west of the river. However, the fact that the Mesha Inscription makes no reference to the tribe of Reuben in Transjordan but refers only to the Gadites as having 'long dwelt in the land of Ataroth' (cf. v. 34; *DOTT*, p. 196) would seem to support Noth's conclusion. It is probable that at some stage in the later period of the judges, the clan of Machir migrated east of the Jordan into the region of Gilead, and this tradition is referred to in vv. 39f., and is reflected in the statement found in some *OT* genealogies that Machir was the 'father' of Gilead (cf. Jos. 17:3; 1 Chr. 2:21, 23).

Another problem concerning the historicity of the account contained in this chapter arises from the discrepancy between the description contained in vv. 34–38 and that encountered in Jos. 13:15ff. concerning the area of Transjordan allotted to the two Israelite tribes. Both accounts agree that Reuben and Gad were given territory in Transjordan within the area from approximately the southern end of the Sea of Galilee to the river Arnon, but while Num. 32 locates Gad further south than Reuben, Jos. 13:15ff. seems to reverse their positions. This ambiguity concerning their precise settlement area has led some scholars to conclude that these two tribes were never confined to a specific territory, but were permitted to range widely with their flocks (cf. Miller and Hayes, *History*, pp. 102f.). On the whole, however, it seems preferable to regard the tradition incorporated in 32:34–38 as reflecting the actual conditions of colonization in Transjordan, and to view Jos. 13:15ff. as a later construction by the Deuteronomistic historian, based on the ancient material contained in the present chapter and in 21:21ff. (cf. Noth, *ZDPV* 58 [1935], pp. 230–5; *ZAW*, N.F., 19 [1944], pp. 11ff.).

1. Now the sons of Reuben and the sons of Gad: This is the order in which the two tribes are usually listed in the genealogical traditions of the *OT* (cf. Dt. 3:12ff.; Jos. 22:1ff.), and it reflects their relative positions of seniority. Elsewhere in the present chapter, however, this order is reversed (cf. vv. 2, 6, 25, 29, 31, 33), and this probably reflects the fact that the story originally belonged to a time when the strength and significance of Reuben (cf. Gen. 49:3) had begun to decline, and the tribe of Gad had attained a position of pre-eminence (cf. Dt. 33:20f.). LXX (except in vv. 6, 33), Sam. (except in v. 2) and Syr. retain the order Reuben/Gad throughout

vv. 1–33, but it seems more probable that in the original narrative the more unusual sequence Gad/Reuben was deployed, and that this was altered by a scribe in v. 1 in deference to the customary genealogical order. How the tribes of Reuben and Gad had come to possess **a very great multitude of cattle** in the wilderness is not explained, but it is in keeping with references elsewhere which suggest that the Israelites were richly endowed with flocks and herds during their desert sojourn (cf. 14:33; Exod. 12:38; 17:3; 34:3). The desire of these two tribes to settle in Transjordan was prompted by their observation that **the land of Jazer and the land of Gilead** was **a place for cattle**, i.e., was a region which would provide ample grazing for their herds. As a matter of fact, the predominantly pastoral character of the tribes of Reuben and Gad was probably the *result* of their settlement in the fertile countryside to the east of the Jordan rather than the reason for their settlement in this region (cf. Gray). Rudolph (p. 133, n. 2) regards the reference to the 'land of Jazer' as an addition based on 21:32, while Mittmann (*op. cit.*, p. 95, n. 7) regards the reference to the 'land of Gilead' as secondary, based on vv. 26 and 29; however, there are no compelling reasons for regarding either as later accretions to the text. Jazer appears elsewhere in the *OT* as the name of a town (see on 21:24), but here it seems to designate its surrounding district, i.e., the northern half of the territory between the rivers Jabbok and Arnon to the east of the Jordan. The 'land of Gilead' must here presumably refer to the southern half of this area. The term 'Gilead' is not, however, used with any consistency in the present chapter, for in v. 29 it refers to the whole area between the two rivers, while in vv. 39–42 (which reflects a different tradition again) it seems to designate the area north of the Jabbok (cf. Jos. 17:1, 5f.). Elsewhere in the *OT*, the term 'Gilead' is used in a comprehensive sense to refer to the entire Transjordanian territory held by Israel (cf. Dt. 3:12f.; Jos. 12:2, 5; 13:31; 22:9, 13). See Simons, *Texts*, pp. 36–38.

3. The list of towns in this verse is probably a later addition, based on vv. 34–38, where they all reappear, although three of them are there found in a slightly different form. For their probable locations, see on vv. 34–38, below. **Beon** is possibly a scribal error for Meon, which appears in v. 38 as Baal-meon.

5–7. The request of Gad and Reuben to settle to the east of the Jordan is peremptorily turned down by Moses, who was only too aware of the adverse effect their action may have on the rest of the

Israelites: **Shall your brethren go to the war while you sit here?**
These words, reminiscent of the accusation made against Reuben
and Gilead (= Gad) in the Song of Deborah (Jg. 5:16f.), imply that
the proposal of Gad and Reuben involved a blatant disregard for
the unity of Israel and a contemptuous repudiation of Yahweh's
promise of a home for the entire people in the promised land.

8–15. These verses contain a summary of chs. 13f. in their present, composite form. Moses reminds the people that the adverse
reports of the spies concerning the land of Canaan had discouraged
their fathers from entering the promised land, and that this had
provoked Yahweh's anger and had resulted in the annihilation of
all the Israelites (except Caleb and Joshua) in the wilderness. If the
present generation were to be similarly discouraged by the action
of Gad and Reuben, then the people would inevitably be consigned
to a further prolonged period of wilderness wandering, and Gad
and Reuben would ultimately have been responsible for their
destruction.

14. Moses accuses the petitioners of being no better than their
fathers, and he addresses them, in contemptuous fashion, as **a brood
of sinful men**: The Heb. word for 'brood' (*tarbût*) occurs only here
in the *OT*, but the root from which it is derived, *rābāh* (= to be
many), is common enough (cf. *BDB*, pp. 915f.).

16–19. A compromise is here reached. Gad and Reuben, having
built **sheepfolds** (i.e., drystone walled enclosures) for their flocks,
and cities for their **little ones** to the east of the Jordan, would then
be only too ready to assist the other tribes to conquer the land of
Canaan, and would remain with them until the conquest was complete. Paterson (p. 64; cf. Noth, p. 238) suggests that the Heb.
ṭappēnû, rendered 'little ones' in *RSV*, would in this instance (cf.,
also, v. 24) have included wives as well as children (cf. *NIV*); if this
is so, then 'households' or 'dependents' (*NEB*) would be a more
appropriate translation. **but we will take up arms, ready to go
before the people of Israel**: The Heb. word *ḥušîm*, rendered by
RSV 'ready to go' means, lit., 'in haste', but the expression 'we will
arm ourselves hastening' is awkward, and *BHS* suggests emending
ḥušîm to *ḥᵃmušîm* (cf. *G–K* § 72*p*). *ḥᵃmušîm* was a technical military
term (cf. Exod. 13:18; Jos. 1:14; 4:12; Jg. 7:11) which perhaps originally meant 'in groups of fifty' (though cf. de Vaux, *AI*, pp. 216f.),
but which later came to have a more general sense, such as 'in battle
array' (*BDB*, p. 332*b*) or 'as a fighting force' (*NEB*). The words

'before the people of Israel', if understood literally, suggest that the tribes of Gad and Reuben were prepared to lead the invasion of the promised land and bear the brunt of any attack.

20-24. Moses, having been satisfied with the assurance given by Gad and Reuben, now formally repeats the terms of the agreement. If the two tribes fulfil their promise to participate fully in the forthcoming invasion of Canaan, then they would be permitted to dwell in Gilead and would be **free of obligation to the LORD and to Israel**, i.e., they would be exempt from any further military service (cf. Dt. 24:5). If, on the other hand, Gad and Reuben were tempted to renege on their agreement, then they would have sinned against Yahweh, and **your sin will find you out**. These words, which have become proverbial in common parlance, conceive of sin not in abstract terms, but as a quasi-personal force, capable of exacting its own retribution (cf. Gen. 4:7). The meaning, quite simply, is that there will be no escape for Gad and Reuben from the consequences of their action (cf. von Rad, *OT Theology*, i, p. 266).

25-27. Gad and Reuben agree to abide by the conditions outlined by Moses, and confirm the promise which they had already made in vv. 16-19.

28-30. Since Moses himself would not live to see the promise fulfilled (cf. 27:12-14), he charges Eleazar the priest, Joshua, and the leaders of the various tribes to ensure that Gad and Reuben keep to the terms of the agreement. If Gad and Reuben proved faithful to their promise, they could look forward to returning to Transjordan with a good conscience, and would be given the land of Gilead as their possession; but if they failed in their duty, they would be forced to live among the other Israelite tribes on the west of the Jordan. According to the tradition recorded in Jos. 4:12f.; 22:1ff. the two tribes were as good as their word, for they played a leading part in the invasion of Canaan and engaged in battle until the enemy was finally subdued and the land was distributed among the tribes.

33. Moses is here reported to have allocated to the Gadites and Reubenites and to the **half-tribe of Manasseh the son of Joseph** the agreed areas of Transjordan. The reference to the half-tribe of Manasseh here is unexpected, since there is no mention of this tribe earlier in the narrative (though Sam. includes a reference to it in vv. 1, 2, 6, 25, 29, 31, no doubt to harmonize the rest of the chapter with the present verse). Consequently, many commentators are of the view that this clause is a later interpolation designed to accommodate the chapter to the tradition, frequently encountered in the *OT*, that Moses distributed the territory east of the Jordan to the Manassites as well as to the Reubenites and Gadites (cf. Dt. 3:12f.; 4:43; 29:7f.; Jos. 12:6; 13:29, 31; 14:3; 18:7). The addition of this clause may well have been precipitated by the later insertion into the chapter of vv. 39–42, which conceive of the conquest of Gilead as the result of the independent action of various Manassite clans. Gray (p. 432) prefers to regard the whole of v. 33 as a later addition, since here Moses himself appears to allocate the land, and does so unconditionally, whereas earlier in the narrative, Joshua and Eleazar are charged with this responsibility, and the land is only to be allocated if certain specified conditions are fulfilled (cf. vv. 28–30). For attempts to defend the authenticity of v. 33, however, see Segal, *PEFQS* 50 (1918), pp. 126f.; Wenham, p. 215.

34–38. These verses list fourteen towns which were built (or, rather, 'rebuilt'; cf. *REB*) by the Gadites and the Reubenites. Of these, nine have already appeared, in roughly the same order and with a few alterations, in v. 3. These towns, most of which have been identified with some probability, are assigned between the Gadites (who have eight; cf. vv. 34–36) and the Reubenites (who have six; cf. vv. 37f.). According to this allocation, the Gadites appear to have occupied the southern, northern and north-western parts of the region, while the Reubenites seem to have occupied only an enclave within Gadite territory, round about the ancient city of Heshbon. The unevenness of the distribution of the towns between the two tribes suggests that the list may well reflect an authentic tradition of settlement in Transjordan, and Noth (p. 240) concedes that these verses probably reveal the actual circumstances of colonization in the area. A very different tradition concerning the colonization of the region is reflected in Jos. 13:15ff., where a dividing line running east from the northern point of the Dead Sea separates the two tribes, and the territory of Reuben is regarded as being situated in the south and that of Gad in the north. While there is nothing intrinsically improbable in the idea that certain fluctuations occurred in the territorial relations between Reuben and Gad, and that some of the towns mentioned in vv. 34–38 may have changed ownership in the course of time (e.g., Dibon changing from Gadite into Reubenite hands; cf. Jos. 13:17), there is much to be said for the view that the Joshua passage reflects a later, idealistic view of the portions of territory occupied by the two tribes. The towns 'built' (for *bānāh* in the sense of 'rebuild, repair', cf. Isa. 58:12; 61:4; Ezek. 36:36) by the Gadites included the following: **Dibon**: This is the modern Dhībān, 4 miles (6 km.) north of the Arnon, and 12 miles (19 km.) east of the Dead Sea. In the *OT* it is variously regarded as belonging to Gad (as here), to Reuben (Jos. 13:17) and to Moab (21:30; Isa. 15:2; Jer. 48:18, 22). Mesha, king of Moab, made Dibon his capital, and it was here that the Mesha Inscription (now housed in the Louvre) was discovered in 1868. For the excavations carried out here, which indicate a settlement during the Early Bronze Age, and subsequent periods, see Tushingham, *AASOR* 40 (1972), *passim*. **Ataroth**: This is the modern 'Aṭṭarûs, approx. 8 miles (13 km.) north of Dhībān, and 8 miles east of the Dead Sea. It is mentioned in the Mesha Inscription (l. 10), which records that 'the men of Gad had long dwelt in the land of Ataroth'. The inscription also notes that the 'king of Israel' had 'built' Ataroth for himself, but that Mesha had subsequently conquered it and massacred its inhabitants (*DOTT*, p. 196). **Aroer**, modern 'Ara'ir, was situated close to the Arnon, some 3 miles (5 km.) south of Dhībān. In Jos. 13:16 it belongs to Reuben, and is regarded as a southern boundary town in the territory east of the Jordan. Like Ataroth, this town is mentioned in the Mesha Inscription (l. 26), where it is stated that Mesha 'built' it in connection with a road which had been constructed near the Arnon. On the excavations carried out here, which show evidence of Late Bronze Age settlement, see Olávarri, *EAEHL*, i, 1975, pp. 98ff.; *RB* 76 (1969), pp. 230ff.; cf. *RB* 72 (1965), pp. 77ff. **Atroth-shophan**: The name occurs only here, and its site is unknown. **Jazer**: For its location, see on 21:24. **Jogbehah**: This is usually considered to be the modern Jubeihât, 5 miles (8 km.) north-west of Rabbath-Ammon, the modern 'Ammân, although some scholars prefer to locate it in nearby Khirbet Umm Oseij or Tell Ṣafût (cf. Oded, *PEQ* 103 [1971], p. 34). **Beth-nimrah**: In v. 3 it is called, simply, Nimrah. Its site is uncertain; it is identified by some with Tell Nimrin, approx. 6 miles (10 km.) east of the Jordan and 8 miles (13 km.) north of the Dead Sea (cf. Wüst, *op. cit.*, p. 148, n. 491), and by others with Tell Bleibil, some 10 miles (16 km.) north-west of Heshbon (cf. Noth, p. 240; Simons, *Texts*, p. 122; Aharoni, *Land*, p. 374). **Beth-haran** (spelt Beth-haram in Jos. 13:27) is sometimes identified with Tell er-Rāme, a few miles south of Tell Nimrin, though others prefer to locate it at Tell Iktanū. Cf. Simons, *Texts*,

p. 122, and the discussion by Wüst, *op. cit.*, pp. 148f., n. 492. The cities 'built' by the Reubenites included: **Heshbon**: This is the modern Ḥesbân, some 13 miles (21 km.) east of the northern extremity of the Dead Sea. This city seems to have changed hands frequently in *OT* times. It is here said to belong to Reuben (cf. Jos. 13:17); in Jos. 21:38f. it belongs to Gad; in Isa. 15:4; 16:9; Jer. 48:2 it is in the possession of Moab, and according to Jer. 49:3 it belonged to Ammon. **Elealeh**: This is usually identified with modern el-'Al, situated some 2 miles (3 km.) north-east of Heshbon; the town always appears in connection with Heshbon in the *OT* (cf. v. 3; Isa. 15:4; 16:9; Jer. 48:34). **Kiriathaim**: Its location is uncertain (cf. Gray, p. 436), but it is usually identified with the modern Khirbet el-Qureiyât, some 6 miles (10 km.) north-west of Dhibān (cf. Simons, *Texts*, p. 118), although a location at Qaryat el-Mekhaiyet is tentatively suggested by Aharoni (*Land*, p. 380). **Nebo**: Its location is unknown, though it is thought that it was situated near Mt. Nebo (Dt. 32:49), which is identified with the modern Mt. Nebâ, some 5 miles (8 km.) south-west of Ḥesbân. Nebo is mentioned in the Mesha Inscription, where it is stated that Mesha captured it from Israel and massacred its population of 7,000. **Baal-meon**: This is identified with the modern Ma'în, 10 miles (16 km.) south-south-west of Ḥesbân, and 10 miles east of the Dead Sea (cf. de Vaux, *Bible et Orient*, p. 123). In Jer. 48:23 it is called Beth-meon, and in Jos. 13:17 (and in the Mesha Inscription, l. 30) the fuller form Beth-baal-meon appears. **(their names to be changed)**: These words in parenthesis should probably be regarded as a marginal note intended to inform the reader that the two preceding place-names (Nebo and Baal-meon) should not be pronounced as written lest the names of two heathen deities, the Babylonian Nebo and the Canaanite Baal, should be inadvertently uttered (cf. Eissfeldt, *Fest. Thomas*, p. 70). This may explain why Baal-meon appears in v. 3 simply as Beon. **Sibmah**: This is the form in which the name appears in v. 3 in LXX and Sam., though MT there reads Sebam. Its location is unknown, though one possibility is that it should be identified with Khirbet Sumiyeh, 5 miles (8 km.) north-west of Ḥesbân.

39–42. These verses are generally regarded as part of an isolated fragment, for there is nothing in the preceding part of the chapter which would justify their presence here apart from the reference in v. 33 to the 'half-tribe of Manasseh, the son of Joseph', which, as has been indicated, is itself probably a later addition. Moreover,

the independent action here ascribed to the three Manassite clans,
Machir, Jair and Nobah, is clearly at variance with the emphasis
upon the concerted action of all Israel presupposed in the rest of
the chapter. The origin of this fragment is unknown. Burney (*Judges*,
pp. 47ff.) argued that the narrative contained in Jos. 17:14ff. once
served as its introduction, but this must be regarded as highly speculative. The most that can be said is that the individual traditions of
conquest presupposed in vv. 39–42 are redolent of the conquest
traditions contained in Jg. 1, and that these verses provide supplementary information to the material found in such passages as
Dt. 3:14f.; Jos. 13:8–13, 31. These verses record the successful raid
of three Manassite clans upon the territory of Gilead. That Machir
managed to conquer the land of Gilead and take up residence there
(v. 39) is a statement that finds confirmation in several passages in
the *OT*. The settlement of Jair and Nobah in the area (vv. 41f.) is
presented in the form of an aetiology: Jair captured a number of
villages and called them Havvoth-jair ('the villages of Jair'), and
Nobah succeeded in capturing Kenath, and called it after his own
name.

40. This verse may be editorial, since it seems intrusive and
redundant in the present context; it was probably a belated attempt
to accommodate the fragment contained in vv. 39, 41f. to its present
context. That Machir's settlement of Gilead was sanctioned by
Moses is a view echoed in Dt. 3:15.

41. Jair is mentioned in Jg. 10:3 as 'Jair the Gileadite', and he
is there represented as one of the 'minor judges' of Israel. **their
villages**: Since 'their' has no immediate antecedent, Bergman
(*JPOS* 16 [1936], p. 235; cf. de Vaux, *History*, pp. 588, 786; Simons,
Texts, p. 124) suggests emending *ḥawwōṭêhem* to read *ḥawwōṭ hām*,
i.e., 'the villages of Ham' (cf. *NEB*). As Snaith (p. 334) points out,
a place of this name is mentioned in Gen. 14:5, and was located 25
miles (40 km.) east of the Jordan and north-west of Ramoth Gilead.
However, it seems preferable to retain the reading of *RSV* and to
regard 'their villages' as a reference to the villages of the Amorites
mentioned in v. 39, an interpretation which seems entirely plausible
if v. 40 is regarded as a secondary addition. The Heb. word *ḥawwōṭ*,
here rendered 'villages', occurs only in connection with the name
Jair in the *OT* (cf. Dt. 3:14; Jos. 13:30; Jg. 10:4; 1 Kg. 4:13; 1 Chr.
2:23), and its meaning is by no means certain. It may be connected
with the Arab. *ḥiwāʾ* = 'a cluster of tents' (cf. *BDB*, p. 295*b*), in

which case 'encampments' (*JB*), 'settlements' (*NIV*) or 'tent-villages' may well reflect the correct meaning of the Hebrew. See, further, Frick, *City*, p. 59. The number of such villages may well have varied considerably at different periods, for sixty of them are mentioned in Jos. 13:30; 1 Kg. 4:13, but only thirty in Jg. 10:3f., and twenty-three in 1 Chr. 2:22.

42. Kenath is identified by some commentators (e.g., Binns, following Eusebius and Jerome) with Kanatha, modern Ḳanawāt, situated on the north-western slopes of the Hauran mountains (cf., also, Aharoni, *Land*, pp. 148, 192). If this is correct, the **Nobah** referred to cannot be the same as that mentioned in Jg. 8:11, for it is there presupposed that Nobah lay near Jogbehah (cf. v. 35), but Ḳanawāt was situated too far east (approx. 68 miles or 110 km.) for any close association with Jogbehah to have been possible. Many commentators, however, *are* inclined to identify the Nobah of the present verse with the town of the same name in Jg. 8:11 (cf., e.g., Noth, Sturdy), and since this was near Jogbehah, Nobah is located somewhere in the region to the west or north-west of modern 'Ammān.

(i) THE WILDERNESS ITINERARY
33:1–49

Vv. 1–49 purport to trace the journey of the Israelites from Rameses in Egypt to the border of the promised land. Although no fewer than forty stopping-places are mentioned in the itinerary (making it the largest and most complete example of the genre found in the *OT*), the fact remains that only a very general impression can be gained from the text concerning the direction of the march, since few of the places named can be located with any certainty. The list is sometimes interrupted by brief references to specific events that occurred in the place in question (vv. 3f., 8, 9, 38f., 40), but it is doubtful whether these references can be of any real value in identifying the places concerned, for it is almost certain that they were appended to the itinerary at a later stage (cf. Noth, p. 243). The original form of vv. 1–49 thus probably consisted merely of a list of place names, introduced by a formula repeated in stereotyped fashion ('and they set out from A and encamped in B; and they set out from B and encamped in C' etc.). Itineraries formulated in this way are known to have existed elsewhere in the ancient world, and a particularly close parallel to the form of the present list has been found in Assyrian annals of the ninth century BC (cf. Davies, *TynB*

25 [1974], pp. 57ff., 78f.; Maarsingh, Sturdy). The existence of such parallels, together with the fact that Moses himself is stated to have compiled the list (v. 2), has been taken by some commentators as evidence of the general antiquity and reliability of the present section (cf. Wenham, pp. 219f.); however, the fact that some well-known places on the journey (e.g., Massah, Meribah, Taberah) are omitted from the itinerary, and that the route described seems to differ in some important respects from that presupposed in Num. 20f. (cf. Kallai, *JJS* 33 [1982], pp. 175ff.) tends to cast some doubt on its reliability. Moreover, a few of the places mentioned (e.g., Pi-hahiroth, Mount Hor, Oboth) are known only to the Priestly source, and this makes it somewhat doubtful that the list can, in its present form, be regarded as very ancient. The general lateness of the section appears to be further confirmed by the fact that the compiler, in vv. 5–15, appears to have drawn upon a section of the Pentateuchal narrative (Exod. 12:37–19:2) in which the collation of sources is already presupposed (cf. Noth, pp. 242–44).

One striking feature of the itinerary is that sixteen of the places listed are not mentioned anywhere else in the *OT*. The fact that these places are grouped together (vv. 18b–30a, 41b–47a) has been taken as an indication that they originally derived from an independent and self-contained document (cf. Lagrange, *RB* 9 [1900], p. 65). The origin of such a document is unclear, but Noth has suggested that it may represent an itinerary of a well-known 'pilgrim route' to and from Sinai (*Pentateuchal Traditions*, p. 221, and, in more detail, in *PJB* 36 [1940], pp. 5ff.). This theory, however, must be regarded as improbable (cf. de Vaulx, pp. 376f.; Zuber, *Vier Studien*, pp. 62ff.), for, if there ever was a regular pilgrimage to and from Sinai, the comparative oblivion into which this place sank during the period of the monarchy, and the uncertainty that continues to surround its location, would be difficult to explain (cf. de Vaux, *History*, ii, pp. 560f.). It seems more probable that the material contained here was derived from official court archives, and that it was intended to record a route either for travellers in general or for trade and commerce in particular (cf. Budd, p. 356).

The journey described in vv. 5–49 may be divided into four sections: (i) from Egypt to the wilderness of Sinai (vv. 5–15); (ii) from the wilderness of Sinai to Ezion-geber (vv. 16–35); (iii) from Ezion-geber to the wilderness of Zin (= Kadesh; v. 36); (iv) from Kadesh to Moab (vv. 37–49). For a detailed analysis of the itinerary, and attempts to locate some of the places mentioned, see Davies, *Way*, pp. 79ff.; Noth, *PJB* 36 (1940), pp. 5ff.

Commentators generally view the itinerary as having originated in Priestly circles. Elements characteristic of the Priestly style include the constant repetition of a simple formula ('and they set out from ... and encamped at ...'), the superscription and expression 'by their hosts' in v. 1, and the dates of the exodus and Aaron's death in vv. 3, 38. Moreover, all the stopping-places mentioned elsewhere in P (apart from the wilderness of Paran) are incorporated in the present itinerary. The fact that the section is regarded as a very late composition has inclined commentators to attribute it to one of the final stages of the redaction of P^s (cf. Holzinger, p. 160).

(i) *The departure from Egypt:* **33:1–4**

1–2. The itinerary begins with a heading (vv. 1–2), the style of which is regarded by Gray (p. 444) as 'awkward and redundant'. However, there is certainly no need to follow Noth (p. 243) in regarding v. 2*a* (in which the itinerary is said to have been compiled by Moses) as a later addition, for the compiler may well have wished to give the composition an air of verisimilitude by suggesting that it was derived from an ancient source written by Moses himself.

3–4. They set out from Rameses: Rameses (or Raamses) is the Hebrew transcription of the Egyptian *(pr)-r'-ms-sw* (= 'house of Rameses'), and this was one of the two cities which the Hebrew slaves are said to have built for Pharaoh in the eastern Nile delta (Exod. 1:11; cf. Redford, *VT* 13 [1963], pp. 408ff.). Its location is disputed, but it is usually identified either with Avaris-Tanis (the biblical Zoan), or with Qantir, some 15 miles (24 km.) to the south. The date of the Israelites' departure is given as **the fifteenth day of the first month**, which was the day after they had celebrated the Passover (cf. Exod. 12:2, 6). They set out **triumphantly** (lit., 'with a high hand'; *NEB*, 'defiantly'; *NIV, NRSV*, 'boldly'; cf. 15:30) in full view of the Egyptians, while the latter were still burying their dead (cf. Exod. 12:29f.).

(ii) *From Egypt to the wilderness of Sinai:* **33:5–15**

All the places referred to in this section (apart from Dophkah and Alush; vv. 12–14) are mentioned also in Exod. 12:37–19:2, and there is every reason to believe that the compiler of the present itinerary has made use of the Exodus text in what must, effectively, have been its final form (see above).

5. The first place of encampment was **Succoth** (cf. Exod. 12:37). It is not clear whether this is a true Semitic name, meaning 'booths', or a Hebraized form of the Egyptian *Tkw(t)*. Its location is uncertain. Some identify it with Pithom (= Tell el-Maskhuta) in the eastern area of the Wadi Tumilat, while others locate it at the neighbouring site of Tell el-Retabe.

6. After leaving Succoth, the Israelites encamped at **Etham** (cf. Exod. 13:20), which was located **on the edge of the wilderness**. The name Etham, in Egyptian, means 'wall' or 'fortification', and it is probable that Etham was the site of a fortress which lay somewhere on the eastern frontier of Egypt; such fortresses, however, were so common that the location of this particular one is uncertain.

7. Since the Israelites were presumably unable to pass this Egyptian fortress, they were compelled to turn back to **Pi-hahiroth** (cf. Exod. 14:2). The precise location of Pi-hahiroth is unknown, but it is here said to have been situated to the east of **Baal-zephon**. The location of Baal-zephon is also uncertain, but one possibility is that it is to be identified with the Graeco-Roman Casium (modern Ras Qasrun) which was situated on the western end of the strip of land separating the Mediterranean Sea from Lake Sirbonis (modern Lake Bardawil). The Israelites then encamped before **Migdol**, which is usually identified with Tell el-Her, although this was some 30 miles (48 km.) from Ras Qasrun. For a discussion of the problems relating to the identification of Baal-zephon and Migdol, see Davies, *Way*, pp. 80–82.

8. The Israelites then travelled **from before Hahiroth** (almost certainly an error for 'from Pi-hahiroth', as was recognized by the ancient Vsns), and **passed through the midst of the sea**. If this is a reference to the miraculous deliverance of the Israelites recorded in Exod. 14f., then the sea in question must be the Red Sea or the Sea of Reeds. The difficulty with this, however, is that, according to the present itinerary, the Israelites did not reach the Red Sea until after they had set out from Elim (v. 10). Noth (pp. 243f.) therefore conjectures that the reference here to the passage of the Israelites through the sea, and the subsequent allusion to their three days' journey in the wilderness of Etham, are later additions; this seems not implausible in view of the fact that the Israelites are already depicted as having encamped at Etham in v. 6.

Alternatively, the present itinerary may reflect two separate traditions concerning the place of deliverance, one (v. 10; cf. Exod. 15:4) placing it at the Red Sea, and the other situating it further north (cf. Davies, *Way*, pp. 72–74). The people then moved on to **Marah**. Its location is uncertain, but it has traditionally been identified with the modern 'Ain Hawara, some 50 miles (80 km.) south of the northern end of the Gulf of Suez. Marah means 'bitter', and Exod. 15:22ff. contains an aetiological legend designed to explain the origin of the name.

9. After leaving Marah the Israelites came to **Elim** (cf. Exod. 15:27). The name means 'terebinth-trees', and since these were commonly regarded as sacrosanct (cf. Gen. 12:6), it is sometimes suggested that Elim was an oasis with sacral associations. Its location is uncertain, but it is usually identified with the oasis of Wadi Gharandel, some 60 miles (96 km.) south-east of the town of Suez. At Elim there were **twelve springs of water and seventy palm trees**: These phenomena (mentioned also in Exod. 15:27) were invested with a symbolic significance by Jewish exegetes, the twelve springs representing the twelve tribes of Israel, and the seventy palm trees signifying the seventy elders (cf. 11:16).

10. The Israelites then encamped at the **Red Sea**: Here, the reference is probably to the Gulf of Suez (see on 14:25). This place of encampment is not mentioned in the Exodus narrative, where Elim is followed directly by the wilderness of Sin (Exod. 16:1). That the Red Sea should be placed after Elim is somewhat surprising, and Noth suggests that the present text is based on a misunderstanding of Exod. 15:27, which states that the Israelites, after reaching Elim, encamped 'by the water'.

12–13. Neither of the two places referred to in these verses, **Dophkah** (LXX Raphaka) and **Alush**, is mentioned elsewhere, and their location is unknown. Attempts to identify Dophkah with Serābît el-Khâdim, and Alush with Wadi el-'Eshsh (cf. Snaith, p. 336; Simons, *Texts*, pp. 252f.) must be regarded as very tentative (cf. Davies, *Way*, p. 84).

14. The next place of encampment was **Rephidim**, the location of which is uncertain, but which is usually identified with Wadi Refayid in the southern part of the Sinai peninsula.

15. From Rephidim, the Israelites journeyed to the **wilderness of Sinai**: The location of the wilderness clearly depends on the site

of Mount Sinai itself, but if the traditional location of the mountain
is accepted, the reference here must be to the general vicinity of
Jebel Musa.

(iii) *From the wilderness of Sinai to Ezion-geber:* **33:16—35**
None of the twelve places listed in vv. 18*b*—29 are mentioned elsewhere in the *OT*, and thus any attempt to identify their geographical
location must be regarded as highly speculative.

16—17. For **Kibroth-hattaavah** and **Hazeroth**, see on 11:34f.
According to 12:16, the Israelites moved from Hazeroth to the
'wilderness of Paran', but the latter is not mentioned in the
present itinerary.

30—34. The four stopping-places mentioned in these verses
appear also in Dt. 10:6f., and it is suggested by some commentators
(Snaith, Sturdy) that the Priestly tradition is here directly dependent
on the Deuteronomic passage. However, the fact that differences
exist in the form and sequence of the places mentioned makes it
probable that there is no direct relationship between the two passages, but that both were drawing on a common source.

31. The location of **Moseroth** is unknown. Dt. 10:6 states that
this place (or Moserah) was where Aaron died and was buried, but
the Priestly tradition locates Aaron's death at Mount Hor (v. 38;
cf. 20:22—9).

(iv) *From Ezion-geber to Kadesh:* **33:36**
Ezion-geber was a port situated at the head of the Gulf of Akaba
(cf. 1 Kg. 9:26; 22:48). It is identified by some (e.g., Snaith) with
the modern Tell el-Kheleifeh, near the modern port of Elath, and
by others (e.g., Soggin, *IJH*, p. 343) with Jezirat Faraun, which was
in the same vicinity, but farther to the south-west. See, further,
Davies, *Way*, pp. 85f. From Ezion-geber, the people journeyed to
the **wilderness of Zin (that is, Kadesh)**. Before the reference to
Kadesh, LXX adds 'and they set out from the wilderness of Zin, and
encamped in the wilderness of Paran'; this presumably represents
a secondary harmonization of the passage with statements found
earlier in the book of Numbers (cf. 10:12; 12:16; 13:26). A problem
arises at this juncture in the itinerary, for it is implied that the
distance between Ezion-geber and Kadesh was covered in a single
march, without any stop in between; however, if Ezion-geber was
situated at the head of the Gulf of Akaba, and Kadesh at 'Ain Qadeis

or nearby 'Ain Qudeirat (see on 13:26), then these two encampments would have been some 90 miles (144 km.) apart. One possible solution to the difficulty is that the compiler simply lacked detailed information about this part of the route (cf. Budd, pp. 353, 356); alternatively, this section of the journey may have been regarded as so familiar that it needed to be described only in cursory fashion. For the latter possibility, and other proposed solutions, see Davies, *Way*, pp. 6of.

(v) *From Kadesh to Moab*: 33:37–49

38–39. The usual brief record of the stages of Israel's journey through the wilderness is interrupted at this point by a note concerning the death of Aaron. It is generally agreed that these two verses are a gloss based on 20:22–29, but with the added details (found only here in the *OT*) of the date of Aaron's death (the first day of the fifth month of the fortieth year of the exodus) and his age (**a hundred and twenty-three years old**). The event is reported to have occurred at **Mount Hor**; for its location, see on 20:22.

40. This fragmentary statement, which appears strange in the present context, is probably a gloss based on 21:1, which stands immediately after the Priestly account of Aaron's death.

41. After Mount Hor, the next place of encampment was **Zalmonah**, the location of which is unknown; the suggestion that it is to be identified with Calamona, a Roman station mentioned in the *Notitia Dignitatum* (cf. de Vaux, *History*, ii, p. 562) is most improbable (cf. Davies, *Way*, p. 90).

42–49. For the most plausible locations of the places mentioned in this part of the itinerary, see Noth, *PJB* 36 (1940), pp. 9ff. **Punon** (or, with Sam., Syr., Phinon), may be the same as the Pinon of Gen. 36:41; it is probably the modern Khirbet Feinan, situated approx. 30 miles (48 km.) south of the southern end of the Dead Sea. **Oboth** is often identified with the modern 'Ain el-Weibeh (cf. Simons, *Texts*, pp. 259f.), some 15 miles (24 km.) from the southern end of the Dead Sea, though Davies, *Way*, p. 90, suggests that a more likely location would be to the north of Khirbet Feinan, on the way to Khirbet Ay (= Iye-abarim, the next station in the itinerary). For the view that the Heb. *'iyyê hā'ăbārîm* does not refer to a specific site but should rather be rendered, 'the ruins on the other side', see Miller, *JBL* 108 (1989), pp. 581, 589. **Dibon-gad** is to be identified with Dhībān (see on 32:34); the name 'Gad' is derived from the

Israelite tribe that occupied it (cf. 32:34–38). **Almon-diblathaim** is usually identified with the Beth-diblathaim mentioned in Jer. 48:22, and referred to in the Mesha Inscription (l. 30; cf. *DOTT*, p. 197). Noth suggests a location near Khirbet et-Tēm (*PJB* 36 [1940], pp. 12f.). The **mountains of Abarim** were in the vicinity of Mount Nebo, overlooking the Dead Sea on the east. **Beth-jeshamoth** is usually identified with the modern Tell el-'Azeimeh, near the northern shore of the Dead Sea. The Israelite encampment stretched from here to **Abel-shittim** (the fuller form of the simpler Shittim of 25:1). This is perhaps the modern Tell el-ḥammām, which is situated at the point where the Wadi Kefrein enters the Jordan valley (cf. Noth, p. 196; Glueck, *BASOR* 91 [1943], pp. 17ff.); others, however, have favoured a site a short distance to the east of Tell el-ḥammām, at Tell Kefrein (cf. Snaith).

(j) COMMANDS REGARDING THE SETTLEMENT
33:50–56

The Israelites are here commanded to expel the inhabitants of Canaan, to destroy their idols, and demolish their sanctuaries (vv. 51f.). The land would then be ready to be occupied (v. 53) and divided between the tribes by lot (v. 54). The section concludes with a dire warning: if the people refused to obey Yahweh's command, they would be tormented continually by the inhabitants of the land, and Israel would suffer the same punishment which Yahweh had intended to inflict upon the Canaanites (vv. 55f.).

The style of the passage is somewhat perplexing, for it seems to combine elements characteristic of the Priestly writer, the Holiness Code and the Deuteronomist. Vv. 50–51*a* are couched in the style of the Priestly writer, and the command in v. 54 to divide the land by lot is also expressed in language characteristic of P (cf. 26:52–56). The reference to the destruction of the 'figured stones' (Heb. *maśkît*) and the 'high places' (Heb. *bāmôṯ*; v. 52), on the other hand, is redolent of certain passages in H (cf. Lev. 26:1, 30), as is the conditional curse which would come into effect if Israel failed to annihilate the inhabitants of the land (Lev. 26:14ff.; cf. Haran, *Temples*, p. 20, n. 11). Finally, the general concern of the passage, namely, the need to rid the land of the Canaanites and their religion, is typical of the Deuteronomist as, indeed, is the reason given for such drastic action, viz., that their presence would pose a perennial threat to Israel's life and well-being (cf. Dt. 7:1ff.; 12:2f., 29ff.; Noth, p. 248).

Closer analysis of the text, however, reveals that the link with the Holiness Code is more apparent than real. The characteristic expressions of H (e.g., 'I am the LORD your God') are here lacking, and some of the words thought to emanate from this source (e.g., *bāmôṯ*) are common in the Deuteronomistic literature (e.g., 2 Kg. 23:8; Jer. 7:31). On the whole, therefore, it seems preferable to view the passage as a blend of Deuteronomistic and Priestly features (cf. Auld, *Joshua*, pp. 74f.).

52. The Israelites, after entering the promised land, are required to drive out its inhabitants and to destroy all their **figured stones**: The precise meaning of the word rendered here 'figured stones' (*maśkîṯ*) is difficult to establish. The ancient Vsns can hardly be said to support the rendering of *RSV*, for LXX has *skopos* (something on which one looks), Vulg. has *tituli* ('tablets'), while Targ. and Syr. suggest it means 'cult, worship'. The use of the word in Lev. 26:1, however, lends some support to the translation of *RSV*, for it there occurs in conjunction with *'eḇen*, 'stone', and the fact that it appears in the present verse in connection with 'molten images' (on which, see Barr, *BJRL* 51 [1968-9], pp. 20ff.) makes it not at all improbable that the stones in question would have been carved with a picture of a Canaanite deity. **and demolish all their high places**: The 'high places' (*bāmôṯ*; *NEB*, 'hill shrines') were a characteristic feature of Canaanite worship, and they were to prove a constant source of temptation to the Israelites (cf. Dt. 12:2f.). For a full discussion of the term, see Vaughan, *Bama, passim*.

54. The land was to be divided between the families by lot, and in the process of distribution due account was to be taken of the relative size of the various tribes. The verse is based on 26:52-56, and may well have been inserted at this point to prepare for the account of the distribution of the land in the next chapter.

55. If the Israelites were to fail to expel the Canaanites from the land, the latter would remain **as pricks in your eyes and thorns in your sides**: Similar imagery is encountered in Jos. 23:13. The notion that the Canaanites who were allowed to remain in the land would be a constant 'snare' to Israel is frequently encountered in the *OT* (cf. Exod. 23:33; Dt. 7:16).

(k) THE DIVISION OF THE LAND
34:1–29

Having been given the command to enter the promised land (33:53), Moses is now given instructions concerning its boundaries. The borders of the country, to the south, west, north and east are described at some length in vv. 1–12. Vv. 13–15 have every appearance of being a redactional addition inserted to take account of the Transjordanian traditions reflected in ch. 32. The remainder of the chapter (vv. 16–29) is concerned with the appointment of ten officers to supervise the distribution of the tribal territories.

The eastern and western boundaries of the country pose little difficulty, for they consist, respectively, of the river Jordan and the Mediterranean (the 'Great Sea'; vv. 6, 7); however, the northern and southern limits are much less clear, for there is considerable uncertainty regarding the identification of many of the places mentioned. It is generally agreed that the description of the borders contained in this chapter does not correspond to the boundaries of the promised land during any period of Israel's occupation. Nevertheless, it has been argued by some scholars that the outline here presented is by no means the product of the writer's imagination, for the borders of Canaan here described were essentially those which existed during the period of Egyptian control at the end of the thirteenth century BC (cf. Aharoni, *Land*, pp. 68f.; de Vaux, *JAOS* 88 [1968], pp. 28f.; Weippert, *IDBSup*, p. 126a). It is therefore supposed that the Priestly writer was here drawing upon an ancient source which reflected the pre-conquest traditions concerning the extent of the land of Canaan. But the difficulty with this view is that it is by no means clear how or why such an ancient document should have been preserved until the time of the Priestly writer; consequently, it seems preferable to suppose that the description given here of the boundaries on the west of the Jordan is idealistic, reflecting the dimensions of the land which it was considered fitting that Israel should possess. Similar expansionistic ideals are reflected in expressions such as 'from the entrance of Hamath to the Brook of Egypt' (cf. 1 Kg. 8:65; 2 Chr. 7:8) and 'from the river of Egypt [i.e., the Nile] to the great river, the river Euphrates' (cf. Gen. 15:18). A far more realistic appraisal of Israel's boundaries is found in the phrase 'from Dan to Beersheba', which occurs frequently in the *OT* (cf. 2 Sam. 3:10; 17:11; 1 Kg. 4:25 etc.).

Noth (pp. 248f.) argues that the delimitation of the borders of the promised land in the present chapter is presented in a style similar to that encountered in Jos. 15ff., and he observes that the description of the southern border in vv. 3–5 is identical with the southern border of Judah as defined in Jos. 15:1–4, except that one border point, Karka, mentioned in Jos. 15:3, is omitted in Num. 34:3–5, and that two separate border points in Jos. 15:3 (Hezron and Addar) are combined as one (Hazar-addar) in Num. 34:4. On this basis, Noth claims that there can be no doubt that the details found in vv. 3–5 are derived from Jos. 15. However, as Auld (*Joshua*, p. 76) has observed, there is an unmistakable difference in presentation between the two texts which makes it probable that neither was dependent upon the other, but that both drew upon a common list of names. No mention is made in Joshua of the northern boundary, but a comparable description to that found in vv. 7–9 of the present chapter appears in Ezek. 47:15–17; 48:1 as the northern border of the tribe of Dan. According to some commentators, the similarities are such as to suggest a dependence on Ezekiel (cf. Sturdy, p. 235), but here, too, there are some variations between the two passages and it is, perhaps, preferable to think in terms of a mutual dependence on a common source.

Analysts have no difficulty in assigning the chapter to the Priestly source (cf. Baentsch, Holzinger), and it probably derives from a comparatively late strand of Priestly editing.

3–5. The southern boundary of the promised land is described in summary fashion in v. 3*a*, and in more detail in vv. 3*b*–5. Kallai (*VT* 37 [1987], pp. 438ff.) suggests that this 'dual description' constitutes a fixed literary pattern in *OT* historiographical texts. The southern border ran from the south end of the **Salt Sea** (i.e., the Dead Sea) up the ascent of **Akrabbim** (lit., 'scorpions'; probably the modern Naqb eṣ-Ṣafā), and continued in a southwesterly direction until it reached a point **south of Kadesh-barnea** (modern ʿAin Qadeis or ʿAin Qudeirat). This represented the most southerly point of the boundary. From Kadesh-barnea it proceeded in a northwesterly direction by way of **Hazar-addar** and **Azmon** (neither of which can be located) to the **Brook of Egypt** (modern Wadi el-ʿArîsh), and ended at the sea (i.e., the Mediterranean). See, further, Simons, *Texts*, pp. 135–7.

6. The western boundary was formed by the **Great Sea**, i.e., the Mediterranean, usually referred to simply as 'the sea' (cf. 13:29).

The description of this boundary confirms its idealistic nature, for, in fact, Israel did not occupy any area on the coastal plains of the Mediterranean until the Maccabees captured Joppa in the latter half of the second century BC (1 Mac. 14:5).

7−9. The northern boundary began at an unidentified point on the Mediterranean coast and ran east as far as **Mount Hor**. The location of Mount Hor is unknown, but it is certainly not to be confused with the mountain of the same name on the border of Edom, where Aaron died (cf. 20:22). From Mount Hor, the boundary extended northwards to **the entrance of Hamath** (see on 13:21), and from there it ran through **Zedad** and **Ziphron** and as far as **Hazar-enan** (which appears in Ezek. 47:17 as Hazar-enon). The location of the northern boundary has proved to be the most problematic of all the borders, and it has engendered much scholarly discussion. Some exegetes advocate a line extending from the mouth of the Nahr el-Qāsimiyeh, just north of Tyre, to the sources of the Jordan and Mount Hermon, while others favour a line much further north which would include within its boundary a large part of the Lebanon and would terminate in the area of Palmyra. The view taken will depend largely on whether the **entrance of Hamath** (or, with *NEB*, Lebo-hamath) is located in the plateau between Lebanon and Antilebanon (cf. Noth, p. 250), or whether it is identified with Lebweh on the Upper Orontes, north of Ba'albek (cf. Aharoni, *Land*, pp. 65ff.). For a full discussion, see, further, Simons, *Texts*, pp. 98ff.; Mackay, *JTS* 35 (1934), pp. 22ff.

10−12. The upper part of the eastern boundary began at **Hazar-enan** and extended to the eastern slopes of the **sea of Chinnereth** (known in *NT* times as the sea of Galilee or lake Gennesaret; cf. Lk. 5:1); its precise delimitation, however, must remain uncertain, for the locations of the intermediate boundary-points, viz., **Shepham**, **Riblah** and **Ain** are unknown. The lower part of the eastern boundary stretched from the sea of Chinnereth down to the Jordan and then ran directly south, terminating at the Dead Sea. See Simons, *Texts*, pp. 102f.

13−15. Since Reuben, Gad and the half-tribe of Manasseh had already received their inheritance portion on the east of the Jordan (ch. 32), the land was to be divided between the nine and a half tribes which were to settle to the west of the river.

16−29. Moses is commanded to appoint ten leaders (*nāśî'*), one from each of the nine and a half tribes, to help Eleazar and Joshua to supervise the allotment of land between the tribes. Apart from **Caleb the son of Jephunneh** (v. 19), the names of the leaders are different from those found in previous lists of tribal representatives in Numbers (cf. 1:5ff.; 13:4ff.); this is, of course, entirely in keeping with the fact that none of the previous generation, except Caleb and Joshua (cf. 26:65), had been permitted to survive the wilderness wanderings (cf. 14:26ff.). Some of the names (e.g., Elidad, Ahihud; vv. 21, 27) give the impression of being archaic, but many are attested in late texts (cf. Budd, pp. 365f., 368f.), and the list as a whole may well be the construction of the Priestly writer. The tribes are listed in the order of their eventual geographical settlement in Canaan (cf. Jos. 18f.), the four southern tribes (Judah, Simeon, Benjamin, Dan) being named first (vv. 19–22), followed by the two central tribes (Manasseh, Ephraim; vv. 23f.), and, finally, the four northern tribes (Zebulun, Issachar, Asher, Naphtali; vv. 25–28). See, further, Weippert, *VT* 23 (1973), pp. 76ff. Significantly, Dan is placed beside Benjamin as one of the southern tribes, in deference to the tradition that Dan originally settled in the south and only later migrated to the north (Jos. 19:40ff.; Jg. 18:1ff.).

(1) LEVITICAL CITIES AND CITIES OF REFUGE
35:1–34

This chapter contains two distinct ordinances: (i) the provision of forty-eight cities, with a portion of land attached to each, for the support of the Levites (vv. 1–8); (ii) the provision of six cities of refuge for those found guilty of accidental murder (vv. 9–15). In connection with the latter, some general guidelines are given to help distinguish between murder and manslaughter (vv. 16–23), and the legal procedure to be followed in cases of homicide is prescribed (vv. 24–32). The chapter concludes with an explanation of the religious motive which lies behind the law (vv. 33f.).

Commentators have no difficulty in attributing the chapter to the Priestly source. There is some evidence to indicate that vv. 9–32 may derive substantially from P^g (cf. Baentsch), but certain peculiarities of vocabulary, style and content suggest that vv. 1–8 should be attributed to the later stratum, P^s (cf. Gray, p. 464).

(i) *The Levitical cities:* **35:1–8**
Arrangements having been made for the division of the land of Canaan among the secular tribes (34:1ff.), the special needs of the

Levites now receive attention. In all, forty-eight cities, with their surrounding land, were to be set aside for them, of which six were to be cities of refuge (v. 6). Jos. 21, which contains a brief account of the fulfilment of this command, states that the priests received thirteen cities from Judah, Simeon and Benjamin, while the Kohathites received ten cities from Ephraim, Dan and west Manasseh, the Gershonites thirteen cities from Issachar, Asher, Naphtali and east Manasseh, and the Merarites twelve cities from Reuben, Gad and Zebulun. The account in Jos. 21 is clearly highly schematic, with four cities listed for each tribe, the only exceptions being Judah/Simeon (who have nine cities between them) and Naphtali (who has three), but even these offset each other, allowing for the grand total of forty-eight (= 4 x 12) cities in all.

The schematic nature of the list in Jos. 21 led earlier scholars, such as Wellhausen (*Prolegomena*, pp. 159ff.), to question its authenticity and to conclude that the entire notion of a provision of special cities for the Levites was nothing more than a fiction which never had any real historical basis. Several factors were thought to confirm this view. In the first place, the scheme presupposed in Jos. 21 was difficult to reconcile with other texts from the pre-exilic period which suggested that some priests were resident in places not mentioned at all in the list, e.g., Shiloh (1 Sam. 1-4), Nob (1 Sam. 21:1) and Bethel (Am. 7:10). Secondly, the measurements given in Num. 35:4f. for the land attached to each city (an exact square of 2,000 cubits) had every appearance of being contrived and artificial, and in a mountainous country like Israel, it would have been virtually impossible, on a purely practical level, to have measured off forty-eight square plots of land in the way here envisaged. Moreover, some of the cities mentioned in the list were so close to one another that their surrounding lands (each estimated to consist of over 200 acres) would almost inevitably have overlapped (e.g., Hebron and Holon, Anathoth and Almon), and in the case of Hammoth-dor, its land would have extended into the Sea of Galilee! Finally, the notion that specific cities and their surrounding lands were to be given to the Levites was in direct conflict with other *OT* passages, which suggested that the Levites had been prevented from acquiring any share in the inheritance of Canaan (cf. 18:21-24; 26:62; Dt. 10:9; 18:1-5), and were therefore to be included among the landless and impoverished members of the community, and commended (along with the widow, orphan and stranger) to the charity of the people at large (cf. Dt. 14:27, 29). Such considerations as these led Wellhausen to argue that the account of the Levitical cities in Jos. 21 belonged to one of the latest strata of P, and that the concept was a purely utopian one based partly on the distant memory that many cities in Israel were originally cultic centres, and partly on Ezekiel's vision of the temple and its surrounding precincts (Ezek. 45:1-5; 48:8-22).

Wellhausen's arguments proved to be very influential, although a few scholars did attempt to modify some of his conclusions. Kaufmann, e.g., while sharing Wellhausen's general approach, argued that the ideal enshrined in the concept of 'Levitical cities' was not a late innovation, but belonged to the earliest stages of Israel's existence as a nation, and could be traced to the beginning of the period of the conquest (*Conquest*, pp. 40ff.). But despite such modifications of Wellhausen's position, scholars were, by and large, in agreement with his theory that the scheme envisaged in Jos. 21 was merely wishful thinking on the part of the Priestly writers, and Gray's observation (p. 465) that the Levitical cities were 'merely the objects of desire in certain circles' and that they 'never passed out of the realm of theory into that of fact' may be regarded as fairly typical of the view adumbrated by earlier commentators.

A significant challenge to the prevailing consensus, however, was posed by Alt (*Kleine Schriften*, ii, pp. 306ff.), who observed that the list in Jos. 21 did not, in fact, mention many of the known cultic centres of Israel, such as Gilgal, Bethlehem, and Mizpah, as might have been expected if the scheme were a purely fictitious construction. Moreover, Alt noted that the cities which were enumerated were not evenly distributed throughout the land; none was to be found in the centre of Judah, between Jerusalem and Hebron, and none was located either in the centre of the northern kingdom; rather, most seem to have been positioned on the periphery of the two kingdoms. This observation led Alt to conclude that the list contained in Jos. 21 belonged to the time of Josiah's reform and reflected his policy of centralization, which involved the destruction of the 'high places' and the expulsion of all the priests who resided in the cities of Judah 'from Geba to Beersheba' (2 Kg. 23:8). As a result of his reform, the Levites would have been forced to live in the outlying parts of the kingdom, and the Levitical cities would, therefore, of necessity, have been located at some distance from the central sanctuary in Jerusalem.

While Alt's arguments in favour of the historicity of the list were broadly welcomed, scholars had certain reservations concerning his dating of the list in the period of Josiah's reform (cf. Cazelles, *PEQ* 87 [1955], p. 171). Albright, for example, undertook a detailed analysis of the list, comparing it with 1 Chr. 6:54–81, and concluded that it should be dated in the period of the united monarchy (*L. Ginzberg Jubilee Volume*, pp. 49ff.; *Archaeology*, pp. 121ff.). Proof of this dating was further corroborated by a study of the fortunes which befell the cities mentioned in the list. Since some of them (e.g., Gezer, Taanach, Nahalol; cf. Jg. 1:27–30) did not pass into Israel's possession until the time of David, and since others (e.g., Anathoth, Alemeth) were not even built until that time, the list could hardly be dated earlier than David's reign; on the other hand, since some of the cities (e.g., Golan, Ashtaroth, Jahaz) were lost to Israel by the ninth century BC, the list could not plausibly be assigned to a date much later than David. Albright's arguments were generally regarded as convincing, and although some scholars, such as Noth (*Das Buch Joshua*, pp. 127, 131f.) favoured a much later date for the list, its early provenance and its basic historicity gradually came to be accepted by an increasing number of *OT* scholars (cf. Aharoni, *Land*, pp. 269ff.; Mettinger, *Solomonic State Officials*, pp. 98f.; Bright, *History*, p. 202; Mazar, *IEJ* 10 [1960], pp. 70f.).

Once it was established that the origin of the Levitical cities could be traced to an early period in Israel's history, it was inevitable that speculation should arise concerning the purpose and function of such an institution in the context of Israel's social organization. This was basically the problem addressed by B. Mazar in an influential study published in 1960 (*VTS* 7 [1959], pp. 193ff.). He favoured dating the list of Levitical cities to the time of Solomon, a period when significant changes were taking place in the organization of the kingdom. Drawing attention to the statement in 1 Chr. 26:29–32 that the Levites were appointed in Hebron 'for all the work of the LORD and for the service of the king', Mazar suggested that, during the early period of the monarchy, these functionaries were charged with both cultic and secular duties in various parts of the Israelite state. The Levitical cities, he argued, represented administrative and fiscal centres, and the Levites who dwelt in them would have been responsible not only for the official cult, but also for such duties as collecting taxes and supervising the royal estates. According to Mazar, this was why the cities were situated at the frontiers of the empire rather than in the strongholds of the kingdom itself, for it was precisely in these difficult regions that such administrative centres would have been most needed. This was an area predominantly occupied by a non-Israelite or mixed population which continued to adhere steadfastly to the old Canaanite traditions, and it was here that the services of the Levites were required to promulgate Yahweh-worship and to establish a national identity and loyalty to the king (cf. Aharoni, *Land*, pp. 272f.). In support of this theory, Mazar drew on parallels from Egypt, where each city had a temple staffed by priests who were occupied with both cultic and secular duties (cf. *ANET*, pp. 26off.); since Solomon was in other respects open to the influence of the higher culture and organization of Egypt, Mazar regarded it as inherently probable that he would also have been so influenced in the matter of establishing in his kingdom special cities in which the Levites could dwell.

Although some recent studies have again tended to cast doubt on the antiquity of the list contained in Jos. 21 (cf. Zvi, *JSOT* 54 [1992], pp. 77ff.) and to question its historical value (cf. Spencer, *Levitical Cities*, pp. 210ff.), the balance of probability still favours the view that the list in Jos. 21 is early, and that the institution of Levitical cities does have a firm historical basis. This does not, of course, mean that the descriptions of the Levitical cities in the *OT* are entirely devoid of idealistic elements, for they undoubtedly do contain some utopian features. The exact measurements given for the surrounding lands in vv. 4f., e.g., are probably artificial, and the impression given that the cities in question were the exclusive preserve of the Levites is probably quite misleading. On the other hand, the fact that such idealistic elements are present should not be taken to imply that the accounts of the Levitical cities are completely divorced from historical reality (cf. Haran, *JBL* 80 [1961], pp. 156ff.; *Temples*, pp. 122ff.; de Vaux, *AI*, pp. 366f.; Frick, *The City*, p. 140). The institution was undoubtedly rooted in history, and its continued survival was probably facilitated by the fact that it functioned to the mutual advantage of the king and the Levites: from the point of view of the monarchy, it was useful in securing government control in areas where the king's authority appeared to be at its weakest; from the point of view of the Levites, it provided meaningful employment for a group living on the edge of poverty, while at the same time enabling them to continue their normal duties *vis à vis* the cult.

2. The Israelites are commanded to give to the Levites **cities to**

dwell in and **pasture lands round about the cities**: The fact that the cities were to be given for the Levites to 'dwell in' is taken by some commentators (e.g., Budd, p. 376) to imply that the Levites were not given *possession* of the cities as such, but were merely permitted to reside in them; similarly, they were not given ownership of the surrounding pasture land, but merely permitted to enjoy its usufruct (cf. Haran, *Temples*, pp. 116f.). However, the most natural reading of the text is that the Levites were to be given ownership of the cities and their surrounding lands, and this interpretation is confirmed by Lev. 25:32–34, which clearly asserts that both were to be regarded as their inalienable possession. But although the impression given is that the cities in question were intended for the exclusive use of the Levites, it is probable that, in practice, the Levites were merely allocated specific quarters within the city wall; indeed, in the context of the entire population of the towns in which they resided, the Levites themselves would probably have constituted a relatively small minority (cf. Haran, *Temples*, pp. 124, 130f.; Albright, *Archaeology*, p. 123). The precise meaning of the Heb. term *migrāš*, rendered 'pasture lands' in *RSV*, is unclear. *RV* reads 'suburbs', but this is based on Vulg.'s *et suburbana earum*. Most commentators derive the word from the root *grš* = 'to drive out', and assume that *migrāš* originally referred to a place where cattle could be 'driven out' to graze (hence *RSV*'s 'pasture lands') and that it later came to be used in a more general sense of 'common land' (*NEB*), which could be used by all the inhabitants of the town (cf. McNeile, Gray; *BDB*, p. 177). Barr, however, has recently questioned whether *migrāš* originally meant 'pasture land', for none of the ancient Vsns implies such a restricted understanding of the term, and although the word may be derived from the root *grš*, 'to drive out', this verb is never used in the *OT* in connection with cattle or, indeed, with any other animal. He therefore suggests that the term originally designated a demarcated zone extending outside the walls of a city, the purpose of which may have been to define legally the city's boundaries or, more esoterically, to invest the city with a special numinous quality. Each city, according to Barr, would have had its *migrāš*, and the purpose of the present legislation was to define precisely what portion of this land should be allotted for the use of the Levites (*JSS* 29 [1984], pp. 15ff.).

4–5. The size of the pasture land has long proved problematical, for it is impossible to reconcile the measurements given in v. 4, where the land is to extend 1,000 cubits (approx. 500 yards) from the wall of the city, with those found in v. 5, where the land is stated to be that of a square of which each side was 2,000 cubits (approx. 1,000 yards). As has often been pointed out by commentators, the data in v. 5 can only be reconciled with those in v. 4 by reducing the city and its wall to a single point. Greenberg (*JAOS* 88 [1968], pp. 59ff.; cf. Milgrom, *JJS* 33 [1982], pp. 185ff.) seeks to resolve the contradiction by referring to the second century AD Tannaitic regulations (based on the present passage) concerning the distance (2,000 cubits) which one was entitled to walk from one's residence on the Sabbath. According to Greenberg, the rabbis, in their calculation, effectively disregarded the size of the town (or reduced it to a mathematical point) thus avoiding the complications that would inevitably arise if, for example, the city was irregularly shaped. He therefore suggests that the author of the present passage deliberately omitted the dimensions of the city, regarding them as an unnecessarily complicating factor, and that in doing so he was able to give directions for the layout of the land in the most economical and practical way possible. For other attempts to harmonize the measurements in vv. 4 and 5, see Delekat, *VT* 14 (1964), pp. 15f.; Haran *JBL* 80 (1961), p. 157, n. 1; and for a discussion of some of the solutions proposed by earlier scholars, see Gray, pp. 467f. LXX seeks to resolve the contradiction by reading 2,000 cubits in v. 4 (cf. Josephus, *Ant.* IV.4.3f.), but this is clearly an inferior reading, designed to harmonize two conflicting statements.

6. Included among the forty-eight cities were to be **six cities of refuge**: This reference provides the connecting link with the next section (vv. 9ff.), where the function of these cities is described in detail.

8. The principle by which the cities should be yielded by the secular tribes to the Levites is here clearly enunciated: **from the larger tribes you shall take many, and from the smaller tribes you shall take few**, i.e., the cities were to be contributed by each tribe in numbers proportionate to its size. This principle is the same as that adopted in the original distribution of the land (26:54; 33:54), although it differs somewhat from the one envisaged in Jos. 21 (cf. Gray).

(ii) *Cities of refuge and the law of homicide:* **35:9-34**
Of the forty-eight Levitical cities, six were to function also as cities of refuge, i.e., as places of asylum to which a person who had killed

another by accident could retreat. If the manslayer managed to reach the city of refuge before the 'avenger of blood' caught up with him, then he was protected by law until a trial could be arranged and objective judgment could be passed by 'the congregation' (v. 12). If he was then deemed to have killed his victim deliberately, he would be handed over to the 'avenger of blood' who had the right (and, indeed, the duty) to take his life; if, on the other hand, he was deemed to have killed unintentionally and without premeditation, he was returned to the city of refuge, where he was to remain until the death of the high priest (v. 25).

The present passage was generally regarded by earlier scholars as representing the latest development in the *OT* of the law of asylum (cf. Wellhausen, *Prolegomena*, p. 33; Horst, *EvTh* 16 [1956], pp. 59f.; Nicolsky, *ZAW*, N.F., 7 [1930], pp. 146ff.). According to this view, Israelite legislation initially provided the manslayer with asylum at any local altar (cf. Exod. 21:13f.; 1 Kg. 1:50; 2:28) but, with the abolition of the local sanctuaries under Josiah, alternative provisions had to be made for those who sought refuge. Dt. 19:1ff. thus provided that special cities were to be set aside for this purpose. Three such cities were deemed to be sufficient at first (Dt. 19:2), but a provision was added to the effect that, should Israel's borders increase, another three were to be added (Dt. 19:8f.). The legislation contained in the present chapter was regarded as reaffirming the Deuteronomic law, while at the same time refining some of its details by stating, for example, that the cities were to be formally designated as 'cities of refuge' (*'ārê miqlāṭ*) and that, of the six to be established, three were to be located on each side of the Jordan.

Such a view of the development of the institution has, however, been increasingly questioned in recent years. While it is true that all extant references to the 'cities of refuge' in the *OT* are Deuteronomic or post-Deuteronomic, there are grounds for supposing that their establishment was by no means a Deuteronomic innovation. Firstly, the manner in which the law of asylum is promulgated in Dt. 19:4f., 11f. (an impersonal formulation cast in casuistic style) suggests that the provision was originally based on pre-Deuteronomic traditions, and this would seem to favour a fairly early date for the institution (cf. Mayes, *Deuteronomy*, p. 284). Moreover, the altars originally provided at the local shrines would, at best, only have afforded the manslayer with temporary asylum, and it seems intrinsically probable that even in early pre-exilic times some additional provision must have been made to protect the man-slayer on a more long-term basis (cf. Greenberg, *IDB*, i, p. 639; von Rad, *Deuteronomy*, p. 128; cf., already, Dillmann, p. 218). Finally, it is possible that Hos. 6:8f. refers to Gilead and Shechem as 'cities of refuge', in which case the institution may have been in existence at least as early as the eighth century BC (cf. Phillips, *Law*, pp. 101f.). Thus, the establishment of the cities of refuge is no longer seen as a logical and necessary outcome of the centralization of the cult; rather, the institution is now widely regarded as one of great antiquity, and considered as a natural adjunct to, rather than a replacement of, the local altars (cf. Frick, *City*, pp. 137ff.).

The right of asylum is a concept which is encountered in various cultures from the time of the Greeks and Romans down to the close of the Middle Ages (cf. Baentsch, p. 693), although there is evidence to suggest that it was not always connected with holy shrines (cf. Nicolsky, *op. cit.*, pp. 160ff.). Clearly, the institution was designed originally to control personal vendettas and to place restrictions on the practice of blood vengeance. The present legislation may be regarded as modifying the ancient custom of blood-vengeance in three ways: (i) In early times, no distinction was drawn between accidental and wilful murder, and, in either case, the avenger of blood was responsible for ensuring that any loss of life suffered by a member of his family was duly compensated for. The present law, on the other hand, seeks to distinguish between the two types of crime, demanding death for the murderer but some measure of leni-ency in the case of one guilty of manslaughter. (ii) In ancient custom, the loss of life could be compensated for by the death of any member of the murderer's kin group (cf. 2 Sam. 21:1ff.); here, however, it is tacitly presupposed that only the murderer himself should forfeit his life. (iii) In early Israel, murder was regarded as a private matter to be settled between the families of the two parties concerned, but here such family feuds are no longer entertained, and the present legislation directs that public justice should arbitrate between the slayer and the avenger of blood. Despite these modifications, how-ever, the present law had still not reached its final stage of develop-ment, for the role of the 'avenger of blood' is merely restricted and regulated, not abolished, and justice had yet to become entirely the duty of the state (cf. Gray, p. 471).

11. When the Israelites had crossed the Jordan into Canaan, they were to **select cities to be cities of refuge for you**: The verb here rendered 'select' (*qārāh* in the Hiphil) is nowhere else used in this sense in the *OT*. In Gen. 24:12; 27:20 it means 'to cause [the right thing, good fortune] to occur', and it may, therefore, here have the connotation of selecting 'suitable' or 'appropriate' cities (cf. *BDB*, p. 899*b*). The technical term 'cities of refuge' (Heb. *'ārê miqlāṭ*) occurs only in this chapter and in Jos. 20f.; 1 Chr. 6:57, 67 in the *OT*. Jos. 20:1ff. describes how the Israelites fulfilled the command of the present verse; on the links between vv. 11–15 and Jos. 20, see Auld, *Joshua*, p. 80. **that the manslayer who kills any person without intent may flee there**: For the Heb. term *biš'gāgāh*, rendered by *RSV* 'without intent', see on 15:24. The idea of unintentionality is also emphasized in Dt. 19:4, although a different expression is there used.

12. The cities were intended as a place of refuge **from the avenger** (Heb. *gō'ēl*): LXX and Targums read the fuller form 'avenger of blood' (Heb. *gō'ēl haddām*) here, thus harmonizing the expression with that found elsewhere in this chapter (cf. vv. 19, 21, 24f., 27). The *gō'ēl* was usually a person's next-of-kin, and it is clear from the *OT* that his duties were many and varied (cf. Ringgren, *TDOT*, ii, pp. 351f.; Leggett, *Levirate, passim*). He might be called upon, e.g., to marry the widow of his deceased brother, if the latter had died without producing male offspring (Dt. 25:5–10; Ru. 3:13), or he may be required to redeem a relative who had been forced to sell himself into slavery (Lev. 25:47ff.), or to repurchase his relative's land if the latter had been forced, through poverty, to part with it (Lev. 25:25; Ru. 4:1ff.; Jer. 32:6ff.). In the present case, his duty was to avenge the murder of his relative by finding and killing the person responsible. It has been suggested by Phillips (*Law*, pp. 102ff.; *Deuteronomy*, pp. 129f.) that a clear distinction should be drawn between the *gō'ēl* and the *gō'ēl haddām*: the former was a person's relative or next-of-kin, but the latter was a technical expression designating an officer ('the Protector of blood') appointed by the local community to act on its behalf in vindicating the rights of a man who had been wilfully murdered by another. In effect, he functioned as a type of public executioner, and since he was regarded as a representative of the community at large, death at his hands would have been entirely appropriate. However, this interpretation is not without its difficulties. In the first place, the description of the *gō'ēl haddām* in Dt. 19:6 as pursuing the murderer 'in hot anger' would be more appropriate if understood in the context of a kinsman intent upon blood vengeance rather than of an officer dispassionately performing his legitimate duty on behalf of the community. Moreover, the fact that the term *gōʾēl* is used in the present verse without the qualifying *haddām* (assuming that MT has preserved the original reading) suggests that the *gōʾēl* and the *gōʾēl haddām* were one and the same person, namely a close relative of the deceased. Thus *NEB*'s rendering of *gōʾēl haddām* in Dt. 19:6 as 'the next-of-kin who had the duty of vengeance', although somewhat cumbersome, probably accurately reflects the proper meaning of the term. See, further, Leggett, *op. cit.*, pp. 134ff. **that the manslayer may not die until he stands before the congregation for judgment**: While the manslayer remained in the city of refuge, he was legally protected from the 'avenger of blood' until the proper judicial proceedings could be set in motion. The expression 'stand before' is here used in a technical, forensic sense (cf. *NEB*, 'standing his trial'); for a similar use of the idiom *ʿāmad lipʿnê*, see 27:2; Jos. 20:6; Zech. 3:1. The term *ʿēdāh*, 'congregation', in P usually refers to the theocratic community, but it here evidently designates a representative body chosen to arbitrate in judicial matters; perhaps, as Budd (pp. 382f.) suggests, the implication here is that the individuals officiated as representatives of the sacred congregation of Yahweh. The 'congregation' in this instance was probably that of the manslayer's own city (cf. Dt. 19:12) rather than that of the city in which he had taken refuge (*contra* Baentsch, p. 693), for v. 25 implies that he had been summoned away from the city of refuge to stand his trial, and this perhaps indicates that he had been taken to his own city to appear before representatives of his own people (cf. Dillmann, McNeile). Such representatives would no doubt have been better placed than most to decide whether there had been any enmity between the manslayer and his victim in the past (v. 21).

13–14. The people were to appoint, in all, **six cities of refuge** three **beyond** (i.e., east of) **the Jordan** and three **in the land of Canaan**. The names of the cities are not listed here (as was appropriate in view of the fact that the land had yet to be conquered), but they are given in Jos. 20:7f. as Kedesh, Shechem and Kiriath-arba, to the west of the Jordan, and Bezer, Ramoth and Golan to the east. The location of these cities, in so far as they can be determined (see Snaith, pp. 343f.), suggests that they were distributed in the south, the centre and the north, on each side of the river, thus ensuring that at least one of the cities would be within easy reach of the manslayer, regardless of where the fatal accident had occurred.

15. The cities of refuge were intended not only for the native Israelite, but also for **the stranger and for the sojourner among them**: For the term *gēr*, 'stranger', see on 9:14, and on the rather blurred distinction between the *gēr* and the *tôšāḇ*, 'sojourner', see de Vaux, *AI*, pp. 75f.; van Houten, *Alien*, pp. 124ff. The institution of asylum was clearly designed for the benefit of all the inhabitants of the land, irrespective of their status, provided, of course, that they had killed **without intent**.

16−23. These verses contain specimen cases which were designed to illustrate the difference between deliberate (vv. 16−21) and accidental (vv. 22f.) murder, and they were evidently intended as a means of guidance for those who might be called upon to distinguish between such acts. The crucial factor was clearly the element of intent (cf. Phillips, *JJS* 28 [1977], p. 114, n. 34) or premeditation (cf. Jackson, *Essays*, pp. 91f.; Wenham, p. 237, n. 1) in the perpetration of the offence. If the death of the victim was not the result of advance planning (v. 22) or malice aforethought (v. 23), then even an ostensibly violent or aggressive act could, to some extent, be exonerated (cf. Dt. 19:4f.). If, on the other hand, the act was wilful and the result of previous hatred or ill-feeling between the assailant and his victim, then the former was deemed to be guilty of murder, and was to be put to death by the 'avenger of blood' (v. 19).

16−18. The type of weapon used was evidently regarded as an indication of murderous intent. For example, the use of an **instrument of iron** was in itself suggestive of a clear intention to cause grievous harm. The instruments listed in vv. 17f. are each qualified by the words **by which a man may die** (*NEB*, 'capable of causing death'); the lack of any such qualification with regard to the 'instrument of iron' suggests that a blow with this weapon was automatically assumed to prove fatal.

19. If the man was guilty of wilful murder, it was the duty of the 'avenger of blood' to **put him to death** (cf. v. 21*b*). This verse presupposes the results of the judicial investigation described in vv. 24f., and may well be misplaced in the present context.

20−21. These verses note other possible causes of death. **And if he stabbed him from hatred**: The verb used here, *hāḏap*, implies, rather, a pushing or shoving action (*BDB*, p. 213*b*; cf. 2 Kg. 4:27; Ezek. 34:21), and *NRSV*'s rendering, 'if someone pushes another' (cf. *NIV*), is to be preferred. The situation envisaged is that of a man who pushes another in such a way as to cause his death, e.g., by causing him to fall over a cliff (cf. McNeile). **or hurled at him**: the object is indeterminate in MT, but is supplied by LXX (*pan skeuos*, 'anything'; cf. v. 22) and some modern translations (cf. *NRSV*, *NIV*, 'something'; *NEB*, *JB*, 'missile').

24–28. These verses describe in detail the legal procedure to be followed by the congregation in cases where proof of intent could not be established. The manslayer was to be returned, after the trial, to the city of refuge to which he had fled, and he was to remain there, protected from the 'avenger of blood', until the death of the high priest. If, for some reason, he were to leave the city prematurely he would, in effect, be renouncing the protection provided by the asylum, and the 'avenger of blood' was entitled to slay him with impunity. If, on the other hand, the manslayer remained in the city of refuge for the prescribed period then, as soon as the high priest had died, he would be free to return home and resume his normal life, without any further recriminations.

24–25. The congregation, on the basis of the specimen cases noted in vv. 16–23 (**in accordance with these ordinances**), was to decide upon the guilt or innocence of the manslayer. If it was deemed that the case was one of accidental homicide, the manslayer was to be returned to the city of refuge **to which he had fled** and was to remain there **until the death of the high priest who was anointed with the holy oil**. Some commentators take the reference to the anointing with holy oil as indicative of the fact that the high priest had now assumed the role formerly occupied by the king as 'Yahweh's anointed'; consequently, the high priest's death is interpreted as the occasion for a general amnesty, such as occurred whenever there was a change in the occupancy of the throne (cf. Wellhausen, *Prolegomena*, p. 150, followed by Baentsch, p. 695; Noth, p. 255; David, *OTS* 9 [1951], pp. 40ff.; de Vaux, *AI*, p. 162). However, this interpretation must be regarded as dubious, for the evidence usually marshalled in favour of the existence of such an amnesty in Israel is very ambiguous and inconclusive (cf. the discussion by Whitelam, *Just King*, pp. 144ff.). Moreover, this interpretation fails to take into account the *religious* presupposition of the law of asylum. As McKeating (*VT* 25 [1975], pp. 64f.) has observed, homicide was regarded by the Priestly writer as essentially a sacral offence (cf. vv. 33f.), and some form of expiation was required to expunge the manslayer's guilt (cf. Sturdy, Budd). The manslayer, though innocent of wilful murder, was not regarded as entirely free of blame, since even the unintentional shedding of blood involved bloodguilt, for which atonement had to be made. The only person whose religious importance might endow his death with such atoning significance was the high priest; as the sacral representative of the people, his death would have been regarded as efficacious in obliterating the stain caused by bloodguilt, and this was doubtless why the manslayer had to remain in the city of refuge until the high priest had died (cf. Greenberg, *JBL* 78 [1959], pp. 127ff.). This interpretation of the significance of the high priest's death has the advantage of being in keeping with the general tenor of the present law, and is, at the same time, entirely consistent with the way in which ancient exegetes interpreted the passage under discussion (Bab. Talmud, *Makkoth*, 11b). For a different, although not altogether convincing, explanation of the significance of the high priest's death in the present passage, see Delekat, *Asylie*, pp. 290ff. The word *haggāḏōl*, 'high', in the expression 'high priest' is regarded by some commentators (e.g., Dillmann) as a gloss, for v. 32 in MT refers simply to the 'priest', which is the usual term used by P to refer to Aaron and his successors; however, it is more probable that v. 32 originally read 'high priest' (cf. LXX, Syr., Sam.) and that the qualifying *haggāḏōl* has either accidentally dropped out of the text, or been deliberately omitted as unnecessary after its appearance in vv. 25, 28.

29. And these things (i.e., the foregoing enactments) were to be regarded as a permanent **statute and ordinance**, i.e., they were to serve as 'legal precedents' (*NEB*), just as was the decision in the case of the daughters of Zelophehad (27:8b–11).

30. No person accused of murder was to be **put to death on the testimony of one witness**: This is in keeping with the principle enshrined in Dt. 17:6, which states that more than one witness was required to substantiate an accusation of apostasy, a ruling which is applied in Dt. 19:15 to any charge brought against the accused. Since early Israelite legal practice laid the burden of proof largely upon the accused, perjured evidence could clearly have a pernicious effect on the verdict, and it was in order to guard against such possible miscarriages of justice that the law demanded that evidence should be corroborated by the testimony of at least two witnesses. A false witness would suffer the punishment which would have been inflicted upon the accused, if he had been found guilty (Dt. 19:18f.), a principle also encountered in extra-biblical law (cf. *CH* §§ 1–4; *ANET*, p. 166).

31–32. No **ransom** (Heb. *kōper*) was to be accepted **for the life of a murderer, who is guilty of death**, i.e., no one found guilty of wilful murder was to be allowed to commute his death sentence by the payment of money (presumably to the relatives of the victim). The taking of human life was regarded as such a heinous offence in Israel, that no one was permitted to escape the proper penalty prescribed by law (cf. Greenberg, *Kaufmann Jubilee Volume*, pp. 13ff.; *ScrHier* 31 [1986], pp. 1ff.). In this regard, the Israelite legal system differed from other ancient Near Eastern law codes, where the payment of a 'ransom' to avoid the death penalty was permitted (cf. Hittite Law §§ 1–5; *MAL* A § 10 and B § 2; *ANET*, pp. 181, 185, 189; Paul, *Studies*, pp. 61f.; Driver and Miles, *Assyrian Laws*, pp. 33ff.). There is only one instance in *OT* law where the payment of compensation for causing death was allowed, and that was in the case of the owner of an ox whose beast was known to have a propensity to gore (Exod. 21:29f.); however, as Phillips (*JJS* 28 [1977], pp. 109f., 116f.) has demonstrated, even this was not an exception to the general rule, for the 'murderer' (in this case, the ox) *was* put to death, and only its owner, as the indirect accomplice, was permitted to save his life by the payment of monetary compensation (cf. Schenker, *Bib* 63 [1982], p. 32ff.). The rule which applied to the wilful murderer also applied, in principle, to the man found guilty of accidental homicide, for he was prohibited from paying a ransom in lieu of his detention in the city of refuge. As many commentators have observed, this precept illustrates the punitive character of the manslayer's confinement, a fact recognized by Josephus (*Ant.* IV.7.4) and Philo (*De spec. leg.* III.123), both of whom regarded his enforced detention as a kind of 'banishment'. According to some scholars, the present legislation represents a transformation in the concept of 'asylum' in Israel, whereby the purely humanitarian concern of the original institution has given way to a concept of it as a form of punishment, as well as a means of protection (cf. David, *op. cit.*, pp. 44f.).

33–34. The chapter concludes by explaining why murder was regarded as a particularly serious crime, and why the proper penalty had to be inflicted upon the person found guilty: the blood of the murdered victim **pollutes the land**, and atonement could only be

effected by the death of the murderer **who shed it** (cf. Gen. 4:10).
To leave murder unrequited, or to accept a monetary payment in
compensation, would be tantamount to leaving the land polluted,
and this, in turn, would have deprived the people of the presence
of Yahweh in their midst, for he could not dwell in a land which
had been defiled, without compromising his own holiness. Thus
murder had to be punished, and the purity of the land preserved,
for I the LORD dwell in the midst of the people of Israel.

(m) THE INHERITANCE OF MARRIED DAUGHTERS
36:1-13

The law of 27:1-11 permitted a man's daughters to inherit his property in the absence of any male heirs. This ruling, however, meant
that, should the daughters marry, there was a risk that the property
of their father would pass into the possession of another tribe. The
present law, therefore, sought to guard against this contingency by
obliging an heiress to marry within her own tribe (v. 6). The imposition of this restriction effectively closed the loophole in the provision of 27:8*b*-11 and ensured that, irrespective of any matrimonial
arrangements, each tribe would preserve its original heritage for
future generations. Although the enactment of the present chapter
was intended, in the first instance, to benefit the daughters of Zelophehad, it is here given wider application by being made binding
on all the Israelite tribes (v. 8).

There can be no doubt that the chapter comes from the Priestly
source and that it belongs, like 27:1-11, to a comparatively late
stage in the Priestly redaction of the Pentateuch. It is probable,
however, that the concluding formulation in v. 13 is earlier, and
some commentators (e.g., Holzinger) are prepared to assign this
verse to P^g. Although there are obvious points of similarity between
the present chapter and 27:1-11, there is much to be said for the
view that the two sections are the work of two different authors (cf.
Gray, p. 477).

1. Attention is drawn to the danger inherent in the enactment of
27:8*b*-11 by **the heads of the fathers' houses** (see on 1:2) **of the
families of the sons of Gilead**, i.e., by representatives of the family
or clan most closely concerned with the matter. The fact that such
senior tribal members are depicted as making a formal petition
before Moses (LXX, Syr. add 'and before Eleazar the priest'; cf.

27:2) **and before the leaders**, indicates the importance of the matter under consideration.

4. And when the jubilee of the people of Israel comes, then their inheritance will be added to the inheritance of the tribe to which they belong: The term 'jubilee' is formed from the Heb. *yôḇēl*, which means 'ram's horn' or 'trumpet', and the 'year of the jubilee' was so called because it was ushered in by the blowing of trumpets. One of the primary provisions of the jubilee was that all land which had been purchased had to be returned, in the fiftieth year, to its original owner or to his descendants, thus giving each family in Israel the opportunity to return to its ancestral estate (Lev. 25:8ff.; see North, *Sociology, passim*; Westbrook, *Property*, pp. 38ff.). The reference to the jubilee in the present context, however, is unexpected, for this institution was concerned only with land that had been sold, not with land that had been inherited. Moreover, the verse does not contemplate the restoration of the land to the tribe of Manasseh, as might have been expected, but anticipates, rather, its permanent alienation to the tribe into which the daughters would marry. It is therefore suggested by some commentators that this verse must refer to a special ruling concerning land acquired through marriage, which is not documented in Lev. 25:8ff., namely, that if a sudden change in the woman's circumstances (e.g., death, or the loss of a child) occurred *before* the jubilee year, the land was to return to the woman's family, but that at the jubilee it would pass definitively to the family of her husband (cf., e.g., de Vaulx, p. 405). However, this interpretation is not altogether convincing, for it is unclear why such a provision, if it was, indeed, a part of the jubilee legislation, was not included in the otherwise detailed enactments contained in Lev. 25. It is more probable that the present verse should be regarded as a mistaken gloss, and the fact that it breaks the sequence of thought between vv. 3 and 5 seems to confirm Noth's view (p. 257) that the verse is an 'irrelevant addition' to the chapter (cf. Baentsch, p. 698).

5–7. Moses concedes that **the tribe of the sons of Joseph** has a legitimate grievance, and so it is decreed that henceforth daughters who inherit their father's property must marry **within the family of the tribe of their father**. The enactment thus ensured that, even if an heiress *were* to marry, the property which she had inherited would be retained within the tribe to which it had originally belonged. In this way, the inheritance of the Israelites was prevented from being arbitrarily **transferred from one tribe to another**. (For the technical use of the verb *sābab* here to refer to the legal transference of property, see Sasson, *ZAW* 94 [1982], pp. 108f.; cf., also, 1 Chr. 10:14; Jer. 6:12.) Although it is not explicitly stated in the present text, it may be presumed that an heiress who married a man from another tribe would have lost all claims to her father's inheritance, and that any property which had been bequeathed to her would have returned forthwith to her father's tribe (cf. Josephus, *Ant.* IV.7.5).

11–12. In accordance with the law, the daughters of Zelophehad (here listed in a different order to that encountered in 26:33; 27:1 and Jos. 17:3, Noah and Tirzah having exchanged places) marry their cousins on their father's side, and in this way their inheritance was kept within the tribe of Manasseh, where it rightfully belonged. A further example of the observance of this law is found in 1 Chr. 23:22, where the sons of Kish marry the daughters of Eleazar, their uncle, who, like Zelophehad, had died without leaving male offspring (cf., also, Tob. 6:12; 7:1ff.).

13. It is not clear whether the subscription contained here was intended to refer to the legislation of chs. 27–36 (Snaith, Sturdy), or to the entire body of laws contained in chs. 22–36 (McNeile, Gray), or, indeed, to the book of Numbers as a whole (Binns, Budd). A similar subscription is found in Lev. 27:34 appended to the laws given at Sinai, although it is not particularly well placed in that context, since further Sinaitic laws follow in Num. 1ff. The present verse serves as a fitting conclusion to the book, emphasizing that all the commands and regulations given to the people of Israel ultimately came from Yahweh, and were formulated at a period prior to Israel's entry into Canaan. The end of the book of Numbers, however, merely marked the conclusion of one stage of Israel's pilgrimage; another, no less decisive stage, was now about to begin, as the chosen people, under God's guidance, prepared to cross the Jordan and take possession of the promised land.

GENERAL INDEX

INDEX OF AUTHORS